GREAT FIRST WORLD WAR STORIES

Bounty
Books

First published in Great Britain in 1930 by Eyre and Spottiswoode
under the title *Great Short Stories of the War*

First published as *Great First World War Stories* in 1994 by
Chancellor Press (Bounty Books)

This edition published in 2014 by Bounty Books,
a division of Octopus Publishing Group Ltd
Endeavour House, 189 Shaftesbury Avenue,
London WC2H 8JY
www.octopusbooks.co.uk

An Hachette UK company
www.hachette.co.uk

ISBN: 978-0-753727-21-8

A CIP catalogue record for this book is available from the
British Library.

Printed and bound in China

GREAT FIRST WORLD WAR STORIES

ACKNOWLEDGEMENTS

The Publishers wish to thank the following for use of previously printed material in this collection. Every effort has been made to trace the owners of the copyright material in this book. In the case of any question arising as to the use of any such material, the editor would be pleased to receive notification of this.

The Estate of Richard Aldington and Chatto and Windus for "Introduction to the Trenches" from *Death of a Hero* by Richard Aldington

"In Another Country" from *Men Without Women* by Ernest Hemingway, copyright © Ernest Hemingway, reproduced by permission of the Curtis Brown Group Ltd, London

"Among the Trumpets" by Leonard Nason, copyright ©1927, reprinted by permission of *The Saturday Evening Post.*

"Prentice" from *The Baker's Cart* by Gerald Bullett reprinted by permission of Mrs Rosemary Seymour

A.P. Watt Ltd and the Estate of Sheila Reeves for "Cain's Atonement" by Algernon Blackwood

William Heinemann Ltd for "The Traitor" from *Ashenden* by W. Somerset Maugham, used by permission.

The Estate of Liam O' Flaherty, and the publisher, Jonathan Cape, for "The Alien Skull" from *The Mountain Tavern* by Liam O' Flaherty

"One Hundred Per Cent" by Leo V. Jacks is reprinted with the permission of Charles Scribner's Sons, an imprint of Macmillan Publishing Company, from Scribner's Magazine

CONTENTS

THE HOME FRONT

DEFEAT

by
John Galsworthy

SHE had been standing there on the pavement a quarter of an hour or so after her shilling's worth of concert. Women of her profession are not supposed to have redeeming points, especially when—like May Belinski, as she now preferred to dub herself—they are German; but this woman certainly had music in her soul. She often gave herself these "music baths" when the Promenade Concerts were on, and had just spent half her total wealth in listening to some Mozart and a Beethoven symphony.

She was feeling almost elated, full of divine sound, and of the summer moonlight that was filling the whole dark town. Women "of a certain type" have, at all events, emotions—and what a comfort that is, even to themselves! To stand just there had become rather a habit of hers. One could seem to be waiting for somebody coming out of the concert, not yet over—which, of course, was precisely what she *was* doing. One need not for ever be stealthily glancing and perpetually moving on in that peculiar way, which, while it satisfied the police and Mrs. Grundy, must not quite deceive others as to her business in life. She had only "been at it" long enough to have acquired a nervous dread of almost everything—not long enough to have passed through that dread to callousness. Some women take so much longer than others. And even for a woman "of a certain type" her position was exceptionally nerve-racking in war-time, going as she did by a false name. Indeed, in all England there could hardly be a greater pariah than was this German woman of the night.

She idled outside a book-shop humming a little, pretending to read the titles of the books by moonlight, taking off and putting on one of her stained yellow gloves. Now and again she would move up as far as the posters outside the hall, scrutinising them as if interested in the future, then stroll back again. In her worn and discreet dark dress, and her·small hat, she had nothing about her to rouse suspicion, unless it were the trail of violet powder she left on the moonlight.

For the moonlight this evening was almost solid, seeming with its cool still vibration to replace the very air; in it the war-time precautions against light seemed fantastic, like shading candles in a room still full of daylight. What lights there were had the effect of strokes and stipples of dim colour laid by a painter's brush on a background of ghostly whitish-blue. The dreamlike quality of the town was perhaps enhanced for her eyes by the veil she was wearing—in day-time no longer white. As the music died out of her, elation also ebbed. Somebody had passed her, speaking German, and she was overwhelmed by a rush of nostalgia. On this moonlit night by the banks of the Rhine—whence she came—the orchards would be heavy with apples; there would be murmurs and sweet scents; the old castle would stand out clear, high over the woods and the chalky-white river. There would be singing far away, and the churning of a distant steamer's screw; and perhaps on the water a log raft still drifting down in the blue light. There would be German voices talking. And suddenly tears oozed up in her eyes, and crept down through the powder on her cheeks. She raised her veil and dabbed at her face with a little, not-too-clean handkerchief, screwed up in her yellow-gloved hand. But the more she dabbed the more those treacherous tears ran. Then she became aware that a tall young man in khaki was also standing before the shop-window, not looking at the titles of the books, but eyeing her askance. His face was fresh and open, with a sort of kindly eagerness in his blue eyes. Mechanically she drooped her wet lashes, raised them obliquely, drooped them again, and uttered a little sob. . . .

This young man, captain in a certain regiment, and discharged from hospital at six o'clock that evening, had entered Queen's Hall at half-past seven. Still rather brittle and sore from his wound, he had treated himself to a seat in the grand circle, and there had sat, very still and dreamy, the whole concert through. It had been like eating after a long fast—something of the sensation Polar explorers must experience when they return to their first full meal. For he was of the New Army, and before the war had actually believed in music, art, and all that sort of thing. With a month's leave before him, he could afford to feel that life was extraordinarily joyful, his own experiences particularly wonderful; and, coming out into the moonlight, he had taken what can only be described as a great gulp of it, for he was a young man with a sense of beauty. When one has been long in the trenches, lain out wounded in a shell-hole twenty-four hours, and spent three months in hospital, beauty has such an edge of novelty, such a sharp sweetness, that it almost gives pain. And London at night is very beautiful. He strolled slowly towards the Circus, still drawing the moonlight deep into his lungs, his cap tilted up a little on his forehead in that moment of unmilitary abandonment; and whether he stopped before the book-shop window because the girl's figure was in some sort a part of beauty, or because he saw that she was crying, he could not have made clear to anyone.

Then something—perhaps the scent of powder, perhaps the yellow glove, or the oblique flutter of the eyelids—told him that he was making what he would have called " a blooming error," unless he wished for company, which had not been in his thoughts. But her sob affected him, and he said :

" What's the matter?"

Again her eyelids fluttered sideways, and she stammered :

" Not'ing. The beautiful evening—that's why! "

That a woman of what he now clearly saw to be a " certain type " should perceive what he himself had just been perceiving, struck him forcibly, and he said :

" Cheer up."

She looked up again swiftly. " All right! But you are not lonelee like me."

For one of that sort she looked somehow honest; her tear-streaked face was rather pretty, and he murmured :

" Well, let's walk a bit and talk it over."

They turned the corner and walked east, along streets empty and beautiful, with their dulled orange-glowing lamps, and here and there the glint of some blue or violet light. He found it queer and rather exciting—for an adventure of just this kind he had never had. And he said doubtfully :

" How did you get into this? Isn't it an awfully hopeless life?"

" Ye-es, it ees——" her voice had a queer soft emphasis. " You are limping—haf you been wounded?"

" Just out of hospital."

" The horrible war—all the misery is because of the war. When will it end?"

He looked at her, and said :

" I say—what nationality are you?"

" Rooshian."

" Really! I never met a Russian girl."

He was conscious that she looked at him, then very quickly down. And he said suddenly :

" Is it as bad as they make out?"

She slipped her yellow-gloved hand through his arm.

" Not when I haf anyone as nice as you; I never haf yet, though;" she smiled—and her smile was like her speech, slow, confiding.

"You stopped because I was sad; others stop because I am gay. I am not fond of men at all. When you know, you are not fond of them."

"Well! You hardly know them at their best, do you? You should see them at the front. By George! they're simply splendid—officers and men, every blessed soul. There's never been anything like it—just one long bit of jolly fine self-sacrifice; it's perfectly amazing."

Turning her blue-grey eyes on him, she answered:

"I expect you are not the last at that. You see in them what you haf in yourself, I think."

"Oh! not a bit—you're quite out. I assure you when we made the attack where I got wounded there wasn't a single man in my regiment who wasn't an absolute hero. The way they went in—never thinking of themselves—it was simply superb!"

Her teeth came down on her lower lip, and she answered in a queer voice: "It is the same too, perhaps, with—the enemy."

"Oh, yes, I know that."

"Ah! You are not a mean man. How I hate mean men!"

"Oh! they're not mean really—they simply don't understand."

"Oh! you are a baby—a good baby, aren't you?"

He did not quite like being called a baby, and frowned; but was at once touched by the disconcertion in her powdered face. How quickly she was scared!

She said clingingly:

"But I li-ike you for it. It is so good to find a ni-ice man."

This was worse, and he said abruptly:

"About being lonely? Haven't you any Russian friends?"

"Rooshian! No! The town is so beeg! Haf you been in the concert?"

"Yes."

"I, too—I love music."

"I suppose all Russians do."

She looked up at his face again, and seemed to struggle to keep silent; then she said quietly :

"I go there always when I haf the money."

"What! Are you so on the rocks?"

"Well, I haf just one shilling now." And she laughed.

The sound of that little laugh upset him—she had a way of making him feel sorry for her every time she spoke.

They had come by now to a narrow square, east of Gower Street.

"This is where I lif," she said. "Come in!"

He had one long moment of violent hesitation, then yielded to the soft tugging of her hand, and followed. The passage-hall was dimly lighted, and they went upstairs into a front room, where the curtains were drawn, and the gas turned very low. Opposite the window were other curtains dividing off the rest of the apartment. As soon as the door was shut she put up her face and kissed him— evidently formula. What a room! Its green and beetroot colouring and the prevalence of cheap plush disagreeably affected him. Every-thing in it had that callous look of rooms which seem to be saying to their occupants : "You're here to-day and you'll be gone to-mor-row." Everything except one little plant, in a common pot, of maid-enhair fern, fresh and green, looking as if it had been watered with-in the hour; in this room it had just the same unexpected touch-ingness that peeped out of the girl's matter-of-fact cynicism.

Taking off her hat, she went towards the gas, but he said quickly :

"No, don't turn it up; let's have the window open and the moon-light in." He had a sudden dread of seeing anything plainly—it was stuffy, too, and, pulling the curtains apart, he threw up the window. The girl had come obediently from the hearth, and sat down opposite him, leaning her arm on the window-sill and her chin on her hand. The moonlight caught her cheek where she had just renewed the powder, and her fair crinkly hair; it caught the plush of the furniture, and his own khaki, giving them all a touch of unreality.

"What's your name?" he said.

"May. Well, I call myself that. It's no good askin' yours."

"You're a distrustful little soul, aren't you?"

"I haf reason to be, don't you think?"

"Yes, I suppose you're bound to think us all brutes?"

"Well, I haf a lot of reasons to be afraid all my time. I am dreadfully nervous now; I am not trusting anybody. I suppose you haf been killing lots of Germans?"

He laughed.

"We never know, unless it happens to be hand to hand. I haven't come in for that yet."

"But you would be very glad if you had killed some?"

"Glad? I don't think so. We're all in the same boat so far as that's concerned. We're not glad to kill each other. We do our job —that's all."

"Oh! it is frightful. I expect I haf my broders killed."

"Don't you get any news ever?"

"News! No indeed, no news of anybody in my country. I might not haf a country; all that I ever knew is gone—fader, moder, sisters, broders, all—never any more I shall see them, I suppose, now. The war it breaks and breaks—it breaks hearts." Her little teeth fastened again on her lower lip in that sort of pretty snarl. "Do you know what I was thinkin' when you came up? I was thinkin' of my native town and the river there in the moonlight. If I could see it again I would be glad. Were you ever homeseek?"

"Yes, I have been—in the trenches; but one's ashamed, with all the others."

"Ah! ye-es!" It came from her with a hiss. "Ye-es! You are all

comrades there. What is it like for me here, do you think, where
everybody hates and despises me, and would catch me, and put me
in prison, perhaps?"

He could see her breast heaving with a quick breathing painful
to listen to. He leaned forward, patting her knee, and murmuring : "So sorry."

She said in a smothered voice :

"You are the first who has been kind to me for so long! I will
tell you the truth—I am not Rooshian at all—I am German."

Hearing that half-choked confession, his thought was : "Does
she really think we fight against women?" And he said :

"My dear girl, who cares?"

Her eyes seemed to search right into him. She said slowly :

"Another man said that to me. But he was thinkin' of other
things. You are a veree ni-ice boy. I am so glad I met you. You see
the good in people, don't you? That is the first thing in the world
—because there is really not much good in people, you know."

He said, smiling :

"You're a dreadful little cynic!" Then thought : "Well—of
course!"

"Cyneec? How long do you think I would live if I was not a
cyneec? I should drown myself to-morrow. Perhaps there are good
people, but, you see, I don't know them."

"I know lots."

She leaned forward eagerly.

"Well now—see, ni-ice boy—you haf never been in a hole, haf
you?"

"I suppose not a real hole."

"No, I should think not, with your face. Well, suppose I am
still a good girl, as I was once, you know, and you took me to some
of your good people, and said : 'Here is a little German girl that

has no work, and no money, and no friends.' Your good people
they will say: 'Oh! how sad! A German girl!' and they will go
and wash their hands."

Silence fell on him. He saw his mother, his sister, others—good
people, he would swear! And yet——! He heard their voices,
frank and clear; and they seemed to be talking of the Germans. If
only she were not German as well!

"You see!" he heard her say, and could only mutter:

"I'm sure there *are* people."

"No. They would not take a German, even if she was good.
Besides, I don't want to be good any more—I am not a humbug
—I have learned to be bad. Aren't you going to kees me, ni-ice
boy?"

She put her face close to his. Her eyes troubled him, but he drew
back. He thought she would be offended or persistent, but she
was neither; just looked at him fixedly with a curious inquiring
stare; and he leaned against the window, deeply disturbed. It was
as if all clear and simple enthusiasm had been suddenly knocked
endways; as if a certain splendour of life that he had felt and seen
of late had been dipped in cloud. Out there at the front, over here
in hospital, life had been seeming so—as it were—heroic; and yet
it held such mean and murky depths as well! The voices of his
men, whom he had come to love like brothers, crude burring voices,
cheery in trouble, making nothing of it; the voices of doctors and
nurses, patient, quiet, reassuring voices; even his own voice, in-
fected by it all, kept sounding in his ears. All wonderful somehow,
and simple; and nothing mean about it anywhere! And now so
suddenly to have lighted upon this, and all that was behind it—
this scared girl, this base, dark, thoughtless use of her! And the
thought came to him: "I suppose my fellows wouldn't think twice
about taking her on! Why, I'm not even certain of myself, if she

insists!" And he turned his face and stared out at the moonlight.
He heard her voice:

" Eesn't it light? No air-raid to-night. When the Zepps burned
—what a horrible death! And all the people cheered—it is natural.
Do you hate us veree much?"

He turned round and said sharply:

" Hate? I don't know."

" I don't hate even the English—I despise them. I despise my
people too—perhaps more, because they began this war. Oh, yes!
I know that. I despise all the peoples. Why haf they made the world
so miserable—why haf they killed all our lives—hundreds and
thousands and millions of lives—all for not'ing? They haf made
a bad world—everybody hating, and looking for the worst everywhere. They haf made me bad, I know. I believe no more in anything. What is there to believe in? Is there a God? No! Once I was
teaching little English children their prayers—isn't that funnee? I
was reading to them about Christ and love. I believed all those
things. Now I believe not'ing at all—no one who is not a fool or
a liar can believe. I would like to work in a hospital; I would like
to go and help poor boys like you. Because I am a German they
would throw me out a hundred times, even if I was good. It is the
same in Germany and France and Russia—everywhere. But do
you think I will believe in love and Christ and a God and all that?
—not I! I think we are animals—that's all! Oh! yes—you fancy it
is because my life has spoiled me. It is not that at all—that's not
the worst thing in life. These men are not ni-ice, like you, but it's
their nature, and," she laughed, " they help me to live, which is
something for me, anyway. No, it is the men who think themselves
great and good, and make the war with their talk and their hate,
killing us all—killing all the boys like you, and keeping poor
people in prison, and telling us to go on hating; and all those

dreadful cold-blooded creatures who write in the papers—the same in my country, just the same; it is because of all them that I think we are only animals."

He got up, acutely miserable. He could see her following him with her eyes, and knew she was afraid she had driven him away. She said coaxingly: "Don't mind me talking, ni-ice boy. I don't know anyone to talk to. If you don't like it, I can be quiet as a mouse."

He muttered:

"Oh! go on, talk away. I'm not obliged to believe you, and I don't."

She was on her feet now, leaning against the wall, her dark dress and white face just touched by the slanting moonlight; and her voice came again, slow and soft and bitter:

"Well, look here, ni-ice boy, what sort of a world is it, where millions are being tortured—horribly tortured, for no fault of theirs at all? A beautiful world, isn't it? 'Umbug! silly rot, as you boys call it. You say it is all 'Comrade!' and braveness out there at the front, and people don't think of themselves. Well, I don't think of myself veree much. What does it matter?—I am lost now, any-way; but I think of my people at home, how they suffer and grieve. I think of all the poor people there and here who lose those they love, and all the poor prisoners. Am I not to think of them? And if I do, how am I to believe it a beautiful world, ni-ice boy?"

He stood very still, biting his lips.

"Look here! We haf one life each, and soon it is over. Well, I think that is lucky.

He said resentfully:

"No! there's more than that."

"Ah," she went on softly, "you think the war is fought for the future; you are giving your lives for a better world, aren't you?"

"We must fight till we win," he said between his teeth.

"Till you win. My people think that, too. All the peoples think that if they win the world will be better. But it will not, you know; it will be much worse, anyway."

He turned away from her and caught up his cap; but her voice followed him.

"I don't care which wins, I despise them all—animals—animals! Ah! Don't go, ni-ice boy—I will be quiet now."

He took some notes from his tunic pocket, put them on the table, and went up to her.

"Good-night."

She said plaintively:

"Are you really going? Don't you like me enough?"

"Yes, I like you."

"It is because I am German, then?"

"No."

"Then why won't you stay?"

He wanted to answer: "Because you upset me so;" but he just shrugged his shoulders.

"Won't you kees me once?"

He bent, and put his lips to her forehead; but as he took them away she threw her head back, pressed her mouth to his and clung to him.

He sat down suddenly, and said:

"Don't! I don't want to feel a brute."

She laughed. "You are a funny boy, but you are veree good. Talk to me a little, then. No one talks to me. I would much rather talk, anyway. Tell me, haf you seen many German prisoners?"

He sighed—from relief, or was it from regret?

"A good many."

"Any from the Rhine?"

"Yes, I think so."

"Were they very sad?"

"Some were—some were quite glad to be taken."

"Did you ever see the Rhine? Isn't it beautiful? It will be wonderful to-night. The moonlight will be the same here as there; in Rooshia too, and France, everywhere; and the trees will look the same as here, and people will meet under them and make love just as here. Oh! isn't it stupid, the war?—as if it was not good to be alive."

He wanted to say : "You can't tell how good it is to be alive till you're facing death, because you don't live till then. And when a whole lot of you feel like that—and are ready to give their lives for each other, it's worth all the rest of life put together." But he couldn't get it out to this girl who believed in nothing.

"How were you wounded, ni-ice boy?"

"Attacking across open ground—four machine-gun bullets got me at one go off."

"Weren't you veree frightened when they ordered you to attack?" No, he had not been frightened just then! And he shook his head and laughed.

"It was great. We did laugh that morning. They got me much too soon, though—a swindle!"

She stared at him.

"You laughed?"

"Yes, and what do you think was the first thing I was conscious of next morning—my old colonel bending over me and giving me a squeeze of lemon. If you knew my colonel, you'd still believe in things. There *is* something, you know, behind all this evil. After all, you can only die once, and if it's for your country all the better."

Her face, with intent eyes just touched with dark, had in the moonlight a most strange, other-world look. Her lips moved :

"No, I believe in nothing. My heart is dead."

"You think so, but it isn't, you know, or you wouldn't have been crying when I met you."

"If it were not dead, do you think I could live my life—walking the streets every night, pretending to like strange men—never hearing a kind word—never talking for fear I will be known for a German. Soon I shall take to drinking, then I shall be '*kaput*' very quick. You see, I am practical; I see things clear. To-night I am a little emotional, the moon is funny, you know. But I live for myself only now. I don't care for anything or anybody."

"All the same, just now you were pitying your people, and prisoners, and that."

"Yes, because they suffer. Those who suffer are like me—I pity myself, that's all; I am different from your Englishwomen. I see what I am doing; I do not let my mind become a turnip just because I am no longer moral."

"Nor your heart either."

"Ni-ice boy, you are veree obstinate. But all that about love is umbug. We love ourselves, nothing more."

Again, at that intense soft bitterness in her voice, he felt stifled and got up, leaning on the window-sill. The air out there was free from the smell of dust and stale perfume. He felt her fingers slip between his own, and stay unmoving. If she was so hard and cynical, why should he pity her? Yet he did. The touch of that hand within his own roused his protective instinct. She had poured out her heart to him—a perfect stranger! He pressed it a little, and felt her fingers crisp in answer. Poor little devil! This was a friendlier moment than she had known for years! And after all, fellow-feeling was bigger than principalities and powers! Fellow-feeling was all-pervading as this moonlight, which she had said would be the same in Germany—as this white ghostly glamour wrapping the trees, making the orange lamps so quaint and decoratively useless out in the narrow square, where emptiness and silence reigned. He looked round into her face—in spite of kohl and powder, and the red salve on her lips, it had a queer, unholy, touching beauty. And he had suddenly the strangest feeling, as if they stood there—the two of them—proving that kindness and human fellowship were stronger than lust, stronger than hate; proving it against meanness and brutality, and the sudden shouting of newspaper boys in some neighbouring streets, whose cries, passionately vehement, clashed into each other, and obscured the words—what was it they were calling? His head went up to listen; he felt her hand rigid within his arm—she too was listening. The cries came nearer, hoarser, more shrill and clamorous; the empty moonlight seemed of a sudden crowded with figures, footsteps, voices, and a fierce distant cheering. "Great victory—great victory! Official! British! Severe defeat of the 'Uns! Many thousand prisoners!" So it sped by, intoxicating, filling him with a fearful joy; and leaning far out, he waved his cap and cheered like a madman; and the whole night seemed to him to flutter and vibrate and answer. Then he turned to rush down into the street, struck against something soft, and recoiled. The girl! She stood with hands clenched, her face convulsed, panting, and even in the madness of his joy he felt for her. To hear this —in the midst of enemies! All confused with the desire to do something, he stooped to take her hand; and the dusty reek of the table-cloth clung to his nostrils. She snatched away her fingers, swept up the notes he had put down, and held them out to him.

"Take them—I will not haf your English money—take them." And suddenly she tore them across twice, three times, let the bits flutter to the floor, and turned her back to him. He stood looking at her leaning against the plush-covered table which smelled of dust, her head down, a dark figure in a dark room with the moonlight

sharpening her outline—hardly a moment he stayed, then made
for the door. . . .

When he was gone, she still stood there, her chin on her breast
—she who cared for nothing, believed in nothing—with the sound
in her ears of cheering, of hurrying feet, and voices; stood in the
centre of a pattern made by fragments of the torn-up notes, staring
out into the moonlight, seeing, not this hated room and the hated
square outside, but a German orchard, and herself, a little girl,
plucking apples, a big dog beside her; a hundred other pictures,
too, such as the drowning see. Her heart swelled; she sank down
on the floor, laid her forehead on the dusty carpet, and pressed her
body to it.

She who did not care—who despised all peoples, even her own
—began, mechanically, to sweep together the scattered fragments
of the notes, assembling them with the dust into a little pile, as of
fallen leaves, and dabbling in it with her fingers, while the tears
ran down her cheeks. For her country she had torn them, her country in defeat! She, who had just one shilling in this great town of
enemies, who wrung her stealthy living out of the embraces of her
foes! And suddenly in the moonlight she sat up and began to sing
with all her might—"*Die Wacht am Rhein.*"

A RAID NIGHT

by
H.M. Tomlinson

SEPTEMBER 17, 1915. I had crossed from France to Fleet Street, and was thankful at first to have about me the things I had proved, with their suggestion of intimacy, their look of security; but I found the once familiar editorial rooms of that daily paper a little more than estranged. I thought them worse, if anything, than Ypres. Ypres is within the region where, when soldiers enter it, they abandon hope, because they have become sane at last, and their minds have a temperature a little below normal. In Ypres, whatever may have been their heroic and exalted dreams, they awake, see the world is mad, and surrender to the doom from which they know a world bereft will give them no reprieve.

There was a way in which the office of that daily paper was familiar. I had not expected it, and it came with a shock. Not only the compulsion, but the bewildering inconsequence of war was suggested by its activities. Reason was not there. It was ruled by a blind and fixed idea. The glaring artificial light, the headlong haste of the telegraph instruments, the wild litter on the floor, the rapt attention of the men scanning the news, their abrupt movements and speed when they had to cross the room, still with their gaze fixed, their expression that of those who dreaded something worse to happen; the suggestion of tension, as though the Last Trump were expected at any moment, filled me with vague alarm. The only place where that incipient panic is not usual is the front line, because there the enemy is within hail and is known to be another unlucky fool. But I allayed my anxiety. I leaned over one of the still figures, and scanned the fateful document which had given its reader the aspect of one who was staring at what the Moving Fin-

ger had done. Its message was no more than the excited whisper of
a witness who had just left a keyhole. But I realised in that moment
of surprise that this office was an essential feature of the War; without it, the War might become Peace. It provoked the emotions
which assembled civilians in ecstatic support of the sacrifices, just
as the staff of a corps headquarters, at some comfortable leagues
behind the trenches, maintains its fighting men in the place where
gas and shells tend to engender common sense and irresolution.

I left the glare of that office, its heat and half-hysterical activity,
and went into the coolness and quiet of the darkened street, and
there the dread left me that it could be a duty of mine to keep hot
pace with patriots in full stampede. The stars were wonderful. It
is such a tranquillising surprise to discover there are stars over London. Until this War, when the street illuminations were doused,
we never knew it. It strengthens one's faith to discover the Pleiades
over London; it is not true that their delicate glimmer has been
put out by the remarkable incandescent energy of our power stations. As I crossed London Bridge the City was as silent as though
it had come to the end of its days, and the shapes I could just make
out under the stars were no more substantial than the shadows of
its past. Even the Thames was a noiseless ghost. London at night
gave me the illusion that I was really hidden from the monstrous
trouble of Europe, and, at least for one sleep, had got out of the
War. I felt that my suburban street, secluded in trees and unim-
portance, was as remote from the evil I knew of as though it were
in Alaska. When I came to that street I could not see my neighbours' homes. It was with some doubt that I found my own. And
there, with three hours to go to midnight, and a book, and some
circumstances that certainly had not changed, I had retired thank-
fully into a fragment of that world I had feared we had completely
lost.

"What a strange moaning the birds in the shrubbery are making!" my companion said once. I listened to it, and thought it was strange. There was a long silence, and then she looked up sharply. "What's that?" she asked. "Listen!"

I listened. My hearing is not good.

"Nothing!" I assured her.

"There it is again." She put down her book with decision, and rose, I thought, in some alarm.

"Trains," I suggested. "The gas bubbling. The dog next door. Your imagination." Then I listened to the dogs. It was curious, but they all seemed awake and excited.

"What is the noise like?" I asked, surrendering my book on the antiquity of man.

She twisted her mouth in a comical way most seriously, and tried to mimic a deep and solemn note.

"Guns," I said to myself, and went to the front door.

Beyond the vague opposite shadows of some elms, lights twinkled in the sky, incontinent sparks, as though glow lamps on an invisible pattern of wires were being switched on and off by an idle child. That was shrapnel. I walked along the empty street a little to get a view between and beyond the villas. I turned to say something to my companion, and saw then my silent neighbours, shadowy groups about me, as though they had not approached but had materialised where they stood. We watched those infernal sparks. A shadow lit its pipe and offered me its match. I heard the guns easily enough now, but they were miles away.

A slender finger of brilliant light moved slowly across the sky, checked, and remained pointing, firmly accusatory, at something it had found in the heavens. A Zeppelin!

There it was, at first a wraith, a suggestion on the point of vanishing, and then illuminated and embodied, a celestial maggot stuck to the round of a cloud like a caterpillar to the edge of a leaf. We gazed at it silently, I cannot say for how long. The beam of light might have pinned the bright larva to the sky for the inspection of interested Londoners. Then somebody spoke. " I think it is coming our way."

I thought so too. I went indoors, calling out to the boy as I passed his room upstairs, and went to where the girls were asleep. Three miles, three minutes! It appears to be harder to waken children when a Zeppelin is coming your way. I got the elder girl awake, lifted her, and sat her on the bed, for she had become heavier, I noticed. Then I put her small sister over my shoulder, as limp and indifferent as a half-filled bag. By this time the elder one had snuggled into the foot of her bed, resigned to that place if the other end were disputed, and was asleep again. I think I became annoyed, and spoke sharply. We were in a hurry. The boy was waiting for us at the top of the stairs.

" What's up?" he asked with merry interest, hoisting his slacks.

" Come on down," I said.

We went into a central room, put coats round them, answering eager and innocent questions with inconsequence, had the cellar door and a light ready, and then went out to inspect affairs. There were more search-lights at work. Bright diagonals made a living network on the overhead dark. It was remarkable that those rigid beams should not rest on the roof of night, but that their ends should glide noiselessly about the invisible dome. The nearest of them was followed, when in the zenith, by a faint oval of light. Sometimes it discovered and broke on delicate films of high fair-weather clouds. The shells were still twinkling brilliantly, and the guns were making a rhythmless baying in the distance, like a number of alert and indignant hounds. But the Zeppelin had gone. The firing diminished and stopped.

They went to bed again, and as I had become acutely depressed, and the book now had no value, I turned in myself, assuring everyone, with the usual confidence of the military expert, that the affair was over for the night. But once in bed I found I could see there only the progress humanity had made in its movement heavenwards. That is the way with us; never to be concerned with the newest clever trick of our enterprising fellow-men till a sudden turn of affairs shows us, by the immediate threat to our own existence, that that cleverness has added to the peril of civilised society, whose house has been built on the verge of the pit. War now would be not only between soldiers. In future wars the place of honour would be occupied by the infants, in their cradles. For war is not murder. Starving children is war, and it is not murder. What treacherous lying is all the heroic poetry of battle! Men will now creep up after dark, ambushed in safety behind the celestial curtains, and drop bombs on sleepers beneath, for the greater glory of some fine figment or other. It filled me, not with wrath at the work of Kaisers and Kings, for we know what is possible with them, but with dismay at the discovery that one's fellows are so docile and credulous that they will obey any order, however abominable. The very heavens had been fouled by this obscene and pallid worm, crawling over those eternal verities to which eyes had been lifted for light when night and trouble were over-dark. God was dethroned by science. One looked startled at humanity, seeing not the accustomed countenance, but, for a moment, glimpsing instead the baleful, lidless stare of the evil of the slime, the unmentionable of a nightmare. . . .

A deafening crash brought us out of bed in one movement. I must have been dozing. Someone cried, "My children!" Another rending uproar interrupted my effort to shepherd the flock to a lower floor. There was a raucous avalanche of glass. We muddled down somehow—I forget how. I could not find the matches. Then in the dark we lost the youngest for some eternal seconds while yet another explosion shook the house. We got to the cellar stairs, and at last there they all were, their backs to the coals, sitting on lumber.

A candle was on the floor. There were more explosions, somewhat muffled. The candle-flame showed a little tremulous excitement, as if it were one of the party. It reached upwards curiously in a long, intent flame, and then shrank flat with what it had learned. We were accompanied by grotesque shadows. They stood about us on the white and unfamiliar walls. We waited. Even the shadows seemed to listen with us; they hardly moved, except when the candle-flame was nervous. Then the shadows wavered slightly. We waited. I caught the boy's eye, and winked. He winked back. The youngest, still with sleepy eyes, was trembling, though not with cold, and this her sister noticed, and put her arms about her. His mother had her hand on her boy's shoulder.

There was no more noise outside. It was time, perhaps, to go up to see what had happened. I put a raincoat over my pyjamas, and went into the street. Some of my neighbours, who were special constables, hurried by. The enigmatic night, for a time, for five minutes, or five seconds (I do not know how long it was), was remarkably still and usual. It might have been pretending that we were all mistaken. It was as though we had been merely dreaming our recent excitements. Then, across a field, a villa began to blaze. Perhaps it had been stunned till then, and had suddenly jumped into a panic of flames. It was wholly involved in one roll of fire and smoke, a sudden furnace so consuming that, when it as suddenly ceased, giving one or two dying spasms, I had but an impression of flames rolling out of windows and doors to persuade me that what I had seen was real. The night engulfed what may have been an illusion, for till then I had never noticed a house at that point.

Whispers began to pass of tragedies that were incredible in their incidence and craziness. Three children were dead in the rubble of one near villa. The ambulance that was passing was taking their father to the hospital. A woman had been blown from her bed into the street. She was unhurt, but she was insane. A long row of humbler dwellings, over which the dust was still hanging in a faint mist, had been demolished, and one could only hope the stories about that place were far from true. We were turned away when we would have assisted; all the help that was wanted was there. A stranger offered me his tobacco pouch, and it was then I found my rainproof was a lady's, and therefore had no pipe in its pocket.

The sky was suspect, and we watched it, but saw only vacuity till one long beam shot into it, searching slowly and deliberately the whole mysterious ceiling, yet hesitating sometimes, and going back on its path as though intelligently suspicious of a matter which it had passed over too quickly. It peered into the immense caverns of a cloud to which it had returned, illuminating to us unsuspected and horrifying possibilities of hiding-places above us. We expected to see the discovered enemy boldly emerge then. Nothing came out. Other beams by now had joined the pioneer, and the night became bewildering with a dazzling mesh of light. Shells joined the wandering beams, those sparks of orange and red. A world of fantastic chimney-pots and black rounds of trees leaped into being between us and the sudden expansion of a fan of yellow flame. A bomb! We just felt, but hardly heard, the shock of it. A furious succession of such bursts of light followed, a convulsive opening and shutting of night. We saw that when midnight is cleft asunder it has a fiery inside.

The eruptions ceased. Idle and questioning, not knowing we had heard the last gun and bomb of the affair, a little stunned by the maniacal rapidity and violence of this attack, we found ourselves gazing at the familiar and shadowy peace of our suburb as we have always known it. It had returned to that aspect. But something had gone from it for ever. It was not, and never could be again, as once we had known it. The security of our own place had been based on the goodwill or indifference of our fellow-creatures everywhere. To-night, over that obscure and unimportant street, we had seen a celestial portent illuminate briefly a little of the future of mankind.

THEM OTHERS

by
Stacy Aumonier

IT is always disturbing to me when things fall into pattern form, when, in fact, incidents of real life dovetail with each other in such a manner as to suggest the shape of a story. A story is a nice neat little thing with what is called a "working-up" and a climax, and life is a clumsy, ungraspable thing, very incomplete in its periods, and with a poor sense of climax. In fact, death—which is a very uncertain quantity—is the only definite note it strikes, and even death has an uncomfortable way of setting other things in motion. If, therefore, in telling you about my friend Mrs. Ward, I am driven to the usual shifts of the story-teller, you must believe me that it is because this narrative concerns visions: Mrs. Ward's visions, my visions, and your visions. Consequently I am dependent upon my own poor powers of transcription to mould these visions into some sort of shape, and am driven into the position of a story-teller against my will.

The first vision, then, concerns the back view of the Sheldrake Road, which, as you know, butts on to the railway embankment near Dalston Junction Station. If you are of an adventurous turn of mind you shall accompany me, and we will creep up on to the embankment together and look down into these back yards. (We shall be liable to a fine of £2, according to a bye-law of the Railway Company, for doing so, but the experience will justify us.)

There are twenty-two of these small buff-brick houses huddled together in this road, and there is surely no more certain way of judging not only the character of the individual inhabitants but of their mode of life than by a survey of these somewhat pathetic yards. Is it not, for instance, easy to determine the timid, well-ordered mind of little Miss Porson, the dressmaker at number nine, by its garden of neat mud paths, with its thin patch of meagre grass, and the small bed of skimpy geraniums? Cannot one read the tragedy of those dreadful Alleson people at number four? The garden is a wilderness of filth and broken bottles, where even the weeds seem chary of establishing themselves. In fact, if we listen carefully—-and the trains are not making too much noise—we can hear the shrill crescendo of Mrs. Alleson's voice cursing at her husband in the kitchen, the half-empty gin bottle between them.

The methodical pushfulness and practicability of young Mr. and Mrs. Andrew MacFarlane is evident at number fourteen. They have actually grown a patch of potatoes, and some scarlet-runners, and there is a chicken-run near the house.

Those irresponsible people, the O'Neals, have grown a bed of hollyhocks, but for the rest the garden is untidy and unkempt. One could almost swear they were connected in some obscure way with the theatrical profession.

Mrs. Abbot's garden is a sort of playground. It has asphalt paths, always swarming with small and not too clean children, and there are five lines of washing suspended above the mud. Every day seems to be Mrs. Abbot's washing day. Perhaps she " does " for others. Sam Abbot is certainly a lazy, insolent old rascal, and such always seem destined to be richly fertile. Mrs. Abbot is a pleasant " body," though.

The Greens are the swells of the road. George Green is in the grocery line, and both his sons are earning good money, and one daughter has piano lessons. The narrow strip of yard is actually divided into two sections, a flower-garden and a kitchen-garden. And they are the only people who have flower-boxes in the front.

Number eight is a curious place. Old Mr. Bilge lives there. He spends most of his time in the garden, but nothing ever seems to come up. He stands about in his shirt-sleeves, and with a circular paper hat on his head, like a printer. They say he was formerly a corn merchant, but has lost all his money. He keeps the garden very neat and tidy, but nothing seems to grow. He stands there staring at the beds, as though he found their barrenness quite unaccountable.

Number eleven is unoccupied, and number twelve is Mrs. Ward's.

We come now to an important vision, and I want you to come down with me from the embankment and to view Mrs. Ward's garden from inside, and also Mrs. Ward as I saw her on that evening when I had occasion to pay my first visit.

It had been raining, but the sun had come out. We wandered round the paths together, and I can see her old face now, lined and seamed with years of anxious toil and struggle; her long bony arms, slightly withered, but moving restlessly in the direction of snails and slugs.

"Oh dear! Oh dear!" she was saying. "What with the dogs, and the cats, and the snails, and the trains, it's wonderful anything comes up at all!"

Mrs. Ward's garden has a character of its own, and I cannot account for it. There is nothing very special growing—a few pansies and a narrow border of London Pride, several clumps of unrecognisable things that haven't flowered, the grass patch in only fair order, and at the bottom of the garden an unfinished rabbit-hutch. But there is about Mrs. Ward's garden an atmosphere. There is something about it that reflects in her placid eye the calm, somewhat contemplative way she has of looking right through things, as though they didn't concern her too closely. As though, in fact, she were too occupied with her own inner visions.

"No," she says in answer to my query. "We don't mind the trains at all. In fact, me and my Tom we often come out here and sit after supper. And Tom smokes his pipe. We like to hear the trains go by."

She gazes abstractedly at the embankment.

"I like to hear things . . . going on and that. It's Dalston Junction a little further on. The trains go from there to all parts, right out into the country they do . . . ever so far. . . . My Ernie went from Dalston."

She adds the last in a changed tone of voice. And now perhaps we come to the most important vision of all—Mrs. Ward's vision of "my Ernie."

I ought perhaps to mention that I had never met "my Ernie." I can only see him through Mrs. Ward's eyes. At the time when I met her, he had been away at the War for nearly a year. I need hardly say that "my Ernie" was a paragon of sons. He was brilliant, handsome, and incredibly clever. Everything that "my Ernie" said was treasured. Every opinion that he expressed stood. If "my Ernie" liked anyone, that person was always a welcome guest. If "my Ernie" disliked anyone they were not to be tolerated, however plausible they might appear.

I had seen Ernie's photograph, and I must confess that he appeared a rather weak, extremely ordinary looking young man, but then I would rather trust to Mrs. Ward's visions than the art of any photographer.

Tom Ward was a mild, ineffectual-looking old man, with something of Mrs. Ward's placidity but with nothing of her strong individual poise. He had some job in a gas works. There was also a daughter named Lily, a brilliant person who served in a tea-shop, and sometimes went to theatres with young men. To both husband and daughter Mrs. Ward adopted an affectionate, mothering, almost pitying attitude. But with " my Ernie," it was quite a different thing. I can see her stooping figure, and her silver-white hair gleaming in the sun as we come to the unfinished rabbit-hutch, and the curious wistful tones of her voice as she touches it and says :

" When my Ernie comes home. . . ."

The War to her was some unimaginable but disconcerting affair centred round Ernie. People seemed to have got into some desperate trouble, and Ernie was the only one capable of getting them out of it. I could not at that time gauge how much Mrs. Ward realised the dangers the boy was experiencing. She always spoke with conviction that he would return safely. Nearly every other sentence contained some reference to things that were to happen " when my Ernie comes home." What doubts and fears she had were only recognisable by the subtlest shades in her voice.

When we looked over the wall into the deserted garden next door, she said :

" Oh dear ! I'm afraid they'll never let that place. It's been empty since the Stellings went away. Oh, years ago, before this old war."

II

It was on the occasion of my second visit that Mrs. Ward told me more about the Stellings. It appeared that they were a German family, of all things! There was a Mr. Stelling, and a Mrs. Frow Stelling, and two boys.

Mr. Stelling was a watchmaker, and he came from a place called Bremen. It was a very sad story Mrs. Ward told me. They had only been over here for ten months when Mr. Stelling died, and Mrs. Frow Stelling and the boys went back to Germany.

During the time of the Stellings' sojourn in the Sheldrake Road it appeared that the Wards had seen quite a good deal of them,

and though it would be an exaggeration to say that they ever became great friends, they certainly got through that period without
any unpleasantness, and even developed a certain degree of intimacy.

" Allowing for their being foreigners," Mrs. Ward explained,
" they were quite pleasant people."

On one or two occasions they invited each other to supper, and
I wish my visions were sufficiently clear to envisage those two
families indulging this social habit.

According to Mrs. Ward, Mr. Stelling was a kind little man
with a round fat face. He spoke English fluently, but Mrs. Ward
objected to his table manners.

" When my Tom eats," she said, " you don't hear a sound—I
look after that! But that Mr. Stelling. . . . Oh dear!"

The trouble with Mrs. Stelling was that she could only speak a
few words of English, but Mrs. Ward said " she was a pleasant
enough little body," and she established herself quite definitely in
Mrs. Ward's affections for the reason that she was so obviously
and so passionately devoted to her two sons.

" Oh, my word, though, they do have funny ways—these foreigners," she continued. " The things they used to eat! Most peculiar! I've known them eat stewed prunes with hot meat! "

Mrs. Ward repeated, " Stewed prunes with hot meat!" several
times, and shook her head, as though this exotic mixture was a
thing to be sternly discouraged. But she acknowledged that Mrs.
Frow Stelling was in some ways a very good cook; in fact, her
cakes were really wonderful, " the sort of thing you can't ever buy
in a shop."

About the boys there seemed to be a little divergence of opinion.
They were both also fat-faced, and their heads were " almost shaved
like convicts." The elder one wore spectacles and was rather noisy,

but :

"My Ernie liked the younger one. Oh yes, my Ernie said that young Hans was quite a nice boy. It was funny the way they spoke, funny and difficult to understand."

It was very patent that between the elder boy and Ernie, who were of about the same age, there was an element of rivalry which was perhaps more accentuated in the attitude of the mothers than in the boys themselves. Mrs. Ward could find little virtue in this elder boy. Most of her criticism of the family was levelled against him. The rest she found only a little peculiar. She said she had never heard such a funny Christian name as Frow. Florrie she had heard of, and even Flora, but not *Frow*. I suggested that perhaps Frow might be some sort of title, but she shook her head and said that that was what she was always known as in the Sheldrake Road, "Mrs. Frow Stelling."

In spite of Mrs. Ward's lack of opportunity for greater intimacy on account of the language problem, her own fine imaginative qualities helped her a great deal. And in one particular she seemed curiously vivid. She gathered an account from one of them—I'm not sure whether it was Mr. or Mrs. Frow Stelling or one of the boys—of a place they described near their home in Bremen. There was a narrow street of high buildings by a canal, and a little bridge that led over into a gentleman's park. At a point where the canal turned sharply eastwards there was a clump of linden-trees, where one could go in the summer-time, and under their shade one might sit and drink light beer, and listen to a band that played in the early part of the evening.

Mrs. Ward was curiously clear about that. She said she often thought about Mr. Stelling sitting there after his day's work. It must have been very pleasant for him, and he seemed to miss this luxury in Dalston more than anything. Once Ernie, in a friendly

mood, had taken him into the four-ale bar of "The Unicorn" at
the corner of the Sheldrake Road, but Mr. Stelling did not seem
happy. Ernie acknowledged afterwards that it had been an unfortunate evening. The bar had been rather crowded, and there was a
man and two women who had all been drinking too much. In any
case, Mr. Stelling had been obviously restless there, and he had
said afterwards :

"It is not that one wishes to drink only . . ."

And he had shaken his fat little head, and had never been
known to visit "The Unicorn" again.

Mr. Stelling died quite suddenly of some heart trouble, and
Mrs. Ward could not get it out of her head that his last illness was
brought about by his disappointment and grief in not being able to
go and sit quietly under the linden-trees after his day's work and
listen to a band.

"You know, my dear," she said, "when you get accustomed to
a thing it's *bad* for you to leave it off."

When poor Mr. Stelling died, Mrs. Frow Stelling was heart-
broken, and I have reason to believe that Mrs. Ward went in and
wept with her, and in their dumb way they forged the chains of
some desperate understanding. When Mrs. Frow Stelling went back
to Germany they promised to write to each other. But they never
did, and for a very good reason. As Mrs. Ward said, she was "no
scholard," and as for Mrs. Frow Stelling, her English was such a
doubtful quantity, she probably never got beyond addressing the
envelope.

"That was three years ago," said Mrs. Ward. "Them boys
must be eighteen and nineteen now."

III

If I had intruded too greatly into the intimacy of Mrs. Ward's life, one of my excuses must be, not that I am "a scholard," but that I am in any case able to read a simple English letter. I was, in fact, on several occasions "requisitioned." When Lily was not at home, someone had to read Ernie's letters out loud. The arrival of Ernie's letters was always an inspiring experience. I should perhaps be in the garden with Mrs. Ward when Tom would come hurrying out to the back, and call out:

"Mother! a letter from Ernie!"

And then there would be such excitement and commotion. The first thing was always to hunt for Mrs. Ward's spectacles. They were never where she had put them. Tom would keep on turning the letter over in his hands, and examining the postmark, and he would reiterate:

"Well, what did you do with them, mother?"

At length they would be found in some unlikely place, and she would take the letter tremblingly to the light. I never knew quite how much Mrs. Ward could read. She could certainly read a certain amount. I saw her old eyes sparkling and her tongue moving jerkily between her parted lips, as though she were formulating the words she read, and she would keep on repeating:

"T'ch! T'ch! Oh dear, oh dear, the *things* he says!"

And Tom impatiently by the door would say:

"Well, what *does* he say?"

She never attempted to read the letter out loud, but at last she would wipe her spectacles and say:

"Oh, you read it, sir. The *things* he says!"

They were indeed very good letters of Ernie's, written apparently in the highest spirits. There was never a grumble, not a word. One might gather that he was away with a lot of young bloods on some sporting expedition, in which football, rags, singsongs, and strange feeds played a conspicuous part. I read a good many of Ernie's letters, and I do not remember that he ever made a single reference to the horrors of war, or said anything about his own personal discomforts. The boy must have had something of his mother in him in spite of the photograph.

And between the kitchen and the yard Mrs. Ward would spend her day placidly content, for Ernie never failed to write. There was sometimes a lapse of a few days, but the letter seldom failed to come every fortnight.

It would be difficult to know what Mrs. Ward's actual conception of the War was. She never read the newspapers, for the reason, as she explained, that "there was nothing in them these days except about this old war." She occasionally dived into *Reynolds' Newspaper* on Sundays to see if there were any interesting law cases or any news of a romantic character. There was nothing romantic in the war news. It was all preposterous. She did indeed read the papers for the first few weeks, but this was for the reason that she had some vague idea that they might contain some account of Ernie's doings. But as they did not, she dismissed them with contempt.

But I found her one night in a peculiarly preoccupied mood. She was out in the garden, and she kept staring abstractedly over the fence into the unoccupied ground next door. It appeared that it had dawned upon her that the War was to do with "these Germans," that in fact we were fighting the Germans, and then she thought of the Stellings. Those boys would now be about eighteen and nineteen. They would be fighting too. They would be fighting against Ernie. This seemed very peculiar.

"Of course," she said, "I never took to that elder boy—a greedy, rough sort of a boy he was. But I'm sure my Ernie wouldn't hurt young Hans."

She meditated for a moment as though she were contemplating

what particular action Ernie would take in the matter. She knew
he didn't like the elder boy, but she doubted whether he would
want to do anything very violent to him.

" They went out to a music-hall one night together," she explained, as though a friendship cemented in this luxurious fashion
could hardly be broken by an unreasonable display of passion.

IV

It was a few weeks later that the terror suddenly crept into Mrs.
Ward's life. Ernie's letters ceased abruptly. The fortnight passed,
then three weeks, four weeks, five weeks, and not a word. I don't
think that Mrs. Ward's character at any time stood out so vividly
as during those weeks of stress. It is true she appeared a little fee-
bler, and she trembled in her movements, whilst her eyes seemed
abstracted as though all the power in them were concentrated in
her ears, alert for the bell or the knock. She started visibly at odd
moments, and her imagination was always carrying her tempestu-
ously to the front door, only to answer—a milkman or a casual
hawker. But she never expressed her fear in words. When Tom
came home—he seemed to have aged rapidly—he would come
bustling into the garden, and cry out tremblingly :

" There ain't been no letter to-day, mother? "

And she would say quite placidly :

" No, not to-day, Tom. It'll come to-morrow, I expect."

And she would rally him and talk of little things, and get busy
with his supper. And in the garden I would try and talk to her
about her clumps of pansies, and the latest yarn about the neighbours, and I tried to get between her and the rabbit-hutch with its
dumb appeal of incompletion. And I would notice her staring
curiously over into the empty garden next door, as though she were
being assailed by some disturbing apprehensions. Ernie would not

hurt that eldest boy . . . but suppose . . . if things were reversed
. . . there was something inexplicable and terrible lurking in this
passive silence.

During this period the old man was suddenly taken very ill.
He came home one night with a high temperature and developed
pneumonia. He was laid up for many weeks, and she kept back
the telegram that came while he was almost unconscious, and she
tended him night and day, nursing her own anguish with a calm
face.

For the telegram told her that her Ernie was " missing and believed wounded."

I do not know at what period she told the father this news, but
it was certainly not till he was convalescent. And the old man
seemed to sink into a kind of apathy. He sat feebly in front of the
kitchen fire, coughing and making no effort to control his grief.

Outside the great trains went rushing by, night and day. Things
were " going on," but they were all meaningless, cruel.

We made inquiries at the War Office, but they could not ampli-
fy the laconic telegram.

And then the winter came on, and the gardens were bleak in
the Sheldrake Road. And Lily ran away and married a young
tobacconist, who was earning twenty-five shillings a week. And
old Tom was dismissed from the gasworks. His work was not
proving satisfactory. And he sat about at home and moped. And
in the meantime the price of foodstuffs was going up, and coals
were a luxury. And so in the early morning Mrs. Ward would go
off and work for Mrs. Abbot at the wash-tub, and she would earn
eight or twelve shillings a week.

It is difficult to know how they managed during those days, but
one could see that Mrs. Ward was buoyed up by some poignant
hope. She would not give way. Eventually old Tom did get some

work to do at a stationer's. The work was comparatively light, and the pay equally so, so Mrs. Ward still continued to work for Mrs. Abbot.

My next vision of Mrs. Ward concerns a certain winter evening. I could not see inside the kitchen, but the old man could be heard complaining. His querulous voice was rambling on, and Mrs. Ward was standing by the door leading into the garden. She had returned from her day's work and was scraping a pan out into a bin near the door. A train shrieked by, and the wind was blowing a fine rain against the house. Suddenly she stood up and looked at the sky; then she pushed back her hair from her brow and frowned at the dark house next door. Then she turned and said :

"Oh, I don't know, Tom; if we've got to do it, we *must* do it. If them others can stand it, we can stand it. Whatever them others do, we can do."

And then my visions jump rather wildly. And the War becomes to me epitomised in two women. One in this dim doorway in our obscure suburb of Dalston, scraping out a pan, and the other perhaps in some dark high house near a canal on the outskirts of Bremen. Them others! These two women silently enduring. And the trains rushing by, and all the dark, mysterious forces of the night operating on them equivocally.

Poor Mrs. Frow Stelling! Perhaps those boys of hers are " missing, believed killed." Perhaps they are killed for certain. She is as much outside " the things going on " as Mrs. Ward. Perhaps she is equally as patient, as brave.

And Mrs. Ward enters the kitchen, and her eyes are blazing with a strange light as she says :

" We'll hear to-morrow, Tom. And if we don't hear to-morrow, we'll hear the next day. And if we don't hear the next day, we'll hear the day after. And if we don't . . . if we don't never hear . . .

again . . . if them others can stand it, we can stand it, I say."

And then her voice breaks, and she cries a little, for endurance has its limitations, and—the work is hard at Mrs. Abbot's.

And the months go by, and she stoops a little more as she walks, and—someone has thrown a cloth over the rabbit-hutch with its unfinished roof. And Mrs. Ward is curiously introspective. It is useless to tell her of the things of the active world. She listens politely but she does not hear. She is full of reminiscences of Ernie's and Lily's childhood. She recounts again and again the story of how Ernie when he was a little boy ordered five tons of coal from a coal merchant to be sent to a girls' school in Dalston High Road. She describes the coal carts arriving in the morning, and the consternation of the head-mistress.

"Oh dear, oh dear," she says; "the things he did!"

She does not talk much of the Stellings, but one day she says meditatively :

"Mrs. Frow Stelling thought a lot of that boy Hans. So she did of the other, as far as that goes. It's only natural like, I suppose."

V

As time went on Tom Ward lost all hope. He said he was convinced that the boy was killed. Having arrived at this conclusion he seemed to become more composed. He gradually began to accustom himself to the new point of view. But with Mrs. Ward the exact opposite was the case.

She was convinced that the boy was alive, but she suffered terribly.

There came a time—it was in early April—when one felt that the strain could not last. She seemed to lose all interest in the passing world and lived entirely within herself. Even the arrival of Lily's baby did not rouse her. She looked at the child queerly, as though she doubted whether any useful or happy purpose was served by its appearance.

It was a boy.

In spite of her averred optimism she lost her tremulous sense of apprehension when the bell went or the front door was tapped. She let the milkman—and even the postman—wait.

When she spoke it was invariably of things that happened years ago.

Sometimes she talked about the Stellings, and one Sunday she made a strange pilgrimage out to Finchley and visited Mr. Stelling's grave. I don't know what she did there, but she returned looking very exhausted and unwell. As a matter of fact she was unwell for some days after this visit, and she suffered violent twinges of rheumatism in her legs.

I now come to my most unforgettable vision of Mrs. Ward.

It was a day at the end of April, and warm for the time of the year. I was standing in the garden with her and it was nearly dark. A goods train had been shunting, and making a great deal of noise in front of the house, and at last had disappeared. I had not been able to help noticing that Mrs. Ward's garden was curiously neglected for her for the time of year. The grass was growing on the paths, and the snails had left their silver trail over all the fences.

I was telling her a rumour I had heard about the railway porter and his wife at number twenty-three, and she seemed fairly interested, for she had known John Hemsley, the porter, fifteen years ago, when Ernie was a baby. There were two old broken Windsor chairs in the garden, and on one was a zinc basin in which were some potatoes. She was peeling them, as Lily and her husband were coming to supper. By the kitchen door was a small sink. When she had finished the potatoes, she stood up and began to pour the water down the sink, taking care not to let the skins go too. I was noticing her old bent back, and her long bony hands gripping the sides of the basin, when suddenly a figure came limping round the bend of the house from the side passage, and two arms were thrown around her waist, and a voice said :

"Mind them skins don't go down the sink, mother. They'll stop it up!"

VI

As I explained to Ernie afterwards, it was an extremely foolish thing to do. If his mother had had anything wrong with her heart, it might have been very serious. There have been many cases of people dying from the shock of such an experience.

As it was, she merely dropped the basin and stood there trembling like a leaf, and Ernie laughed loud and uproariously. It must have been three or four minutes before she could regain her speech, and then all she could manage to say was :

"Ernie! . . . My Ernie!"

And the boy laughed and ragged his mother, and pulled her into the house, and Tom appeared and stared at his son, and said feebly :

"Well, I never!"

I don't know how it was that I found myself intruding upon the sanctity of the inner life of the Ward family that evening. I had never had a meal there before, but I felt I was holding a sort of watching brief over the soul and body of Mrs. Ward. I had had a little medical training in my early youth, and this may have been one of the reasons which prompted me to stay.

When Lily and her husband appeared we sat down to a meal of mashed potatoes and onions stewed in milk, with bread and cheese, and very excellent it was.

Lily and her husband took the whole thing in a boisterous, high comedy manner that fitted in with the mood of Ernie. Old Tom sat there staring at his son, and repeating at intervals:

"Well, I never!"

And Mrs. Ward hovered round the boy's plate. Her eyes divided their time between his plate and his face, and she hardly spoke all the evening.

Ernie's story was remarkable enough. He told it disconnectedly and rather incoherently. There were moments when he rambled in a rather peculiar way, and sometimes he stammered, and seemed unable to frame a sentence. Lily's husband went out to fetch some beer to celebrate the joyful occasion, and Ernie drank his in little sips, and spluttered. The boy must have suffered considerably, and he had a wound in the abdomen, and another in the right forearm which for a time had paralysed him.

As far as I could gather, his story was this:

He and a platoon of men had been ambushed and had had to surrender. When being sent back to a base, three of them tried to escape from the train, which had been held up at night. He did not know what had happened to the other two men, but it was on this occasion that he received his abdominal wound at the hands of a guard.

He had then been sent to some infirmary, where he was fairly well treated; but as soon as his wound had healed a little, he had been suddenly sent to some fortress prison, presumably as a punishment. He hadn't the faintest idea how long he had been confined there. He said it seemed like fifteen years. It was probably nine months. He had solitary confinement in a cell, which was like a small lavatory. He had fifteen minutes' exercise every day in a yard with some other prisoners, who were Russians, he thought. He spoke to no one. He used to sing and recite in his cell, and there were times when he was quite convinced that he was "off his chump." He said he had lost "all sense of everything" when he was suddenly transferred to another prison. Here the conditions were somewhat better and he was made to work. He said he wrote six or seven letters home from there, but received no reply. The letters certainly never reached Dalston. The food was execrable, but a big improvement on the dungeon. He was only there a few weeks when he and some thirty prisoners were sent suddenly to work on the land at a kind of settlement. He said that the life there would have been tolerable if it hadn't been for the fact that the Commandant was an absolute brute. The food was worse than in the prison, and they were punished severely for the most trivial offences.

It was here, however, that he met a sailor named Martin, a Royal Naval Reservist, an elderly, thick-set man with a black beard and only one eye. Ernie said that this Martin "was an artist. He wangled everything. He had a genius for getting what he wanted. He would get a beef-steak out of a stone." In fact, it was obvious that the whole of Ernie's narrative was coloured by his vision of Martin. He said he'd never met such a chap in his life. He admired him enormously, and he was also a little afraid of him.

By some miraculous means peculiar to sailors, Martin acquired a compass. Ernie hardly knew what a compass was, but the sailor explained to him that it was all that was necessary to take you straight to England. Ernie said he "had had enough of escaping. It didn't agree with his health," but so strong was his faith and belief in Martin that he ultimately agreed to try with him.

He said Martin's method of escape was the coolest thing he'd ever seen. He planned it all beforehand. It was the fag-end of the day, and the whistle had gone, and the prisoners were trooping back across a potato field. Martin and Ernie were very slow. They lingered apparently to discuss some matter connected with the soil.

There were two sentries in sight, one near them and the other perhaps a hundred yards away. The potato field was on a slope; at the bottom of the field were two lines of barbed wire entanglements. The other prisoners passed out of sight, and the sentry near them called out something, probably telling them to hurry up. They started to go up the field when suddenly Martin staggered and clutched his throat. Then he fell over backwards and commenced to have an epileptic fit. Ernie said it was the realest thing he'd ever seen. The sentry ran up, at the same time whistling to his comrade. Ernie released Martin's collar-band and tried to help him. Both the sentries approached, and Ernie stood back. He saw them bending over the prostrate man, when suddenly a most extraordinary thing happened. Both their heads were brought together with fearful violence. One fell completely senseless, but the other staggered forward and groped for his rifle.

When Ernie told this part of the story he kept dabbing his forehead with his handkerchief.

"I never seen such a man as Martin, I don't think," he said. "Lord! he had a fist like a leg of mutton. He laid 'em out neatly on the grass, took off their coats and most of their other clothes, and flung 'em over the barbed wire, and then swarmed over like a cat. I had more difficulty, but he got me across too, somehow. Then we carted the clothes away to the next line.

"We got up into a wood that night, and Martin draws out his compass and he says : 'We've got a hundred and seven miles to do in night shifts, cully. And if we make a slip we're shot as safe as a knife.' It sounded the maddest scheme in the world, but somehow I felt that Martin would get through it. The only thing that saved me was that—that I didn't have to think. I simply left everything to him. If I'd started thinking I should have gone mad. I had it fixed in my mind, 'Either he does it or he doesn't do it. I can't help it.' I reelly don't remember much about that journey. It was all a dream like. We did all our travellin' at night by compass, and hid by day. Neither of us had a word of German. But Gawd's truth! that man Martin was a marvel! He turned our trousers inside out, and made 'em look like ordinary labourers' trousers. He disappeared the first night and came back with some other old clothes. We lived mostly on raw potatoes we dug out of the ground with our hands, but not always. I believe Martin could have stole an egg from under a hen without her noticing it. He was the coolest card there ever was. Of course there was a lot of trouble one way and another. It wasn't always easy to find wooded country or protection of any sort. We often ran into people and they stared at us, and we shifted our course. But I think we were only addressed three or four times by men, and then Martin's methods were the simplest in the world. He just looked sort of blank for a moment, and then knocked them clean out and bolted. Of course they were after us all the time, and it was this constant tacking and shifting ground that took so long. Fancy! he had never a map, you know, nothing but the compass. We didn't know what sort of country we were coming to, nothing. We just crept through the night like cats. I believe Martin could see in the dark. . . . He killed a dog one night with his hands. . . . It was necessary."

VII

It was impossible to discover from Ernie how long this amazing journey lasted—the best part of two months, I believe. He was himself a little uncertain with regard to many incidents, whether they were true or whether they were hallucinations. He suffered greatly from his wound and had periods of feverishness. But one morning, he said, Martin began " prancing." He seemed to develop some curious sense that they were near the Dutch frontier.

And then, according to Ernie, "a cat wasn't in it with Martin."

He was very mysterious about the actual crossing. I gather that there had been some "clumsy" work with sentries. It was at that time that Ernie got a bullet through his arm. When he got to Holland he was very ill. It was not that the wound was a serious one, but, as he explained:

"Me blood was in a bad state. I was nearly down and out."

He was very kindly treated by some Dutch Sisters in a convent hospital. But he was delirious for a long time, and when he became more normal they wanted to communicate with his people in England, but this didn't appeal to the dramatic sense of Ernie.

"I thought I'd spring a surprise packet on you," he said, grinning.

We asked about Martin, but Ernie said he never saw him again. He went away while Ernie was delirious, and they said he had gone to Rotterdam to take ship somewhere. He thought Holland was a dull place.

During the relation of this narrative my attention was divided between watching the face of Ernie and the face of Ernie's mother.

I am quite convinced that she did not listen to the story at all. She never took her eyes from his face, and although her tongue was following the flow of his remarks, her mind was occupied with the vision of Ernie when he was a little boy, and when he ordered five tons of coal to be sent to the girls' school.

When he had finished, she said:

"Did you meet either of them young Stellings?"

And Ernie laughed rather uproariously and said no, he didn't have the pleasure of renewing their acquaintance.

On his way home, it appeared, he had reported himself at headquarters, and his discharge was inevitable.

"So now you'll be able to finish the rabbit-hutch," said Lily's husband, and we all laughed again, with the exception of Mrs. Ward.

I found her later standing alone in the garden. It was a warm spring night. There was no moon, but the sky appeared restless with its burden of trembling stars. She had an old shawl drawn round her shoulders, and she stood there very silently with her arms crossed.

"Well, this is splendid news, Mrs. Ward," I said.

She started a little, and coughed, and pulled the shawl closer round her.

She said, "Yes, sir," very faintly.

I don't think she was very conscious of me. She still appeared immersed in the contemplation of her inner visions. Her eyes settled upon the empty house next door, and I thought I detected the trail of a tear glistening on her cheeks. I lighted my pipe. We could hear Ernie, and Lily, and Lily's husband still laughing and talking inside.

"She used to make a very good puddin'," Mrs. Ward said suddenly, at random. "Dried fruit inside, and that. My Ernie liked it very much. . . ."

Somewhere away in the distance—probably outside The Unicorn—someone was playing a cornet. A train crashed by and disappeared, leaving a trail of foul smoke which obscured the sky. The smoke cleared slowly away. I struck another match to light my pipe.

It was quite true. On either side of her cheek a tear had trickled. She was trembling a little, worn out by the emotions of the evening.

There was a moment of silence, unusual for Dalston.

"It's all very . . . perplexin' and that," she said quietly.

And then I knew for certain that in that great hour of her happiness her mind was assailed by strange and tremulous doubts. She was thinking of "them others" a little wistfully. She was doubting whether one could rejoice—when the thing became clear and actual to one—without sending out one's thoughts into the dark garden to "them others" who were suffering too. And she had come out into this little meagre yard at Dalston, and had gazed through the mist and smoke upwards to the stars, because she wanted peace intensely, and so she sought it within herself, because she knew that real peace is a thing which concerns the heart alone.

And so I left her standing there, and I went my way, for I knew that she was wiser than I.

BEHIND THE FRONT LINE

COMING HOME

by
Edith Wharton

THE young men of our American Relief Corps are beginning to come back from the front with stories.

There was no time to pick them up during the first months—the whole business was too wild and grim. The horror has not decreased, but nerves and sight are beginning to be disciplined to it. In the earlier days, moreover, such fragments of experiences as one got were torn from their setting like bits of flesh scattered by shrapnel. Now things that seemed disjointed are beginning to link themselves together, and the broken bones of history are rising from the battle-fields.

I cannot say that, in this respect, all the members of the Relief Corps have made the most of their opportunity. Some are obtuse or perhaps simply inarticulate; others, when going beyond the bald statistics of their job, tend at once to drop into sentiment and cinema scenes; and none but H. Macy Greer has the gift of making the thing told seem as true as if one had seen it. So it is on H. Macy Greer that I depend, and when his motor dashes him back to Paris for supplies, I never fail to hunt him down and coax him to my rooms for dinner and a long cigar.

Greer is a small, hard-muscled youth, with pleasant manners, a sallow face, straight, hemp-coloured hair, and grey eyes of unexpected inwardness. He has a voice like thick soup, and speaks with the slovenly drawl of the new generation of Americans, dragging his words along like reluctant dogs on a string, and depriving his narrative of every shade of expression that intelligent intonation gives. But his eyes see so much that they make one see even what his foggy voice obscures.

Some of his tales are dark and dreadful, some are unutterably sad, and some end in a huge laugh of irony. I am not sure how I ought to classify the one I have written down here.

II

On my first dash to the Northern fighting line—Greer told me the other night—I carried supplies to an ambulance, where the surgeon asked me to have a talk with an officer who was badly wounded and fretting for news of his people in the East of France.

He was a young Frenchman, a cavalry Lieutenant, trim and slim, with a pleasant smile and obstinate blue eyes that I liked. He looked as if he could hold on tight when it was worth his while. He had had a leg smashed, poor devil, in the first fighting in Flanders, and had been dragging on for weeks in the squalid camp hospital where I found him. He didn't waste any words on himself, but began at once on his family. They were living, when the War broke out, at their country place in the Vosges; his father and mother, his sister, just eighteen, and his brother Alain, two years younger. His father, the Comte de Réchamp, had married late in life and was over seventy; his mother, a good deal younger, was crippled with rheumatism; and there was, besides—to round off the group—a helpless but intensely alive and domineering old grandmother, about whom all the others revolved. You know how French families hang together, and throw out branches that make new roots but keep hold of the central trunk, like that tree— what's it called?—that they give pictures of in books about the East.

Jean de Réchamp—that was my Lieutenant's name—told me his family was a typical case. "We are very *province*," he said.

"My people live at Réchamp all the year. We have a house at Nancy—rather a fine old *hôtel*—but my parents go there only once in two or three years, for a few weeks. That is our 'season.' . . . Imagine the point of view! Or, rather, don't because you can't. . . ." (He had been about the world a good deal and known something of other angles of vision.)

Well, of this helpless, exposed little knot of people he had had no word—simply nothing—since the first of August. He was at home, staying with them, when the War broke out. He was mobilised the first day and had only time to throw his traps into a cart and dash to the station. His depôt was on the other side of France, and communication with the East by mail and telegraph was completely interrupted during the first weeks. His regiment was sent at once to the fighting line, and the first news he got came to him in October, from a communique in a Paris paper a month old, saying: "The enemy yesterday retook Réchamp." After that, dead silence: and the poor devil left in the trenches to digest that "*retook*"!

There are thousands and thousands of just such cases; and men bearing them, and cracking jokes, and hitting out as hard as they can. Jean de Réchamp knew this, and tried to crack jokes too—but he got his leg smashed just afterwards, and ever since he'd been lying on a straw pallet under a horse-blanket, saying to himself: "Réchamp retaken."

"Of course," he explained, with a weary smile, "as long as you can tot up your daily bag in the trenches it is a sort of satisfaction—though I don't quite know why; anyhow, you're so dead beat at night that no dreams come. But lying here staring at the ceiling one goes through the whole business once an hour, at the least: the attack, the slaughter, the ruins . . . and worse. . . . Haven't I seen and heard things enough on *this* side to know what has been

happening on the other? Don't try to sugar the dose. I *like* it
bitter."

I was three days in the neighbourhood, and I went back every
day to see him. He liked to talk to me because he had a faint hope
of my getting news of his family when I returned to Paris. I
hadn't much myself, but there was no use telling him so. Besides,
things changed from day to day, and when we parted I promised
to get word to him as soon as I could find out anything. We both
knew, of course, that that wouldn't be till Réchamp was taken a
third time—by his own troops; and perhaps, soon after that, I
should be able to get there, or near there, and make inquiries myself. To make sure that I should forget nothing, he drew the
family photographs from under his pillow, and handed them
over: the little witch-grandmother with a face like a withered
walnut; the father, a fine broken-looking old boy with a Roman
nose and a weak chin; the mother, in crêpe, simple, serious, and
provincial; the little sister, ditto; and Alain, the young brother—
just the age the brutes have been carrying off to German prisons
—an overgrown, thread-paper boy with too much forehead and
eyes, and not a muscle in his body. A charming-looking family,
distinguished and amiable; but all, except the grandmother, rather
usual. The kind of people who come in sets.

As I packed the photographs I noticed that another lay face
down by his pillow. "Is that for me too?" I asked.

He coloured and shook his head, and I felt I had blundered.
But after a moment he turned the photograph over and held it
out.

"It is the young girl I am engaged to. She was at Réchamp
visiting my parents when War was declared; but she was to leave
the day after I did." He hesitated. "There may have been some
difficulty about her going. . . . I should like to be sure she got

away. . . . Her name is Yvonne Malo."

He did not offer me the photograph, and I did not need it. That girl had a face of her own! Dark and keen and splendid; a type so different from the others that I found myself staring. If he had not said " *ma fiancée*," I should have understood better. After another pause, he went on: "I will give you her address in Paris. She has no family; she lives alone—she is a musician. Perhaps you may find her there." His colour deepened again as he added: "But I know nothing—I have had no news of her, either."

To ease the silence that followed I suggested: "But if she has no family, wouldn't she have been likely to stay with your people? and wouldn't that be the reason of your not hearing from her?"

"Oh no—I don't think she stayed." He seemed about to add, "If she could help it," but shut his lips and slid the picture out of sight.

As soon as I got back to Paris I made inquiries, but without result. The Germans had been pushed back from that particular spot after a fortnight's intermittent occupation; but their lines were near by, across the valley, and Réchamp was still in a net of trenches. No one could get to it, and apparently no news could come from it. For the moment, at any rate, I found it impossible to get in touch with the place.

My inquiries about Mlle. Malo were equally unfruitful. I went to the address Réchamp had given me, somewhere off in Passy, among gardens, in what they call a " square," no doubt because it is oblong—a kind of long, narrow court with rather æsthetic studio buildings round it. Mlle. Malo lived in one of them, on the top floor, the *concierge* said, and I looked up and saw a big studio window and a roof-terrace with a dead gourd dangling from a pergola. But she wasn't there, she hadn't been there, and they had no news of her. I wrote to Réchamp of my double failure; he sent me back a line of thanks; and, after that, for a long while I heard no more of him.

By the beginning of November the enemy's hold had begun to loosen in the Argonne and along the Vosges, and one day we were sent off to the east with a couple of ambulances. Of course, we had to have military chauffeurs, and the one attached to my ambulance happened to be a fellow I knew. The day before we started, in talking over our route with him, I said: "I suppose we can manage to get Réchamp now?" He looked puzzled—it was such a little place that he'd forgotten the name. "Why do you want to get there?" he wondered. I told him, and he gave an exclamation. "Good God! Of course—but how extraordinary! Jean de Réchamp's here now, in Paris, too lame for the front, and driving a motor." We stared at each other, and he went on: "He must take my place—he must go with you. I don't know how it can be done, but done it shall be."

Done it was, and the next morning I found Jean de Réchamp at the wheel of my car. He looked another fellow from the wreck I had left in the Flemish hospital; all made over, and burning with activity, but older, and with lines about his eyes. He had had news from his people in the interval, and had learnt that they were still at Réchamp, and well. What is more surprising was that Mlle. Malo was with them—had never left. Alain had been got away to England, where he remained; but none of the others had budged. They had fitted up an ambulance in the château, and Mlle. Malo and the little sister were nursing the wounded. There were not many details in the letter, and they had been a long time on their way; but their tone was so reassuring that Jean could give himself up to unclouded anticipation. You may fancy if he was grateful for the chance I was giving him; for, of course, he could not have seen his people in any other way.

Our permits, as you know, did not as a rule let us into the firing line: we only take supplies to second-line ambulances and carry back the wounded in need of delicate operations. So I wasn't in the least sure whether we should be able to go to Réchamp—though I had made up my mind to get there, anyhow.

We were about a fortnight on the way, coming and going in Champagne and the Argonne, and that gave us time to get to know each other. It was bitter cold, and after our long runs over the lonely frozen hills we used to crawl into the café of the inn—if there was one—and talk and talk. We put up in fairly rough places, generally in a farmhouse or cottage packed with soldiers; for the villages have all remained empty since the autumn, except when troops are quartered in them. Usually, to get warm, we had to go up after supper to the room we shared and get under the blankets with our clothes on. Once some jolly sisters of charity took us in at their hospice, and we slept two nights in an ice-cold white-washed cell—but what tales we heard around their kitchen fire! The sisters had stayed alone to face the Germans, had seen the town burn, and had made the Teutons turn the hose on the singed roof of their hospice and beat the fire back from it. It is a pity those sisters of charity can't marry. . . .

Réchamp told me a lot in those days. I don't believe he was talkative before the War, but his long weeks in hospital, starving for news, had unstrung him. And then he was mad with excitement at getting back to his own place. In the interval he'd heard how other people, caught in their country houses, had fared—you know the stories we all refused to believe at first, and that we now prefer not to think about. . . . Well, he'd been thinking about those stories pretty readily for some months; and he kept repeating: "My people say they're all right, but they give no details."

"You see," he explained, "there never were such helpless

beings. Even if there had been time to leave they couldn't have done it. My mother had been having one of her worst attacks of rheumatism—she was in bed, helpless, when I left. And my grand-mother, who is a demon of activity in the house, won't stir out of it. We haven't been able to coax her into the garden for years. She says it is draughty, and you know how we all feel about draughts! As for my father, he hasn't had to decide anything since the Comte de Chambord refused to adopt the Tricolour. My father decided that he was right, and since then there has been nothing particular for him to take a stand about. But I know how he be-haved just as well as if I had been there—he kept saying: ' One must act—one must act,' and sitting in his chair and doing noth-ing. Oh, I'm not disrespectful: they were *like* that in his genera-tion! Besides—it is better to laugh at things, isn't it?" And sud-denly his face would darken. . . .

On the whole, however, his spirits were good till we began to traverse the line of ruined towns between Sainte Menehould and Bar-le-Duc. "This is the way the devils came," he kept saying to me; and I saw he was hard at work picturing the work they must have done in his own neighbourhood.

"But since your sister writes that your people are safe!"

"They may have made her write that to reassure me. They'd heard I was badly wounded. And, mind you, there's never been a line from my mother."

One day, when we had passed through a particularly devastated little place, and had got from the curé some more than usually abominable details of things done there, Réchamp broke out to me over the kitchen fire of our night's lodging. "When I hear things like that I don't believe anybody who tells me my people are all right!"

"But ·you know well enough," I insisted, "that the Germans

are not all alike—that it all depends on the particular officer. . . ."

"Yes, yes, I know," he assented, with a visible effort at impartiality. "Only, you see—as one gets nearer. . . ." He went on to say that, when he had been sent from the ambulance at the front to a hospital at Moulins, he had been for a day or two in a ward next to some wounded German soldiers—bad cases, they were—and had heard them talking. They didn't know he knew German, and he had heard things. . . . There was one name always coming back in their talk—von Scharlach, Oberst von Scharlach. One of them, a young fellow, said: "I wish now I'd cut my hand off rather than do what he told us that night. . . . Every time the fever comes I see it all again. I wish I'd been struck dead first." They all said "Scharlach" with a kind of terror in their voices, as if he might hear them even there and come down on them horribly. Réchamp had asked where their regiment came from, and had been told, from the Vosges. That had set his brain working, and whenever he saw a ruined village, or heard a tale of savagery, the Scharlach nerve began to quiver. At such times it was no use reminding him that the Germans had had at least three hundred thousand men in the east in August. He simply did not listen. . . .

III

The day before we started for Réchamp his spirits flew up again, and that night he became confidential. "You've been such a friend to me that there are certain things—seeing what is ahead of us—that I should like to explain." And, noticing my surprise, he went on: "I mean about my people. The state of mind in my *milieu* must be so remote from anything you are used to in your happy country. . . . But perhaps I can make you understand. . . ."

I saw that what he wanted was to talk to me of the girl he was engaged to. Mlle. Malo, left an orphan at ten, had been the ward of a neighbour of the Réchamps, a chap with an old name and a starred château, who had lost almost everything else at baccarat before he was forty, and had repented, had the gout, and studied agriculture for the rest of his life. The girl's father was a rather brilliant painter, who died young, and her mother, who followed him in a year or two, was a Pole. You may fancy that, with such antecedents, the girl was just the mixture to shake down quietly into French country life with a gouty and repentant guardian. The Marquis de Corvenaire—that was his name—brought her down to his place, got an old maid sister to come and stay, and really, as far as one knows, brought his ward up rather decently. Now and then she used to be driven over to play with the young Réchamps, and Jean remembered her as an ugly little girl in a plaid frock, who used to invent wonderful games and get tired of playing them just when the other children were beginning to learn how. But her domineering ways and searching questions did not meet with his mother's approval, and her visits were not encouraged. When she was seventeen her guardian died and left her a little money. The maiden sister had gone dotty. There was nobody to look after Yvonne, and she went to Paris to an aunt; broke loose from the aunt when she came of age, set up her studio, travelled, painted, played the violin, knew lots of people, and never laid eyes on Jean de Réchamp till about a year before the War, when her guardian's place was sold and she had to go down there to see about her interest in the property.

The old Réchamps heard she was coming but didn't ask her to stay. Jean drove over to the shut-up château, however, and found Mlle. Malo lunching on a corner of the kitchen table. She exclaimed: "My little Jean!" flew to him with a kiss for each cheek, and made him sit down and share her omelet. . . . The ugly little girl had shed her chrysalis and you may fancy if he went back once or twice!

Mlle. Malo was staying at the château all alone, with the farmer's wife to come in and cook her dinner : not a soul in the house at night but herself and her brindled sheep-dog. She had to be there a week, and Jean finally suggested to his people to ask her to Réchamp. But at Réchamp they hesitated, coughed, looked away, said the spare rooms were all upside down, and the *valet de chambre* laid up with the mumps and the cook short-handed—till finally the irrepressible grandmother broke out : " A young girl who chooses to live alone—probably prefers to live alone!"

There was a deadly silence, and Jean didn't raise the question again; but I can imagine his blue eyes getting obstinate.

Soon after Mlle. Malo's return to Paris he followed her and began to frequent the Passy studio. The life there was unlike anything he had ever seen—or conceived as possible, short of the prairies. He had sampled the usual varieties of French womenkind, and explored most of the social layers, but he had missed the newest, that of the artistic-emancipated. I don't know much about that side myself, but from his descriptions I should think they were a good deal like intelligent Americans, except that they didn't seem to keep art and life in such watertight compartments. But his great discovery was the new girl. Apparently he had never known any before but the traditional type, which predominates in the provinces, and still persists, he tells me, in the last fastnesses of the Faubourg St. Germain. The girl who comes and goes as she pleases, reads what she likes, has opinions about what she reads, who talks, looks, and behaves with the independence of a married woman—and yet has kept the Diana freshness—think how she must have shaken up such a man's inherited view of things! Mlle. Malo did far more than make Réchamp fall in love with her : she turned his world topsy-turvy and prevented his ever again squeezing himself into his little old pigeon-hole of prejudices.

Before long they confessed their love—just like any young couple of Anglo-Saxons—and Jean went down to Réchamp to ask permission to marry her. Neither you nor I can quite enter into the state of mind of a young man of twenty-seven who has knocked about all over the globe, and been in and out of the usual sentimental coils—and who has to ask his parents' leave to get married! Don't let us try: it is no use. We should only end by picturing him an incredible ninny. But there is not a man in France who would not feel it his duty to take that step, as Jean de Réchamp did. All we can do is to accept the premise and pass on.

Well—Jean went down and asked his father and his mother and his old grandmother if they would permit him to marry Mlle. Malo; and they all with one voice said they wouldn't. There was an uproar, in fact; and the old grandmother contributed the most piercing note to the concert. Marry Mlle. Malo! A young girl who lived alone! Travelled! Spent her time with foreigners, with musicians and painters! *A young girl!* Of course, if she had been a married woman—that is, a widow—much as they would have preferred a young girl for Jean, or even, if widow it had to be, a widow of another type—still it was conceivable that, out of affection for him, they might have resigned themselves to his choice. But a young girl—bring such a young girl to Réchamp! Ask them to receive her under the same roof with their little Simone, their innocent Alain. . . .

He had a bad hour of it; but he held his own, keeping silent while they screamed, and stiffening as they began to wobble from exhaustion. Finally he took his mother apart and tried to reason with her. His arguments were not much use, but his resolution impressed her, and he saw it. As for his father, nobody was afraid of M. de Réchamp when he said: "Never while I live and there is a roof on Réchamp!" They all knew he had collapsed inside. But the grandmother was terrible. She was terrible because she was so old, and was clever at taking advantage of it. She could bring on a valvular heart attack by just sitting and holding her breath, as Jean and his mother had long since found out; and she always treated them to one when things weren't going as she liked. Madame de Réchamp promised Jean that she would intercede with her mother-in-law; but she hadn't much faith in the result, and when she came out of the old lady's room she whispered: "She's just sitting there holding her breath."

The next day Jean himself advanced to the attack. His grandmother was the most intelligent member of the family, and she knew he knew it, and liked him for having found it out; so when he had her alone she listened to him without resorting to any valvular tricks. "Of course," he explained, "you're much too clever not to understand that the times have changed, and manners with them, and that what a woman was criticised for doing yesterday she is ridiculed for not doing to-day. Nearly all the old social thou-shalt-nots have gone: intelligent people nowadays don't give a fig for them, and that simple fact has abolished them. They only existed as long as there was someone left for them to scare." His grandmother listened with a sparkle of admiration in her ancient eyes. "And, of course," Jean pursued, "that can't be the real reason for your opposing my marriage with a young girl you've always known, who has been received here——"

"Ah, that's it—we've always known her!" the old lady snapped him up.

"And what of that? I don't see——"

"Of course you don't. You are here so little: you don't hear things. . . ."

"What things?"

"Things in the air . . . that blow about. . . . You were doing your military service at the time. . . ."

"At what time?"

She leant forward and laid a warning hand on his arm. "Why did Corvenaire leave her all that money—*why?*"

"But why not—why shouldn't he?" Jean stammered, indignant. Then she unpacked her bag—a heap of vague insinuations, baseless conjectures, village tattle, all, at the last analysis, based, as he succeeded in proving, and making her own, on a word launched at random by a discharged maidservant who had retailed her grievances to the curé's housekeeper. "Oh, she does what she likes with M. le Marquis, the young miss! *She* knows how. . . ." On that single phrase the whole neighbourhood had raised a slander built of adamant.

Well, it will give you an idea of what a determined fellow Réchamp is when I tell you he pulled it down—or thought he had. He kept his temper, hunted up the servant's record, proved her to be a liar and dishonest, cast grave doubts on the discretion of the curé's housekeeper, and poured such a flood of ridicule over the whole clumsy fable, and those who had believed in it, that for sheer shamefacedness at having based her objection on such grounds, his grandmother gave way, and brought his parents toppling down with her.

All this happened a few weeks before the War, and soon afterwards Mlle. Malo came down to Réchamp. Jean had insisted on her coming; he wanted her presence there, as his betrothed, to be known to the neighbourhood. As for her, she seemed delighted to come. I could see from Réchamp's tone, when he reached this part of his story, that he rather thought I should have expected its heroine to have shown a becoming reluctance—to have stood on her dignity. He was distinctly relieved when he found that I expected no such thing.

"She is simplicity itself—it is her great quality. Vain complications don't exist for her, because she doesn't see them. . . . That is what my people can't be made to understand. . . ."

I gathered from the last phrase that the visit hadn't been a complete success, and this explained his having let out, when he first told me of his fears for his family, that he was sure Mlle. Malo would not have remained at Réchamp if she could help it. Oh no, decidedly, the visit was not a success. . . .

"You see," he explained, with a half-embarrassed smile, "it was partly her fault. Other girls as clever, but less—how shall I say?—less proud, would have adapted themselves, arranged things, avoided startling allusions. She talked to my family as naturally as she did to me. You can imagine, for instance, the effect of her saying: 'One night, after a supper at Montmartre, I was walking home with two or three pals.' It was her way of affirming her convictions, and I adored her for it—but I wished she wouldn't!"

And he depicted, to my joy, the neighbours rumbling over to call in heraldic barouches (the mothers alone, with embarrassed excuses for not bringing their daughters), and the agony of not knowing, till they were in the room, whether Yvonne would receive them with lowered lids and folded hands, sitting by in a *pose de fiancée* while the elders talked; or if she would take the opportunity to air her views on the separation of Church and State, or the necessity of making divorce easier. "It's not," he explained, "that she really takes much interest in such questions: she is much more absorbed in her music and painting. But anything her eye lights on sets her mind dancing—as she said to me once: 'It's your mother's friends' bonnets that make me stand up for divorce!'" He broke off abruptly to add: "Good God, how far off all that nonsense seems!"

IV

The next day we started for Réchamp, not sure if we could get there, but bound to, anyhow! It was the coldest day we had had, the sky still, the earth iron, and a snow-wind howling down on us from the north. The Vosges are splendid in winter. In summer they are just plump, puddingy hills; when the wind strips them they turn to mountains. And we seemed to have the whole country to ourselves—the black firs, the blue shadows, the beech-woods cracking and groaning like rigging, the bursts of snowy sunlight from cold clouds. Not a soul in sight except the sentinels guarding the railways, muffled to the eyes, or peering out of their huts of pine-boughs at the cross roads. Every now and then we passed a long string of ·75's, or a train of supply wagons or army ambulances, and at intervals a cavalry patrol cantered by, his cloak bellied out by the gale; but of ordinary people about the common jobs of life, not a sign.

The sense of loneliness and remoteness that the absence of the civilian population produces everywhere in eastern France is increased by the fact that all the names and distances have been scratched out and the signposts at the cross roads thrown down. It was done, of course, to throw the enemy off the track in September: and the signs have never been put back. The result is that one is for ever losing one's way, for the soldiers quartered in the district know only the names of their particular villages, and those on the march can tell you nothing about the places they are passing through. We had got badly off our road several times during the trip, but on the last day's run Réchamp was in his own country, and knew every yard of the way—or thought he did. We had turned off the main road and were running along between rather featureless fields and woods, crossed by a good many wood-roads with nothing to distinguish them; but he continues to push ahead, saying: "We don't turn till we get to a manor house on a stream, with a big paper mill across the road." He went on to tell me that the millowners lived in the manor and were old friends of his people: good old local stock who had lived there for generations and had done a lot for the neighbourhood.

"It's queer I don't see their village steeple from this rise. The village is just beyond the house. How the devil could I have missed the turn?" We ran on a little farther, and suddenly he stopped the motor with a jerk. We were at a cross road, with a stream running under the bank on our right. The place looked like an abandoned stoneyard. I never saw a completer ruin. To the left, a gate gaped on emptiness; to the right, a mill-wheel hung in the stream. Everything else was as flat as your dinner-table.

"Was this what you were trying to see from that rise?" I asked; and I saw a tear or two running down his face.

"They were the kindest people: their only son got himself shot the first month in Champagne——"

He had jumped out of the car and was standing staring at the level waste. "The house was there—there was a splendid lime in the court. I used to sit under it and have a glass of *vin gris de Lorraine* with the old people. . . . Over there, where that cinder heap is, all their children are buried." He walked across to the graveyard under a blackened wall—a bit of the apse of the vanished church—and sat down on a gravestone. "If the devils have done this *here*—so close to us," he burst out, and covered his face.

An old woman walked toward us down the road. Réchamp jumped up and ran to meet her. "Why, Marie-Jeanne, what are you doing in these ruins?" The old woman looked at him with unastonished eyes. She seemed incapable of any surprise. "They left my house standing. I am glad to see monsieur," she simply said. We followed her to the one house left in the waste of stones. It was a two-roomed cottage, propped against a cow-stable, but fairly decent, with a curtain in the window and a cat on the sill. Réchamp caught me by the arm and pointed to the door panel. " Oberst von Scharlach " was scrawled on it. He turned as white as your table-cloth and hung on to me for a minute; then he spoke to the old woman. " The officers were quartered here : that was the reason they spared your house?"

She nodded. " Yes; I was lucky. But the gentlemen must come in and have a mouthful."

Réchamp's finger was on the name. " And this one—this was their Commanding Officer?"

"I suppose so. Is it somebody's name?" She had evidently never speculated on the meaning of the scrawl that had saved her.

"You remember him—their Captain? Was his name Scharlach?" Réchamp persisted.

Under its rich weathering the old woman's face grew as pale as his. " Yes, that was his name—I heard it often enough."

"Describe him then. What was he like? Tall and fair? They're all that—but what else? What in particular?"

She hesitated, and then said : " This one wasn't fair. He was dark and had a scar that drew up the left corner of his mouth."

Réchamp turned to me. " It's the same. I heard the men describe him at Moulins."

We followed the old woman into the house, and while she gave us some bread and wine she told us about the wrecking of the village and the factory. It was one of the most abominable stories I have heard yet. Put together the worst of the typical horrors and you will have a fair idea of it. Murder, outrage, torture : Scharlach's programme seemed to be fairly comprehensive. She ended off by saying : " His orderly showed me a silver-mounted flute he always travelled with, and a beautiful paint-box mounted in silver, too. Before he left he sat down on my doorstep and made a painting of the ruins."

Soon after leaving this place of death we got to the second lines, and our troubles began. We had to do a lot of talking to get through the lines, but what Réchamp had just seen had made him eloquent. Luckily, too, the ambulance doctor, a charming fellow, was short of tetanus serum, and I had some left; and while I went over with him to the pine-branch hut, where he hid his wounded, I explained Réchamp's case and implored him to get us through. Finally, it was settled that we should leave the ambulance there— for in the lines the ban against motors is absolute—and drive the remaining twelve miles. A sergeant fished out of a farmhouse a toothless old woman with a furry horse harnessed to a two-wheeled trap, and we started off by roundabout wood-tracks. The horse was in no hurry, nor the old lady either; for there were bits of road that were pretty steadily curry-combed by shell, and it was to everybody's interest not to cross them before twilight. Jean de Réchamp's excitement seemed to have dropped: he sat beside me dumb as a fish, staring straight ahead of him. I didn't feel talkative either, for a word the doctor had let drop had left me thinking. "That poor old crony mind the shells? Not she!" he had said when our crazy chariot drove up. "She doesn't know them from snowflakes any more. Nothing matters to her now, except trying to outwit a German. They're all like that where Scharlach's been—you've heard of him? She had only one boy—half-witted: he cocked a broom-handle at them, and they burnt him. Oh, she'll take you to Réchamp safe enough."

"Where Scharlach's been"—so he had been as close as this to Réchamp! I was wondering if Jean knew it, and if that had sealed his lips and given him that flinty profile. The old horse's woolly flanks jogged on under the bare branches and the old woman's bent back jogged in time with it. She never once spoke or looked around at us. " It isn't the noise we make that'll give us away," I said at last; and just then the old woman turned her head and pointed silently with the osier-twig she used as a whip. Just ahead of us lay a heap of ruins : the wreck, apparently, of a great château and its dependencies. " Lermont!" Réchamp exclaimed, turning white. He made a move to jump out and then dropped back into the seat. " What's the use?" he muttered. He leant forward and touched the old woman's shoulder.

" I hadn't heard of this—when did it happen?"

" In September."

" They did it?"

" Yes. Our wounded were there. It's like this everywhere in our country."

I saw Jean stiffening himself for the next question. " At Réchamp, too?"

She relapsed into indifference. " I haven't been as far as Réchamp."

" But you must have seen people who'd been there—you must have heard."

" I've heard the masters were still there—so there must be something standing. Maybe, though," she reflected, " they are in the cellars."

We continued to jog on through the dusk.

V

" There is the stable," Réchamp burst out.

Through the dimness I could not tell which way to look; but I suppose in the thickest midnight he would have known where he was. He jumped from the trap and took the old horse by the bridle. I made out that he was guiding us into a long village street edged by houses in which every light was extinguished. The snow on the ground sent up a pale reflection, and I began to see the gabled outline of the houses and the stable at the head of the street. The place seemed as calm and unchanged as if the sound of war had never reached it.

In the open space at the end of the village Réchamp checked the horse.

"The elm—there is the old elm in front of the church!" he shouted, in a voice like a boy's. He reached back and caught me by both hands. "It was true, then—nothing's touched!" The old woman asked: "Is this Réchamp?" and he went back to the horse's head and turned the trap toward a tall gate between park walls. The gate was barred and padlocked, and not a gleam showed through the shutters of the porter's lodge; but Réchamp, after listening a minute or two, gave a low call twice repeated, and presently the lodge door opened, and an old man peered out. Well —I leave you to brush in the rest. Old family servant, tears and hugs, and so on. I know you affect to scorn the cinema, and this was it, tremolo and all. Hang it! This War's going to teach us not to be afraid of the obvious.

We piled into the trap and drove down a long avenue to the house. Black as the grave, of course; but in another minute the door opened and there, in the hall, was another servant, screening a light—and then more doors opened on another cinema scene: fine old drawing-room with family portraits, shaded lamp, domestic group about the fire. They evidently thought it was the servant coming to announce dinner; not a head turned at our approach. I could see them all over Jean's shoulder: a grey-haired lady knitting with stiff fingers, an old gentleman with a high nose and a weak chin sitting in a big carved armchair and looking more like a portrait than the portraits; a pretty girl at his feet, with a dog's head in her lap, and another girl who had a Red Cross on her sleeve, at the table with a book. She had been reading aloud in a rich veiled voice, and broke off her last phrase to say: "Dinner. . . ." Then she looked up and saw Jean. Her dark face remained perfectly calm, but she lifted her hand in a just perceptible gesture of warning, and instantly understanding he drew back and pushed the servant forward in his place.

"Madame la Comtesse—it is someone outside asking for Madame."

The dark girl jumped up and ran out into the hall. I remember wondering: "Is it because she wants to have him to herself first—or because she's afraid of their being startled?"

I wished myself out of the way, but she took no notice of me, and going straight to Jean flung her arms about him. I was behind him and could see her hands about his neck, and her brown fingers tightly locked. There wasn't much doubt about those two. . . .

The next minute she caught sight of me, and I was being rapidly scanned by a pair of the finest eyes I ever saw—I don't apply the term to their setting, though that was fine, too, but to the look itself, a look at once warm and resolute, all-promising and all-penetrating. I really can't do with fewer adjectives . . . .

Réchamp explained me, and she was full of thanks and welcome; not excessive, but—well, I don't know—eloquent! She gave every intonation all it could carry, and without the least emphasis: that is the wonder.

She went back to "prepare" the parents, as they say in melodramas; and in a minute or two we followed. What struck me at first was that these insignificant and inadequate people had command of the grand gesture—had *la ligne*. The mother had laid aside her knitting—*not* dropped it—and stood waiting with open arms. But even in clasping her son she seemed to include me in her welcome. I don't know how to describe it; but they never let me feel I was in the way. I suppose that is part of what you call distinction; knowing instinctively how to deal with unusual moments.

All the while, I was looking about me at the fine, secure, old room, in which nothing seemed altered or disturbed, the portraits smiling from the walls, the servants beaming in the doorway— and wondering how such things could have survived in the trail of death and havoc we had been following.

The same thought had evidently struck Jean, for he dropped his sister's hand and turned to gaze about him, too.

" Then nothing's touched—*nothing?* I don't understand," he stammered.

Monsieur de Réchamp raised himself majestically from his chair, crossed the room, and lifted Yvonne Malo's hand to his lips. " Nothing is touched—thanks to this hand and this brain."

Madame de Réchamp was shining on her son through tears. " Ah, yes—we owe it all to Yvonne."

" All, all! Grandmamma will tell you!" Simone chimed in; and Yvonne, brushing aside their praise with a half-impatient laugh, said to her betrothed : " But your grandmother! You must go up to her at once."

A wonderful specimen, that grandmother : I was taken to see her after dinner. She sat by the fire in a bare panelled bedroom, bolt upright in an armchair, a knitting-table at her elbow with a shaded lamp on it. She was even more withered and ancient than she looked in her photograph, and I judge she'd never been pretty; but she somehow made me feel as though I'd got through with prettiness. I don't know exactly what she reminded me of : a dried bouquet or something rich and clovy that had turned brittle through long keeping in a sandal-wood box. I suppose her sandal-wood box had been Good Society. Well, I had a rare evening with her. Jean and his parents were called down to see the curé, who had hurried over to the château when he heard of the young man's arrival; and the old lady asked me to stay on and chat with her. She related their experiences with uncommon detachment, seeming chiefly to resent the indignity of having been made to descend into the cellar—"to avoid French shells, if you'll believe it: the Germans had the decency not to bombard us," she observed impartially. I was so struck with the absence of rancour in her tone that finally, out of sheer curiosity, I made an allusion to the horror of having the enemy under one's roof. "Oh, I might almost say I didn't see them," she returned. "I never go downstairs any longer; and they didn't do me the honour of coming beyond my door. A glance sufficed them—*une vieille femme comme moi!*" she added with a phosphorescent gleam of coquetry.

"But they searched the château, surely?"

"Oh, a mere form; they were *très bien—très bien*," she almost snapped at me. "There was a first moment, of course, when we feared it might be hard to get Monsieur de Réchamp away with my young grandson; but Mlle. Malo managed that very cleverly. They slipped off while the officers were dining." She looked at me with the smile of some arch old lady in a Louis XV. pastel. "My grandson Jean's *fiancée* is a very clever young woman: in my time no young girl would have been so sure of herself, so cool and quick. After all, there is something to be said for the new way of bringing up girls. My poor daughter-in-law, at Yvonne's age, was a bleating babe: she is so still, at times. The convent doesn't develop character. I am glad Yvonne was not brought up in a convent." And this champion of tradition smiled on me more intensely.

Little by little I got from her the story of the German approach :
the distracted fugitives pouring in from the villages north of
Réchamp, the sound of the distant cannonading, and suddenly,
the next afternoon, after a reassuring lull, the sight of a single
spiked helmet at the end of the drive. In a few minutes a dozen
followed : mostly officers; then all at once the place hummed with
them. There were supply waggons and motors in the court, bundles of hay, stacks of rifles, artillerymen unharnessing and rubbing
down their horses. The crowd was hot and thirsty, and in a moment the old lady, to her amazement, saw wine and cider being
handed about by the Réchamp servants. " Or, say, at least I was
told," she added, correcting herself, " for it's not my habit to look
out the window. I simply sat here and waited." Her seat, as she
spoke, might have been a curule chair.

Downstairs, it seemed, Mlle. Malo had instantly taken her
measures. *She* didn't sit and wait. Surprised in the garden with
Simone, she had made the girl walk quietly back to the house and
receive the officers with her on the doorstep. The officer in command—Captain, or whatever he was—had arrived in a bad temper, cursing and swearing, and growling out menaces about spies.
The day was intensely hot, and possibly he had had too much
wine. At any rate, Mlle. Malo had known how to " put him in
his place "; and when he and the other officers entered they found
the dining-table set out with refreshing drinks and cigars, melons,
strawberries, and iced coffee!

The effect had been miraculous. " The Captain—what was his
name? Yes, Charlot, Charlot—Captain Charlot had been specially
complimentary on the subject of the whipped cream and the cigars.
Then he asked to see the other members of the family, and Mlle.
Malo told him there were only two—two old women! He made
a face at that, and said all the same he should like to meet them;

and she answered: 'One is your hostess, the Comtesse de Réchamp, who is ill in bed'—for my poor daughter-in-law was lying
in bed paralysed with rheumatism—'and the other her mother-in-
law, a very old lady who never leaves her room.'"

"But aren't there any men in the family?" he had then asked;
and she had said: "Oh yes—two. The Comte de Réchamp and
his son."

"And where are they?"

"In England. Monsieur de Réchamp went a month ago to take
his son on a trip."

The officer said: "I was told they were here to-day"; and
Mlle. Malo replied: "You had better have the house searched and
satisfy yourself."

He laughed and said: "The idea *had* occurred to me." She
laughed, also, and sitting down at the piano struck a few chords.
Captain Charlot, who had his foot on the threshold, turned back
—Simone had described the scene to her grandmother afterwards. "Some of the brutes, it seems, are musical," the old lady
explained; "and this was one of them. While he was listening,
some soldiers appeared in the court carrying another who seemed
to be wounded. It turned out afterwards that he'd been climbing
a garden wall after fruit, and cut himself on the broken glass on
the top; but the blood was enough—they raised the usual dreadful cry of an ambush, and a Lieutenant clattered into the room
where Mlle. Malo sat playing Stravinsky." The old lady paused
for her effect, and I was conscious of giving her all she wanted.

"Well——?"

"Will you believe it? It seems she looked at her watch-bracelet
and said: 'Do you generally dress for dinner? *I* do—but we've
still time for a little Moussorgsky'—or whatever wild names they
call themselves—'if you will make those people outside hold their

tongues.' Our Captain looked at her again, laughed, gave an order that sent the Lieutenant right about, and sat down beside her at the piano. Imagine my stupor, dear sir: the drawing-room is directly under this room, and in a moment I heard two voices coming up to me. Well, I won't conceal from you that his was the finest. But then I always adored a baritone." She folded her shrunken hands among their laces. "After that, the Germans were *très bien—très bien*. They stayed two days, and there was nothing to complain of. Indeed, when the second detachment came, a week later, they never even entered the gates. Orders had been left that they should be quartered elsewhere. Of course, we were lucky in happening on a man of the world like Captain Charlot."

"Yes, very lucky. It's odd, though, his having a French name."

"Very odd. It probably accounts for his breeding," she answered placidly; and left me marvelling at the happy remoteness of her age.

VI

The next morning early Jean de Réchamp came to my room. I was struck at once by the change in him: he had lost his first glow, and seemed nervous and hesitating. I knew what he had come for; to ask me to postpone our departure for another twenty-four hours. By rights, we should have been off that morning; but there had been a sharp brush a few kilometres away, and a couple of poor devils had been brought to the château whom it would have been death to carry further that day and criminal not to hurry to a base hospital the next morning. "We have simply *got* to stay till to-morrow: you're in luck," I said, laughing.

He laughed back, but with a frown that made me feel I had been a brute to speak in that way of a respite due to such a cause.

"The men will pull through, you know—trust Mlle. Malo for

that!" I said.

His frown did not lift. He went to the window and drummed on the pane.

"Do you see that breach in the wall, down there behind the trees? It's the only scratch the place has got. And think of Lermont! It's incredible—simply incredible!"

"But it's like that everywhere, isn't it? Everything depends on the officer in command."

"Yes; that's it, I suppose. I haven't had time to get a consecutive account of what happened: they are all too excited. Mlle. Malo is the only person who can tell me how things went," he swung about on me. "Look here, it sounds absurd, what I'm asking; but try to get me an hour alone with her, will you?"

I stared at the request, and he went on, still half-laughing: "You see, they all hang on me; my father and mother, Simone, the curé, the servants. The whole village is coming up presently: they want to stuff their eyes full of me. It's natural enough, after living here all these long months cut off from everything. But the result is I haven't said two words to her yet."

"Well, you shall," I declared; and with an easier smile he turned to hurry down to the mass of thanksgiving which the curé was to celebrate in the private chapel. "My parents wanted it," he explained; "and after that the whole village will be upon us. But after——"

"Later I will effect a diversion; I swear I will," I assured him.

By daylight, decidedly, Mlle. Malo was less handsome than in the evening. It was my first thought as she came toward me, that afternoon, under the limes. Jean was still indoors, with his people, receiving the village; I rather wondered she had not stayed there with him. Theoretically, her place was at his side; but I knew she was a young woman who did not live by rule, and she had already struck me as having a distaste for superfluous expenditure of feeling.

Yes, she was less effective by day. She looked older, for one thing; her face was pinched, and a little sallow, and for the first time I noticed that her cheek-bones were too high. Her eyes, too, had lost their velvet depth : fine eyes still, but not unfathomable. But the smile with which she greeted me was charming : it ran over her tired face like a lamplighter kindling flames as he runs.

"I was looking for you," she said. "Shall we have a little talk? The reception is sure to last another hour, every one of the villagers is going to tell just what happened to him or her when the Germans came."

"And you've run away from the ceremony?"

"I'm a trifle tired of hearing the same adventures retold," she said, still smiling.

"But I thought there *were* no adventures—that that was the wonder of it?"

She shrugged. "It makes their stories a little dull, at any rate. We've not a hero or a martyr to show." She had strolled further from the house as we talked, steering me in the direction of a bare horse-chestnut walk that led towards the park.

"Of course, Jean's got to listen to it all, poor boy; but I needn't," she explained.

I didn't know exactly what to answer, and we walked on a little way in silence; then she said : "If you'd carried him off this morning he would have escaped all this fuss." After a pause, she added slowly : "On the whole, it might have been as well."

"To carry him off?"

"Well, yes." She stopped and looked at me. "I wish you would."

"Would? Now?"

"Yes, now; as soon as you can. He's really not strong yet—he's drawn and nervous." ("So are you," I thought, parenthetically.) "And the excitement is greater than you can perhaps imagine——"

I gave her back a look. "Why, I think I *can* imagine."

She coloured up through her sallow skin, and then laughed away her blush. "Oh, I don't mean the excitement of seeing *me!* But his parents, his grandmother, the curé, all the old associations——"

I considered for a moment; then I said: "As a matter of fact, you're about the only person he *hasn't* seen." She checked a quick answer on her lips, and for a moment or two we faced each other silently. A sudden sense of intimacy, of complicity almost, came over me. What was it the girl's silence was crying out to me?

"If I take him away now he won't have seen you at all," I continued.

She stood under the bare trees, keeping her eyes on me. "Then take him away now!" she reiterated; and as she spoke I saw her face change, decompose into deadly apprehension and as quickly regain its usual calm. From where she stood she faced the courtyard, and glancing in the same direction I saw the throng of villagers coming out of the château. "Take him away—take him away at once!" she passionately commanded; and the next minute Jean de Réchamp detached himself from the group and began to limp down the walk in our direction.

What was I to do? I cannot exaggerate the sense of urgency Mlle. Malo's appeal gave me, or my faith in her sincerity. No one who had seen her meeting with Réchamp the night before could have doubted her feeling for him: if she wanted him away it was not because she did not delight in his presence. Even now, as he approached, I saw her face veiled by a fine mist of emotion: it was like watching a fruit ripen under a midsummer sun. But she turned sharply from the house and began to walk on.

"Can't you give me a hint of your reason?" I suggested, as I followed.

"My reason? I have given it!" I suppose I looked incredulous, for she added in a lower voice: "I don't want him to hear—yet —about all the horrors."

"The horrors? I thought there had been none here."

"All around us——" Her voice became a whisper. "Our friends . . . our neighbours . . . everyone. . . ."

"He can hardly avoid hearing of that, can he? And, besides, since you are all safe and happy. . . . Look here," I broke off, "he is coming after us. Don't we look as if we were running away?"

She turned around, suddenly paler; and in a stride or two Réchamp was at our side. He was pale, too; and before I could find a pretext for slipping away he had begun to speak. But I saw at once that he didn't know or care if I was there.

"What was the name of the officer in command who was quartered here?" he asked, looking straight at the girl.

She raised her eyebrows slightly. "Do you mean to say that after listening for three hours to every inhabitant of Réchamp you haven't found that out?"

"They all call him something different. My grandmother says he had a French name: she calls him Charlot."

"Your grandmother was never taught German: his name was Oberst von Scharlach." She didn't remember my presence either: the two were still looking straight in each other's eyes.

Réchamp had grown white to the lips; he was rigid with the effort to control himself.

"Why didn't you tell me it was Scharlach who was here?" he

brought out at last, in a low voice.

She turned her eyes in my direction. "I was just explaining to Mr. Greer——"

"To Mr. Greer?" He looked at me, too, half-angrily.

"I know the stories that are about," she continued quietly; "and I was saying to your friend that, since we had been so happy as to be spared, it seemed useless to dwell on what had happened elsewhere."

"Damn what happened elsewhere! I don't know yet what happened here."

I put a hand on his arm. Mlle. Malo was looking hard at me, but I wouldn't let her see I knew it. "I'm going to leave you to hear the whole story now," I said to Réchamp.

"But there isn't any story for him to hear!" she broke in. She pointed at the serene front of the château, looking out across its gardens to the unscarred fields. "We are safe; the place is untouched. Why brood on other horrors—horrors we were powerless to help?"

Réchamp held his ground doggedly. "But the man's name is a curse and an abomination. Wherever he went he spread ruin."

"So they say. Mayn't there be a mistake? Legends grow up so quickly in these dreadful times. Here"—she looked about her again at the peaceful scene—"here he behaved as you see. For heaven's sake be content with that!"

"Content?" He passed his hand across his forehead. "I'm blind with joy . . . or should be, if only . . ."

She looked at me entreatingly, almost desperately, and I took hold of Réchamp's arm with a warning pressure. "My dear fellow, don't you see that Mlle. Malo has been under a great strain? *La joie fait peur*—that's the trouble with both of you!"

He lowered his head. "Yes, I suppose it is." He took her hand

and kissed it. "I beg your pardon. Greer's right: we're both on edge."

"Yes: I will leave you for a little while, if you and Mr. Greer will excuse me." She included us both in a quiet look that seemed to me extremely noble, and walked slowly away toward the château. Réchamp stood gazing after her for a moment; then he dropped down on one of the benches at the edge of the path. He covered his face with his hands. "Scharlach—Scharlach," I heard him repeat.

We stood there side by side for ten minutes or more without speaking. Finally I said: "Look here, Réchamp—she's right and you're wrong. I shall be sorry I brought you here if you don't see it before it's too late."

His face was still hidden; but presently he dropped his hands and answered me. "I do see. She's saved everything for me—my people and my house, and the ground we're standing on. And I worship it because she walks on it!"

"And so do your people: the War's done that for you, any-how," I reminded him.

VII

The morning after we were off before dawn. Our time allow-ance was up, and it was thought advisable, on account of our wounded, to slip across the exposed bit of road in the dark.

Mlle. Malo was downstairs when we started, pale in her white dress, but calm and active. We had borrowed a farmer's cart in which our two men could be laid out on a mattress, and she had stocked our trap with food and remedies. Nothing seemed to have been forgotten. While I was settling the men Réchamp turned back into the hall to bid her good-bye; anyhow, when she fol-lowed him out a moment later he looked quieter and less strained.

He had taken leave of his parents and his sister upstairs, and Yvonne Malo stood alone in the dark doorway watching us as we drove away.

There was not much talk between us during our slow drive back to the lines. We had to go at a snail's pace, for the roads were rough; and there was time for meditation. I knew well enough what my companion was thinking about, and my own thoughts ran on the same lines. Though the story of the German occupation of Réchamp had been retold to us a dozen times, the main facts did not vary. There were little discrepancies of detail, and gaps in the narrative here and there; but all the household, from the astute ancestress to the last bewildered pantry-boy, were at one in saying that Mlle. Malo's coolness and courage had saved the château and the village. The officer in command had arrived full of threats and insolence: Mlle. Malo had placated and disarmed him, turned his suspicions to ridicule, entertained him and his comrades at dinner, and contrived during that time—or, rather, while they were making music afterwards (which they did for half the night, it seemed)—that Monsieur de Réchamp and Alain should slip out of the cellar in which they had been hidden, gain the end of the gardens through an old hidden passage, and get off in the darkness. Meanwhile, Simone had been safe upstairs with her mother and grandmother, and none of the officers lodged in the château had—after a first hasty inspection—set foot in any part of the house but the wing assigned to them. On the third morning they had left, and Scharlach, before going, had put in Mlle. Malo's hands a letter requesting whatever officer should follow him to show every consideration to the family of the Comte de Réchamp, and if possible—owing to the grave illness of the Countess—avoid taking up quarters in the château, a request which had been scrupulously observed.

Such were the amazing but undisputed facts over which Réchamp and I, in our different ways, were now pondering. He hardly spoke, and when he did it was only to make some casual references to the road or to our wounded soldiers; but all the while I sat at his side I kept hearing the echo of the question he was asking himself, and hoping to God he wouldn't put it to me. . . .

It was nearly noon when we finally reached the lines, and the men had to have a rest before we could start again; but a couple of hours later we landed them safely at the base hospital. From there we had intended to go back to Paris; but as we were starting there came an unexpected summons to another point of the front, where there had been a successful night attack, and a lot of Germans taken in a blown-up trench. The place was fifty miles away, and off my beat, but the number of wounded on both sides was exceptionally heavy, and all the available ambulances had already started. An urgent call had come for more, and there was nothing for it but to go; so we went.

We found things in a bad mess at the second line shanty hospital where they were dumping the wounded as fast as they could bring them in. At first we were told that none were fit to be carried further that night; and after we had done what we could we went off to hunt up a shakedown in the village. But a few minutes later an orderly overtook us with a message from the surgeon. There was a German with an abdominal wound who was in a bad way, but might be saved by an operation if he could be got back to the base before midnight. Would we take him at once and then come back for the others?

There is only one answer to such requests, and a few minutes later we were back at the hospital, and the wounded man was being carried out on a stretcher. In the shaky lantern gleam I caught a glimpse of a livid face and a torn uniform, and saw that he was an officer, and nearly done for. Réchamp had climbed to the box and seemed not to be noticing what was going on at the back of the motor. I understood that he loathed the job and wanted not to see the face of the man we were carrying; so when we had got him settled I jumped into the ambulance beside him and called out to Réchamp that we were ready. A second later an *infirmier* ran up with a little packet and pushed it into my hand. "His papers," he explained. I pocketed them and pulled the door shut, and we were off.

The man lay motionless upon his back, conscious, but desperately weak. Once I turned my pocket-lamp on him, and saw that he was young—about thirty—with damp dark hair and a thin face. He had received a flesh wound above the eyes, and his forehead was bandaged, but the rest of the face was uncovered. As the light fell on him he lifted his eyelids and looked at me: his look was inscrutable.

For half an hour or so I sat there in the dark, the sense of that face pressing close on me. It was a damnable face—meanly handsome, basely proud. In my one glimpse of it I had seen that the man was suffering atrociously, but as we slid along during the night he made no sound. At length the motor stopped with a violent jerk that drew a single moan from him. I turned the light on him, but he lay perfectly still, lips and lids shut, making no sign; and I jumped out and ran round to the front to see what had happened.

The motor had stopped for lack of gasolene and was stock still in the deep mud. Réchamp muttered something about a leak in his tank. As he bent over it, the lantern flame struck up into his face, which was set and businesslike. It struck me vaguely that he showed no particular surprise.

"What is to be done?" I asked.

"I think I can tinker it up; but we've got to have more essence to go on with."

I stared at him in despair; it was a good hour's walk back to the lines, and we weren't so sure of getting any gasolene when we got there! But there was no help for it; and as Réchamp was dead lame, no alternative but for me to go.

I opened the ambulance door, gave another look at the motion-less man inside, and took out a remedy which I handed over to Réchamp with a word of explanation. "You know how to give a hypo? Keep a close eye on him and pop this in if you see a change—not otherwise."

He nodded. "Do you suppose he'll die?" he asked below his breath.

"No, I don't. If we get him to the hospital before morning I think he'll pull through."

"Oh, all right." He unhooked one of the motor lanterns and handed it over to me. "I'll do my best," he said as I turned away.

Getting back to the lines through that pitch-black forest and finding somebody to bring the gasolene back for me was about the worst job I ever tackled. I couldn't imagine why it wasn't daylight when we finally got to the place where I'd left the motor. It seem-ed to me as if I'd been gone twelve hours when I finally caught sight of the grey bulk of the car through the thinning darkness.

Réchamp came forward to meet us, and took hold of my arm as I was opening the door of the car. "The man's dead," he said.

I had lifted up my pocket-lamp, and its light fell on his face, which was perfectly composed, and seemed less gaunt and drawn than at any time since we had started for Réchamp.

"Dead? Why—how? What happened? Did you give him the hypodermic?" I stammered, taken aback.

"No time to. He died in a minute."

"How do you know he's dead? Were you with him?"

"Of course, I was with him," Réchamp retorted, with a sudden harshness that made me realise I had grown harsh myself. But I had been almost sure the man wasn't anywhere near death when I left him. I opened the door of the ambulance and slipped in with my lantern. He didn't appear to have moved, but he was dead sure enough—had been for two or three hours, by the feel of him. It must have happened not long after I left. . . . Well, I'm not a doctor, anyhow. . . .

I don't know that Réchamp and I exchanged a word during the rest of that run. But it was my fault and not his if we didn't. By the mere rub of his sleeve against mine as we sat outside on the motor I knew he was conscious of no bar between us: he had somehow got back, in the night's interval, to a state of wholesome stolidity, while I, on the contrary, was tingling all over with exposed nerves.

I was glad enough when we got back to the base at last, and the grim load we carried was lifted out and taken into the hospital. Réchamp waited in the courtyard beside his car, lighting a cigarette in the cold early sunlight; but I followed the bearers and the surgeon into the whitewashed room where the dead man had to be undressed. I had a burning spot at the pit of my stomach while his clothes were ripped off him and the bandages undone; I couldn't take my eyes from the surgeon's face. But the surgeon, with a big batch of wounded on his hands, was probably thinking more of the living than the dead; and, besides, we were near the front, and the body before him was an enemy's.

He finished his examination and scribbled something in a notebook. "Death must have taken place nearly five hours ago," he merely remarked. It was the conclusion I had come to myself.

"And how about the papers?" the surgeon continued. "You

have them, I suppose? This way, please."

We left the half-stripped body on the blood-stained oil-cloth, and he led me into an office where a functionary sat behind a littered desk.

"The papers? Thank you. You haven't examined them? Let's see, then."

I handed over the leather note-case I had thrust into my pocket the evening before, and saw for the first time its silver-edged corners and the coronet in one of them. The official took out the papers and spread them on the desk between us. I watched him absently while he did so.

Suddenly he uttered an exclamation. "Ah—that's a haul!" he said, and pushed a bit of paper towards me. On it was engraved the name—Oberst Graf Benno von Scharlach. . . .

"A good riddance," said the surgeon over my shoulder. . . . I went back to the courtyard and saw Réchamp still smoking his cigarette in the cold sunlight. I don't suppose I had been in the hospital ten minutes; but I felt as old as Methuselah.

My friend greeted me with a smile. "Ready for breakfast?" he said good-humouredly; and a little chill ran down my spine. . . .

But I said: "Oh, all right—come along. . . ." For, after all, I *knew* there wasn't a paper of any sort on that man when he was lifted into my ambulance the night before: the French officials attend to their business too carefully for me not to have been sure of that. And there wasn't the least shred of evidence to prove that he hadn't died of his wounds during the unlucky delay in the forest; or that Réchamp had known his tank was leaky when we started out from the lines.

"I could do with a *café complet,* couldn't you?" Réchamp suggested looking straight at me with his good blue eyes; and arm-in-arm we started off for the nearest hotel.

MARIE-LUISE

by
Karl Wilke

GEHRMANN was in charge of the canteen of our war prisoners' company in France. He slept next to me in the tent. He came from Berlin, and was engaged to a girl there, about whom he used to talk to me a lot in the evening before going to sleep. But I was favoured with even more about the girl whom he had in tow at St. Quentin. She was the daughter of Madame Bouffon, who supplied our canteen, and her name was Marie-Luise.

Gehrmann was a merchant in civil life, a wholesale merchant, as he was sometimes wont to emphasise, explaining to me that for this higher grade of commerce it was essential to have matriculated. So he had given this modest evidence of intelligence, and after two years of training had become a *Kriegsfreiwillige,* and had hoped speedily to get his commission—if nothing were to interfere, as unfortunately it did, for he had just got his second stripe when the French took charge of his further destiny by making him a prisoner.

He once showed me a photograph of the girl in Berlin, which had come with a letter, and asked me what I thought of her. It was a beautiful face, frank, but perhaps a little cold; it suggested sincerity and great purity.

"She will be true to you," I said at once.

"She is," he replied; "true as gold."

"Much too good for you," I said, handing back the picture after I had studied it for a while longer, held by this curiously lovely face. The becoming large hat which she was wearing also testified to her good taste.

Gehrmann turned round in his bed so that he faced me; the wire mattress creaked under the weight of his heavy body. He nipped the candle out with his fingers. It was the last candle alight in our tent, and the sentry had already called his familiar "La lumière kaput!" We continued to talk in a whisper, so that the others should not overhear.

"She suits me all right," said Gehrmann, "just because I am rather more easygoing in many ways. Opposites always get on well together; besides, fidelity is not so difficult for women as for us. . . . I've had three years of it, old boy."

"Hence Marie-Luise, I suppose."

He was silent and thoughtful for a while, then he said slowly: "Hence Marie-Luise? No. That's my dilemma—in point of fact, I'm thinking of marrying her."

"You're mad," I exclaimed indignantly. "Fancy thinking of leaving your pretty German girl in the lurch for a French woman."

He tossed about. "Mad? Well—you go to·Madame Bouffon and have a look at Marie-Luise, and then say if I'm mad. The Berlin girl can get ten others to take my place."

He had often suggested that I should go round to Madame Bouffon's, but I was not keen on making the acquaintance of my fellow-prisoner's French love. During the following days he grew more insistent. Marie-Luise was a beautiful girl, he said, not at all the ordinary type. In the end I yielded out of sheer curiosity, for I really had not seen a French woman who could be called beautiful.

We belonged to the so-called Town Company; most of us had been taken prisoner at the beginning of the War, we were well dressed and the majority of us could speak French. Apart from the camp staff, to which I belonged, we were engaged by private people in the town as clerks and as interpreters. We were not kept under

any kind of surveillance and each man had his pass. Gehrmann's
chit, which covered me, was made out from the camp to the Rue
Cordelière, where Madame Bouffon lived.

We were not supposed to walk on the pavement; but this regulation did not trouble Gehrmann. He had told a French officer
who had wanted to drive him off the pavement that as a man of
kultur his place was not down where the horses walked. He had
put the point suavely in his best French, and the officer had
smiled and had let him alone.

Gehrmann's whole manner was expressive of this convinced
superiority; that may have been why nobody stopped us. I had
often noticed that, as he walked along with his confident stride,
it was the French who side-stepped rather than he. He seemed to
impress the feminine population especially; he was tall and broad
and had bright blue eyes. I could understand that he was a success.

Madame Bouffon's shop contained a medley of every kind of
thing that is bought and sold, and everything that prisoners of
war might possibly want from a canteen. Gehrmann took me
through the miscellaneous stock of goods to the back room, where
a few favoured guests were sitting drinking wine. But he did not
stop here. "Go through there," he said over his shoulder, "and
open the next door." We found ourselves in the kitchen, one corner
of which was arranged as a sitting-room. There was a broad sofa
behind the table and there was even a piano next to it.

As we passed through the outer shop we had greeted Madame
Bouffon. Marie-Luise was not to be seen; a plump little maid was
fussing about the stove in the dark background. Gehrmann immediately sat down at the piano and began to play a Strauss waltz.
The maid smiled at me invitingly, and Gehrmann winked at me,
indicating that I ought to dance with her. I explained that I was
not conversant with that art.

Possibly if it had been Marie-Luise——

At that moment she entered. That lucky fellow Gehrmann was right. She was strikingly beautiful; slender and elegant, a thoroughbred, like the kitten which she carried on her arm. There was a warm glow in her cheeks, and she had dark, melting eyes.

I jumped up; Gehrmann continued to play a few bars until I nudged him. I was interested to see how the two would meet, but there was no special familiarity noticeable. Gehrmann bowed in courtly fashion over her little hand; there was a half smile on the lovely creature's mouth, which vanished as she turned to me.

" My friend," he said, introducing me. I saw only her wonderful dark eyes; like velvet, I thought. . . .

Then the German lesson began. Gehrmann had not told me that he was teaching her German. Marie-Luise seemed rather dense; and she was certainly lacking in concentration. After five minutes she took up the kitten again and went out. Gehrmann sat down to the piano. He did not look at me; perhaps he was ashamed of her stupidity.

The maid took up the carpet. Her skimpy skirt exposed her ridiculously short legs. My friend looked at me and nodded his head in her direction. Then Marie-Luise suddenly appeared behind him; had she noticed something? Her eyes had a surprised or severe expression; they were quite unfathomable.

She tapped the pianist on the shoulder; he subdued his playing somewhat and half turned round to her.

" Wie heisst Ge—burts—tack?" she asked in German.

" Birthday."

Marie-Luise reflected for a moment, and then she pressed her dark head into the warm fur of the kitten and disappeared again. As the piano resounded again to the industrious fingers of the prisoner of war I reflected quietly in my sofa corner on the strange

relationship between these two persons. It was obvious that nothing sensible would ever come of it. I believe that a Franco-German
reconciliation was more likely than a successful union between
these two particular representatives of the two nations. I felt I had
to argue him out of it. He had once made a point of the fact that
Marie-Luise was his eleventh love, so that it was to be hoped she
would not be his last. On the other hand, I knew well that he had
a strong vein of obstinacy, especially when he felt himself opposed.
It was not for nothing that the French had entered on his pass the
honorary title, "Tête carrée." I could well understand that this
strange girl would attract him. She had suddenly entered the room
again without a sound, and tapped him on the shoulder with the
same swift, confident gesture which had affected me unpleasantly
before.

"The Adjutant has forbidden music here," she said. Gehrmann
stopped abruptly, and said we had to go, in any case.

"You know who she means by the Adjutant?" he said as we
walked along. "That's our friend Boulanger. And he's my rival
in her affections. That's how matters stand."

"Well, you're asking for trouble."

"That's just what makes it interesting, my dear fellow. Of
course, she doesn't want to have anything to do with him, but he's
awfully keen on her. It's a pity that I can't just tell him plainly
that he doesn't cut any ice with her. . . . I'm the only one that
does. How do you like her?"

"Very well," I said, rather hesitating, "but——"

"No buts about it," he put in at once, "I can't do better than
marry her. She's got money; the business is doing splendidly. She
wants to marry somebody in the wholesale business if possible.
When the War's over I shall be in clover. What's the good of
Germany to me?"

" I thought that your main interest in this affair was something rather different," I suggested.

He saw my point. " Well, I don't want to buy a pig in a poke, but I do mean to marry her."

He was as fickle as a child. At one moment he decided in favour of the Berlin girl, the next for Marie-Luise. Every evening I was favoured with an account of his love-pangs until I told him bluntly that he was a cad, and that I had lost all interest in the whole business. He didn't bear me any resentment, and we had indeed told each other plainer home truths. Although he said nothing more about the matter, I thought that was for other reasons. The canteen orderlies, too, noticed the sudden gloom that had descended upon his exuberant nature.

One evening he confided in me: " The Adjutant is on my tracks," he said.

" So he knows that you're the man?" I asked in alarm.

" He doesn't actually know that it's me. He only knows that a prisoner is constantly pursuing Marie-Luise, but he has sworn to shoot him on the spot if he catches him. He watches like a lynx, but he's not yet discovered that I'm the man."

" Let the girl alone," I advised him for the umpteenth time.

" Certainly not now," he answered aggressively. " Of course, I won't be able to be with her so much during the day. I'll have to wangle things a bit. I'll just go there at night, and you will be a sport and say I've gone out to the lavatory if anybody comes to inspect. You will, won't you?"

I promised to oblige him. We were a specially favoured company, and there was no real risk in remaining away occasionally even at night, provided that the German sergeant-in-charge was made wise. He was responsible for defaulters.

The following evening Gehrmann told me that the Adjutant

did seem to be suspicious of him. He had been in the back room that day where the customers were sitting, and had looked at him sharply. Gehrmann, however, had refrained from gratifying him by going into the kitchen, and Marie-Luise had pretended complete indifference. No doubt I had noticed on the other occasions how well she could do this.

That evening he crawled through the "mole's alley," which a love-sick prisoner in our tent, who was always abroad at night, had laboriously burrowed. This approach to the outside world started under the shoemaker's bed, and was concealed during the day by a box. It ended on the other side of the barbed wire fence in a mass of litter under an old railway truck. I kept guard, pressed close up against the tent, until the sentry had passed that point, when I tapped the ground several times with my boot. Directly afterwards my friend was scurrying through the trees of the Champs Elysées, unnoticed by the sentry. He came back without my assistance, it being about midnight when he lay down.

"Did it all go off well?" I asked.

"Splendidly. It was a good evening, my lad. A pity the Adjutant couldn't see us, he'd have gone blue with fury. *Sacré nom de Dieu!*"

For a week it worked all right, and then Gehrmann stayed out all night. I didn't worry about this particularly; perhaps he was having a specially good time with Marie-Luise, and had decided not to leave and would come through the gate the next day just like any ordinary man who had been to the canteen. He did come in the next morning immediately after the fatigue parties had left. He was looking deadly pale and immediately sank on his bed.

"What's up?"

He sighed heavily. "Get the medical orderly—with bandages —I have been shot at—but not the doctor," he shouted after me as I dashed off to the hospital.

He had been shot through the upper portion of the right arm. As we carefully took his coat off, he called for the tailor. " Are you good at invisible mending?" he asked. " I want you to deal with my sleeve as quickly as possible. I'll make it worth your while."

It was a clean shot; hardly any blood had flowed. " We won't need the doctor," said the orderly, " but you must take things easy for a couple of days."

" Out of the question," exclaimed Gehrmann, " I must get to the canteen again at once. The Adjutant must know nothing about it. Was there any inspection at night?" I told him there was none. " Yes, but he might come at any moment; hurry up so that I can get across."

The tailor took some time, and we put a man at the door to warn us if the Adjutant came, in which case Gehrmann would have put on someone else's tunic. " I dare say he won't come at all for the next few days," Gehrmann remarked when the medical orderly had gone and we were left alone for a moment. " I believe I landed him a good one. The night was on my side: I have always gone through the courtyard lately, but he had found that out too, and last night, when I was on my way home, a man was standing outside—I didn't recognise him, but I would bet it was that swine. He collared me and gave me one in the chest; but I was too quick for him and planted my fist in his face. If it was he, he won't be able to show himself in the street for some time. He fell flat on the ground and I was up and off in a moment. Then the swine fired at me; I felt that I was hit and thought I'd better not come back to the camp until the fatigue parties were out, so I hid in a ruined house. Then I crawled in. Give me a drink, old man, I'm feeling a bit faint. . . ."

I got him some wine, which cheered him up, and after that he insisted on going to the canteen. The tailor had mended his tunic so well that there wasn't the slightest trace of the hole. He got a five franc note for his skill. The bandage had also been very skilfully put on so as not to make it too awkward for him to move, and strong-smelling antiseptics had been avoided.

I went with my friend to the canteen. He held himself well and there was no sign that there was anything the matter with him except that his arm hung a little awkwardly. "If the Adjutant should look in I can even move it about a bit," Gehrmann said.

The canteen had a back room, with a sofa which had been requisitioned from the town. By agreement with the other inmates the sofa was left to Gehrmann, who reclined on it while someone was detailed in return for a drink to keep a lookout in case the enemy should come into sight.

I went to visit him at midday and on my way I saw the Adjutant bearing down on the camp. I hurried along, but Gehrmann had already been warned, and he came out of the back room, his face flushed with sleep, as I entered the canteen. The Adjutant was inside already; he looked sharply at Gehrmann and asked him for a drink. I could hardly repress my laughter when I saw the Frenchman's black eye as he turned to the light, and Gehrmann also found it hard to control himself. His lips quivered sarcastically. Apart from this there was nothing to notice about him as he handed his rival a glass of wine and said:

"*Votre santé,* mon Adjutant!"

"*Merci*—you look very pale, Monsieur Gehrmann."

"Had a bit of a binge last night," mumbled the prisoner, and looked meaningly at the other's black eye. He paled noticeably, and I saw that he had difficulty in standing straight.

Thereupon an orderly dashed in and told the Adjutant that he was wanted by the Commanding Officer. The Adjutant went out quickly with an oath. The prison guards told us later that he was severely reprimanded for being seen in the street with a black eye. The interpreters stated definitely that he was put under arrest.

Gehrmann slept himself well, and when his enemy reappeared in the camp he had fully regained the use of his arm. He naturally made for Marie-Luise again, but Madame Bouffon informed him that she had gone away on a visit and was not coming back for some time. Meanwhile, the time for our return home was approaching, and it was not until the evening before we left that he met her again. It seemed that his passion for her had cooled considerably in the meantime.

"How did the farewell go off?" I asked him chaffingly.

"Oh, so-so. I confined myself principally to discussing business with the old woman. I am coming back again as a civilian. I'll get another one in on the Adjutant then."

I advised him not to do anything foolish as it might involve the whole company. He shook his head and said that he would see to it that it happened on the other side of the frontier. Perhaps he would let the Adjutant off, only he would like to tell him that it was he who had given him the black eye, "and then I'll invite him to my marriage with Marie-Luise."

He was not able to carry out his intentions because the French escort marched us back too quickly to Düsseldorf. After we had got home it was a long time before I heard anything further from him. One day he paid a surprise visit and told me that he was engaged to a girl near my home; he showed me her photograph, she was very pretty.

When I reminded him of Marie-Luise he said: "It was sport more than love with her. I only wanted to prevent the Frenchman from winning."

RETREAT

by
Werner Beumelburg

DURING the morning of November 10th, 1918, two officers were riding on their exhausted horses, which for weeks had not seen the inside of a stable or had a decent ration of oats, through a magnificent park near the city of Mons in Belgium. Ancient poplars hid their heads in a damp veil of mist, and there was a gentle dripping in the air as from invisible, damp draperies. Like monstrous discontented hedgehogs, great solitary cypresses stood in the dewy meadows, and fir-trees stretched hands to one another as for the dance of a gloomy measure. The mist embraced all with melancholy arms, and in the near distance assumed the consistency of a grey wall. . . .

Anyone noting the faces of the two officers would have received a shock. Privation, fatigue, and the dull despair of utter hopelessness were met there. Their nags ambled with dragging hoofs along the gravel paths that wound through the poplars.

" That's where the map shows the château," said the taller of the two; " let's ride across the meadows." He made a left incline, and the other followed him, without paying much attention to what his companion said. He was too much immersed in his own thoughts.

" To-day will be no different from yesterday and the day before, and to-morrow will be like to-day," the first continued after a short pause. " At night we shall march . . . in the morning we shall dig ourselves in and lie for a few hours in heavy sleep. The rain will soak through us and the frost will keep us awake; by eleven o'clock at the latest they will be after us and catch us up, and by midday the battle will be in progress. We shall not be able

to hold our position, and at four o'clock we shall resume the retreat with heavy losses, and their artillery will harry us until night-
fall. The remnant will go on retreating through the darkness. . . .
I've had enough of it," he suddenly roared, and snatched at the
bridle of his horse, which made an ineffective, half-hearted attempt to rear. He calmed down as quickly and then trotted on
over the meadows.

The horsemen said nothing more. Veils of dampness drizzled
down, and the poplars draped their heads with grey streamers. . . .

The gloomy walls of the château rose darkly out of the wreaths of
mist. Slowly the two men rode the length of the deserted frontage.

Suddenly, and almost simultaneously, they both snatched at
their horses' bridles, and stopped motionless as though struck by
lightning. They had looked through one of the large windows
into a lofty room, and what they saw there seemed to them like
a long-forgotten fairy tale. In the centre of the room, which was
filled with gloomy portraits, heavy Gobelin tapestry, figures of
black marble and dark hangings, there was a rocking-chair, and
in the chair was reclining a dark-haired girl, who was certainly
not more than seventeen; she had dark, Italian eyes, a red mouth,
and gleaming white teeth. Her eyes gazed in happy unconcern at
the motionless strangers, whose origin mystified her. To her they
may have seemed like figures in a romance, which one may observe, but cannot set in motion. As, however, the two horsemen,
forgetful of all the rules of good manners, continued to gaze at
her with a strange persistence, her whole face was suddenly suffused in a deep blush. She got up hurriedly, and vanished in a
few easy strides, as though the dark walls had swallowed her up.
Had it not been for the chair that was still rocking, the strangers
might well have thought that they had been the victims of a lovely
hallucination.

Stephan, the smaller of the two, had gone pale as a sheet; Claus, the elder, gave a laugh and then remembered his business. He jumped quickly from his horse and exclaimed: "Come on . . . we must speak to the owner and arrange for accommodation for the battalion."

Of the fairy-tale, however, they said not a word. . . .

They knocked at the iron portal of the château, and after a long time a battered old servitor opened it. He showed not the slightest surprise at the curious visit, receiving the strange officers with the manner that was probably habitual to him when receiving his master's guests. He led them to a lofty room that was half in darkness. The scent of ancient splendour clung to the heavy velvet of the seats. From the walls silent oil portraits gazed down with melancholy eyes, dark clothes, pale faces, and white ruffs.

The owner of the château entered the room. Hair that was almost white framed a waxen yellow face that at first sight resembled the portraits on the walls. He introduced himself as Comte de L., and spoke in a slow voice that was hushed almost to solemnity: "My house is at your disposal . . . please give your instructions. . . ."

Claus stammered something about the inexorability of war, his sincere regret, and other remarks such as are usual when one must inflict hardship on anyone against one's personal inclination. The Count, however, cut the officer short, remarking with a casual wave of the hand: "It's war . . . I know it. Do as your duty towards your country requires. . . ."

The rest of the business was speedily concluded; Claus carried through the negotiations alone. Stephan was still pale, and to his spirit, which had just emerged from privation and the presence of death, it all seemed like a terrible, torturing unreality, which he was unable, despite all his efforts, to shake from him. . . .

About midday the mist rose and cleared away. The château lay bright in the sunshine, and its gloomy walls were bathed in an autumnal light. At the western end of the park the men were digging themselves in; patrols were wandering about in the foreground, and hid themselves behind trees and walls.

The Major, the medical officer, Claus, and Stephan went into the château and billeted the men. When this had been done, the old servant invited them into the dining-room. There the Count received the strangers and bade them take their seats at the table. This was covered with a snow-white damask cloth and the Burgundy sparkled in crystal goblets. An enormous mirror, which filled almost the whole of the back wall of the room, revealed to the officers their faces, distorted by hardship, pale, hollow, and weary, with tufts of beard on their chins and disordered hair.

An overmastering oppression fell upon the Germans. Perhaps within an hour the howling furies of war would have been let loose upon table and glasses, the Burgundy would flow like red blood over the carpet, and the damask cloth would be torn into filthy shreds—the Count, however, entertained them with his best wine! Was he mad?

"Gentleman," said their host, "let us empty our glasses, each drinking to the victory of his own country—may Heaven grant it."

His voice sounded hushed and quite solemn, and the pale oil paintings on the walls seemed to listen breathlessly to his words. A barely perceptible smile passed over his features, and as he finished speaking there was a slight tremor as though of secret malice. Beyond a doubt he was scoffing at the intruders.

The Major set down the glass, which he had raised to his lips, and stared at the old gentleman. Claus dashed his goblet to the ground, so that it broke into a thousand fragments and the Burgundy was spattered on the floor like drops of blood. Stephan bent his head low over the damask and groaned. . . .

Before the Count could reply, or even make a movement, a shell was heard outside in the distance, whose echo rebounded sharply from the castle wall like the crack of a whip. . . .

Over the hills in the distance hung a grey little explosive cloud, which slowly melted into a mist. On the edge of the park, among the cypresses and cunningly trimmed fir-trees, there stood a German field battery. With a terrific hiss the first shell left the barrel and screamed away.

Close to the little cloud of the shell-burst was a bush; as they looked through their field-glasses, the officers could see the bush go up, rent into a thousand fragments. There was a scrambling as though an ants' nest had been disturbed. Ten, twenty, tiny forms ran down the hill as though possessed, and vanished into a farmstead. . . .

The next shot sped away.

A little black cloud danced immediately in front of the farm; before it had risen from the ground there was another crash in the park. For some seconds there was a howling and roaring . . . then a thick, inert, sulphurous mass issued from the walls . . . rafters and walls crashed as in a far-away puppet stage.

Then shot after shot wailed across; from the black throats of the guns at the park edge came a roaring, as though a whole pack of savage dogs were lurking there; the air was noisy as though with the jingle of thousands of metallic veils. There was a wild devil's dance about the farm, and occasionally one of the bombarding shells would crash right into the gables and tear out of the rafters a flaming yellow banner. . . .

In the end they came out of their hole. There was a desperate running to and fro about the house. With a shrill screaming the machine-guns on the edge of the park hurled themselves upon their prey. The little men in the distance tumbled over like rabbits, and but a few of them made any effort to get up from the ground. . . .

Then . . . all in the space of a thought . . . a monstrous hissing descended straight from above . . . a deafening splittering and crashing . . . a rattling down of stones, panes, and pieces of furniture . . . outside, in front of the windows, which suddenly made all the noises seem uncannily close, a yellow wall and a terrible oppression on lungs and temples. All the work of two seconds . . . and then a second to grasp what had occurred. . . .

The officers leapt back. The Count went pale as a corpse, and trembled like an aspen. The damask cloth was strewn with innumerable glass splinters, and the Burgundy spread over the floor in great red pools. . . .

Ten seconds passed before the second blow. Some oil paintings crashed from the walls . . . the whole room filled with a fine suffocating dust. The Gobelins hung in tatters to the ground. . . .

Claus shouted to the Count that he should leave the room; but he was unable to understand. Thereupon Claus seized him by the arm and took him out into the hall. He came almost without resistance, but in his eyes there was the terror of the beast that is to be slaughtered. Stephan was outside already, and was searching for someone.

At this moment the third shell struck the front of the château, causing the heavy walls to shake to their foundations. From the park came a confused noise; shouts rang out, shells crashed and aroused a feverish yelling. The four guns outroared one another in the rage of battle. . . .

There was a wild terror in Stephan's eyes. He turned to Claus entreatingly and mumbled: "The fairy-tale, Claus . . . the fairy-tale. . . ."

The old servitor came towards them. His hair was all disordered, and there was an idiot gleam in his eyes. Blood was dripping persistently from his left arm, which hung limp. It dripped upon the snow-white frock of the fairy, who was supported in a faint on his right arm. Her eyes were closed and her forehead pale as chalk. . . .

Stephan, who did not know whether she had been struck by a shell fragment, or by a falling stone, or whether it was merely terror that had caused her to faint, hurried up to the old man to relieve him of his burden. The latter, however, remained motionless, baring his teeth like some monstrous ape. . . .

At this moment the next shell came. The wall collapsed under the terrible impact; the air pressure hurled the whole group into confusion, and darkness spread with frightful suddenness. . . .

"Get a move on!" shouted the Major, as he pressed through the fumes. "Get a move on!" shouted Claus, clutching at Stephan's arm. The latter looked at his friend with a curiously absent expression. Then an unpleasant smile of embarrassment passed over his face, and he looked shyly to one side, where the old man was dragging the fairy off. He took a couple of steps up to them. . . .

"Stephan!" shouted Claus, "the English are attacking . . . what are you playing at?"

Stephan collapsed as though he had been shot from the back. Outside the machine-gun fire was raging. The noise increased to an infernal din. . . .

A word of command rang through the park.

"No. 4 Company occupy the park edge and open rapid fire. . ."

Stephan roused himself with a violent effort and turned again.

. . . Breathing heavily, the old man dragged the fairy along, and disappeared with his burden down a dark passage. Her white dress still fluttered like a ghost in the distance. . . .

The battery at the park edge offered a sorry spectacle.

The first gun had been knocked over. The shattered barrel had buried itself in the earth; the limber stared up at the sky. Black, burnt corpses lay beside it. Behind the shield of the second gun a gunner lay across the barrel with his right hand at the breech. The shield was riddled like a sieve, and the man was dead. Two guns were still firing, sadly mutilated and half burst to pieces.

The air was sharply streaked with twittering, wailing, crackling bullets. The bursting shells kept up a horrid accompaniment. At the park edge lay the infantry, their heated rifles in front of them, with whole handfuls of ammunition poured out beside them, and fired . . . fired . . . fired. The machine-guns whipped and hammered out their bursts of fire in between. From an immeasurable distance the hissing goblins went wailing overhead, and burst with furious impact against the front of the groaning château. A weary cloud rolled over the park. . . .

The foreground was swarming with tiny figures. Singly and in small groups they stumbled through the seething lead fragments and nerve-racking hurricane. In little holes, behind hedges and walls, they collected in small groups, and went forward in short leaps across the field. With grim determination they dragged their machine-guns forward, dug them in, and let loose bursts of searching fire, the bullets crackling over the meadow as from a hosepipe. Wherever a little group of men collected together raging death came amongst them and cast them to the ground. They tumbled and went head over heels like shot rabbits . . . they leapt right up and clutched at the earth . . . they suddenly threw up their arms and collapsed . . . in rows they were mown down by screaming death. . . .

Speedily the crawling field was emptied. . . .

Gradually the machine-guns became silent, and only the heavy thuds of shells occasionally beat through the twilight. Soon these also ceased. . . .

The officers returned to the ruined château. No sound disturbed the silence. It was as though it had been an unearthly visitation, a destructive whirlwind that had produced a heap of ruins in half an hour.

The four men were sitting in the same room, through whose empty window frames the cool of evening came. Dust lay everywhere thick, and splinters covered the floor. . . .

They were all weary and oppressed. Their heads sank upon their arms, their eyes kept closing . . . but mad pictures chased one another through their brains. Like thick drops of a viscous liquid the minutes passed. The evening wind slowly moved through the trees. Like hungry birds of prey the mists hung about the park in isolated groups.

For a long time not a word was spoken. Claus was the first to break the silence.

"I should like to see the Rhine again. . . ."

The sudden idea almost terrified him, and he listened eagerly to see whether anyone would offer a comment. But his words died away in the gloom like flowers on a frosty night. But after a time they awoke a chord.

"We are told," said the Major, as though he were quite alone, "that nearly two thousand years ago a golden eagle sank in the Rhine, and that he will rise again when his time is fulfilled. Then he will set out on his flight to the west, where the sun sets red in the evenings. His golden pinions will gleam in the evening light, so that all shall see it far and wide. But there are still a hundred years ere the two thousand are accomplished. I should like to see that eagle. . . ."

Claus was roused from deep thought.

"Yes . . . if there were someone to raise the eagle! But he who bore him perished under the burden. . . ."

"Then another must raise him," said the doctor, and listened to the mysterious stillness without. The ghostly gleam of a Verey light for a few moments revealed monstrous, quivering shadows in the park.

A moan escaped from Stephan's breast, as though from a cry that could find no outlet.

"What ails you?" asked the Major, and slowly turned his face towards Stephan. . . .

Stephan sank again into dreams. . . .

He wandered through dark corridors and reached no end. A tittering in the darkness frightened him. Perhaps it came from one of the dark oil paintings that hung upon the walls. He stopped and endeavoured to identify the picture. There was tittering on the other side. Light steps brushed past him, and he saw how the shadows were suddenly leaving the frames of the pictures and stealing past him timorously. He heard them laughing together as they went further away, a ghostly sound that went through the château.

Stephan followed the shadows, which attracted him with a mysterious power. A gleam of light at the end of the passage revealed where they were. As he went, a white form joined him. Stephan recognised it and his breath stopped.

"Countess," he whispered, "please wait . . . take me with you.

. . . I am such a stranger in your house . . . in fact, I am really frightened. . . ."

She stopped with a laugh. But her laugh made the blood run cold. She put her arm through Stephan's, and he shuddered. Her light footsteps gave no sound, and he could not see her face. He wanted to stop and speak, but neither his limbs nor his mouth would obey him. On her arm he had to wander, wander. . . .

"Come," she whispered; "there, where the light shines, my father is waiting for us . . . there you can tell him all that you feel in your heart. . . ."

As she said this, she laughed again mysteriously and quietly.

At last the two reached the light. A number of dark forms were seated about a bright fire, which, however, gave out no heat. The little flames conjured monstrous shadows of the crouching forms upon the walls. In a low voice they were all speaking to one in their midst.

"Still alive? Still alive? Disgrace to our race! A curse upon our degenerate son!"

Stephan recognised him whom they were thus chiding. It was the Count. His face was as pale as those of the portraits that had come to life, but about his mouth there was a mocking smile.

"You dolts . . . ," he whispered, withdrawing his head so deep between his shoulders that it almost seemed as though he had suddenly lost it, and as though his voice were forcing its way out of the swamp of his neck, "hanging on the walls all this time has addled your brains. . . . Why do you want to interfere in these matters when you understand nothing about them? Let me carry on . . . let me carry on . . . I don't need your help. You've no idea what my little daughter, the Countess, can do."

The fairy on Stephan's arm suddenly gave a silvery laugh. Like a spotted, yellow salamander the fire leapt into the air, and shot

out at her face. Stephan was seized with horror as he looked at her
. . . she had neither lips nor flesh . . . from empty eye-sockets and
gumless teeth grinned death . . . .

As though hounded by Furies, Stephan tore back through the
corridors. The shapes at the fire rose from the floor and rushed
after him, the Count leading with long strides. He panted like a
rabid wolf. New shapes kept descending from the picture frames
to block his way or to join in the chase. There was a rushing
through the corridors like the beating of bats' wings. Like a shrill
bell the dead fairy kept clanging at him, fiercer and more persistent
the farther he went. Suddenly, from one of the side passages a
searing blast of heat rushed to meet him. The walls swayed and
opened . . . from all sides poured yellow fire, through which he
had to wade with painful feet, the laughter following him, and the
hoarse grunts of the dead about him. *The château was burning*.
There was no escape from the flames now . . . the spirits shouted
in wild triumph . . . the bell tolled wildly . . . the fairy was all
ablaze . . . in the picture frames grinning devils' masks glowed
There was a hissing and boiling and bursting and crackling . . .
into the seething caldron . . . the fairy nodded, the fairy shouted.
. . .

Stephan made a convulsive effort before he sank into the flames.
. . .

He heard his name being called. He struck out; strong arms
seized him. At last he recovered consciousness. . . .

It was Claus who was holding him.

"You've been dreaming of the Countess . . . poor fellow, in half
an hour we shall be on the road again . . . marching orders have
already been received."

Another night of marching.

The dark columns of the marching troops stood out ghostly in the weak light of the moon. Far away on the horizon a couple of Bengal lights flickered. . . . Verey lights. Boots crunched on the road. The moonlight shed its pale beams over the steel helmets. Entrenching tools rattled rhythmically to the movement of the men. The mists gathered in the meadows. . . .

Claus and Stephan rode for a long time side by side without speaking.

In the end Claus, who was finding the stillness intolerable, broke the silence: " Each night sees us a bit nearer the Rhine. Shall we see it again?"

" The Rhine!" Stephan uttered the word with a dreamy bitterness, suggestive of hopeless remoteness.

" I should like to ask the Major," Claus continued persistently, " what he meant about the eagle that is supposed to have sunk two thousand years ago. I've never read anything about it; but I have a feeling as though I might have dreamt of it."

" The Major is a dreamer himself. He has imagined it all. How could the eagle rise out of the river after two thousand years?"

" But the doctor spoke about it too . . . there must be something in it."

" He dreamt like the Major and you. I shall never see the Rhine again. Each morning a couple of us die; it's my turn next."

Claus became peevish. " You seem to have it all cut and dried."

A murmur went through the weary ranks. A strange glow, quite different from the pale illumination of the moon, sped over the column, and the faces flickered yellow. Claus turned round. At their back a yellow pillar of flame shot clumsy tongues out into the night.

" *The castle is on fire,*" Claus said dully, and snatched at Stephan's arm. Stephan uttered not a word, but even the uncertain glare of the fire did not succeed in hiding the deadly pallor of his face. The devils' masks in the portrait frames shone before him . . . the fairy blazed with the grinning hollows in her face . . . the bell clanged with a mad shrillness. . . .

Claus had an intuition of what was passing in Stephan's mind, although he did not know the dream. A sudden sense of oppression constricted his throat.

"Stephan . . .," he whispered hoarsely, bending over to his friend, " the Rhine . . . we shall soon see the Rhine . . . then everything must change. . . ."

A groan issued from Stephan's mouth, and it seemed as though he swayed in the saddle. . . .

The column continued to advance. Soon the eastern sky was streaked by the first pink of dawn. . . .

It was November the eleventh.

At noon, when orders were given for the general cessation of hostilities, Claus was at regimental headquarters awaiting instructions. There was an expression of infinite relief on all faces, for the certainty of once more seeing home alive was as yet of vastly greater significance than the fact that the War had been lost.

The Colonel produced a carefully treasured bottle of red wine, stuffed it into Claus' coat-pocket, and told him to drink the contents with his friends to the health of those at home.

Claus thanked him and put spurs to his horse.

The terrible feeling of oppression overcame him again, and caused him to hurry. In the end he felt as though he were riding a race with death . . . and yet he had already a feeling of constriction, as though it were impossible for him to win. Terror almost robbed him of his senses. He did not see the victory flags hung out by the inhabitants, nor did he understand the joyful excitement on all sides. He never noticed that the thunder of artillery and the rattle of machine-guns had ceased. Not for one moment did the terrific feeling that the war had expended all its murderous energy affect him. He thought, indeed, of nothing but his own fear, and he was incapable of countering it with any rational arguments. The stumbling of his exhausted mount roused him to paroxysms of rage.

Claus could now recognise the British sentries, who were walking slowly to and fro with fixed bayonets a hundred yards from the Germans.

The Major and the doctor were standing talking together in front of a house. Claus shouted something to them.

The Major slowly turned towards him; there was a look of compassion in his eye.

Claus felt his limbs refusing to work, and all his blood rushed to his heart.

"Is he alive?" he hissed, although he already felt a terrible certainty.

The Major shook his head. Claus slipped from his horse, making a sound like a wild beast. The Major and the doctor caught him in their arms.

As though from an immeasurable distance Claus heard their words. He had ridden back secretly half an hour before noon . . . the whole morning he had seemed peculiar . . . gone the same way as the battalion had marched that night . . . horse came back alone . . . the sentries saw him shot when he was about fifty yards in front of the line . . . obviously shot through the head or the heart, for he did not move again. . . .

The nearer the army came to the Rhine on its march home, the more silent Claus became. The news about the terms of the armis-

tice and events at home—fresh blows every day—left him almost
unmoved. He did not remember at all that he had looked forward
to seeing the Rhine, and he did not even pay any attention when
one evening in mess the Major said: "To-morrow at noon we
shall cross the bridge . . . and then we shall not see the Rhine again
for a long time. . . ."

Ceaselessly the columns rattled over the bridge, from early
morning until late in the evening. And when the new day came,
it began again. . . .

Detachment was linked to detachment by an invisible hand to
an endless chain that never broke.

Starting back in the hills, the rattling seemed to be transmuted
into a monotonous chant over the stream.

They came from Flanders, from Champagne, from Argonne,
from the Oise and the Scheldt, and all wore the same grey cloth
and had the same weary lines about the mouth.

The rifles, from which the last shot had been fired, rested in
long rows on their shoulders. The guns, which had spoken for the
last time, passed like surly watch-dogs over the water, as though
they were preparing for a long sleep. The machine-guns already
slept the sleep of death under their coverings, and let themselves
be dragged on without resistance, they who had been used to bark
in sudden anger when approached even from afar.

Company after company, battery after battery, squadron after
squadron, they filed past . . . more and more of them . . . always
more . . . as though there would be no end.

All those who had been populating the crumbling battlefields,
invisible in their holes, now looked at one another like wanderers
returning home from a distant shore full of dread secrets.

Yes . . . they wondered, each one at his fellow, that just he had lived to see this day while so many others had remained behind.

For beside the visible army was marching an unseen army, whose bodies would not emerge from the hidden holes. They were, however, recognisable only to those who sought in vain a comrade, a son, a brother, or a father among the ranks of the visible. They carried no rifle, nor did they sit on horses or limbers. Rather they flitted about the columns of the living, in anxious haste lest they should lose contact, for they feared to remain alone in their distant graves. And it was well that one could not see them, for they were not a pleasant sight. . . .

Ceaselessly the columns rattled over the bridge, from early morning until late at night. And when light returned it began again. . . .

As Claus' company reached the middle of the bridge, the columns came to a stop. An axle had broken, and the waggon had to be got out of the way.

The infantry halted, pushed back their heavy helmets, took the rifles from their shoulders, and rested their packs on them.

Claus went to the bridge railing and looked down at the river.

The dark waves passed tirelessly under the bridge. He discerned a subdued plashing, which had hitherto been muffled by the clatter of the army. As his eyes rested on the water he felt more and more that the bridge itself was beginning to move, to glide slowly against the course of the stream.

Claus' thoughts merged with the stream and penetrated to its bed. Down there it was almost dark; only a faint gleam fell from above as through a glass wall. Mysterious shapes were about him, and moved with an inept monotony. They approached close to him, and made way for others. As they did so, they looked for a moment into his eyes, and it seemed to Claus as though there were an infinite melancholy in their faces because he did not recognise them, and addressed them no word of farewell. He recognised them all well enough, as they passed him silently and asked him to go with them; only he could not exactly place them. He felt that he had only to say that he would wander with them, towards the great sea, always on the dim bed of the river, and he would know them all by name. But something still held him back from acquiescing in this invitation.

Until one of them, who had already passed him, suddenly turned round and took his hand. "Come," he said, "come, Claus ... why are you still worrying? How long am I to wait for you?"

Claus at once recognised the voice and the face. It was Stephan. On Stephan's forehead gleamed a circular hole, or rather it seemed as though a fat, blood-red spider were squatting there, which had spun her fine threads in all directions over the marble brow. The suffering on the dead man's face was terrible. . . .

Just as Claus was about to seize Stephan's hand, to enter the ranks of the dead at his side, he felt himself lifted by the bed of the river. Stephan vanished in the dim hollow. . . .

Claus raised his eyes from gazing at the surface of the stream and looked straight ahead, where the mists of the distance merged together hills, banks, and water—merged in the mists of distance.

The mist seemed to be condensing to form a second bridge. It was built not of stone and iron like the one on which he was standing, but rested upon wooden piles. Claus now perceived that over that bridge, too, an army was passing, not from west to east, but in the opposite direction. He heard clearly the rumbling of transport and the subdued rattle of weapons. The bright helmets of the legionaries glittered through the mist, and the points of the *pila* gleamed like a cornfield with shining ears. The centurions rode at the head of the detachments, and the boards of the bridges gave a low roar under the horse's hoofs. The legionaries wore laurel wreaths on their brows. The endless train disengaged from the thick woods on the right bank and crawled shrilly over the bridge. Two thousand years were embraced in a single hour, and merged with the present day to form one picture. In both directions the army processions moved, from west to east and from east to west. Here the army of home-coming Germans . . . there the army of home-coming Romans, fleeing from the German forests and the avenging swords of their enemies. The rattling of the two processions mingled to form a single web of sound, which spread over the river like a cloud of destiny. . . .

Claus stared across at the procession of misty forms, and he felt for the first time since the weeks of dull oppression an excitement stirring within him. It was not fear but the solemn expectation of great tidings.

Then it happened. A distant light broke through the mist . . . the wooden bridge parted asunder as though melting in the new fire. A radiant fiery circle rose out of the centre of the river and mounted heavenwards. The light kept increasing in intensity, a glowing sphere shimmering like a million pearls.

Then it divided into two wings . . . a head rose out of the centre . . . the vision was vouchsafed . . . the eagle!

As Claus, shading his dazzled eyes with his hand, looked to see who was raising the eagle from the river, he believed he recognised the arms and face of a young German who was shaking the water drops from his blond hair and gazed laughing at the departing legionaries. . . .

Claus felt himself enveloped by a marvellous sense of peace. Heaving a deep sigh, he turned from the bridge railing. Words of command were ringing out; the infantrymen pushed their steel helmets over their foreheads, took their rifles on their shoulders, and resumed the march. The rattling resumed its monotonous melody; ceaselessly the column marched eastward across the river that was gliding peacefully down the open valley.

IN THE FRONT LINE

INTRODUCTION TO THE TRENCHES

by
Richard Aldington

WINTERBOURNE had an easy initiation into trench warfare. The cold was so intense that the troops on both sides were chiefly occupied in having pneumonia and trying to keep warm. He found himself in a quiet sector, which had been fought over by the French in 1914 and had been the scene of a fierce and prolonged battle in 1915, after the British took over the sector. During 1916, when the main fighting shifted to the Somme, the sector had settled down to ordinary trench warfare. Trench raids had not then been much developed, but constant local attacks were made on battalion or brigade fronts. A little later the sector atoned for this calm.

To Winterbourne, as to so many others, the time element was of extreme importance during the war years. The hour goddesses who had danced along so gaily before, and have fled from us since with such mocking swiftness, then paced by in a slow, monotonous file as if intolerably burdened. People at a distance thought of the fighting as heroic and exciting, in terms of cheering bayonet charges or little knots of determined men holding out to the last Lewis gun. That is rather like counting life by its champagne suppers and forgetting all the rest. The qualities needed were determination and endurance, inhuman endurance. It would be much more practical to fight modern wars with mechanical robots than with men. But then, men are cheaper, although in a long war the initial outlay on the robots might be compensated by the fact that the quality of men deteriorates while they cost more in upkeep. But that is a question for the War Departments. From the point of view of efficiency in war, the trouble is that men have feelings; to attain the perfect soldier we must eliminate feelings. To the human

robots of the last war, time seemed indefinitely and most unpleasantly prolonged. The dimension then measured as a "day" in its
apparent duration approached what we now call a "month." And
the long series of violent stalemates on the Western front made any
decision seem impossible. In 1916 it looked as if no line could be
broken, because so long as enough new troops were hurried to
threatened points the attacker was bound to be held up; and the
supplies of new troops seemed endless. It became a matter of which
side could wear down the other's man-power and moral endurance. So there also was the interminable. The only alternatives
seemed an indefinite prolongation of misery, or death, or mutilation, or collapse of some sort. Even a wound was a doubtful blessing, a mere holiday, for wounded men had to be returned again
and again to the line.

For the first six or eight "weeks," Winterbourne, like all his
companions, was occupied in fighting the cold. The Pioneer company to which he was attached were digging a sap out into No
Man's Land and making trench-mortar emplacements just behind
the front line. They worked on these most of the night and slept
during the day. But the ground was frozen so hard that progress
was tediously slow.

The company were billeted in the ruins of a village behind the
reserve trenches, over a mile from the front line. The landscape
was flat, almost treeless except for a few shell-blasted stumps, and
covered with snow frozen hard. Every building in sight had been
smashed, in many cases almost level with the ground. It was a
mining country, with great queer hills of slag and strange pit-head
machinery in steel, reduced by shell-fire to huge masses of twisted
rusting metal. They were in a salient, with the half-destroyed,
evacuated town of M—— in the elbow-crook on the extreme right.

The village churchyard was filled with graves of French soldiers; there were graves inside any of the houses which had no cellars, and graves flourished over the bare landscape. In all directions were crosses, little wooden crosses, in ones and twos and threes, emerging blackly from the frozen snow. Some were already askew; one just outside the ruined village had been snapped short by a shell-burst. The dead men's caps, mouldering and falling to pieces, were hooked on to the tops of the crosses—the grey German round cap, the French blue and red kepi, the English khaki. There were also two large British cemeteries in sight—rectangular plantations of wooden crosses. It was like living in the graveyard of the world—dead trees, dead houses, dead mines, dead villages, and dead men. Only the long steel guns and the transport waggons seemed alive. There were no civilians, but one of the mines was still worked about a mile and a half further from the line.

Behind Winterbourne's billet were hidden two large howitzers. They fired with a reverberating crash which shook the ruined houses, and the diminishing scream of the departing shells was strangely melancholy in the frost-silent air. The Germans rarely returned the fire—they were saving their ammunition. Occasionally a shell screamed over and crashed sharply among the ruins; the huge detonation spouted up black earth or rattling bricks and tiles. Fragments of the burst shell-case hummed through the air.

But it was the cold that mattered. In his efforts to defend himself against it, Winterbourne, like the other men, was strangely and wonderfully garbed. Round his belly, next the skin, he wore a flannel belt. Over that, a thick woollen vest, grey flannel shirt, knitted cardigan jacket, long woollen under-pants, and thick socks. Over that, service jacket, trousers, puttees, and boots; then a sheep-skin coat, two mufflers round his neck, two pairs of woollen gloves, and over them trench gloves. In addition came equipment—box respirator on the chest, steel helmet, rifle, and bayonet. The only clothes he took off at night were his boots. With his legs wrapped in a greatcoat, his body in a grey blanket, a ground-sheet underneath, pack for pillow, and a dixie of hot tea and rum inside him, he just got warm enough to fall asleep when very tired.

Through the broken roof of his billet Winterbourne could see the frosty glitter of the stars and the white rime. In the morning, when he awoke, he found his breath frozen on the blanket. In the line his short moustache formed icicles. The boots beside him froze hard, and it was agony to struggle into them. The bread in his haversack froze greyly; and the taste of frozen bread is horrid. Little spikes of ice formed in the cheese. The tins of jam froze and had to be thawed before they could be eaten. The bully beef froze in the tins and came out like chunks of reddish ice. Washing was a torment. They had three tubs of water between about forty of them each day. With this they shaved and washed—about ten or fifteen to a tub. Since Winterbourne was a late-comer to the battalion, he had to wait until the others had finished. The water was cold and utterly filthy. He plunged his dirty hands into it with disgust, and shut his eyes when he washed his face. This humiliation, too, he accepted.

He always remembered his first night in the line. They paraded in the ruined village street about four o'clock. The air seemed crackling with frost, and the now familiar bloody smear of red sunset was dying away in the south-west. The men were muffled up to the ears, and looked grotesquely bulky in their sheep or goat skin coats, with the hump of box respirators on their chests. Most of them had sacking covers on their steel helmets to prevent reflection, and sacks tied round their legs for warmth. The muffled officer came shivering from his billet as the men stamped their feet on the hard, frost-bound road. They drew picks and shovels from a dump, and filed silently through the ruined street behind the officer. Their bayonets were silhouetted against the cold sky. The man in front of Winterbourne turned abruptly left into a ruined house. Winterbourne followed, descended four rough steps, and found himself in a trench. A notice said:

HINTON ALLEY
To the Front Line.

To be out of the piercing cold wind in the shelter of walls of earth was an immediate relief. Overhead shone the beautiful ironic stars.

A field-gun behind them started to crash out shells. Winterbourne listened to the long-drawn wail as they sped away and finally crashed faintly in the distance. He followed the man ahead of him blindly. Word kept coming down: "Hole here; look out." "Wire overhead." "Mind your head—bridge." He passed the messages on, after tripping in the holes, catching his bayonet in the field telephone wires, and knocking his helmet on the low bridge. They passed the reserve line, then the support, with the motionless sentries on the fire-step, and the peculiar smell of burnt wood and foul air coming from the dug-outs. A minute later came the sharp message: "Stop talking; don't clink your shovels." They were now only a few hundred yards from the German front line. A few guns were firing in a desultory way. A shell crashed outside the parapet about five yards from Winterbourne's head. It was only a whizz-bang, but to his unpractised ears it sounded like a heavy. The shells came in fours—Crump, CRUMP, CRRUMP; the Boche was bracketing. Every minute or so came a sharp ping!—fixed rifles firing at a latrine or an unprotected piece of trench. The duck-boards were more broken. Winterbourne stumbled over an unexploded shell, then had to clamber over a heap of earth where the side of the trench had been smashed in a few minutes earlier. The trench made another sharp turn, and he saw the bayonet and helmet of a sentry silhouetted against the sky. They were in the front line.

They turned sharp left. To their right were the fire-steps, with a sentry about every fifty yards. In between came traverses and dug-out entrances, with their rolled-up blanket gas-curtains. Winterbourne peered down them—there was a faint glow of light, a distant mutter of talk, and a heavy stench of wood and foul air. The man in front stopped and turned to Winterbourne:

"Halt! Password to-night's 'Lantern.'" Winterbourne halted, and passed the message on. They waited. He was standing almost immediately behind a sentry, and got on the fire-step beside the man to take his first look at No Man's Land.

"'Oo are you?" asked the sentry in low tones.

"Pioneers."

"Got a bit o' candle to give us, chum?"

"Awfully sorry, chum, I haven't."

"Them muckin' R.E.s gets 'em all."

"I've got a packet of chocolate, if you'd like it."

"Ah! Thanks, chum."

The sentry broke a bit of chocolate and began to munch.

"Muckin' cold up here, it is. Me feet's fair froze. Muckin' dreary, too. I can 'ear ole Fritz coughin' over there in 'is listenin' post—don't 'arf sound 'ollow. Listen."

Winterbourne listened, and heard a dull, hollow sound of coughing.

"Fritz's sentry," whispered the man. "Pore ole ——. Needs some liquorice."

"Move on," came the word from the man in front. Winterbourne jumped down from the fire-step and passed on the word.

"Good-night, chum," said the sentry.

"Good-night, chum."

Winterbourne was put on the party digging the sap out into No Man's Land. The officer stopped him as he was entering the sap.

"You're one of the new draft, aren't you?"

"Yes, sir."

"Wait a minute."

"Very good, sir."

The other men filed into the sap. The officer spoke in low tones :

"You can take sentry for the first hour. Come along, and don't stand up."

The young crescent moon had risen and poured down cold, faint light. Every now and then a Verey light was fired from the German or English lines, brilliantly illuminating the desolate landscape of torn, irregular wire and jagged shell-holes. They climbed over the parapet and crawled over the broken ground past the end of the sap. The officer made for a shell-hole just inside the English wire, and Winterbourne followed him.

"Lie here," whispered the officer, "and keep a sharp lookout for German patrols. Fire if you see them and give the alarm. There's a patrol of our own out on the right, so make sure before you fire. There's a couple of bombs somewhere in the shell-hole. You'll be relieved in an hour."

"Very good, sir."

The officer crawled away, and Winterbourne remained alone in No Man's Land, about twenty-five yards in front of the British line. He could hear the soft, dull thuds of picks and shovels from the men working the sap, and a very faint murmur as they talked in whispers. A Verey light hissed up from the English lines, and he strained his eyes for the possible enemy patrol. In the brief light he saw nothing but the irregular masses of German wire, the broken line of their parapet, shell-holes and debris, and the large stump of a dead tree. Just as the bright magnesium turned in its luminous parabola, a hidden machine-gun, not thirty yards from Winterbourne, went off with a loud crackle of bullets like the engine of a motor-bicycle. He started, and nearly pulled the trigger of his rifle. Then silence. A British sentry coughed with a deep hacking sound; then from the distance came the hollow coughing of a German sentry. Eerie sounds in the pallid moonlight. "Ping!" went a sniper's rifle. It was horribly cold. Winterbourne was shivering, partly from cold, partly from excitement.

Interminable minutes passed. He grew colder and colder. Occasionally a few shells from one side or the other went wailing overhead and crashed somewhere in the back areas. About four hundred yards away to his left began a series of loud, shattering detonations. He strained his eyes, and could just see the flash of the explosion and the dark column of smoke and debris. These were the German trench-mortars, the dreaded "minnies," although he did not know it.

Nothing different happened until about three-quarters of an hour had passed. Winterbourne got colder and colder, felt he had been out there at least three hours, and thought he must have been forgotten. He shivered with cold. Suddenly he thought he saw something move to his right, just outside the wire. He gazed intently, all tense and alert. Yes, a dark something was moving. It stopped, and seemed to vanish. Then near it another dark figure moved, and then a third. It was a patrol, making for the gap in the wire in front of Winterbourne. Were they Germans or British? He pointed his rifle towards them, got the bombs ready, and waited. They came nearer and nearer. Just before they got to the wire,

Winterbourne challenged in a loud whisper:

"Halt, who are you?"

All three figures instantly disappeared.

"Halt, who are you?"

"Friend," came a low answer.

"Give the word or I fire."

"Lantern."

"All right."

One of the men crawled through the wire to Winterbourne, followed by the other two. They wore balaclava helmets and carried revolvers.

"Are you the patrol?" whispered Winterbourne.

"Who the muckin' 'ell d'you think we are? Father Christmas? What are you doin' out here?"

"Pioneers digging a sap about fifteen yards behind."

"Are you Pioneers?"

"Yes."

"Got a bit o' candle, chum?"

"Sorry, I haven't; we don't get them issued."

The patrol crawled off, and Winterbourne heard an alarmed challenge from the men working in the sap and the word "Lantern." A Verey light went up from the German lines just as the patrol were crawling over the parapet. A German sentry fired his rifle and a machine-gun started up. The patrol dropped hastily into the trench. The machine-gun bullets whistled cruelly past Winterbourne's head—zwiss, zwiss, zwiss. He crouched down in the hole. Zwiss, zwiss, zwiss. Then silence. He lifted his head and continued to watch. For two or three minutes there was complete silence. The men in the sap seemed to have knocked off work, and made no sound. Winterbourne listened intently. No sound. It was the most ghostly, desolate, deathly silence he had ever experienced.

He had never imagined that death could be so deathly. The feeling of annihilation, of the end of existence, of a dead planet of the dead arrested in a dead time and space, penetrated his flesh along with the cold. He shuddered. So frozen, so desolate, so dead a world —everything smashed and lying inertly broken. Then "crack— ping!" went a sniper's rifle, and a battery of field-guns opened with salvoes about half a mile to his right. The machine-guns began again. The noise was a relief after that ghastly dead silence.

At last the N.C.O. came crawling out from the sap with another man to relieve him. A Verey light shot up from the German line in their direction just as the two men reached him. All three crouch- ed motionless as the accurate German machine-gun fire swept the British trench parapet. Zwiss, zwiss, zwiss, the flights of bullets went over them. Winterbourne saw a strand of wire just in front of him suddenly flip up in the air where a low bullet had struck it. Quite near enough—not six inches above his head.

They crawled back to the sap, and Winterbourne tumbled in. He found himself face to face with the platoon officer, Lieutenant Evans. Winterbourne was shivering uncontrollably; he felt utterly chilled. His whole body was numb, his hands stiff, his legs one ache of cold from the knees down. He realised the cogency of the Adjutant's farewell hint about looking after feet, and decided to drop his indifference to goose grease and neat's-foot oil.

" Cold?" asked the officer.

"It's bitterly cold out there, sir," said Winterbourne through chattering teeth.

"Here, take a drink of this "; and Evans held out a small flask.

Winterbourne took the flask in his cold-shaken hand. It chinked roughly against his teeth as he took a gulp of the terrifically potent army rum. The strong liquor half choked him, burned his throat, and made his eyes water. Almost immediately he felt the deadly chill beginning to lessen. But he still shivered.

"Good Lord, man! you're frozen," said Evans. "I thought it was colder than ever to-night. It's no weather for lying in No Man's Land. Corporal, you'll have to change that sentry every half hour—an hour's too long in this frost."

"Very good, sir."

"Have some more rum?" asked Evans.

"No, thanks, sir," replied Winterbourne; "I'm quite all right now. I can warm up with some digging."

"No; get your rifle and come with me."

Evans started off briskly down the trench to visit the other working parties. About a hundred yards from the sap he climbed out of the trench over the parados; Winterbourne scrambled after, more impeded by his chilled limbs, his rifle, and heavier equipment. Evans gave him a hand up. They walked about another hundred yards over the top, and then reached the place where several parties were digging trench-mortar emplacements. The N.C.O. saw them coming, and climbed out of one of the holes to meet them.

"Getting on all right, sergeant?"

"Ground's very hard, sir."

"I know, but——"

Zwiss, zwiss, zwiss, zwiss, came a rush of bullets, following the rapid tat-tat-tat-tat-tat-tat-tat of a machine-gun. The sergeant ducked double. Evans remained calmly standing. Seeing his unconcern, Winterbourne also remained upright.

"I know the ground's hard," said Evans, "but those emplacements are urgently needed. Headquarters were at us again to-day about them. I'll see how you're getting on."

The sergeant hastily scuttled into one of the deep emplacements, followed in a more leisurely way by the officer. Winterbourne remained standing on top, and listened to Evans as he urged the men to get a move on. Tat-tat-tat-tat-tat. Zwiss, zwiss, zwiss, very close this time. Winterbourne felt a slight creep in his spine; but since Evans had not moved before, he decided that the right thing was to stand still. Evans visited each of the four emplacements, and then made straight for the front line. He paused at the parados.

"We're pretty close to the Boche front line here. He's got a machine-gun post about a hundred and fifty yards over there."

Tat-tat-tat-tat-tat-tat. Zwiss, zwiss, zwiss.

"Look! Over there."

Winterbourne just caught a glimpse of the quick flashes.

"Damn!" said Evans. "I forgot to bring my prismatic compass to-night. We might have taken a bearing on them, and got the artillery to turf them out."

He jumped carelessly into the trench, and Winterbourne dutifully followed. About fifty yards further on he stopped.

"I see from your paybook that you're an artist in civil life."

"Yes, sir."

"Paint pictures and draw?"

"Yes, sir."

"Why don't you apply for a draughtsman's job at Division? They need them."

"Well, sir, I don't particularly covet a hero's grave, but I feel very strongly I ought to take my chance in the line along with the rest."

"Ah! Of course. Are you a pretty good walker?"

"I used to go on walking tours in peace time, sir."

"Well, there's an order that every officer is to have a runner. Would you like the job of platoon runner? You'd have to accompany me, and you're supposed to take my last dying orders! You'd have to learn the lie of the trenches, so as to act as guide, take my orders to N.C.O.s, know enough about what's going on to help them if I'm knocked out, and carry messages. It's perhaps a bit more dangerous than the ordinary work, and you may have to turn out at odd hours, but it'll get you off a certain amount of digging."

"I'd like it very much, sir."

"All right; I'll speak to the Major about it."

"It's very good of you, sir."

"Can you find your way back to the sap? It's about two hundred yards along this trench."

"I'm sure I can, sir."

"All right. Go back and report to the corporal, and carry on."

"Very good, sir."

"You haven't forgotten the password?"

"No, sir—'Lantern.'"

About thirty yards along the trench there was a rattle of equipment, and Winterbourne found a bayonet about two feet from his chest. It was a gas sentry outside a company H.Q. dug-out.

"Halt! Who are yer?"

"Lantern."

The sentry languidly lowered his rifle.

"Muckin' cold to-night, mate."

"Bloody cold."

"What are you—Bedfords or Essex?"

"No; Pioneers."

"Got a bit of candle to give us, mate? It's muckin' dark in them dug-outs."

"Very sorry, chum, I haven't."

Rather trying, this constant demand for candle-ends from the Pioneers, who were popularly supposed by the infantry to receive immense "issues" of candles. But without candles the dug-outs were merely black holes, even in the daytime, if they were of any depth. They were deep on this front, since the line was a captured German trench reorganised. Hence the dug-outs faced the enemy instead of being turned away from them.

"Oh, all right; good-night."

"Good-night."

Winterbourne returned to the sap, and did two more half-hour turns as sentry, and for the rest of the time picked or shovelled the hard clods of earth into sandbags. The sandbags were then carried back to the front line and piled there to raise the parapet. It was a slow business. The sap itself was camouflaged to avoid observation. Winterbourne hadn't the slightest idea what its object was. He was very weary and sleepy when they finally knocked off work about one in the morning. An eight-hour shift, exclusive of time taken in getting to and from the work. The men filed wearily along the trench, rifles slung on the left shoulder, picks and shovels carried on the right. Winterbourne stumbled along, half asleep with the cold and the fatigue of unaccustomed labour. He felt he didn't mind how dangerous it was—if it was dangerous—to be a runner, provided he got some change from the dreariness of digging and filling and carrying sandbags.

After they passed the support line, the hitherto silent men began to talk incessantly. At reserve they got permission to smoke. Each grabbed in his pockets for a fag, and lighted it as he stumbled along the uneven duck-boards. After what seemed an endless journey to Winterbourne, they reached the four steps, climbed up, and emerged into the now familiar ruined street. It was silent and rather ghostly in the very pale light of the new moon. They dumped their picks and shovels, went to the cook to draw their ration of hot tea, which was served from a large black dixie and tasted unpleasantly of stew. They filed past the officer, who gave each of them a rum ration.

Winterbourne drank some of the tea in his billet, then took off his boots, wrapped himself up, and drank the rest. Some real warmth flushed into his chilled body. He was angry with himself for being so tired, after a cushy night on a cushy front. He wondered what Elizabeth and Fanny would say if they saw his animal gratitude for tea and rum. Fanny? Elizabeth? They had receded far from him; not so far as all the other people he knew, who had receded to several light years, but very far. "Elizabeth" and "Fanny" were now memories and names at the foot of sympathetic but rather remote letters. Drowsiness came rapidly upon him, and he fell asleep as he was thinking of the curious zwiss, zwiss made by machine-gun bullets passing overhead. He did not hear the two howitzers when they fired a dozen rounds before dawn.

THE LAST KINDNESS

by
Frank Harris

IN the early days of the War two men were walking casually along the streets of Boulogne towards the jetty, evidently to meet the Folkestone mail boat.

Boulogne had already assumed the aspect of an English town containing a few French inhabitants. Khaki was the prevailing colour, rain the most familiar element. All the larger hotels had been converted to military service, and the usual atmosphere of an important war-base prevailed.

Our two friends, both clad in khaki, the one an army chaplain and the other a Lieutenant in the Welsh Fusiliers, did not therefore arouse even a passing interest. They were deep in argument. One, the Lieutenant, a small wiry man of about thirty, with clear eyes of steel and a bulging, prominent forehead, did most of the talking, and emphasised his words with forcible and impatient gestures. He possessed the gift of concentration. He neither saw nor cared what went on around him; his mind was occupied to the exclusion of everything else with the subject under discussion. His companion, on the other hand, said very little. He often shook his head, and sometimes smiled tolerantly. He did not agree with what his friend was saying, but listened patiently all the time. Also about thirty years old, he wore his uniform with a certain dapper air, as if he preferred the military tunic to the surplice. His good-humoured Irish eyes looked all about him, missing nothing.

" I do not agree with a word you say," he said at length; " that, of course, you knew already. I am not good at argument, though perhaps I ought to be. Still, I hope confidently that you will see your mistake now that we are about to come to grips with life, so to speak. These things are better realised in times of danger. But come along; you stand still so often that we shall miss your brother."

The Lieutenant walked on for a few yards in silence. The son of a Belfast solicitor, he had been brought up a strict Presbyterian, but on reaching the years misnamed of discretion, with his lawyer's mind he had refused to admit the supernatural; he had carefully weighed the Christian faith, studied its proofs and the arguments against it, the benefits and disadvantages it had brought in its train, weighed it all carefully, and found it wanting. He therefore rejected it root and branch. We may be sorry for him and his like; we do not blame them; belief is not a matter of will. But John Milligan did not stop at disbelief. He insisted on discussing ticklish questions at all times and on all occasions, appropriate or inappropriate, whenever he found himself with a disputant. He had the aggressive persistence of the disbeliever with none of the usual Celtic tact. It is not surprising that he was not popular in his regiment. Englishmen don't talk much about religion, but they usually cherish some faith, and they resent attacks on it profoundly. The padre was the only man in the regiment who could stand Milligan's conversation for long.

"Do you mean to say," Milligan persisted, "that on account of some obscure and unnatural or supernatural precept of your religion you would refuse to a fellow-creature a simple kindness that you would not deny to any dog, or cat, or horse?"

The chaplain looked at him inquiringly. "Of course, if an animal, a dog, a cat, or a horse, as you say, were so wounded that there was not the least hope of his recovering, yet if allowed to live he might linger on for days in agony, any man would put the poor brute out of his suffering in some painless way."

"Naturally," replied the Lieutenant. "Yet you would not do as much for a human being?"

"Certainly not."

"Why?"

"Well, the man might recover—the resources of surgery——"
Milligan broke in:

"You are deliberately begging the question. My supposition was that there was no chance of recovery, all the doctors being agreed ——"

Argument was not the kindly chaplain's strong point. He was painfully conscious of his own weakness.

"I am sure," he said, "that you yourself would not act upon your theories. An immortal soul may rise to higher heights through suffering, and no one has a right to commit murder."

"Bosh!" cried Milligan; "I hope I may never be put to the proof. But if it was anyone I really loved I should force myself to act in the best interest of my friend and do to him what I'd wish him to do to me."

Further argument was not possible, as they had arrived at the landing-stage. The boat was already in, and the Paris passengers, stepping off the gangway, were being hurried over the railway lines into the Customs-house. Everybody seemed to be talking at once. Porters, burdened with hand luggage, were pushing and shouting at each other. French soldiers, lining the route, tried to regulate the stream of hurrying travellers. Milligan caught sight of a tall, slim figure in khaki, leaning over the rail of the boat waving to him. A change seemed to come over him. He thawed and softened perceptibly. He was no longer the tiresome, argumentative fanatic, but the most devoted of brothers. Poor Milligan had many faults, but one redeeming feature, the love he cherished for his brother, five years his junior. Motherless from boyhood, Walter had only his brother to lean on for that help and guidance fathers so often neglect or forget. He had been given a commission in the same regiment as his brother, but ill-health had prevented him leaving England when the others did. He had always been delicate—in khaki he looked almost fragile—yet the War often taught us that a stout heart may be found in a weak body. Until the excitement of the greeting had passed, the padre, forgotten, rested himself upon a large packing-case and smiled on the world and the dwellers therein, whom he loved instinctively.

*　　　*　　　*　　　*　　　*

It was about an hour before dawn—already a thin line, as if made by a red pencil, marked the leaden sky. The silence, only disturbed by occasional shouts and far-off calls, seemed all the more intense after the hell of a few hours earlier. The excitement and exhilaration of battle had given place to agony and horror. The scent of death was everywhere, the indescribable reek of blood which we may pray that our children and our childen's children may never know. John Milligan raised himself painfully and looked about him, but he could see nothing and hear nothing. He sank back again exhausted, and tried to close his eyes. His head ached dreadfully, and he guessed both his sight and hearing were impaired, at all events for a time. But the sharpest pain came from his foot. Laboriously he tried to feel in the dark what damage he had sustained. He succeeded in pulling away the remains of his boot, and, ever practical, he tried vainly to recall what had been taught him in his lessons of first aid. His hand, sticky with blood, fumbled at his shirt. He tried to tear off a strip to bind round his wounded heel. There had been a night attack. Orders had been received to take the enemy's position at all costs. They had succeeded, but the enemy's retreat had been protected as usual by their artillery, which had wrought fearful havoc in the attacking ranks. Milligan himself had been wounded as far as he remembered very early in the fight, and lay now at the base of a wooded hill, waiting for the stretcher bearers. At the present moment they were fully occupied where the fight had been hottest on the other side of the hill. Milligan found the waiting unendurable, and he tried painfully to crawl in the direction from which he imagined succour would come. He wondered with a heavy heart how his brother had fared. He envied for the first time the believers in that great consolation, prayer. As he crawled along, he stumbled every now and then, sometimes against the root of a tree, sometimes against a prostrate form. Complete silence reigned, interrupted by an occasional groan of agony, which made him shudder. Yet he might have been worse off, he told himself. He might have been killed or, worst of all, suffered some awful wound that had not killed him outright. As it was, he might be lame for the rest of his life, but he would certainly be invalided home.

A faint light now enabled him at length to distinguish objects and to avoid obstacles in his path. His tunic, torn and caked with mud, was grey rather than brown. He had long ago lost his cap, but still had his revolver in its case. He thought of this, lest he should be fired at by some wounded Boche; but he remembered that it was unlikely that there were any in that part of the wood. On he crept; a form lay in his path which he proceeded to skirt. Something—was it instinct?—made him pause. He waited, it seemed centuries, for the light to get brighter to enable him to banish his fears. Then suddenly a great cry escaped him—all his own suffering and pain were in a moment forgotten: he was kneeling by his brother, who, alas! would have been hardly recognisable even in the full light of day. An appalling wound he had received in the abdomen would have proved fatal itself, but in addition one side of his head had been blown away and part of his brain lay on the ground. Yet he was not dead, but suffering awful torture, greater than the human mind is capable of realising. Foam, flecked with blood, dripped from the corner of his mouth, and he even retained the use of one eye, which, as he could not speak, looked in mute appeal at his brother. Did he recognise him? John thought not. What could he do?

As in a dream his conversation with the padre returned to his brain, and his whole body quivered. So this was to be the test, and, of course, he could not act up to his theory. He could do absolutely nothing, that was the awful part, and his brother might live through the day, but certainly on the morrow he would die. And all the time John knelt by his brother, powerless, helpless, in agony. Silence, dead silence! He tried to shout, but the words stuck in his parched throat. There was no one near him alive except his brother. Suddenly a quiver shook his spare frame. He determined, cost what it might, to carry his theory into practice. It would be a last kindness; he could not refuse it to the only person he loved. The mute appeal in that eye was unanswerable.

Slowly, almost mechanically, he proceeded to take his brother's pocket-case from his pocket, as he knew he would wish him to do; he felt in the other pocket to see if there were other papers he could take charge of. Then he took out his revolver and deliberately pointed it at the shapeless features that confronted him. His nerve failed him. It was more than he could do. His arm sank, but the appeal in that eye seemed to change to a look of reproach. Again he raised his weapon, pointed, and, turning his head away, fired. . . .

"By Jove! do you see that chap? Must be a Boche deliberately robbing one of our wounded?"

An R.A.M.C. officer, descending the hill, was speaking to the subaltern who accompanied him.

"Are you sure it is a Boche?"

"Of course it is. Don't you see his grey coat? Wish I had my glasses, though, the light is so bad——"

He broke off with an exclamation of horror and indignation.

"My God! did you see that?" he cried. "Shot him after rifling his pockets." As he seized his rifle and took careful aim, the subaltern made a movement of restraint; but the other shook his head impatiently and fired.

The R.A.M.C. officer reached the two bodies first, and as he came upon them he gave a great cry. "John Milligan!" he exclaimed, puzzled.

"And his brother, I think," added the subaltern.

The English are not a talkative people at any time, and on such an occasion as this words were obviously superfluous.

"We had better say nothing about this," said the officer after a pause; " it is the simplest way, though I don't understand——"

"I think I understand everything," said the subaltern slowly, "but I shall say nothing."

"For the sake of the regiment, you know," added the officer.

"Yes," replied the junior, " for the sake of the regiment."

And, as if in mockery, the warm rays of the morning sun shone down on that scene of desolation and death.

THE MAN IN THE NEXT BED

by
Paul Alverdes

ONE autumn evening in 1915, while the Allies were delivering a violent attack on the German positions to the south of La Bassée, a raw recruit, who was little more than a boy, was alone in one of his battery's dug-outs. In accordance with orders he had been boiling soup at an iron stove for the other men in his battery outside, who had been loading and firing ceaselessly since the attacks by Moroccan and Indian divisions, which had unexpectedly developed immediately after lunch. He was just about to dish out the steaming fluid with a large ladle into the dixies on the ground, when a bearded face appeared between the tent-flaps, at the entrance to the dug-out, and looked down at him nervously. Directly afterwards the flaps opened completely, and a strange militiaman in coat and helmet, carrying a full pack, slowly descended the steps.

His sudden appearance dismayed and confused the youth for a moment in a manner which he himself could not understand. It was as though he had known the man for a long time and had only been waiting for him to come again, but at the same time it was in vain that he racked his memory as to how he knew him; he could not think what they had had to do with one another. The images which he conjured up passed across his mind's eye with lightning rapidity again and again. Shapes kept on giving place to one another, young and old, handsome and distorted, with which he had run through the misty fields of shell-holes or wandered about in the nightly labyrinth of graves. But this one, which drew him as with the strength of a father's love, with a powerful and mysterious force, was not among them.

When he had reached the bottom of the steps the stranger remained standing before him. He was of gigantic size, so that everything which he had about him seemed like a kind of toy, although he was very heavily burdened. He had thick, straw-coloured hair, which bunched out of the rim of his helmet that had slipped to the back of his head, and a broad beard of the same colour. His eyes, under their bushy, white brows, were small and of a very light blue. Their glance was searching and uneasy, but not as though he were afraid of any danger, but as though he were in constant expectation of being called upon to perform some duty which he did not wish to refuse. His pack was adjusted very high on his back, and his rifle, the breech of which was carefully wrapped about with rags, hung obliquely across his chest, while six or eight chains of closely packed clips of cartridge cases, which he had disposed about his neck and shoulders, drew his weight somewhat forward. A knotted stick with a long, very flat-polished crook hung from his wrist in a leather sheath.

"I say," he remarked in a tone that was half apologetic and half confidential, as he took off his helmet and dangled it like a hat in his hands—"I say, it's all right here." He gazed at the steaming dixies.

"Yes, you've struck it all right here," answered the youth, and bent lower over his cooking utensils; "they're all good fellows here."

The militiaman now also bent down low and drew his chin in, for at that very moment it seemed again as though one of the naval shells that kept howling over the position in a flat trajectory were poising in the air directly over the dug-out in order the more certainly to hit its objective.

He was coming back from leave, he murmured almost into the youth's ear, after waiting for the explosion, and he had had a long way to march. He belonged to a Prussian militia regiment, which must be somewhere in front. He wanted to rejoin his company that night. He wanted to ask for a dish of soup, because he hadn't had anything to eat.

Without a word the youth passed one of the dixies to him, and the militiaman, grasping this helmet between his knees, raised it with both fists to his mouth. He emptied it in long gulps without setting it down and without taking his eyes off the face of the other. Then he returned the pot, wiped his beard as he passionately murmured, "Many thanks, old boy," and began to look about the dug-out with a kind of polite interest.

"Don't misunderstand me," he then uttered with an insistent look, when he saw that the other did not catch the drift of his meaning—"don't misunderstand me, but I wonder whether I ought to give myself up?" He explained that he was, so to speak, a double size, but could generally only get rations for one. That was terrible, and sometimes he thought that he would not be able to stick it much longer.

The youth filled the dixie again, somewhat reluctantly, and with a nervous glance at the entrance of the dug-out; for at that time provisions were beginning to run short, and the thoughtless sharing of rations with members of strange units had already been punished in some instances by the authorities, as being unfair to one's own.

The stranger refreshed himself once more, then he put on his helmet, fastened the chin-strap, and was about to go up the steps again with an embarrassed "Good luck to you, old boy." But the youth suddenly recollected a box containing cake, which his aunt had sent him a few days previously; he had been keeping it on a shelf at the head of his bunk. He called the militiaman back again, got up an earth-step in front of him, and tied the box to the straps of his pack by a string. The large man remained motionless, looked down at the boy's hands, and shook his head the while, seeming with heartfelt sighs to express his regret at taking away such precious things. Suddenly he looked up, raised his enormous hand to his helmet by way of farewell, and remained for some time in that position, while he smiled at the youth with the purest expression of admiring and devoted love. The latter slowly blushed all over and returned his smile. Directly afterwards the stranger disappeared through the flaps into the outside world.

A little later, when the recruit also stepped out, carrying in both hands the dixies which were tied together, a cloud of shrapnel was again screaming over the battery, which was still firing madly. The four guns, dug in only up to their carriage axles, were standing fairly close together on the marshy meadow ground over to the left; the bombardiers were massed close up behind the shield, while the telephonists were dug in further back with the sergeant, who was constantly shouting ranges and fire orders. The flickering lights of the attack showed them all up clearly, now in a red light as of distant conflagrations, and now sharp, black shadows in the white blaze of munition dumps that were going up on the flank, or again bathed in a dazzling brightness as bunches of Verey lights came slowly gliding to earth, illuminating the foliage and grasses so that for seconds they gleamed as green as by daylight. The militiaman was still leaning on his stick in the shadow of the farm ruins under which the dug-out was; he gazed up at the sky, shaking his head, as though he were wondering what the weather was going to do, and plaintively sighing again and again: "O God! O Christ Jesus!" Then he went up once more to the youth, who was just getting his breath before making a dash through the firezone with the soup, and gazed long in poignant silence at his face. Finally, he turned away, scrambled up the bank of the road to the right of the battery, and, swaying under his load, broke into a double in the direction where the infantry fire was at its hottest.

Not long afterwards the battery ceased firing, as the attack seemed to have collapsed. A man remained on guard with the guns; the others threw themselves fully clad and in their boots on the mattresses in their dug-outs, and the youth also lay down beside his fellows. But, although he was utterly exhausted, he could not get to sleep; the memory of his strange visitor began to trouble him, and again he ransacked his memory in vain for a similar voice, face, and form. He is in difficulties, he thought, listening anxiously, as a confused din came across from the trenches; they are doing him in. He had the face of a man who is soon to die, and now I know how I recognised it. Finally, however, in order to hear no more, he drew his thick woollen cap over his ears and fell asleep, but he had a strange dream.

In the grey of morning he saw a monstrous flat field, on which innumerable soldiers were standing next to one another in grey coats and grey helmets. It was surely the whole army; they were ranged all in circles, facing inwards as for a game of ring of roses. The game seemed to be starting, and they raised their hands to their helmets in salutation, and bowed to one another. They all looked just the same, for each one of them had the face of the flaxen bearded militiaman. But suddenly the sky flamed with tongues of light, a terrific thunderclap shattered the air, the groups broke up into a chaotic mass of men swinging their weapons, and in an instant they were changed, each one assuming a different form.

At this moment the dreamer awoke completely, the guard shouted the alarm, the bombardiers rushed cursing up the steps into the open, where the crashing of hand grenades, the rattle of infantry fire, and the confused noise of men shouting words of command already filled the air. As he stumbled along to his gun behind the others, the recruit thought that he detected something like blue sky above the dawn mists of the grey morning; we shall have fine weather again, he thought, and above and about him swarms of birds were singing. But he perceived directly that it was the whistling of rifle bullets. They were coming thick, in a fairly flat trajectory across the hollow, and the top of a willow behind whose trunk he flung himself, waiting until an oncoming shell should have burst, scattered a silent, constant rain of leaves and twigs upon him. Suddenly, as though it had long been settled and decided, and it had merely slipped his mind for the time, it occurred to him that to-day he was to die. In point of fact he had never thought of such a thing, but had confidently attributed a virtue greater than the force of any bullet to the blessing which his father had given him with his farewell embrace. Now, however, it seemed to him the simplest and most natural thing in the world to die here in the meadow by the ruins of the French farm, and to his own astonishment the idea no longer terrified him, although many and many a time he had not been able to master a wild fear of death. From that moment the day passed in a state of expectation that had no element of fear, but mere curiosity as to when and how his death would occur.

He had taken the place at his gun of the loading bombardier, who had been killed shortly after dawn—with a bullet in his hip the man had staggered a few yards to the side, crouching and pressing both hands to the front of his body. He now lay flat on his back in the grass with slightly parted lips, as though he were only asleep; for there had been no time to carry him away. At his place behind the shield, close to the gun-barrel, the recruit was now standing, wearing a blue woollen jacket, his cap askew on his head, with the sweat pouring down his face and mingling with the oil and gun fumes.

"Get a move on! Same elevation! Another round! Another round!" the sergeant kept shouting again and again, leaping like a man possessed from gun to gun. "Fire!" shouted No. 1 as he sprawled over the sights; the youth bent from his hips and snatched out the detonator by its leather thong. The howitzer leapt with a thunderous report, the thick short barrel speeding backwards deep between the thighs of the limber, as though it would bury itself in the earth, and it was only slowly and with reluctant growling that it reverted to its former position. Even before it had completely done so the youth tore open the breech again. A puff of smoke belched out, driving the empty shell case to the rear; its place was taken by a new one. He raised his free arm and pressed his hand to his ear, and even as the breech was rattled to, the new word of command rang out. This lasted hour after hour until the burnt-out cartridges mounted to hills and the empty wicker baskets for shell cases rose mountain high behind the guns. More and more frequently a high-explosive shell, bursting right among the guns, or a cloud of shrapnel just above the shield, drove them all to the ground, and more and more of the section remained afterwards lying on their faces or ran off suddenly with staring eyes, staggering like drunken men and covered with blood. But nothing happened to the youth.

It was already near evening when the battery had fired off all its ammunition; there were no fresh supplies to be got, and the remnant of the section collected in one of the dug-outs in an exhausted condition, expecting to be taken prisoners or to receive orders to leave the position. But all of a sudden, just as the rattle of machine-gun fire in the immediate vicinity and the shrill shouts of native troops who were attacking again seemed to herald the immediate approach of the end, the recruit was overcome with a wild fit of uneasiness, and he pushed into the open past the sergeant, who was on the lookout for the eagerly awaited munition columns. He observed on the bank of the road to the right of the battery a man crawling back painfully on all fours, whom he believed that he recognised. The man was bareheaded, and his yellow hair hung right down into his eyes. The sergeant had seen him too, and was gesticulating and shouting at him to crawl under the cover of the remains of a wall, which skirted the road there. At the same time, however, he held the youth, who wanted to go across, back by the belt, for the British machine-gun bullets kept pelting across the street, and the battery had already lost several men that day, who had wanted to get across to help the man to make his way back.

The wounded man must have heard the shouts; he stopped moving, raised his head, and stared across in perplexity. Then suddenly he crumpled up and rolled over on his side. Then, with his face turned away, he made a movement with his arms indicating that he badly wanted a drink. The youth wrenched himself free, and got across in great bounds. But while he knelt beside him, and pulled at the stopper of his water-bottle with his teeth, he saw that he had made a mistake. The wounded man was not the militiaman after all; he was wearing the badges of a different regiment. The youth pushed his hand under his neck, and put the bottle to his mouth. Greedily the wounded man smacked his lips like a child and tried to drink; but suddenly an anxious look came on his face, and with his muddy hand he pushed the bottle from him. He seemed to wish to say something, but he only shook his head and looked at the recruit with a wistful embarrassment, as though he profoundly regretted having caused so much trouble, and now to be unable even to drink. His head-shaking changed to a rolling movement; he gave a pathetic sigh, made one gesture of negation with his hand, and lay still with failing eyes. At the same moment a bullet from the flank went through the throat of the young man, who was just going to raise himself, and he flung himself upon the dead man, pressing his face upon his. He got up again, however, at once, staggered back, and collapsed at the feet of the sergeant, who was cursing and lamenting.

By the most extraordinary chance the arteries of the neck had not been hurt, or at any rate they were not bleeding at the moment, and so, breathing with difficulty and at first completely bereft of speech, he was able that very night to reach the nearest field hospital behind that sector of the German position. The doctors immediately took steps to ease his breathing, and were moderately successful.

When he awoke on the following afternoon he found himself in a large room, which had been the waggon-shed of a farm and had been converted into a hospital. Two long rows of rough-hewn beds stood facing one another, and behind each one hung a black board, bearing in white letters the name, unit, and age of its wounded occupant. It was deathly still, as though they were all asleep, or as though they were already dead. The sun shone in obliquely.

When the youth turned over on his side he saw the militiaman sitting in the bed next his own. He recognised him at once, although he seemed very much altered. His hair had been cut in accordance with military requirements and his beard trimmed, no doubt in order to get at his wound more easily, which he, too, must have received in the neck or the lower part of the jaw. Supported by a few pillows he was sitting upright in bed with his neck heavily bandaged and breathing with difficulty; but he seemed to pay no attention to this or to be deliberately concealing it, for he looked straight ahead, not moving his face. His eyes now seemed big and had completely lost all restlessness.

In order to attract his attention, the youth tapped at his bedstead. The other slowly turned his face; he showed no surprise, but just smiled wanly, and as he cast down his eyes, made a soothingly affirmative gesture, as though he had known everything for a long time, and what was going to happen too, and as though the other should just leave things to him. Then he looked straight ahead, laid his finger on his lips, and gazed into the distance again with a clear, resolute expression. The recruit lay back again comforted, and immediately fell once more into a deep sleep.

He did not wake until the middle of the night, when he was roused by a noise, which he could not at once interpret. It was a whistling and hissing and rattling, which was constantly repeated in quick, wild gasps, and he now realised that it was the man in the next bed, fighting with death. In the dim light of the lamps he saw the assistants standing about his bed, he heard the clatter of instruments, and the quiet voice of the doctor giving his instructions. A horrid terror overcame him. I must die, he thought, and I must go off with him; it cannot be otherwise. He wrung his hands and raised them to his face, over which sweat and tears were running; he wanted to pray, but he was unable to do so, for the pious words turned on his lips to desperate railing and cursing. Then he drew the rug over his head and buried his face deep in the pillows; he would have welcomed unconsciousness, even death itself, only to make an end. But it was of no avail. His breath, too, began to rattle, his heart fluttered in his breast, and the room began to sway about him in longer and ever quickening pulsations, and to turn backwards and forwards in a circle. But quite suddenly there was quiet next to him, the light went out, and the figures went away. He listened: the man's breath was coming wholesomely and quietly.

He has got over it, he thought; we have got over it. He stretched himself and closed his eyes. Sleepily, he groped with his hand at his naked breast over the heart. It was going in regular, strong beats.

Next morning, when he awoke, wonderfully refreshed, with a cool skin and a feeling of absolute conviction that he would soon recover, he saw two soldiers taking a long form from the bed next to him and carrying it out. It was wrapped from top to toe in the white bed-cover, and did not stir. He jumped up and stretched out his arms; his lips moved as though he wanted to shout something, but no sound issued from his lips. Then he sat down with burning eyes. When, after a little while, one of the two orderlies returned and began to sponge out the name and regimental number on the board above the empty bed, he sank back and laid both hands over his face. It was now certain that he would return home, and he was ashamed, although perhaps not before men.

He was in due course transferred to a hospital in Germany, where he got well.

A TOUCH OF IRONY

by
André Maurois

CHORUS: " What, Jupiter not so strong as these goddesses?"
PROMETHEUS: " Yes, even he cannot escape destiny."

WHEN young Lieutenant Warburton, temporarily commanding B Company of the Lennox Highlanders, took over his
trench, the Captain he came to relieve said to him:

" This part is not too unhealthy; they are only thirty yards off,
but they are tame Boches. All they ask is to be left alone."

" We will wake things up a bit," said Warburton to his men,
when the peaceable warrior had departed.

When wild beasts are too well fed, they become domesticated;
but a few well-directed rockets will make them savage again. In
virtue of this principle, Warburton, having provided himself with
a star shell, instead of sending it straight up fired it horizontally
towards the German trenches.

A distracted Saxon sentry cried, " Liquid-fire attack!" The
Boche machine-guns began to bark. Warburton, delighted, replied
with grenades. The enemy called the artillery to its assistance. A
telephone call, a hail of shrapnel, and immediate reprisals by the
British big guns.

The next day the German *communiqué* said: " An attack by
the British under cover of liquid-fire at H—— was completely
checked by the combined·fire of our infantry and artillery."

0275 Private Scott, H.J., who served his King and country under
the strenuous Warburton, disapproved heartily of his officer's
heroic methods. Not that he was a coward, but the War had taken
him by surprise when he had just married a charming girl, and,
as Captain Gadsby of the Pink Hussars says, " a married man is

only half a man." Scott counted the days he spent in the trenches, and this one was the first of ten, and his chief was reckless.

The god who guards lovers intervened the next day by the simple means of a scrap of paper asking for a man from the regiment, mechanic by trade, to look after a machine at P—— for disinfecting clothes. P—— was a pretty little town at least eight miles from the front line, rather deserted by the inhabitants on account of *marmites*, but all the same a safe and comfortable retreat for a troglodyte of the trenches.

0275 Private Scott, mechanic by trade, put his name down. His Lieutenant abused him, his Colonel recommended him, and his General nominated him. An old London omnibus painted a military grey took him away to his new life, far from Warburton and his perils.

The machine which Scott had to look after was in the yard of a college, an old building covered with ivy; and Abbé Hoboken, the principal, received him, when he arrived, as if he were a General.

" Are you a Catholic, my son?" he asked him in the English of the college.

Luckily for Scott, he did not understand, and answered vaguely. "Yes, sir."

This involuntary renunciation of the Scotch Presbyterian Church procured him a room belonging to a mobilised Belgian professor and a bed with sheets.

Now, at that very moment, Hauptmann Reineker, who commanded a German battery of heavy artillery at Paschendaele, was in a very bad temper.

The evening post had brought him an ambiguous letter from his wife in which she mentioned too often, and with an affectation of indifference, a wounded officer of the Guards whom she had been nursing for several days.

During the night he surveyed his gun emplacements on the outskirts of a wood, then he said suddenly :

" Wolfgang, have you any shells available?"

" Yes, sir."

" How many?"

" Three."

" Good! Wake up Theresa's crew."

He then verified his calculations by his map.

The men, half awake, loaded the enormous gun. Reineker gave the order, and, shaking up everyone and everything, the shell started forth, hurtling through the night.

0275 Private Scott, then, who adored his wife and had accepted a post without honour for her sake, was sleeping peacefully in the bedroom of a mobilised Belgian professor; and Captain Reineker, whose wife no longer loved him, and whom he mistrusted, was striding furiously up and down among the frozen woods. And these two circumstances, widely apart from one another, were developed independently in an indifferent world.

Now the calculations of Reineker, like most calculations, went wrong. He was four hundred yards out. His landmark was the church. From the church to the college was four hundred yards. A light wind increased the deviation by twenty yards, and from that moment the Reineker and the Scott situation began to have points in common. At this particular point the chest of 0275 Private Scott received the full force of the ·305 shell, and he was blown into a thousand bits, which, amongst other things, put an end to the Scott situation.

SOUVENIRS

by
W. F. Morris

A MALTESE cart drawn by a chestnut horse, harnessed in the military fashion without a collar, was jogging along one of the straight, tree-bordered roads of France. Side by side on the plank seat under the canvas tilt sat a young officer and a private soldier. Behind them in the back of the cart was an unsoiled Wolesley valise resembling a huge brown roly-poly.

The private soldier, who had been a country postman in civilian life, was holding forth disparagingly on French agricultural methods, and the young officer was murmuring " quite " and " really " appropriately and even inappropriately in a manner which suggested that on this sunny afternoon in June, 1916, his interest lay in things other than agriculture.

Secretly he was experiencing much the same feelings of excitement and solemnity as he had known on his first day at school not so many years before. He was on the threshold of what the illustrated papers at home in England called " The Great Adventure," and to this youth of eighteen, who found himself, after six months training on his way to join a battalion in the field, the War *was* a great adventure. It was *the* great adventure.

It was not surprising, therefore, that he was not very interested in his companion's disquisition on roots and lucerne and binders; but politeness and that new-boy feeling of not knowing precisely what was " done " and what was " not done " restrained him from interrupting to ask questions about that in which he was interested.

The little Maltese cart jogged unhurriedly on its way. Lorries passed in low rolling clouds of white dust, and G.S. waggons, whose drivers dropped their arms and jerked their heads in salute like mechanical dolls. The road switch-backed uncompromisingly across the low, corn-covered hills of Picardy; and its bordering trees, whose blue shadows lay diagonally across the white surface, could be seen ahead and behind cresting the rollers of the hedgeless country like the wake of a ship. From each crest the road fell away to a valley, and then ran tape-like up the slope beyond; and from each crest the young officer looked eagerly ahead for some change in the landscape that would announce that he was nearing the barrier that stretched from Switzerland to the Channel.

His eagerness was rewarded when the surmounting of a slope showed the road ahead swooping over a low, intermediate crest towards a tall, ruddy church tower that rose from a medley of roofs and chimneys glimmering in the heat haze beyond. There seemed to be something odd about this little town, though at that distance it was difficult to say what it was.

The driver broke off a one-sided discussion on artificial fertilisers to point with his whip at a glittering bar of light that appeared to jut almost horizontally from the top of the tower. "That's the 'Anging Virgin of Albert," he announced, "what the 'Uns can't knock down. They say when it do come down that'll be the end of the War. And," he added cynically, "if that's true, it's a perishin' marvel to me that some bloke 'asn't been up there afore now and pulled it down."

The young officer seized the opportunity to ask a question that had been uppermost in his mind for the past hour. "How far away are the trenches?"

"Up on them hills beyont the town—about four kilos."

The young officer stared eagerly at the low skyline dimly visible through the haze above the roofs.

A long-drawn whistle on a descending note rose suddenly above the klipity-klop of the horse's hoofs. "'Ark at Jerry!" exclaimed the driver.

The young officer was trying to account for the sound when suddenly a reddish-black cloud bellied out in the town ahead. A sound like a blow on a huge brass tray followed.

"Was that a shell?" he asked. His voice betrayed the excitement he was trying to conceal.

The driver nodded. "And here we come again!" he exclaimed, as that long-drawn, descending whistle rose again out of the distance.

The young officer watched the town with galloping pulses. The seat beneath him gave a little jump. He saw a red fountain spout suddenly by the distant church tower and that black, bellying cloud materialise in the clear air. A long, rumbling roar, like coals being tipped down a chute, followed.

"Five-nine," diagnosed the driver professionally. "In the square."

The young officer nodded. His eyes were very bright. He had seen a shell burst, and the experience had been more thrilling and far less terrifying than he had anticipated. Really, it was rather fun to hear that curious whistling sound and then try to guess where the black, rolling balloon of smoke would appear. He would see if he could guess the next one correctly by the sound. But to his regret no more came.

As the cart crossed a bridge above weed-grown railway lines and approached the outlying houses, he saw what it was that had appeared odd about this town. It was a mere shell. Roofs were full of holes or tileless, and windows were without glass. Dark brick walls were pitted with star-shaped hollows as though splashed with red paint. Here and there a roof had collapsed and a ragged hole gaped in a wall. On the right, where a factory had once stood, was a tangle of rusty metal like a huge bramble bush. Weeds sprouted between the stones of the pavements, and circular holes in the *pavé* of the road had been filled with brick ends.

The church, seen close at hand, was a ruin. The nave was roofless and gutted; the great tower gaped like a broken cardboard box, its ornate brick and stonework gashed and pitted as though slashed by the hammer of a frenzied giant; and the huge gilded figure of the Virgin on top was bent downwards, so that the child she had held aloft now spread its flashing arms like a diver above the shattered houses.

It reminded the young officer of those silent, ruined cities of the jungle that had captured his boyish imagination, and he would have liked to have gone exploring through these brick-littered streets; but he caught only a tantalising glimpse of a shattered, shell-pocked square before the cart turned off down a street that led back to the open country.

Regret, however, was soon forgotten in the interest evoked by his surroundings; for instead of the green corn that had formerly flanked the road, rank grass and weeds grew on the unhedged fields, and here and there, marked by the yellow weed which seemed to choose them for its home, were holes of varying circumference and depth which even his inexperienced eye recognised as shell craters. Signs of military occupation were now abundant. Horse lines, huts of various kinds, and dumps were scattered about the slopes or tucked snugly away in the tributary valleys, and when the driver left the road for a rutted track between two gentle slopes, the sudden turning of a corner brought into view an amphitheatre crowded like a fair ground. Every inch of the barren ground on either side of the dusty track was occupied by horse lines, waggon lines, forage dumps, and tarpaulins; and the surrounding slopes were terraced with huts, shacks, and bivouacs of every shape and size.

The driver pulled up by a large tarpaulin filled with water. "That's A Company office up there, sir," he said, pointing towards the slope. The young officer, in all the panoply of revolver holster, field-glasses, water-bottle, and haversack, climbed down to the dusty, sunbaked track and mopped his face with a khaki handkerchief. The driver hoisted the valise on to his shoulder and led the way between a tarpaulin shack and a huge mound of trusses of hay. He dumped his burden between a Stevenson hut and a shack built of ammunition boxes. "In there, sir," he said, with a jerk of his head towards the shack. "You'll find the Captain inside."

The young officer stooped and went through the narrow doorway. Three or four rope-handled ammunition boxes, a blanket-covered table, and a black japanned despatch box with A Company painted on it in white letters, occupied nearly all the space inside. A dark moustached young man wearing captain's badges of rank sat on an upturned box at the table. The young officer pressed his left arm as close to his body as his bulging equipment would permit, clicked his heels, and saluted.

The young Captain looked up and exclaimed : "Hullo! What can I do for you?"

The newcomer, standing stiffly to attention, said : "I have been ordered to report for duty, sir."

The other leaned back on his box and took up a long-stemmed pipe that lay on some papers before him. "Oh, I see. You're a reinforcement." He put the pipe in his mouth and felt in his pocket for a match. "That's good. What is your name?"

"Eastwell, sir."

The Captain nodded as he drew at his half-smoked pipe. "Eastwell—I see." He threw away the match and held out a hand.

"Mine's Jervis. I run A Company. Been out before?"

"No, sir," answered Eastwell.

Jervis nodded towards the other's cumbersome equipment. " I expect you would like to get rid of that junk, anyway. Dump it in the corner there."

Eastwell slipped off his harness and rebuttoned his shoulder straps.

"Got your kit with you?"

"It's outside, sir."

"Good." Jervis glanced at his wrist-watch and stood up. "Well, I'll just show you where to put your kit and then we'll have some tea. Come along."

II

Tea, consisting of bread, butter, and jam, was spread on a box outside the Stevenson hut. "We always feed on the 'terrace,'" grinned Jervis. "You don't eat so many flies."

A young officer wearing a web belt was introduced as Stokes. "Mouldy jam," he growled as he fished a purplish mass out of the tin and inspected it on the end of a knife. "Do you know, Charles, I have dark suspicions that Daddy keeps back all the strawberry for headquarters."

"You don't know our canny Quartermaster, do you?" he added to Eastwell.

"Is he the grey-haired Scotch officer with a lot of medal ribbons?"

Stokes nodded with his mouth full. "That's him—round and ruddy like a haggis."

"I saw him at battalion headquarters," said Eastwell. "Do you know, I—I thought he was the C.O., and——"

"I know," laughed Jervis. "His grey hairs and Piccadilly ribbons are rather imposing. But he's quite harmless unless you lose your disc identity with string, or some damn thing; then he talks backwards at you and eats his young."

"Just come out?" asked Stokes.

"I crossed last night," admitted Eastwell.

"Just in time for the big push."

"Really!"

Jervis nodded. "At seven-thirty ack emma to-morrow the band begins. But of course it's a secret."

"Yes, of course," said Eastwell seriously.

Stokes nodded emphatically with his mouth full of bread and jam. "Rather! Why, we only heard it officially last night when a chit came in labelled all over 'Secret and Confidential' and 'Very Urgent,' though, of course, we had it from the civilians weeks ago."

"It is to be the real thing this time," put in Jervis. "Non-stop to Berlin."

"Same as Loos," grinned Stokes.

"Shut up, George. It's going to be a good show. The cavalry are all up ready and bags of reserves." He pointed towards a rectangular barbed wire enclosure on the opposite slope. "See that gadget? That's for prisoners."

"I say, is it really?" exclaimed Eastwell.

"And do you see all that water down there?" asked Stokes solemnly, pointing with a jammy knife at the tarpaulin water reservoir below them. "Well, that's for the German Navy."

Eastwell grinned. "I say, what on earth is that?" he exclaimed suddenly. Something huge, glistening, and yellow was slowly rising from behind the opposite slope.

Jervis cocked an uninterested eye upon it over the top of his mug of tea. "That's the old sausage balloon going up. Spotting for the heavies. Gets good visibility this time of day with the sun behind."

Eastwell watched the huge yellow bag rise slowly till it hung far above, glistening in the sun like a bloated slug.

"I say, it's—it's awfully interesting about to-morrow," he said presently. "What do we do, sir? Or is it all a secret?"

"Oh, we are just waiting for the Boche collapse to push through. We are not in to-morrow's show. The platoons are all on detachment—O. Pips and things. George here lives in a hole on the Peronne Road—like the night watchman. That is, when he's not catching fish in the Somme."

"Is he a great fisherman?" asked Eastwell conversationally.

"Well, you see, he's the company bombing expert," said Jervis. And then they both laughed at Eastwell's mystified face. "He drops bombs in the river," explained Jervis, "and stuns the fish so that they float to the top. Then he collects the poor miserable little blighters before they come round. Not my idea of sport—still!"

"Still, his sportsmanship does not interfere with his appetite," put in Stokes drily.

Suddenly it seemed to Eastwell that an express train was tearing across the sky above them. He looked up, but there was nothing to be seen. And then the sound ended in mid-career with a stunning thunderclap right overhead, and he saw a thick woolly black cloud materialise as if by magic in the clear air.

"Jerry sniping the old sausage," commented Jervis.

"What about the fellow in the basket?" asked Eastwell, who had his eyes on the black speck that swung below the glistening yellow bag.

"He is probably wishing he had joined the Navy," grinned Stokes.

"Here we come again!" exclaimed Jervis, as the train-like roar hurtled out of the distance. "Ah, that's a nasty one!" The thick woolly smoke which just preceded the stunning thunderclap was just above and in front of the balloon.

"Thought that would shift him," commented Stokes, as the balloon swung round and moved slowly back.

Eastwell turned his eyes back to the coming and going of horses and waggons and men in the motley town below him. "All this is awfully interesting!" he exclaimed.

Jervis was pressing tobacco into the bowl of his pipe. "War is damned boring really, but you have come out just at the most interesting time. To-morrow in that cage you will probably see more Germans in half an hour than I have seen the whole eighteen months I've been out."

"But in the trenches surely——" began Eastwell.

Jervis grinned and shook his head.

"It's—it's all rather different," said Eastwell. "I thought that one always——"

"I know," broke in Stokes. "But one doesn't. I was out months before I saw a Hun. And then it was only a little twirp of a fellow washing his neck in a bucket. It was one morning when the mist lifted suddenly, and then it came down again before I could have a pot at him.

"You know, Charles, it's my belief we could walk into Fricourt any time we liked. I don't believe there is anybody there except a machine-gun or two and a fellow running up and down putting up lights and firing a round occasionally. I believe Fritz keeps all his troops back in support. Millington and I went over one night, and we walked along his parapet for a hell of a distance and never saw a Boche. I don't believe there is anyone there."

"Well, we shall know to-morrow, anyway," said Jervis.

"Where are the trenches?" asked Eastwell.

Jervis waved a hand over his shoulder. "Over there. What time are you going back to your hole, George?"

"Not till dusk."

"You might take Eastwell up as far as Bronfay Farm and show him where the communicating trench begins. What do you say, Eastwell?"

"Oh, I—I'd like to awfully, sir."

"Right-o, then. He can find his own way back, or perhaps Stockton will give him a lift back to Sapper Corner in his car."

III

Excitement and a sobering sense of the solemnity of the occasion were the conflicting feelings that possessed Eastwell later on that evening as he struggled into his equipment in the Stevenson hut, where his valise had been spread out by his newly appointed servant. He was going up to the trenches; perhaps even into them. A veteran like Stokes might regard such a journey with bored indifference, but it was not to be expected that a newcomer could contemplate it without a little flutter of the pulses. Though nearly everyone might be a soldier nowadays, there were, after all, varying degrees of soldiership, and the trenches was the summit of those stages of efficiency and experience which one begun to climb with one's first clumsy efforts at forming fours. This was the end of one's apprenticeship; one was about to be initiated into the final mystery.

"Good God! you look like Ragtime Cowboy Joe with all that revolver and stuff hung round you!" was Stokes' greeting as Eastwell emerged from the Stevenson hut.

Eastwell blushed to the roots of his fair hair. "What do I take?" he asked.

"Just your gas gadget and tin hat. You never wear a revolver except in the front line, and then you shove it in your pocket."

Dusk was falling as they crossed the Bray-Albert road by a big dump of engineers' stores and took a narrow road running up the slope eastwards. Behind them a line of trees was fretted against the after-sunset glow. "Red at night is the shepherd's delight," quoted Stokes. "I really believe we shall have a fine day for to-morrow."

On either hand was the rank jungle grass that flourished over all the forward area, and the yellow weed that grew profusely in the shell-holes seemed to glow in the fast failing light. A long range shell waddled lazily across the sky and died away. And then a dull, distant crunch told that it had landed far back behind the lines. The hill crest ahead was outlined fitfully against the greenish glow of Verey lights, and occasionally a light itself rose above the crest like some new and splendid planet, sank slowly, and expired.

A sudden explosion close beside him in the darkness startled Eastwell, and instantly the unsuspected gun beneath its canopy of netting sprinkled with leaves leapt out of the dark, vivid in every detail like theatrical scenery, and was gone again.

Stokes pointed to a shattered roof that loomed darkly against the sky. "That's Bronfay Farm," he said. "And that's the trench. We use it only in daylight."

Eastwell peered at the low irregular bank of chalk that zig-zagged away from the road, and he was conscious of a feeling of slight disappointment in his first view of a real trench.

Limber and G.S. waggons passed up the road, dark, slowly moving shapes except for the glow of a cigarette or a spark from a descending hoof. Guns banged to right and left, and their flashes danced like summer lightning among the hills. A sudden paroxysm of sound accompanied by vivid flashes came from the left.

"There, do you hear that?" cried Stokes. "That's a battery of

French seventy-fives. I was watching 'em at it this morning. Potty looking little cannon they are, but they deliver the goods all right."

A line of trees lifted slowly above the dark crest ahead and stood out black and clear cut against the greenish glow that waxed and waned.

A steel-hatted officer wearing staff badges appeared suddenly beside them. " Hullo, Stokes!"

" Hullo, sir. Going to be fine, I believe."

" Looks like it. If so, we will put it across 'em to-morrow."

" I say, sir, could you give Eastwell a lift back to Sapper Corner?"

" If he does not mind waiting a bit."

" Not he. He wants to see the war. He has only just come out."

" Well, he can come along with me if he likes; I'm just going down into Carnoy."

" I'll leave you to it then. Cheerio, sir. Cheerio, Eastwell." And Stokes' form was swallowed up in the darkness.

Eastwell and the staff officer walked on and reached a tree-bordered road littered with twigs that crackled underfoot. One fallen giant lay darkly across the straight pale ribbon, and its shivered stump showed like a broken tooth in the gap in the line of trees whose branches were etched upon the night sky.

They descended a steep, pot-holed track into the darkness of a little valley and found themselves in a hive of industry. Waggons were being unloaded with feverish speed. As soon as one waggon was emptied of its rations or ammunition, it jolted off and another took its place. Long files of men were passing field-gun ammunition from hand to hand in the dark; others were staggering under the weight of the big toffee-apples which were the projectiles of the heavy trench mortars; and a party of men, encouraged by long drawn " heaves," were hauling a howitzer into position, and the cautiously used flashlight of an officer revealed their bare, dripping backs and straining arms.

All this purposeful coming and going in the darkness held a suggestion of big things afoot that set the pulses galloping, and the thunder of the bombardment which went on ceaselessly seemed a fitting accompaniment to the ant-like activity. All too soon for Eastwell, Stockton turned and said : "Well, young fellow, we must be getting back, I suppose. Up bright and early to-morrow."

IV

Eastwell was awake early, and his first thought was the weather. Jervis, in shirt-sleeves, was shaving in the grey light of dawn before a cracked mirror propped on a box. A smell of wood smoke drifted up from the gipsy town of huts below. Eastward, the hills were hidden beneath wrappers of mist, but already the sky was growing rosy.

Jervis waved his safety razor at Eastwell's tousled head appearing from the Stevenson hut. "Hullo, young fellow! Topping morning. The mist will all be gone in an hour or two. Hark at the guns tuning up for the last lap! Poor old Jerry, he's for it to-day."

From behind the mists eastwards came a rapid undercurrent of sound as though thousands of wooden hammers were beating on balks of timber.

"I'm going up to Maricourt," continued Jervis; "and you are to report to Kennedy—he's the R.A.M.C. wallah who's running the dressing station and aid posts on our bit. You will find him in some shelters at the bottom of the road you went up last night."

Eastwell found the shelters and reported. "I would just cruise up and down the road if I were you and see what is going on," said Colonel Kennedy. "If I want you, I will send a runner." He glanced at his watch again. "Another five minutes now and they go over. I am going to ring up headquarters presently and get the news."

Eastwell walked slowly up the road. One or two orderlies wearing new red cross armlets hung about expectantly in the bright morning sunshine; otherwise the road was almost deserted. It seemed peculiarly peaceful in spite of the rumble of the barrage.

Eastwell glanced at his watch for the twentieth time. "They are going over now," he told himself breathlessly, and gazed eagerly eastwards where the road disappeared over the crest of the hill. But there was nothing to be seen except a half limber jogging slowly towards him.

He walked on, and only when the broken roof of Bronfay Farm lifted above the crest did he turn reluctantly and retrace his steps. He longed to go on and see something of the battle that must now be raging beyond that peaceful hill crest, but it would not do to go too far. He might be wanted.

Back at the dressing station Colonel Kennedy was standing on the roadside. "I have rung up headquarters," he said. "We went over ten minutes ago, and all is going well."

Eastwell wandered off again. Some twenty yards to the right of the road a French howitzer was in action. He stopped to watch the gun numbers at work. The heavy breech was swung open and the shell and charge pushed home. The short ugly nose of the weapon rose. Then came a spurt of flame, a slobber of smoke, and a detonation that smacked the ear-drums like a blow as the barrel slid back on its recoil buffers. He heard the shell sizzling away into the distance, and discovered that by watching along the line of fire he could even see the shell itself as a tiny black receding dot high up in the sky.

He went off again up the road, and this time he ventured further. He reached the farm. The yard was stacked with shells and stores.

Some of the shells stood nearly four feet in height and were painted yellow. Two motor ambulances stood in the lee of the wall. On the left, by the outer wall, the communicating trench with its bordering mounds of excavated earth zigzagged away over the crest. A steel-hatted sentry with fixed bayonet stood on guard at the end of it. Away to the right was a small wood in which concealed field-guns were booming, but ahead nothing was visible except the trees on the twig-strewn road he had crossed the night before.

Three men were coming down the road towards him. Something odd about them held his attention. Their arms were about each other's shoulders, and the sound of their voices raised in a lusty chorus came fitfully between the booming of the barrage. They carried neither rifle nor equipment, and as they drew near he saw that they were wounded. Their tunics were open at the neck, and a little white label dangled from the third button of each.

The middle man had one leg of his breeches cut away just above the puttee, revealing a broad white bandage bound round the thigh. The man on his right had one sleeve of his tunic ripped off and a field dressing bound round the upper arm. The third man had no puttee on one leg, and the bandage round the shin had a dark red stain in front. They hobbled cheerfully along, singing at the top of their voices.

Two men in fatigue dress strolled from the farm to speak to them, and Eastwell joined the little group. He tried to avoid looking at the bandages, but they fascinated him. There was nothing shocking about them, however, and the men themselves seemed careless of their injuries.

"How are we getting on up there, boys?" asked one of the men in fatigue dress.

"Old Jerry's getting it in the bleedin' neck," replied one of the wounded.

"Got a fag, chum?" asked he of the bandaged arm.

Eastwell fumbled for his cigarette case and passed it round. These men had passed the supreme test; they had been "over the top," and he basked in the reflected glory.

"'Ow far 'ave we got?" demanded the other man in fatigue dress.

"I copped this packet on Jerry's parapet," answered he of the bandaged thigh, puffing luxuriously at his cigarette. "We're in their second line now and going fine. Kaiser Bill won't 'arf be vexed."

"'O says we're Fred Karno's army?" demanded the third.

"Come on, me lucky lads, where's this dressin' station?"

Eastwell eagerly pointed out the way.

"Are we down'earted? No," they roared. "Is Jerry down-'earted? Yes." And they hobbled off singing lustily.

More walking wounded appeared in twos and threes. One man wore a German pickelhaube on his bandaged head, and strutted along in imitation of the goose step whenever he passed a knot of onlookers. Men in fatigue dress came from their burrows and shacks and sat on the banks at the roadside to watch, and much good-natured chaff passed between the wounded and the onlookers.

The road became busy with traffic. Lorries and limber waggons passed up it; ambulances came slowly down. Then came the first batch of prisoners, half a dozen men in faded field grey and black, shin-high boots, shepherded by a jaunty Tommy, cigarette in mouth, bayoneted rifle slung over one shoulder, and an inexhaustible fund of back chat to the chaff of the onlookers.

Eastwell gazed at them much as he would have gazed at exhibits in a menagerie. These were the Germans who had turned the world upside down, the exponents of blood and iron, whose atrocities had sent a shudder through Europe. He had never seen a German soldier in the flesh, though he had seen countless sketches and caricatures of the spike-helmeted blonde beast with a machine-gun. But these men looked harmless enough. They looked like very poor and rather stupid country labourers. They were so much less imposing than he had imagined they would be. With their ill-fitting, dirt-stained clothes, narrow chests, and shuffling walk, they did not even look like soldiers. If they were all we were up against, then the whole thing was a vast bluff.

And an officer prisoner, whom he saw later, did not agree with his preconceived idea of the ruthless, efficient Prussian. He was a little squit of a fellow in an absurd tight-waisted top coat with plum-coloured facings. He wore a cap with an enormous shiny black peak that made him look like a bird under an extinguisher, and he gazed about him through his ridiculous monocle with such an air of affectation that Eastwell wanted to pick him up and spank him.

He went back to the camp in the valley for lunch, but Jervis had not returned. The cage on the opposite slope was nearly full of prisoners. A green-tabbed intelligence officer was questioning some of them, and others stood with hands raised above their close cropped heads while a sergeant-major searched them. A crowd of Tommies in grey shirt-sleeves lounged outside the wire and looked on.

Later in the afternoon he met the contents of the cage winding in a long, slowly moving column out of the valley, shepherded by half a dozen cavalrymen with drawn swords; and he was very amused when the cavalry officer in front shouted some order in German and the dreary column of field grey goose-stepped a dozen yards and eyes righted to an English Colonel who was passing.

V

After dusk the traffic on the road increased. It seemed as though the whole British Army was moving forward that night. Limbers, G.S. waggons, Maltese carts, gun waggons, water carts, and guns crowded up the road, the horses with their noses over the tail-boards of the waggon in front; ambulances, lorries, and tenders coming down had difficulty in passing. Mounted military police rode here and there striving to keep the mass of vehicles on the move. Occasionally the stream was dammed to allow a long bar-relled sixty-pounder gun with its team of eight huge, straining hairies to pull off the road. Caterpillar tractors rattled and clanked, dragging behind them six-inch howitzers or the huge steel mount-ings and squat barrels of nine-point-twos. By the wood to the right some sixty-pounders were in action, and at each salvo the night was lit as though a bonfire had been uncovered.

Beyond the farm stood Stockton, the A.P.M., pipe in mouth, steel helmet tilted over one eye, watching one of his men control-ling the stream of traffic at the cross roads. He recognised East-well by the light of the sixty-pounder flashes.

"Bit of a scrum, sir," said Eastwell.

Stockton nodded. "Rather like the Mansion House—what! But that fellow is used to this sort of thing. He's a City police-man," he said, with a nod towards the traffic control man, who was manipulating the stream of vehicles with professional skill. "Fortunately, the Boche is too busy getting his own batteries back to worry about us, or he might have made it very unpleasant."

"News still good, sir?"

"I believe so. We were hung up at Fricourt this morning. But there is a rumour that we got into it after dark. We will go along to brigade headquarters here in a moment and get the latest news."

Fifty yards back along the road the lights of an aid post twinkled in the darkness, and, nearby, the red lamp of a brigade head-quarters was propped on a mound of chalk. Stockton climbed over the tumbled earth and rank grass, and led the way down the dozen odd steps of a timber revetted shaft that led underground. It was Eastwell's first visit to a dug-out, and this one fulfilled his rather romantic expectations. The narrow pit-propped passage at the foot of the sloping shaft gave entrance to three or four compartments. From those on the left came the click of a typewriter and the hum of a buzzer, but that facing him was crowded with officers. The smoke of many pipes drifted in wreaths about the electric bulbs that hung from coloured cables on the roof timbers. Regardless of the laughter and buzz of voices about him, the red-tabbed Brigade Major was at work at a table piled with papers; the Brigadier was talking to a group of officers in the centre of the dug-out. He caught sight of Stockton in the doorway, and called: "Hullo, Stockton! Come in."

Stockton saluted and went in, followed by Eastwell. The Brigadier took his long-stemmed pipe from his mouth and said with a grin: "Get him a drink somebody; he looks positively overworked."

Stockton grinned and said: "Thank you, sir."

The Brigadier tilted his gold-laced cap over his eyes and assumed an expression of mock ferocity. "Do you know, one of your damned fellows turned Everett back on the Peronne Road tonight," he growled.

"Did he, sir?" said Stockton with a smile.

"Did he!" echoed the General, giving a hitch to the gas respirator that hung over one shoulder. "You damn well know he did."

"Well, we are rushing up guns and ammunition chiefly, sir. And the corps heavies——"

The Brigadier clapped Stockton on the shoulder. "Oh, I dare say. Meantime Everett took nearly an hour to get to Maricourt."

Stockton took the glass handed to him and said: "Cheerio, sir.

How is the war going?"

"Bon! My fellows are well up on the western edge of Montauban and full of buck. They are all out to give Master Jerry another shove in the face to-morrow. They have just reported some people moving across their front. We are not sure whether they are Boches retiring or our own fellows moving east from Fricourt. We are just ringing up division to find out."

Eastwell was rather awed by the presence of a General, but the prevailing spirit of optimism and good-fellowship put him at his ease. He sipped the whisky-and-soda that was put into his hands and took stock of his surroundings. It was rather like a scene on a stage, he thought. The confusing buzz of conversation, the uniforms, the scarlet and gold of the General's gorgets, and the bright electric bulbs shining on the heavy timbers of the low roof and the expanding metal revetment of the earth walls, were all a trifle theatrical and unreal. He must try to describe it all in his first letter home—that and the guns and limbers streaming through the night outside and the ghostly Verey lights rising and falling among the low hills.

A hand dug him suddenly in the ribs, and he turned to find Stokes behind him. "Finish that up and come out," said Stokes with a jerk of his head towards the door; and before Eastwell could ask why he was gone. Eastwell gulped down his drink and followed.

Out in the narrow timbered passage at the foot of the shaft Stokes stood with two other young officers. "We are going over to the old Boche front line," he whispered. "I want one of those German bivouac gadgets. And there's any amount of stuff in their dug-outs—field-glasses, helmets, Mauser pistols. . . . Are you game?"

Eastwell was very much game.

"Right-o, then. Got a flash-lamp?"

"No."

"I'll borrow one for you."

Stokes went back into the crowded brigade dug-out and return-ed a few moments later with an electric torch. He thrust it into Eastwell's hands. "Come on, and not a word."

They climbed the steps into the night and stumbled along over the rough earth parallel with the road. Presently the now familiar line of trees loomed ahead. The stream of traffic had stopped. Horses tapped the road impatiently with their feet, and cigarettes glowed in the darkness. At the cross roads they saw the cause of the blockage. One of the tall trees lay across the road, and the dark figures of a party of men sweating to remove the obstacle could be seen against the glow of a fire in some distant village.

They crossed the obstacle and descended into the darkness of the little Carnoy valley. Here, as on the previous night, all was movement and bustle. The narrow road was badly pot-holed. Hum-mocks of jagged masonry and brickwork on either side proclaimed that they were passing through the village, and they overtook files of dark, trudging figures bearing strange-shaped burdens on their shoulders. The Verey lights came again into view as they ascended the slope, and Stokes led the way off the road. The going was rough. Unseen shell-holes were everywhere in the darkness, and their feet clattered old tins and became entangled in rusty wire. Occasionally Eastwell heard that thrilling aerial whistle, followed by a bump and the sound as of a sack of coals being tipped down a chute.

They fell into single file along a narrow track through the rank grass and wire. They crossed two or three trenches by narrow plank bridges, and Eastwell, peering curiously down at the slit of dark-ness he was crossing, found there was nothing to be seen except the sandbags of the parapet and the rusty tangles of wire and knife rests among the rank grass beyond. Not far distantly he heard the crack of a rifle and the clack-clack-clack of a machine-gun. That first letter home would be a long one, he thought.

"You are now in the old No Man's Land," Stokes told him.

They seemed to be in a shallow valley, for the Verey lights ahead revealed a near dark horizon behind which they rose and fell. Underfoot were the same rank grass, uneven ground, old tins, and scraps of wire. One of Stokes' companions stumbled and recovered himself with a muttered "damn." He. flashed his torch behind him, and Eastwell saw a pair of upturned boots and puttees in the brief bright circle of light. "One of our fellows," said Stokes, and they went on.

Half right a pale grey line glimmered faintly. They turned towards it and found a breast-high barrier of chalk. Eastwell followed Stokes up the slippery incline of loose rubble and drew back precipitately at the top. Beyond it there was nothing. The grey chalk sloped steeply to a vast funnel-shaped pit, so deep that the tumbled chalky boulders at the bottom glimmered but faintly in the almost exhausted beam of the torch.

"Mine crater," announced Stokes, and switched off the light.

They skirted the curving bank of chalk that marked the perimeter of the mine crater and reached a lower bank of trampled earth. Stokes directed the beam of his torch downwards. At his feet was a broad, deep trench cut in the chalk, the bottom duck-boarded and littered with scraps of equipment, clothing, and chalky rubble.

"Here we are," he said, and dropped lightly down to the firestep. The others followed. They turned and leaned against the parapet, looking out across the darkness of the old No Man's Land.

"Queer, isn't it!" exclaimed one of Stokes' companions after a short silence.

Stokes grunted. "To think of the number of times we've looked out from across there and wondered what Jerry was doing over here; and now—here we are!"

It was very dark and quiet there in the trench. The direct rays of the Verey lights were cut off by the slope behind them, and only a faint greenish, moonlight-like glow told when they rose and fell. Faintly they could hear the clink of tins from a carrying party moving along a track away to their left, and the clank of a caterpillar tractor came distantly from the dark ridge facing them. On the same dark ridge a brief, lightning-like flash was followed by the bang of a gun, and they heard the shell sailing mournfully over their heads to detonate grumpily in the distance. The long, muffled cr-r-r-ump of a German five-nine far away to the right served only to accentuate the silence.

"Well, let's get on with the washing," cried Stokes, as he dropped from the fire-step. He rounded a traverse bulking hugely against the sky and threw the beam of his torch down the black-timbered shaft of a dug-out. "See how Jerry had built his dug-outs facing his rear so that our shells can't possibly land in the shaft as his sometimes do in ours!" he exclaimed. He started down the steps. "Come on, you fellows, but bags I the first bivvy sheet we see."

In single file they stumbled down the steep narrow shaft.

"Much the same as ours," commented one of Stokes' companions as the four torch beams moved over the earthen walls of the burrow below.

"Only a damn sight deeper and better built," growled Stokes. "Trust old Jerry! Look at that post. You might blow the top of the shaft in, but the biggest stuff would never touch this." He began rummaging with his foot among some broken boxes and rubbish beside a wire-netting bunk. He stopped suddenly and picked up something.

"What is it?" asked Eastwell, staring at the round grey object.

"Hark at him! 'What is it? Why, a pickelhaube, you fool."

"But I thought——" began Eastwell.

"This is the canvas cover they keep 'em in," said Stokes. He turned the helmet round to show the green cloth numbers stitched on the front. "I'll show you." He stripped off the cover and revealed a shiny black leather helmet decorated in front with the Imperial eagle.

"But where is the spike?" asked one of his companions.

"Lying about somewhere, I expect," said Stokes. "Look for it, you slackers. It fits into this notch arrangement on top."

They found it after a short search, and Stokes put on the German helmet and goose-stepped up and down the dug-out with a ten centimes stuck in his eye for a monocle. They found a round German gas-mask, which one of the other two appropriated, and a smutty German postcard.

"Come on, there's nothing more here. Let's try the next," said Stokes.

They tramped up the steps back into the trench and went on to the next shaft. Eastwell was coveting the pickelhaube. What a souvenir to send home with that letter describing his adventures! But if Stokes went down first each time he would get all the plums.

In the next dug-out one of the other officers appropriated a German pioneer saw bayonet, and Stokes got his bivouac sheet. There was nothing else there except lousy blankets and a few grey linen bandoleers of small arms ammunition.

Eastwell was determined to get something. He was first out of the dug-out and led the way along the trench to the next shaft. "Bags I the next," he said over his shoulder.

"Right-o," agreed Stokes good humouredly. "You and Green take the next dug-out; Anderson and I will go on to the one after that."

Eastwell flashed his torch down the next shaft and started to descend. Stokes and Anderson passed on along the trench. Stokes halted suddenly and called back : " I say, Green, chuck me one of those cigarettes of yours."

Green turned on the second step and went up again into the trench. " Right-o. But give me a fill of baccy."

Eastwell hurried on down the steps. He would make sure of anything here for himself.

He reached the bottom of the shaft and swung the light round the dug-out. It was a large one, but there did not seem to be much there. Four or five bunks in tiers on the side nearest the shaft, a roughly carpentered table overturned on the floor, and the other timbered walls bare except for a nail or two on which hung a great-coat and one of the round grey· German caps. It was very quiet down there underground, and the place had a stale, pungent, gar-licky smell like the lair of a wild beast.

He appropriated the little grey cap with its gay red band, and swung the light round on one last inspection. It was then that he noticed in the end wall to his right a low, timbered opening. Two steps led down from it, evidently to a small burrow beyond. Stoop-ing in the low entrance, he inspected it with his torch. The circle of light slid slowly along the damp clay wall, rested a moment on a rough shelf containing a candle end and a jagged meat tin, and moved on to the corner and along the opposite wall. It reached the other corner, and remained like a circle of yellow paper pinned on a black screen.

The head and shoulders of a man were in the centre of the circle —a man with short, earth-encrusted hair and pale, dirt-stained face. His fixed eyeballs glittered in the strong light. Upon the lower edge of the circle, across the faded grey uniform, projected a hand clutch-

ing a short glittering trench dagger. The figure was motionless
like a bust modelled in wax; only the tautness of the lean face and
the madness of fear and desperation in the eyes showed that it was
alive and, like a trapped animal, waited to spring.

Eastwell's trembling finger released its pressure on the button.
The light wavered and went out. Seconds passed. He recovered
himself sufficiently to draw back a pace from the low archway.
His heart was pounding against his ribs, and in that intense silence,
as he held his breath, he heard the watch ticking on his wrist. He
pressed it against the back of his leg to muffle the sound. He pictured that terrifying figure creeping silently up the steps and springing upon him.

He held his breath and took another cautious step sideways. If
he went straight back across the dug-out he would bump into that
overturned table. Thank God, the walls on one side were clear of
obstructions.

He put out his hand and touched the wall. He took another pace
back. Still no sound. His heart was pounding so hard that he could
hear it, and he was half suffocated with the effort to keep his breathing noiseless. He held the torch by the very end; he was terrified
lest he should touch the button and give a tell-tale flash of light.

His back touched a wall behind him : he had reached the corner.
Inch by inch in an agony of silence he started back along the long
wall that faced the shaft. To his right distantly he discerned a
slight lessening of the intense darkness. That must be the bottom
of the shaft in the opposite wall. But he dared not cross to it. That
paleness, faint though it was, would betray him. He was crouching. He would have a better chance when the man sprang upon
him suddenly from the wall of darkness ahead, though he knew
that when that happened he would scream and drop without resistance.

Faintly he heard a voice in the trench above. It was remote; it came from another world. He was like a diver in the dark, silent depths of the ocean.

Another long agony of suspended breathing and silent movement brought his back against the wall. He had reached the second corner. Then suddenly he knew what he would do. He would move in the same silent fashion along this wall to the third corner, and so along the next wall till he stood by the foot of the shaft. Then a deep breath and a dash up the steps before the trapped madman could spring upon him.

He went along this wall sideways, with his back to it, keeping his face towards the length of the dug-out and that opening in the far wall. He heard no sound, but he knew that the other had left the burrow and was not far from him. Inch by inch he moved along and reached the third corner. Crouching low, he moved on again with the tips of his fingers hovering over the wall to his right.

His fingers touched the post, the big post at the foot of the shaft, and he paused. After æons of silence it was not easy to break it now with that frantic rush up the steps. But it had to be done. He nerved himself for the effort. He would go when he had counted three. He began to count.

A faint sound from the shaft arrested him. It was a high-pitched drone, as though up there in the trench above a circular saw was cutting through timber. The drone rose to a scream and then rapidly expanded to a roar, as though an express train were coming down the shaft. A vivid orange flame slit the darkness; and as Eastwell's eyes went blind, he saw facing him on the other side of the shaft that pale, earth-stained mask and staring, desperate eyes.

Then one side of the face went suddenly dark and shapeless; the grey form lifted like a dancer and curved through the air to the floor. Some great force swept up Eastwell also and hurled him to the ground. There came a crashing roar that shook the dug-out like an earthquake, and then darkness and silence, broken only by the tinkle of stones and earth down the steps.

He lay dazed and motionless. Then something soft beneath him twitched once convulsively and was still. He leapt wildly to his feet and rushed like a madman through the choking fumes and smoke up the steps. He tumbled panting into the trench at the top as two dark figures came round the traverse beside him.

"Hullo, young fellow!" cried the voice of Stokes. "Did that one put the breeze up you!"

Eastwell leaned panting against the wall of the trench, his eyes closed against the glare of Anderson's torch.

"Come on, pull yourself together," said Stokes. "That's nothing. You wait till you get mixed up in a proper strafe or have to hare backwards and forwards round a traverse all day dodging minnies."

"Hullo, he's stopped a bit!" exclaimed Anderson, as the lowered beam of his torch glistened on two thick trickles of blood on Eastwell's hand.

Stokes gently raised the wrist, and then for the first time Eastwell became aware that his shoulder burned as though it had been branded. Stokes produced a knife and neatly slit the seam of the sleeve. "Hold the light here—that's right." He slit the khaki shirt. "Um-m! Get his dressing out, Andy."

Anderson ripped the first field dressing from the skirt of Eastwell's tunic. Another figure appeared round the traverse. "Hullo, anybody stopped one?" asked the voice of Green.

"Eastwell. Got a nice little knock on the shoulder. No serious damage as far as I can see."

"Cheer up, old son," cried Anderson. "You'll be in Blighty in a couple of days. They are bunging everyone right through to England, I'm told. Where's the nearest aid post?"

"There's one up an old Boche communicating trench on the right here. I'll take him along," volunteered Green.

Stokes lit a cigarette as the two figures moved off round the traverse. "That's quick work," he growled. "A Blighty one on his first day out! And here have I been dodging 'em for eighteen months.

"They will put him on to lecturing on the fighting on the Western front, I expect," said Anderson with a grin.

"But think of it, Andy: a Blighty one on his first day! He's never been in the line, and he's never even seen a Boche—except a tame one in a cage."

"Some people have all the luck," agreed Anderson.

Stokes bent down and picked up something from the floor of the trench. "And, damn it," he cried, "he's bust that torch I lent him."

MISAPPLIED ENERGY

by
William T. Scanlon

I WAS sitting in my hole reading by a home-made candle made out of bacon grease and old rag wick. Murphy was lying on his back not far away.

Murphy said: "What are you reading?"

"The Bible. Did you ever read it?" (I had a pocket-size Testament.)

Murphy said: "I looked at one back in Tours when Hancock was shooting his head off about the Kaiser being the whore that sat on seven hills and caused the war. . . ."

"That was a lot of cheap stuff," I said. "Hancock read it in some paper. . . ."

Murphy: "Well, if it's in the Bible I suppose it's true. . . . Still I leave all that up to the priests. . . . That's what they get paid for. . . ."

I said: "Remember how we used to argue with Hancock up in the old trenches about 'He that kills by the sword shall perish by the sword'? . . ."

Murphy: "Yes, and I still stick to what I always said—we haven't got any swords . . . and it doesn't say anything about machine-guns and rifles. . . ."

Just then one of the fellows came up and said Captain Ladd wanted to see me, so I went over to his dug-out.

He said: "Corporal, I have here some very important documents that the Intelligence Section just sent up." He pointed to a bundle of papers on the ground. He picked up a sheet and passed it to me. It was written in German.

He said: "Can you read it?"

"No, sir."

He said: "Well, it doesn't make any difference. . . . Neither can I, but here is what I want you to do with them. Pick out a detail of men—five or six—and to-night, about eleven o'clock, take these papers and distribute them inside the German lines in as open a space as you can find. We want the Germans to find them. Come in later and I'll give you the papers."

I picked out six men—Young, Dale, White, Quinn, Bretherton, and Carney. I told them to be ready at ten-forty-five. No equipment was to be worn, I told them, except gas-masks, and they were to be tied on securely so they wouldn't make a noise. No weapons were to be carried except an automatic revolver. Revolvers were furnished only to corporals and sergeants, so I had to dig around to borrow six of them, but I did. Extra clips would be carried in the pocket, as no belts could be worn. We were not a combat group or patrol and it was up to us to avoid any encounter.

A little before eleven I called in at the Captain's hole and he gave me the bundle of papers. They were about the size of a regular book leaf, and were cheap paper, like newspaper stock.

The captain told us to go down the ravine to where the last man was posted and then cut across the field until we hit a main road which ran between Soissons and Château-Thierry. We would have to be careful along that road, as the Germans used it at night and our artillery usually shelled it at regular intervals, but to-night they would not shell this part of the road in front of our positions between the hour of eleven-thirty and twelve-thirty. The Captain suggested that along this road and the sides of the road would be a good place to distribute the papers.

It was about eleven-fifteen when I left and close to eleven-thirty by the time I reached the last man in the ravine. This was Hancock. I left my gas-mask with him. It was always a bother, as no matter how you tied it down it would flop up, and, besides, it would hinder me crawling on my belly through the grass. The other men wanted to keep their masks, so I let them. I knew the lines were too close together to use gas.

We started across the field toward the road on our hands and knees, and as we got farther out we dropped flat and wriggled the rest of the way on our bellies. I was leading, the rest following fairly close behind. The German lines seemed restless. Star shells were going up right along; also signal lights for batteries—green and red. The artillery on both sides were firing away, trying to bust each other up.

We were snaking through grass which was about six or eight inches high and heavy with dew. We were soaking wet. It was slow work, as we had to stop crawling when the star shells were up.

I was looking straight ahead through the grass when all at once I found my head sticking out over a small embankment. About ten feet ahead was a road. I stopped. This road was inside the German lines and they had outposts in back of us, although their main line was on the other side of the road in a wood similar to ours. I could hear a waggon creaking in the distance and soon a French two-wheeled waggon went by drawn by one horse. It was off the road on the grassy part alongside. It was headed north.

I gradually lowered myself down over the embankment. I told the next man to crawl along about ten feet and then come over. I sent one man one way and the next man the other and told them to get about ten feet apart before letting themselves down on the side of the road. Each one had some of the papers. I told them to keep down and scatter the papers out in front. Two of us crept out to the road and distributed the stuff as best we could for about two hundred feet along the road.

It did not take very long and we were soon crawling back. The path was easy to pick out, as the grass was all flattened out. It was about twelve-fifteen when we got back. I got my gas-mask from Hancock and reported back to the captain.

I had saved one of the sheets, and the next day I got Eberle to translate it. It went something like this:

To the German Soldier

The people of the United States are still friends of the people of Germany. The United States did not enter the War to fight the German people. We are at war with the German Military Power which is trying to murder the people of the world the way they are murdering you. You are being deceived by them. Here is an offer that we make to you. Every German soldier who will lay down his arms and enter our lines of his own free will will be furnished free transportation to the United States and will be given a large piece of rich farm land that he can work for himself. We have plenty of good land and can take care of you all.

I can't remember how it was signed.

That night I heard Murphy getting a patrol together. He came to borrow my automatic for one of his men. I told him I would be on guard from 1 to 3 a.m. and would need the gun, so he said he would have it back to me by that time.

About a quarter to one I went down to the top sergeant's hole to see if he had any orders. His hole was right next to the Captain's and there was an opening between them just as between Murphy's and mine. I was just about to go when I heard somebody slide into the hole next to me and start to talk in an excited voice. It was Murphy.

He said: "Lookit, Captain! . . . I picked up a whole bunch of German orders that somebody dropped along the road!"

There was a rattling of papers for a minute. I looked through the hole and saw Murphy pulling little papers out of all his pockets.

Then the Captain spoke. "German orders, hell! These are the papers I sent out last night to be distributed in the German lines. And you had to go out and pick them up again——!"

"Well, my orders were to pick up any information about the German lines I could, and as soon as I spotted these papers along the road and saw that they were written in German, I figured some despatch runner had dropped them."

"Did you get any information about the German positions?"

"No, sir, nothing but these papers. It took us quite a while to pick them up."

"I guess you got them all all right."

Murphy went out and I followed. When I caught up with him I started to bawl him out.

I said: "What did you want to go and pick up all those German papers for when I had such a hard time scattering them along the road?"

Murphy said: "So you're the guy that did it?"

"Yes, didn't we do a good job?"

"Too damned good! We crawled along that road for over an hour on our hands and knees picking them up. Next time put them all in one pile."

THE RED LIGHT OF MORNING

by
Josef Magnus Wehner

THIS is the story of my friend, Ivan Savov, a senior subaltern in the third Bulgarian Army, who fell before my eyes in the Serbian mountains between Ibar and Morava. It was the late autumn of the second year of the Great War, the day after my birthday, which I was celebrating there on the outskirts of the wood between two dead beech-trees. I can still see the camp fire, and the occasional snowflakes fluttering into the flames from a grey sky, deepening the sense of complete desolation, and I remember that the situation suddenly struck me as rather comic. What on earth could it matter to a soldier on active service on the day before a battle that he was born just twenty-four years previously? Yet it seemed just as absurd to think of death; one does not die the day before one's birthday. And so I wrapped myself more closely in my cloak, made myself snug in the heaped-up foliage and looked at the stars twinkling through the bare entwining branches of the friendly trees.

At three o'clock in the morning the alarm was sounded. The first infantry battalion of the Bavarian Guards was to attack. As I crept sleepily out of the wet foliage, Ivan Savov passed by with the staff officers of the Alpine corps. He had a G.H.Q. map in his hand and pointed to the south. I was about to jump up and rush over to him and say: "Ivan Savov, don't you remember me? Don't you remember Jena, where we met? I know you're an officer and I'm only a private, but I must come and shake hands." The other officers would perhaps be startled and step back; for it isn't usual for two friends to meet after years of separation on the morning of a battle.

But I didn't emerge from my two trees; I remained where I was with my hands pressed against the wet trunks. I was a soldier and had learnt how to wait. Ivan Savov disappeared with the others into the mist and the battalion moved off.

But while those grey soldiers descended into the wild gorge, wading through a brown torrent, pressing on through the mist, with the sparse shrubs on the bleak uplands taking shape in the first light of morning, I thought of Ivan Savov.

I was not thinking of those ecstatic nights at Jena, when we sang " Schumi Maritza " as we drank our red wine, philosophised and embraced, and terrified the peaceful burghers as we passed through the streets. No, I was not thinking of him thus, the young Bulgarian painter with his steely blue hair, the stiff black lashes in his olive coloured face and his long, firm hands. To the others with whom we danced until the stars faded out as the birds burst into song, he was the gay, brilliant cavalier, burning the candle at both ends, working all day at his technical drawings in the factory of Zeiss and Schott for his living, and rioting through the night contemptuous of mere sleep. I, however, was privileged to see another side of him.

One day he took me to his den, a tumble-down attic, in which bed, table, chair, and easel took all the available space. After casually throwing me his sketch-books full of the usual landscapes, human figures, and buildings, he drew back a curtain that concealed an enormous canvas attached to the whitewashed wall. What I saw—well, it was his life-work, the utmost that he had to give. Against a red sky, outlined by saw-toothed mountains, were two wrestlers, fighting to the last breath. The two naked men, giants of mythical size and strength, lit up the firmament with their flaming rage. The earth blazed to the sky, and the curves of the fighters' limbs seemed to straddle across a globe whose axis threatened to split. I remember now how it impressed me, but Ivan Savov said: "It's all wrong, Jossin! That red should be flame, fire, the red light of morning . . ."

I alone know how Savov sweated to get that colour. His suffering was demonic, unreasoning, and hopeless; he could not contrive such a red from his modest palette, and at last he said to me one day that he would never be able to paint that picture until he had seen another sunrise in his home in Bulgaria. That same summer the War came. I tore myself from my friend and his unfinished picture, which suddenly seemed to be the ordained symbol of the time—and now . . .

Four days after I first met him again, I was on guard in front of a Serbian village when two Bulgarian officers rode up. They were riding side by side at a slow trot, and one of them had his arm across the other's shoulders. After they had passed me I recognised Ivan Savov. That morning, as we set out for the unknown, for the battle on the Amsel, I saw him again, but I did not speak.

My heart throbbed as the bugles sounded the attack. We had gained the top of a hill, and over against us on the other side of the valley were the Serbians. We fixed bayonets while the enemy bullets passed leisurely over us, like birds of passage, then suddenly the command rang out, "Advance!" We rushed forward to the attack, shouting as the bullets whistled past us. We did not know the names of the mountains, but we knew that Bulgaria and Macedonia were on our left, Montenegro to our right, and the enemy to the south. We swept through a field of maize, then through the valley and up the hillside, trampling down the heather and crashing through the fern. Two men in the Serbian crooked-caps threw hand-grenades and hit one of our men, but we carried the hill and put the Serbs to flight. We continued to fire spasmodically as we went on; the ground was rising all the time, and we stumbled through abandoned trenches. One man stopped to cut off a dead Serbian's haversack, looking for bread or tobacco in it. So we came up the second hill, with the brownish-green swarms of the Serbians massed on the slope. There we were checked by a stone wall some three hundred yards in front of the enemy; we were ordered to lie down in front of it and continue our firing. The enemy fired convulsively; his bullies split the stones and shattered the boughs of the undergrowth around us. Then we were once more ordered to advance, and we leapt forward with a savage joy. The Serbian lines wavered and broke; strange bearded faces surrounded us, their rifles broken or discarded. The transport men rounded up the prisoners while we pursued the flying enemy into the river.

That day we stormed seven hills. We did not count the hours, we thought neither of father or mother, and it was not until evening that we saw where we were. We were at the edge of a steep, wooded hill, without cover of any kind. On the sky-line of the hill opposite were the Serbian reserves. They were still maintaining a continual fire, but the victory was ours. Now for the first time our officers took out their maps, and discovered that we had advanced beyond the line ordered. So we retired an hour's march and lit the camp fires.

Then we found that we had forgotten one officer. Young Captain P., commanding No. 2 Company, had scrambled down with only one man into the valley, as we were lying at the edge of the steep hill, to take a mill from which the enemy were firing. When we retired in the evening we forgot this brave man, so the Colonel asked for volunteers to fetch the Captain back. It all went like lightning; men jumped up offering to go, and I saw Ivan Savov offering to take charge of the party, to which the Colonel finally agreed under protest. We set out through the silent, mysterious night, keeping close together.

Ivan Savov knew the way well, that was why he had offered himself as leader. Soon I was next to him, having felt my way along the chain of my companions. I said to him, " Jena, Jossin," and then he laughed in his deep, husky voice and we fell into one another's arms. Distant shots were ringing out in the night as I told him that four weeks ago my brother had fallen in France, and that he must now be my brother in this country. We went slowly through the trailing mist, up hill and down; our hands firmly clasped, then suddenly we began again to philosophise as in the old days; we discussed the picture, the two wrestlers and the flaming sky. " I still haven't painted it," he whispered, as we stepped out upon the ghostly upland " —after the War. We must be together again—at Jena or Munich or Sofia."

Suddenly we found that we were on the wrong track. We got no light from a sky that was completely overcast, and when we tried to follow the compass we came to gorges and ravines, but not to the deep valley where the mill stood. The many echoes of enemy firing misled us, and it was not until the mist grew brighter, about five o'clock in the morning, that we saw the evil paddle-wheel of the Serbian mill lying below us.

We scrambled cautiously down while the Serbian bullets ceaselessly whistled over us from the high ground beyond. Strangely enough the mill-wheel was still turning, driven by the wild mountain torrent. We crawled closer—nothing stirred—but we saw a man seated under the mill-wheel. We released our safety catches and shouted to him. He was Corporal K., of No. 2 Company, and at his feet lay Captain P., shot through the thigh; he had bled to death. It was a long time before we could bring the man who was guarding the body to his senses. Then we dug a grave and laid the dead man in it, with his face towards the enemy and his legs pointing southwards along the slope of the barren mountain. The ground was hard and stony, and our spades were still at work when the first sickly light of morning showed. As we ran the wooden cross into the hillside the dead man's helmet was lit up by a delicate red. We should have dispersed immediately to take cover, but the sun was more powerful than we. It rose slowly from the serrated hills to the east, from the dreaming homeland, Bulgaria; it flooded the Macedonian mountains. The red glow of that morning between Ibar and Morava forced us old, hard soldiers to our knees.

At that moment I saw Ivan Savov like a man in a trance of prayer. There was expectation in his eyes and a veil over them— that veil which dims the eyes to approaching death. He could not feel death approach; it was unknown to him. But I, his friend, knew it only too well. . . . Ivan Savov raised himself right up, his face turned towards his home. He saw the terrible, blissful red of the morning, and as he turned to me he said: "See, the new day. That is the red——" He was struck by a bullet from beyond the ridge. I saw him smile almost contemptuously, but the shot had pierced his heart. He had seen his home in the red light of morning. If only he had been able to paint it. . . .!

So we had to dig a second grave. But we laid Ivan Savov close beside the German officer; there could be no barrier between those comrades in arms sharing the same few feet of soil. The sods of the German's grave rolled on to the Bulgarian's breast, and we placed them hand in hand. There was no shot as we went away in the red light of morning. The last bullet had been fired.

THE SACRIFICE

by
Jean Bernier

"COME on, get up!"

Favigny opened his eyes. Yes, that was what they said, "Get up" . . . and he supposed he must. He could see just the dim outline of Martin, the liaison orderly, whose job it was to awaken them, perched on the edge of the trench, croaking out his orders:

"Come on, get up!"

The soldiers, sunk in the ox-like slumber of complete exhaustion, did not budge.

Favigny pretended not to hear. He knew that he could thus count on lying there for a few seconds more, and he held on to those moments as desperately as a man clings to the last breath of pleasure. The harsh voice of the orderly, more imperative now, cut jarringly across his muddled dreams.

"Come on, get up, for God's sake!"

Favigny dragged himself up, slowly and heavily. Then, to show his authority, he too began to growl.

"Come on, damn you, get up!"

There was a general confused movement as the men began to stir, and, his job there being finished, Martin passed on to the other companies, to rouse them to life.

Snores and groans and oaths resounded in the darkness as, without an articulate word, the half-conscious men staggered to their feet. Their clumsy hands fumbled with their kit, those wretched bundles that comprised all their meagre possessions.

Favigny, as chief of the section, was animated solely by the desire to get ready first without forgetting anything. So he hurried on, rolling his coverlet and ground-sheet as tightly as possible. But there wasn't room for them in his haversack after all, and instead of one compact parcel, he found himself, to his intense annoyance, burdened with several clumsy bundles. And then the straps of his knapsacks were all tangled up, his dixie bulged out in the middle of one of them so that he couldn't fasten it, and he fumbled vainly with the buckle, swearing all the time.

"Oh, blast it! damn the —— thing! . . . it'll have to do as it is . . . I'll settle it later on." Then at last he managed to pull it together. "That's got it," he said in triumph, as though nothing else in the world mattered.

All round him the other men were feverishly packing their belongings, grumbling and swearing. All they cared about was getting their things together, and nothing would go right. The air was full of curses and complaints.

"Oh, hell! where's my can?"

"Damn! that's not my haversack. Where the devil is mine?"

"Heave your carcass off my ground-sheet, can't you? How the hell d'you think I can roll it?"

Favigny buckled his straps across his sore and chafing shoulders. Yes, they were all complete, those three accursed bundles. Provisions on this side, a change of clothes on that, and here, where he could get at them easily, his gas-mask and first-aid equipment—lint, iodine, cottonwool. Then he passed the straps through his two cans, his flashlight, his periscope, assembling them all mechanically, reflection mercifully suspended by this dull necessity. A mute resignation had engulfed him almost without resistance; he could feel nothing any more. His imagination was dead; he could apprehend nothing but a vague and formless menace of disaster, divorced from personal feeling.

Something inside him said mechanically over and over again: "This time you're for it. But what does it matter? Why worry any more?" Whatever he did the wheel would roll on remorselessly to crush him. You could not stop that Juggernaut with one finger . . . or two . . . or three.

He forced himself to adjust his pack properly, making sure before he clasped his belt that his flask was slung conveniently within reach of his mouth. Then he drew his bayonet from its sheath.

Mechanically he ran his fingers along the blade, and the chill of the steel struck into his heart, reawakening the horror and the fear.

"Oh, God! the bayonet. Once more I've got to fix it ready . . . ready . . . for what?"

Twice before he had had to go through that sinister preparation. Twice before, at Carnoy and Perthes-les-Herlus. He retasted once more the bitterness of those moments, fraught with the chill expectancy of death.

Carnoy and Perthes-les-Herlus. . . .

The names detonated through his brain, their hideous significance tearing through his soddened memory. He saw once again the levelled rifle and the naked, hungry steel, and his anguish overpowered him.

The fixed bayonet . . . that meant the attack, the final, desperate throw, the horror of No Man's Land and the hail of the machine-guns, the death struggle of man to man in the trenches, and then, and then. . . . There was no escape from it, no escape from the naked, hungry blade.

He shuddered in shame and fear; the blood sang in his ears. He struggled to regain control.

"Well, what of it? You've been through it all before. Anyhow, you've got a little life left."

He worked feverishly to stop himself from thinking. He rested his kit on the level ground and stuck his rifle against the wall of the trench. Then he crawled painfully out of his dug-out, covered from head to foot with the chalky soil, and galvanised himself into activity. For activity was the only thing that could keep him sane.

He tramped heavily along the trench, growling at his men to get them together. "Hurry up, for God's sake! What the hell are you messing about for? Hurry up, damn you! We're supposed to be ready now."

Black as the night itself, the men crawled out of the earth and gathered together.

Discipline still held sway over him; he was trembling with fright in case his section should be the last to be ready. He barked out his orders—" Roll call!"

The corporals called out the names mechanically; the men made lifeless replies.

"Fabre?" "Present." "Crosse?" "Present." "Ignace?" "Present!" The routine proceeded as regularly as if they were in barracks.

"Fifth squad, all present."

"Sixth squad, all present."

"Seventh squad, all present."

One of them, a newcomer, went so far as to click his heels and salute.

A sensation of gratification and relief stole over Favigny as he realised that they were ready. The other half of the company behind them was not ready yet; although he couldn't see them he could hear the growling and cursing which proclaimed the fact. He wished that the Lieutenant would come.

Standing at ease in silence, the men shuffled uneasily, amid coughing and spitting and sniffing, resting first on one foot and then on the other, the butts of their rifles against their chins.

The threat of battle was the more terrifying by the silence which prevailed. An occasional German shell sped on its way with a warning whistle that seemed unnaturally prolonged; the shells were so scarce that they seemed almost impotent, their very explosions dying feebly away. The earth seemed to merge into the heavy sky: they were mist and cloud together.

The tall, slim figure of the Lieutenant, swathed in packages and clothes, loomed up out of the blackness.

"Are you ready, Favigny?"

Favigny saluted and replied: "Yes, sir."

"Everybody here?"

"Yes, sir."

"All right. Get the men who are going to mop up the trenches. They will form the left wheel of the company, and they will unite with the moppers-up of the other sections to make a separate section, which will fall into line immediately behind us."

"Very well, sir."

That was something he had forgotten . . . the men who were to mop up the trenches. And he had picked them out himself, on the night of that ghastly vigil of the 24th, six men from each section, six of the best. It was their job to follow after the attack and dispose of any Germans showing fight in the captured trenches. Those trenches had been captured, and from them they were now to go on. Doubtless the barbed wire had melted in the night . . . he sneered to himself.

But he obeyed all the same, and called out the men whom he had nominated—"the gizzard-slitters," as they were called in the company. They were nearly all young men, and they were proud of having been chosen—proud to carry, sheathed in their puttees, the immemorial insignia of the assassin.

"Now then, boys. You're to form up on the left, you understand? Don't take any notice of what we do; your job is to come on after."

All the while he spoke, his mind, shattered by rage and fear, gibbered a contemptuous commentary:

"Yes, you're to come on after. Get that, you lucky swine? When we've gone over the top you'll come on after; you'll come on after us, lying there shot to bits or screaming in agony. You'll have a bloody fine mess to mop up, you will. Don't worry yourselves; we're going out first, and if we get shot up it doesn't matter. Plenty more silly bastards like us. Don't *you* worry; when the blood-letting is over and the gods are gorged there's a good time coming for you. Until they get thirsty again. But you're a lucky lot of swine; you *have* got a chance."

The "gizzard-slitters" trickled out, wretched and forlorn at leaving their mates, and filled with a vague fear of the unknown future. But Favigny could hardly swallow his bitterness. Why they and not he? He had only one chance in the world—that before they were launched into the ghastly hand-to-hand death struggle of the trenches they might be saved by the mere failure of the attack itself.

It was a foul thought, and he rejected it, quickly and with shame. After all, that would only mean shooting up a lot of the poor swine for nothing. To tell the truth, he still felt a sort of perverted pride at being reckoned among those whom he called poor swine.

*   *   *   *   *

The minutes passed by. Favigny picked up the bulky knapsack off the ground and passed his left shoulder through the strap, as automatically as you put your arm into a coat-sleeve. Sensitive by long experience, he realised that the kit-bag was badly slung, and he shifted his body so that the weight should be more evenly distributed. Then he passed his right arm through the second shoulder-strap, fastened it under his arm, braced his body, and slung the pack free. Ah, that was better. He had got it now.

"In single file, forward march."

It was the Lieutenant ordering them to advance, and the company spread out into the usual parallel lines. From the black mass in front of Favigny a thin line of men filtered out into the night. The mass dwindled gradually, almost imperceptibly, as one by one the men dropped off into that fatal Indian file. Favigny was waiting for the last man to fall in. The group in front of him had melted now; he could see the individual figures, five, four, three, two. Piard, the sergeant of the second half section, brought up the rear. They were ready.

"In single file, forward."

It was Favigny giving the order now, as he stepped into line behind Piard. At his word his section poured out from the company, like soda-water from a siphon.

Inexorably linked, a blind leader of the blind, he marched on, at once the leader and the led. And every man followed alike, blind and ignorant, leading and led, even as he. They followed. He followed. They must all follow. The idea obsessed him.

The line must not be broken—at all costs it must not be broken. They must not break, they must not divide, they must not falter. They were a fragment of that inexorable ascent mounting towards the attack, yet they were led only by one man, he who walked first. Mechanically he murmured the phrases of that nightmare litany : "Keep together, men. Keep together. March as close as you can to the man in front of you. Keep together, for God's sake!"

The tired bodies pressed on, the mere effort dulling all reflection. Now and then the man in front would call the next man's attention to a shell-hole, and the man behind would pass the warning on. And so it would go all down the line. Favigny could hear them saying, one by one: "Look out for the hole. Mind the hole."

Destiny, pitiless and unfaltering, marched in step with that single file. Neither poet nor painter can depict that shadowy march of the doomed soldiers, climbing on and on—climbing towards death and flinching before its threat, yet unable to do anything but pass it along to their fellows.

They came to the ridge. It was a chaos of gaping holes where the crumbling soil refused a foothold, where they struggled upwards with bent backs and lowered heads, stumbling and sliding downwards in a vain endeavour to dig their heels in the unstable soil. The bayonets clanked monotonously as they made the ascent, the cans and the kettles banged and clattered on the earth.

Suddenly the line wheeled to the left where the sky shivered over a black gulf of nothingness. From this nameless horror the beneficent ridge had protected them, but now they were naked before it, there was neither mound nor stump between it and they. For all his terror, Favigny was aware of a certain curiosity. What was it? What on earth was it? Well, he would know soon. They were drawing near. He had lost all sense of direction and stumbled on vaguely, not knowing why or where. Darkness and menace enshrouded them; ahead there loomed that sinister duel where men crouched behind their barricades of earth, their rifles levelled to their ears, while the machine-guns panted to loose their hail of bullets, a hail that could shatter the most ardent advance.

He had wanted to see for himself those dread traverse emplacements of which he had heard so much since the infantry first encountered them in the offensive of the 27th. They had come to be regarded as some invulnerable enchanted monster—"You know, we could do absolutely nothing. We were up against it. They've got traverse emplacements for machine-guns in their trenches."

Well, he would see them now. He, too, would be " up against it."
He, too, fell under the spell of that dreaded concrete monster, and
he felt himself trembling without hope. Ah, well, they would be
for it soon enough now.

The colonial infantry had made the previous attack there; he
knew that. He imagined their shapeless bodies exposed on the gaping earth, shattered, disembowelled, rotting. He could see all the
foul litter of broken guns, bayonets red with blood rust, exploded
grenades, broken helmets, packs, tools, weapons—all the abandoned jetsam that marked the aftermath of the receded flood. Ah,
well, very soon they and their belongings would be nothing more
than rags and scrap iron in that Gargantuan dust-bin.

If they could only see it wouldn't be so bad. Oh, God, if only
they could see! His straining eyes scalded and pricked; he was
gibberingly, idiotically afraid of crying out, like a frightened child
in the dark.

The heavy breathing of the men was punctuated only by the
clatter of bayonets and utensils as they plodded on and on, hud-
dling close together, each man against the man next to him. For
each man knew that had he been alone. . . .

Monfrant stumbled against Favigny's foot and jerked him from
his abyss of terror. He turned on his mate with savage relief:
" Why don't you look where you're going, you clumsy swine."

The ground sloped downwards continually, and behind him he
could just see a regularly descending line of heads. Suddenly his
nostrils became aware of something unusual. Probably he only
imagined it; but, no, there *was* something, a faint chemical odour,
a reeking, choky hospital smell coming unmistakably towards him.
It made him cough. In front of him and behind him the men were
all coughing and spluttering, and the warning ran instantly all
down the line.

"Hell! it's gas."

And at the same time the nameless fear took hold of them again, paralysing their weary limbs in a torpor of terror, while they cursed and swore in panic and confusion.

"If we make a row they'll be able to locate us. And there isn't a hole to crawl into."

It was Favigny who recovered himself first. "Shut your row, you bloody fools! Shut up, for Christ's sake! D'you want to be shot to bits? If it is gas it's a damn long time choking you. It's only the remains of an old tear shell, that's all. It'll only make your eyes water and bung up your noses for a bit. Shove your handker-chiefs in your mouths, and in five minutes it'll have cleared off."

The men quietened down, secretly ashamed. The air cleared in a few minutes and the ground began to rise now. And then Favigny felt his nightmare taking hold of him again: "Oh, God, we're getting near now! What is going to happen to us? Well, it won't be long now, it won't be long." And then came a lightning shaft of sudden and particular apprehension: "My God! suppose some-body sends up a light!"

But the moment passed, and once more he held his fear under control.

A sudden burst of firing brought them to a halt. Heads were thrust out from bodies like snails from their shells, helmets struck against kit-bags as each man bent forward to ward off the charge from behind. They halted instinctively, snuffling, spitting, breath-ing heavily.

Favigny jostled Piard, who was next to him. "Well, what the devil are you stopping for? Go on, or we'll lose our bearings. Aren't you going to get on?"

"You go to hell. Can't you see we're held up? They're climb-ing into the trenches now; give 'em time to get down."

" Ah," murmured Favigny to himself, " so they're climbing into the trenches. It's all going on just the same."

One by one, clumsily and heavily, the soldiers scrambled down,
their feet resounding on the earth as they struck the bottom. Favigny jumped blindly in the darkness and grazed his leg against the
wall of the trench. All round him the men, finding that their
bulging packs literally wedged them in the narrow passage, were
tearing them off hastily, and even so, in some places, they could
only walk sideways. But they bent their heads and went on, curiously calmed and strengthened by this regained contact with the
earth, their habitation and their element.

They came to a cross-cutting—it was a traverse trench—and
Piard turned to the left. Favigny hesitated for a moment.

" Ah, Favigny, is that you?"

Favigny looked up; he could just distinguish the form of the
Lieutenant, side by side with another shadow, the guide presumably.

" Yes, sir."

" We are here now. Get your men together and mass them as
closely as possible in the left-hand trench; that's the parallel facing
the enemy."

He raised his long arm to point the direction.

Favigny called out Ser, the sergeant of the first half-section, a
hardened old soldier whose age and experience entitled him to respect.

" Ser, lead your men off to the left and see that they stick close
together. I'll bring up the rear with Rainette and the Lieutenant."

" Good-bye, then." They shook hands.

" Good-bye," repeated old Ser, in his sing-song Southern accent,
and he disappeared into the night, his son and his men behind him.
Favigny did not see them again until after the attack, and then

. . poor devils!

In a hoarse, jerky voice he called out their names. "Go on, boys; keep together. Go on, Fabre. Go on, Crosse. Go on, daddy Ignac; shake yourself up. Go on and stick together. Stick together all the time."

Rainette, the sergeant of the second half-section, brought up the rear, and behind him, on the Lieutenant's orders, the second half-company turned to the right. Favigny fell in after Rainette, and in a moment they halted. Like all the others, he took off his kit-bag and sat on it at the bottom of the trench. He didn't have to stumble under its weight any more, and he stretched his body in exquisite appreciation of the relief. They had only to wait. There was nothing else to do. But it was comfortable here, waiting. They might have to wait a good while before the attack started. It could hardly take place until well on in the morning, perhaps not until the afternoon, and anything might happen before then. There were so many possibilities. But since they knew nothing now there might, in fact, be nothing to know. There might even be counter-orders. That had happened before, at Perthes, and since the 25th of September. . . .

Supine in the stillness, he began to pick up the thread of his reverie, arguing with himself. For a brief moment a flicker of hope revived in him, fanned by his passionate rejection of death. This life of his, so firmly held, so bitterly cherished, asserted itself once more among the choking embers of despair. He could not imagine himself dead, he could not die. No! No! It was too horrible. It simply could not be.

Fortified by the reassurance, he took two biscuits and a bar of chocolate out of his haversack. It was his last bar but one. Groping in the dark, he marked it carefully into squares with his knife, first wiping the blade free of the dirt and dust. He ate with relish, while around him the Lieutenant, Rainette, and Crosse, who was sitting next to Rainette, were eating too. The others he could not see in the darkness, but he could hear them crunching steadily away.

The night, although dark, was clear and still. Their own artillery was silent, and only an occasional low-calibre German shell rose out of the remoter darkness, spouting into a trail of sparks and disseminating its characteristic odour of burnt horn or red-hot iron being beaten on the anvil. Seventy-sevens evidently, and nobody cared a damn about *them*.

They all kept quiet; there was no sound except munching and breathing. The presence of the Lieutenant imposed a restraint on the men. In his dark corner, unseen and unseeing, Favigny felt curiously peaceful. Then his misgivings began again as he thought to himself: " But I expect *he* knows all about it, although he says nothing."

And aloud he said to the Lieutenant:

" Are there any orders, sir?"

" No, Favigny, nothing."

" Perhaps we're not going to attack after all, sir?"

" Oh yes, we are. I'm sure of that at least."

In the darkness Favigny flushed at the death of his hopes. Raising his eyes, he thought he saw an almost imperceptible lessening of the solid blackness between the narrow trench walls. The night was fading. " Daylight," he said to himself; and then, remembering that delusive mirage so common in the infantry, he asked Rainette:

" It's getting light, isn't it?"

" Yes, I think it is."

It really was getting light. The solid sky began to break up; they could distinguish the black furrow of the trench where they were. Warily, cautiously, heads were raised, eyes strained, and nostrils dilated in the keen air. Favigny looked all round him, crowding a lifetime in that look.

In front of him the ground sloped upwards. It was bathed in a fantastic grey light; not the familiar grey of moonless nights, but an unnatural haze through which he could just perceive on his right a group of meagre truncated trees, probably firs, but he could see no more details.

He peered at his wrist watch and managed to make out the time at last. It was twenty-five minutes past four.

The sky was lightening steadily now, but it was still a uniform grey, and presently he found out the reason for this pallid night-mare dawn. The muzzle of his rifle was clammy with fog. The branches of the fir-trees, their foliage as yet intact, undulated slow-ly in a fluttering rise and fall; it was daylight, yet they couldn't see forty yards ahead. That place of doom still kept its secret. Evident-ly the Germans were somewhere there, in front of them, but there was nothing to reveal their presence, neither the confused clamour of the trenches nor the bristling hedge of barbed wire.

He recorded these things calmly, impressing on his brain every detail of the place where he and his life were to be parted. Pro-saically he said to himself : " It's useful to know where you are, to get your landmarks . . . ah, there's a shell-hole; that gives you a chance to save your neck."

Suard, the company commander's liaison orderly, was speaking to the Lieutenant.

" The seventh, that's right, sir. The seventh, that's the order, sir."

The wave of terror engulfed Favigny once more. " Already, oh, God, already." Now it was all over. There was no hope, no chance. No, there was no hope at all. The Lieutenant was speaking to him as calmly as ever :

"Our orders are to go out at twenty minutes past five. The official time is now five o'clock."

The fatal news ran all down the line, a murmuring torrent of doom—twenty past five, twenty past five, twenty past five. Favigny put his watch right to five o'clock. His mouth was parched, but he managed to speak clearly, following the officer's lead.

"Get ready to make your way over the top."

Resignedly the spades dug into the loose earth, hacking out rough steps in the high wall of the trench. Showers of dirt and rubbish fell down on them as they worked.

Twenty minutes, twenty minutes more—only twenty minutes. That was all the life he had now, just twenty minutes. The Lieutenant ordered them to put their kit on their backs, and "on your backs," "on your backs" echoed all down the line. Left arms came out, testing the weight, fingers struggled with straps and buckles, fastening them as best they could.

Suddenly Favigny stopped. "What was that? What the devil's that? Our artillery?"

And, as if in answer to him, the familiar sounds began. Whiz, tch, whiz, tch . . . one, two, three, four seventy-fives passed over his head, "shaving the ceiling," and exploded a good way off, two hundred, three hundred, or perhaps four hundred yards away. Whiz, tch, whiz, tch, crash, crash, crash, crash; soon he couldn't count them, they came so thickly. Whiz, crash, whiz, crash—how the devil could anybody think in this racket?—whiz, crash, whiz, crash, crash, crash, crash. . . .

The treacherous fog hid the trench walls in the wavering slimy shroud that Favigny was to remember always . . . for ever.

Then the Germans began. Tsing, boom, tsing, boom. That was the seventy-seven. War . . . ar . . . ar . . . crash. That was a one-fifty. The ground shuddered, and the acrid vapours of the explosion stung their nostrils.

Five past five, six, seven, eight, nine minutes past five. Favigny's eyes were glued to the dial of his wrist watch, doubled up under his chin as he crouched there. He squinted in trying to follow the hands in the dim light, walled up alone with his horror and his fear.

Ten past five. Ten minutes more. Still ten minutes. He tried to bolster himself up with the soldier's ironic humour: "God, it's going to be bloody comfortable going out in that packet!"

Eleven minutes past five, twelve minutes past five . . . the fury of the French guns died down suddenly, and now nothing came over but an occasional isolated shell. They could hear the individual explosions. The Germans followed suit; one could count the shells now and place them. They continued to fall just like that, regularly but sparsely.

The Lieutenant straightened himself up; Favigny also rose and stretched himself. The men seemed to return to life, the human contact restored now that the blasting storm had passed over.

Thirteen minutes past five. Favigny was growling, cursing, giving orders.

"Get on with your digging; come on, get on, get on."

Spade in hand he slaved away, digging furiously at the parapet, the men, bent almost double, following his example.

Sixteen minutes past five. "Fix bayonets!" commanded the Lieutenant. And Favigny drew the blade from its sheath, pressed the bolt with his thumb, and slid the knife into place as he repeated, "Fix bayonets!"

It was no longer he himself who spoke; it was his empty body responding to the habit of discipline, the mere hulk from which the spirit had fled. It was strange to think that his own body could be inhabited by this alien parasite, and that he should be agitated and impelled by it when he himself was dead. For he was dead. He must remember that he was dead. He must hold on to this annihilation with all his might.

On his left he could hear the re-echoing click, click of the bayonets as they went into the barrels.

Now the men were putting on their helmets and fastening them beneath their chins, those dehumanising helmets that severed the haggard eyes from the sunken, hollow jaws. The faint glimmer of the bared steel flickered among the sombre mass of crouching figures, hunched up over their rifles, the blue of their overcoats a dull grey in the shadow.

Favigny casually looked behind him. Thirty yards behind, the 8th company, in just such another trench, were waiting too. They also were getting ready, for the last time.

All at once he ceased to be an empty hulk. He could feel the onrush of his own living spirit invading his body once more. It surged into his blood, his ears, and his eyes, filling them with tears that he savagely restrained.

Their heads sunk between their shoulders by the weight of the burden they must carry, the men of the 8th elbowed their way out of the earth, coalescing into the thickness of the fog. Their helmets hid their faces. All along the dim formation of their line, regularly spaced from man to man, gleamed the cold white bayonets, dozens and dozens of them, sardonically topped with cans like mocking coronets.

On the level ground ahead, in front of them all, the leader of the company stood immobile, unflinching. His face was hidden by his helmet, but Favigny knew that it was rigid. In that moment Favigny saw him as the master of all men living, endowed with absolute power over their senses, their actions, and their fate. His own nerves were giving way; he wanted to leap forward and to cry out: "Oh, my God! get it over quickly, get it over quickly."

Then, out of the comparative silence, rose the methodical clac, clac, clac, clac of a solitary machine-gun, one only, rapping out its shots precisely and monotonously, without any acceleration, without any change of tone.

Clac, clac, clac, clac; you couldn't mistake that. It was a German gun. Clac, clac, clac, clac . . ., then suddenly three more joined in the monotonous enemy solo, each a little behind the other till they swelled into an unsynchronised chorus of hate and fear.

Bsing, bsing, bsing, bsing. High over their heads the shells passed, with the same meticulous regularity of the shots.

"Good-bye, Favigny." The Lieutenant held out his hand. Favigny pressed it. "Good-bye, sir." Then the Lieutenant silently mounted the parapet and threw himself flat on the plain.

Nineteen minutes past five. Clac, clac, clac, clac, clac, clac, clac, clac, clac, clac, clac, clac, clac, clac, clac, clac, clac clac for ever . . . the machine-guns flayed the valley, whipping up the fog like cream. Then some more shells fell, but Favigny hardly noticed them. He was hypnotised by that implacable clac, clac.

In front of him, on the barren slope, vague and unidentifiable shadows met and parted, a thin shaft of pale light darting and wavering to the left of their heads. The bayonets!

The third battalion, the third battalion who had been ordered to lead the attack, were going out now. Yes, they were going; he was certain of it. And he shouted it aloud, "The third battalion's moving; get ready, the third battalion's moving," as the Lieutenant rose up from the earth in front of him.

With his rifle in his left hand, pulling himself up with his right, Favigny scrambled over the parapet. He was launched forward in a barren frenzy without volition, his nerves quivering in his spine, the tears streaming down his furrowed, ravaged cheeks.

Then he flung out the order with the full power of his voice, that terrible irrevocable order, " Advance!"

There stood the Lieutenant, facing his men, his back exposed to the enemy. Favigny was wedged in among them, riveted indissolubly to his fellows. Vibrating in every part, like a clock that has just ceased striking, a living clock that still throbbed with every spent emotion that once could move mankind . . . racked, exhausted, and unstrung, he looked out beyond. . . .

His section rose in an uplifted line, like one man. They stuck their rifles in the ground above them, their knees bent to their chin as they scrambled up. Against the bulky misshapen kit-bags the cans and the bayonets emitted a spectral gleam in the wan daylight.

" They're going over the top, they're going over the top!" A ferocious exultation, a savage joy divorced from all human feeling, transported him as he yelled aloud, " They're going over the top!"

The gulf of shadow stretched across them, blotted out their dim, dehumanised faces, as, welling up with them from the trenches, a hideous, obscene clamour arose. It swelled and drowned even the sound of the machine-guns; a furious retch of fathomless horror, as though afar off, away from their empty bodies, they were vomiting forth their broken, tortured lives. Ah . . . ah . . . ah . . . ah . . . ah . . . ah . . . ah . . . h!

In a sudden bound of sanity, remembering his orders in the overwhelming confusion, Favigny tried to cry out, " Keep the line there, keep the line!"

Two, three, four men crumpled up suddenly, their faces striking the earth, but he could not recognise them.

Ah . . . ah . . . ah . . . ah . . . ah . . . ah . . . ah . . . ah!

The surging howl continued, triumphant over all.

Two yards ahead of him the ground heaved suddenly, clouds of earth were tossed up and scattered, then on the right Favigny saw the Liteutenant. Ah, how well he remembered him, that tall, spare figure. But now he was swaying feebly, his arms flapping uselessly up and down; then he collapsed into a flabby, supine heap. Where his head had been there was a bleeding, gaping hole.

And over above the inarticulate roaring Favigny's lament arose: "The Lieutenant is dead; they've killed our Lieutenant."

It was the last thing he was ever to know or see or feel.

Overwhelmed, unheeded, forgotten even of himself, he was swept forward in the flood. His screaming unheard in his deafened ears, his consciousness abandoned, he ran on and on, taking refuge in that cry. . . .

Ah . . . ah . . . ah . . . ah . . . ah . . . ah . . . ah . . . ah! . . .

BATTLE, RAID AND PATROL

THE END OF AN EPOCH

by
F. Britten Austin

IN the bleak conventionalism of nomenclature made necessary by the complete obliteration of every minor topographical feature, battalion headquarters for the night of the 14/15th September, 1916, had been fixed at S. 11b 4.9—in a shattered ex-German trench system between the two patches of splintered tree-stumps known familiarly as High Wood and Devil's Wood, on the bare downs north of the Somme. The fitfully illumined midnight darkness permitted only staccato silhouette views of the locality, as, having ascertained that the four companies were duly gone to ground in the fragmentary trenches and more or less linked shell-holes they were temporarily to occupy, the Adjutant returned stumblingly and cursingly to the Colonel and the Major, second-in-command. Those two officers, their faces dimly visible by the glowing cigarette ends under the flattish shrapnel helmets, were seated at the timbered orifice to an ex-German dug-out, an attempted investigation of the interior having induced a unanimous and emphatic preference for the open air; the still possessive occupants of that retreat had been dead a month.

"All O.K., sir," reported the Adjutant.

"Good," said the Colonel. "Now we've nothing to do but wait."

"They've got us here early this time," remarked the Major. "I hate this confounded waiting, but it's better than scrambling into position five minutes before zero-hour like we did a fortnight ago."

The Adjutant seated himself on a pile of the plentifully strewn semi-eviscerated earth sacks that had made a barricade, filled his pipe, lit it cautiously in the concealment from the enemy afforded by the former parados of this all but flattened trench. He also hated that confounded waiting—that waiting in which it was better not to think. To the westward, their own artillery was engaged in a methodic bombardment which had already lasted three days; near and far the blackness was torn by guns firing in stabs of flame and a slamming as of iron doors, by howitzers discharging in a great livid blaze and heavy double detonation. To the eastward, the enemy artillery replied perfunctorily in similar flashes, similar slams and detonations. Overhead, uncanny wailing crossed each other under the splendour of the stars. Every now and then one of those wailings changed its note to an ugly hissing rush, descended to terminate in a sudden brevity of reddish flame, a deafening crash, more or less close to them. Their own shells were falling on a diversity of map-deduced targets, some far away in a closely calculated search for the hostile batteries, for suspected concentra- tion points, for the roads and tracks and communication trenches by which reliefs and ration parties would be in nocturnal activity; others, the majority, disrupting in ever renewed twinkles of flame, in vindictive multiplied explosions, along the enemy position whence the flares tossed upward nervously and incessantly. From where the Adjutant sat he could see those flares innumerably re- peated to right and left, from horizon to horizon, the nearer ones shedding a milk-white, ghastly glare as they popped into intense incandescence and hung driftingly, those more remote dwindling into the semblance of low, bright stars that dropped and soared again. So every night for two fantastic years those baleful lights had risen and dropped and risen, illuminating the rigid horrors of a narrow No Man's Land, on a contorted line that stretched from Switzerland to the North Sea—a line that, despite fearful and prolonged intensifications of conflict, now here, now there, monstrous paroxysms of effort from now one side and now the other, was still unbroken and scarcely modified. To the Adjutant, puffing at his pipe in a stomach-sinking tension of the nerves (God! how he hated these waits before zero-hour!), the immensity of that unending battle in which he was but one of millions of ciphers imposed itself not for the first time in an overwhelming awe. It seemed a conflict as of invisible space-filling gods, transcending the mere humanity they used as agents.

A flat-helmeted soldier arose in the darkness from the adjacent shell-hole where the headquarters signallers had established themselves, saluted in a stolid normality of discipline.

" Brigade wants to speak to Adjutant, sir."

He got up stiffly, went into the shell-hole, squatted to exchange a few words over the field telephone. With a fierce downward rush, a violent crash, a random high-explosive shell burst a dozen yards away, blew acrid smoke over him. He cursed irritably, rose to stumble back to the Colonel.

" Brigade has just had aircraft report, sir. They say there are three more suspected machine-gun nests in S. 6c—warn us to look out for them." He switched on the shaded electric lamp at his belt, picked up the folded-back map in its leather case, likewise at his belt. " No change in zero-hour, sir," he added, as he bent down to the map.

" Ruddy machine-guns," murmured the Major. " They're stiff with 'em again, I suppose."

" Deuced hard to spot, too," said the Colonel equably. " Particularly their latest dodges. Typical bit of Boche thoroughness those deep shafts with a counterpoise lift to shoot man and gun up to the surface the moment the barrage passes. I give full marks to brother Fritz for doing his job properly."

" Damn him!" added the Major, with emphatic sincerity. In a

former existence he was anxious to resume at the earliest possible moment he had been a stockbroker, and he was unable to share the regular soldier's detached professional admiration for the pains-taking efficiency of the enemy.

The Adjutant looked up from his map.

" Here we are, sir," he said. " Between their first and second lines. That makes eight nests reported there—and God knows how many more besides! I'll warn the companies." He scribbled four notes on his message-pad, addressed them, called sharply : " Runner ! "

Another flat-helmeted soldier appeared out of the darkness, took the messages, saluted, vanished.

" Show me where they are," said the Colonel. " Confound them ! " He looked with interest on the torch-illuminated map filled with a complicated network of red and blue lines amid which the Adjutant had made a number of pencilled crosses. " Let's hope our barrage puts them out of business."

" We'll hope so, sir," agreed the Adjutant with a dutiful affecta-tion of optimism.

" Can't help it if it doesn't," said the Colonel. " We've got to make a job of it and break through this time—G.H.Q.'s deter-mined on it, so Brigade tells me."

" It always is," growled the Major. " It's been determined on it for the last two and a half months—ever since this show started. I see they've got the cavalry up again for the dash to Berlin—divi-sions of 'em, brought up from their holiday home by the sea. And all they'll do is just what they have done before, promenade around for three or four days, blocking up the roads and getting in every-one's way—and then go back again. I don't believe G.H.Q. has ever been to have a look at this war. It reads about it in the news-papers, and the dear old Balaclava Generals recite ' The Charge of the Light Brigade' over the mess port. *Cavalry!*" He finished in a short laugh of bitter sarcasm. "Why not bows and arrows?"

"The principle is all right," replied the Colonel, with a touch of asperity. It was in his blood to defend the wisdom of hierarchical authority against the impertinent criticisms of "amateur" soldiers. "If ever we're going to break through it must be with an arm that combines mobility with offensive power. The trouble is that cavalry horses can't lie down and take cover from machine-gun fire."

"And you can't very well get them to gallop in gas masks, sir," put in the Adjutant. It was something to have a topic of conversation in this nerve-racking wait for zero-hour. "With every month both sides are using gas more and more. I wouldn't mind betting the battlefields are flooded with it before we're finished."

"Very likely," agreed the Colonel. "I'll admit that personally I don't see where cavalry are ever going to come in—less than ever with gas added to all the other unpleasantnesses. And, on balance, gas helps the machine-gunner. With both sides wearing masks, it makes the attack on him more difficult. The machine-gun is the dominant weapon of this war—and the side that first finds an answer to it is going to win. So far I don't see that answer."

"There won't be any answer," said the Major vindictively. "The poor old infantry will just go on exposing its extremely vulnerable skins to bullets sent at six hundred a minute by a comfortably camouflaged Hun squatting in a hole in the ground. And when we're all scuppered, G.H.Q. says: 'Break through? Who ever meant to break through? This is a war of attrition.' 'Attrition' is a good word for the newspapers. What it really means is that the machinery for killing has become so perfect that neither side can do anything except get itself killed in heaps. This isn't a war—war means getting something for your money and your casualties—this is civilisation committing suicide. For thousands of years humanity has been making war, and now it has become so clever at it that neither side can win. Attack and defence is the irresistible force meeting the immovable obstacle. War, as humanity has always understood it, has become impossible. This is the end of an epoch, my friends." He spoke like a man who has been long brooding over a problem.

"You want a spot of leave, Major." The Colonel smiled at him in the darkness. "It's the best cure for pessimism."

"It isn't pessimism," retorted the Major, "it's common sense. I don't pretend to know anything about high strategy—I'm only a plain business man who is accustomed to get his living by the use of common sense. Look at the history of this war so far—whether the Boche makes a push or we make a push, it's all the same. In an effort to knock out the machine-guns, an immense concentration of artillery blows everything off the map—except the machine-guns. And then the infantry goes forward over ground so churned up as to be almost impassable—a floundering target for those machine-guns and the equally intense shelling of the enemy. The whole thing has become a contradiction in terms—infantry can't advance except by such artillery fire as makes the ground impossible to advance over. Look at this show. We've been at it two and a half months, and bit by bit we've blasted the enemy off a few square miles—but always before we can get up guns and supports to the shelled area he has had time to organise a new line. It must have cost us a quarter of a million casualties already—and it's getting worse. The divisions are now only lasting three days in the forward area. They come out shot to skeletons. In the last show we had sixty per cent. casualties, and we never saw the enemy. It's just as bad for the Hun. He had the same experience at Verdun. Modern weapons have made war impossible, though, naturally, you can't expect the professional soldiers to realise it. Men will still fight in the air and on the sea, of course; but between two nations equipped with all the resources of civilisation, land warfare as it has been traditional for thousands of years has come to stalemate. It's the end of an epoch, I tell you."

"There's something in what you say," said the Colonel reluctantly, "unless someone invents a neat answer to the machine-gun. It all comes back to that."

"What's this new machine-gun stunt we're supposed to be co-operating with, sir?" asked the Adjutant. "Who are the Heavy Branch, Machine-gun Corps? I've never heard of 'em."

"Hanged if I know," replied the Colonel. "Something so hush-hush that even the Brigade hasn't been told—although it's been ordered to advance in close support of their machines, whatever they may be. Another one of those patent stunts that never materialise, in all probability."

Far away to the southward there was a sudden outburst of fierce battle in the night, a rapid thudding thunder of artilleries awakened to desperately intense action, a furious crackling of distant machine-gun fire. They rose to their feet in curiosity. Miles off the dark sky was suffused with vivid and incessant sheet-lightnings.

"What is it, Colonel?" asked the Major. "Are we attacking?"

The Colonel shook his head.

"I don't think so. It's probably Fritz trying to forestall us on some sector he's nervous about—coming up against our machine-guns for a change."

For some minutes they watched that fight of whose vicissitudes they could deduce nothing. Then the Colonel yawned. He glanced at the phosphorescent dial of his wrist watch.

"Well, it doesn't concern us," he said. "We've still got an hour or two. I'm going to have a little shut-eye."

He pulled his short overcoat about him, lay down on the earth, his head pillowed on a sandbag, was apparently instantly asleep.

The Major yawned also.

"I think I'll do likewise," he said. "I've been up since four ack-emma."

He laid himself similarly to repose in the angle of a shell-shattered traverse.

Fatigued though the Adjutant was by a long day's marching over the dusty roads from the lost Paradise of the rest area, by the harassments of steering the battalion up through complicated communication trenches encumbered with every kind of unit, by the final supervision of the companies, now officered largely by fresh arrivals and more than half composed of new drafts, as they took up their "jumping-off" positions for the attack where they would advance in second line, he could not imitate the wisdom of that snatched sleep. Nervously tense in anticipation of the fateful dawn (not yet had he recovered from the suppressed neurosis inflicted by the last horror-filled attack, had an accumulation of such neuroses behind him), he sat acutely awake listening to the confused violence of that distant conflict, listening to the slamming of the guns, the overhead rush, the savage shell-bursts, of the still methodic bombardment in their own sector. From the enemy lines the flares still soared in ceaseless renewal, and at irregular intervals a machine-gun hammered spasmodically in suspicion of some movement in the wire-tangled No Man's Land. Every now and then, as the enemy's less frequent shells exploded at hazard in this dark, flickeringly silhouetted landscape, there came a sharp cry for stretcher-bearers. He could hear the vague murmur of other bodies of men in movement, had occasional briefly lit glimpses of figures stumbling among craters and chaotic excavations as of some grotesque circle of the Inferno. They were also taking up their positions for the attack.

Concealed in the darkness, scores of thousands of men were floundering over the shell-smitten ridge, were crowding up the zigzag duckboarded communication trenches, concentrating for the great " push " which was to be made on a three corps front. He found himself imagining the secret apprehension which surely gripped every one of those multitudes struggling uncomplainingly, obediently, disciplined into a selfless sincerity of effort, towards an appalling quasi-certainty of death or mutilation. By this time to-morrow more than half of them would be casualties.

He thought of his own battalion. It had been dreadful to see it when it came out of the last " push " all but officerless, reduced to less than half its strength. In the leafy rest area where the entire division had been sent to fatten up again, the survivors had sat around listlessly, white-faced and haggard, every man mourning the loss of a pal, every man haunted by the thought that next time it would be his turn. It had been part of his job to make them play games, to make them forget the horror from which they had emerged, the horror to which they must inexorably return. If only leave home had not been cancelled! He could see again those poor wretches who came to him begging for it, each with his pathetic tale, his tragedy—the sergeant with the dreadful eyes whose wife had just had a child—" haven't been home for eighteen months, sir." For none of them could he do anything. Not even the officers could get home. How he had hungered to see his own wife (bless her!) in the little book-filled house where, in a remote, incredibly happy past he had written journalism for a living, and delicately exquisite poetry for love and for her fond appreciation. (Extraordinary how his life had changed, how the lives of all these myriads had changed, in that madness of warfare which had so unexpectedly, so violently, metamorphosed a placid world!) If only he could have seen her dear, true eyes looking into his, have felt her arms around him, have renewed the ecstasy of her kisses—just once more—perhaps for the last time! It had been impossible. Day after day the distant thunder of the battle had muttered unceasingly, and while it continued all leave was stopped. The new drafts had come in—some enthusiastic, some anticipatively scared. They had drilled and drilled, had filled the village estaminets, had bought rubbish from the village shops to send home to their dear ones, had written sackfuls of poignantly inarticulate letters he had had to help censor. And then at last the orders had arrived. The division was once more " going in." It was wonderful how the men had pulled themselves together to meet that heart-searching certainty. Singing its favourites, "Keep the Home Fires Burning," "Pack up Your Troubles in Your Old Kit-Bag," its "tin-hats" jauntily askew, its rifles irregularly at the slope but its fours correctly aligned, the battalion had swung again along the dusty roads —with the other battalions of the brigade, of the division. It brought a choke into the throat to see them. They were all volunteers (soon now the politicians would have to bring in conscription for the shirkers!), all picked for physique and intelligence from the eager crowds which had besieged the recruiting offices two years ago. Never, he felt, would Britain have such an army as that magnificent Kitchener Army which routine-bound Regular staffs, enmeshed in their own orthodoxies grown monstrous, sent again and again to futile massacre on the blood-soaked ridges of the Somme. Perhaps the Major was right. Victorious warfare had become impossible. A scientific civilisation was merely committing gigantic suicide in a blind frenzy of scientific destruction where equal met equal. When it awoke from that madness never again would there be such a war. It was the end of an epoch, and the flower of its manhood was perishing with it.

He looked up sharply from these bitter meditations, was instantly again the alert soldier these last two years had made him. What was that? Through a somewhat increased vehemence of their own artillery fire, through a sudden sound-swallowing engine-roar of aeroplanes flying low in the night, he could hear a strange noise, altogether unwonted in the forward area of a battle-field, the clattering, metallic noise of machinery in motion, the popping detonations of motor exhausts. It was a noise that approached slowly from behind their own lines. He could not imagine what could cause it on this trackless desolation of soft earth where no vehicle could pass—was sharply anxious lest the nervously vigilant enemy should hear it also, should send a shower of shells on this area now crowded with crater-lurking troops. The enigmatical noise continued, became louder—ceased. He listened for it, heard only the persistent cannonade, the engine-roar of the invisibly circling aeroplanes, and then—as the aeroplanes passed to a comparative remoteness—the faint murmur of human voices in the obscurity.

A couple of dark figures silhouetted themselves against the stars, standing above him on the edge of the trench. One of them spoke.

"Here's the battalion headquarters, sir."

He rose from his pile of sandbags.

"Yes. What is it? I'm the Adjutant."

The other man answered, in the voice of an officer :

"Good-evening. I wonder whether you could lend me a few of your men with spades. One of my machines is badly ditched."

"Machines"—the idea of such was oddly incongruous in this closeness to the enemy. It brought a recollection.

"Oh, you're these hush-hush people, I suppose?"

"Heavy Branch, M.G.C.—that's our label for the present, anyway. I should be awf'ly obliged to you——" The strange officer was a pleasantly mild-spoken young man.

"Certainly. We've been told to assist you. Where are you?"

"Fifty or sixty yards down the slope." The officer pointed in the darkness. "We struck a particularly bad hole—just a little too big, or not quite big enough."

The Adjutant called up one of the headquarters runners, sent him with an order to the nearest company.

"I'll come and have a look at you," he said, in an idle curiosity. Anything was better than to sit there brooding. "What's this gadget of yours?"

"It's a little surprise for Fritz, the thing that's going to win this war—at least, we believe so," replied the young officer, as they stumbled together through the spasmodically illuminated blackness. "You'll see for yourself."

Conversation was difficult over this soft ground shelled into innumerable pitfalls. The Adjutant reserved his breath for their fatiguing progress, reserved his scepticism. "Win the war"—ever since he had been at the front they had been going to win the war in the next five minutes. He declined to be excited.

"Here you are!" said the officer, a touch of pride in his tone. "Ever seen anything like that before?"

Revealed in the leaping gun-flashes, the Adjutant perceived a large vague shape—a shape which seemed that of some weird prehistoric monster, wallowing in its primeval slime. It was motionless, looked like a huge squat toad lurched sideways and nose-down in a big shell-crater. At a little distance from it was a companion, also motionless, its snout stuck up in the air. Men were busy about them.

"Good Lord!" ejaculated the Adjutant. "What do you call those things?"

"Some of us call 'em 'Willies' and some of us call 'em 'Tanks,'" replied the officer. "We've been so very hush-hush we haven't got a name fixed for 'em yet. We're only just starting, you know."

" And what are they for? "

" Well, they'll push down a house if it's in their way, and they'll go straight over any normal trenches. They're armoured against anything but a direct hit with H.E. shell. As for machine-guns, they might as well be pea-shooters against 'em. When we see a nest, we shall just roll over it and squash it flat. There are two kinds—differently armed—male and female. The one that's ditched is a ' male '—it's got a 6-pounder Hotchkiss as well as machine-guns. The ' female' has machine-guns only. Nasty things to see coming for you in the grey of dawn—what! "

" I should say so," agreed the Adjutant. " You'd think you'd got the jim-jams. How many of them are there? "

" That's the pity," said the officer. " They ought to have waited till we had five hundred machines and use 'em in mass to make a surprise break-through. But you can't expect imagination in the Army. It doesn't like us and it doesn't believe in us—it did its best to prevent us coming into existence—and now it insists on using us before we're properly ready. We've got forty-nine machines, but only about thirty will get into action—and those split up in driblets all along the front. Not enough to do any real good, and just enough to let Fritz know all about it. Never mind—this is only the beginning. We'll have thousands before this war is over —and when they come into action, it's finish to trench warfare. It's finish to old-fashioned warfare altogether. We don't like shells —but infantry and machine-gunners are casualties in advance when we come along. The best they can do is to put their hands up quickly. It's engine-power against muscle-power, armour-proof steel against human skins. We go over barbed wire as if it were thread and no trench can stop us. I don't suppose you realise it, my friend, but you're looking at the beginning of an epoch-making revelation!" He spoke with a specialist's enthusiasm, which left the Adjutant sceptically unconverted.

"What crew do they carry?" he asked, in a tactful avoidance of discussion.

"Eight men—rather crowded and uncomfortable. Like to see inside?"

While the just-arrived infantrymen dug around the ditched Tank, the two officers went across to its companion. A steel door in her side was open, and the Adjutant peered into an interior lit by dim electric bulbs. A large motor-engine in the centre took up most of a confined steel-walled space where there was just room for the gunners to sit on bicycle seats at the breeches of their weapons. Up in the nose was another seat for the driver and the subaltern in command. The officer pointed out the narrow slits of thick glass through which alone they could see what was around them. The air inside was fearfully hot, and thick with petrol fumes. The Adjutant felt devoutly glad he had not to go into battle in such a contraption.

"We're only experimental, of course, as yet," said the officer, enthusiasm still in his voice. "We don't really want this clumsy wheeled tail, and the new ones being built have got a better engine—are better altogether——" He was interrupted by the deafening starting-up of the engine of the ditched Tank. The monster heaved convulsively, crawled with an ear-shattering roar and clatter from the shell-hole which had been just too big for it, stopped.

"All aboard!" shouted the officer. The crew of the other Tank ran towards it, scrambled in through the steel door, which was shut after them. He turned to the Adjutant. "I'm showing 'em the way with a flashlight," he said. "Good-night—and many thanks."

"Good luck to you!" He achieved a human cordiality despite

his scepticism, stood aside to watch.

With sudden violent detonations from exhausts that spouted bluish flame, with an appalling clatter from the endless steel tracks that passed under and over them (surely the enemy must hear!), dragging their clumsy wheeled tails, the uncouth monsters moved off into the darkness, were silhouetted against the enemy flares. He could see them pitching and lurching over the inequalities of the ground, nosing their way forward like weird creatures emerged from an antediluvian past. . . .

*   *   *   *   *

It wanted two minutes to zero-hour. The dawn had already broken to a clear sky that would be brilliantly blue when the sun came up. From the shell-hole where, with the Colonel and the Major, he lay concealed, the Adjutant peered over a landscape of lunar desolation. In front of him, the shells of a steadily maintained bombardment burst in geysers of black smoke among the twisted and contorted wire in front of the enemy trenches, burst in the trenches themselves in violent gouts of up-flung debris; it was not yet the barrage. Nearer to him, he could just discern the crouching crater-sheltered khaki figures who would presently spring up in the first line of the attack. Nearer still, similarly concealed, were the four companies of his battalion. He could not see those monstrous machines. They were camouflaged somewhere out of vision. He had told the Colonel and the Major of them, had been met with cynical, even vigorous scepticism. It would be the P.B.I. who did the job—as usual. The enemy trenches seemed untenanted. Save for a few watchers in concreted emplacements, their garrisons were sheltering in deep dug-outs from the bombardment. It was all very orthodox—and very unpleasant to the nerves. He had had experience enough to know precisely the value of that fallacious quiescence of the enemy—to imagine precisely what sort of reception would meet those khaki-clad thousands the moment they rose for the assault.

One minute! The Major, revealed in the morning light as a robustly built man, a black moustache on the usually ruddy but now pale face under the flat shrapnel helmet, was drumming nervously on his map-case. The Colonel, grey-moustached, haggard in an overstrained middle age, lay peering through his field-glasses, trying to spot the enemy machine-gun posts. He himself made sure, with a hand that trembled involuntarily, that his heavy revolver was fully loaded, that the gas-mask hanging from his neck was susceptible of instant use if required. High up in the sky, sun-suffused at that altitude, aeroplanes were wheeling like gnats. Far away in the enemy back area, anti-aircraft batteries were dotting the heaven with little smoke-puffs extending in a long belt. A very ordinary morning. . . .

Thirty seconds! He had a vivid little vision of his wife still sleeping in the bedroom whose window opened on to the garden where birds piped happily—he mustn't let himself think of such things—hoped to Heaven those new company commanders were up to their job. Pity the last lot had gone—good fellows. They'd be in it long before his wife waked; he might be dead, and she still sleeping—shut up! He glanced at the signallers in the next shell-hole, stolid at their instruments, ear-pieces on their heads—nothing more would come from Brigade now. He could imagine the Brigadier, characteristically biting at his white moustache in his anxiety. What a lot of old men there were—throwing youth into the furnace—doing their best though. . . .

Ten seconds! The thudding of his heart was uncomfortable. The bombardment of the enemy trenches diminished. A haze of smoke drifted over the broken wire, here and there completely blown away in broad channels. He glanced again at his wrist watch—kept his eyes on it—three seconds—two—one——

There was an appalling world-splitting crash and roar behind him—a manifold shrieking in the air. Almost simultaneously the entire length of enemy trench went up in a wall of black-brown smoke, of high-tossed earth vomited in shattering, continuous detonations. The roar persisted in a feverish violent drumming, hundreds of batteries firing at their maximum, maintaining those Valkyrie shrieks in the air, that multitudinously detonating wall of smoke. From their own front line trench-mortars and Stokes-guns had also suddenly opened fire—he could see their missiles soaring over into the smoke—the noise of their discharge and their explosion alike indistinguishable in the bewildering chaos of noise. The ceaseless shells of the barrage were now falling a little farther away, well beyond the wire. From the tumbled earth between him and that spouting inferno had arisen a multitude of khaki-clad, flat-helmeted figures. They plodded and stumbled forward in little groups of specialists—bombers and bayonet-men, Lewis-gunners, machine-gunners with the heavy weapon dismounted and divided among the squad, cumbrously burdened Stokes-gunners, stretcher-bearers—moving, it seemed, with a curious deliberation. He watched them in a dry-throated suspense, an acute anxiety, as they went into the whelm of fumes, through the lanes between the tangled wire. The battalion was to follow at three minutes' interval——

From the opposite horizon came another immense crash prolonged to a roar. The enemy counter-barrage fell with a shriek, shot up in a cataclysmic multitudinous detonation, in a long eruption of smoke and twinkling flame between him and the first wave of the attack, continued in a violent drumming similar to that thunderous drumming which never ceased behind him. In the air was an incessant succession of sharp cracks followed by a menacing drone—shrapnel bursting in handfuls of suddenly produced balls of smoke whence darted snake-like, uncoiling heads. Suddenly he heard—with a shock of apprehension not less unnerving because he had been listening acutely for just that—a rapid methodic hammering, tiny in the universal din. The enemy machine-gunners were popping up from their deep holes, behind the barrage which had failed to destroy them.

He glanced at his wrist watch. Yet another minute! The Colonel had put away his field-glasses, crouched with a whistle ready at his lips. The Major scowled under his flat helmet. In the adjacent shell-hole the signallers had already packed up their instruments, and a man held the reel of wire ready to uncoil in their advance. Away in front of them—beyond the continual eruption of the counter-barrage, not now quite so violent since their own counter-batteries had got on to the enemy guns—the hammering of the machine-guns was a rattling fury, was interspersed with the petty thuds of bombs, just audible in the appalling uproar of the vehemently drumming artilleries, the ceaseless crash and crack of shells arriving in inexhaustible flights. He saw an aeroplane circling boldly at a low altitude above the thick smoke—a contact machine reporting progress. Again he glanced at his watch. It was amazing how quickly that minute had passed! He took a deep breath to still the violence of his heart, willed his knees to firmness as he bent for the spring erect. He was the Adjutant—must set a good example. He refused to contemplate that sudden little vision of his wife leaning over a baby's cot——

The Colonel's whistle shrilled, and simultaneously he could faintly hear the whistles of the four companies, the whistles of other battalions. Instantly he was on his feet, had automatically commenced to walk forward over the loose crumbling soil of the crater-field. It clung heavily to his boots, made anything but the most deliberate pace impossible. Ahead of him, the purposeful little groups of the battalion—machine-gun sections labouring with the heavy barrel, the tripod, the boxes of spare belts; Lewis-gunners with their blunderbuss-like weapons, attendant men carrying the ammunition-drums; bombers with bags of grenades at the waist, accompanied by an equal number of bayonet-men; rifle-bombers; Stokes-gunners; signallers; stretcher-bearers—were in motion through the smother. They plodded straight into the exploding menace of the enemy barrage. It was a triumph of training, of discipline, of teeth-set stolid courage, of desperately loyal endeavour.

Terrible though was that barrier of incessantly bursting shells, it was not so completely destructive as it appeared. That infantry formation had been expressly designed for passing through it. If here and there one of those groups vanished utterly in a spout of black smoke, a riving crash—if from all of them individuals reeled and staggered and fell—yet the most of them emerged on the other side, to that comparative clarity where the lanes had been cut through the tangled masses of rusty barbed wire. Walking as quickly as he could with the Colonel and the Major, the signallers following close, he also emerged unharmed, though around them shell after shell had descended with a screeching rush to disrupt in shattering violence. Ahead he could just see figures of the preceding wave, isolated groups in quick activity amid the drifting smoke—men who threw bombs, who flung themselves down with Lewis-guns that rattled instantly, who stabbed with bayonets at objects beneath them in holes and trenches, who threw up their arms or lurched suddenly forward in collapse. His own battalion was now in among the wire. If only they could pass this dangerous zone—get to close quarters! He balanced his heavy revolver in his hand—shouted to a lagging group in front of him to get on. The next instant there was a rapid vindictive hammering, quite close.

The group went down as though it had been scythed.

Someone must have settled that machine-gun. It ceased abruptly. But others, more distant, were in furious action. On! On! He shouted at the top of his voice that was scarely audible to himself in this din, ran to leadership of some stumbling men in front who had no officer. The hammering was incessant, maddening—the bullets swished and hummed and whip-cracked around him. It was a nightmare, an unreal horror of men who tumbled and writhed upon the ground. On! On! He saw the Colonel likewise urging onward men who had stopped as though paralysed. Where was the Major? On! On! He himself was beyond the wire, was over the all but obliterated parapet of the first trench.

All around him flat-helmeted khaki-clad men were swarming over the shell-blasted heaps that had been the hostile trench system. Except for three deep-helmeted, grey-uniformed men with their hands in the air, stumbling along with a bayonet held close to their backs, he saw none of the enemy. The men who far and near were hurling bombs, were discharging rapid bursts of Lewis-gunfire, seemed engaged with imaginary adversaries. But always that terrible furious hammering continued—in front, and to right and left —and he saw those bombers, those Lewis-gunners, those bayonet-men fall wherever he looked. Ahead, the first wave of the attack seemed to have been swallowed up. He could discern only a few scattered men of it here and there—dodging from concealment to concealment, firing rapidly from behind cover. He kept close to the Colonel, struggling through wrecked trenches, over still smoking debris, towards the point previously indicated on the map as a provisional command post. He agonised to see the companies melting away, becoming mere handfuls of survivors momentarily more reduced. Once more the familiar tragedy was being repeated. He fought down a sickening sense of hopelessness. The "break-

through " was a mockery—but they must do their best. They overtook a group of "moppers-up"—men who flung bombs down
the shaft of a deep dug-out, told him there was a crowd down
there. It was some slight satisfaction.

Just to the right of him, from a little mound almost indistinguishable from the myriad identical mounds of that heaped and
disordered earth, he saw a quick misty spurting. Machine-gun! As
he shouted the warning, dived for cover, the bullets cracked around
them; the Colonel lurched and pitched, lay motionless. Crouching
in the protection of a half-demolished traverse, the Adjutant looked round to the half-dozen similarly crouching men who had followed them, signallers and headquarters runners. One he sent to
crawl and dodge in search of O.C. No. 1 Company, if not himself
a casualty the next senior officer after the Colonel and the Major,
second-in-command. Others he dispatched to find, if possible, a
Stokes-mortar section, bombers, rifle-bombers, and Lewis-gunners.
A grim vindictiveness filled him. He was going to "get" that
machine-gun.

In ones and twos those his messengers had been able to round-
up began to arrive along the shattered trench—breathless, fluster-
ed, smoke-begrimed men whose faces were haggard with strain.
A couple incautiously exposed themselves, were flung headlong
in a quick hammering. He set his teeth, curtly organised his
attack. He had three men with a Stokes-mortar, half a dozen
bombers, three rifle-bombers, and a couple of Lewis-guns. While
the Stokes-mortar and the rifle-bombers sent their missiles on to
the emplacement, the Lewis-gunners and hand-bombers would
try and work round to catch the crew if they made a bolt for it.
Carefully and warily he wriggled himself up to the edge of the
trench, lay so that he could just peer over it. The fatal mound
was twenty yards away.

In the trench the Stokes-mortarmen adjusted their simple weapon to the range he gave them—it was a metal tube with a spike in the bottom upon which a shell, based with a perforated metal cartridge, was dropped to the automatic discharge which propelled it. There was a gruff report, and the missile soared curvingly to fall neatly on the target, exploded in a crash. A flight of rifle-bombs followed, their sticks twirling in the air, detonated one after the other. The emplacement was silent. He ordered out the hand-bombers and Lewis-gunners. They scrambled from the trench as another Stokes projectile finished its curved flight in an explosion. Instantly there was again a quick spurting, a quick hammering from the emplacement. It was of concrete, was undamaged. The men who had emerged from the trench lay prone, motionless. He raged, impotently. It was the old story, familiarly and succinctly described in official reports as "attack finally hung up by machine-gun fire"—so he himself, if he survived, would later on report to Brigade.

What could one do against these all but invulnerably concealed weapons that could singly annihilate a battalion in a few minutes? The Major was right. War had become a hopeless deadlock where the bravest but committed suicide. He had better get back a bit, use his survivors to "consolidate" that trench, put up a barricade.

That emplacement was still firing—other now suddenly revealed emplacements were also firing in a furious unusually prolonged hammering—but the bullets no longer came in his direction. He delayed for a glance at their target. Was another attack following? He saw no rush of men who stumbled and fell. The desolation was empty of human beings. What was it? Fritz was shelling too—shelling his own trenches. From a smoke-smother of shell-bursts he saw something emerge—a weirdly monstrous shape that crawled snoutingly onwards, lurching into shell-holes and trenches, climbing out of them, wallowing over the soft ground. One of the machines he had seen last night! More than ever it was like some prehistoric pachyderm, blind-eyed, sniffing its way, ponderously dragging itself over every obstacle. He could hear the clatter of its steel tracks as they passed down on either side of its unlifted nose, could see the bullets of those frenziedly firing machine-guns splashing bright on its fantastically painted sides. A gun protruded from each flank, and every now and then they spurted in a whiff of smoke and a loud report. It came on like a sentient thing, now as it were hesitating, now resuming a slow but relentless progress uncannily suggestive of some small-brained primeval monster awakened to a dull vindictiveness against a puny humanity that had usurped the earth.

It became at last aware of those furiously raging machine-guns. It stopped, and then with a mighty roar—one track not moving— it turned, began to crawl towards them. The Adjutant watched breathlessly, fascinated. Its camouflage mottling was streaked and scored, splashed all over, by that hail of bullets. It ignored them in a contemptuous invulnerability, disdained to reply with its similar weapons. Ominously purposeful, exhaling as it were angry puffs of vapour from behind its head, roaring and clattering, it lurched and wallowed straight towards the nearest emplacement. The machine-gun within it continued to hammer desperately. The monster approached, was only a yard or two away. It reared a little to climb the mound—very little—rolled over it. Behind it the machine-gun was silent. Roaring and clattering it swung towards the next. That also continued to fire. It fired until the monster heaved and lurched and left it flattened. The Adjutant sprang recklessly to his feet, waved and pointed to that murderous machine-gun nest he had failed to silence. It also was still firing. A brain within the monster perceived and understood. Again the great bulk swung ponderously, commenced to crawl deliberately upon its prey. The Adjutant called up some riflemen from the trench ready in case that doomed machine-gun crew should attempt to bolt. They did not. Their weapon continued to hammer until the great snout lifted above the little mound, until the noisily running steel tracks came down upon it and the huge squat body slithered and lurched. The Adjutant waved and cheered as never before in his life he had waved and cheered. By his side his men cheered and waved also, as though demented with delight.

The monster turned again, moved along the edge of the trench towards the enemy position. The Adjutant yelled and gesticulated. "Follow on, men! Follow on behind!" Cheering, shouting, and laughing like a crowd of excited schoolboys, they followed this roaring, clattering, grotesquely formidable marvel along the trench— not only the original few men with the Adjutant, but a constantly increasing throng. It was extraordinary how many isolated individuals, how many little groups, had been hiding themselves in the shell-holes, waiting until night or another attack should deliver them from those deadly machine-guns vigilant to hammer out annihilation at the first sign of life upon that corpse-strewn craterfield. Now, assured of a local security, they streamed across in a wild enthusiasm, eager for close proximity with this weirdly novel machine which rolled over machine-gun nests as though they were ant-heaps. The Adjutant led them, in a soldierly impulse to gain and consolidate as much ground as possible. They ran suddenly into men in deep-fitting helmets and grey uniforms——

The enemy was massing for a counter-attack. There was a recoil, a moment of confusion among the khaki-clad enthusiasts. It was a moment only. Instantly the monster opened a devastating fire with her machine-guns, with her quick-firing six-pounders, came slithering heavily down into the trench. There was a wild shriek of

horror and astonishment. Some few brave men rushed close in under her weapons, hurled bombs that exploded pettily, harmlessly.
There were those who tripped and fell, failed to get from under
as she clambered in deafening noise up to the farther and firmer
bank. The most turned to rush away, crowding and jamming
around the traverses of this trench comparatively untouched by the
bombardment. The machine-gun bullets, the six-pounder shells,
overtook them. The survivors put up their hands. The Adjutant
hurriedly detailed escorts for squads of prisoners, rushed on again.
All the way up the trench the enemy was surrendering in batches.
It was a triumphal progress.

The trench was empty of any enemy. The monster stopped. A
steel door opened and an officer, his clothes soaked in oil, his face
black, crawled out. The Adjutant ran up to him. It was the officer
of last night. Now, sweating and blowing, he mopped his face
with a dirty rag. He grinned, white-teethed, at the Adjutant.

"I think that'll do for the present," he said. "We're pretty far
forward and we haven't got much in the way of supports. Also we
haven't too much petrol. I should hang on and consolidate if I
were you."

The Adjutant congratulated him, reminded him of their talk
the previous night.

"You were quite right!" he exclaimed excitedly. "This thing
alters everything. Epoch-making isn't the word for it! There's
nothing to prevent us going on and on!"

The officer grinned again.

"Except that we haven't enough machines. But that'll come.
This is only the beginning."

*   *   *   *   *

That morning of September 15th, 1916, when for the first time

the Tank appeared upon the battlefield, indeed signalised the end
of one epoch and the beginning of another. Yet nearly two years
were to elapse before conservative orthodoxy could begin to com-
prehend the proper employment of this novel weapon which, before the war ended, was to supersede all others in primacy of function on the one side and primacy of fear upon the other. Not
until July 18, 1918, would the French and Americans, preceded by
a swarm of 321 Renault Tanks, burst on the German salient at
Chateau-Thierry and carry all before them. Not until August 8th,
1918, the day which for General Ludendorff was the "black day
of the War," would the British fight their first battle in which the
Tank was allowed to show fully what it could do—the day when
435 Tanks broke the German line to a depth of ten miles, and the
infantry marched in column of route behind them. September 15th,
1916, introduced more than a new weapon, it introduced a new
principle into land warfare which for thousands of years had relied
in the last resort upon animal muscle as the generator of the ener-
gies at clash. Crude in design and insufficient in numbers though
they were, the Tanks which that day overran the astonished Germans demonstrated the superiority of engine-power over muscle-
power, the superiority of plate-armour over the human skin as a
protection against bullets. From that day will date the decline and
eventual disappearance of infantry and cavalry and all field artillery that cannot fire as it moves. From that day will date the genesis
of the vastly different land battles of the future. An era almost as
old as humanity has come to an end.

THE SIXTH DRUNK

by
"Sapper"

"NO. 10379 Private Michael O'Flannigan, you are charged, first, with being absent from roll-call on the 21st instant until 3.30 a.m. on the 22nd, a period of five hours and thirty minutes; second, being drunk; third, assaulting an N.C.O. in the execution of his duty."

The Colonel leant back in his chair in the orderly room and gazed through his eyeglass at the huge bullet-headed Irishman standing on the other side of the table.

The evidence was uninteresting, as such evidence usually is, the only humorous relief being afforded by the sergeant of the guard on the night of the 21st, who came in with an eye of cerulean hue which all the efforts of his painstaking wife with raw beefsteak had been unable to subdue. It appeared from his evidence that he and Private O'Flannigan had had a slight difference of opinion, and that the accused had struck him in the face with his fist.

"What have you got to say, Private O'Flannigan?"

"Shure, 'twas one of the boys from Waterford, sorr, I met in the town yonder, and we put away a bit of the shtuff. I would not be denying I was late, but I was not drunk at all. And as for the sergeant, sure, 'twas messing me about he was and plaguing me, and I did but push him in the face. Would I be hitting him, and he a little one?"

The Colonel glanced at the conduct sheet in his hand; then he looked up at O'Flannigan.

"Private O'Flannigan, this is your fifth drunk. In addition to that you have struck a non-commissioned officer in the execution of his duty, one of the most serious crimes a soldier can commit. I'm sick of you. You do nothing but give trouble. The next drunk you have I shall endeavour to get you discharged as incorrigible and worthless. As it is, I shall send you up for court-martial. Perhaps they will save me the trouble. March out."

"Prisoner and escort—right turn—quick march!" The sergeant-major piloted them through the door; the incident closed.

＊   ＊   ＊   ＊   ＊

Now all that happened eighteen months ago. The rest is concerning the sixth drunk of Michael O'Flannigan and what he did; and it will also explain why at the present moment, in a certain depot mess in England, there lies in the centre of the dinner-table, every guest night, a strange jagged-looking piece of brown earthenware. It was brought home one day in December by an officer on leave, and it was handed over by him to the officer commanding the depot. And once a week officers belonging to the 13th and 14th and other battalions gaze upon the strange relic and drink a toast to the Sixth Drunk.

It seems that during November last the battalion was in the trenches round Ypres. Now, as all the world knows, at that time the trenches were scratchy, the weather was vile, and the Germans delivered infantry attacks without cessation. In fact, it was a most unpleasing and unsavoury period. In one of these scratchy trenches reposed the large bulk of Michael O'Flannigan. He did not like it at all—the permanent defensive which he and everyone else were forced into. It did not suit his character. Along with O'Flannigan there were a sergeant and three other men, and at certain periods of the day and night the huge Irishman would treat the world to an impromptu concert. He had a great deep bass voice, and when the mood was on him he would bellow out strange seditious songs

—songs of the wilds of Ireland—and mingle with them taunts and jeers at the Germans opposite.

Now these bursts of song were erratic, but there was one period which never varied. The arrival of the rum issue was invariably heralded by the most seditious song in O'Flannigan's very seditious repertory.

One evening it came about that the Huns tactlessly decided to deliver an attack just about the same time as the rum was usually issued. For some time O'Flannigan had been thirstily eyeing the traverse in his trench round which it would come, when suddenly the burst of firing all along the line proclaimed an attack. Moreover, it was an attack in earnest. The Huns reached the trenches and got into them, and, though they were twice driven out, bit by bit the battalion retired. O'Flannigan's trench being at the end and more or less unconnected with the others, the Germans passed it by, though, as the sergeant in charge very rightly realised, it could only be a question of a very few minutes before it would be untenable.

"Get out," he ordered, "and join up with the regiment in the trenches behind."

"And phwat of the issue of rum?" demanded Michael O'Flannigan, whose rifle was too hot to hold.

"You may think yourself lucky, my bucko, if you ever get another," said the sergeant. "Get out."

*　　　*　　　*　　　*　　　*

O'Flannigan looked at him. "If you're after thinking that I would be leaving the rum to them swine you are mistaken, sergeant."

"Are you going, O'Flannigan?"

"Bedad, I'm not! Not if the King himself was asking me."

At that moment a Boche rounded the traverse. With a howl of joy O'Flannigan hit him with the butt of his rifle. From that moment he went mad. He hurled himself over the traverse and started. It was full of Germans, but this wild apparition finished them. Roaring like a bull and twisting his rifle round his head like a cane, the Irishman fell on them; and as they broke, he saw in the corner the well-beloved earthenware pot containing the rum. He seized the thing in his right hand and poured most of the liquid down his throat, while the rest of it ran over his face and clothes. And then Michael O'Flannigan ran amok. His great voice rose high above the roar of the rifles as, with the empty rum jar in one hand and his clubbed rifle in the other, he went down the trench.

What he must have looked like with the red liquid pouring down his face, his hands covered with it, his clothes dripping with it, in that eerie half-light, Heaven knows. He was shouting an old song of the Fenian days, and it is possible they thought he was the devil. He was no bad substitute, anyway. And then of a sudden his regiment ceased to shoot from the trenches behind, and a voice cried, "O'Flannigan!" It passed down the line, and, as one man, they came back howling "O'Flannigan!" They drove the Germans out like chaff and fell back into the lost trenches—all save one little party, who paused at the sight in front of them. There stood O'Flannigan astride the Colonel, who was mortally wounded. They heard rather than saw the blow that fetched home on the head of a Prussian officer—almost simultaneously with the crack of his revolver. They saw him go down with a crushed skull, while the big earthenware jar shivered to pieces. They saw O'Flannigan stagger a little and then look round—still with the top of the rum jar in his hand.

"You are back," he cried. "It is well, but the rum is gone."

And then the Colonel spoke. He was near death and wandering. "The regiment has never yet lost a trench, has it, O'Flannigan, you scoundrel?" And he peered at him.

"It has not, sorr," answered the Irishman.

"I thought," muttered the dying officer, "there were Prussians in here a moment ago."

"They were, sorr, but they were not liking it, so they went."

Suddenly the Colonel raised himself on his elbow. "What's the matter with you, O'Flannigan? What's that red on your face? It's rum, you blackguard. You're drunk again." His voice was growing weaker. "Sixth time . . . discharged . . . incorrigible and worthless." And with that he died.

They looked at O'Flannigan, and he was sagging at the knees. "Bedad; 'tis not all rum, the red on me, Colonel dear."

He slowly collapsed and lay still.

And that is the story of the strange table adornment of the depot mess, the depot of the regiment who have never yet lost a trench.

WINGULT

by
R.J. Binding

THERE are few who can have encountered that extraordinary apparition, Wingult. He came on the scene in the first year of the Great War, and held the stage for a while, an uncouth hero of strange significance. He went his way as one who came from a far country and from a remote antiquity. He was like those legendary warriors and heroes of old, who performed the deeds of giants, and another age would easily have made of his doings a myth, whereby, quitting the men whom he served, he would have gone over to the gods.

Towards the end of the first great movements of the War, when the opposing armies were settling down into their two endless fronts, digging themselves into the earth and rock, to contest for months the possession of some scrap of land or little hillock, instead of trying for a decisive result, a singular fellow arrived in a French village with a small draft of reinforcements for a German squadron of dragoons. Like the others, he was leading his horse by the bridle, for they had detrained at a convenient distance from the front and had had a long way to go. The squadron commander, who had billeted his squadron in the village, came out of his courtyard on to the village street on the arrival of the new draft. He asked the men their names and ages.

"Wingult," answered the singular one, when it came to his turn, "thirty-five."

The officer paused to look at the man. The fellow's neck was bent forward, he had gigantic shoulders and a powerful back, long arms and monstrous hands; resting, as though wedged into his strong legs, he suggested a bridge pier left behind when the rest of

the bridge had been taken away. Slow, heavy movements revealed
a superhuman strength.

"So you're a volunteer? When did you do your service? What's
your profession?"

He had never been a soldier, Wingult answered.

"How's that?" asked the Captain. "Why weren't you called
up?"

Wingult grinned somewhat sheepishly, grasped at his back with
one of his hands, and said: "I didn't fit into a parade, I believe."

That was true enough: a bridge pier like that was not easy to
fit into a smart company marching in line.

Wingult was by trade a stevedore on the Rhine. The weights
which he had been accustomed to load and unload had, no doubt,
from an early age developed in his shoulders those layers of muscle
which now made them look so prodigious. His mind was occupied
with no other thought but to consider what could be achieved with
the strength of one's body. Year in, year out, day in, day out, he
had lifted ever heavier weights, bearing them upon the iron masses
of his shoulders to the place where they belonged. He had grown
to this service and indifferent to the efforts which it required.
But he had grown proud that he was stronger than others.

The Captain asked whether he had taken the oath. Wingult did
not know what this meant, and it was explained to him that it was
the oath of allegiance to Emperor and Country. Wingult did not
understand; he was only entering a service; he was doing his job
for board and pay. It was explained to him that he had to swear to
the Emperor, and Wingult asked whether the Emperor would
also swear to him. As a precautionary measure he crossed himself,
when, following the example of the others, he raised his hand to
take the oath. Would that affect his having a job? He only wanted
to do his job, he protested, having in mind a simple relationship

which he understood and could appreciate. And he wanted a service book in which everything should be entered. This was promised him; he would have his paybook, and with that Wingult seemed to be satisfied.

Quite as a matter of course, as though it were automatically his job, Wingult proceeded to take on all the heavy duties in his squadron that he could. He groomed six horses instead of one; he carried the whole of the squadron's ration of oats from the cart; alone he shouldered the enormous heavy chests of clothing that arrived almost daily, hitching them into position on his neck without anyone having to lend a hand; and in the smithy he would snatch the legs of the most refractory horses from the ground, when they refused to be shoed, so that they never thought of kicking or lying down. But all this didn't count, and after a few days Wingult began to grieve that no scope was given for warlike deeds, or indeed for work of some other kind, such as would have brought his giant strength into play. The squadron was resting, and apart from routine, police, and fatigue duties there were no laurels to be won. Moreover, during this phase of the War, with its constantly reviving hopes of a big push or a break through, no one had decided what to do with the cavalry. When he had taken the few sacks from the ration cart and seen to his horses, Wingult would run around disconsolately like a veritable Atlas, who had been robbed of his globe and did not know what to do without his accustomed burden.

The first time after his arrival that he was on parade for kit inspection, it was noticed that he had attached a small round, almost spherical, stone bottle or jar with a short neck to his bayonet. The bottle was closed with a large greasy cork, and the mouth of the bottle had an oily gleam. He was ordered not to take the article with him, as it was not part of his equipment and would only get in the way. Two service flasks containing coffee or tea or whatever he might want were permissible.

Thoughtfully Wingult took the offending object back to his quarters and detached it; but at the next kit inspection he again appeared with the greasy stone jar on a strap. The sergeant, irritated at this disregard of orders, asked him what on earth was in the bottle. "Petroleum," answered Wingult. What was the good of that? the sergeant asked. Did he carry a lamp too? But Wingult replied that it was not for a lamp that he wanted the petroleum but for the fire-spitting mountain. The sergeant asked him angrily what on earth that was, but he was quite unable to get any explanation out of Wingult except that the petroleum was used for some trick. He needed it and it gave him pleasure. Others carried a mouth organ or something of the kind, and this was the same sort of thing. The other dragoons laughed at the simpleton's obstinacy and the insistence with which he fought for his hobby against the young N.C.O.; and as there could not be any question of Wingult's powerful limbs being burdened by such a small object he kept his stone jar.

As his days and nights passed in an inactivity which drew from Wingult more sighs than any weight which had ever pressed upon his back, he would clutch spasmodically at the mysterious jar that hung from his belt. It seemed as though he were considering a resolution to free himself decisively somehow. But he would always push the stone bottle back as though he had decided not to resort to extreme measures. One evening, however, he could restrain himself no longer. The other men, although not so fidgety as Wingult, were sitting in weary boredom around a solitary candle in a large, empty inn parlour. "Hi, you chaps," he suddenly shouted to them—"watch the fire-spitting mountain." There was a pause and Wingult crossed himself. Then he took an enor-

mous pull at the jar and blew through the flame of a match
which he had struck quickly on the palm of his hand. A heavy
cloud of flame proceeded from his face and dissipated itself in
tongues of fire running in all directions.

The dragoons, although they were pretty hardened old soldiers,
leapt to their feet in surprise and alarm. The exhibition may have
been Wingult's own invention or he may have picked it up from
a stevedore on the Rhine, but none of them had seen it before.
The air was hot and thick with the stink of burnt petrol. They
all had a bitter, unpleasant taste in their mouths. Many of them
were quite shaken and no one uttered a word. Wingult, however,
roared in unrestrained ecstasy. He had been a success, and as he
left he felt as Apollo may have done after transporting himself
and the assembled gods with the harp. He had exercised great
restraint in resorting to the consolations of the stone jar, as though
he feared that repetition might cause it to lose virtue. The fire-
spitting mountain was a last resource, a wild, fierce sacrament
only to be invoked at the highest pitch of spiritual exacerbation.
The first exhibition seemed to calm him for a few days, but this
calm did not last for long. "Give me something to do and to eat,"
he shouted, "or I'll run away." And he confirmed this threat
with the most obscene and filthy oaths that have ever issued from
the mouth of man. He felt he had been ordained to perform warlike deeds, and every evening he would report to the N.C.O. in
charge, demanding his right as though it were a personal obligation of the latter. "If it weren't for the Lieutenant I should have
run away long ago," said Wingult after these discussions, as he
looked towards the front.

As Wingult spoke in such deadly earnest, and as he was truly
formidable when he prowled restlessly about after finishing his
work, which he polished off with the greatest ease, his remarks

were reported to the squadron commander. The Captain tried to pacify him by pointing out that in the War each man had to remain at his post, and that Wingult would get his chance in due course. "Yes, but I have not got a post," Wingult replied. He had been told that war demanded extreme effort and he was disappointed at being given tasks which made no real call on his strength. "I can do a great deal more," he said plaintively, standing like a humble giant. Could he shoot straight? Had he had any training at the rifle range? the Captain asked, seeking for some way out. This question took Wingult by surprise. He had had that kind of casual training in the elementary use of a rifle which was all that was thought necessary before sending troops to the front, but he really despised it. Anyone could shoot; it had no attraction for him. "If I can get near enough I don't need to shoot," he said finally, after some hesitation.

He certainly would have run away had it not been for Salzach, the junior subaltern, who inspired in Wingult a curious and tender affection. Salzach was still in the first bloom of youth, and the schoolroom seemed a more appropriate place for him than the battlefield. His delicate build was ill-fitted to deal with the hard work of campaigning, and this made a special appeal to Wingult, who derived enormous satisfaction from such occasional services as he could render. He would groom the officer's horse from head to tail and put the saddle with all its equipment in place, which the young lad was never able to do alone. And in the evening he would always come to see that his officer had all the blankets he needed, for it was a cold time of the year, and if Wingult thought that the weather was too cold he would wrap the lad in a second rug of his own and go to sleep himself with nothing to cover him. All of what might be called love in that great rude soul was given to the subaltern, and it was

in him alone that Wingult confided. Thus Salzach learned that
Wingult had a woman at home on the Rhine with whom he
seemed to run a household. They would always go up or down
the Rhine on Sundays in a steamer. Never anywhere except on
the Rhine, and that had been Wingult's conception of pleasure.
But now he felt impelled to do deeds of heroism. He never got a
letter from the woman and he never wrote himself; no doubt they
would find writing too difficult. But once a month a hard black
sausage arrived for Wingult. When Salzach offered to write a
letter for him he declined, explaining that it was understood between them that everything was all right as long as the old woman
sent the sausage.

In no way could Wingult more clearly have demonstrated his
devotion to the subaltern than by the readiness with which he
would offer to perform the dark rite to comfort him. When he
saw his officer secretly weeping as he thought of his sisters at home
and his brothers at the front, his spirit exhausted and broken by
all the bitterness of the War, then Wingult would proceed to try
to cheer him up by the well-known expedient that had never
failed on himself. " Sir," he would say, looking at him sadly, and
with all the tenderness that he could muster—" Sir, shall I do the
fire-spitting mountain?" and he would beam at him. But Salzach,
who had been privileged to be present at the reeking ceremony
when Wingult first astonished his comrades with the perform-
ance, did not share the belief in its beneficial effect upon his spirit
and declined. "No, Wingult," he would answer, not without
emotion, "we must not cheapen it." He smiled, and Wingult
would feel comforted that by the mere mention of his precious
turn he had cheered the boy up.

After hanging round for a few more weeks the squadron was
at last ordered off with some other troops to the front. Wingult

became more cheerful. For the first few days certain clearing-up operations were to be carried out over newly won territory; afterwards the squadron was to be divided into two sections and go into the trenches. Wingult threw himself into the work with a foretaste of heroic deeds to come.

On this section of the front the Germans had made no inconsiderable advance, and had won a good deal of new ground. Young and inexperienced Canadian troops were endeavouring to regain these positions, which enjoyed great natural advantages and dominated a flat valley. Those were the memorable days towards the end of May, which dealt havoc among the Canadian Divisions. In bright daylight the Canadians went forward in close formation to be greeted by countless greedy German machine-guns, and to die blissfully like madmen, who know nothing of death. New regiments followed one another, hour after hour, and when night came the moon illuminated a sleeping host in front of the German line, lying regularly man by man, never to wake again. By the end of the following day, the enemy being unable to offer any serious resistance, the Germans had advanced their line to the low ground without any trouble, leaving the dead army behind them. But by the fifth day the enemy dead were still unburied, for new battles had taken place. The enemy trenches were reversed, new strong points were formed, communication trenches were dug, and what had been won almost without bloodshed had now to be defended by hard fighting. One's own dead and wounded needed every available man and stretcher.

As Wingult, walking by the side of the little subaltern, who was in command of the section, moved into the wide shallowy valley, he surveyed the battlefield with the eyes of a giant to whom alone fell the duty of action. The moon was bright enough to reveal that, even in the small section which had been allotted to the dragoons, many hundreds of corpses were lying. These days of May, following upon many cold weeks, had been very hot. The nights were oppressive. A ghastly miasma of putrefaction lay upon the field and stank to heaven. The men sweated at every pore; they almost fainted at the odour of dead bodies.

But the job had to be done and they set to work. It soon became obvious that it was impossible to give each man a separate grave, and those terrible graves were thrown up bearing the following legends : "Here lie 8 Canadians; here lie 23 Canadians; here lie 45 Canadians; here lie 70 Canadians." Wingult and those who had stretchers, or improvised them out of tent canvas, carried the corpses; the others dug. Wingult lifted his corpses alone, shouldered them crosswise, carried them across, and then let them slip over his powerful neck into the communal grave. He spoke not a word; he never looked up, sighed, or shuddered, giving each body to the earth as though he were working in the service of Death himself.

Thus two nights passed. No one would have ventured to show himself in the valley by day. Although on the second night those who had been out the night before were relieved, Wingult returned to his job. He slipped hundreds of corpses across his neck; his muscles were taut like twisted ropes, his breath came regularly, and he carried on in his businesslike way. By the end of that night they were all buried.

When he got back to his quarters next morning he went up to the subaltern, who was still fast asleep, exhausted by the first night's work. He let him rest, but before lying down himself he did the fire-spitting mountain all over the courtyard to commemorate the triumphant conclusion of his terrible handiwork. Then he watered the horses in the stable and lay down to sleep.

For some reason or other the entry of the dragoons into the

trenches was delayed by a week. Wingult was craving for fresh deeds. His fellows laughed at him; they told him that at the front he would just have to sit down under the shells and the lice, and in any case he wasn't interested in rifle shooting. Only an attack would appeal to him. Wingult said he would find something to do all right. When at last the men chosen for the trenches—a certain number had to remain behind with the horses—arrived at the section allotted to them, they found that they were stationed on the edge of a flat, marshy piece of ground through which a slow stream ran. This stream had been almost completely dammed by the enemy by an oblique embankment, which they kept under constant fire, converting the ground into an impassable morass, although the water was not of any great depth except in the actual bed of the stream. Wingult surveyed the low ground, looking across the stretch of water, through which the tops of the tall reeds just appeared, at the rising ground on the other side, where the enemy barbed wire was. It seemed that he was condemned to inactivity.

He asked to be sent on patrol the following evening. The Captain laughed, saying that they would not get beyond the stream without drowning; it would be impossible even to swim in the reeds. They might perhaps find an easy passage, answered Wingult. As soon as it was quite dark they went down to the bed of reeds, but they found themselves getting stuck in the marshy ground everywhere and stood there water-logged. Wingult looked about him in displeasure. After some futile wading he beckoned to the others to remain where they were, and without a word disappeared downstream in the darkness up to his waist in the water. The dragoons waited patiently for a long time. Then suddenly there was a distinct movement over the flooded area; the water was beginning to flow off in slow circles. Shortly afterwards Wingult appeared again. Nobody knew what he had actually succeeded in doing, but it must have been a gigantic effort. He was black with slimy mud, blowing marshy water from his nose and mouth, his whole body quivering with the exertion he had made. At last he said that he had moved a stone out of position; but from the result he had achieved he must certainly have made a breach in the embankment.

Uneasy at the change in the water level, the enemy kept the marsh under heavy fire during the following day. As a new attack was being planned by the Germans, the troops were ordered to throw a narrow bridge across the stream, and in any case to have trestles, planks, and piers in readiness. During the following night the material required was brought to the edge of the reeds in a four-horse waggon and dumped there inconspicuously. The subaltern and Wingult had been detailed for this operation, and while the waggon was being unloaded two of the horses were killed by a shell. Wingult, who wanted to cross, said it would be better to build the bridge at once. The first piers were firm, and the planks laid across them carried as far as the edge of the marshy stream. To his dismay, however, Wingult observed that the next piers could not be secured to the bed of the stream; there was a patch of open water in the reeds which could not be sounded. Wingult looked about him, and had a wild inspiration for some kind of a floating bridge. He got off the planks and ordered two dragoons to help him. Lying almost prostrate, he pushed his head and neck under the chest of one of the dead horses. He put the front legs across his shoulders; supported behind by the two dragoons, the enormous carcass was carried on his back to the end of the bridge. Then Wingult dropped it over his neck into the marsh.

The little subaltern, who had stepped back with all the others, shuddered slightly, not so much at the sight itself as at the terrific idea which had emanated from such prodigious strength. The carcass, gently resting on the breaking reeds as on a bed, floated a tiny way downstream until it was held in position by the reeds.

Wingult proceeded to test whether the horse's body would bear the weight; and although it gave a little this floating pier carried two planks and the weight of a man, and when the man stepped off it rose again.

Wingult, however, was not satisfied. He repeated the operation, and bore the second dead horse on his back, slipping it over his neck into the reeds to lie beside the other. Then with poles and boards he pushed the whole conglomerate mass outwards and lay the two planks side by side across the intervening space, binding them securely to the planks which were resting on firm ground. The pier held and did not budge; the actual deep spot had been passed, and on the other side the piers got a grip in the soil.

Six times Wingult walked backwards and forwards across the bridge alone, as though to take formal possession. It was protected by the reeds, and even by day it would not have been detected.

Wingult took up a rifle and looked at the subaltern. At last he had got forward, he said, and he was not going to the rear again. The subaltern, who was in command of the little squad that had been working on the bridge, understood what was in his mind, but he asked what his intentions were. "I want to get across," Wingult said, his mind full of vague deeds. "Alone?" asked Salzach, not prepared to allow the others to go. "Alone," said Wingult.

The young officer looked at him with undisguised admiration. To him this seemed an almost impossible act of daring in which he could hardly hope to share. He was suddenly inspired to say, "Only if I come too," blushing in the pride of rivalry.

Wingult turned away and said nothing. He took two loaves from the cart and, mindful of his young friend, took also a rug off one of the horses. In the morning before dawn and in the evening after dusk other members of the squad were to bring food up to the bridge. It would not be necessary for them to cross it, they would merely have to place the provisions at the end of the bridge. Wingult indicated the precise place. Then he made way for the young officer to cross the bridge in front of him with an air as though Salzach were a spectator who had no practical concern in the matter.

Leaving the reeds and the low-lying ground behind, they slowly mounted the gentle incline. Wingult settled himself into an old shell-hole behind a bush which had been uprooted by the explosion. When the night came he would be able to see from this spot what could be done. Little Salzach thrilled at the calm fearlessness with which his friend's great bodily strength fortified him; Wingult had no shudders of terror or disgust to fight down.

So far Wingult had gone his way unchecked, but the ration arrangements broke down. On the following morning, it is true, he found two well-filled bowls of soup that was still warm when he returned to the bridge after an uneventful night, but in the evening the spot where the food should have been was empty.

An hour before Salzach had been shot. The enemy may have noticed some incautious movement, or something else may have aroused his suspicions. In any case, the bush and the roots behind which they were lying were suddenly riddled with a burst of machine-gun fire, and one bullet lodged in the little subaltern's brain. In vain Wingult held his clumsy finger to the little round opening; it was the blood of a dead man that flowed from it.

When he returned to the bridge Wingult took his dead friend with him. How light he is, he thought; none of the hundreds of dead whom he had carried had been so light. He placed the body in the reeds, stretched out like a slim candle. They would come and fetch it, he thought. Then he looked for the rations, but the spot where they should have been was bare.

Wingult looked towards the German lines in dismay. All was quiet there; an occasional flare went up, to sink slowly and die out over the hollow. He supposed that there must have been some accidental delay, and hung the empty pans, out of which he and his officer had eaten, on the bridge post, returning with leisurely steps to his post. The next morning, too, he found nothing; the desolate pans hung there empty, and the subaltern's corpse was untouched. Again he looked over to the German trenches; they were not a quarter of an hour away. He was feeling hungry, the loaves were finished, but he never moved from the bridge. He wanted to know whether he had been forgotten and how far they would go. How could he know that the squadron had been hastily taken out of the line on the previous evening for other duties, and that different troops were occupying the trenches in which he supposed his companions to be; that they had received special instructions from those they were relieving to bring food for two men each day to the bridge in the hollow; and that the officer commanding the relieving troops had flatly forbidden this, as he was not going to risk a man for a couple of pots of food? It was incredible that there should be anyone over there, and if anyone was hungry he would come back all right. Of all this Wingult was certainly in complete ignorance; indeed, he returned to the spot which he had selected, and he kept pondering all day on the question why he was not brought any food. Time and again he went through his paybook to see to what duties the Emperor had committed him. But the book laid down no regulations, and if it had he would not have been able to read them. He tried to think whether they had neglected him before, but he remembered that one morning he had found his cooker filled full with fresh milk, which his companions had got at night by milking the peasants' cows; they must have gone a long way for it.

By the evening of the second day, when he went down to the bridge—he went late, lest he should arrive too early—his body was craving food and his mood was black. He found everything unchanged. He looked incredulously into the pots: they were as empty as on the day before. He turned them up and looked inside them again: they remained empty.

Then Wingult groaned—a deep, savage moan. Holding the pots in his enormous hands, he turned to the darkness, where were the German sentries, the advance troops, the armies, and away behind the land in which he had once been a child. He stretched himself and roared into the night like a monstrous wild beast. Then he dropped the pots.

After this he went to the dead body of the little subaltern at the end of the bridge. It was stiff with the rigor of death. Wingult raised it out of the reeds, and took it under his arm like a board; he turned about and crossed the swaying bridge of carcasses. Near the centre he stopped for a moment. Cautiously he placed the body in front of him on the planks, turned round clumsily, and looked back. As one about to make a fine farewell, he took a long pull at the bottle by his side. For a moment the sentries, who had been startled by his roar, saw the monstrous form of a man rising above the water; then the apparition vanished. But Wingult drove the stopper home into the bottle-neck with the flat of his hand, took up the dead body, and turned his back upon the people whom he had served. He would seek other service, he thought sullenly. Slow and brooding he passed across with his dead friend under his arm; towards the enemy—into the darkness.

THE LAST SQUAD

by
James B. Wharton

"LIEUTENANT, here's a runner with orders!"

The company runner's helmet is awry. His eyes glisten in the candlelight. Steadier now, he takes off his helmet and wipes the sweat off his face with his sleeve.

"Holy, jumpin' Jesus, but it's awful out there. Better stick to th' rear o' th' houses. I'd never got here if I'd stepped out on th' street. Ther' shells an' bullets all over. My God, it's awful!"

The Lieutenant comes into the dug-out through a communicating passage way. The rest of the platoon is at his heels.

"Sir, orders are to take up position to meet a counter-attack!" says the company runner.

"Load and lock pieces—fix bayonets!—the Lieutenant turns towards the soldiers, jammed into the one chamber and with equipment already on their backs—"an' follow me!"

At the head of the stairway, daylight is shut out suddenly by a figure that jumps through the cellar hatch simultaneously with the burst of a shell in the courtyard outside.

"Who's that?" asks the Lieutenant tensely.

"It's Holloway. That you, Osgood? Listen, quick! Message's just come from battalion sayin' th' Boches 're oozin' into town across th' river—under cover o' this hellish barrage—we're going to meet the attack along the line o' these houses—you're on th' extreme left flank o' th' company sector—take up position on that corner where we came in to-day—at th' junction o' th' two streets —but for Christ's sake don't go out on th' main street—it's enfiladed—death out there—go through the rear of th' houses—along here! For Christ's sake, hold—you've got th' pivotal posi-

tion . . . that's all—good luck—send a runner back when you're
in position—I'll be here . . . now—get off!"

Out in the open, the town disintegrates. No longer does anything remain fixed. Explosions tear off corners of dwellings, open
up roofs, burst out through the faces, tear away rafters and joists
which crash entire houses. Everywhere are jets of black smoke,
geysers of stone, plaster, and white dust. The bursts come so close
together they sound like one massive, uninterrupted roar. The
volume of the detonations is so great that it obliterates the screams
of shells passing through the air.

Across the courtyard and over a low, stone wall, over the roofs
of outhouses, through dishevelled kitchens and out through another courtyard, the soldiers stream. At the base of walls and other
obstructions they bunch. Across open spaces they spread out. Sometimes they flatten themselves against the ground, dart under cover
of a wall, dive into a ditch or around the door of a house. Stones,
chunks of shell cases, and bits of plaster fall about them. They go
without thought, madly, in the Lieutenant's wake.

"Gray, take that gate!" he shouts and points, "an' barricade
it! Williams and Ives, take your squads through that house and
stand by th' front door an' windows! Jones and Catman, in th'
barn there! McGuinness and Dennowitz, take cover in th' barn
an' stand by to reinforce when I tell you! Jackson, take th' two
squads in th' house! Bamberger, th' squad in th' barn! I'll command here at th' gate!"

The last squad fills up the open gateway.

"Anything you can find!" shouts Gray.

They drag beds, mattresses, tables, chairs, bureaus, out of the
adjoining houses; pile up boxes, timbers, stones and rubble. The
mass of barricade grows quickly, until it reaches about the level of
the eye. Loopholes are poked through, low down for the two auto-

matic rifles, while the ordinary riflemen rest their pieces overtop.

"It's good now!" shouts Gray. "We've got enfilading fire both ways along the main street and down that cross street towards the bridge! Eyes everywhere!"

"Look sharp everywhere!" cries the Lieutenant. "Th' minute th' shelling let's up, they'll come! Look for 'em close behind th' barrage."

The din is so great that Gray has to go to each man and shout the Lieutenant's warning into every ear.

The roar goes on. Fountains of black smoke and particles of earth geyser into the air behind the tense line of soldiers. Across the street, white dust bursts out of the houses, with bits of plaster, timbers, and tiles. At the barricade the soldiers duck their helmets against the rubble that strikes about them. The white dust settles over their uniforms and packs.

Suddenly the curtain of shell-fire lifts and numbed ears ring in the apparent silence. Gradually that silence ceases as another sound impinges on ears, another uninterrupted score:

Pss-pss-pss-pss-pss.

Dzing-dzing-dzing-dzing-dzing.

That comes from close overhead, while from farther away sounds the incessant rat-tat-tat-tat of innumerable machine-guns.

"Stand to, everywhere!" shouts the Lieutenant. "They'll be comin' now!"

Far overhead aeroplanes circle against a clear sky, like vultures drawn to and poised above a place of death.

Artillery in rear of infantry opens fire. The shells pass overhead with a siren of sound and burst in a broad line that climbs the face of a hill, across the bridge and river, a kilometer distant. The neat line of bursts rakes the hill, down and up, up and down.

"Ain't that purty! Now they're gettin' theirs!"

The supporting machine-guns tap into the orchestration of fire. The bullets drone overhead, indistinguishable from the enemy lead.

The last squad leans against its barricade. Whittaker, with a rifle, presses himself into the angle between the barricade and the house on its right. Below him, Marzulak lies on the ground, staring fixedly along the barrel of his Chauchat, trained down the cross street towards the bridge. Novelli crouches beside him, with extra pans of ammunition piled between him and the automatic rifle. O'Connor lies a yard to the left, another Chauchat pressed against his shoulder, and Waglith hugs his side with ammunition. Gray, rifleman, stands at the extreme left of the barricade.

The Lieutenant weaves restlesssly behind the squad. He bends low, opens and closes his hands nervously. He looks like a quarter-back behind a football line-up.

" Where are they? Where are they? Aren't they goin' to come?" he mutters aloud.

" Light me a cigarette, Mose," says O'Connor.

" That's right," Gray puts in quickly, glad of the distraction.

He reaches in his blouse pocket with his right hand and extracts a single, bent cigarette. He asks Waglith to light it for him. He never takes his eyes away from along his rifle-barrel. With a deep inhalation, he draws the smoke down into his lungs.

" Maybe that'll be th' last smoke." His lips form the syllables, but he doesn't actually speak.

They seem surrounded, hemmed in by the riveting machine-guns. The bullets whisk overhead ceaselessly. Out forward, as far as they can see, there is no life. The main street, to the right and left, is bare. So is the cross street, down which they can see as far as the bridge a hundred yards distant. Across the street, and stretching down towards the bridge, the broken houses seem vacant. Occasionally a rafter or a stone gives way and rubble slides.

" How're they likely to come? " asks Waglith.

" Don't know," replies Gray. " Up that cross street, I guess . . . but keep your eyes to the left, too, down the main street. They'll come fast, I guess, and in a bunch."

" Look sharp! Look sharp! " the Lieutenant keeps saying.

" I'm doin' that, awright," Marzulak growls, without taking his eyes off his Chauchat barrel.

No one has seen anything, when suddenly a Potato Masher flips through the air and explodes just in front of the barricade. Down the cross street a grey arm withdraws into the window of one of the houses.

" Open fire—you Chauchats—into the windows of those houses! " screams the Lieutenant. " They're seeping through. . . ."

His words are lost in the clack of Chauchats and the snap of rifles. Lead pours down the cross street and splashes against the house fronts.

A momentary pause, while the Chauchat feeders slip fresh pans under the automatics and the riflemen open the bolts of their pieces and jam full clips into the breeches.

No sign of life appears out forward. Then, from the corner of the roof of a house diagonally across the street, another grey arm waves upward against the sky. Another clumsy Potato Masher hurtles, end over end, towards the barricade . . . over the barricade . . . at Gray.

He ducks, then straightens up as if he realises a mistake. He swings his rifle at the object and catches it full, as one would a baseball. It hurls the grenade to one side of the barricade, where it explodes harmlessly in the air.

" Good . . ." shouts the Lieutenant, but again his words are lost in the clatter of the Chauchats. He pulls a hand grenade off his belt, jerks the pin and lobs it up over the corner of the roof. It bursts full over the top, shedding its unseen bits of metal against the tiles and through the holes. A grey arm is flung out, over the edge of the roof. It jerks a bit, and then lies still.

While Novelli clips a fresh pan under the automatic, Marzulak twists round and winks at the Lieutenant.

Other grey arms are flung out of the windows, and the tiny, black bores of Maxims are poked out of the corners. Now there is a criss-cross of fire between the houses along the one edge of the cross street and that particular corner of the town occupied by the Fourth Platoon.

The smoke soon renders everything blind-fire. The windows are blotted out. But lower down, where the smoke has lifted, a German jumps through a doorway out into the street. He goes down immediately, pitching forward headlong and throwing his arms out wide before his body. For a few moments he twists about over the cobbles, then lies quiet.

"Come on, you reserve squads, man the barricade!" shouts the Lieutenant. "They're trying to rush it!"

Bent over, the two extra squads rush on to the barricade and double the fire that goes out from it.

The Lieutenant lies on the ground, behind the base of the barricade. From time to time he tosses bandoliers of cartridges and musette bags full of loaded Chauchat pans to the squads. Once he raises himself too high, as he chucks a heavy musette, and a burst of machine-gun fire catches him in the shoulder. The impact swings him round in a semicircle.

"They've got me, Gray!" he yells. "You take command!"

He crawls into the shelter of the barn and lies there quietly, gritting his teeth, while blood soaks through the shoulder of his blouse. He extracts his first-aid kit from his belt, but can't open the tin with only one hand. He tries to tear it open with his teeth but can't. He lies there and swears.

"Lieutenant's got it!" shouts Gray. "We've gotta hold now!"

"What's dat? Lootenant hit?" Marzulak asks Novelli, who nods his head. "De basdards!"

He draws the Chauchat out of its loophole and rises to his feet.

"Where are you goin', for Christ's sake?" asks Gray.

"Too slow dat way," the Serb answers.

He puts the stock of the automatic against his shoulder, leans up over the edge of the barricade and sprays fire down the street, swinging the gun from side to side. His helmet topples off, bumps across the barricade and rolls over the cobbles. His black hair is tumbled over his head. His dark eyes blaze.

"Oh, you basdards—basdards—basdards!" he grits out. "I'll pay you fer it all—de hikin'—de night work an' de empty bellies."

He climbs on to the barricade and calls to Novelli for another pan of ammunition. He twists himself from side to side . . . until, all at once, he collapses. His body crumples, falls on to the parapet, and somersaults out forward. The Chauchat clatters against the barricade, against the cobbles of the street.

It is suddenly quieter. The smoke commences to lift. No more grey arms are flung out of the windows. The tiny bores of the Maxims disappear inside the bullet-pocked faces of the houses.

"They're givin'! Keep up the fire!" Gray shouts. "By God, Jim did it! They must 'a' thought we were comin' over with th' bay'nit!"

Novelli, who no longer has an automatic to serve, straddles the barricade, leans down, and takes Marzulak's body under the shoulders. He drags him over the parapet and lays him on the ground at the base of the barricade. There is a small hole in the centre of his forehead. Out of it, bluish bubbles ooze and burst. His eyes are closed. He is silent, although his lips move, open and close, for a few moments.

"Gone—nothin' do," said Novelli helplessly.

"All right, Novelli, then look to the Lieutenant, by the barn," says Gray.

Novelli disappears through the smoke.

"Stand to, everywhere! They may come on again!"

The smoke clears and all fire ceases. Out forward there is no sign of life. The German who stepped out of the doorway lies across the pavement, his head in the gutter. Another leans out of a ground-floor window, buckled over the sill. Up over the corner of the roof that arm hangs. The blood from it has made a stain on the white face of the house, and another on the pavement below. Alertly the last squad stands at its post.

"God, it's all over," says Gray.

Novelli comes up.

"I took Lieutenant to Captain—he says Sergeant Jackson command platoon."

Jackson appears at the kitchen door of the adjoining house. He rests there, with his hands clutching the jambs on either side.

"Where's th' Lieutenant?" he asks.

"Wounded," Gray answers. "An' the skipper says you're in charge of the platoon."

"All right, what're the orders?" He turns round and shouts into the house: "Watkins, go back to company headquarters and ask Captain Holloway for the orders." He turns to Gray:

"Any casualties?"

"Marzulak's knocked off"—and he points to the body beside the barricade.

"Tough. I had two wounded, but no one killed. Wonder how the other squads made out? Purty hot there for a while, huh?"

"God, yes!" fervently.

Captain Holloway, face streaked with sweat and filth, comes along :

"You did good. We held all along the line." He looks appreciatively at the squads at the barricade.

"Many casualties?"

Gray points to Marzulak.

"No one else?"

"Don't know about Sergeant Bamberger, on the left," Jackson answers. "I'll send for him."

"Can't wait. We've got to go forward. The only way we can hold against another attack like that is to occupy the town up to the river. Take the platoon forward and occupy all houses down that street as far as the bridge. Listen for my whistle. Don't go forward until you hear it. An' be careful. Don't let yourself get enfiladed on any of these streets."

He goes off as he came. Bamberger appears.

"How'd you make out, Bamby?" asks Jackson.

"Not so good." He shakes his head. "Two killed an' three wounded—all by one shell before we ever saw a German. Hear th' Lieutenant got it in th' shoulder?"

"Yeah, I'm in charge. Th' skipper's just been here an' says we've gotta go forward as far as th' bridge down there—when his whistle blows. Send your wounded back to company headquarters. Leave th' dead where they lie—I guess."

The aeroplanes are gone out of the sky. No more shells scream through the air and burst. No more bullets whisk overhead, and the riveting of the machine-guns is gone. Quietness everywhere. The platoon assembles at the barricade and tensely awaits the whistle.

It blows.

"All right," says Jackson. "Take it slow, now. Take advantage of all th' cover you can get. Two at a time. Bamby, you lead off."

Cautiously, in the half-light, they go forward. They hold rifles at the ready, so that the bayonets stick out like feelers. Two at a time, with a long distance between each couple, they file along the edge of the houses and wind in and out of the doorways.

Twilight and darkness. Marzulak, the Serb—the Serbian son-of-a-bitch the others sometimes called him—lies alone beside the barricade. The bluish blood has clotted over his broad, low forehead.

OVER THE TOP

by
Ludwig Tugel

MY friend Paul had been writing to his girl and, as I bent over his candle to light my cigarette, I read what he had written.

"DARLING,

"The enemy has cut the dykes; the canals have risen to their banks, and the earth is already saturated. The whole country will be flooded in two or three hours. We are ordered to attack in the early morning. Prisoners have reported that all bridges, dykes, dugouts, and observation posts have been mined during the last fortnight, and men have been detailed to fire the charges. So that when we advance everything will go up into the air.

"There will only be a short preliminary bombardment, and that is to start in an hour. According to our reports, the enemy has four times as much artillery massed behind his position as we have. It is certain that we shall all be killed; we shall either be blown up into the air while crossing a bridge, reduced to pulp in a trench or dug-out, or drowned in the marsh.

"I try to tell myself, darling, that all this cannot destroy our love. You love me and I love you. My friend, who has been with me all the time this last fortnight, knows all about us. I felt that I had to tell him everything that was in my mind, and so he has come to know you although he has never seen you. My friend won't have anything to do with love; he doesn't believe in it, or at least so he says. He has just woken me up (although we ought to be resting, and Heaven knows we need to) to help drive off the rats, who have got very lively since the water started rising. The water gauge which we have stuck in front of our dug-out is quite unnecessary; the rats are a perfectly reliable gauge. We can always tell by their antics whether the water has risen again.

"Darling, for the first time I am letting myself write to you as I feel. These are my last words to you, and so I shall be quite frank. My friend says that it is no longer necessary to pretend, to tell lies and to try and score off the other fellows. Yesterday Frohlich the bombardier had an attack of madness, and my friend had to tie him down in the dug-out. He called me up to show me the best way of doing it—to slip an arm under his shoulder, tie his hands behind, and push a gag in his mouth—and then he said quite calmly : 'I'm just telling you in case you have to do it to me.'

"Darling, can I make you understand that I have never thought of you so intensely as I do now? Every time a mine explodes I think of you. The dull explosions are gas mines, and when I hear them I put on my gas-mask to shield my cheeks and lips, the lips which you have kissed and which have kissed you. For I shall cherish those kisses when we go over the top in the early morning; they are my dearest memory, for I have never had any greater experience. I have never slept with you. I shall sleep in mud while the water rises over me, and you will be far away, dressing, perhaps, or drinking your morning coffee.

"I don't know whether I would have you weeping or happy when you hear that I am gone. It must be as it will. But you need not worry about my death, for I may tell you that to-day, or rather yesterday (it's already past midnight), the doctor came round. He gave my friend and I each a little roll of morphium tablets, saying that he was not really supposed to do so, but that friendship was more important than regulations. On the roll is printed 'Medical Stores, 9th Army Corps.' That is our final resting-place, the 9th Army Corps. For this is the end.

"No, my dear, I haven't finished yet. I've never felt so deeply about you as now. I have always written you cheery letters, even in the most disgusting filth, even when I've felt like dying, and how often I have felt like that! I've always told you lies, but I told them because I always thought I should see you again, and I didn't want you to shrink from me, to feel me a stranger. I wanted you to love me, and so I told lies when I was on leave, when we were together. I pretended I was proud of your woman's courage that would never let the tears flow when we parted; I pretended to be a hero when I walked through the streets on your arm. But God only knows what this stoicism cost me; I don't know how it was that I didn't die each time I came on leave, just as I don't know how my friend can lie sleeping here now, when in four hours we shall be dead.

"Your people will tell you that it is a good thing we were only engaged and not married. But that is just what hurts me; if only I could feel that you were bearing a son of mine I believe I could go over the top with confidence. Not because you would be any more faithful to me, but because I should at least have fulfilled myself. I could die feeling that there would be something left of me to carry on my undying hatred of this War; there would be a son who would curse it every time you spoke of his father. I will tell the truth now, I have told lies since this War started, but I will tell them no more.

"But I cannot end yet. My darling, I am a coward. I am terrified of this attack. I can't let you mourn me as a hero. Yet neither you nor your friends nor anyone will ever know how I died, for this letter will never reach you. It will sink with me as the water rises, lying on a heart which is bursting with hatred and rebellion. For I loathe this death. I loathe this War with its inhuman, unnatural torture. I cannot bear to die; I am afraid—my God! how can I make you understand how much I am afraid?—of those ghastly machine-guns; I am shaking with terror; I am a miserable, abject coward. I would rather lose my limbs, I would rather lose my reason—anything rather than to die. Let my legs be shot off and my arms shattered, let me lose my hearing and my sight, but only let me live. As a cripple, as a living corpse, I want my seventy years in the world. I cannot bear to die now. I cannot. I will not. Oh, my beloved, if only I could make you feel this and realise it! It is awful to think that you know nothing about it at all. For you do not know it, and because you do not know it you cannot really love me. Not me as I am. Your sorrow is for another. Your tears flow for another, not for me. This is terrible. It is much worse than death. For it means that in death I shall be swallowed up in a greater desolation even than here, in these abominable trenches. I shall die, and you will wear white for me, to show that you are mourning for a hero."

That is what Paul had written to his girl before he fell asleep. As I finished reading, a rat ran over my foot, and I aimed at it with my revolver, just as it was sniffing at his greatcoat pocket. The report made him spring up, wild-eyed, and at that very moment the barrage started outside, shaking the dug-out about us.

Paul snatched his revolver from his pocket, screaming, "Help, the enemy!" and gabbling incoherently, staring at me with vacant eyes.

I pointed to my watch. "It's quite all right," I said; "the firing was to start precisely at 1.35. We don't go over till four o'clock."

"What!" he screamed wildly, and turned his revolver on me.

I snatched his letter from the table and made a grab for the revolver, but he got the letter away from me and thrust it into his breast coat-pocket. Then he pointed the revolver at me again, seized me by the throat, and shouted: "You've been reading it, haven't you? You've been reading it?"

"Yes," I managed to gasp, and I saw him pull the trigger. The bullet flew past my ear; we struggled and rolled over together. Chest to chest, head to head, we were lying locked against each other.

I don't know what happened. We were trying to bite each other's throats like savage beasts, and our lips met harshly, then relaxed and remained together. We murmured brokenly, incomprehensibly, as we wept and kissed and clung. Outside in front of the dug-out they were shouting: "Take cover! Take cover!"

Paul pressed closely against me, and I sheltered him in my arms as once I might have sheltered a woman whom I loved.

"All right, old man. All right." We said no more.

Shattering explosions filled the air; the dug-out seemed continually to rise and fall around us. The rats ran over our feet. It seemed as though we were already dead; no one bothered about us any more. We said nothing, but lay there, hand-in-hand.

At 2.45 there was a slackening off in the firing, to spare the ammunition. The guns, of course, not the men. It was quiet for about fifteen minutes. Paul got up, drew his letter from his pocket, and burnt it to ashes in the candle-flame. Then he came back to my side and we clung together.

*   *   *   *   *

That life at home seems so far away; it is unreal, a painted harlot with a powder-puff for a heart. From the victory reports she has cut herself a garment that leaves her breasts exposed, and of the casualty lists has she made soles for the shoes in which she dances. War profiteers of the flesh and of the spirit sniff around her; they have built a barbed wire fence in front of the stage upon which they enjoy her.

But we are the front line swine, and we know everything about getting through barbed wire. We know that the enemy barbed wire is easier to get through than the barbed wire at home; that is the only reason we keep pushing on; that is why we endure these desolate stinking shell-holes, with the artillery stationed behind to play appropriate music for the burial parties.

The time stands still, and yet it flies so quickly. Why are we here? Why must we attack? Why is there a war? Why is there home and the front?

The front is a world full of ghosts. Birds of death flutter over torn fields, ravaged woods, and broken cities, stroking with their wings the faces of those whose hearts are torn out and shattered. Once you were with me, my beloved, with your light-hearted laughter. How gay we were when you sprang up to dance, singing a song in your heart. And I, who once used to walk round worms and beetles for fear I might kill them! . . .

The rustle of your woods, warm earth. The moan of your breakers, holy sea. The light and shade of human speech, the flowing tide of the cities, joy and sorrow, workday and holiday, the rhythm of life and peace. Peace! Peace!

I remember you, my own earthly mother. You would come to my bedside and stroke my forehead and my hair with your soft-slender hand. What need was there of God with your warm, gentle eyes watching over me? How blissful to be ill or in distress when you were so near! For then you would not leave my bedside; when I awoke from my fevered dream your face was always there, smiling at me. I am again a boy of three, and you have just given birth to my brother. That is my earliest memory; we were brought into your room, and you were lying pale in your bed. I could not help crying as I looked at you, and I threw myself on the bed and kissed you, understanding nothing, but perhaps realising unconsciously that life gives love and that only love can give life.

* * * * *

Paul bent over me, his face like a cut-out silhouette against the darkness. His words came as though from a great way off: "We are going to die, old man. I feel certain of it, and so there is no more use in talking. If we talk our hearts will give us away, hanging out their fears like flags of surrender. And I don't want to do that. Let's forget all about our lives and make a decent end together."

We clasped hands, silently.

At 3.45 the first line was standing at the steps to the parapet. Paul was next to me. The enemy, having guessed that we were about to attack, covered the exits with devastating fire. Shrapnel was bursting all round, and I dodged sideways to take cover, bumping against the ladder on which Paul stood as I did so. The ladder shook and rattled, my heart leapt and swelled, but I clenched my teeth, and tried to shout above the roar of the battle: "Are you all right, Paul?"

The shrapnel scattered fragments in our eyes; everyone cursed to relieve the tension. We were ordered to keep quiet.

I dared not look at Paul. I glued my eyes to the shining dial of my watch, waiting. There were shouts on my left; they came nearer. Visualised in front of me was the page in Field Service Regulations, with a paragraph about passing along the command in the front line trench. The message was shrieked at me: "Advance, squad two, and stand by. Pass it along."

I shouted it along: "Advance, squad two, and stand by. Detail six men from the left. Bombardier Frohlich will take command. Pass it on."

I shouted it again, above the clamour. Then, through the rage

of the whistling, howling, and crashing of shells came the rattle of
the machine-guns. Yes, the enemy has guessed, and he has blocked all ways, leaving only one open, the way of death. The siren
song of the machine-guns lures the poor soldiers, so hungry for
rest, as the nightingale's voice lures its mate on the love night.

I looked at my watch. Was it time yet? The sirens screamed
out, and I shouted above them: "Ready! Over the parapet!"

We rushed into that shrieking hell. I stumbled and fell into a
shell-hole, and my revolver was jerked out of my hand. I picked it
up and ran forward again, but Paul caught me up and snatched it
hastily away. I did not understand at first, but then I realised that
the muzzle was choked with mud, and that, at the first shot, it
would have exploded in my hand. Paul gave me his own revolver,
and so, hand-in-hand, we ran on.

The world is no longer vast and unconfined. It is a narrow
tomb, which is closing in on us; we can hardly breathe.

I got stuck in the barbed wire, and Paul wrenched me free. If
he had torn my veins to shreds I should not have felt it. We can
love even if we must die, and can we die if we love? It is madness,
perhaps, but with this thought flaming through us we leapt into
the enemy's trenches. There was a moment's hesitation. Then the
horrible certainty. We were being fired on by our own artillery.
We had advanced too soon.

Impotently I shouted out, "Stop! stop," but my screams were
cut off by an exploding shell. Paul is staggering, he has fallen, and
I . . . I can hear nothing. He is trying to speak to me; I can see
his lips move. But I cannot catch his words. I bend down. I throw
myself flat on the ground, straining my hearing until I feel that I
am nothing but an ear. But I can hear nothing.

"Paul, Paul, old man," I stammer. Feverishly I rub the trench
mud in my ears to clean them and wipe it out again. It is no good;

I can hear nothing.

Then I see that Paul is closing his eyes. My heart strains out to him: "Paul, Paul!"

I can bear no more. I jump up and shout out to the attacking squad: "Forward! Advance! . . ."

We rush on . . . I will die! I must die!

AMONG THE TRUMPETS

by
Leonard Nason

" He paweth in the valley, and rejoiceth in his strength: he goeth on to meet the armed men. He mocketh at fear. . . . He saith among the trumpets, Ha, Ha; and he smelleth the battle afar off, the thunder of the captains, and the shouting. The glory of his nostrils is terrible."—Job xxxix.

THE morning was well advanced; that is to say, it was some time after nine o'clock. Westward the high-banked clouds that were the remnants of those that had deluged the countryside with rain the night before were still black and menacing, but eastward the sky was blue, and the sun already gave promise of unpleasant heat later on.

From the black woods on the right, gloomy and sinister beneath the clouds, to the rolling hills of the horizon stretched a wavy band of newly ploughed earth. It was wide, it was irregular, it ran up and down hill and squirmed along the side of crests as if the man that had furrowed it had been either drunk or blind. That wavy band of earth, though made with steel, had not been ploughed. It marked the German front line in front of Richecourt; it showed where the defence system that the French had crowned with such names as the Trench of the Goths, Trench of the Vandals, and Trench of the Barbarians had once frowned on Seichprey and Jury Wood. The system was no more. Parapet and parados had been flattened into one uneven heap of mangled earth; the wire had been plucked up by shells, tossed about, rolled up, and flattened again by the passage of tanks. Dug-outs and strong-points that had defied assault for four years had gone as the snows of yesteryear.

The American attack that had begun at dawn had crossed this band of ploughed ground in one jump, found no resistance, and had gone on across the fields to the north, where they were already out of range.

The American artillery, most of its guns outranged, and the others unable to direct the barrage at such a distance from the target, had ceased firing. The Germans, their guns abandoned or in retreat, had done likewise. Deep silence had fallen where so short a time before thunderbolts had crashed, and the ground had trembled with the recoil of a thousand guns. Where all had been smoke and shouts and frantic rockets were now only peaceful fields and quiet, shady woods, except for that long, waving, sinister gash that was like a wound that had killed this countryside.

From a hollow suddenly appeared a group of horsemen. They drew rein before their silhouettes cut the skyline and hurriedly examined the ground to the right flank with their field-glasses. The fields, through a field-glass, were not at all deserted.

The leader of the horsemen, a Captain of United States cavalry, could see men stringing telephone wire, prisoners in groups of three and four coming back, ambulances being loaded with wounded, and, far away northward, white puffs of smoke that came from bursting grenades, and that showed where the American advance was bombing its way toward an objective it had not hoped to reach until the morrow.

"We're through the first line," said the Captain decisively; "the road will be about there." He pointed to his left front, then looked curiously at Mont Sec, a sugar-loaf hill that rose abruptly a thousand feet from the surrounding plain. Its summit was crowned with smoke, from which came the continuous flash of bursting shells. "I doubt if any Boche up there can see us," said the Captain. "We'll assume not. Can you make out the road, Lieutenant? We'd better locate it before we start across."

The officer addressed wore the blue of the French Army. He had a round, bullet head and moustaches that were much too long. He polished his field-glasses with a white handkerchief, breathing upon them, wiping them carefully, and holding them to the light to see if they were clean.

The Captain tightened his lips impatiently. Behind him he heard the stamping of a horse, and, turning about, saw a sergeant who had just ridden up.

" Where the hell have you been?" barked the Captain.

" Sir, I had to come in from the extreme left, and this horse ain't much of a horse."

The sergeant panted slightly. It was apparent from his flushed countenance that he had been having difficulties with his mount.

" Well, if you can't ride him, turn him in," snapped the Captain, and turned back to the French officer.

An enlisted man, his legs seemingly lost behind the high pommel of his packed saddle, under-slicker, gun boot, sabre, saddle-pockets, blanket roll, and two days' grain ration, moved his horse over next to the sergeant's.

" Hey, goldbrick!" he whispered. " Where yuh been?"

The sergeant turned. " Hey, Mac!" he cried. He suddenly paused. He noted that the other wore a trumpet slung across his shoulders, and on the sleeve of his blouse, plainly discernible, was the scar of recently removed chevrons.

" You been busted?" went on the sergeant. " Huh? Drunk? A.W.O. loose? A guy with your service! Yuh oughta know better!"

" Naw, naw," grinned the trumpeter, " I got caught with a pair o' leather putts on. 'N' by the corps commander, too, no less. Don't worry; I got a better job blowin' horn. Why dinyuh join up with us at Mandrees? Where yuh been, anyway, the last three months?"

" At Besançon, learnin' machine-rifle. I'm commandin' the

machine-gun troop. How come else I got invited to a council of war? Whaddyuh think, kid? See any other sergeants around?"

The trumpeter grinned a slow grin, then ejected tobacco juice. "Machine-gun troop, huh? You an' them two machine-rifles! Well, if you get from here to them woods with 'em I'll buy yuh a drink."

"You think that's the entrance then?"

The Captain's voice came clearly in the silence that followed.

"Very well; I think I'll move them across there in echelon of double columns. I don't think we'll meet any resistance yet. The infantry would never have got by the woods if there were any square-heads in a fighting mood there.

"Troop commanders! You will cross the open space by troops, in echelon of platoons in double column. You will regulate the gait according to the nature of the ground and the circumstances, without attempting to maintain the regularity of the squadron formation. On arriving at the woods we'll again resume column formation. I will be with 'H' troop's first platoon. Understand? Posts!"

"Boy," whispered the trumpeter, "if any o' them take up the gallop he won't have a man left in the saddle."

"How come?" demanded the sergeant. "What yuh been doin' all summer?"

"Diggin' a sewer for the Q.M. corps at Gievres," grinned the trumpeter. "Ninety per cent. o' this here 'raggedy pants cadet' outfit ain't never been on a horse before in their lives."

"No kiddin'."

"No kiddin'. If we meet up with any Boche that's on the peck any, there'll be a hot time in the old town, now, what I mean."

"Sergeant Lee!"

"Sir!"

"Where are your machine-rifles?"

"In rear of 'H' troop, sir."

"Good. Ride with me so that I can give you orders for their employment. Off we go!"

The troop commanders—there were but two, and one of them a Lieutenant—rejoined their troops, there was an arm signal, a few moaning whistle blasts, then the squadron, in a formation very similar to that which old-timers used to style "column of bunches," topped the skyline, and, hurriedly descending into the hollow beyond, proceeded at a fast trot toward the distant woods. A fast trot. Too fast, for the slower horses began to canter, whereat the faster ones, hearing tremendous clatter and thumping of hoofs, wanted to canter too; and here and there a bolter began to go from rear to front of a platoon column, to the accompaniment of squeals and kicks from the other horses, and untrammelled language from the riders, who had received a blow from a rifle butt on the thigh, a cinch ring on the knee, or who had been nearly torn from the saddle by the impetuous rush of the bolting horse.

"They'll get over that," observed the trumpeter sagely. "They been fillin' 'em with oats. They won't prance very long under them full packs."

"They didn't waste any oats on mine," panted the sergeant. He had, by dint of voice, heel, and a club he carried, urged his horse into a shambling trot.

"Nor on that Frog Looey's either."

The French officer's horse was one of those who are averse to travelling alone, and who will not leave ranks or picket line for any persuasion. This steed was proceeding at a sort of drifting gait, going sideways like a yacht with no centre-board, and making always toward 'H' troop's second platoon. The French officer kept the horse's head firmly toward the woods, so that the steed could not see his companions; but he knew they were there, and kept ever an ear turned in their direction. Spur and whip prevailed for a time, but the moment the Lieutenant stopped to draw breath or rest his tired leg the drifting began again, accompanied by head tossing and lightning-like thrusts of the neck, which attempts had the effect each time of nearly unseating the French officer.

"That's a nice horse for an officer to ride," observed the sergeant. "You'd think he'd know better than to bring a goat like that with him."

"We give it to him. It's an 'H' troop horse. 'Sidewinder,' they call him. He's like Coke Gillis. He ain't gone straight since he was born."

"We give it to him!" protested the sergeant. "That's a great way to treat an officer and an ally. Give him a star-gazin' goat like that!"

"Huh!" grunted the trumpeter, helping himself to another chew. "The French give him to us in the first place. Let 'em see now how they like their own horses."

They arrived, finally, at the edge of the woods. No sign of life. Not a shot fired. There was a narrow field there, along the edge of which ran a rough track, an old cart path, but now beaten flat by many feet. Beyond, across the field, were more woods, into which this cart path led. There was a trench along the edge of the woods, but empty, and the hurdle that barred the road where it went through the wire had been so hastily put in place that the advance guard had been able to unwire it and drag it clear before the main body had come up.

Across the field went the squadron, skirting a communication trench, then the advance guard was seen to halt, troopers galloped out to left and right, and some indecision was manifested.

"What the matter?" demanded the Captain, riding up.

"There's four roads here," replied one of the troopers of the advance guard.

"Which road, Lieutenant?"

The French officer pulled up his horse and dragged forward his map-case.

"You're not going to look at a map, are you?" demanded the Captain. "I can look at a map myself. I thought you knew this country. Do you realise that I've got a squadron of horse standing here in a field that runs from Apremont halfway to Metz? Do you suppose the Boche are going to sit down and wait for us to cut them off? They're running so fast now we won't catch up with them before night."

"The other end of this field is held by French troops," replied the French Lieutenant. "They won't fire because they have been warned not to. There will be plenty of Boche very soon, don't worry." He bent over his map.

"Very well," snapped the Captain. "I'll make my own decision."

"If you do," replied the other, lifting his long moustache in a sneer, "you are liable to come into an area that is under our own artillery preparation, in which case the responsibility will be yours."

The Captain flushed, but said nothing. After all, this French officer had been sent for just that purpose, to keep this squadron out of areas that the French were pounding. It would not advance the situation to have the squadron destroyed by friendly artillery fire.

The French officer put away his map, took out a cigarette-case, extracted one, and lighted it.

"The road to the right," said he.

The trumpeter tossed his chin meaningly in the direction of the French officer.

"Ah, don't worry about him," replied Sergeant Lee. "The French are probably just as proud of him as we are of some of the mail order wonders we got. Boy, they got 'em in all armies, like coots."

Thick trees but no underbrush, huts, scattered grey overcoats, then, suddenly, long lines of waggons and empty picket lines. Loose horses, many of them wounded, could be seen among the trees, some trotting and whinnying at the sight of the advancing troops, others bounding away, and one or two limping in their direction, as if to ask for help from others of their kind.

Suddenly, at an alley that crossed the main track, the Americans saw men. The Captain, the trumpeter, an orderly, and Sergeant Lee saw them almost simultaneously. There was a group of ten or fifteen that had probably heard the advance guard thud by and had come out of their holes to see what it was all about.

The Captain swung his horse, whipped out his pistol, and charged. " H " troop's leading platoon followed him. Pistols barked, and Sergeant Lee's horse, that up to that time had given but the faintest signs of life, bolted, and, having gotten a firm grip of the bit before the sergeant had recovered himself, was well away into the trees.

It was impossible to circle the runaway in the trees, but the sergeant saw before him an opening in the woods, into which the horse presently tore. Here was the place to reach out, seize the head-stall, and by main strength drag the horse's head around so that he must run in a circle and eventually stop.

Bark!

"Cut out shooting, you damned fool!" shouted the sergeant. "Can't you see this horse——"

Bark! bark!

There was another man there, on a black horse. Flame spat from his hand. It was a German. Lee whipped out his sabre, and, instantly stopping all attempts to control his horse, let him go headlong for the black. The black, however, did not wait for the attack, but leaped aside, and its rider shot at Lee, as he tore by, at point-blank range.

But Lee had pinked him with the sabre. Not badly, he knew, but he had felt resistance as he had lunged out. If only now he could pull this goat down!—but they had crossed the glade and were again amidst the trees.

Bark! Again! The man on the black was pursuing him! Swiftly through the sergeant's mind passed the realisation that he was very probably drawing his last breath. The German was behind, hence Lee would have to either sheathe his sabre—impossible at that gait—let it hang by the sabre-knot while he drew his pistol—impossible, because he had not put his hand through the wrist-loop when he had drawn it—throw it away, and then engage in a pistol combat with the German—impossible, because if he turned around the horse would undoubtedly dash headlong into the first tree—or just lay on the horse's neck, say a prayer, and pour the hooks into him.

How many shots? The German's gun must be nearly empty now. Ah, no, the German pistol held ten. Before him suddenly loomed wire—a parapet. Would the horse jump it? He was done now, anyway.

The horse bucked to a halt. Lee dropped his sabre, tore out his pistol, and, swinging around in the saddle, had one wild shot with it, anyway. He shouted and fired again, more shouts, crashing, then the black horse tore by, saddle empty, and came to a rearing halt at the belt of wire, like a horse that has thrown his rider before the barrier in a riding hall.

There were Americans there—the trumpeter, pistol in hand, two privates of the advance guard.

"Hey, Lee!" cried the trumpeter. "We come down the road! I got that guy on the black!"

He and the two privates rode back to look at the German. He was on his face, but when one had dismounted and turned him over, they saw that he was dead. He was a private, with the black medal that indicates one wound and the light blue and yellow shoulder-straps of a Jaeger zu Pferde, or mounted rifleman.

"Striker, probably," decided the trumpeter, "because this here horse looks like an officer's."

"I'll say," agreed Sergeant Lee. He had ridden over and taken the black's bridle, and then led him back to the others.

"Well, let's go," said the others hurriedly. "This ain't no place to match pennies. These woods are full o' Boche."

"Right!" agreed Lee. "Where's the rest of 'em?"

"On the road. Whachuh dismountin' for?"

"I'm goin' to mount up on this black horse."

"You are?" cried the trumpeter. "Why, if anyone mounts him, I do! I knocked the guy off his back with a ·45."

"How do you know?" demanded the sergeant, picking up the sabre he had dropped. "I had two or three shots at him myself."

"No, it was the trumpeter got him," said one of the privates, looking nervously about him. "We better be gettin' back. I see the Captain out there. No, the trumpeter got that kraut. I seen it."

"Well, this horse is mine," said Sergeant Lee, mounting, "because I'm rankest man. What's the good of having three stripes if you can't rank somebody out of a bunk or a horse or something?"

"What are you men doing in there? See anything?" called a voice from behind the trees.

All wheeled their horses and went out. The alley down which they had charged curved, and the Captain with the rest of the platoon had halted there.

"The trumpeter shot a German, sir," said Sergeant Lee. "He was chasing me. I've captured his horse."

"Nice horse that," remarked the Captain. "Better change saddles the first chance you get. We'll be able to use all the extra horses we can get before we're through. Trumpeter, ride back and tell Lieutenant Bennett to push a patrol forward on the road. I'm going to prospect around in here a little to see what we've run on to, to see if there is any sign of a force here, if this is just a bunch of waggoners and stable orderlies that we've run into. See that that French officer knows what's going on.

"Corporal Petersen, take your squad and see if there are any Germans left in those huts. Write down any regimental numbers you see on the waggons.

"Sergeant Lee, take a set of fours and follow along that trench to see what you find. When you hear three blasts of the whistle, rejoin."

He blew a short blast on his whistle. "Foragers, ho-o-oh!" The platoon, in line of foragers, at "raise pistol" moved off among the trees.

Sergeant Lee, riding the black and leading his own horse, led his four men along the line of the trench that had stopped the runaway rush of his horse. The trench was shallow, and had been newly dug. They found shortly after a small house, a sort of shelter for foresters or shepherds, very strongly built of stone. The trench was evidently part of an attempt to make a strong point out of this house, to prevent, perhaps, the flanking of positions farther back in the woods by attack from the road. The house, however, seemed to be abandoned, for its door hung open.

Sergeant Lee, his pistol ready, rode up, but there was nothing in the interior but scattered bed-clothing and the disorder of boots, belts, and equipment that told of hasty flight.

"Number One," said the sergeant, "take this horse. Don't turn him loose, whatever happens, because he's got everything I own on him. I'm going to ride on a little. Listen for the three whistles and repeat them if you hear them."

He turned over his own horse, and being now free could enjoy the feel of riding the black. The horse was a thoroughbred. Lee had never been on one like him before. It was like sitting on a dynamo. He could feel beneath him the nervous energy and the power of those steel muscles running up and down. A touch of the spur, a flexion of the wrist, and the black was cantering. A turn of the shoulder, a shift of the left leg, and the black had changed leads. What a horse! Schooled, intelligent, powerful. Lee, without pressure on the reins, closed his legs and leaned slightly back. The horse slowed his gait. He leaned farther back. The black halted.

"Ah, boy! That's a horse!" breathed the sergeant to himself. What couldn't a man do with a mount like that? He saw himself leading a charge, outstripping Lieutenants, Captain, everyone, hurling himself upon the enemy, capturing their commander, their flags, raging about among them on that black horse——

"Hey, sergeant! Three whistles!"

There was, alas! a war on. The sergeant, taking one last look about him, moved his hand ever so slightly to the left, and the black, coming around beautifully, cantered back to the others. The sun, higher, began to glitter through the trees. No sign of the enemy, no crash of shell, no crackle of machine-guns.

"Come on with that set of fours!" called someone faintly. "Rejoin! Rally! Ralle-e-e!"

Lee gathered his four men and, trotting through the under-brush, rejoined the platoon, which the Captain was leading back in the direction of the road they had left. They came out, in a minute or two, into the sunlight, and found there the head of the column, the trumpeter, and the French Lieutenant.

"What did you see, sergeant—anything?" demanded the Captain.

"No, sir, only blankets and stuff lying around. That trench hadn't even been finished."

"We're losing time," said the Captain quickly. "There was no force in there. We'll probably be seeing stragglers and orderlies and first-aid men and all sorts of goldbricks running loose in these woods, but that's not what we're here for. Now then, we'll push forward vigorously. Pass the word back that if any isolated enemy are seen to shoot at them, but not to delay the advance to try to capture them. Leave that for the doughboys. That agree with your thoughts, Lieutenant?"

The French officer nodded. "Quite right, Captain," said he. He did not turn his face, however, in the Captain's direction. His eye was upon the black horse that Sergeant Lee rode. "Captain," he went on, "I think I shall have to ask you to give me that horse that man is riding."

"Huh? Give you that horse? That's a German horse. He captured it."

"I see that by the equipment, but it is a much better horse than mine. I want it."

"Perhaps you do," said the Captain, gathering his reins, "but we don't take horses away from non-commissioned officers in this man's army."

"Do you mean to say, sir," cried the French officer, "that you will not give an officer of an Allied army a captured horse simply because some soldier found it first? Which is the most important for the success of our mission—that he should be well mounted, or that I, who am the guide and the officer of liaison and the interpreter, should have the best horse? I think that Higher Authority would not take very long to decide the question."

It was in the Captain's mind to make no reply but to order the advance to be resumed. But then this French officer would make a report of it when he returned, which report would come drifting down from corps headquarters, gathering indorsements and bitterness like a descending snowball, until it came into the hands of the squadron commander's immediate superiors. He would get Hades. And he would get no more details to command provisional squadrons.

"Give him the horse, sergeant," ordered the Captain.

The sergeant's face hardened, and for just a second his blazing eyes met the Captain's, whereat that officer's jaw muscles stood out like cords.

"DISMOUNT!" he barked.

The sergeant obeyed, as well as some half-dozen troopers, who thought that the captain had meant them, too. In the slight confusion attendant on these men being cursed back into their saddles by their respective corporals, Sergeant Lee was able to turn over the black, go to Number One and get his own horse, and mount. The column moved forward again, at a rapid trot.

Sergeant Lee and the trumpeter were once more side by side, Lee muttering under his breath his opinion of some nameless person. His language was picturesque, for he decorated it with idioms learned in bar-room, barrack, and camp, from Jolo in the days of the Sultan of Sulu to the Camp de Valdahon at the present moment.

"You talkin' about that French Looey?" inquired the trumpeter.

"Well, who the hell else would you think?" demanded Lee.

The trumpeter spat expertly between his horse's ears. "Well, I dunno. You ain't got any kick against him. He was just rankest man. What's the use o' bein' rankest man if you can't rank some-one out of a bunk or a horse or somethin'?"

The sergeant's reply was horrible, whereat the trumpeter grinned so widely that he lost his chew.

There were signs now of distress from the squadron. The gait of the head of the column was too fast for that of the rear, so that the last third was at a slow gallop. The smothered admonitions of platoon leader, sergeant, and corporal to "Keep that horse back!" or "Four feet from head to croup, you—you know what that means?" or "Tully! you ridin' that horse or is he ridin' you? Git him into ranks!" were becoming louder and more frequent.

The pack of a man in the second set of fours had come undone, so that the shelter half trailed behind him like an old-fashioned caparison, and his blankets he was carrying over his free arm in a most unsoldierly manner. Finally, a poorly cinched saddle turned, the rider was thrown, and the horse, the saddle under its belly, went the length of the column, kicking and squealing, until it caught one foot in the trailing stirrup, fell, and had two men hurl themselves from their saddles and sit on its head. The column per-force halted, for one of the men was the acting troop commander of "H" troop and the other Sergeant Lee.

"And the rest of the dash blanked Johns sitting in their saddles looking at us!" exclaimed Lee.

"Get the saddle off him!" ordered the squadron commander. "Who's horse is it? Take his name, sergeant. Give him a month in the kitchen and all the spare horses to saddle up. Maybe he'll learn to cinch properly. Have 'H' troop dismount and look over their equipment. When they've finished, have 'I' troop do the same. This will be your last chance. I'm not going to stop again until I run into the enemy. Time flies. They'll all be in Berlin if we don't show more progress than this."

Sergeant Lee took the opportunity to have a look at his machine-rifles, riding in rear of "H" troop. He met, on his way there, the French Lieutenant, prancing along on the black horse. Lee ground his teeth. He had not ridden a McClellan saddle for a long time, and stirrup-buckle and gun-boot were beginning to rub sores on his unaccustomed shins.

How much more pleasure he would have had riding the beautiful officer's saddle on that black! Saddle! That wasn't the half of it! He would have ridden that horse bareback! It grinds a man to have his horse taken away from him. The mildest man will fly into a murderous rage. Lee thought of a man he had known with a clear record during three enlistments that had deserted because his horse had been taken for the polo team. Well, that bird had the right idea. When the march was resumed Lee still thought of him. He, Lee, would go "over the hill." He would find an outfit where a guy was appreciated.

"Forget it," said the trumpeter finally, wearied of Lee's silence. "Don't worry about it no more. The Frog's gone an' good riddance."

"He's not gone," replied Lee, spurring his horse savagely. "He's riding with 'I' troop."

"What for?"

"How the hell should I know?"

"Well, cheer up, anyway. Maybe we'll run into somebody that'll rank that horse away from *him*."

They continued the march through the silent woods. They passed collections of huts, then a rustic village built about a tiny lake that was obviously a recreation centre, a narrow-gauge railway yard, more waggons, more loose horses, and one or two isolated wandering men that took to their heels, pursued by random pistol bullets, as soon as they had identified the nationality of the horse-men.

The column crossed hurriedly a surfaced road that cut through the forest from east to west. At one end, in the hazy distance, they could see the roofs and steeple of a town, and to the west, against the foot of the forest-covered hills, another. But in between all was deserted. Across this road they found fewer huts, then, after a while, nothing. The brush grew thicker on both sides.

The Captain suddenly reined up his horse. Lee, startled out of his black thoughts, raised his head. The advance guard had halted where the road came to the edge of the woods. It was only a grove, because Lee could see the trees where the road entered the forest again farther on. But two of the advance guard had dismounted, and one was wildly pumping his rifle up and down above his head in the old army signal that means "Enemy in large number."

"Hold the squadron in readiness!" ordered the Captain hurriedly. "Trumpeter, Sergeant Lee, follow me!"

The three of them went down to the advance guard as swiftly as their horses could carry them. They did not need to have the enemy pointed out to them.

There was a wide circular cut in the woods here, made by an open field, across which the road they were on took its way to enter the forest once more. This field sloped sharply down on the right, and at the bottom of the slope was another road, wide and sur-faced, with a narrow gauge track running along.

On this road was a column of infantry, perhaps a battalion, marching steadily along, in good order, and with their rifles slung, German fashion, across their breasts. In front were two mounted officers. Behind the infantry, rapidly approaching, was a truck column, eight, ten, perhaps more—they could not see the end of them. There were eight hundred Germans there at least, and they were not to be charged with one-quarter that number.

"Bring up the auto-rifles, trumpeter," whispered the Captain, "and fast. Everyone dismount. Put the led horses in the brush. Now, sergeant, where shall we put the guns?"

"They've got to be fired prone," said the sergeant hurriedly. "The grass—now that will be all right." He threw himself on the ground. "You can't see over the slope here," he decided. "They'll have to be moved downhill—maybe along the edge of the woods. I'll have a look."

"Don't let any of those square-heads spot you. Don't waste too much time, now."

The German infantry continued to advance, unsuspecting. They had no advance guard out, no flankers. The Captain's heart swelled. The classic rôle of the cavalryman was to be his, to drive far behind the enemy's lines and fall upon unsuspecting troops. That truck column should be his, too, and the smoke of its burning would spread terror and alarm! On the heels of this panic the squadron would be on to Vigneulles, destroy the railway-station there, and cut off the retreat of all the mass of troops along the heights of the Meuse. But first, destroy this infantry.

"Hold the rifles here," ordered the Captain, as the gunners with their ammunition bearers appeared. "There's no rush. We'll site them together, let the column pass, and then each gun take half with traversing fire. Now damn those trucks! They'll get here at just the wrong time."

The trucks, however, did not pass the infantry, but halted. Perhaps the road was too narrow, perhaps those trucks contained the battalion's baggage. The Germans came on, while the Americans watched with beating hearts, holding their breath so that the enemy would not hear them. The Germans would pass at less than a hundred yards!

"When I give the signal," hissed the Captain, "rush out, flop, set up the guns, and turn loose."

The column drew near, and the dismounted Americans flattened themselves in the brush. The enemy marched by, boots slumping, bayonets rattling, the harsh coughing of the men coming clearly to the ears of the watchers. Waggons creaked past, one of the drivers idly cracking his whip. Then, the second company.

There was a thud of hoofs from behind the Americans. The Captain swung around. Who was this that had left the squadron without permission? It was the French officer, on the shining black, galloping up from "I" troop to see what the halt was about.

"Get off that horse!" husked the Captain. "Get him back out of sight!"

The black halted. He was alone. Far behind him the squadron waited impatiently. The black tossed his head. He smelled the concealed horses of the advance guard and the machine-rifle men in the brush, or did he see an old stable fellow down there on the road? Did he smell his countrymen? He tossed his head again, then neighed shrilly. The horses in the brush and another in the squadron answered him.

White faces from the marching troops looked up the hill, curious at the sound. Not many, but enough. The Captain, wordless, but thinking many things, rose out of the bush and leaped for the black's head. The black, like all thoroughbreds, was nervous. The sudden rush of the officer from the bushes frightened him. He reared and bolted, and in two jumps was in the meadow. His rider flung himself clear, but too late. The Germans below, open-mouthed, had first heard horses neigh in those woods, and had then seen, clearly against the dark background, a figure in the horizon-blue uniform of the French Army hurl itself from the saddle and run back into the woods again.

"Out with the guns!" shouted the Captain. "Action front! At enemy in road! Fire at will!"

The guns spat, but the road was already half empty. Two seconds more, and the whole column had taken refuge in the ditch on the other side. Waggons, mounted officers, all disappeared.

But the blast of firing that had begun could not have come from the machine-rifles alone! The air crackled, the ear drums rang with the sudden pound of heavy firing. Astonished, the Captain turned about. From the alley in the woods came a thunder of hoofs. Horses reared, others were down and kicking. Dismounted men ran about. There was smoke and the flash of pistols, but the noise was so great that the Captain could not hear the bark of the ·45's.

He looked behind him at the road below. The machine-rifles roared, but the road was empty. There were packs there and bundles that the marching troops had dropped in their haste to get to cover, but the Captain could see no bodies.

The German infantry were now in position behind the road. The only thing for two troops of cavalry in front of a battalion of entrenched infantry is to withdraw. The squadron seemed to have already made up its mind to this.

In just the three seconds that the Captain had spent in looking at the road his men had stampeded. They were going, tails high, saddle-bags flying, hell for leather down the road. Even as he watched, dark figures in bucket-shaped helmets appeared from the woods, shot down a dismounted trooper, and began to plunder the saddle-pockets of the dead horses.

There still remained to him, however, the auto-rifles. He leap-

ed back, threw himself down beside the gunners, and shouted in
their ears:

"Cease firing!"

The gunners heard and complied. With the roar of the auto-
rifles stilled, a sudden hush seemed to fall.

"You! Number One gun! Action rear. Searching, in those
woods, two clips! Commence firing! Number Two gun——" He
stopped.

Below and to the left, in the centre of that white road, head
high, tail outstretched like a plume, stood the black horse. Rifles
cracked, men shouted, machine-guns roared, but the horse paid no
attention. He pawed the ground, and the Captain could have
sworn that he neighed again the shrill, proud shriek that had alerted the Germans and ruined the squadron. That was the horse that
had been frightened by the Captain's rising from the brush!
Never! He had bolted purposely! He was a German horse; he
had known!

"Number Two gun!" ordered the captain. "Get me that horse
on the road, damn his black soul!"

He was not himself, for he had seen his men butchered from
ambush, his squadron destroyed, and he knew that the span of his
own life could be measured in minutes.

The muzzle of the gun shifted ever so slightly, and the gunner's
body thumped the ground as he wiggled himself into his new
position. The gun roared. The horse tossed his head quickly, for
he must have heard bullets crack by. A German dashed from the
shelter of the ditch to seize the trailing bridle, but he seemed to
slip in the mud and then fall, a flat, shapeless, motionless heap.

"The horse!" cried the Captain. "Never mind the men; get the
horse."

Another burst. Tchk! Silence. "Gimme another clip," panted

the gunner.

"Hey, for crysake, bring up that other gun!" shouted Sergeant Lee. "We got an opening here."

"Take up your rifle!" ordered the Captain. "Fall back and report to Sergeant Lee!"

Then the Captain, drawing his pistol, dropped on one knee, and, supporting his right hand on his left arm, took aim at the black horse.

"Hey, Captain!"

The shout in his ear disturbed the officer's aim, and the bullet went skyward.

"What the hell is the matter with you?" he snarled. But it was Sergeant Lee.

"They had machine-guns in the brush," panted the sergeant. "We put one of 'em down. They don't seem to be firin' now. If we're ever gonna get out of here we better go."

From the road below came a deep shout, "Hoch!"

On the heels of it a thin line of the enemy leaped up and, crossing the road, took shelter in the grass at the lower edge of the field.

The Captain emptied his pistol at them, then rose and reloaded. The Germans saw him, for fire crackled along their line.

"Let's get the hell out of here!" said the Captain.

The black horse had turned and, trotting down the road, now faced the German infantry, as though he carried on his back an officer who urged his men on. The Captain would have taken one more shot at him, but bullets whispered about his ears, or cracked overhead like whips. At the edge of the woods the men had already mounted. The Captain, stifling a curse, rejoined them.

Poorly fed horses in full pack, even when stampeded, will not run far, and the Captain, riding off down the woods with his chin on his breast, like Napoleon retreating from Moscow, found the squadron at the cross roads, from whence they had been able to see the two towns.

It had been a rear or flank guard that had ambushed them, and there had been no pursuit. Non-commissioned officers were already displaying their vocabularies, saddles were being transferred from wounded horses to well ones, men were binding up each other's wounds or refilling empty pistol clips.

Into this scene arrived the Captain like an avenging angel. He was a man of few words, but those to whom he addressed himself would remember his remarks to their dying day.

Sergeant Lee, having the care of his auto-rifles first in mind, withdrew them to one side, questioned the gunners, overhauled the ammunition supply, and inspected the horses. His own mount was nearly foundered. Seeing at a little distance a man holding three horses, he went in his direction, thinking he might make an exchange. The other man was the trumpeter, ruefully examining his trumpet that had been punctured by a bullet.

"It'll blow," said the trumpeter, as Lee approached, "but I have to keep my finger over the hole. It don't look military to blow a trumpet that way."

"How's chances on one o' those horses?" demanded Lee. "Mine's about outta breath."

"Naw. One's mine, one's the skipper's, and one's for the Frog Lootenant. He's goin' back."

"Goin' back?"

"Yuh. The Old Man says to him: 'What was the grand idea to gallop out in front where all the Boche would see you? Want them to admire your horsemanship or something?' And the Looey says: 'We rode into an ambush. We went too far without reconnaissance. We haven't lost any ground because this here is the

Heudicourt-Nonsard road that we're on now, and we weren't supposed to be here for half an hour yet.' 'Awright,' says the skipper; 'you know the country so well, you go back and report our progress and where we run into the enemy.' 'But I'm your guide!' says the Looey. 'Well, we'll try to struggle along without you!' bites the Old Man. So then—psst!"

The French officer, his bullet-shaped face like a thundercloud, strode toward the two men. They paid not the slightest attention as he took his old horse, mounted, and rode off.

"You mighta held his stirrup for him, at least," observed the trumpeter.

"Who was his dog-robber last year? Anyway, I'm a sergeant. I don't hold nobody's stirrup."

The trumpeter hitched his pistol-belt higher and tilted his helmet just a little farther over his left eye.

"John Lee," said he, "did it ever occur to you you owe that Looey a whole lot? Suppos'n he hadn't ranked you off that black horse? Wouldn't he nickered just the same and give us away to the Boche?"

"Hey?" gasped the sergeant.

Wouldn't the horse have nickered with him? Oh, man! Yes, he would have. And then what would the skipper have done to Lee? He was not an officer but a buck sergeant. He choked at the thought. If it had been his horse that had nickered—well, the least they would have done would have been to hang him. His name would have been a mock and a disgrace throughout the mounted arm of the United States Army from that day forth. Gone would be his stripes! Gone his pistol and sabre! He would wield nothing but a dish-rag for the rest of his military career!

"Naw," said he to the trumpeter, "that black wouldn't have done it with me. I'd ha' *ridden* him."

"Uh-huh!" remarked the trumpeter. "Well, if you're lookin' for a horse, try Corporal Scully's. Scully's hit. That's a good horse for a sergeant."

"No," said the sergeant, "I guess I'll stick to the one I got. He ain't much on looks, but he's no nickerer."

NO QUARTER

by
W. Townend

MOST ruthless of all fighting men is the soldier who goes into action having in his heart a deep and burning hatred of the enemy. To such a man killing is no mere duty, performed in blind obedience to the orders of his superiors, but the direct expression of his whole being, the one immediate aim in life.

MacCorbin, who was twenty and came from the South, hated the Germans, individually and collectively, as a Kentucky mountaineer might hate the slayers of his kinsmen in a family feud.

This is the story of his first engagement.

It was evening once more—July and hot. The sun had set. The sky was still flushed with pink.

There was no actual front line, but in rifle pits and shell holes and hastily dug trenches, on the fringe of a shattered wood of pines and beeches, men in steel helmets and khaki crouched and waited for what fresh horrors the night might bring. Their faces were tanned and lined, plastered with white chalk and sweat; their eyes were strained and anxious; their mouths hard; their uniforms torn and slovenly.

In front of the wood they held was a wide stretch of white, sandy ground, covered with patches of sparse brush, sloping upward gradually to another wood, through which before morning they would have to force their way or die, as those others had died who now lay in the open where they had fallen.

For a time the fighting had lulled. On either side the guns were silent, save where far off, miles distant to the north, the men waiting could hear the dull throb of drum fire and knew that another attack was being launched.

In one end of a stretch of dry ditch that had been deepened into some semblance of a trench were six privates.

Four of them, MacBride, Hennessey, Bridger, and Thompson, survivors of the original platoon that had left New York in the fall, squatted on the trunk of a young birch-tree that had toppled into the ditch and had been trimmed of its branches. They talked listlessly in low voices. Their rifles, with bayonets fixed, rested against the parapet, handy in case there might emerge from the wood opposite men in grey whom they would proceed to kill, without undue waste of energy or ammunition, killing being their business.

Another of the six, Marshall, a boy of nineteen, stood in the extreme corner of the trench, shielded from observation by the limbs of a tree and a tangle of broken branches and brushwood. He watched the German position intently.

At a point where the trench twisted back at an angle of about 135 degrees, skirting the front of the wood, the sixth man, Bates, knelt and adjusted a puttee that was loose. He was a fair, sallow man with thin features, a moustache, and sleepy eyes that seemed to miss nothing of what happened. From time to time he glanced to his left at the four men on the tree trunk and smiled to himself.

MacBride, a long, lank Texan, yawned.

"Could sleep fer a month, I guess, if I had the chanst!"

"After I'd had some chow, me too!" said Bridger, who was Middle Western, from Iowa.

Thompson, a hard bitten, red headed Californian from the desert country up Ludlow way, grinned and then sighed: ·

"Gosh! Any sign them damn' ration carriers gittin' up this-aways to-night, hey?"

"Nary a sign," said Hennessey; an ex-sergeant, with a fondness for whisky, he was Boston Irish. "We're Reg'lars—we don' wanna eat; they says we fight!"

"Et me iron ration two days ago, Gawd help me!" said Mc-
Bride. "Nawthin' yesterday, as I'm a livin' sinner; nawthin' to-
day! Three dawgone nights without sleep."

"Guys," said Thompson, "I gotta eat."

"To hear you bums talk," said Bates, "you wouldn't think
there was a war, nawthin'."

The four men on the tree trunk regarded him in silence. They
did not like Bates. He talked too much.

"To hear you talk, Bates, you'd think you owned the dawgone
war!" said Bridger. He broke off quickly. "Say, listen to this
what's comin'!"

The boy, Marshall, ducked.

Overhead there was a high, wailing sound that grew louder and
louder, passed, and ended in the loud *crump* of a heavy shell bursting back where the supports would be awaiting orders to move up.

"S'long as the ol' Boche keeps that range I ain't worryin' none,"
said MacBride.

Marshall was smiling uncertainly, his face white in the twilight.

"Thought it was nearer," he said.

"No need to apologise," said Bates. "Considerin' you wasn't
taught that disappearin' movement on no parade ground, you done
it right smart!"

"Fellers," said Thompson, "war ain't all it's cracked up to be!
I got cooties breedin' all over me, I ain't had a wash since Pete
knows when, nor nawthin' to eat. I ain't slept in a bed so long I
can't remember if you put yer head or yer feet on the pillow. An'
top of everythin' else, I got the chanst o' goin' to Kingdom Come
any minute, expeditious."

"Bo," said MacBride, "you said a heap o' sense! They ain't bad
soldiers, the Heinies, what I've seen of 'em!"

"I'll say they ain't! Brave as you'd find anywheres."

"Sure they're brave! Too damn' brave, some o' them guys! D'ye mind that feller we bumped off coupla days ago? Stuck to his machine-gun, he did, an' knocked out Gawd only knows how many of us chaps, an' wouldn't surrender, though we was wishin' him!"

"That's so! Good fightin' man, the ol' Boche!"

"Kinda feel sorry for 'em sometimes," said MacBride. "Gittin' it in the neck good an' plenty, ain't they?"

A voice that was new to the men in the trench said—

"What made you say that?"

They turned their heads quickly and saw a thin, boy's face and angry eyes under a steel helmet.

"It's an orf'cer," said Hennessey. "Beg pardon, sir."

"That's all right," said the officer. "Don't get up!"

At that the four men on the tree trunk grinned.

Behind the officer was the platoon sergeant, old Culbriddy, with the row of medal ribbons on his blouse and the scar of a bolo slash across his cheek.

"This salient is the most advanced part of our position, isn't it, Sergeant?"

"It is, sir," said Culbriddy.

"H'm! You're keeping a good lookout, I hope."

"Yes, sir," said Marshall.

"I've taken over the platoon," said the young officer gruffly.

He looked not much more than a lad, younger than Marshall, even : a little self-conscious and embarrassed, possibly, but friendly and apparently eager to do the right thing.

"My name's MacCorbin. Perhaps you'd better tell me yours!"

Rather startled by the request, they told him.

MacBride, Hennessey, Bridger, Thompson. Each spoke in turn.

The officer who had given his name as MacCorbin nodded toward the man crouching down at the corner where the trench twisted back along the front of the wood.

"Yours?"

"Bates, sir."

"Yours?"

He spoke to the boy next him.

"Mine, sir—Marshall."

"Been out long?"

"Two weeks, sir. Two weeks with the regiment, sir."

"I see. Getting on all right?"

"Yes, thank you, sir," said Marshall.

"We tote him along as a kinda mascot," said Bates. "He's ornamental, if he ain't nothin' else."

MacCorbin glanced at him with a frown and spoke to MacBride.

"What made you say you felt sorry for the Germans?" he said. "You can't expect to win battles if you're sorry for the crowd you're up against, can you?"

He gazed toward the German position, silent and sinister in the dusk, the shattered pine-trees, dark against the sky, the hillside and the first dead he had ever seen. He shivered suddenly, though the night was hot, and then turned and studied the grim and tired faces of the men who were with him in the trench. Hennessey, Bridger, Thompson, and MacBride, unshaven, bronzed, covered with the grime and muck of three days' fighting, were, he felt, soldiers—men who would push on to the bitter end, against odds, or hold on, with no thought of retreat.

Bates, the narrow-faced, sallow man with the fair moustache and the cruel, sleepy eyes and the tigerish mouth, puzzled him. He did not trust him. Yet Bates, too, was a soldier; perhaps the best soldier in that short trench. In battle, where other men might show mercy, Bates would kill for the lust of killing. The man was a killer. Brave, of course; cruel, no doubt; but worth a dozen of young Marshall. Glancing at Marshall's angular profile under the steel helmet, MacCorbin was suddenly doubtful. He knew instinctively, watching him, that Marshall was scared. He gave the impression of being broken in spirit by what he had suffered.

And to-morrow these men were some of the men he must lead across the open into the wood. And they were sorry for the Germans. God Almighty!

"I want to tell you about my brothers," MacCorbin said. "My eldest brother was in Paris when war broke out. He joined up with the French and became an airman; he was shot down and crashed behind the German lines in the spring of '15. He died in hospital. They treated him badly, neglected him, didn't forward his letters home, didn't let anyone know where he was. Maybe you'd say that wasn't the fault of the Germans. Well, it was the fault of one damn' German, anyway. That we know for a fact. He died of neglect. Right, that's the first of 'em!

"The second brother crossed to England in the autumn of 1914 and joined the Gordon Highlanders. He was with the Gordons in the advance after the German retirement on the Somme last year. He went down into a dug-out with a couple of other men because they heard a cat crying. They found the cat tied so that it could hardly move. My brother cut the string and set off a mine that blew him to bits. That makes two.

"The third brother was killed in No Man's Land in the spring down Verdun way. He was with the Marines. He was out on patrol at night and was helping a wounded German who'd been lying between the lines a couple of days and a German sniper put a bullet through his head. All right, then, that's the lot! But maybe you understand now how I feel about the Germans. I've got a personal interest in this War because of what I've told you. I'm the last of the crowd and I want to get even. Maybe I'll go the same way as the others, maybe I won't; but I want to do some damage or see some damage done first.

"Anyhow, that's why I don't like to hear you fellows talking about feeling sorry for the Germans. We've got to fight to-morrow and fight like hell!"

"We have the reputation, sir," said Sergeant Culbriddy.

The men grinned.

"I know that, Sergeant," said MacCorbin, "but what I'm trying to impress on you all is, don't stop to take any prisoners! This war's going to be won by killing. Understand what I mean, MacBride? It is MacBride, isn't it? You can't kill if you feel sorry for the man you're fighting. That's why I don't like to hear you say you're sorry for the Germans! That's why I don't want you to take prisoners. Killing's your job, MacBride, and everyone else's job, too."

Bates laughed.

"Killing's what we come out for, ain't it?"

"Killing!" Marshall uttered a harsh noise, deep in his throat. "Sure, that's what we come out for, killing!"

"Who in hell's the fool talking about killing?" said another voice.

Darkness was falling but MacCorbin could see the lean, haggard face and dark eyes of the man who had just made his way through the brush into the trench.

"What are you?" he asked sharply. "Where've you been?"

"Mr. Searle took me off, sir, to help bring up some ammunition that had been dumped at the reg'mental P.D., sir."

"I see. What's your name?"

"Rutherford, sir." The man spoke respectfully enough, but

roughly, as if impatient at being questioned. "I didn't know there was an orf'cer here, sir."

"That's all right," said MacCorbin.

This man, Rutherford, was of a different type from the other men in the trench. He was powerfully built, not tall but lean and wiry; capable, probably, of enduring any amount of hardship without harm, yet from his manner not such a good fighter as Bates. He seemed sullen and morose, bitter almost—a man likely to be sensitive to shell-fire or the sight of death and not so cheerful when things went wrong as MacBride or Hennessey or Thompson or Bridger; but a sound man, notwithstanding; best, perhaps, fighting with his back to the wall, in defence, not in attack. This, at least, was the impression he gave in those first few minutes. MacCorbin continued—

"You were saying something about killing!"

"Didn't mean nawthin', sir," said Rutherford.

"He's another that wants the War over," said Bates.

"Mebbe the War 'll be over soon enough for most of us," said Rutherford, "without a hero like you sayin' so!"

"I ain't trying to be killed," said Bates. "You are."

MacCorbin, feeling rather perplexed, spoke to Culbriddy.

"Let's be going on, Sergeant. And you men, remember what I said. We've got to kill if we want to win the War, so don't you birds worry your heads about taking prisoners!"

He moved along the trench, followed by Culbriddy.

"Who's he?" said Rutherford presently.

"Dunno," said MacBride. "He blew in durin' the heat of the combat to teach us the meanin' of love yer enemies!"

"No prisoners, hey!" said Rutherford. "Who in hell wants to take prisoners? Better be killed straight off than be took prisoner, too!"

"What d'you know about it, hey?" said Bates. "Ever been in prison yet, Rutherford, or is that a pleasure to come?"

Rutherford spoke without heat or emotion.

"One o' these days, Bates, you'll git a bullet through you and it won't be a German bullet, neither."

"Say," said Hennessey, "you guys cut it out! Rutherford, you talk too much for the good o' yer health!"

In all battalions there will be men who are mysteries to other men. Rutherford was one. An old soldier, who had rejoined his regiment at the outbreak of war, he was a silent, sombre man. Queer tempered, likely to fly into fierce rages without adequate cause, a heavy drinker, yet in spite of MacCorbin's hasty summing up, as fine a soldier as there was in the company. At the best of times a man who had little to say, he had of late been silent, more unapproachable than ever before. He seemed to be suffering, physically as well as mentally. His face was drawn and peaked, his eyes were worn. Although he said himself that nothing could ever tire him, he had the appearance of being exhausted. Uneasy and restless and quarrelsome, he was most composed and cheerful when under shell-fire or in an attack.

Men respected him but did not care for him. Like Bates, he had no friends in the company. Unlike Bates, however, he made no attempt to be friendly.

"Whadja make of the little Loot?" said Thompson.

"Nice boy, I dare say," said MacBride, "but wait till to-morrer an' see what he does when we gits to movin' up ag'in' that wood!"

"Talk about gall!" said Hennessey. "Well, say! Seen nawthin' an' comes along talkin' just like a grown man! Take no prisoners, says he! Wish the ol' Colonel could 'a' heard him!"

Marshall spoke to Bates over his shoulder.

"What did you wanna say that about me for?"

"I said nawthin', kid," said Bates.

"You did. I won't stand fer much more yer damn' kiddin'!"

"Say, to-morrer, don't you git to hangin' back same as last time!" said Bates. "No lettin' other fellers do your fightin' for you, young Marshall, an' don't you forget it!"

"Seems to me I heard someone talkin' about a twisted ankle only yesterday," said Rutherford. "Bates, where was you when we got into that wood? An' last week you was sick an' takin' pills! Doggone funny how many times you been out of it, ain't it?"

"I don't understand what in hell you think you're drivin' at!" said Bates.

"No," said Rutherford. "No, mebbe not. But you will understand if you're anywheres near me to-morrer, Bates, which you won't be! You're a helluva talker, sure, but I've gotta see yet what kinda fighter you are!"

"Damn funny!" said Bates. "That kind o' bein' funny don't cut no ice with me. Listen, fellers . . ."

Sergeant Culbriddy crept through the thick undergrowth at the back of the trench.

"You birds gotta cut out the yappin'! Next thing you'll have someone turnin' a machine-gun on you to quiet you."

"Don't believe there's no one left in that wood at all," said Bridger. "We ain't had so much as a chirp outa them since long 'bout four o'clock. They've gone back, I bet."

"Mebbe you'll have the pleasure later o' crawlin' out on combat patrol to investigate," said MacBride.

"Mebbe not," said Culbriddy. "That bit o' wood's goin' to git hell mighty soon now; all the guns they can lay their hands to."

"No chanst of any chow before next week, is there?" said Thompson.

"Yeh. Seen the ration carriers on their way up."

"Thank Gawd fer that!" said Bridger.

"Huh! I bet five bucks they forget us stuck here, anyways!" said Hennessey. "Say, Sarje, what about sendin' one of us with our canteens an' mess kits fer our coffee an' slum, hey?"

A flare lit up the sloping, brush covered ground between the lines, making the dusk brighter than midday; but with queer, blue-black shadows; it waned gradually and faded into twilight once more.

"An' now fer business," said Rutherford.

The short summer night was passing. In the east the first faint sign of dawn was visible between the dying down of one flare and the upward flight of the next.

At other times men might have gloried in the freshness of the air, the peace and beauty of the countryside, the stars, the clear sky, the scent of the pine-woods. Now, with the reek of death and high explosive in their nostrils, their ears deafened by heavy gunfire, they crouched in their shelters and watched the great shells bursting with flashes of flame and black clouds of smoke in the shattered wood opposite.

MacCorbin, once more in the section of advanced trench held by Sergeant Culbriddy and the seven privates, MacBride, Hennessey, Bridger, Thompson, Marshall, Bates, and Rutherford, peered through the screen of brush across the open ground at the German position and shuddered.

There were men, perhaps, in that hell, dying, being maimed, torn limb from limb. It was terrible, yet he had no pity. They must pay the price, just as he, too, and the men with him, might pay the same price at any instant.

Marshall, by whose side he stood, groaned.

"Is anything the matter?" said MacCorbin.

No one was near enough to hear what he said.

"I'm scared," Marshall whispered.

"The Germans?"

"Scared of myself, sir. Scared I'll turn and run. I wanted to ask you, sir, if I can't face it, if I run, or anything, I'd like you to promise this, sir——" his voice was so low that MacCorbin could scarcely hear him—"I'd like you to put a bullet through me. I would."

MacCorbin was troubled. What he had felt earlier in the night was true, after all.

"You'll be all right, Marshall, I'm sure."

"You've not been over yet, sir. I have. Last time I just managed to keep going. To-morrow I won't be able. My God! I hate this War. It's jus' killin' me."

"You're making things harder for yourself by thinking you're bound to fail. Marshall, there isn't a single man of us who isn't afraid at heart. Do you mean to say you're not so good a man as " —he was going to say Rutherford, but changed his mind—" as anyone else? You are. What's the absolute worst that can happen? Turning back, isn't it? Well, suppose you don't! What's the next worst? Being killed! What's that amount to, anyway? You've acknowledged that much, haven't you, by what you asked me to do! You're not afraid of being killed; you've proved it!" He patted his shoulder. "You'll be all right, Marshall, I know."

"I wish I knew it, too, sir."

MacCorbin, despairing of bringing him any comfort, moved along the trench.

MacBride was leaning over the parapet, watching the wood opposite and the bursting shrapnel and high explosive.

"Everything all right, MacBride?"

"They're catching it over there, sir, ain't they?" MacBride

stroked the stock of his Springfield. "Maybe they'll all 've gone before we can git to grips with 'em!"

Thompson, the lean, red-headed Californian, said :

"This time to-morrer, wonder what the company's gonna look like! The quicker we git across the open the better."

"The bayonet's the only way," said Hennessey.

"You need the helluva long bayonet to reach them guys from here," said Bridger. "It's the gittin' so you can use the bayonet hurts most."

"You'll get there all right," said MacCorbin. "And when you do, remember what I said—no prisoners. You've got to kill."

And then he heard above the crash of the shells opposite a high wailing sound approaching through the air, growing louder and deeper in note, roaring like a heavy train emerging from a tunnel, rushing straight down at him from the sky.

His heart felt weak and empty. Fear choked him.

The men had flung themselves down into the bottom of the trench.

There was a crash like thunder, worse than thunder, the crash of the end of the world, a flash of yellow flame. The earth shivered and rocked with the concussion. MacCorbin was hurled back and then forward again, against the parapet of the trench. He claw-ed with his finger-nails at the chalky soil and bent his head. His steel helmet was tilted over his face. Stones and earth fell on him. A tree toppled to the ground. The air was filled with the pungent reek of hot metal and high explosive and smoke.

When presently he straightened himself up he laughed.

"Nothing in that," he said, and shuddered.

"Nothing in that, did ye say, sir?" He saw by the light of a flare Sergeant Culbriddy by his side. "It's the like o' them nine inchers can lose ye the number of yer mess, just by the blast of its passing, without it so much as touching yez!"

MacCorbin knew that Culbriddy had reproved him and he was annoyed and ashamed. He felt that the reproof was justified.

He moved on to the bend in the trench.

Rutherford, leaning back, his rifle on the parapet, pointing toward the German lines, chewed solemnly. MacCorbin had an impression that he alone of all the men in the trench was unaffected by the shell that had burst so near. He felt that he had kept his feet and waited for death and was startled that he was still alive.

Almost without intention he asked him the question he had asked Marshall.

"Anything the matter, Rutherford?"

The man glanced at him quickly and then turned once more and gazed toward the wood.

"Big shell that, sir."

His voice was harsh and stern.

"There's something worrying you," said MacCorbin.

"It ain't this, then," said the man.

And then he brought his face very near the officer's and whispered—

"Ever been drunk, sir?"

"Drunk!" said MacCorbin. He was indignant. "Is that how you talk to an officer?"

"Guess I didn't mean that, exactly, sir; no. But I was drunk last week, back at Maubray-le-Petit before we come into the line again. I got a girl at home—Baltimore. If I'm killed to-morrer that's the best way out for all of us, her an' me, both! I'm going to be put under arrest as soon as we're through with the fighting."

"For being drunk?"

"No," said Rutherford. "There was trouble in one of them

estaminets. Little place, kept by an old woman and her grown-up son who was a half-wit and not in the Army. A U.S. soldier, one of our crowd, stole the old woman's money. The son give the alarm just as he was gittin' away an' he turned and hit him. Seems I'm the man."

"But were you?" said MacCorbin.

"No. I wasn't. But I was in the estaminet that evenin' an' next day they found a letter on the floor, addressed to me an' post-marked Baltimore."

"That's no proof," said MacCorbin. "It'll be easy enough to clear yourself, won't it?"

"No," said Rutherford. "I was drunk somewheres else. No alibi. I got back to my billet early in the mornin'. Where had I been? Asleep in a field. I'm for arrest, if I come out of this alive. It wasn't me stole the money, I swear, but I can't prove it. And then sometimes I wonder. Was it me? I'm mean when I get two-three drinks in me. No dawgone good. I oughta quit. Well, that's my weakness—booze. They say the half-wit's dead."

MacCorbin was startled by his placidity.

"Who told you?"

"I heard when I was fetchin' that ammunition up. One of the headquarter crowd heard it from someone who'd come up from Maubray-le-Petit with the transport. Maybe it ain't true. More likely it is. I'm the guy what's responsible. I didn't do it, I swear! But did I? Queer the things a man will do when he's drunk, ain't it?"

MacCorbin sighed. It was terrible that just when all his energy should be directed toward killing Germans he should have had this other problem thrust on to him.

"All they've got against you is that envelope," he said.

"One of our fellers seen me comin' out the estaminet, he said,

at the time the money was bein' stolen. I didn't ask if he give me
away to the M.P.s; that's nawthin' to do with me. But he seen
me, he said, an' spoke to me."

"Who was it? Anyone I've met?"

"Yes, sir. Bates."

Dawn was at hand. The shells still pounded the wood.

"There can't be none o' them left alive!" said MacBride.

"Them poor fellers layin' out in the open," said Marshall softly,
"are mebbe waitin' on us. Last night I felt to-day there'd be a
full company to march in with 'em."

Bates cackled a shrill laugh.

"Hear him! Say, kid, you oughta be paid for talkin'!"

"What d'you make of it, Mac?" said Hennessey.

"They've gone," said MacBride. "We'll have the first part of
our *pasear,* mebbe, in peace an' comfort with time to admire the
view!"

"They're still there," said Marshall. "I know they are. An',
my God, you'll know it, too, soon enough!"

"Feelin' bad, son?" said Thompson.

"He's scairt," said Bates. "Didn't I say so?"

"You want the butt of a rifle shoved down your ugly trap; or
what?" said Bridger.

MacCorbin, alone in the trench with Culbriddy and the seven
men, one of whom was a murderer and one a coward, prayed
that he would do them credit, the murderer and the coward no
less than the others.

But did the men he was going to lead across the open understand what he understood? It seemed to him that men who could
talk so lightly of what lay before them, who treated the War as
merely an episode in their lives, of less importance than the food
they craved, who sympathised with the enemy, it seemed that

such men were not the men to push home an attack and kill.

And yet these men had reputation enough as fighters, God knew! He thought of his three brothers—David, with his laugh and his ready wit, dead in a German prison hospital, neglected, alone, broken; Andrew, the Gordon Highlander, killed by that senseless piece of cruelty that brought tears to one's eyes and hate to one's heart; Stewart, killed on patrol, helping the wounded German. And then he thought of himself, the last of four brothers, so soon perhaps to follow them!

Tired of inaction, he walked the full length of the trench held by the platoon, spoke to the two corporals and one or two of the men and presently turned and walked slowly back to the nose of the salient where he stood between Rutherford and Sergeant Culbriddy and tried to distinguish in the dim light the route he would have to take across the open to the wood still shrouded in smoke and the flashes of bursting shells.

He glanced at the faces of the men in the short stretch of trench near him, just as he had done the evening before. Culbriddy, the grizzled sergeant with the medal ribbons on his blouse. MacBride, the long, lank Texan, who was sorry for the Germans. Thompson, the red-headed, hard-bitten Californian, who thought more of his chow than he did of winning the War. Bridger, the burly Middle Westerner with the nasal drawl. Hennessey, the ex-sergeant, short and thick-set and stern. Bates, the fair haired, sallow man with the cruel eyes, a fighter from the toes up. Marshall, the boy, white faced and afraid. And Rutherford, the man who perhaps had killed the half-wit, grim, tragic, and silent. To his right, other men, who had made less impression on his mind, whose names he had scarcely memorised—Smith, MacBeith, Harrison, Prentiss, Malone. There weren't so many of them. The platoon was only a skeleton of its full war-time strength.

He realised that the Germans were showing signs of life. Shells were whistling overhead and bursting behind the wood where they were, back among the supports.

In five minutes, he reflected, he would clamber out of the ditch where he stood and, cane in one hand, pistol in the other, walk across the open toward the German machine-guns.

He wondered how it would feel to be shot at. He wondered whether he could hide the fear he knew would creep over him. He smiled grimly. He thought once more of his dead brothers. He must kill or he would never again know peace. He felt coldly efficient. A little impatient; a little nervous—but not very.

He looked at his watch again. God, how time did fly!

"Thirty seconds more!" he said.

The hands crawled slowly on. God, how time did drag!

"Twenty seconds!"

If he lived long enough to reach the wood and set his men an example he would be satisfied.

"Fifteen seconds!" he said.

His voice shook. He wasn't afraid, surely. He reached for his pistol. The feel of the butt steadied him.

"Ten seconds!" he said.

The men began to count.

"Nine, eight, seven, six, five, four, three, two, one!"

"Up you go!" he said, and scrambled out over the sandy, crumbling parapet of the ditch that had served them as a trench.

The guns had lifted. For a moment the wood in front, the sinister, shattered wood, was silent, still shrouded in smoke already drifting away on the light morning breeze.

MacCorbin, glancing quickly right and left, saw the assault waves deployed, long lines of infantrymen in khaki, tramping stolidly across the open, laden like beasts of burden, with rifles

and equipment, steel helmets, chaut-chaut automatic rifles, bandoleers, gas-masks, grenades, two hundred and twenty rounds of
ammunition each man.

He saw the dead, the white sandy soil, the scattered brush, the
broken trees with their green foliage wilted. He saw beyond the
wood the flashes of shells bursting. He heard his own busky voice
saying—

"Don't bunch there!"

He heard someone laugh; Rutherford, he thought; but was not
sure. He heard, next, a burst of sound, like thunder, a cataclysm
of sound, the roar of a typhoon, a sound not to be compared with
any sound his ears had ever heard. Machine-guns massed, hundreds of machine-guns, their individual *tocka-tocka-tocka-tocka-
tocka-tocka* blended into a devastating roar. He heard the bullets
whipping over his head; he saw men dropping, stumbling, lying
still; he saw the bayonets.

He was alive still. Christ! But for how long! His neck and
back were damp with sweat. His throat was parched. There was
a tightness in his chest, a burning pain across his forehead. His
limbs were without strength. He shouted :

"Come on! Come on!"

He bent his head and quickened his pace.

Men, he noticed now, were running, intent on reaching the
wood whence came the storm of bullets. The ground was rough,
scarred with dry rain channels and gullies, pitted with shell-holes.
It was difficult to keep going without tripping.

He heard above the machine-guns' roar Rutherford's voice.

"Get on, you, Bates, or I'll bayonet you!"

"Come on!" he yelled. "Come on! Into 'em!"

God Almighty! how they were falling!

He was afraid now, in grim earnest; not of being killed—he

would be killed, he was sure—but of being killed too soon.

"Get on, you, Bates, damn you! Get on!"

Rutherford again. What the devil was the man up to?

MacCorbin turned his head and saw Culbriddy's honest, red face at his elbow; Marshall, pale and distressed, but moving ahead quickly; Rutherford, still alive, fierce looking and hard and angry; Bates, white like Marshall, stumbling, gasping for breath, whimpering; Hennessey, Bridger, MacBride, Thompson. He saw them all. Others of the platoon as well—Harrison, Prentiss, Jacobs, Bradley, Smith, Hughes, Robinson, Malone. He saw Jackson, the company commander—Jackson! What in hell was he doing so far ahead? And his orderly, away on the left. He saw the commander fall and the orderly, bending over him, fall, too. Nearer, Thompson, the red-headed Californian, hurled his rifle away from him, doubled up, his hands clasped to his belly, and rolled over like a shot rabbit.

Damn those machine-gunners! Damn them! Wouldn't they ever let up?

"Come on!" he shouted. "Come on!"

And then MacCorbin knew that the attack was breaking down. All impetus had gone. Too many men had been killed.

His foot caught in a hole; he tripped and pitched forward.

Culbriddy threw himself down by his side.

"Stay where ye are, sir! Wait!"

"We've got to get on," he said, panting.

"Give them time, sir. If it wasn't fer the dip in the groun', sir, that's saved us, we'd none of us be here now!"

They lay on a flat sandy piece of ground, sheltered by a steep bank a yard high. With them were Marshall and MacBride, Bridger, his face smeared with blood, Hennessey, smiling a tight lipped smile, and others.

It was full dawn at last. The sun had risen, but the open space across which they had struggled was still in shadow. In front of them, behind the wood, the sky was pink. Back of them, the German shells were crashing, sending up huge masses of smoke and earth, smashing down big trees. The bullets of the massed machine-guns whistled overhead.

"Damn them!" said Hennessey. "Damn them to hell!"

He sprawled at full length to the right of the bank that sheltered them, cuddled his cheek against the stock of his rifle and began firing.

"Helluva lot o' good, that!" said Bridger.

There was a strangled cry. MacCorbin turned his head and saw Bates crawling toward him, his face livid, damp with sweat and lined and old looking, stark terror in his eyes, bareheaded and with his fair hair plastered over his forehead. Rutherford, bleeding from a wound in the neck, his lips parted in a grin, crawled after him.

"I'll git you into the German line, you white livered skunk, if I have to bayonet you every yard o' the way!"

"For Gawd's sake, let me be!" Bates whimpered. "I'm sick."

"Yeller from the toes up. Tripped he did, fellers, an' lay on his face, so he wouldn't be made move! Git up this livin' minute, Bates, or I'll make you!"

He prodded him with the point of his bayonet. Bates shrieked.

"Damn you, lemme be!" He wept. "I can't, I tell you."

He reached across and dragged at MacCorbin's arm. "Sir, make him stop! I'm hurt. Can't you see I'm hurt, damn you! I ain't fitten to die, neither! Let up, Rutherford, fer Gawd's sake!"

He squirmed and screamed. The survivors of the platoon, dirty, tired men, huddled under the bank, watched in silence.

Rutherford caught hold of Bates by the back of his neck.

"What's that you say? You ain't fitten to die! Believe me, you ain't, sweetheart! No more ain't I. But if I can die, guess you can. Up you git, dearest! We two gonna reach the Germans, if the others ain't. D'jer hear me? Up with you!"

"I can't. Christ, lemme get outa this! I'm gonna give myself up, damn you! I stole that money, I tell you. Rutherford, I gotta give myself up. It was me took that money. He fought, damn him! I didn't mean to do him no harm, but he took a knife to me, an' fought."

Rutherford let go of his neck and twisted him about and stared at him with a look of blank amazement in his eyes.

"What's he yappin' about?" said MacBride.

"God!" said Rutherford. "You seen me comin' out that estaminet, you said. You dawgone liar! You killed that poor halfwit an' let me be blamed!" He clenched his fist and struck him on the face. "You Judas!"

"That'll do," said Culbriddy. "Are yez crazy?"

"Do you hear what he said, Sarje?"

MacCorbin, sickened, roused himself from the stupor that had held him and said gruffly:

"Cut it out, Rutherford! We've got to be moving on."

Bates turned and on hands and knees began to crawl down the slope, bareheaded still, without his rifle, toward the wood from which they had advanced.

Suddenly he screamed, rose to his feet and began to run, then leaped in the air, dropped, and lay still.

"I hope he's got some kinda excuse when they git him on to the carpet where he's gone to," said Rutherford. "He'll tell 'em a pack o' lies, I bet, but they won't listen! He blamed me for what he done, but cleared me in front of all you fer witnesses! I don't care now if I die or live!"

"Look!" said Culbriddy. "Look there, sir!"

From the trees that were being shelled by the Germans long lines of men in khaki deployed in combat groups were advancing.

"The supports are up," said MacBride. "Look, the poor fellers are gittin' it! Lookit! God! See them fallin'!"

From the left there came a roar of cheering.

"We're in on 'em over yonder!" said Bridger through bandaged jaws. "Good ol' roughnecks!"

"You're damn' right," said Culbriddy, "we're in the wood."

"How we gonna stop them machine-guns in front of us, hey?" said MacBride.

MacCorbin wriggled forward and lay near where Hennessey was shooting at the right of the bank which sheltered them and peered through a tangle of brush at the wood.

A voice called to him—

"Sir, Mr. MacCorbin!"

He turned his head and to his surprise saw Marshall in a shallow gully farther still to the right and some four or five yards in advance of where he lay.

"Sir," he said, "I can see the gunners workin' that gun jus' ahead, plain as anythin'. If someone could knock it out it would clear the way, like, fer the rest of us."

"All right, Marshall, we'll do our best right now."

"Believe I got one them guys!" said Hennessey. "Two, mebbe." He fired again. "Believe they got a sniper layin' out somewheres in front."

MacCorbin shouted to the men sheltered by the bank:

"You fellows ready! When I jump to my feet, follow!"

He glanced back at the waves of men moving up the slope. They were very near now. There was something, he felt, majestic, almost stately, in their advance. But, Lord! To see men drop forward and lie huddled up and know that they were dead!

He waited. Another minute and he and the platoon would join in their final rush.

"Mother o' God!" said Hennessey. "Look!"

MacCorbin turned and saw Marshall crawling on hands and knees up the dry rain channel between sparse and scattered bushes toward the wood.

A lump rose to his throat. Marshall, of all men!

He jumped to his feet.

"Up!" he yelled. "Up, the lot of you!" He scrambled over the edge of the bank and ran forward through the brush.

Only another fifty yards and he would reach the machine-guns. Fifty yards, but the worst fifty of all. Would he last? God, just to have one chance at them. Alive, still.

"Up! Up!"

Rutherford was by his side, red faced, grinning.

"Not so dawgone fast, that orf'cer!" someone shouted.

"Come on, then! Come on!"

A bullet snicked the edge of his steel helmet; he staggered, recovered himself and plunged forward.

He saw Marshall in front of him rise out of the ground, race up the side of a steep slope of white earth and, poised for an instant, arm uplifted, fling a grenade. There was the crash of an explosion, black smoke, screams. And then Marshall fell and slid down the slope into the brush.

"They got him!" said Rutherford.

MacCorbin pushed on. His heart was thumping fiercely. He was close up to the machine-guns now and he was not yet dead. One gun had been put out by Marshall; that was why he was still alive, perhaps! Another gun—he could see the blunt ugly snout —swung about. He was finished. How could they miss him at so short a range? There was no burst of firing. He could see the rounded helmets of the gunners. Jammed perhaps, or out of ammunition! He heard himself yelling:

"Come on! Come on! Give 'em hell!"

Rutherford thrust himself in front of him.

"Out of it, you!"

His bayonet flashed. There was a wild scream from a rifle pit almost at his very feet.

"Got him!" said Rutherford.

He grunted and lurched forward across the body of the German he had killed.

MacCorbin cursed. Rutherford gone. He scrambled up the last steep slope. He could hear the yells of the men who followed. Nothing could stop them now, he knew.

He reached the crest of the slope. He saw before him broken tree trunks and dead Germans. He smelt high explosive and raw, fresh blood. A cold rage possessed him. He was alive and could kill. He gazed down into the broken machine-gun emplacement and raised his pistol.

And then, before he could shoot, before he could avenge the first of his dead brothers, there rose out of the ground in front of him dead men—dead men with yellow, corpselike faces, and red eyes and hollow cheeks; men in round steel helmets that came down over their ears; men in dirty grey uniforms that stank of sweat and dirt and wet cloth; men in an agony of fear; dead men; corpses whose faces were the faces of men who have lived in hell and torment.

"*Kameraden! Kameraden!* Mercy! Surrender!"

They held their hands above their heads and whimpered. The machine-guns were silent at last. A deathlike stillness had settled on the wood. The yells of the advancing infantrymen sounded thin and unreal.

"*Kameraden!*"

MacCorbin hesitated, stunned, horrified. He wanted to shoot. He had his chance. Why didn't he shoot, then?

How could he shoot poor broken devils like these!

They had surrendered. Damn them! They had kept fighting their damned guns to the very last, pouring their bullets in on the men attacking them across the open, and then when they were cornered they held their hands up! Damn them!

MacCorbin turned.

He saw the men in khaki racing forward; he saw the long bayonets glinting in the first rays of the sun; he heard the wild yells; he saw MacBride, Culbriddy, Bridger, Hennessey. He saw men he did not know, men from the 2nd Battalion; hard, sunburnt faces, streaked with sweat and white dust.

"Kill them! Let me git at them!"

MacCorbin heard himself shout:

"Stop that! You, MacBride, put that rifle down! Hennessey, Bridger, damn you! They've surrendered! They're prisoners!"

He raised his pistol. There was no other officer living, only himself.

"Get back!" he said hoarsely. "Sergeant Culbriddy, these men are prisoners! We must get them sent back at once!"

He saw men surging up the slope toward him. He saw as through a mist angry faces, flushed faces, scowls, jeering grins, eyes that expressed hate and resentment, the faces of soldiers who have endured much punishment and are robbed of their right to kill. He had defrauded them, he felt. He had gone back on his word. He had saved the Germans from the death they deserved. He had done what was right.

"The first man that tries to kill these prisoners, I'll shoot!" he said. " Stop where you are!"

" The fact is," said a voice, " he's gone bugs!"

There was a shout of laughter and something, a clenched fist, the butt of a Springfield—he did not know what—crashed against his chest. He had an impression that he was falling from a great height, down and down and down. He passed into unconsciousness easily, peacefully.

" Hello! He's comin' to. Look at him!"

MacCorbin lay on his back and stared at the blue sky above him. With an effort he raised his head. Near him were men he knew. Bridger, his face bandaged; Culbriddy, with a shattered arm, smoking a cigarette, his face grey; MacBride, the Texan, sullen and tired looking! Hennessey, his eyes closed, leaning forward, bareheaded, breathing heavily; Prentiss, Harrison, Malone, a corporal whose name he did not know, two other men of the platoon, Jacobs and Bradley—or was one Hughes?

He saw they were watching him. He saw no pity in their looks. He saw contempt and suspicion and rage.

" You're a pack of damned cowards!" he said. " You shot them down after they'd surrendered! What kind of men are you?"

They looked at him uneasily.

" Who shot 'em down!" said Culbriddy. " They're prisoners."

" Lucky stiffs!" said MacBride.

" We got 'em rounded up, the dawgone lot of 'em!" said Bridger. " They're on their way to the cages now."

MacCorbin felt very weak.

" But I thought," said Culbriddy, " you told us not to take any prisoners! Wasn't that the gospel you was preachin' last night, sir?"

" My God!" said MacCorbin, and thought of his dead brothers and shivered. " I'm no damn' good, am I?"

"You're as damn' good as anyone," said Culbriddy. "Where would we be now, sir, if it wasn't for you leadin' us up that draw in the ground where them machine-guns couldn't rache us an' restin' us there by the bank under cover till the supports come up? The Colonel's pleased with you, sir. He's afther goin' past not tin seconds ago!"

And that needed thought, too.

"Well," he said after a time, "whoever it was knocked me out did the right thing. Only—only you see how it was, don't you? They'd surrendered. And now, we've got to be pushing on to our objectives!"

They laughed.

"You'll stay where you are, sir," said Culbriddy.

"We've got to go on!"

"There's about thirty left out the whole battalion," said Mac-Bride.

"We're bein' taken out the line," said Hennessey. "The attack's gone on the best part of half an hour!"

"An'," said Bridger, "nobody knocked you out!"

"Someone hit me!"

"Git away with you, sir!" said old Culbriddy, smiling at him. "You're makin' fun of us. The nose cap of a shell ricocheted an' took you in the breast-bone. You're for hospital an' across the water!"

THE LIGHTER SIDE OF WAR

THE SQUARE EGG

by
"Saki"

ASSUREDLY the badger is the animal that one most resembles in this trench warfare, that drab-coated creature of the twilight and darkness, digging, burrowing, listening; keeping itself as clean as possible under unfavourable circumstances, fighting tooth and nail on occasion for possession of a few yards of honeycombed earth.

What the badger thinks about life we shall never know, which is a pity, but cannot be helped; it is difficult enough to know what one thinks about it oneself in the trenches. Parliament, taxes, social gatherings, economies, and expenditure, and all the thousand and one horrors of civilisation seem immeasurably remote, and the War itself seems almost as distant and unreal. A couple of hundred yards away, separated from you by a stretch of dismal, untidy looking ground and some strips of rusty wire entanglement, lies a vigilant, bullet-spitting enemy; lurking and watching in those opposing trenches are foemen who might stir the imagination of the most sluggish brain, descendants of the men who went to battle under Moltke, Blücher, Frederick the Great, and the Great Elector, Wallenstein, Maurice of Saxony, Barbarossa, Albert the Bear, Henry the Lion, Witekind the Saxon. They are matched against you there, man for man and gun for gun, in what is perhaps the most stupendous struggle that modern history has known, and yet one thinks remarkably little about them. It would not be advisable to forget for the fraction of a second that they are there, but one's mind does not dwell on their existence. One speculates little as to whether they are drinking warm soup and eating sausage, or going cold and hungry; whether they are well supplied with copies of the

Meggendorfer Blätter and other light literature, or bored with un-
utterable weariness.

Much more to be thought about than the enemy over yonder or
the war all over Europe is the mud of the moment, the mud that at
times engulfs you as cheese engulfs a cheesemite. In the Zoological
Gardens one has gazed at an elk or bison loitering at its pleasure
more than knee-deep in a quagmire of greasy mud, and one has wondered what it would feel like to be soused and plastered, hour-long,
in such a muck-bath. One knows now. In narrow-dug support
trenches, when thaw and heavy rain have come suddenly a-top of
a frost; when everything is pitch dark around you, and you can
only stumble about and feel your way against streaming mud
walls; when you have to go down on hands and knees in several
inches of soup-like mud to creep into a dug-out; when you stand
deep in mud, lean against mud, grasp mud-slimed objects with mud-
caked fingers, wink mud away from your eyes, and shake it out of
your ears, bite muddy biscuits with muddy teeth, then at least you
are in a position to understand thoroughly what it feels like to wal-
low. On the other hand, the bison's idea of pleasure becomes more
and more incomprehensible.

When one is not thinking about mud one is probably thinking
about estaminets. An estaminet is a haven that one finds in agreeable plenty in most of the surrounding townships and villages, flour-
ishing still amid roofless and deserted houses, patched up where
necessary in rough-and-ready fashion, and finding a new and profitable tide of customers from among the soldiers who have replaced
the bulk of the civil population. An estaminet is a sort of com-
pound between a wine-shop and a coffee-house, having a tiny bar
in one corner, a few long tables and benches, a prominent cooking-
stove, generally a small grocery store tucked away in the back prem-
ises, and always two or three children running and bumping about

at inconvenient angles to one's feet. It seems to be a fixed rule that estaminet children should be big enough to run about and small enough to get between one's legs. There must, by the way, be one considerable advantage in being a child in a war-zone village; no one can attempt to teach it tidiness. The wearisome maxim, " A place for everything and everything in its proper place," can never be insisted on when a considerable part of the roof is lying in the backyard, when a bedstead from a neighbour's demolished bedroom is half buried in the beetroot pile, and the chickens are roosting in a derelict meat-safe because a shell has removed the top and sides and front of the chicken-house.

Perhaps there is nothing in the foregoing description to suggest that a village wine-shop, frequently a shell-nibbled building in a shell-gnawed street, is a paradise to dream about; but when one has lived in a dripping wilderness of unrelieved mud and sodden sandbags for any length of time, one's mind dwells on the plain furnished parlour with its hot coffee and *vin ordinaire* as something warm and snug and comforting in a wet and slushy world. To the soldier on his trench-to-billets migration the wine-shop is what the tavern rest-house is to the caravan nomad of the East. One comes and goes in a crowd of chance-forgathered men, noticed or unnoticed, as one wishes; amid the khaki-clad, be-putteed throng of one's own kind one can be as unobtrusive as a green caterpillar on a green cabbage-leaf; one can sit undisturbed, alone or with one's own friends, or if one wishes to be talkative and talked to one can readily find a place in a circle where men of divers variety of cap badges are exchanging experiences, real or improvised.

Besides the changing throng of mud-stained khaki there is a drifting leaven of local civilians, uniformed interpreters, and men in varying types of foreign military garb, from privates in the Regular Army to Heaven-knows-what in some intermediate corps that only an expert in such matters could put a name to; and, of course, here and there are representatives of that great army of adventurer purse-sappers that carries on its operations uninterruptedly, in time of peace or war alike, over the greater part of the earth's surface. You meet them in England and France, in Russia and Constantinople; probably they are to be met with also in Iceland, though on that point I have no direct evidence.

In the estaminet of the Fortunate Rabbit I found myself sitting next to an individual of indefinite age and nondescript uniform, who was obviously determined to make the borrowing of a match serve as a formal introduction and a banker's reference. He had the air of jaded jauntiness, the equipment of temporary amiability, the aspect of a foraging crow, taught by experience to be wary and prompted by necessity to be bold; he had the contemplative downward droop of nose and moustache and the furtive, sidelong range of eye—he had all those things that are the ordinary outfit of the purse-sapper the world over.

" I am a victim of the war," he exclaimed, after a little preliminary conversation.

" One cannot make an omelette without breaking eggs," I answered, with the appropriate callousness of a man who had seen some dozens of square miles of devastated country-side and roofless homes.

" Eggs!" he vociferated, " but it is precisely of eggs that I am about to speak. Have you ever considered what is the great drawback in the excellent and most useful egg—the ordinary, everyday egg of commerce and cookery?"

" Its tendency to age rapidly is sometimes against it," I hazarded. " Unlike the United States of North America, which grow more respectable and self-respecting the longer they last, an egg gains nothing by persistence; it resembles your Louis the Fifteenth, who declined in popular favour with every year he lived—unless the historians have entirely misrepresented his record."

"No," replied the Tavern Acquaintance seriously, "it is not a question of age. It is the shape, the roundness. Consider how easily it rolls. On a table, a shelf, a shop counter, perhaps, one little push, and it may roll to the floor and be destroyed. What catastrophe for the poor, the frugal!"

I gave a sympathetic shudder at the idea; eggs here cost six sous apiece.

"Monsieur," he continued, "it is a subject I had often pondered and turned over in my mind, this economical malformation of the household egg. In our little village of Verchey-les-Torteaux, in the Department of the Tarn, my aunt has a small dairy and poultry farm, from which we drew a modest income. We were not poor, but there was always the necessity to labour, to contrive, to be sparing. One day I chanced to notice that one of my aunt's hens, a hen of the mop-headed Houdan breed, had laid an egg that was not altogether so round-shaped as the eggs of other hens; it could not be called square, but it had well-defined angles. I found out that this particular bird always laid eggs of this particular shape. The discovery gave a new stimulus to my ideas. If one collected all the hens that one could find with a tendency to lay a slightly angular egg and bred chickens only from those hens, and went on selecting and selecting, always choosing those that laid the squarest egg, at last, with patience and enterprise, one would produce a breed of fowls that laid only square eggs."

"In the course of several hundred years one might arrive at such a result," I said; "it would more probably take several thousands."

"With your cold Northern conservative, slow-moving hens that might be the case," said the Acquaintance impatiently and rather angrily; "with our vivacious Southern poultry it is different. Lis-

ten. I searched, I experimented, I explored the poultry-yards of our
neighbours, I ransacked the markets of the surrounding towns and
wherever I found a hen laying an angular egg I bought her; I collected in time a vast concourse of fowls all sharing the same tendency; from their progeny I selected only those pullets whose eggs
showed the most marked deviation from the normal roundness. I
continued, I persevered. Monsieur, I produced a breed of hens that
laid an egg which could not roll, however much you might push
or jostle it. My experiment was more than a success; it was one of
the romances of modern industry."

Of that I had not the least doubt, but I did not say so.

"My eggs became known," continued the *soi-disant* poultry farmer; " at first they were sought after as a novelty, something curious,
bizarre. Then merchants and housewives began to see that they
were a utility, an improvement, an advantage over the ordinary
kind. I was able to command a sale for my wares at a price considerably above market rates. I began to make money. I had a monopoly.
I refused to sell any of my ' square-layers,' and the eggs that went
to market were carefully sterilised, so that no chickens should be
hatched from them. I was in the way to become rich, comfortably
rich. Then this War broke out, which has brought misery to so
many. I was obliged to leave my hens and my customers and go to
the Front. My aunt carried on the business as usual, sold the square
eggs, the eggs that I had devised and created and perfected, and received the profits. Can you imagine it? She refuses to send me one
centime of the takings! She says that she looks after the hens, and
pays for their corn, and sends the eggs to market, and that the
money is hers. Legally, of course, it is mine; if I could afford to
bring a process in the courts I could recover all the money that the
eggs have brought in since the War commenced, many thousands
of francs. To bring a process would only need a small sum; I have

a lawyer friend who would arrange matters cheaply for me. Unfortunately, I have not sufficient funds in hand; I need still about eighty francs. In war-time, alas! it is difficult to borrow."

I had always imagined that it was a habit that was especially indulged in during war-time, and said so.

"On a big scale, yes, but I am talking of a very small matter. It is easier to arrange a loan of millions than of a trifle of eighty or ninety francs."

The would-be financier paused for a few tense moments. Then he recommenced in a more confidential strain.

"Some of you English soldiers, I have heard, are men with private means; is it not so? It is perhaps possible that among your comrades there might be someone willing to advance a small sum —you yourself, perhaps—it would be a secure and profitable investment, quickly repaid——"

"If I get a few days' leave I will go down to Verchey-les-Torteaux and inspect the square egg hen farm," I said gravely, "and question the local egg merchants as to the position and prospects of the business."

The Tavern Acquaintance gave an almost imperceptible shrug to his shoulders, shifted in his seat, and began moodily to roll a cigarette. His interest in me had suddenly died out, but for the sake of appearances he was bound to make a perfunctory show of winding up the conversation he had so laboriously started.

"Ah, you will go to Verchey-les-Torteaux and make inquiries about our farm. And if you find that what I have told you about the square eggs is true, Monsieur, what then?"

"I shall marry your aunt."

SEQUEL TO A BATTLE

by
Charles MacArthur

IT was a mistake to win the battle of St. Mihiel. All it got us was a piece in the papers, three or four dud towns, and several thousand acres of marshy woods, worth five dollars an acre at the most. However, General Pershing got the idea that this duck pond was important and ought to be defended. Orders shortly came down to consolidate. Consolidate means dig. Dig means work.

A brand-new trench system was ordered. We scooped it out. Roads were needed. We made them. Gun-pits and *abris* were necessary. We dug, and dug some more. Our officers sought to speed work by pretending the Germans were sore about getting kicked out and intended coming right back with their gang. Apple sauce.

Those Dutchmen knew when they were well off. They knew those woods too. We couldn't have coaxed them back if we had opened a beer garden and admitted ladies free. So we dug away and remembered how happy we had been before the battle started.

Meanwhile rumours spread that the Rainbow was stuck in the bog for the winter. The men blew up, for a lot of good, honest-to-God reasons. There was talk of fighting in the north, and the toughest aggregation of star-spangled bums in the A.E.F. was spading up a lousy front that could have been held by any good football team—all because we had been suckers enough to take St. Mihiel in the first place.

Stories that Pershing had it in for us because we had shown up his pet Regular Army divisions were renewed. Well, if there was anything in precedent, the minute anything happened to those little Rollos, we would be on our way to the fire again—*toots sweet.*

Awaiting the call—it came sooner than we expected—we prepared to make ourselves comfortable. Our woods stood several miles back of the original front line, in the enemy S.O.S.

Evidently the Heinies had been using it for a *turnverein*. With real home-loving instinct they had built a flock of rustic tables and benches, suitable for small dinners, etc. If we wanted to get strong there were any number of horizontal bars about, and a trapeze or two. Also the woods were dotted with bungalows, where the officers ran to tell each other secrets and play House.

Scouts beat the Captain to several of these shanties and returned with everything that made life worth while. We acquired a piano, several stoves, a few Bavarian pipes in fair condition, a collection of superb *steins,* a file of funny papers, and a stack of rude photographs. Art subjects. Even an accordion was discovered, and George Savage learned to manipulate it beautifully between hands of Three Card Monte. Stores of lumber, tar paper, and tin roofing led up to little homes with shelves in them. Imagine shelves. After working hours we lived like millionaires.

Moreover, we ate like millionaires for a couple of weeks, due to the cunning of Porch Climber MacMillan, who discovered an officers' ration dump down the road. Every morning he hitched up the supply waggon and drove it boldly to the dump. Assisted by other blithe spirits, he picked out the choicest delicacies and— bellyaching loudly at the injustice of carrying officers' dainties on a diet of privates' slum—piled them into the waggon. Every night we dined on canned peaches, beans, corned-beef hash, and real coffee—in order. Every night, until success turned his head and made him attempt the impossible. In brief, he sought to remove the entire dump to our diggings; but our hardy trio made the fatal blunder of carrying two boxes at once. At this show of zeal the officer in charge of the dump dropped dead. He had hitherto been forced to yell his heart out before six privates would carry one box. The three were immediately arrested, and there was big talk of shooting them. We went back to monkey meat and goldfish.

The Y.M.C.A. arrived and converted one of the German log barracks into a get-together hut. That was a novelty for us; and when the word went out that chocolate, cakes, cigarettes, and writing-paper would be passed out on the opening night there was a panic. The doors were opened finally, and everybody not on guard fought and bit and kicked to get in. The men at the guns were represented by delegates, which was a bit optimistic on their part. The prospect of chocolate—free—was far and away the high moment of the war to date. But instead of stacks of chocolate a benevolent secretary stood on the platform, waving his handkerchief and beaming benignly. He announced right off the bat that he was happy to see us and now wished to recite a little poem by Robert W. Service. With no further warning he cleared his throat and commenced. The poem had to do with a soldier who was very depressed about something and about to commit suicide. The secretary acted it out with much shadow boxing and hands to the heart and brow. His voice sank to a hoarse whisper and rose triumphantly as the soldier decided not to die after all, but stick it out for the sake of the Little Woman and the Fifty-second Congress. On reaching the moral, Mr. Secretary stepped heavily on the gas and choked up. He began to weep.

" *Where's that chocolate?*" bawled the loudest voice in the outfit. It began to look as if the chocolate had been a ruse. There was talk of eating the secretary. *He* looked sweet.

Lieutenant-Colonel A. V. Smith, who had been sobbing quietly in a corner, leaped to the platform and averted a pogrom. The muttering died down. We were very fond of Smith. Yet he was no diplomat. Blind to the pulsing issue, he went on from where the secretary had left off. For no reason he announced that we were not so badly off in comparison with the suffering of Washington at Valley Forge. As if anybody gave a damn about Washington and Valley Forge, or Lincoln, or William Jennings Bryan.

"Where's that chocolate?" insisted Mr. McGraw and glee club.

The Lieutenant-Colonel begged to be heard. Washington was a fine fellow, he said, and a real credit to America. The demands for chocolate became deafening. Again Smith raised his hand. A sinister silence fell. If the Y.M.C.A. had been using chocolate as a bait for the Better Things of Life some wise secretary was going to be hamburger.

"Comrades!" cried the Lieutenant-Colonel. "And I am *proud* to call you comrades!"

This was an alarming statement. He might just as well have confessed that there wasn't a bar of chocolate within fifty miles. An ugly murmur ran through the room, rising in ominous crescendo. The French Revolution began just like that. (*Cf.* Carlyle.)

In the nick of time Lieutenant-Colonel Smith grasped the situation. He was a lawyer and knew his stuff. He yelled suddenly that there was chocolate for all. Moreover, if anybody wanted to write home for forbidden boxes he personally would sign all requests. Thirdly, as he had mentioned before, he was *proud* to call us comrades.

The resultant cheer revealed the fickleness of human nature. It was immediately decided that Smith was the greatest officer in the Army, and should be a General, by rights. We unbelted with a few good opinions of the Y.M.C.A. as well.

Hitherto the initials had been interpreted as meaning "You Must Come Across," on account of excessive prices asked by the secretaries for their wares. Now it was a good institution. The chocolate was distributed. A grave crisis of the War was averted.

This episode almost reconciled us to the tedium of digging; especially as a hot rumour indicated that we were destined for another front more worthy of our talents. We prepared for the move by trading our skinny, drooping nags for some fat and frisky ponies belonging to a French battery down the road. Those French were a little careless about the way they guarded their picket lines, although the boys who made the swap could have stolen their Frog eyes if we had wanted them.

Quite a scene took place the next day when the Frogs called and tried to get their horses back. We were amazed at their claims, and patiently pointed out—by certain markings—that our new horses were genuine American mustangs, fresh from the Woolly West. When they remained unconvinced we tweaked a couple of moustaches and asked them if they wanted to make anything out of it. Nobody could call *us* liars and get away with it.

There was no new front in stock, so the General thought up something just as good. He decided it would be a slick idea if the battery sneaked out into No Man's Land and fired a few shots at point-blank ranges. It certainly was an original idea. People have been put in the Nut House for less.

It is barely possible that men, women, and children not connected with Battery F., 149th Field Artillery, may glance over this record some day. For their benefit, a slight description of the General's plans with comment on same :

It was proposed by the General and seconded by his sycophantic admirers that the battery should leave its safe little woods on the night of September 21st and mosey up to the front line trenches, crossing them as if they were roller-skating rinks; after which we were to line up the guns—at a neat dress—in No Man's Land and shoot such Germans as we saw fit. The theory was that such unprecedented procedure would scare the wits out of the enemy and teach them not to start any more wars.

From our point of view there were several slight objections to the scheme : (*a*) We might get killed. (*b*) Very likely we *would* get killed. (*c*) We couldn't escape getting killed. And for no reason. We could hit whatever targets the General had in mind just as hard and twice as accurately from our regular positions.

Moreover, the General's plan assumed that the Germans were going to sit still while we sent several hundred shells into their little stomachs from a distance of a few hundred feet. We knew better. At that time the Germans had good machine-guns, elegant cannon, and no sense of humour. It was fairly certain that they would put up with our tomfoolery for just so long and then get good and mad. They might even shoot back.

When the order came down, therefore, it looked as if the General had invented a contest for the goofiest idea of the War— and then had set out to win it himself. However—

> Theirs not to make reply,
> Theirs not to reason why,
> Theirs but to do and die.
> PERSHING.

Another call for volunteers. Another touching rush to be killed. Captain Stone mournfully picked out a platoon. The woods shuddered with drama, and private opinions of all generals caused the sweet green leaves to curl up and die. Such handshaking went on between the select few and their potential survivors! A thousand expressions of good luck fell flat in the mud. The little Greek said a prayer.

The practical side of the matter received some attention. Axles were thoroughly greased to take out the squeak. The clank of the harness was deadened with rags. The guns sneaked out at set of sun. Why the General gave us the break of doing our stuff in the dark is a mystery. The Germans would have much better pickings by daylight. The parade crept through the inky woods, the men cursing in whispers when a horse snorted or a stick broke under the wheels. We reached the front line, indistinguishable from any other part of the line in the darkness, except for the click of a bayonet and an occasional doughboy humming a song. Captain Stone and Fred Somant rode ahead and flitted back and forth with whispered directions. A steel waggon tyre rang against a rock. Wild echoes woke the silent valley. Oh, oh! That was bum coffee. No back talk from the Krauts, however. So far we were playing in elegant luck. But one star-shell would have caused some handsome hash.

Midway in No Man's Land lay a little hollow. The horses were led—very gently—over the rim. We unlimbered in five seconds flat and turned the guns towards Germany. Our target was Merin-Bois Farm, supposedly impregnable. The brick farm buildings loomed in the dark blue night like Gibraltar. Caissons were silently unloaded, shells piled in rows. Each accidental clash of iron on iron brought a hiss of hard-boiled reproach. The horses were led to a patch of pine back of the first line. The cannoneers dug their flops—shovels burning. No digging ever was done so fast or so well. Captain Stone crept over the rise of ground to direct fire. At once a full moon shot from a cloud on a bob-sled. The farm lighted up like a Christmas tree. Three quick ranges came down, then :

"Fire!"

A murderous salvo, instantly repeated as the shells ripped into the building and tore it apart. We were loading on the recoil now. Dotted lines of death streamed from every gun to the farm. There were so many explosions that our target was obscured by smoke.

The Germans ran around like monkeys in a ninety-mile blizzard. A dozen rockets hissed out of their little hell, breaking red and white and green over our heads. That meant a few return packages at any minute. We got ready to duck. Several machine-guns began to rattle : our nerves were spared by all the noise we ourselves were making. Only when snip-snips filled the cracks of sound were we conscious of possibilities.

Wham! We were faded! Big guns, too. The Katzenjammer Kids didn't know where we were yet. The closest shells were a hundred feet away. It's pretty tough, firing at flashes.

Bong! That one clipped the crest. Getting warmer. Germans. Some nosey *Oberlieutenant* was giving them the right address. Big buckets of high explosive hammered the hollow. Some of them were bad news. We took to firing from our hands and knees as fragments whirred like pigeons past our ears. Two or three honeys landed twenty feet from the second piece. We got on our faces, popping up like jacks-in-the-box, at every battery right. A fragment sliced Wilbur Wood in the arm. He kept on serving the gun. The Germans got real rough, slinging iron like confetti. Result : they began to have the same trouble we were having—they couldn't see us for shell bursts. We laid off for a second and got a new line on the farm, passing the salt and pepper every time our Dutch cousins stuck their snoots out of the wreckage. Meanwhile a smudge of dawn streaked the sky. We began to get nervous. This sort of thing couldn't go on for ever.

Nevertheless, through many tough campaigns one natural law had revealed itself : *If* we got through the first fifteen minutes of fire without serious damage we were reasonably safe from harm thereafter. This law had operated beautifully for seven months. On the strength of its continued operation some of the boys got frisky. Walter Birkland, in particular, ran around the second gun during a regular cyclone of shell fragments. It was for luck, he explained.

Night began to fade—perceptibly. So did our ammunition. Between shots we discussed what we would do by the dawn's early light—when all those fun-loving Katzenjammers got a look at us. Someone suggested that we pretend we were waxworks. The rest thought of apologising and clung to those who had studied German in college.

Worry vanished with the sudden appearance of the drivers racing through the smoke drifts. Three cheers for the Red, White, and Blue! Hooray for Lloyd George! Bravo, Clemenceau! By some process of nerves the guns were hooked to the limbers. We tore across the field, one side or a leg off. Considerable scrap-iron pounded in our tracks. A good mile back of the first line we stopped running, feeling that we were still ten miles too near.

So there *was* a God.

A terrific reunion took place at the old position. Those who had been left behind were thoroughly Ritzed by the death dodgers. The stunt was discussed from every angle. Among other things we took it all back about the General. Shooting from No Man's Land was an elegant idea. The General was a genius. He knew his oats, that boy; and he knew whom to pick for the tough jobs too.

A little later the expedition was warmly commended through the Colonel. Our opinions of the General went up another eight notches. There was a man who would amount to something in the War. The Captain did the handsome thing and cited all who took part in the mission for their conduct under fire. We reminded the Captain that he had been very brave too. It was all like Christmas in the Harem. Further, the Intelligence Department reported that our fire had completely demolished the enemy positions, annihilating the defenders. A few of them, deprived of the

Y.M.C.A.'s heartening counsel, had committed suicide. On the other hand, we were intact and apparently immune. No German could hurt us from now on. Several of the boys attempted to cut out their Army insurance. Obviously there was no sense in shelling out ten dollars every month when the War was all a big joke.

Then came the discovery of General Pershing that his best troops were playing kiss-the-pillow in the woods of Essey. This was three weeks after the battle of St. Mihiel. Immediately orders came thick and fast. It was rumoured that we were scheduled to crack the line north of Verdun. That was O.K. with us. There was glamour about Verdun, already the graveyard of a million brave men.

We rolled out of our beer garden on the double. The doughboys flashed past in motor trucks, yelling, " See you later!" They were sitting pretty, riding from front to front like bank presidents, while we hiked on swollen feet.

The regiment became separated, due to some brainy work on the part of a Major and a Lieutenant. The latter's idea of being a great officer was to threaten stragglers with death, on the theory that any officer could shoot an enlisted man whenever he felt like it. And get a bounty from Congress, to boot.

" That's what *I* call army diss-*sip*-lin!" he would bawl, in support of his permit to kill. Of course, we never took the threat seriously. In spite of army regulations, there must be a law somewhere against shooting people.

All the way we were bothered by various pests, chiefly Marine M.P.s. One General, who thought he was a tough guy, amused himself by dressing up in a private's slicker and hammering our buzzing ear-drums with :

" What *out*-fit, buddy?"

You can't fool a horse-fly. *We* knew he was a General. The

answers came back like rubber bands:

"Buffalo Bill, you big sap!"

"Nine Hunert and Eighty-eighth Dental Supply. Dismounted. Remounted on horseback."

"Hunert and One Ranch! Y.M.C.A. Replacements! What's it *to* you?" etc.

The General met this razz with words that are never used by Generals or gentlemen. We threatened to wash his mouth out with soap and water. In a fine blaze of fury he ripped off the slicker and stood revealed in all his silver stars. Now that he could prove he was a General it was not fair insulting him. We shut up.

After twenty long hours—boots, boots, boots, going up and down again, and occasional opportunities to trade places with the drivers—we hit a collection of wooden barracks and paused for the afternoon. A sack of potatoes was immediately switched from a National Army ration dump, and someone promoted a gallon of bacon grease. We ate French potatoes and the last of our reserve rations.

Captain Stone went completely military and ordered us to wash the carriages and guns, which did away with any foolish notions of sleep. Work was interrupted several times by his loud snores. At night we hit the trail again, tired and sore as hell; shooting tobacco juice at the officers as they snooped up and down the column in the hope of catching somebody hanging on to a carriage for support.

Morning brought us to the dust piles around Verdun. Once they were towns. We swung into the wide white road called the Holy Way in remembrance of the thousands upon thousands of dead men who had tramped over the hill and on out of the world. Countless corpses. In the first cemetery were twenty thousand tidy graves. The French are a neat people. Thirty thousand lay in the next. In all we passed more than twenty graveyards. Well, there were still more than 1,500,000,000 people in the world with approximately the same dreams and jobs and jokes.

We steamed up a long hill. Those monotonous crosses stuck out of the slope like cloves from a ham. The hill was as burned and barren-looking. We halted at the summit in what passed as a woods. Barracks here, and mail. We hung out a "Not to be Disturbed" sign for an hour and didn't start the crap game until late in the afternoon. Some diversion was furnished by a green division, hot from the States. They twitted us for fellow newcomers because we had neglected to sew on our service stripes. Shiners were hung on a couple of them.

The little Greek thought he saw a woman and burned down the road with a set of tempting chops. His quarry turned out to be a priest. Mr. Papolis returned, a bitter Scotch Presbyterian.

Sunset and evening star; and one clear call for us. We dragged our badly swollen dogs down the hill and hit it out for the War.

A long and horrible hike on bleeding feet. Avocourt at last. This was a pile of dirty flour-like dust at a cross roads. A broken milestone was the one remainder of the town. In the early morning light it began to look as if we were just poking our noses into a lot of trouble. We proceeded to the bloody Bois de Montfaucon and had a chair.

So this was the Argonne! A bunch of doughboys snored on the ground. They informed us that the American Army had suffered overwhelming defeat; that the Allies were trapped; that the Germans were making sandwiches out of one and all. This was staggering news until we learned that the rumours had their origin in the plight of the now famous Lost Battalion, cut off directly ahead. We were there to help get them out.

The sun appeared, and we gave our new surroundings the once-over. It was hardly a garden of roses. The woods were splintered into small bits, green with mustard gas. There wasn't a live leaf in twenty miles. Thousands of dead men sprawled in the ulcerated fields. Horses, their legs awkwardly pointing up, and a general litter of junk. Waggons, rifles, socks, rations, love-letters. What bum soldiers those boys must have been, God rest their pretty souls! Everything pointed to panic and massacre.

One of the kids lay on the ground dying with a bullet in his guts. He had been yanked from a stenographer's job in New York, trained (as they say) and exposed to his first fire—all in thirty-seven days. He was slightly bewildered by it all.

The doughboys told of being marched in a column of fours right down to the trenches in full sight of the German gunners. More Sears-Roebuck officers. One gang of artillerymen told us of firing for thirty-six hours without effect. It turned out that they hadn't used fuses. Apparently their officers thought shells went off by themselves and had been pegging iron cucumbers through the entire battle. It became clear why we had run all the way from St. Mihiel.

One of the boys expressed the general sentiment when he gazed upon the piles of the gaping dead, scratched his nose, and re-marked:

"Something tells me we ain't going to be happy here."

STRANGE STORIES

THE TRAITOR
by
Somerset Maugham

NOTE.—Ashenden, a British Secret Service Agent, has received orders to go into Switzerland on a mission from his chief R.

HAVING taken a room at the hotel at which he had been instructed to stay, Ashenden went out; it was a lovely day, early in August, and the sun shone in an unclouded sky. He had not been to Lucerne since he was a boy, and but vaguely remembered a covered bridge, a great stone lion, and a church in which he had sat, bored yet impressed, while they played an organ; and now, wandering along a shady quay (and the lake looked just as tawdry and unreal as it looked on the picture postcards), he tried not so much to find his way about a half-forgotten scene as to re-form in his mind some recollection of the shy and eager lad, so impatient for life (which he saw not in the present of his adolescence but only in the future of his manhood), who so long ago had wandered there. But it seemed to him that the most vivid of his memories was not of himself but of the crowd; he seemed to remember sun and heat and people; the train was crowded and so was the hotel; the lake steamers were packed, and on the quays and in the streets you threaded your way among the throng of holiday makers. They were fat and old and ugly and odd, and they stank. Now, in war-time, Lucerne was as deserted as it must have been before the world at large discovered that Switzerland was the playground of Europe. Most of the hotels were closed, the streets were empty, the rowing boats for hire rocked idly at the water's edge and there was none to take them, and in the avenues by the lake the only persons to be seen were serious Swiss taking their neutrality, like a dachshund, for a walk with them. Ashenden felt exhilarated by the solitude, and, sitting down on a bench that faced the water, surrendered himself deliberately to the sensation. It was true that the lake was absurd, the water was too blue, the mountains too snowy, and its beauty, hitting you in the face, exasperated rather than thrilled; but all the same, there was something pleasing in the prospect, an artless candour, like one of Mendelssohn's "Songs Without Words," that made Ashenden smile with complacency. Lucerne reminded him of wax flowers under glass cases and cuckoo clocks and fancy work in Berlin wool. So long, at all events, as the fine weather lasted he was prepared to enjoy himself. He did not see why he should not at least try to combine pleasure to himself with profit to his country. He was travelling with a brand-new passport in his pocket, under a borrowed name, and this gave him an agreeable sense of owning a new personality. He was often slightly tired of himself, and it diverted him for a while to be merely a creature of R.'s facile invention. The experience he had just enjoyed appealed to his acute sense of the absurd. R., it is true, had not seen the fun of it : what humour R. possessed was of a sardonic turn, and he had no facility for taking in good part a joke at his own expense. To do that you must be able to look at yourself from the outside and be at the same time spectator and actor in the pleasant comedy of life. R. was a soldier, and regarded introspection as unhealthy, un-English, and unpatriotic.

Ashenden got up and strolled slowly to his hotel. It was a small German hotel of the second class, spotlessly clean, and his bedroom had a nice view; it was furnished with brightly varnished pitch-pine, and though on a cold, wet day it would have been wretched, in that warm and sunny weather it was gay and pleasant. There were tables in the hall, and he sat down at one of these and ordered a bottle of beer. The landlady was curious to know why in that dead season he had come to stay, and he was glad to satisfy her curiosity. He told her that he had recently recovered from an attack of typhoid, and had come to Lucerne to get back his strength. He was employed in the Censorship Department, and was taking the opportunity to brush up his rusty German. He asked her if she could recommend to him a German teacher. The landlady was a blond and blowsy Swiss, good humoured and talkative, so that Ashenden felt pretty sure that she would repeat in the proper quarter the information he gave her. It was his turn now to ask a few questions. She was voluble on the subject of the War, on account of which the hotel, in that month so full that rooms had to be found for visitors in neighbouring houses, was nearly empty. A few people came in from outside to eat their meals *en pension,* but she had only two lots of resident guests. One was an old Irish couple who lived in Vevey and passed their summers in Lucerne, and the other was an Englishman and his wife. She was a German, and they were obliged on that account to live in a neutral country. Ashenden took care to show little curiosity about them— he recognised in the description Grantley Caypor—but of her own accord she told him that they spent most of the day walking about the mountains. Herr Caypor was a botanist and much interested in the flora of the country. His lady was a very nice woman, and she felt her position keenly. Ah, well, the War could not last for ever. The landlady bustled away and Ashenden went upstairs.

Dinner was at seven, and, wishing to be in the dining-room before anyone else, so that he could take stock of his fellow-guests as they entered, he went down as soon as he heard the bell. It was a very plain, stiff, whitewashed room, with chairs of the same shiny pitch-pine as in his bedroom, and on the walls were oleographs of Swiss lakes. On each little table was a bunch of flowers. It was all neat and clean and presaged a bad dinner. Ashenden would have liked to make up for it by ordering a bottle of the best Rhine wine to be found in the hotel, but did not venture to draw attention to himself by extravagance (he saw on two or three tables half-empty bottles of table hock, which made him surmise that his fellow-guests drank thriftily), and so contented himself with ordering a pint of lager. Presently one or two persons came in, single men with some occupation in Lucerne and obviously Swiss, and sat down each at his little table and untied the napkins that at the end of luncheon they had neatly tied up. They propped newspapers against their water-jugs and read while they somewhat noisily ate their soup. Then entered a very tall, bent man, with white hair and a drooping white moustache, accompanied by a little old white-haired lady in black. These were certainly the Irish Colonel and his wife of whom the landlady had spoken. They took their seats, and the Colonel poured out a thimbleful of wine for his wife and a thimbleful for himself. They waited in silence for their dinner to be served to them by the buxom, hearty maid.

At last the persons arrived for whom Ashenden had been waiting. He was doing his best to read a German book, and it was only by an exercise of self-control that he allowed himself only for one instant to raise his eyes as they came in. His glance showed him a man of about forty-five with short, dark hair, somewhat grizzled, of middle height but corpulent, with a broad, red, clean-shaven face. He wore a shirt open at the neck, with a wide collar and a grey suit. He walked ahead of his wife, and of her Ashenden only caught the impression of a German woman, self-effaced and dusty. Grantley Caypor sat down and began in a loud voice explaining to the waitress that they had taken an immense walk. They had been up some mountain the name of which meant nothing to Ashenden, but which excited in the maid expressions of astonishment and enthusiasm. Then Caypor, still in fluent German, but with a marked English accent, said that they were so late they had not even gone up to wash, but had just rinsed their hands outside. He had a resonant voice and a jovial manner.

"Serve me quick; we're starving with hunger, and bring beer —bring three bottles. *Lieber Gott,* what a thirst I have!"

He seemed to be a man of exuberant vitality. He brought into that dull, over-clean dining-room the breath of life, and everyone in it appeared on a sudden more alert. He began to talk to his wife in English, and everything he said could be heard by all; but presently she interrupted him with a remark made in an undertone. Caypor stopped, and Ashenden felt that his eyes were turned in his direction. Mrs. Caypor had noticed the arrival of a stranger and had drawn her husband's attention to it. Ashenden turned the page of the book he was pretending to read, but he felt that Caypor's gaze was fixed intently upon him. When he addressed his wife again it was in so low a tone that Ashenden could not even tell what language he used; but when the maid brought them their soup Caypor, his voice still low, asked her a question. It was plain that he was enquiring who Ashenden was. Ashenden could catch of the maid's reply but the one word *lander.*

One or two people finished their dinner and went out picking their teeth. The old Irish Colonel and his old wife rose from their table, and he stood aside to let her pass. They had eaten their meal without exchanging a word. She walked slowly to the door; but the Colonel stopped to say a word to a Swiss who might have been a local attorney, and when she reached it she stood there, bowed and with a sheep-like look, patiently waiting for her husband to come and open it for her. Ashenden realised that she had never opened a door herself. She did not know how to. In a minute the Colonel, with his old, old gait, came to the door and opened it; she passed out and he followed. The little incident offered a key to their whole lives, and from it Ashenden began to reconstruct their histories, circumstances, and characters; but he

pulled himself up : he could not allow himself the luxury of crea-
tion. He finished his dinner.

When he went into the hall he saw tied to the leg of a table a
bull-terrier, and, in passing, mechanically put down his hand to
fondle the dog's drooping, soft ears. The landlady was standing
at the foot of the stairs.

"Whose is this lovely beast?" asked Ashenden.

"He belongs to Herr Caypor. Fritzi he is called. Herr Caypor
says he has a longer pedigree than the King of England."

Fritzi rubbed himself against Ashenden's leg, and with his nose
sought the palm of his hand. Ashenden went upstairs to fetch his
hat, and when he came down saw Caypor standing at the entrance
of the hotel talking with the landlady. From the sudden silence
and their constrained manner he guessed that Caypor had been
making inquiries about him. When he passed between them into
the street, out of the corner of his eye he saw Caypor give him a
suspicious stare. That frank, jovial red face bore then a look of
shifty cunning.

Ashenden strolled along till he found a tavern where he could
have his coffee in the open, and, to compensate himself for the
bottle of beer that his sense of duty had urged him to drink at
dinner, ordered the best brandy the house provided. He was
pleased at last to have come face to face with the man of whom
he had heard so much, and in a day or two hoped to become
acquainted with him. It is never very difficult to get to know anyone who has a dog. But he was in no hurry; he would let things
take their course. With the object he had in view he could not
afford to be hasty.

Ashenden reviewed the circumstances. Grantley Caypor was an
Englishman, born, according to his passport, in Birmingham, and
he was forty-two years of age. His wife, to whom he had been

married for eleven years, was of German birth and parentage. That was public knowledge. Information about his antecedents was contained in a private document. He had started life, according to this, in a lawyer's office in Birmingham and then had drifted into journalism. He had been connected with an English paper in Cairo and with another in Shanghai. There he got into trouble for attempting to get money by false pretences and was sentenced to a short term of imprisonment. All trace of him was lost for two years after his release, when he reappeared in a shipping office in Marseilles. From there, still in the shipping business, he went to Hamburg, where he married, and to London. In London he set up for himself in the export business, but after some time failed and was made a bankrupt. He returned to journalism. At the outbreak of war he was once more in the shipping business, and in August, 1914, was living quietly with his German wife at Southampton. In the beginning of the following year he told his employers that owing to the nationality of his wife his position was intolerable; they had no fault to find with him, and, recognising that he was in an awkward fix, granted his request that he should be transferred to Genoa. Here he remained till Italy entered the War, but then gave notice, and with his papers in perfect order crossed the border and took up his residence in Switzerland.

All this indicated a man of doubtful honesty and unsettled disposition, with no background and of no financial standing; but the facts were of no importance to anyone till it was discovered that Caypor, certainly from the beginning of the War and perhaps sooner, was in the service of the German Intelligence Department. He had a salary of forty pounds a month. But, though dangerous and wily, no steps would have been taken to deal with him if he had contented himself with transmitting such news as he was able to get in Switzerland. He could do no great harm there, and it

might even be possible to make use of him to convey information
that it was desirable to let the enemy have. He had no notion that
anything was known of him. His letters, and he received a good
many, were closely censored; there were few codes that the people
who dealt with such matters could not in the end decipher, and
it might be that sooner or later through him it would be possible
to lay hands on the organisation that still flourished in England.
But then he did something that drew R.'s attention to him. Had
he known it, none could have blamed him for shaking in his
shoes: R. was not a very nice man to get on the wrong side of.
Caypor scraped acquaintance in Zürich with a young Spaniard,
Gomez by name, who had lately entered the British Secret Service,
by his nationality inspired him with confidence, and managed to
worm out of him the fact that he was engaged in espionage.
Probably the Spaniard, with a very human desire to seem important, had done no more than talk mysteriously; but on Caypor's
information he was watched when he went to Germany, and one
day caught just as he was posting a letter in a code that was eventually deciphered. He was tried, convicted, and shot. It was bad
enough to lose a useful and disinterested agent, but it entailed besides the changing of a safe and simple code. R. was not pleased.
But R. was not the man to let any desire of revenge stand in the
way of his main object, and it occurred to him that if Caypor was
merely betraying his country for money it might be possible to get
him to take more money to betray his employers. The fact that
he had succeeded in delivering into their hands an agent of the
Allies must seem to them an earnest of his good faith. He might
be very useful. But R. had no notion what kind of man Caypor
was; he had lived his shabby, furtive life obscurely, and the only
photograph that existed of him was one taken for a passport.
Ashenden's instructions were to get acquainted with Caypor and

see whether there was any chance that he would work honestly for the British. If he thought there was, he was entitled to sound him, and if his suggestions were met with favour to make certain propositions. It was a task that needed tact and a knowledge of men. If, on the other hand, Ashenden came to the conclusion that Caypor could not be bought, he was to watch and report his movements. The information he had obtained from Gustav was vague but important; there was only one point in it that was interesting, and this was that the head of the German Intelligence Department in Berne was growing restive at Caypor's lack of activity. Caypor was asking for a higher salary, and Major von P. had told him that he must earn it. It might be that he was urging him to go to England. If he could be induced to cross the frontier Ashenden's work was done.

" How the devil do you expect *me* to persuade him to put his head in a noose?" asked Ashenden.

" It won't be a noose, it'll be a firing squad," said R.

" Caypor's clever."

" Well, be cleverer, damn your eyes!"

Ashenden made up his mind that he would take no steps to make Caypor's acquaintance, but allow the first advances to be made by him. If he was being pressed for results it must surely occur to him that it would be worth while to get into conversation with an Englishman who was employed in the Censorship Department. Ashenden was prepared with a supply of information that it could not in the least benefit the Central Powers to possess. With a false name and a false passport he had little fear that Caypor would guess that he was a British agent.

Ashenden did not have to wait long. Next day he was sitting in the doorway of the hotel, drinking a cup of coffee and already half asleep after a substantial *mittagessen,* when the Caypors came out of the dining-room. Mrs. Caypor went upstairs and Caypor released his dog. The dog bounded along and in a friendly fashion leaped up against Ashenden.

" Come here, Fritzi," cried Caypor, and then to Ashenden : " I'm so sorry. But he's quite gentle."

" Oh, that's all right. He won't hurt me."

Caypor stopped at the doorway.

" He's a bull-terrier. You don't often see them on the Continent." He seemed while he spoke to be taking Ashenden's measure; he called to the maid : " A coffee, please, fräulein. You've just arrived, haven't you?"

" Yes, I came yesterday."

" Really? I didn't see you in the dining-room last night. Are you making a stay?"

" I don't know. I've been ill, and I've come here to recuperate."

The maid came with the coffee, and, seeing Caypor talking to Ashenden, put the tray on the table at which he was sitting. Caypor gave a laugh of faint embarrassment.

" I don't want to force myself upon you. I don't know why the maid put my coffee on your table."

" Please sit down," said Ashenden.

" It's very good of you. I've lived so long on the Continent that I'm always forgetting that my countrymen are apt to look upon it as confounded cheek if you talk to them. Are you English, by the way, or American?"

" English," said Ashenden.

Ashenden was by nature a very shy person, and he had in vain tried to cure himself of a failing that at his age was unseemly, but on occasion he knew how to make effective use of it. He explained now, in a hesitating and awkward manner, the facts that he had the day before told the landlady and that he was convinced she had already passed on to Caypor.

"You couldn't have come to a better place than Lucerne. It's an oasis of peace in this war-weary world. When you're here you might almost forget that there is such a thing as a war going on. That is why I've come here. I'm a journalist by profession."

"I couldn't help wondering if you wrote," said Ashenden, with an eagerly timid smile.

It was clear that he had not learnt that "oasis of peace in a war-weary world" at the shipping office.

"You see, I married a German lady," said Caypor gravely.

"Oh, really?"

"I don't think anyone could be more patriotic than I am. I'm English through and through, and I don't mind telling you that in my opinion the British Empire is the greatest instrument for good that the world has ever seen; but having a German wife I naturally see a good deal of the reverse of the medal. You don't have to tell me that the Germans have faults, but, frankly, I'm not prepared to admit that they're devils incarnate. At the beginning of the War my poor wife had a very rough time in England, and I for one couldn't have blamed her if she'd felt rather bitter about it. Everyone thought she was a spy. It'll make you laugh when you know her. She's the typical German *hausfrau*, who cares for nothing but her house and her husband and our only child Fritzi." Caypor fondled his dog and gave a little laugh. "Yes, Fritzi, you are our child, aren't you? Naturally, it made my position very awkward. I was connected with some very important papers, and my editors weren't quite comfortable about it. Well, to cut a long story short I thought the most dignified course was to resign and come to a neutral country till the storm blew over. My wife and I never discuss the War, though I'm bound to tell you that it's more on my account than hers. She's much more tolerant than I am, and she's more willing to look upon this terrible business from my point of view than I am from hers."

"That is strange," said Ashenden. "As a rule women are so much more rabid than men."

"My wife is a very remarkable person. I should like to introduce you to her. By the way, I don't know if you know my name. Grantley Caypor."

"My name is Somerville," said Ashenden.

He told him then of the work he had been doing in the Censorship Department, and he fancied that into Caypor's eyes came a certain intentness. Presently he told him that he was looking for someone to give him conversation lessons in German, so that he might rub up his rusty knowledge of the language; and as he spoke a notion flashed across his mind. He gave Caypor a look, and saw that the same notion had come to him. It had occurred to them at the same instant that it would be a very good plan for Ashenden's teacher to be Mrs. Caypor.

"I asked our landlady if she could find me someone, and she said she thought she could. I must ask her again. It ought not to be very hard to find a man who is prepared to come and talk German to me for an hour a day."

"I wouldn't take anyone on the landlady's recommendation." said Caypor. "After all, you want someone with a good North-German accent, and she only talks Swiss. I'll ask my wife if she knows anyone. My wife's a very highly educated woman, and you could trust her recommendation."

"That's very kind of you."

Ashenden observed Grantley Caypor at his ease. He noticed how the small, grey-green eyes, which last night he had not been able to see, contradicted the red, good-humoured frankness of the face. They were quick and shifty, but when the mind behind them was seized by an unexpected notion they were suddenly still. It gave one a peculiar feeling of the working of the brain. They were not eyes that inspired confidence; Caypor did that with his jolly, good-natured smile, the openness of his broad, weather-beaten face, his comfortable obesity, and the cheeriness of his loud, deep voice. He was doing his best now to be agreeable. While Ashenden talked to him, a little shyly still but gaining confidence from that breezy, cordial manner, capable of putting anyone at his ease, it intrigued him to remember that the man was a common spy. It gave a tang to his conversation to reflect that he had been ready to sell his country for no more than forty pounds a month. Ashenden had known Gomez, the young Spaniard, whom Caypor had betrayed. He was a high-spirited youth, with a love of adventure, and he had undertaken his dangerous mission not for the money he earned by it but from a passion for romance. It amused him to outwit the clumsy German, and it appealed to his sense of the absurd to play a part in a shilling shocker. It was not very nice to think of him now, six feet underground in a prison yard. He was young and he had a certain grace of gesture. Ashenden wondered whether Caypor had felt a qualm when he delivered him up to destruction.

" I suppose you know a little German?" asked Caypor, interested in the stranger.

"Oh yes, I was a student in Germany, and I used to talk it fluently; but that is long ago, and I have forgotten. I can still read it comfortably."

" Oh yes, I noticed you were reading a German book last night."

Fool! It was only a little while since he had told Ashenden that he had not seen him at dinner. He wondered whether Caypor had observed the slip. How difficult it was never to make one! Ashenden must be on his guard; the thing that made him most nervous was the thought that he might not answer readily enough to his assumed name of Somerville. Of course, there was always the chance that Caypor had made the slip on purpose to see by Ashenden's face whether he noticed anything. Caypor got up.

" There is my wife. We go for a walk up one of the mountains every afternoon. I can tell you some charming walks. The flowers even now are lovely."

" I'm afraid I must wait till I'm a bit stronger," said Ashenden with a little sigh.

He had naturally a pale face and never looked as robust as he was. Mrs. Caypor came downstairs and her husband joined her. They walked down the road, Fritzi bounding round them, and Ashenden saw that Caypor immediately began to speak with volubility. He was evidently telling his wife the results of his interview with Ashenden. Ashenden looked at the sun shining so gaily on the lake; the shadow of a breeze fluttered the green leaves of the trees; everything invited to a stroll. He got up, went to his room, and, throwing himself on his bed, had a very pleasant sleep.

He went into dinner that evening as the Caypors were finishing, for he had wandered melancholy about Lucerne in the hope of finding a cocktail that would enable him to face the potato salad that he foresaw, and on their way out of the dining-room Caypor stopped and asked him if he would drink coffee with them. When Ashenden joined them in the hall, Caypor got up and introduced him to his wife. She bowed stiffly, and no answering smile came to her face to respond to Ashenden's civil greeting. It was not hard to see that her attitude was definitely hostile. It put Ashenden at his ease. She was a plainish woman, nearing forty, with a muddy skin and vague features; her drab hair was arranged in a plait round her head like that of Napoleon's Queen of Prussia, and she was squarely built, plump rather than fat, and solid. But she did not look stupid; she looked, on the contrary, a woman of character, and Ashenden, who had lived enough in Germany to recognise the type, was ready to believe that though capable of doing the housework, cooking the dinner, and climbing a mountain, she might be also prodigiously well informed. She wore a white blouse that showed a sunburned neck, a black skirt, and heavy walking boots. Caypor, addressing her in English, told her in his jovial way, as though she did not know it already, what Ashenden had told him about himself. She listened grimly.

"I think you told me you understood German," said Caypor, his big red face wreathed in polite smiles but his little eyes darting about restlessly.

"Yes, I was for some time a student in Heidelberg."

"Really?" said Mrs. Caypor in English, an expression of faint interest for a moment chasing away the sullenness from her face. "I know Heidelberg very well. I was at school there for one year."

Her English was correct but throaty, and the mouthing emphasis she gave her words was disagreeable. Ashenden was diffuse in praise of the old university town and the beauty of the neighbourhood. She heard him, from the standpoint of her Teutonic superiority, with toleration rather than with enthusiasm.

"It is well known that the valley of the Neckar is one of the beauty places of the whole world," she said.

"I have not told you, my dear," said Caypor then, "that Mr. Somerville is looking for someone to give him conversation lessons while he is here. I told him that perhaps you could suggest a teacher."

"No, I know no one whom I could conscientiously recommend," she answered. "The Swiss accent is hateful beyond words. It could do Mr. Somerville only harm to converse with a Swiss."

"If I were in your place, Mr. Somerville, I would try and persuade my wife to give you lessons. She is, if I may say so, a very cultivated and highly educated woman."

"*Ach*, Grantley, I have not the time. I have my own work to do."

Ashenden saw that he was being given his opportunity. The trap was prepared, and all he had to do was to fall in. He turned to Mrs. Caypor with a manner that he tried to make shy, deprecating, and modest.

"Of course, it would be too wonderful if you would give me lessons. I should look upon it as a real privilege. Naturally, I wouldn't want to interfere with your work. I am just here to get well, with nothing in the world to do, and I would suit my time entirely to your convenience."

He felt a flash of satisfaction pass from one to the other, and in Mrs. Caypor's blue eyes he fancied that he saw a dark glow.

"Of course, it would be a purely business arrangement," said Caypor. "There's no reason that my good wife shouldn't earn a little pin-money. Would you think ten francs an hour too much?"

"No," said Ashenden, "I should think myself lucky to get a first-rate teacher for that."

"What do you say, my dear? Surely you can spare an hour, and you would be doing this gentleman a kindness. He would learn that all Germans are not the devilish fiends that they think them in England."

On Mrs. Caypor's brow was an uneasy frown, and Ashenden could not but think with apprehension of that hour's conversation a day that he was going to exchange with her. Heaven only knew how he would have to rack his brain for subjects of discourse with that heavy and morose woman. Now she made a visible effort.

"I shall be very pleased to give Mr. Somerville conversation lessons."

"I congratulate you, Mr. Somerville," said Caypor noisily. "You're in for a treat. When will you start—to-morrow at eleven?"

"That would suit me very well if it suits Mrs. Caypor."

"Yes, that is as good an hour as another," she answered.

Ashenden left them to discuss the happy outcome of their diplomacy. But when, punctually at eleven next morning, he heard a knock at his door (for it had been arranged that Mrs. Caypor should give him his lesson in his room), it was not without trepidation that he opened it. It behoved him to be frank, a trifle indiscreet, but obviously wary of a German woman, sufficiently intelligent and impulsive. Mrs. Caypor's face was dark and sulky. She plainly hated having anything to do with him. But they sat down, and she began, somewhat peremptorily, to ask him questions about his knowledge of German literature. She corrected his mistakes with exactness, and when he put before her some difficulty in German construction explained it with clearness and precision. It was obvious that though she hated giving him a lesson she meant to give it conscientiously. She seemed to have not only an aptitude for teaching but a love of it, and as the hour went on she began to speak with greater earnestness. It was already only by an effort that she remembered that he was a brutal Englishman. Ashenden, noticing the unconscious struggle within her, found himself not a little entertained; and it was with truth that, when later in the day Caypor asked him how the lesson had gone, he answered that it was highly satisfactory. Mrs. Caypor was an excellent teacher and a most interesting person.

"I told you so. She's the most remarkable woman I know."

And Ashenden had a feeling that when in his hearty, laughing way Caypor said this he was for the first time entirely sincere.

In a day or two Ashenden guessed that Mrs. Caypor was giving him lessons only in order to enable Caypor to arrive at a closer intimacy with him, for she confined herself strictly to matters of literature, music, and painting; and when Ashenden, by way of experiment, brought the conversation round to the War, she cut him short.

"I think that is a topic that we had better avoid, Herr Somerville," she said.

She continued to give her lessons with the greatest thoroughness, and he had his money's worth; but every day she came with the same sullen face, and it was only in the interest of teaching that she lost for a moment her instinctive dislike of him. Ashenden exercised in turn, but in vain, all his wiles. He was ingratiating, ingenious, humble, grateful, flattering, simple, and timid. She remained coldly hostile. She was a fanatic. Her patriotism was aggressive but disinterested, and, obsessed with the notion of the superiority of all things German, she loathed England with a virulent hatred because in that country she saw the chief obstacle to their diffusion. Her ideal was a German world, in which the rest of the nations, under a hegemony greater than that of Rome, should enjoy the benefits of German science and German art and German culture. There was in the conception a magnificent impudence that appealed to Ashenden's sense of humour. She was no fool. She had read much in several languages, and she could talk of the books she had read with good sense. She had a knowledge of modern painting and modern music that not a little impressed Ashenden. It was amusing once to hear her before luncheon play one of those silvery little pieces of Debussy; she played it disdainfully because it was French and so light, but with an angry appreciation of its grace and gaiety. When Ashenden congratulated her she shrugged her shoulders.

"The decadent music of a decadent nation," she said. Then, with powerful hands, she struck the first resounding chords of a sonata by Beethoven; but she stopped. "I cannot play, I am out of practice; and you English, what do you know of music? You have not produced a composer since Purcell."

"What do you think of that statement?" Ashenden asked Caypor, who was standing near.

"I confess its truth. The little I know of music my wife taught me. I wish you could hear her play when she is in practice." He put his fat hand, with its square, stumpy fingers on her shoulder. "She can wring your heart-strings with pure beauty."

"*Dummer Kerl* (Stupid fellow)," she said in a soft voice; and Ashenden saw her mouth for a moment quiver, but she quickly recovered. "You English, you cannot paint, you cannot model, you cannot write music."

"Some of us can at times write pleasing verses," said Ashenden with good humour, for it was not his business to be put out, and—he did not know why—two lines occurring to him, he said them:

"Whither, O splendid ship, thy white sails crowding,
Leaning across the bosom of the urgent West?"

"Yes," said Mrs. Caypor, with a strange gesture, "you can write poetry. I wonder why?"

And to Ashenden's surprise she went on, in her guttural English, to recite the next two lines of the poem he had quoted.

"Come, Grantley, *mittagessen* is ready; let us go into the dining-room."

They left Ashenden reflective.

Ashenden admired goodness, but was not outraged by wickedness. People sometimes thought him heartless because he was more often interested in others than attached to them, and even in the few to whom he was attached his eyes saw with equal clearness the merits and the defects. When he liked people it was not because he was blind to their faults—he did not mind their faults

—but accepted them with a tolerant shrug of the shoulders, or because he ascribed to them excellencies that they did not possess; and since he judged his friends with candour they never disappointed him, and he seldom lost one. He asked from none more than he could give. He was able to pursue his study of the Caypors without prejudice and without passion. Mrs. Caypor seemed to him more of a piece, and therefore the easier of the two to understand; she obviously detested him. Though it was so necessary for her to be civil to him her antipathy was strong enough to wring from her now and then an expression of rudeness; and had she been safely able to do so she would have killed him without a qualm. But in the pressure of Caypor's chubby hand on his wife's shoulder and in the fugitive trembling of her lips Ashenden had divined that this unprepossessing woman and that mean, fat man were joined together by a deep and sincere love. It was touching. Ashenden assembled the observations that he had been making for the past few days, and little things that he had noticed but to which he had attached no significance returned to him. It seemed to him that Mrs. Caypor loved her husband because she was of a stronger character than he and because she felt his dependence on her; she loved him for his admiration of her, and you might guess that till she met him this dumpy, plain woman with her dulness, good sense, and want of humour could not have much enjoyed the admiration of men. She enjoyed his heartiness and his noisy jokes, and his high spirits stirred her sluggish blood; he was a great big bouncing boy, and he would never be anything else, and she felt like a mother towards him. She had made him what he was, and he was her man and she was his woman, and she loved him, notwithstanding his weakness (for with her clear head she must always have been conscious of that); she loved him, *ach, was,* as Isolde loved Tristan. But then there was the espionage. Even

Ashenden, with all his tolerance for human frailty, could not but feel that to betray your country for money is not a very pretty proceeding. Of course, she knew of it—indeed, it was probably through her that Caypor had first been approached; he would never have undertaken such work if she had not urged him to it. She loved him, and she was an honest and an upright woman. By what devious means had she persuaded herself to force her husband to adopt so base and dishonourable a calling? Ashenden lost himself in a labyrinth of conjecture as he tried to piece together the actions of her mind.

Grantley Caypor was another story. There was little to admire in him, but at that moment Ashenden was not looking for an object of admiration; but there was much that was singular and much that was unexpected in that gross and vulgar fellow. Ashenden watched with entertainment the suave manner in which the spy tried to inveigle him in his toils. It was a couple of days after his first lesson that Caypor after dinner, his wife having gone upstairs, threw himself heavily into a chair by Ashenden's side. His faithful Fritzi came up to him and put his long muzzle with its black nose on his knee.

" He has no brain," said Caypor, " but a heart of gold. Look at those little pink eyes. Did you ever see anything so stupid? And what an ugly face, but what incredible charm! "

" Have you had him long?" asked Ashenden.

" I got him in 1914, just before the outbreak of war. By the way, what do you think of the news to-day? Of course, my wife and I never discuss the War. You can't think what a relief to me it is to find a fellow-countryman to whom I can open my heart."

He handed Ashenden a cheap Swiss cigar, and Ashenden making a rueful sacrifice to duty, accepted it.

" Of course, they haven't got a chance, the Germans," said Caypor—"not a dog's chance. I knew they were beaten the moment we came in."

His manner was earnest, sincere, and confidential. Ashenden made a commonplace rejoinder.

"It's the greatest grief of my life that, owing to my wife's nationality, I was unable to do any war work. I tried to enlist the day war broke out, but they wouldn't have me on account of my age; but I don't mind telling you, if the War goes on much longer, wife or no wife, I'm going to do something. With my knowledge of languages I ought to be of some service in the Censorship Department. That's where you were, wasn't it?"

That was the mark at which he had been aiming, and in answer now to his well-directed questions Ashenden gave him the information that he had already prepared. Caypor drew his chair a little nearer and dropped his voice.

"I'm sure you wouldn't tell me anything that anyone shouldn't know, but after all, these Swiss are absolutely pro-German, and we don't want to give anyone the chance of overhearing."

Then he went on another tack. He told Ashenden a number of things that were of a certain secrecy.

"I wouldn't tell this to anybody else, you know, but I have one or two friends who are in pretty influential positions, and they know they can trust me."

Thus encouraged, Ashenden was a little more deliberately indiscreet, and when they parted both had reason to be satisfied. Ashenden guessed that Caypor's typewriter would be kept busy next morning and that that extremely energetic Major in Berne would shortly receive a most interesting report.

One evening, going upstairs after dinner, Ashenden passed an open bath-room. He caught sight of the Caypors.

"Come in," cried Caypor in his cordial way. "We're washing

our Fritzi."

The bull-terrier was constantly getting himself very dirty, and it was Caypor's pride to see him clean and white. Ashenden went in. Mrs. Caypor, with her sleeves turned up and a large white apron, was standing at one end of the bath, while Caypor, in a pair of trousers and a singlet, his fat, freckled arms bare, was soaping the wretched hound.

"We have to do it at night," he said, "because the Fitzgeralds use this bath, and they'd have a fit if they knew we washed the dog in it. We wait till they go to bed. Come along, Fritzi; show the gentlemen how beautifully you behave when you have your face scrubbed."

The poor brute, woebegone but faintly wagging his tail to show that however foul was this operation performed on him he bore no malice to the god who did it, was standing in the middle of the bath in six inches of water. He was soaped all over, and Caypor, talking the while, shampooed him with his great fat hands.

"Oh, what a beautiful dog he's going to be when he's as white as the driven snow! His master will be as proud as Punch to walk out with him, and all the little lady dogs will say : 'Good gracious! who's that beautiful aristocratic-looking bull-terrier, walking as though he owned the whole of Switzerland?' Now stand still while you have your ears washed. You couldn't bear to go out into the street with dirty ears, could you? Like a nasty little Swiss schoolboy? *Noblesse oblige*. Now the black nose. Oh, and all the soap is going into his little pink eyes and they'll smart."

Mrs. Caypor listened to this nonsense with a good-humoured, sluggish smile on her broad, plain face, and presently gravely took a towel.

"Now he's going to have a ducking. Upsie-daisy."

Caypor seized the dog by the fore-legs and ducked him once and ducked him twice. There was a struggle, a flurry, and a splashing. Caypor lifted him out of the bath.

"Now go to mother and she'll dry you."

Mrs. Caypor sat down and, taking the dog between her strong legs, rubbed him till the sweat poured off her forehead. And Fritzi a little shaken and breathless, but happy it was all over, with his sweet, stupid face, white and shining.

"Blood will tell," cried Caypor exultantly. "He knows the names of no less than sixty-four of his ancestors, and they were all nobly born."

Ashenden was faintly troubled. He shivered a little as he walked upstairs.

Then, one Sunday, Caypor told him that he and his wife were going on an excursion and would eat their luncheon at some little mountain restaurant; and he suggested that Ashenden, each paying his share, should come with them. After three weeks at Lucerne, Ashenden thought that his strength would permit him to venture the exertion. They started early, Mrs. Caypor businesslike in her walking boots and Tyrolese hat and alpenstock, and Caypor in stockings and plus-fours, looking very British. The situation amused Ashenden, and he was prepared to enjoy his day. But he meant to keep his eyes open; it was not inconceivable that the Caypors had discovered what he was, and it would not do to go too near a precipice. Mrs. Caypor would not hesitate to give him a push, and Caypor, for all his jolliness, was an ugly customer. But on the face of it there was nothing to mar Ashenden's pleasure in the golden morning. The air was fragrant. Caypor was full of conversation. He told funny stories. He was gay and jovial. The sweat rolled off his great red face, and he laughed at himself because he was so fat. To Ashenden's astonishment he showed a peculiar knowledge of the mountain flowers. Once he went out of the way to pick one he saw a little distance from the path and brought it back to his wife. He looked at it tenderly.

"Isn't it lovely?" he cried, and his shifty, grey-green eyes for a moment were as candid as a child's. "It's like a poem by Walter Savage Landor."

"Botany is my husband's favourite science," said Mrs. Caypor. "I laugh at him sometimes. He is devoted to flowers. Often when we have hardly had enough money to pay the butcher he has spent everything in his pocket to bring me a bunch of roses."

"*Qui fleurit sa maison fleurit son cœur*," said Grantley Caypor.

Ashenden had once or twice seen Caypor, coming in from a walk, offer Mrs. Fitzgerald a nosegay of mountain flowers with an elephantine courtesy that was not entirely displeasing; and what he had just learned added a certain significance to the pretty little action. His passion for flowers was genuine, and when he gave them to the old Irish lady he gave her something he valued. It showed a real kindness of heart. Ashenden had always thought botany a tedious science, but Caypor, talking exuberantly as they walked along, was able to impart to it life and interest. He must have given it a good deal of study.

"I've never written a book," he said. "There are too many books already, and any desire to write I have is satisfied by the more immediately profitable and quite ephemeral composition of an article for a daily paper. But if I stay here much longer I have half a mind to write a book about the wild flowers of Switzerland. Oh, I wish you'd been here a little earlier. They were marvellous. But one wants to be a poet for that, and I'm only a poor newspaper man."

It was curious to observe how he was able to combine real emotion with false fact.

When they reached the inn, with its view of the mountains and the lake, it was good to see the sensual pleasure with which he poured down his throat a bottle of ice-cold beer. You could not but feel sympathy for a man who took so much delight in simple things. They lunched deliciously off scrambled eggs and mountain trout. Even Mrs. Caypor was moved to an unwonted gentleness by her surroundings—the inn was in an agreeably rural spot; it looked like a picture of a Swiss châlet in a book of early nineteenth-century travels—and she treated Ashenden with something less than her usual hostility. When they arrived she had burst into loud German exclamations on the beauty of the scene, and now, softened perhaps, too, by food and drink, her eyes, dwelling on the grandeur before her, filled with tears. She stretched out her hand.

"It is dreadful and I am ashamed; notwithstanding this horrible and unjust war I can feel in my heart at the moment nothing but happiness and gratitude."

Caypor took her by the hand and pressed it, and, an unusual thing with him, addressing her in German, called her little pet-names. It was absurd. but touching. Ashenden, leaving them to their emotions, strolled through the garden and sat down on a bench that had been prepared for the comfort of the tourist. The view was, of course, spectacular, but it captured you; it was like a piece of music that was obvious and meretricious, but for the moment shattered your self-control.

And as Ashenden lingered idly in that spot he pondered over the mystery of Grantley Caypor's treachery. If he liked strange people he had found in him one who was strange beyond belief. It would be foolish to deny that he had amiable traits. His joviality was not assumed, he was without pretence a hearty fellow, and he had real good nature. He was always ready to do a kindness. Ashenden had often watched him with the old Irish Colonel and his wife, who were the only other residents of the hotel; he would listen good-humouredly to the old man's tedious stories of the Egyptian war, and he was charming with her. Now that Ashenden had arrived at terms of some familiarity with Caypor he found that he regarded him less with repulsion than with curiosity. He did not think that he had become a spy merely for the money; he was a man of modest tastes, and what he had earned in a shipping office must have sufficed to so good a manager as Mrs. Caypor, and after war was declared there was no lack of remunerative work for men over the military age. It might be that he was one of those men who prefer devious ways to straight for some intricate pleasure they get in fooling their fellows; and that he had turned spy, not from hatred of the country that had imprisoned him, not even from love of his wife, but from a desire to score off the big-wigs who never even knew of his existence. It might be that it was vanity that impelled him, a feeling that his talents had not received the recognition they merited, or just a puckish, impish desire to do mischief. He was a crook. It is true that only two cases of dishonesty had been brought home to him, but if he had been caught twice it might be surmised that he had often been dishonest without being caught. What did Mrs. Caypor think of this? They were so united that she must be aware of it. Did it make her ashamed, for her own uprightness surely none could doubt, or did she accept it as an inevitable kink in the man she loved? Did she do all she could to prevent it or did she close her eyes to something she could not help?

How much easier life would be if people were all black or all white, and how much simpler it would be to act in regard to them! Was Caypor a good man who loved evil, or a bad man who loved good? And how could such unreconcilable elements exist side by side and in harmony within the same heart? For one thing was clear: Caypor was disturbed by no gnawing of conscience; he did his mean and despicable work with gusto. He was a traitor who enjoyed his treachery. Though Ashenden had been studying human nature more or less consciously all his life, it seemed to him that he knew as little about it now in middle age as he had done when he was a child. Of course, R. would have said to him: "Why the devil do you waste your time with such nonsense? The man's a dangerous spy, and your business is to lay him by the heels."

That was true enough. Ashenden had decided that it would be useless to attempt to make any arrangement with Caypor. Though doubtless he would have no feeling about betraying his employers, he could certainly not be trusted. His wife's influence was too strong. Besides, notwithstanding what he had from time to time told Ashenden, he was in his heart convinced that the Central Powers must win the War, and he meant to be on the winning side. Well, then Caypor must be laid by the heels, but how he was to effect that Ashenden had no notion. Suddenly he heard a voice.

"There you are. We've been wondering where you had hidden yourself."

He looked round and saw the Caypors strolling towards him. They were walking hand-in-hand.

"So this is what has kept you quiet," said Caypor as his eyes fell on the view. "What a spot!"

Mrs. Caypor clasped her hands.

"*Ach Gott, wie schön!*" she cried. "*Wie schön.* When I look at that blue lake and those snowy mountains I feel inclined, like Goethe's Faust, to cry to the passing moment: Tarry."

"This is better than being in England with the excursions and alarums of war, isn't it?" said Caypor.

"Much," said Ashenden.

"By the way, did you have any difficulty in getting out?"

"No, not the smallest."

"I'm told they make rather a nuisance of themselves at the frontier nowadays."

"I came through without the smallest difficulty. I don't fancy they bother much about the English. I thought the examination of passports was quite perfunctory."

A fleeting glance passed between Caypor and his wife. Ashenden wondered what it meant. It would be strange if Caypor's thoughts were occupied with the chances of a journey to England at the very moment when he was himself reflecting on its possibility. In a little while Mrs. Caypor suggested that they had better be starting back, and they wandered together in the shade of the trees down the mountain paths.

Ashenden was watchful. He could do nothing (and his inactivity irked him) but wait with his eyes open to seize the opportunity that might present itself. A couple of days later an incident occurred that made him certain something was in the wind. In the course of his morning lesson Mrs. Caypor remarked:

"My husband has gone to Geneva to-day. He had some business to do there."

"Oh," said Ashenden, "will he be gone long?"

"No, only two days."

It is not everyone who can tell a lie, and Ashenden had the feeling, he hardly knew why, that Mrs. Caypor was telling one then. Her manner, perhaps, was not quite as indifferent as you would have expected when she was mentioning a fact that could be of no interest to Ashenden. It flashed across his mind that Caypor had been summoned to Berne to see the redoubtable head of the German Secret Service. When he had the chance he said casually to the waitress:

"A little less work for you to do, fräulein. I hear that Herr Caypor has gone to Berne."

"Yes. But he'll be back to-morrow."

That proved nothing, but it was something to go upon. Ashenden knew in Lucerne a Swiss who was willing on emergency to do odd jobs, and, looking him up, asked him to take a letter to Berne. It might be possible to pick up Caypor and trace his move-ments. Next day Caypor appeared once more with his wife at the dinner-table, but merely nodded to Ashenden, and afterwards both went straight upstairs. They looked troubled. Caypor, as a rule so animated, walked with bowed shoulders, and looked neither to the right nor to the left. Next morning Ashenden received a reply to his letter. Caypor had seen Major von P. It was possible to guess what the Major had said to him. Ashenden well knew how rough he could be; he was a hard man and brutal, clever, and unscrupu-lous, and he was not accustomed to mince his words. They were tired of paying Caypor a salary to sit still in Lucerne and do noth-ing; the time was come for him to go to England. Guesswork? Of course it was guesswork, but in that trade it mostly was : you had to deduce the animal from its jaw-bone. Ashenden knew from Gustav that the Germans wanted to send someone to England. He drew a long breath; if Caypor went he would have to get busy.

When Mrs. Caypor came into give him his lesson she was dull and listless. She looked tired, and her mouth was set obstinately. It occurred to Ashenden that the Caypors had spent most of the night talking. He wished he knew what they had said. Did she urge him to go or did she try to dissuade him? Ashenden watched them again at luncheon. Something was the matter, for they hard-ly spoke to one another, and as a rule they found plenty to talk about. They left the room early, but when Ashenden went out he saw Caypor sitting in the hall by himself.

"Hulloa!" he cried jovially, but surely the effort was patent, "how are you getting on? I've been to Geneva."

"So I heard," said Ashenden.

"Come and have your coffee with me. My poor wife's got a headache. I told her she'd better go and lie down."

In his shifty green eyes was an expression that Ashenden could not read. "The fact is, she's rather worried, poor dear; I'm thinking of going to England."

Ashenden's heart gave a sudden leap against his ribs, but his face remained impassive.

"Oh, are you going for long? We shall miss you."

"To tell you the truth, I'm fed up with doing nothing. The War looks as though it were going on for years, and I can't sit here indefinitely. Besides, I can't afford it. I've got to earn my living. I may have a German wife, but I am an Englishman, hang it all! and I want to do my bit. I could never face my friends again if I just stayed here in ease and comfort till the end of the War and never attempted to do a thing to help the country. My wife takes her German point of view, and I don't mind telling you that she's a bit upset. You know what women are."

Now Ashenden knew what it was that he saw in Caypor's eyes. Fear. It gave him a nasty turn. Caypor didn't want to go to England, he wanted to stay safely in Switzerland; Ashenden knew now what the Major had said to him when he went to see him in Berne. He had got to go or lose his salary. What was it that his wife had said when he told her what had happened? He had wanted her to press him to stay, but it was plain she hadn't done that; perhaps he had not dared to tell her how frightened he was. To her he had always been gay, bold, adventurous, and devil-may-care; and now, the prisoner of his own lies, he had not found it in him to confess himself the mean and sneaking coward he was.

"Are you going to take your wife with you?" asked Ashenden.

"No, she'll stay here."

It had been arranged very neatly. Mrs. Caypor would receive his letters and forward the information they contained to Berne.

"I've been out of England so long that I don't quite know how to set about getting war work. What would you do in my place?"

"I don't know; what sort of work are you thinking of?"

"Well, you know, I imagine I could do the same thing as you did. I wonder if there's anyone in the Censorship Department that you could give me a letter of introduction to."

It was only by a miracle that Ashenden saved himself from showing by a smothered cry or by a broken gesture how startled he was; but not by Caypor's request, by what had just dawned upon him. What an idiot he had been! He had been disturbed by the thought that he was wasting his time at Lucerne; he was doing nothing, and though, in fact, as it turned out, Caypor was going to England, it was due to no cleverness of his. He could take to himself no credit for the result. And now he saw that he had been put in Lucerne, told how to describe himself and given the proper information, so that what actually had occurred should occur. It would be a wonderful thing for the German Secret Service to get an agent into the Censorship Department; and by a happy accident there was Grantley Caypor, the very man for the job, on friendly terms with someone who had worked there. What a bit of luck! Major von P. was a man of culture and, rubbing his hands, he must surely have murmured : *stultum facit fortuna quem vult perdere*. It was a trap of that devilish R., and the grim Major at Berne had fallen into it. Ashenden had done his work just by sitting still and doing nothing. He almost laughed as he thought what a fool R. had made of him.

"I was on very good terms with the chief of my department. I could give you a note to him if you liked."

"That would be just the thing."

" But, of course, I must give the facts. I must say I've met you here and only known you a fortnight."

"Of course. But you'll say what else you can for me, won't you?"

"Oh, certainly."

"I don't know yet if I can get a visa. I'm told they're rather fussy."

"I don't see why. I shall be very sick if they refuse me one when I want to go back."

"I'll go and see how my wife is getting on," said Caypor suddenly, getting up. "When will you let me have that letter?"

"Whenever you like. Are you going at once?"

"As soon as possible."

Caypor left him. Ashenden waited in the hall for a quarter of an hour so that there should appear in him no sign of hurry. Then he went upstairs and prepared various communications. In one he informed R. that Caypor was going to England; in another he made arrangements through Berne that wherever Caypor applied for a visa it should be granted to him without question; and these he despatched forthwith. When he went down to dinner he handed to Caypor a cordial letter of introduction.

Next day but one Caypor left Lucerne.

Ashenden waited. He continued to have his hour's lesson with Mrs. Caypor, and under her conscientious tuition began now to speak German with ease. They talked of Goethe and Winckelmann, of art and life and travel. Fritzi sat quietly by her chair.

" He misses his master," she said, pulling his ears. " He only really cares for him, he suffers me only as belonging to him."

After his lesson Ashenden went every morning to Cook's to ask for his letters. It was here that all communications were addressed to him. He could not move till he received instructions, but R. could be trusted not to leave him idle long; and meanwhile there was nothing for him to do but have patience. Presently he received a letter from the consul in Geneva to say that Caypor had there applied for his visa and had set out for France. Having read this, Ashenden went on for a little stroll by the lake, and on his way back happened to see Mrs. Caypor coming out of Cook's office. He guessed that she was having her letters addressed there too. He went up to her.

"Have you had news of Herr Caypor?" he asked her.

"No," she said. "I suppose I could hardly expect to yet."

He walked along by her side. She was disappointed, but not yet anxious; she knew how irregular was the post. But next day during the lesson he could not but see that she was impatient to have done with it. The post was delivered at noon, and at five minutes to she looked at her watch and him. Though Ashenden knew very well that no letter would ever come for her, he had not the heart to keep her on tenterhooks.

"Don't you think that's enough for the day? I'm sure you want to go down to Cook's," he said.

"Thank you. That is very amiable of you."

When a little later he went there himself he found her standing in the middle of the office. Her face was distraught. She addressed him wildly:

"My husband promised to write from Paris. I am sure there is a letter for me, but these stupid people say there's nothing. They're so careless; it's a scandal."

Ashenden did not know what to say. While the clerk was looking through the bundle to see if there was anything for him she came up to the desk again.

"When does the next post come in from France?" she asked.

"Sometimes there are letters about five."

" I'll come then."

She turned and walked rapidly away. Fritzi followed her with his tail between his legs. There was no doubt of it; already the fear had seized her that something was wrong. Next morning she looked dreadful; she could not have closed her eyes all night; and in the lesson she started up from her chair.

"You must excuse me, Herr Somerville, I cannot give you a lesson to-day. I am not feeling well."

Before Ashenden could say anything she had flung herself nervously from the room, and in the evening he got a note from her to say that she regretted that she must discontinue giving him conversation lessons. She gave no reason. Then Ashenden saw no more of her; she ceased coming in to meals; except to go morning and afternoon to Cook's she spent apparently the whole day in her room. Ashenden thought of her sitting there hour after hour with that hideous fear gnawing at her heart. Who could help feeling sorry for her? The time hung heavy on his hands too. He read a good deal and wrote a little, he hired a canoe and went for long leisurely paddles on the lake; and at last one morning the clerk at Cook's handed him a letter. It was from R. It had all the appearance of a business communication, but between the lines he read a good deal.

" Dear Sir (it began),

"The goods, with accompanying letter, despatched by you from Lucerne have been duly delivered. We are obliged to you for executing our instructions with such promptness."

It went on in this strain. R. was exultant. Ashenden guessed that Caypor had been arrested, and by now had paid the penalty of his crime. He shuddered. He remembered a dreadful scene. Dawn. A cold, grey dawn, with a drizzling rain falling. A man, blindfolded, standing against a wall, an officer, very pale, giving an order, a volley, and then a young soldier, one of the firing-party, turning round and holding on to his gun for support, vomiting. The officer turned paler still, and he, Ashenden, feeling dreadfully faint. How terrified Caypor must have been! It was awful when the tears ran down their faces. Ashenden shook himself. He went to the ticket-office and, obedient to his orders, bought himself a ticket for Geneva.

As he was waiting for his change Mrs. Caypor came in. He was shocked at the sight of her. She was blowsy and dishevelled, and there were heavy rings round her eyes. She was deathly pale. She staggered up to the desk and asked for a letter. The clerk shook his head.

"I'm sorry, madam, there's nothing yet."

"But look, look! Are you sure? Please look again."

The misery in her voice was heartrending. The clerk, with a shrug of the shoulders, took out the letters from a pigeon-hole and sorted them once more.

"No, there's nothing, madam."

She gave a hoarse cry of despair, and her face was distorted with anguish.

"Oh, God! oh, God!" she moaned.

She turned away, the tears streaming from her weary eyes, and for a moment she stood there like a blind man groping and not knowing which way to go. Then a fearful thing happened. Fritzi, the bull-terrier, sat down on his haunches and threw back his head and gave a long, long melancholy howl. Mrs. Caypor looked at him with terror; her eyes seemed really to start from her head. The doubt, the gnawing doubt that had tortured her during those dreadful days of suspense, was a doubt no longer. She knew. She staggered blindly into the street.

CAIN'S ATONEMENT

by
Algernon Blackwood

SO many thousands to-day have deliberately put Self aside, and
are ready to yield their lives for an ideal, that it is not surprising a few of them should have registered experiences of a novel
order. For to step aside from Self is to enter a larger world, to be
open to new impressions. If Powers of Good exist in the universe
at all, they can hardly be inactive at the present time. . . .

The case of two men, who may be called Jones and Smith,
occurs to the mind in this connection. Whether a veil actually
was lifted for a moment, or whether the tension of long and terrible months resulted in an exaltation of emotion, the experience
claims significance. Smith, to whom the experience came, held
the firm belief that it was real. Jones, though it involved him too,
remained unaware.

It is a somewhat personal story, their peculiar relationship dating from early youth; a kind of unwilling antipathy was born between them, yet an antipathy that had no touch of hate or even
of dislike. It was rather in the nature of an instinctive rivalry.
Some tie operated that flung them ever into the same arena with
strange persistence, and ever as opponents. An inevitable Fate delighted to throw them together in a sense that made them rivals;
small as well as large affairs betrayed this malicious tendency of
the gods. It showed itself in earliest days, at school, at Cambridge,
in travel, even in house-parties and the lighter social intercourse.
Though distant cousins, their families were not intimate, and
there was no obvious reason why their paths should fall so persistently together. Yet their paths did so, crossing and recrossing
in the way described. Sooner or later, in all his undertakings,

Smith would note the shadow of Jones darkening the ground of him; and later, when called to the Bar in his chosen profession, he found most frequently that the learned counsel in opposition to him was the owner of this shadow, Jones. In another matter, too, they became rivals, for the same girl, oddly enough, attracted both, and though she accepted neither offer of marriage (during Smith's lifetime!), the attitude between them was that of unwilling rivals. For they were friends as well.

Jones, it appears, was hardly aware that any rivalry existed; he did not think of Smith as an opponent, and as an adversary, never. He did notice, however, the constantly recurring meetings, for more than once he commented on them with good-humoured amusement. Smith, on the other hand, was conscious of a depth and strength in the tie that certainly intrigued him; being of a thoughtful, introspective nature, he was keenly sensible of the strange competition in their lives, and sought in various ways for its explanation, though without success. The desire to find out was very strong in him. And this was natural enough, owing to the singular fact that in all their battles he was the one to lose. Invariably Jones got the best of every conflict. Smith always paid; sometimes he paid with interest.

Occasionally, too, he seemed forced to injure himself while contributing to his cousin's success. It was very curious. He reflected much upon it; he wondered what the origin of their tie and rivalry might be, but especially why it was that he invariably lost, and why he was so often obliged to help his rival to the point even of his own detriment. Tempted to bitterness sometimes, he did not yield to it, however; the relationship remained frank and pleasant—if anything, it deepened.

He remembered once, for instance, giving his cousin a chance introduction which yet led, a little later, to the third party offering certain evidence which lost him an important case—Jones, of course, winning it. The third party, too, angry at being dragged into the case, turned hostile to him, thwarting various subsequent projects. In no other way could Jones have procured this particular evidence; he did not know of its existence even. That chance introduction did it all. There was nothing the least dishonourable on the part of Jones—it was just the chance of the dice. The dice were always loaded against Smith—and there were other instances of a similar kind.

About this time, moreover, a singular feeling, that had lain vaguely in his mind for some years past, took more definite form. It suddenly assumed the character of a conviction that yet had no evidence to support it. A voice, long whispering in the depths of him, became much louder, grew into a statement that he accepted without further ado : " I'm paying off a debt," he phrased it; " an old, old debt is being discharged. I owe him this—my help and so forth." He accepted it, that is, as just; and this certainty of justice kept sweet his heart and mind, shutting the door on bitterness or envy. The thought, however, though it recurred persistently with each encounter, brought no explanation.

When the war broke out both offered their services : as members of the O.T.C. they got commissions quickly, but it was a chance remark of Smith's that made his friend join the very regiment he himself was in. They trained together, were in the same retreats and the same advances together. Their friendship deepened. Under the stress of circumstances the tie did not dissolve, but strengthened. It was indubitably real, therefore. Then, oddly enough, they were both wounded in the same engagement.

And it was here the remarkable fate that jointly haunted them betrayed itself more clearly than in any previous incident of their long relationship—Smith was wounded in the act of protecting his cousin. How it happened is confusing to a layman, but each apparently was leading a bombing party, and the two parties came together. They found themselves shoulder to shoulder, both brimmed with that pluck which is complete indifference to Self; they exchanged a word of excited greeting, and the same second one of those rare opportunities of advantage presented itself which only the highest courage could make use of. Neither, certainly, was thinking of personal reward; it was merely that each saw the chance by which instant heroism might gain a surprise advantage for their side. The risk was heavy, but there *was* a chance; and success would mean a decisive result, to say nothing of high distinction for the man who obtained it—if he survived. Smith, being a few yards ahead of his cousin, had the moment in his grasp. He was in the act of dashing forward when something made him pause. A bomb in mid-air, flung from the opposing trench, was falling; it seemed immediately above him. He saw that it would just miss himself, but land full upon his cousin, whose head was turned the other way. By stretching out his hand, Smith knew he could field it like a cricket-ball. There was an interval of a second and a half, he judged. He hesitated—perhaps a quarter of a second —then he acted. He caught it. It was the obvious thing to do. He flung it back into the opposing trench.

The rapidity of thought is hard to realise. In that second and a half Smith was aware of many things. He saved his cousin's life unquestionably; unquestionably also Jones seized the opportunity that otherwise was his cousin's. But it was neither of these reflections that filled Smith's mind. The dominant impression was another. It flashed into actual words inside his excited brain : " I must risk it. I owe it to him—and more besides." He was, further, aware of another impulse than the obvious one. In the first fraction of a second it was overwhelmingly established. And it was this :

that the entire episode was familiar to him. A subtle familiarity was present. All this had happened before. He had already—elsewhere—seen death descending upon his cousin from the air. Yet with a difference. The "difference" escaped him; the familiarity was vivid. That he missed the deadly detonators in making the catch, or that the fuse delayed, he called good luck. He only remembers that he flung the gruesome weapon back whence it had come, and that its explosion in the opposite trench materially helped his cousin to find glory in the place of death. The slight delay, however, resulted in his receiving a bullet through the chest—a bullet he would not otherwise have received, presumably.

It was some days later, gravely wounded, that he discovered his cousin in another bed across the darkened floor. They exchanged remarks. Jones was already "decorated," it seemed, having snatched success from his cousin's hands, while little aware whose help had made it possible. . . . And once again there stole across the inmost mind of Smith that strange insistent whisper: "I owed it to him . . . but, my God! I owe more than that . . . I mean to pay it too . . .!"

There was not a trace of bitterness or envy now; only this profound conviction, of obscurest origin, that it was right and absolutely just—full, honest repayment of a debt incurred. Some ancient balance of account was being settled; there was no "chance"; injustice, caprice played no rôle at all. . . . And a deeper understanding of life's ironies crept into him; for if everything was just, there was no room for whimpering.

And the voice persisted above the sound of busy footsteps in the ward: "I owe it . . . I'll pay it gladly . . .!"

Through the pain and weakness the whisper died away. He was exhausted. There were periods of unconsciousness, but there were periods of half-consciousness as well; then flashes of another kind of consciousness altogether, when, bathed in high, soft light, he was aware of things he could not quite account for. He *saw*. It was absolutely real. Only the critical faculty was gone. He did not question what he saw as he stared across at his cousin's bed. He knew. Perhaps the beaten, worn-out body let something through at last. The nerves, overstrained to numbness, lay very still. The physical system, battered and depleted, made no cry. The clamour of the flesh was hushed. He was aware, however, of an undeniable exaltation of the spirit in him as he lay and gazed towards his cousin's bed. . . .

Across the night of time, it seemed to him the picture stole before his inner eye with a certainty that left no room for doubt. It was not the cells of memory in his brain of To-day that gave up their dead, it was the eternal Self in him that remembered and understood—the soul. . . .

With that satisfaction which is born of full comprehension, he watched the light glow and spread about the little bed. Thick matting deadened the footsteps of nurses, orderlies, doctors. New cases were brought in, " old " cases were carried out; he ignored them; he saw only the light above his cousin's bed grow stronger. He lay still and stared. It came neither from the ceiling nor the floor; it unfolded like a cloud of shining smoke. And the little lamp, the sheets, the figure framed between them—all these slid cleverly away and vanished utterly. He stood in another place that had lain behind all these appearances—a landscape with wooded hills, a foaming river, the sun just sinking below the forest, and dusk creeping from a gorge along the lonely banks. In the warm air there was a perfume of great flowers and heavy-scented trees; there were fire-flies, and the taste of spray from the tumbling river was on his lips. Across the water a large bird flapped its heavy wings as it moved downstream to find another fishing place. For he and his companion had disturbed it as they broke out of the thick foliage and reached the river-bank. The companion, moreover, was his brother; they ever hunted together; there was a passionate link between them born of blood and of affection—they were twins.

It was all as clear as though of Yesterday. In his heart was the lust of the hunt; in his blood was the lust of woman, and thick behind these there lurked the jealousy and fierce desire of a primitive day. But, though clear as of Yesterday, he knew that it was of long, long ago. . . . And his brother came up close beside him, resting his bloody spear with a clattering sound against the boulders on the shore. He saw the gleaming of the metal in the sunset, he saw the shining glitter of the spray upon the boulders, he saw his brother's eyes look straight into his own. And in them shone a light that was neither the reflection of the sunset nor the excitement of the hunt just over.

"It escaped us," said his brother. "Yet I know my first spear struck."

"It followed the fawn that crossed," was the reply. "Besides, we came down wind, thus giving it warning. Our flocks, at any rate, are safer——"

The other laughed significantly.

"It is not the safety of our flocks that troubles me just now, brother," he interrupted eagerly, while the light burned more deeply in his eyes. "It is, rather, that *she* waits for me by the fire across the river, and that I would get to her. With your help added to my love," he went on in a trusting voice, "the gods have shown me the favour of true happiness." He pointed with his spear to a camp-fire on the farther bank, turning his head as he strode forward to plunge into the stream and swim across.

For a moment, then, the other felt his natural love turn into bitter hate. His own fierce passion, unconfessed, concealed, burst into instant flame. That the girl should become his brother's wife sent the blood surging through his veins in fury. He felt his life and all that he desired go down in ashes. . . . He watched his brother stride towards the water, the deerskin cast across one naked shoulder—when another object caught his practised eye. In mid-air it passed suddenly, like a shining gleam; it seemed to hang a second, then it swept swiftly forward past his head and downward. It had leaped with a blazing fury from the overhanging bank behind; he saw the blood still streaming from its wounded flank. It must land—he saw it with a secret, awful pleasure—full upon the striding figure whose head was turned away.

The swiftness of that leap, however, was not so swift but that he could easily have used his spear. Indeed, he gripped it strongly. His skill, his strength, his aim—he knew them well enough. But hate and love, fastening upon his heart, held all his muscles still. He hesitated. He was no murderer, yet he paused. He heard the roar, the ugly thud, the crash, the cry for help—too late . . . and when, an instant afterwards, his steel plunged into the great beast's heart, the human heart and life he might have saved lay still for ever. . . . He heard the water rushing past, an icy wind came down the gorge against his naked back; he saw the fire shine upon the farther bank . . . and the figure of a girl in skins was wading across, seeking out the shallow places in the dusk, and calling loudly as she came. . . . Then darkness hid the entire landscape, yet a darkness that was deeper, bluer than the velvet of the night alone. . . .

And he shrieked aloud in his remorseful anguish: "May the gods forgive me, for I did not mean it! Oh, that I might undo . . . that I might repay . . .!"

That his cries disturbed the weary occupants in more than one bed is certain, but he remembers chiefly that a nurse was quickly by his side, and that something she gave him soothed his violent pain and helped him into deeper sleep again. There was, he noticed, anyhow, no longer the soft, clear, blazing light about his cousin's bed. He saw only the faint glitter of the oil-lamps down the length of the great room. . . .

And some weeks later he went back to fight. The picture, however, never left his memory. It stayed with him as an actual reality that was neither' delusion nor hallucination. He believed that he understood at last the meaning of the tie that had fettered him and puzzled him so long. The memory of those far-off days of shepherding beneath the stars of long ago remained vividly beside him. He kept his secret, however. In many a talk with his cousin beneath the nearer stars of Flanders no word of it ever passed his lips.

The friendship between them, meanwhile, experienced a curious deepening, though unacknowledged in any spoken words. Smith, at any rate, on his side, put into it an affection that was a brave man's love. He watched over his cousin. In the fighting especially, when possible, he sought to protect and shield him, regardless of his own personal safety. He delighted secretly in the honours his cousin had already won. He himself was not yet even mentioned in despatches, and no public distinction of any kind had come his way.

His V.C. eventually—well, he was no longer occupying his body when it was bestowed. He had already " left." . . . He was now conscious, possibly, of other experiences besides that one of ancient, primitive days when he and his brother were shepherding beneath other stars. But the reckless heroism which saved his cousin under fire may later enshrine another memory which, at some far future time, shall reawaken as an " hallucination " from a Past that to-day is called the Present. . . . The notion, at any rate, flashed across his mind before he " left."

THE ALIEN SKULL

by
Liam O'Flaherty

WHEN he was within ten yards of the enemy outpost, Private Mulhall lay flat, with his right ear close to the ground. He listened without drawing breath. He strained his ear to catch a word, a cough, or the grating sound of a boot touching the frost-bound earth. There was no sound.

Had they gone?

It was eleven o'clock at night. There was perfect silence along that section of the battle-front. In the distance there was the monotonous and melancholy murmur of heavy guns in action. Here everything was still, as in a tomb. The moon had not risen. But the sky was not dark. It was an angry blue colour. There were stars. It was possible to see the ground for a long distance. It was freezing heavily. Bayonets, lying beside dead men, gleamed. All the huddled figures scattered about between the two lines of trenches were dead men. There had been a battle that day.

They had sent out Mulhall to discover whether the enemy had retired from his front line. If so, an advance was to be made at midnight into the trenches evacuated by him. If possible, Mulhall was to bring back a live prisoner. A man had been seen a little earlier peering over the top of the advanced post, before which Mulhall was now lying.

Irritated by the silence, Mulhall began to curse under his breath. He had ceased to listen and looked back towards his own line. He had come up a slope. He saw the dim shapes of the newly made scattered posts, the rambling wire fences and the heaps of rooted earth. He cursed and felt a savage hatred against his officers. He had now been three years at the front without leave. He was always doing punishment behind the line for insolence and insubordination. In the line he was chosen for every dangerous duty, because of his ferocious courage. But as soon as he came out he was up again before the adjutant, taken dirty on parade, absent, drunk, or for striking a corporal.

Lying flat on the ground, Mulhall thought savagely of the injustice done to him. He thought with cunning pleasure of crawling back towards his own line and shooting one of the officers or sergeants against whom he had a grudge. With pleasure, he rehearsed, in his mind, this act, until he saw the stricken victim fall, writhe, and lie still. Then terrible disciplinary cries rose up before his mind, his own name shouted by the sergeant, and then the giant figure of the sergeant-major, with his pace stick under his arm, heels together, erect, reading out the documentary evidence. A whole lot of shouting and stamping and awe-inspiring words. An enormous, invisible, inhuman machine, made of terrible words, constituted in his mind the terror that gave power to his superiors over him.

Compared to that it was pleasant out here.

He turned his head and looked towards the enemy outpost again. His hatred was now directed against the enemy. Their words were meaningless. Whenever he heard their words, they sounded like the barking of a dog. He was not afraid of them, and his punishment was remitted when he killed one or two of them.

Now he ceased to think and he thrust upwards his lower lip. His body became rigid. He fondled the breech of his rifle. With his rifle folded in his arms, ready for use, he slowly pushed his body forward, moving on his left side. He propelled himself with his left foot. He was listening intently. He moved like a snail, a few inches at a time. He made no sound. Then he stopped suddenly when he had gone half the distance. He had heard a sound. It was the sound of teeth gnawing a crust of hard bread, an army biscuit or a stale piece of bread, hardened by the frost. An enemy! There was an enemy there in front, five yards away.

He turned over gently on his stomach and brought his rifle to the front. Then he slowly touched various parts of his equipment and of his weapon to see that everything was in order. He settled his steel hat a little farther forward on his head, so that its rim shielded his face. Then he raised his back until he was on his elbows and knees. He then raised his feet and hands. He crawled forward as slowly as before and even more silently, breathing gently through his nose. He reached the post and lay still, behind a little knoll that formed the parapet. The enemy was within a yard of him. The enemy snuffled as he chewed at the crust.

Mulhall slowly raised his right knee. He put his right foot to the ground under him. He balanced his rifle in his right hand. He put his left hand on the ground. Then he jumped. He jumped right on top of the man in the hole beyond. But his foot struck something hard as he fell downwards and he tumbled over the man, losing his rifle. His head struck the side of the hole. He was slightly dazed. Almost immediately, however, he raised himself and held out his hands to grope for the enemy.

The enemy had also been tossed by the impact. Just then he was pulling himself up against the side of the hole, his hands supporting him, his mouth and eyes wide open with fright and wonder. There was a piece of black bread in his right hand. There were crumbs of bread on his lips. His face was within a few inches of Mulhall's face.

Mulhall's hands, which he had thrust forward instinctively to grapple with the enemy, instinctively dropped. With the amazing courage of stupid men, Mulhall saw at a glance that the enemy was much bigger and stronger than himself and that he was almost standing up. Mulhall, on the other hand, was huddled on the ground.

Now the enemy was incapable of movement through the paralysis of sudden fear. But if Mulhall touched him the same terror would make him struggle like a madman. Mulhall knew that and lay still. His face imitated the enemy's face. He opened his mouth and dilated his eyes.

They remained motionless, watching one another, like two strange babies. Their rifles lay side by side at the bottom of the hole. The enemy's rifle had been leaning against the side of the hole, and Mulhall had tripped over it, losing his own rifle. Now they were both unarmed. Their faces were so close together that they could hear one another's breathing.

The enemy was a stripling, but fully grown, and of a great size. His cheeks were red and soft. So were his lips. His whole body was covered with good, soft flesh. Mulhall was a squat fellow, thin and hard. His face was pale and marked with scars. He had eyes like a ferret. A drooping, fair moustache covered his lip and curled into his mouth. He looked brutal, ugly, war-worn and humpy compared to the fine young enemy, whose flesh was still soft and fresh on his big limbs.

Although his mouth lay stupidly open, as if with terror, Mulhall's mind remained brutal, calm, and determinedly watching for an opportunity to capture the enemy. If he could only reach his gun or disengage his entrenching tool or release his jack-knife. But he must take the fellow alive and drag him back over the frosty ground by the scruff of the neck, prodding him with his bayonet.

Then the enemy did a curious thing that completely puzzled Mulhall. At first his face broke into a smile. Then he laughed outright, showing his teeth that were sound and white, like the teeth of a negro. He made a low, gurgling sound when he laughed. His eyes remained dilated and full of terror while he laughed. Then, slowly, with a jerky, spasmodic movement, he raised the hand that held the crust until the bread was in front of Mulhall's face. Then his face became serious again and his expression changed.

The look of fear left his eyes. They became soft and friendly. His lips trembled. Then his whole body trembled. Gesticulating with his hands and shoulders, he offered the bread to Mulhall eagerly. He moved his lips and made guttural sounds which Mulhall did not understand. Every other time that Mulhall heard those words he thought they were like the barking of a dog. But now they had a different sound.

Mulhall became confused and ashamed. His forehead wrinkled. At first, he felt angry with the enemy, because he had aroused a long-buried feeling of softness. Then he became suspicious. Was the bread poisoned? No. The enemy had been eating it himself. Then he suddenly wanted to shed tears. He thought, with maudlin self-pity, of the brutal callousness and cruelty of his own comrades and superiors. Everybody despised Mulhall. Nobody would share blankets with him in the hut. He always got the dregs of the tea. They moved away from him in the canteen. When he was tied to the wheel of the cook-house cart fellows used to jeer at him and cry out: " Are they bitin' ye, Mull?" With tears in his eyes, Mulhall wanted to bite the hand that held out the bread. The action brought to a climax the whole ghastly misery of his existence. It robbed him of his only solace, the power to hate somebody whom he could injure with impunity.

He was on the point of striking away the bread when his instinct of cunning warned him. So he took the bread. He fumbled with it uncertainly. Then he stuffed it into the pocket of his tunic. The enemy became delighted and made fresh gestures, gabbling all the while.

Then the enemy stopped gabbling and both became still, watching one another. Their faces became suspicious again. Their eyes wandered over one another's bodies, each strange to the other. Their features became hostile. Their hands jerked uneasily.

Mulhall, slightly unnerved by the enemy's action, began to feel afraid. He became acutely conscious of the enemy's size. So he also began to make guttural sounds imitating the enemy. He touched the enemy's sleeve and said: "Huh. Yuh. Uh. Uh." Then he put his finger in his mouth and sucked it. Then he nodded his head eagerly. The enemy looked on in wonder, with suspicion in his eyes.

Mulhall took off his steel hat. There was a crumpled cigarette in the hat. He took out the cigarette and gave it to the enemy.

The enemy's face relaxed again. He was overcome with emotion. He took the cigarette and then kissed Mulhall's hand.

Then Mulhall surrendered completely to this extraordinary new feeling of human love and kindness. Were it not for his native sense of reserve, he would return the enemy's kiss. Instead of that he smiled like a happy child and his head swam. He took the enemy's hand and pressed it three times, mumbling something inaudible. They sat in silence for a whole minute, looking at one another in a state of ecstasy. They loved one another for that minute, as saints love God or as lovers love, in the first discovery of their exalted passion. They were carried up from the silent and frightful corpse-strewn battle-field into some God-filled place, into that dream state where life almost reaches the secret of eternal beauty.

They were startled from their ecstasy by the booming of a single cannon, quite near, to the rear of the enemy lines. They heard the whizzing of the shell over their heads, flying afar.

The enemy soldier started. His face grew stern. He sat up on his heels and took Mulhall's hand. He began to make guttural sounds as he pressed Mulhall's hand fervently.

Mulhall also awoke, but slowly. His soul had sunk deeply into the tender reverie of human love so alien to him. Like a sick man awaking from a heavy sleep, he scanned the enemy's face, seeking the meaning of the change that had been caused by the boom and the whizzing passage of the shell. Slowly he became aware of the boom. Then his cunning awoke in him. Was it a signal?

Without changing his features he became cruel again.

Still uttering guttural sounds, the enemy crawled out into the bottom of the hole and picked up his rifle. Mulhall struggled between the desire of his cunning to throttle the enemy while his back was turned, and an almost identical desire to throw his arms around the enemy's neck and beg him to remain. The cunning desire lost in the struggle and he felt very lonely and miserable as if he were on the point of losing somebody he had loved all his life. So he remained motionless, watching the enemy with soft eyes. And yet he felt violently angry at not being able to hate the enemy and throttle him.

Having taken up his rifle, the enemy paused and looked at the crumpled cigarette which he still held in his hand. Then he smiled and began to make effusive gestures. He kissed the cigarette. Then he made curious sounds, his face aglow with joy and friendship. Then he put down his rifle, pointed to Mulhall's helmet and then to his own. He laughed. He took off his own helmet, which was shaped differently from Mulhall's helmet.

Immediately, Mulhall started violently. He became rigid. All his savagery and brutality again returned. The enemy's skull was exposed. As soon as he saw it the lust of blood overwhelmed him, as if he were a beast of prey in sight of his quarry. The enemy's bare skull acted on his senses like a maddening drug. Its shape was alien. It was shaped like a bullet. It had whitish hairs on it. It was hostile, foreign, uncouth, the mark of the beast. The sight of it caused his blood to curdle in him. A singing sound started in his head, at the rear of his forehead. His eyes glittered. He wanted to kill. He again felt exalted, gripped by the fury of despair.

The skull disappeared. The enemy put his helmet back on his head and then peered over the top of the hole in both directions. Then he struck his chest a great blow, murmured something, and crawled out back towards his own line.

As quick as a cat Mulhall pounced on his own rifle and arranged the breech. Then he crouched up against the side of the hole, thrust out his rifle and looked. The enemy was already a few yards away, slouching off in a stooping position. Quickly, taking quick aim, Mulhall fired. The enemy grunted, stopped, and expanded his chest. Then he turned his head towards Mulhall as he sank slowly. Baring his teeth, with glittering eye, Mulhall aimed slowly at the wondering, gaping young face of the enemy. He fired. The enemy's face twitched and lowered to the ground. His whole body lowered to the ground, trembled and lay still. The haunches remained high off the ground. The feet were drawn up. One hand was thrown out. The head was twisted around towards Mulhall. The face, now stained with blood, still seemed to look at Mulhall with awe and wonder.

Mulhall suddenly felt an irresistible desire to run away.

He dashed out of the hole in the direction of his own line, careless of taking cover. He had not gone three yards when he threw up his hands and dropped his gun. He got it right between the shoulder blades. Coughing and cursing, he fell backwards on his buttocks. His head was still erect. With maniacal joy he looked up into the cruel blue sky and laughed out fierce blasphemies.

They got him again, three times, around the shoulders and neck. His head fell forward. In that position he lay still, like a grotesque statue, dead.

At dawn, when the sun began to shine, he was still sitting that way, like a Turk at prayer, stiff and covered with frost.

DEATH OF A CAT

by
Axel Eggebrecht

HOUTHOULST FOREST was the heart of that ravaged earth. There all horrors met and flowed together; trickled ceaselessly from a livid sky, flowed through broken dykes and oozed untiringly from an earth which absorbed what it discharged with a depraved thirst.

The horror was wetness. Dryness would have been Paradise, an unimaginable alleviation to demoralised nerves. But nothing was dry. The damp bread went mouldy overnight; the plum and apple jam swelled and burst its tins; worst of all was the greasy leather, which the damp once more resolved into unsavoury strips of dead beasts, exhaling the fetid, sweetish odour of mildewed corpses.

This sodden corner of the earth was also, by the illogical dictates of war, a strategic point on the fighting front. Limbs were blown off and shattered for it, as they were being shattered all over Europe—in Lorraine, in Macedonia, in the Ukraine. But there they were at least embedded in the sheltering earth—that earth which they had never touched in their jerry-built houses, their concrete factories, and their asphalt streets. When they were cast, by sheer physical revolt, upon her whom poets still call mother, she, at least, would not reject them.

But even this comfort was denied us. Flanders was not earth; Flanders was paste. Here even the almighty mother was dissolved, disintegrated, and enfeebled, so that she could support us no longer.

If you threw yourself down, even in those places designated on the maps as "firm ground," you would sense, not that sudden invigorating contact with solid earth, but the sucking embrace of mud cushions with the slimy water flowing endlessly away.

Nevertheless, we did lie down to sleep. The ceaseless trickle of water did not waken us, although our legs swelled and our flesh grew morbid and discoloured. We did not die, we did not even fall sick; only we ceased to talk to each other, passing by with nothing but a grunt. It was as though the spoken word were an unbearable superfluity in an existence so futile and so precarious.

Such was our condition when there came to us the incredible hope of sleeping once more in the dry. One night, as we went forward in single file to relieve a section in an advanced gun outpost, we suddenly collapsed on top of each other in a shock of joy. Our happiness made us once more articulate; we talked, we uttered whole sentences. In front of us was a hole, a dry hole, ten yards long, roofed over. The walls, it was true, dripped with damp, but on the ground yellow straw was strewn thickly for a couch. It was quite evident that we were to sleep there.

The hole proved to be the remains of a tunnelling through a dyke. It was knee-deep in water, but our predecessors had built wooden trestles on which we threw ourselves immediately. The surface of that loathsome element from which we had at last escaped lay three spans below.

All fourteen of us fell asleep and dreamed—fourteen warm, bright dreams of throats that could once more feel thirst, of skins that could once more feel dust and heat, of burning, golden sands with green-blue oases. Hands that had become flaccid and nerveless found sensual pleasure in stroking the fabric of our uniforms, now almost dry.

My head was burning; I was panting along in the dust of an unending road in a welter of dry, pitiless heat. Each moment I was becoming browner, drier, shrivelling in that supernatural sun. The dryness had ceased to be grateful, and then . . . just at the right moment, a finger touched me—a cool, slender finger, like a little fragment of a snake. It was a dark enchantress who had put her finger into her mouth and then trailed its sinister coolness across my throat. The sun's heat had waned, the dust was thickening and swelling into a myriad of sluggish raindrops, and still that cold, snake-like finger stroked my throat and my lips and my face. . . .

Then I started up. Something heavy ran down my legs and fell with a loud plop off the wooden platform. The pointed dark thing that was so strange to me had slid out of my dreams into the water. Someone in the corner shouted: "Hell! Rats!"

And so that night became transmuted into the night of our deepest despair. We had found refuge from the wet, we had escaped to a world where we could once more dream of dryness, but out of that loathsome liquid beneath our sleeping bodies the obscene creatures emerged, rested their weight impudently upon our limbs, and drew their slimy tails across our mouths. They upset the coffee-pot and nibbled at the bread. We put it into a bag and hung it from the roof, that beloved roof which kept the streaming sky from us. But scarcely had we fallen asleep again when once more the running and the scratching began; by twos and threes they leapt up at the desirable bundle, falling with horrid little plops into the water below.

A couple of us decided to remain awake, keeping off sleep by retailing horrid accounts of rats that had eaten off children's hands and the eyes out of living calves, tales of plague and cholera. Suddenly the speaker ceased. He seemed to see, at the end of the wooden bench, a sharp, malignant face, listening with an approving grin while its beady eyes winked an unqualified concurrence.

There was a moment's silence. Then he snatched his revolver and fired it two or three times. We all jumped up in panic, crowding out of the hole, and relieving ourselves with a burst of wild, aimless shooting. Then we quietened down and returned, to find the trestles strewn with patches of wet lime, while our bread dropped lamentably through the holes of the shot-ridden sack. Two dirty-white little taut bellies were floating about in the water; we flung them outside.

Once more I fell asleep, then, a quarter of an hour later, that disgusting familiar pressure once more intruded upon my dreaming consciousness—damp little feet and a pointed, waving tail. I tried not to awaken, although, as a matter of fact, I was awake already. I kept my eyes shut and tried to hold my breath, but in the end my nerves forced me to get up. I groped my way out, threw a coat over me, and squatted down for the rest of the night out there in the rain.

Some nights later, Moogk, who was splashing up and down on sentry duty, noticed something peculiar moving about in the fitful light cast by distant flares. With the usual curiosity of the soldier in the front line he ran after it, saw it run off in a zigzag course and disappear in the ruins of what was once the village, but was now a shapeless heap of bricks. For a moment two green eyes had glared at him, and he suddenly turned round and rushed back to us as fast as the clay and mud would let him. I happened to be the first man he met, and he grabbed me excitedly by the arm, his hoarse voice eager with his great news. *There was a cat in the village.*

Three minutes later we were all scrambling about among the bricks looking for it.

On such a night as this the drenched Flemish carriers must have crowded in at the inn door, invoking the Blessed Virgin as they poured the rough spirit down their chilled throats. With their great heavy boots they probably kicked the little cat out of the way

as she crowded in among them, hating the cold and the wet as
much as they. Perhaps it would rush past them into the warm inn-
parlour, refusing to be scared by any display of violence. They
had gone now, but it remained, roaming among the bricks and
the debris and the shell-holes as though they were the currant
bushes in the garden. It had refused to be driven away by shells
and bullets, but now that fourteen human wraiths were flittering
once more about the remains of that human habitation, trying to
coax it with friendly calls as though all were well again, the animal
huddled in the deepest and most inaccessable cleft of its labyrinth.
We called it and searched for it in vain; it mewed piteously, but it
would not come. At last we withdrew and threw ourselves back
on our wooden couch, beneath which lurked the filthy creatures of
the flood.

But that gave us something to talk about. If the cat had been
there in the flesh we might have felt a little foolish in confessing
that her wholesome fur coat crystallised for us all our longing for
warmth and dryness in that place of loathsome damp; that she
seemed like a guardian appointed to drive off the obscene devils
of that unnatural underworld. But we felt that we could speculate
and indulge our fancies freely while we were still uncertain whether
she were anything but a creature of Moogk's imagination.

The following night she was seen by two others. In fact, we
must have been surrounded by whole battalions of cats, so many
were the conflicting reports about large cats, small cats, coal-black
cats, snow-white cats, spotted cats, and every other strange and
commonplace variety of the animal. Our affection deepened to
positive worship; we expressed it by cutting off bits of our rare and
exiguous meat ration as votive offerings to the goddess, the offerings being placed in prominent places far removed from our pro-
fane dwelling. At first they were spurned, for did we not bear the

brand of Cain, and how could our sacrifice prove acceptable? But in the end the goddess relented, and the dedicated morsels began to vanish. Before dawn she would sometimes even prowl around our hole, while we waited inside breathlessly. But if one of us moved towards her she would disappear in a couple of bounds, contemptuous of our dismay.

So things went on for a few days. The rats wandered about, quite indifferent to the fact that we were darkly planning their extermination. Then we called a council, prompted by Heaven knows what atavistic survival from a primitive past, to discuss whether we might compel the goddess to come to us. Opinion was divided; but when Moogk, the first harbinger of salvation, declared himself in agreement, the holy chase was approved.

In the early morning we circled round the ruins of the inn, armed with all sorts of instruments for noise-making. One of the men actually took a flare, to which, however, he meant to have recourse only in extreme emergency.

We were standing, in the growing daylight, gazing upon the dirty pile of bricks in a state of excitement which we had believed to be long since forgotten. We were waiting for Moogk's shout, and he was standing, like a true militant prophet, with arm upraised in the damp stillness.

We waited tensely for him to lower it, but instead he himself crumpled up on the ground, and at that very moment, at seven thirty-six of that cold, wet morning, the most terrible bombardment of the winter campaign began. Like a striking clock, timed to the second, the British offensive was set in motion, and the pile of bricks that housed our goddess was levelled to the ground.

We ran through a curtain of burning splinters that hummed round our heads. I stumbled and fell among the bricks, and as I lay there I noticed that all the fourteen men were not running back to the hole. Some had been wounded and fallen; I, crawling painfully along, was the last to get in. As I pulled the door to, a ridiculous gesture to heighten the false security of being under cover, a soft thing slipped through my hands and cowered with wild eyes in the corner, where it glanced from one to another.

There, between the six of us who had come through safely, lay the cat, a draggled bundle of pure terror—a terror so acute that it became infectious.

None of us thought of approaching her. Outside the world was collapsing; we sat huddled together without thought. Some time later the door was flung open by men hurrying past. They signed to us to follow, and so we joined in the retreat that had been ordered. At the last moment I wanted to take the cat in my arms, but at the first movement of my outstretched hand she retreated so wildly that she slipped off the wooden platform. I can still see the stark horror in her eyes as she fell, but there was no time to do anything. Torn by remorse, I had to rush out, close the door, and run for my life.

       *   *   *   *   *

Eight or ten hours later the attack was checked. It was night before we returned, and as we approached the hole, dead tired as we were, I was conscious of an extraordinary sense of expectation. I ran on in front of the others, pulled open the door, and flashed a light. A fat rat grinned at my torch, turned slowly round, and dropped off into the water.

We flashed our torches round all the corners, but in vain, and, as though by agreement, all our lights were extinguished suddenly together. We did not say anything about the vanished one, but lay down in sulky silence on the boards. I lay awake for a long time before the rhythm of approaching sleep began to beat upon my senses—I was numbed as if by an anæsthetic—and then, just at the moment when I was sinking into oblivion, turning unconsciously on my other side as I have always done since childhood, I sensed a pressure on my shoulder. I leapt up, wide awake.

I could not keep back the shriek of terror that rose so suddenly, almost before I could draw my breath. All the torches flashed out in panic. My hand grasped a little round white skull.

It was smooth and polished clean, scratched with a thousand little marks like a scalpel. I could still feel the pressure under my shoulder, and now that the lights showed up every corner of the place I could see little white bones strewn all over the straw.

Like a man caught in some monstrous act of betrayal, I held the little white skull in my hands. They trembled as though I should never again be able to control them. One of the men said slowly :

" And she didn't want to fight at all."

We looked at one another, and the unchecked tears were streaming down our cheeks.

CARNIVAL, 1915

by
George Britling

IT was always windy in Flanders; at least, so it seemed during the War. Many roads ran through Flanders, and on either side of the roads stood high trees—poplars, of course—and the poplars bent in the wind like suppliants under the cloudy sky. Once I saw four men on a windy day carrying a stretcher along one of the roads . . . but enough of this; we will change the scene.

Every movement raised clouds of stale dust. Reismuller shouted: "For Christ's sake lie down!" Still the shuffling went on; in a corner of the dark room someone shouted, "Stow it," but the buzz of talk still persisted.

Two reeking oil lamps dangled from the ceiling—a light just too dim to make out other faces. Something crashed in the gallery that ran round the room; it was a pile of chairs that had fallen.

With packs and haversacks as pillows, most of the men lay down on the bare boards and tried to sleep. But sleep did not come very easily, for they were still keyed up with the excitement of the battle in which, two hours previously, they had been engaged.

Reismuller was cursing up stage: "Do get to sleep, you chaps." He was lying in a greenwood clearing. I had made myself snug in the prompter's box—somewhat cramped quarters. Henry was among the dusty properties. I held my hands together like the pages of an open book, and, acting the prompter, hissed at him: "*Heinrich, mir graut vor dir!*"

But Henry, no doubt himself a dabbler in the black arts like his prototype, had suddenly vanished as though by magic. I scrambled out of the box, curious to see what had happened, discovered the door at the back of the stage, and found him on the other side of it swinging a pasteboard helmet like a madman. Pewter mugs, tinsel crowns, and all kinds of theatrical odds and ends were littered about. From rusty nails hung wigs, dusty and dilapidated—grey wigs, dark wigs, fair wigs, and matted beards. In the flickering candlelight it was like a headhunters' hut in the South Seas with enemy scalps dangling from leather strings. A spider had spun his web between a long, pointed, coal-black beard and the blonde pigtails of a girl, and the web quivered in the air, and Henry, exclaiming "blasted bug," held the candle under the motionless creature, which suddenly developed many legs under the point of flame, writhed convulsively, ceased writhing, and melted with the web.

"I'm sleeping here," said Henry; a cheerless place, I thought, but I let him be, among his wigs and pigtails, and went off.

It was cold in the room, and I was hungry, too. I had had nothing to eat, so I made my way to the exit. It was two o'clock in the morning, pitch dark and raining, and the wind was whistling. A horseman was trotting up the road, his collar turned up. He loomed up darkly before me, man and horse merging into one vague form. A hoof struck a spark out of the wet stone—how oddly cheering, that warm, yellow-red, dry little spark of life seemed. I wanted to talk to the rider.

The man on guard was lounging in a straw chair, finding it difficult to keep his eyes open. There was an unsavoury odour of damp uniforms; the many snoring sleepers were a depressing sight as they lay there, some with half-open mouths and others wheezing painfully. Most of them had their knees drawn up and had buried their hands in their pockets, huddled up like dogs. The rifles were piled along one of the sides of the room. In a corner the warrant officer, Kettler, was sleeping on some tents. He was in command of the company, being the only unwounded wearer of a

Sam Browne left.

We had been engaged with the English all day—they had been incredibly tenacious. They wore small saucepan-shaped iron helmets, and had long legs; that's what struck us all, their long legs. Yellow wrappings were wound round the thin calves of their long legs, and they had breast pockets on their close-fitting, stylish overcoats. The breast pockets excited us especially, because we only saw them on Generals' coats. And these long-legged, yellow "Generals" (we seemed to see none that were fat) were all brave. We had lain opposite each other all day in the mud, shooting and being shot at, and when evening came (and we had observed that each day, yes, positively each day, was followed by an evening), well, when evening came, we were relieved, and returned to reserve billets in this little Flemish hole, but any moment things might get lively again. I said good-night to the man on sentry duty, and carefully picked my way to the stage. Someone shouted "Hurrah!" in his sleep, and flung his arms about. I dropped into the gaping, black hole of the box, drew my Balaclava helmet down over my head, and went to sleep.

Then I saw the spider again. She was spinning between two scalps, not a web, but a thick, disgusting rope, and the rope began to sway to and fro, and suddenly it lay about my neck. I struggled, a mass of limbs, like the spider under the candle flame in the lumber-room; I hung as on a gallows, and the dead men's faces grinned, and a chief began to speak, but, of course, I didn't understand a word; he was jabbering in a strange language. The noose about my neck hurt more and more, and the chief's voice grew louder and louder. What on earth did this grinning South Sea Islander want with me? Because I didn't understand anything, he said *tok-tok-tok* to me, and then I understood him, and woke up to the sound of lively British rifle-fire. The warrant officer was standing in the middle of the room, shouting : "Take your rifles, and get out into the street." There was shouting and dust and excitement. A crowd of men, swearing loudly, moved towards the exit. Some hung nervously about in the corners, others looked for their rifles; the sleepers in the gallery staggered down the steps.

To hell with the bastards! They must have broken through, with their long legs and their flat saucepan helmets, and their thin lips in clean-shaven faces. An N.C.O. drove the last of the men out of the room. A lamp was overturned and there was a smell of petrol.

We were out in the street. The terrified inhabitants had taken refuge in their cellars. The bullets whistled through the air, emitting a sound like paper being scratched with a needle. Hand-to-hand fighting had already started. A hulking fellow was leaning up against a corner. Suddenly he fell. He passed his hand over his mouth, which was full of blood. He lay still on the paving stones. The fighting passed on to the end of the village. A section put up a fight there. They had barricaded the street with mattresses, with all kinds of household goods. We attacked them with bombs, but we could not make much headway against them.

Behind us a mad fellow dashed up the street. "A clown!" shouts someone. In his white and red overall he looked as though he had come from a fancy dress ball. All he needed to complete the effect was the pointed sugar-loaf hat. The mad fellow climbed up the barricade. "Hi!" he shouted triumphantly (the damned fool), and threw bombs, and waved and shouted at the English. All this actually happened in the first grey light of dawn, a fellow in white and red. The English who were there, if there be one of them still alive, which is quite possible, will know that I tell the truth. The man in the mask sang something as though he enjoyed singing. No one knew why he sang on that cold March morning in the year 1915. Then, suddenly, there was silence. Not for long, fifteen, twenty seconds, but that seemed a very long time. There was no shot fired on either side. No doubt each man was getting bombs ready, and the man in the red and white cloak sang no more. He stood on top of the fence, and I was below; the red and white markings of the fool's cloak danced before my eyes. The white patches were grey, lighter than the grey of the morning, and the red ones were blood-red. No other comparison occurred to me, during that moment of absolute silence, when a blood-red-white chequered leg was just in front of my nose. And then the clown went double and prepared to leap. In a flash the man was down over the other side of the barricade among the English, with the stylish coats and the impressive breast pockets. Shots rang out wildly from all sides, the grey dawn grew brighter; roaring and laughing, we hopped across after the comic fellow, and then the edge of the village was ours again.

Yes, it was Henry. He had picked out the clown's cloak in the theatre and put it on for warmth, and also as a joke. He had not been able to get it off so easily, and he had fought in that get-up and was now lying with the rest of us in the flat trench which we were digging.

We would not allow him to doff his fool's cloak at once. One of us suddenly remembered that it was Shrove Tuesday. What did we know about the calendar? But it really was Shrove Tuesday, for we worked out the date. In the afternoon the field kitchens brought food, rifle-cleaning stuff, and a terrible, fiery, brown kind of liquor, which we drank.

Later on, I saw a large spider on the edge of the trench; by Jove! it was huge, like an English tin helmet. I wanted to kill it, but when I struck it my fist did not meet the soft, quivering, blood-spurting body I had expected; it struck something hard that squeaked. It was, of course, a tin helmet, but there was no head with a clean-shaven face underneath it. It was just a helmet, and no doubt its owner had been obliged to go to the quartermaster-sergeant at the stores for another one and had been heartily cursed.

We were merry in the trench—in our new and shallow trench —and it didn't rain. The long-legged ones on the other side didn't shoot any more, and we didn't shoot either, chivalrous fellows that we were. Henry the Fearless of the red and white cloak, who had got hold of most of the liquor, was drunk, and kept on shouting: "To-morrow's Ash Wednesday."

Next day was Ash Wednesday, and lived up to its name, too, but we didn't know that then. We had liquor to drink, and it was carnival time in the trenches.

If I had the gift of second sight, which I haven't, I could describe something now, which happened a day later, which I saw with my own eyes, but which I did not see on Shrove Tuesday.

There was a road in Flanders, and one half of the road was paved with round cobbles and the other half was unpaved, and both halves shone in the wet. The round stones were damp, and the earth of the unpaved half was brown and damp, and tall trees, poplars, of course, here in Flanders, stood along the street, and, of course, there was a wind. It bent the poplars so that they all stood bowed in a suppliant position. What were they asking of the grey, overcast sky, for they must have been asking something. The road was long and endless, and in the flat country it was like a sea, a land sea, with farmsteads here and there for ships, drifting without rudders. Four men came along the road carrying a stretcher, and on the stretcher was something covered with brown sacking. The men were going with the wind, which bent them as it bent the poplars, and the long thing, the long thing stretched on the bier, did not stir. It was irrevocably dead. A gust of wind, a particularly violent gust of wind, blew up the road; the poplars swayed and bent, creaking; the men bent forward and the wind lifted a little of the brown sacking, and one saw something red, something square and red, revealed. Those who saw under the sacking believed that the red they had seen was blood.

But it was not blood. A fatal shot through the heart produced no blood, not a drop of blood, only a dry death. It was a red square on Henry's clown's cloak, which a sudden gust of wind revealed on that Ash Wednesday in 1915.

WAR DOG

by
John W. Thomason, Jnr.

GRETA was a war dog in the service of H.M. the Kaiser and King. They bred her in the kennels of a Pomeranian Junker who was reported dead at Contalmaison, on the Somme, in 1916. With the bleak autumn of that year his widow found that she could not endure alone the rambling old estate on the dark North German plain; so she closed it, and went down to Berlin, where, in the bitter war-time, there was at least company for loneliness and misery.

Greta, with other matters pertaining to the house of a landed German gentleman, came up for sale. A purchasing officer of the signal service, waiting for a train in Pommern, saw her and bought her for the Army. She was then five months old, but the signal officer had a good eye.

She went across Germany and into France, boxed up in a military train, and came to Seventh Army Headquarters, behind Laon. On a winter morning they let her out of her crate into a swept courtyard where there were soldiers and dogs, and you heard the guns along the Chemin des Dames sound sharp and angry from the south-west across the new snow; then someone thrust a mess of horse-meat stew under her nose, and she found no concern for the far-off thunder.

The gross *Wachtmeister* of the Seventh Army *Meldehund-Trupp*—on detail from a uhlan regiment because of his handiness with animals—observed the lanky puppy while, all legs and appetite, she wolfed her food. Writing down her points in his book as he noted them, he decided that she had a good head and good legs, and when it caught up with her belly, her chest would be broad and deep enough.

The colour, too, was right—greyish, like the good German uniform; you did not want blacks and tans in this war, where the harder you were to see the longer you lasted. And she was the seventh puppy in this draft, so her name must begin with G— Gertrude—Garda—Gretchen—Greta. Greta would do. Here, having polished her pan, she sat back to ease her stomach, and cocked an amiable ear at the big man in the tight cavalry tunic.

"Attention, you!" he rumbled at her. "Your name is Greta. To begin with, you will learn that name—Greta——" Thereafter, the "Prussian Regulations for the Care, Training, and Handling of War Dogs, 1913: Revised, with Notes on the Recent Fighting, 1915," ordered her life.

More than any other detail of modern battle, the war dog has been swamped in sentimental nonsense. The fact is that the German armies found them useful in a certain limited field and employed them from sound tactical considerations where they were effective; for there was never any sentimentality about the German service.

Of course you saw nondescript and various mascots among the regiments, since there is a natural affinity between soldiers and dogs the world over; and in the trench sectors, where the War settled into routine, the men in the listening-posts in front of the wire used to take out small alert animals that raised a helpful row when people approached from the wrong direction. But the real war dogs, rationed and quartered and borne on the regimental strength, were the clever brutes of the German shepherd breed, selected and trained to carry messages from a regimental headquarters to its battalions on the line.

This German shepherd dog is a northern strain, as old as history, and until late years entirely utilitarian, the colleague of herders and the assistant of the Continental police. He is sturdy and faithful, he takes kindly to discipline, and he is capable of a high degree of training along open-air lines. Commonly he is called the police dog, and he has other names.

His remote ancestors crossed the Rhine with the flocks of the Cimbri and the Teutons, and medieval manuscripts show him exactly in appearance as he is now. More remotely, he is kin to the wolves that roamed the North German plain, and to this day the wolfish look is written large upon him.

In battle, they found that he could replace to a certain extent the regimental runner, that unfortunate whose duty takes him most frequently across the blazing forward zone of combat, maintaining touch between one post and another. Therefore, it was common sense to use him, because you can grow a dog in two years where a man takes twenty, and a dog may get through where a man cannot.

The war dogs, then, in the German service were the affair of the army signal officer, along with radio, telegraph, the field-telephone, carrier-pigeons, flags, and signal-lanterns, and all the diverse means whereby a field army talks between its elements. In battle, everything mechanical has a way of going out of commission : there is a heat at the point of contact which fuses things.

A Colonel in action might be able to talk over his field-telephone to Berlin, and not be able to get through to his forward battalion half a kilometre away. To be certain, therefore, he must fall back on the means of communication that Cæsar used; he must send somebody with his message. The messenger may be a dog.

Buried in the war archives in Potsdam there is the final opinion in the matter : After exhaustive tests it was found that five dogs would do the regimental messenger work of sixteen soldier runners. The arithmetic is plain—five men to look after five dogs, and eleven rifles more for the firing line. So they used dogs when they could.

The army *Meldehund-Trupp*—messenger dog outfit—took Greta and moulded her to pattern in half a year. There were two basic lessons: the first was obedience to orders, and the second concerned the grey-green uniform of the German soldier. A puppy idled in the courtyard of the billet with Drina and Blitz and Eric and a dozen or so others, playing gravely after the fashion of the breed and keeping a watchful eye on the soldiers in the light grey shoulder-straps of the communication troops.

When one called Greta, you went swiftly to receive instruction, paying no attention to any other name. You carried things from one soldier to another, things fastened to your collar. First it was just across the courtyard, then it would be around the corner, and, later, your man would deliberately hide, so that you had to trail and cast about to find him.

Presently the affair took you out into the fields and up and down ravines, and there must be no loitering on the way. They worked you from one place to another place, and they worked you at night. Simple things, done over and over, they came to be second nature. And through every exercise ran the other lesson—respect for the uniform.

" Because, *Liebchen,*" the *Herr Wachtmeister,* with his heavy voice and remarkably gentle hands, would say, " it would be frightful if, when you get Out There, you should take up with the wrong fellows. Those Frenchmen in their dirty blue breeches, or the English *Schwein* in khaki—— So!" There were practical lessons.

The *Feld-grau* fed and cherished you. It cleaned your quarters and dispensed work and play and food and caresses. With civilians a dog had no contacts—dubious, mean persons, passed aloofly on the street. And once, Greta, carrying a message to the young *Gemeiner* on the other end of her run, found him in the place he ought to have been, wearing strange blue clothes.

It was puzzling; but the hands and the face and the smell of this private were familiar, and she accepted his blandishments and made him free of the tin cylinder at her neck. She never forgot what happened to her after that, for the *Wachtmeister* had a way of impressing things.

Again, it was a fellow in an English uniform; and when, the next day, a sorry file of khaki prisoners passed on the street, Greta had to be restrained. The conclusion was inevitable: people in grey-green were all right; otherwise, they were to be avoided if possible and attacked if not. In any case, they meant trouble.

Later, they ran Greta about the firing ranges of the army small-arms schools, and loosed off rifles and machine-guns near her, and exploded things around her. The French planes also helped her education along with the occasional bombing-raids that an army headquarters must expect behind an active front.

Steady nerves and discipline and custom dissipated any gun-shyness she might have had. At the field trials of the new blood, which the *Meldehund-Trupp* held in the early summer, she got a message over a kilometre of broken ground in less than four minutes, which is classed as good in the Prussian service, and she received the compliments of exalted personages, even officers of the General Staff, turned out to observe the event.

She was a grave, upstanding dog, approaching her full growth, with a fine head and clean hard legs, and a close, greyish-tawny coat, when, in the late summer of '17, they certified her fit for field duty and drafted her to the 40th Fusilier Regiment in the 28th Infantry Division, the old Regular division that they called the Conquerors of Lorette.

The 28th Division had been fighting in Caurieres Wood before Verdun and needed replacements of every kind. They went down into Alsace and entered the line north-west of Altkirch, which was a quiet sector and a suitable place for a division to renew itself; and here Greta had her first combat experiences, sharp enough and not too crowded, as is best for recruits, both men and dogs.

The War flicked languidly across the great still valleys of the region. Greta became acquainted with shell-fire and learned to cock an ear and gauge them, proceeding with a contemptuous flick of her tail when the thing howled high or wide, and squatting like a soldier when the whine of it increased to a shattering roar and crashed down near at hand.

Incautiously quartering over a ridge, between reserve and the forward position, she drew long-range machine-gun fire and she deduced from that the wisdom of avoiding the sky-line and keeping away from the open. She watched the war-wise soldiers and patterned her conduct on theirs.

She followed her occasions up and down black ravines in the night, and under the flares of the front line she learned what dead men are like.

When the division, much restored, went up into the Champaigne around the Butte de Mesnil, Greta went competently with them and did good service with the 1st Battalion of the 40th Regiment, which was her particular assignment, in that wilderness of shell-holes and wire and old trenches where the War was always bitter.

Her division was one of those which rushed north for the counter-battle at Cambrai, and Greta saw her first tanks—disconsolate monsters, out of gasoline beyond the Nord Canal—and her first fighting Englishmen, and took the rifle-fire of a platoon of them at bay in the wreck of a wood; and there began to be stories about her in the regiment. The 28th wintered in the Ardennes and had a post of honour in the great March drive that rolled down to the gates of Amiens, and thereafter drew out and practised the arts of open warfare in the country behind Laon, through April and early May of 1918.

Near the last of the month the Seventh Army pounded across the Chemin des Dames, and four days later, in a red sunset full of crackling shrapnel, Greta lapped water from the Marne and heard her dusty soldiers, filling their canteens by the blue river, talk of a place called Paris. Then they went back a little way and rested.

Always keen to the moods of soldiers, Greta sensed the anger and disgust in the ranks when the division was alerted and moved up to the front barely a week afterward. It was not their turn, the grey-green files growled. What was the War coming to, when the 10th Division—which had always been fairly good as front-troops went—lost a town to these Yankee amateurs the beaten French were putting in to plug their holes! However, they added with sour pride, the 28th would show them—and this is the proper and healthy frame of mind for soldiers.

Greta's Fusilier Regiment took over a narrow front, with the 1st Battalion in the corner of a wood through which the right division prolonged the line, and the 2nd facing down on a battered village where shells were always falling. Going in with Regimental Headquarters, you noted that things here were quite lively. The columns did not tramp confidently along the roads, but went in hurrying groups across the fields and kept to the woods where it was possible. There was shelling always and everywhere, and many dead men and horses.

Greta's particular signalman—the stubby little private who always looked after her—was killed taking her over her route the first time. They went from the wood where Headquarters lived in holes, down a gully to the road. Then a ditch covered the way, as far as a railroad embankment.

That had to be crossed; here the enemy got the signalman and came near getting Greta. Bullets flung dust into her nose and ripped into the ground around her, and she fled straight across a wheat-field to the edge of the wood and found her own people, more concerned about her than about the poor *Gemeiner*, who lay now in plain sight on the embankment with his knees drawn up.

She was fired at in the dusk when she went back, and every time afterwards when she had to move in daylight. There were no trenches; and things happened as often and as quickly as they did in the Champaigne.

About the third day matters became very bad. All afternoon and all night the shells crashed down on the woods and along the roads. The telephones went out. Greta, catching cat-naps in her hole, as a war dog must, was awakened by the heavy boots of the reserve battalion, brought up to Headquarters before dawn, from rest billets in the rear area.

They sent her out when the sky was getting grey, and a machine-gun, very near, spat a stream of bullets around her ears when she scuttled across the railroad. She made the shelter of the wood with her tongue out, and was confused. The place had changed its very shape. Some of her best landmarks were gone, and many dead lay about in field-grey uniforms.

In the place where battalion command post should have been, there was nothing but a great shell-hole and an untidy litter of corpses. One of these was the Signal *Feldwebel*, who always took her messages. He lay now partly under a fallen branch, with dew on his yellow moustache, and Greta licked his cold jowl and permitted herself to grieve softly in her throat.

She went on with bristling shoulders and cast about through the wood to find her people, as she had been trained. She came to a narrow clearing, where a body lay in a strange khaki uniform. Stepping around it with distaste, she halted at the edge of the open, some wolfish instinct sounding an alarm.

Private Hense Jordan, of the Fifth Marines, noted with satisfaction that the night was about finished. A sickly bluish light came sifting into the woods. Shredded tree-tops and splintered branches grew sharp against a pale green sky. The flailed and broken timber and trampled underbrush around him took form in the shadows. The dawn chill bit into his bones, and he shifted himself in the shallow hole he had scooped the night before, and drew his salvaged German blanket closer around his shoulders.

An agonising cramp in his thigh jerked him painfully on his feet, to ease the tortured muscle. That spasm passing, he propped his rifle in a convenient crotch and remained standing, hunched over, his hands thrust into his breeches for warmth. He yawned and shivered miserably, his teeth chattering and his bony knees knocking together. It was the time of day when battles start and raids may be expected and réveillé turns you out, and the time of day a man always feels the lowest!

Of all the duty you got, these listening-posts, out in front in a place like this, were the meanest. And double watches, because the Major said there weren't enough men left in the battalion to run regular reliefs. . . . Where, by the way, was that dam' sergeant with his relief? He'd been out here since the Major-General Commandant was a corporal.

Meantime, his trained hard eyes searched restlessly in the brush for any movement; Private Hense Jordan was an old soldier, and he had no intention of dying for his country—not through carelessness, anyway. It was quiet, right here. Over on the left, toward the Veuilly Woods and Hill 142, the guns of the French division were shelling something, and you heard chaut-chauts and Hotchkiss guns. On the eastern face of this wood single rifles were going —snipers, most likely; Heine had good snipers.

Some of our machine-guns were bickering with the Maxims across the fields from Bouresches. A quiet morning. Well, after last night, Private Jordan considered, everybody ought to have his belly full—and here *Minenwerfer* shells began to break regularly in the right rear, where the ravine that bordered the southern edge of the wood led back to the town of Lucy.

"Steppin' 'em up an' down that there gully, where the chow detail has to go," considered Private Jordan sadly. "Heine's on the job, an' Gawd help them poor greaseballs, if they's any of them in there—hope some of them gets through with grub—an' oh, Lawd, let there be coffee." He couldn't remember when he had eaten, and he felt too weak to stand. He reached back and shook his canteen, although he knew it was empty, and he spat cotton from a dry mouth, and small irritations gravelled him.

It was, he decided, no life for a white man. Lying out nights. And being shelled. And fighting blind in the woods, and never getting any rations. "Gettin' us all bumped off like this, they might at least feed us." He hadn't had his shoes off for eleven days. He wished he was back on a battleship, where they piped for chow three times a day an' mornin' coffee before turn-to; and he regretted all the evil things he had said in his time about the Navy.

"Leastways, you wear marine uniform 'board ship." He crooked a torn khaki sleeve and regarded it with disgust. "First thing the Army done was take away our Lewis guns an' give us chaut-chauts—take away our greens an' give us khaki——" That last rankled. Every man in the marine brigade considered it a blow struck at their morale by the envious Army when they were informed that in France they would receive no more of the forester-green winter field uniforms of the marine corps, but would go garbed in olive-drab.

"Same as any odd lot of doughboys—yeh!" What if it was very like the German uniform? "Time a Boche gets near enough to tell the difference, he's in danger, I'll tell the cock-eyed worl'!" Only a few officers in the brigade clung to the old greens of the corps. The Major was one.

Private Jordan considered him briefly, the memory of his last court-martial sour on his mind. A hard son of a dog, but he was up here last night with his little stick, when they reorganised after the attack, looking things over. "Well, if I was a Major, they wouldn't get me in no army O.D., neither. Wouldn't have a chance. Recruitin' Office, Kansas City, Mizzour-i: that would be my billet."

There was, in the brush ahead, something that moved. Private Jordan's rifle was by his knee, and his hands were in his pockets, which was bad; but he was too old a stager to duck and grab. He froze motionless, every sense alert. The weakness flowed out of him, and his eyes narrowed to slits. Which way, and what——

It was a dog, a dust-grey, tall fellow with pointed ears, and when it lifted its wolfish head, pale colour on its throat. It materialised from around a bush a dozen yards away and stood, a fore-foot lifted, considering the next move. Private Hense Jordan remembered the order, reiterated when they came up to this fight: "Kill all dogs. We don't use them, and the French don't. The

Germans use them for messengers. Kill them, wherever seen—
and search the remains—they're usually carrying something."

Private Jordan also reflected that the Boche was very close to
him, on ahead through the woods, and he did not want to shoot
or otherwise demonstrate from his position if he could help it. But
he'd have to get that dog. . . . Looked like the critter might
come on out into the open, where a snap shot would have a better
chance—easy does it. Strictly as an afterthought, he loved dogs.
But orders were orders.

Greta settled it for him. The day before she had been right
through here. There should be a section of her infantrymen and
two light machine-guns just past the clearing. She trotted out, her
head low, taking a confusion of scents from the trampled ground,
and the marine saw that she would come within a yard of him.
Try it with the bayonet—no noise—— He caught up his rifle
and lunged in one motion, sudden as a snake's, but she was a
split-second quicker, and recoiled.

In her schooled brain, as she faced him, the cold face of her
Feldwebel back there, and the little *Gemeiner* on the railroad,
and the mad things that zipped and droned around her in the
wheat, all connected at once with this lean brown man. Here was
the enemy. She flung herself at him, slashing for the thigh, as a
wolf does. He shifted his bayonet and caught her on it; the point
slid inside her fore-leg and back, by the angle of her leap, across
her shoulder-blade.

But her weight overbalanced the man, and they went down
together in a tangle which the rifle dominated. Rolling clear of
her ringing jaws, Private Jordan brought one hobnailed boot down
on her head and considered that it was enough. He got up, wrenched the blade clear, shot a quick glance around, and bent over the
long, crumpled body, which quivered briefly and relaxed.

At her neck, hooked to the leather collar, was a thin aluminium cylinder.

" Active Boche, all right—in the messenger business. . . . Dam' it, I had to do it! An' it's a bitch, too! Arh! But there wasn't no way out of it—guess that got her in the heart." Kneeling, much distressed, he investigated the battered head and felt along her chest.

A sergeant and a private of marines came noiselessly up behind him. They spoke in husky whispers. " Got one, Hense? Seen anything else? If the mutt's got anything on 'im, rush it on back to the skipper. An' report to your platoon—moved it to the right this mornin'—Corporal Kent's in charge; they got some slum up. Here's the lay-out, guy," and the sergeant turned to instruct the relief.

Meantime Private Jordan had noted that the dog's chest still bled, and the flow was bright and not sluggish. " Say," he said, without looking up, " she ain't dead! I never killed her. She——"

" Well, kill it an' get back from here," snapped the sergeant in disgust. " This any place to be sobbin' over our dumb friends, you——" And Private Jordan slung his rifle, picked her up, and dodged into the brush to the rear, where he set her down and clumsily applied his first-aid bandage to stop the flow of blood.

Her skull didn't seem to be smashed, and although she was still entirely limp, he thought her heart went a little. Then he walked swiftly down through the position, along a very thin line of men in holes, who regarded him without curiosity and gulped cold slum and lukewarm coffee.

" Battalion?—down that there trail, fella." For he wasn't going to the company commander, a man not sympathetic to dogs or to irregularities.

" If the skipper says how come I went over his head, I'll tell him I thought orders was to take Boche dope right to the Major. Major used to have a dog," he planned uneasily; and passed through two platoons of the 2nd Engineers, unkempt and competent and constituting the battalion reserve; and found battalion headquarters group disposed in the ravine.

The Major sat on a rock and drank coffee from a canteen cup. He was unshaven, and his eyes were red-rimmed from loss of sleep, and the shine had departed from his field boots; but he wore his stained forester-green uniform with an air, and his helmet, the chin-strap looped up over the brim, was slanted at a cocky angle. He conversed casually with his Adjutant, and did not look around when Private Jordan, strangely burdened, slid down the bank of the ravine and was halted by the important sergeant-major.

"Private Jordan wants permission to speak to the battalion commander—got a Boche dog here, carryin' messages."

The Adjutant, a young man in a soldier's blouse and Quartermaster breeches everywhere too large for him, turned to hear, with a cold, bad-tempered eye.

"Sir, I'm on listenin'-post on the left, back there, an' just now, this here dog—I think she's a Boche messenger-houn', sir, like it says in orders—she tries to get by me, an'——" Then Greta came alive. Her lax body, sagging in the man's arms, quickened. She slashed Private Jordan's wrist wickedly, threw herself down and away from him, rolled over on her wrecked shoulder, and came in frantic haste to her three good feet, every tooth showing and her back hair all on end.

The Adjutant swore and plucked out his pistol, and the battalion gas non-com. clubbed his rifle, and Private Jordan, clutching at his wrist, rocked on his feet and pleaded foolishly: "Aw, don' kill her—don' kill her. She's a bitch, too." The Major walked toward her.

Sick and dizzy, with an unaccountable weakness dragging at her, and surrounded by khaki, Greta whirled on this new enemy, to do what she could. The fire went out of her eye. For the man had on a green uniform and had also the stiff, high look of her own officers. It was all very confusing, but with her people here it would be all right. He held out his hand, and stooped to her, and spoke softly. Greta lunged painfully to him, tried to lick his hand, and collapsed against his boots.

The Major detached the aluminium cylinder, and thrust it at his Adjutant. "See if it's anything, Le Grand. And my compliments to the surgeon—want him here. Now, old lady, did they do you wrong? Damnation! Bayonet—and you've bashed her eye out, you——"

"Sir "—Private Jordan, much distressed, pulled away from the file who was working at his wrist—"I done my best not to kill her. Sir, I never hurt a dawg in my life—I——"

"Oh, all right. All right. Surgeon, give me a hand here—maybe we can patch her up. Dam' fine animal, I think. Yes, what is it?"

The Adjutant, with the aid of a Navy hospital corps man who had studied in Vienna, had a translation. "It's addressed in code and signed in code, sir, but I think it's from Headquarters to battalion. Says KTK Battalion will approach position under cover from the right, pass through you, and attack to recover lost position. Says you will support attack after it has passed through. Says half-hour SMW—must mean heavy *Minenwerfer*—preparation, starting at five-fifteen—a.m., sir. And the time sent is four-thirty-five —don't get that, for it's just after four now—and it says acknowledge with two yellow smokes."

Said the Major, his head on one side: " Their time's an hour ahead of ours. Sergeant-major, you inventoried those captured pyrotechnics, you said. Ought to be yellow smoke rockets among 'em. Go forward a little way and send up two. Pick a place in the clear, so they'll get above the trees." The sergeant-major saluted and set off at a trot. "Where's that engineer officer? Mr. Shank, have your platoons stand by to reinforce the left company in half an hour. Go up there now and look it over; you'll put them in as the company commander directs. Tell him about it; they'll come that way. Work in through the woods and hit the left, I think. Le Grand, get Headquarters. I want some artillery."

A runner said: "Hi! Ol' sergeant-major sure made knots—there go them yellow smokes!" And very soon afterward the *Minenwerfer* shells began to crash into the woods. In the 40th Fusilier Regiment they never understood why their counter-attack failed so disastrously. The Lieutenant-Colonel had a very bad time explaining it.

And Greta lives now in Quantico, when she's at home. Her Major has a regiment there. She carries her years well, although she is one-eyed and has a heavy limp. She is an aloof, unfriendly dog to every other person but her Colonel; yet it is noted that in the fall and winter, when the marines go in forester-green, her temper becomes more genial, and she allows familiarities on the part of the rank and file.

SOLDIERS ON LEAVE

ON LEAVE

by
Henri Barbusse

EUDORE sat down awhile, there by the roadside well, before taking the path over the fields that led to the trenches, his hands crossed over one knee, his pale face uplifted. He had no moustache under his nose—only a little flat smear over each corner of his mouth. He whistled, and then yawned in the face of the morning till the tears came.

An artilleryman who was quartered on the edge of the wood—over there where a line of horses and carts looked like a gipsies' bivouac—came up, with two canvas buckets that danced at the end of his arms in time with his feet. In front of the sleepy un-armed soldier with a bulging bag he stopped short.

"On leave?"

"Yes," said Eudore; "just back."

"Good for you," said the gunner as he made off. "*You've* nothing to grumble at—with six days' leave in your pocket!"

Then four men came down the road, their gait heavy and slow, their boots turned into enormous caricatures of boots by reason of the mud. As one man they stopped on espying the profile of Eudore.

"There's Eudore! Hello, Eudore! Hello, old sport! You're back then!" they cried together, as they hurried up and offered him hands as big and ruddy as if they were hidden in woollen gloves.

"Morning, boys," said Eudore.

"Had a good time? What have you got to tell us, old man?"

"Yes," replied Eudore, "not so bad."

"*We've* been on wine fatigue, and we've finished. Let's go back together—what!"

In single file they went down the embankment of the road; arm-in-arm they crossed the field of grey mud, where their feet fell with the sound of dough being mixed in the kneading-trough.

"Well, you've seen your wife, your little Mariette—the only girl in the world—that you could never open your jaw without telling us a tale about, eh?"

Eudore's wan face winced.

"My wife? Yes, I saw her, sure enough, but only for a little while—there was the best I could do—but no luck, I admit, and that's all about it."

"How's that?"

"How? You know that we live at Villers-l'Abbaye, a hamlet of four houses, neither more nor less, straddling over the road. One of those houses is our café, and she runs it, or rather she is running it again since they gave up shelling the village.

"Now then, with my leave coming along, she asked for a permit to Mont-St.-Eloi, where my old folks are, and *my* permit was for Mont--St.-Eloi. See the move?

"Being a little woman with a headpiece, you know, she had applied for her permit long before the date when my leave was expected. All the same, my leave came before her permit. Spite o' that I set off—for one doesn't let his turn in the company go by, eh? So I stayed with the old people, and waited. I like 'em well enough, but I got down in the mouth all the same. As for them, it was enough that they could see me, and it worried them that I was bored by their company—what else could you expect? At the end of the sixth day—at the finish of my leave, and the very evening before returning—a young man on a bicycle, the son of the Florence family, brings me a letter from Mariette to say that her permit had not yet come——"

"Ah, rotten luck!" cried the audience.

"And that," continued Eudore, "there was only one thing to do—I was to get leave from the Mayor of Mont-St.-Eloi, who would get it from the military, and go myself at full speed to see her at Villers."

"You should have done that the first day, not the sixth!"

"So it seems, but I was afraid we should cross and me miss her—y'see, as soon as I landed, I was expecting her all the time, and every minute I fancied I could see her at the open door. So I did as she told me."

"After all, you saw her?"

"Just one day, or rather, just one night."

"Quite sufficient!" said Lamuse grinning, and Eudore, pale and serious, shook his head under the shower of suggestive remarks that followed.

"Shut your great mouths for five minutes, chaps."

"Get on with it, kid."

"There isn't much to tell," said Eudore.

"Well, then, you were saying you had got the hump with your people?"

"Ah, yes. They had tried their best to make up for Mariette—giving me lovely rashers of our own ham, and peach brandy, and patching up my linen, and all sorts of little spoiled-kid tricks—and I noticed they were still slanging each other in the old familiar way. But talk about a difference! I always had my eye on the door to see if some time or other it wouldn't get a move on and turn into a woman. So I went and saw the Mayor, and set off, yesterday, towards two in the afternoon—towards fourteen o'clock I might well say, seeing that I had been counting the hours since the day before! I had just one day of my leave left then.

"As we drew near in the dusk, through the carriage window

of the little railway that still keeps going down there on some fag-ends of line, I seemed to recognise the country, and yet somehow I didn't. Here and there seemed familiar and sometimes it would come back to me and then it, all at once, melted away again, just as if it was talking to me. Then it shut up. In the end we got out, and I found out—the limit, that was—that we had to go on foot to the last station.

"I have never been in such weather. It had rained for six days. For six days the sky washed the earth and then washed it again. The earth was softening and shifting, and filling up the holes and making new ones."

"Same here; it only stopped raining this morning."

"It was just my luck. And everywhere there were swollen new streams washing away the borders of the fields as though they were lines on paper. There were hills that ran with water from top to bottom. Gusts of wind sent the rain in great clouds flying and whirling about, and lashing our hands and faces and necks.

"So you bet, when I had tramped to the station, if someone had looked nasty at me it would have been enough to make me turn back."

"But when we did get to the place—there were several of us, some more men on leave; they weren't bound for Villers, but they had to go through it to get somewhere else—so it happened that we got there together—five old cronies that didn't know each other.

"I could make nothing of anything. They've been worse shell-ed over there than here, and then there was the water everywhere, and it was getting dark.

"I told you there are only four houses in the little place, only they're a good way away from each other. You come to the lower end of a slope. I didn't know too well where I was any more than they did, though they too belonged to the district and had some notion of the lay of it. And all the time the rain was falling in bucketsful.

"It got so bad that we started to run. We passed by the farm of the Alleux—that's the first of the houses—and it looked like a sort of stone ghost. Bits of wall like splintered pillars standing up out of the water; the house was shipwrecked. The other farm, a little further, was as good as drowned dead.

"Our house is the third. It's on the edge of the road that runs along the top of the slope. We climbed up, facing the rain that beat on us in the dusk almost blinding us—the cold and wet fairly smacked us in the eye, flop!—and broke our ranks like machine-guns.

"Our house! I ran like a greyhound—like an African attacking. Mariette! I could see her with her arms outstretched in the doorway behind that fine curtain of night and rain—of rain so fierce that it drove her back and kept her shrinking between the doorposts like a statue of the Virgin in its niche. I just threw myself forward, but remembered to give the others the sign to follow me. The house swallowed the lot of us. Mariette laughed a little to see me, with tears in her eye. She waited till we were alone together, and then laughed and cried all at once. I told the boys to make themselves at home and sit down, some on the chairs and the rest on the table.

"'Where are they going, these men?' asked Mariette.

"'We are going to Vauvelles.'

"'*Jésus!*' she said, 'you'll never get there. You *can't* do those two miles and more in the night, with the roads washed away and swamps everywhere. You mustn't even try to.'

"'Well, we'll go on to-morrow, then; only we must find somewhere to pass the night.'

"'I'll go with you,' I said, 'as far as the Pendu farm—they're not short of room there. You'll snore in there all right, and you can start at daybreak.'

"'Right! Let's get a move on so far.'

"We went out again. What a downpour! We were wet past bearing. The water poured into our socks through the boot-soles and by the trouser bottoms, and they, too, were soaked through and through up to the knees. Before we got to this Pendu we met a shadow in a big black cloak with a lantern. The lantern was raised, and we saw a gold stripe on the sleeve, and then an angry face.

"'What the hell are you doing there?' said the shadow, drawing back a little and putting one fist on his hip, while the rain rattled like hail on his hood.

"'They're men on leave for Vauvelles—they can't set off again to-night—they would like to sleep in the Pendu farm.'

"'*What* do you say? Sleep here? This is the police station; I am the officer on guard, and there are Boche prisoners in the buildings.' And I'll tell you what he said as well—'You'd better clear off from here in less than two seconds. Hop it!'

"So we right-about-faced and started back again, stumbling as if we were boozed, slipping, puffing, splashing, and bespattering ourselves. One of the boys cried to me through the wind and rain: 'We'll go back with you as far as your home, all the same. As we've nowhere to go we've plenty of time.'

"'Where will you sleep?'

"'Oh, we'll find somewhere, don't worry, for the little time we have to kill here.'

"'Yes, we'll find somewhere all right,' I said. 'Come in again for a minute meanwhile—I won't take no;' and Mariette sees us enter once more in single file, all five of us soaked like bread in soup.

" So there we all were, with only one little room to go round in and go round again—the only room in the house, seeing that it isn't a palace.

" ' Tell me, madame,' says one of our friends, ' isn't there a cellar here?'

" ' There's water in it,' says Mariette; ' you can't see the bottom step and it's only got two.'

" ' Damn!' says the man, ' for I see there's no loft either.'

" After a minute or two he gets up. ' Good-night, old chum,' he says to me, and they get their hats on.

" ' What, are you going off in weather like this, boys?'

" ' Do you think,' says the old sport, ' that we're going to spoil your stay with your wife?'

" ' But, my good man——'

" ' But me no buts. It's nine o'clock, and *you've* got to take your hook before day. So good-night. Coming, you others?'

" ' Rather,' say the boys. ' Good-night, all.'

" There they are at the door and opening it. Mariette and me, we look at each other—but we don't move. Once more we look at each other, and then we sprang at them. I grabbed the skirt of a coat and she a belt—all wet enough to wring out.

" ' Never! We won't let you go—it can't be done.'

" ' But——'

" ' But, nothing,' I reply, while she locks the door."

" Then what?" asked Lamuse.

" Then? Nothing at all," replied Eudore. " We just stayed like that, very discreetly—all the night—sitting, propped up in the corners, yawning, like the watchers over a dead man. We made a bit of talk at first. From time to time someone said, ' Is it still raining?' and went and had a look, and said, ' It's still raining—

and we could hear it, by the way. A big chap who had a moustache like a Bulgarian fought against sleep like a wild man. Sometimes one or two of them would go to sleep, but there was always
one to yawn and keep an eye open for politeness, and to stretch
himself or half get up so that he could settle more comfortably.

"Mariette and me, we never slept. We looked at each other,
but we looked at the others as well, and they looked at us, and
there you are.

"Morning came and cleaned the window. I got up to go and
look outside. The rain was hardly less. In the room I could see
dark forms that began to stir and breathe hard. Mariette's eyes
were red with looking at me all night. Between her and me a
soldier was filling his pipe and shivering.

"Someone beats a tattoo on the window, and I half open it. A
silhouette with a streaming hat appears, as though carried and
driven there by the terrible force of the blast that came with it,
and asks:

"'Hey, in the café there! Is there any coffee to be had?'

"'Coming, sir, coming,' cried Mariette.

"She gets up from her chair, a little benumbed. Without a
word she looks at herself in our bit of a mirror, touches her hair
lightly, and then says quite simply, the good lass:

"'I am going to make coffee for everybody.'

"When that was drunk, we had all of us to go. Besides, customers were turning up every minute.

"'Hey, little mother,' they cried, shoving their noses in at the
half-open window, 'let's have a coffee—or three—or four,' 'And
two more again,' says another voice.

"We go up to Mariette to say good-bye. They knew they had
played gooseberry that night most damnably, but I could see plainly that they didn't know if it would be the thing to say something

about it or just let it drop altogether.

" Then the Bulgarian made up his mind: 'We've made a hell of a mess of it for you, eh, madame?'

" He said that to show he'd been well brought up, the old sport.

" Mariette thanks him and offers him her hand—'That's nothing at all, sir. I hope you'll enjoy your leave.'

" And me, I held her tight in my arms and kissed her as long as I could—half a minute—discontented—my God! I had reason to be—but glad that Mariette had not driven the boys out like dogs, and I felt sure she liked me, too, for not doing it.

" ' But that isn't all,' said one of the leave men, lifting the skirt of his cape and fumbling in his coat-pocket; 'that's not all. What do we owe you for the coffees?'

" 'Nothing, for you stayed the night with me; you are my guests.'

" 'Oh, madame, we can't have that!'

" And how they set to to make protests and compliments in front of each other! Old man, you can say what you like—we may be only poor devils, but it was astonishing, that little palaver of good manners.

" 'Come along! Let's be hopping it, eh?'

" They go out one by one. I stay till the last. Just then another passer-by begins to knock on the window—another who was dying for a mouthful of coffee. Mariette, by the open door, leaned forward and cried: 'One second!'

" Then she put into my arms a parcel that she had ready. 'I had bought a knuckle of ham—it was for supper for us, for us two and a litre of good wine. But—oh, help!—when I saw there were five of you, I didn't want to divide it out so much, and I want still less now. There's the ham, the bread, and the wine. I give them to you so that you can enjoy them by yourself, my boy.

As for them, we have given them enough,' she says.

"Poor Mariette," sighs Eudore. "Fifteen months since I'd seen her. And when shall I see her again? Ever? It was jolly, that idea of hers. She crammed all that stuff into my bag——"

He half opens his brown canvas pouch.

"Look, here they are! The ham here, and the bread, and there's the booze. Well, seeing it's there, do you know what we're going to do with it? We're going to share it out between us, eh, old pals?"

THE STRANGE HOME

by
Erich Maria Remarque

I LIE down on many a station platform; I stand before many a soup-kitchen; I squat on many a bench; then at last the landscape becomes disturbing, mysterious, and familiar. It glides past the western windows with its villages, their thatched roofs like caps pulled over the whitewashed, half-timbered houses, its cornfields gleaming like mother-of-pearl in the slanting light, its orchards, its barns, and old lime-trees.

The names of the stations begin to take on meaning, and my heart trembles. The train stamps and stamps onward; I stand at the window and hold on to the frame. These names mark the boundaries of my youth.

Smooth meadows, fields, farm-yards; a solitary team moves against the sky-line along the road that runs parallel to the horizon —a barrier, before which peasants stand waiting, girls waving, children playing on the embankment, roads leading into the country—smooth roads without artillery.

It is evening, and if the train did not rattle I should cry out. The plain unfolds itself.

In the distance, the soft blue silhouette of the mountain ranges begins to appear. I recognise the characteristic outline of the Dolbenberg, a jagged comb springing up precipitously from the limits of the forests. Behind it should lie the town.

But now the sun streams through the world, dissolving everything in its golden-red light; the train swings round one curve and then another. Far away, in a long line behind the other, stand the poplars, unsubstantial, swaying and dark, fashioned out of shadow, light, and desire.

The field swings round as the train encircles it, and the intervals between the trees diminish; the trees become a block, and for a moment I see one only, then they reappear from behind the foremost tree and stand out a long line against the sky until they are hidden by the first houses.

A street-crossing. I stand by the window. I cannot drag myself away. The others put their baggage ready for getting out. I repeat to myself the name of the street that we cross over—Bremerstrasse—Bremerstrasse——

Below there are cyclists, lorries, men; it is a grey street and a grey subway; it affects me as though it were my mother.

Then the train stops, and there is the station with noise and cries and sentries, I pick up my pack and fasten the straps, I take my rifle in my hand and stumble down the steps.

On the platform I look round; I know no one among all the people hurrying to and fro. A Red Cross Sister offers me something to drink. I turn away; she smiles at me too foolishly, so obsessed with her own importance. "Just look, I am giving a soldier coffee!" She calls me "Comrade," but I will have none of it.

Outside in front of the station the stream roars alongside the street, it rushes foaming from the sluices of the mill bridge. There stands the old square watch-tower, in front of it the great mottled lime-tree and behind it the evening.

Here we have often sat—how long ago it is!—we have passed over this bridge and breathed the cool, acid smell of the stagnant water; we have leaned over the still water on this side of the lock, where the green creepers and weeds hang from the piles of the bridge; and on hot days we rejoiced in the spouting foam on the other side of the lock and told tales about our school-teachers.

I pass over the bridge, I look right and left; the water is as full of weeds as ever, and it still shoots over in gleaming arches. In the tower building laundresses still stand with bare arms as they used to over the clean linen, and the heat from the ironing pours out through the open windows. Dogs trot along the narrow street; before the doors of the houses people stand and follow me with their gaze as I pass by, dirty and heavy-laden.

In this confectioner's we used to eat ices, and there we learned to smoke cigarettes. Walking down the street I know every shop —the grocer's, the chemist's, the tobacconist's. Then at last I stand before the brown door with its worn latch, and my hand grows heavy. I open the door, and a strange coolness comes out to meet me; my eyes are dim.

The stairs creak under my boots. Upstairs a door rattles; some-one is looking over the railing. It is the kitchen door that was opened. They are cooking potato-cakes; the house reeks of it, and to-day of course is Saturday. That will be my sister leaning over. For a moment I am shy and lower my head, then I take off my helmet and look up. Yes, it is my eldest sister.

"Paul," she cries—"Paul——"

I nod; my pack bumps against the banisters, my rifle is so heavy.

She pulls a door open and calls: "Mother, mother! Paul is here."

I can go no further—"Mother, mother! Paul is here."

I lean against the wall and grip my helmet and rifle. I hold them as tight as I can, but I cannot take another step. The staircase fades before my eyes; I support myself with the butt of my rifle against my feet and clench my teeth fiercely, but I cannot speak a word. My sister's call has made me powerless; I can do nothing. I struggle to make myself laugh, to speak, but no word comes, and so I stand on the steps, miserable, helpless, paralysed, and against my will the tears run down my cheeks.

My sister comes back and says: "Why, what is the matter?"

Then I pull myself together and stagger on to the landing. I lean my rifle in a corner, I set my pack against the wall, place my helmet on it, and fling down my equipment and baggage. Then I say fiercely: "Bring me a handkerchief."

She gives me one from the cupboard and I dry my face. Above me on the wall hangs the glass case with the coloured butterflies that once I collected.

Now I hear my mother's voice. It comes from the bedroom.

"Is she in bed?" I ask my sister.

"She is ill," she replies.

I go in to her, give her my hand, and say as calmly as I can: "Here I am, mother."

She lies still in the dim light. Then she asks anxiously:

"Are you wounded?" and I feel her searching glance.

"No, I have got leave."

My mother is very pale. I am afraid to make a light.

"Here I lie now," says she, "and cry instead of being glad."

"Are you sick, mother?" I ask.

"I am going to get up a little to-day," she says, and turns to my sister, who is continually running to the kitchen to watch that the food does not burn. "And put out the jar of preserved whortle-berries—you like that, don't you?" she asks me.

"Yes, mother; I haven't had any for a long time."

"We might almost have known you were coming," laughs my sister; "there is just your favourite dish—potato-cakes, and even whortleberries to go with them too."

"And it is Saturday," I add.

"Sit here beside me," says my mother.

She looks at me. Her hands are white and sickly and frail compared with mine. We say very little, and I am thankful that she asks nothing. What ought I to say? Everything I could have wished for has happened. I have come out of it safely and sit here beside her. And in the kitchen stands my sister, preparing supper and singing.

"Dear boy," says my mother softly.

We were never very demonstrative in our family; poor folk who toil and are full of cares are not so. It is not their way to protest what they already know. When my mother says to me, "Dear boy," it means much more than when another uses it. I know well enough that the jar of whortleberries is the only one they have had for months, and that she has kept it for me; and the somewhat stale cakes that she gives me too. She must have got them cheap some time and put them all by for me.

I sit by her bed, and through the window the chestnut-trees in the beer garden opposite glow in brown and gold. I breathe deeply, and say over to myself: "You are at home, you are at home." But a sense of strangeness will not leave me; I cannot feel at home amongst these things. There is my mother, there is my sister, there my case of butterflies, and there the mahogany piano—but I am not myself there. There is a distance, a veil between us.

I go and fetch my pack to the bedside and turn out the things I have brought—a whole Edamer cheese that Kat provided me with, two loaves of army bread, three-quarters of a pound of butter, two tins of liver-sausage, a pound of dripping, and a little bag of rice.

"I suppose you can make some use of that——"

They nod.

"Is it pretty bad for food here?" I inquire.

"Yes, there's not much. Do you get enough out there?"

I smile and point to the things I have brought. "Not always quite so much as that, of course, but we fare reasonably well."

Erna takes away the food. Suddenly my mother seizes hold of
my hand and asks falteringly : " Was it very bad out there, Paul?"

" Mother, what should I answer to that? You would not understand, you could never realise it. And you never shall realise it.
Was it bad, you ask. You, mother." I shake my head and say :
" No, mother, not so very. There are always a lot of us together,
so it isn't so bad."

" Yes, but Heinrich Bredemeyer was here just lately, and he
said it was terrible out there now, with the gas and all the rest
of it."

It is my mother who says that. She says : " With the gas and all
the rest of it." She does not know what she is saying; she is merely
anxious for me. Should I tell her how we once found three enemy
trenches with their garrison all stiff as though stricken with apop-
lexy? Against the parapet, in the dug-outs, just where they were,
the men stood and lay about, with blue faces, dead.

" No, mother, that's only talk," I answer; "there's not very
much in what Bredemeyer says. You see, for instance, I'm well and
fit——"

Before my mother's tremulous anxiety I recover my composure.
Now I can walk about and talk and answer questions without fear
of having suddenly to lean against the wall because the world
turns soft as rubber and my veins become brimstone.

My mother wants to get up. So I go for a while to my sister in
the kitchen.

IN THE AIR

FED UP

by
Elliott White Springs

HENRY was tired. He got up every morning tired. He wanted to go away to a quiet place where he could sleep for a month. He was so nervous now he couldn't stay in bed five minutes unless he was completely exhausted or dead drunk. Sleep? He would never sleep again.

For months now—it seemed years—he had been doing nothing but flying, drinking, and arguing with dumb girls. The liquor sooner or later went to his head, the girls sooner or later gave in, and the flying sooner or later would bump him off. What was the use?

Five months he had been at the front now. Five months or five years; he'd forgotten which. His ears were ruined, his eyes were strained until he couldn't read, and his heart beat around a hundred in the air and a hundred and forty on the ground.

Somewhere in the back of his head was the picture of a big white house with a wide shady lawn. He used to call it home. And so was there a memory of marble palaces and golden cities and turreted castles from the fairy tales. Was the big white house a part of them? He couldn't remember. His home now was in the clouds. Years ago he had left his girl. His girl? Was that the same one the prince awakened with a kiss in the enchanted castle? He wasn't sure. What difference did it make? He was going on patrol in half an hour. His date was with Atropos. The Fokkers got two yesterday. Whose turn to-day?

That was a bad show yesterday. The Fokkers had a new leader, apparently a man of cunning, who had taken Richthofen's place. He knew how to fight Camels. Judge Wilmot had gone down in flames and Ben Thomas had died in the ambulance after he got back to the field—shot through the stomach and leg, he had flown back to his own field to die among friends.

Henry felt badly about that show. He wasn't leading it but was up above protecting, and he saw the disaster coming. The Hun leader had made a feint with half his patrol and then zoomed up as his other men came down. It was a dangerous thing to do, but it evidently had been carefully planned and rehearsed. It worked and Henry had gotten only one doubtful bird to soothe his injured pride and ease the loss of Ben and Judge. It wasn't his fault—it wasn't anybody's fault—give the Hun credit for something—but it was up to him to see that it didn't happen again. Maybe he might get revenge!

He had just landed after leading a patrol and his feet seemed to drag as he walked into his office to take off his flying clothes. He told his sergeant to shoot the gunnery corporal at once. Every time he'd get on a Fokker's tail his guns would jam. And get him a new buckle for his shoulder yoke so he could unfasten it in the air if he had to. You can't change gun locks if you can't reach forward.

Johnny Warren walked up to join him. Johnny was the Flight Commander of C Flight and had led the top flight of five machines above him.

"Say, for Pete's sake, use your head, Hank," Johnny begged him, "I washed out another plane in that scrap to-day—all full of holes and one through my floorboard. These Fokkers have got something now they haven't had before."

"Yes," Henry agreed, "I believe it's a new motor. There's been a rumour about it for some time. I hopped on some cold meat yesterday and he not only climbed away from me but could turn right along with me. I didn't get a shot at him and he got two cracks at me—if you don't think they're good. I'll say they've got something! And the boy who was leading their formation was all to the mustard. But that stunt they pulled yesterday was overripe. If Judge had been a little quicker and climbed back toward me instead of going down after those first three, we'd have mopped up. I'm not blaming Judge—he's gone now, anyway—and nine times out of ten he'd have been right. He knew I could take care of myself and he didn't know the first ones had a new motor to zoom up so fast. I guess I'd have been sore as hell if he'd let them get away with their feint."

"Well, you know about these new motors now, so don't try to win the war every day. Leave a few Huns for the next generation to scrap with. I haven't got any grudge against the Hun as long as he's got the best motor. And Napoleon said that God was on the side of the most horse-power. He spoke a mouthful."

"Suppose you lead hereafter."

"No. I'd rather you'd lead. I'm not worried about your leading. You're the best patrol leader in this outfit and got the best eyes in France, but for Pete's sake don't be so pugnacious. There's no time limit on this war. Judge got his yesterday because he was trying to keep up with your pace, and he couldn't make the grade. It'll get even you before long. And when you go, you'll snap like a straw. I'll stick by you till hell freezes over, but don't turn my hair grey with any more shows like that one last week. If they'd had these new motors last week, you and me would either be guests of His Imperial Highness or His Plutonic Majesty."

"You need a rest, Johnny; why don't you take it? You're getting stale."

"Who's going to keep the Huns off your tail while I take leave? Tubby is blind as a bat and has done lost what little guts he ever had."

"Well, thanks for sticking if it's on my account, but you'd be better off in the long run."

"If you take a rest, I'd be all right. You're the baby that keeps me awake nights. Take a rest yourself. Ain't you got any nerves at all, you fish?"

"Don't know. I'm afraid to find out."

They walked over to the squadron office to make out combat reports.

Henry was tired. He sank into the chair and couldn't remember what he was going to write. He had to ask Johnny the time, the height, and the number of Fokkers. He knew all this but his mind was too tired to recall it.

Then he strolled down to the mess tent and looked at himself in the mirror behind the bar. His eyes and nose were red with a coating of black carbon from the exhaust and burnt powder from the guns. His chin and cheeks were white where the helmet protected him. God, he was tired. He had a highball and somebody handed him some mail. Four papers and a dozen fat letters. He threw the papers in the wastebasket and stuck the letters into his pocket. Maybe he would read them later. No, he'd be damned if he would! Then he'd have to answer them. As long as he didn't read them he felt no obligation to answer them. He had another highball and started an argument with the Gunnery Officer who came bustling in to explain that the stoppages occurred because he didn't know how to handle his guns—probably let them get cold—opened fire too soon——

He walked off to finish his drink in peace and read *La Vie Parisienne*.

He had another highball and a couple of bottles of beer with lunch and then slept until four. God, he was tired!

At five he was on patrol again. This time he was on top and

Tubby White of A Flight was leading. The sun was with them now and the wind as well. The Huns had enough for the day, and didn't fancy fighting with the sun in the west. Tubby scared up a two-seater underneath the clouds and Henry had to stay up and watch while all five streaked down out of the sun, pounced on it, and shot it down in flames. He landed in disgust.

God, he was tired! He had not walked a mile in six weeks. He didn't even climb in and out of his machine without two men to assist him. He got into bed alone and lifted his own glass. That was all the exercise he got—yet he was dying of exhaustion.

That was the way he felt—tired. Tired all the time. Nervous? No. Just tired. Can't sleep. Can't eat. Drink gives me a headache. Just tired. Frightened? Never. Worried? Hell, no. Just tired. Fight all the time. All night. All day. For ever. My God—won't we ever do anything but fight? Nerves? No. Got nerves like iron. Just tired!

And now he had to have dinner with the British Colonel. That meant another binge. Americans on the British front were expected to binge. They had a reputation to protect.

He and the C.O. arrived at the Colonel's château at eight. The Colonel, his Adjutant, the Wing Gunnery Officer, the Wing Equipment Officer, the Wing Intelligence Officer and the Flight Surgeon were all discussing the day's combat report. Richthofen's old circus had accounted for fourteen British pilots, and there were four missing. Only one Fokker was known to be destroyed and three two-seaters. We had also lost three balloons. That irked the Colonel particularly. Not a very good day.

Henry had five cocktails with the Colonel. The Colonel was crying for vengeance. Henry was mourning for Ben. He could still see Ben being lifted out of his plane. Ben was mad about the matter. He was cursing the Kaiser when he died. Henry somehow felt ashamed that he wasn't mad, too. Why was it he always killed in cold blood? He never took any joy in it. And very little interest now. Months before it had thrilled him—now it only tired him.

The Colonel wanted a whole flight to act as decoy. Henry admitted that as decoy he didn't have his equal except in the German Army, and he wasn't sure about that. The Colonel asked him if he would go over with the flight and stay over long enough to get the whole Hun circus down on him.

"Sure," said Henry, looking about to see where the sixth cocktail was coming from. "If you give me enough planes up above to handle them when they come down. No use having decoys if your gun isn't loaded. Napoleon said never to go into battle with a broken sword. Or was it Casanova? I don't know. Just like taking a girl to walk after the rain."

"How many do you think you'd need?" the Colonel asked. "You can have all you can use."

"Give me fifteen Camels for the trap," Henry told him, "fifteen S.E.s up above the Camels to get the Fokkers, and ten Dolphins at 22,000 to keep anything off the S.E.s."

"All right," said the Colonel, "day after to-morrow morning. I'll have the S.E. and Dolphin Majors bring their Flight Commanders over for a conference to-morrow afternoon. And if you don't get the Fokkers, don't bother to come back."

The General of the brigade came in with his Adjutant. Henry had five cocktails with the General. They were old friends. Either the General had stolen his girl in London or he had stolen the General's girl. It took half an hour to settle it. At any rate, she was a fine girl! Henry magnanimously forgave the General.

Dinner was served at nine and was constantly interrupted by telephone calls from squadrons. There was soup and white fish and chicken livers and salad and champagne—a great deal of champagne.

Henry was called upon for jokes. He told all he knew. Stories he hadn't told since he was in grade school—stories that rustled the shroud of Joe Miller's corpse—stories that hadn't been laughed at in fifteen years. But the British laughed. They enjoyed them. Henry recited them until the champagne overcame his tongue and he could not make sense.

After dinner, they gathered around the piano and sang. The General played and they sang "Keep the Home Fires Burning," "Little Grey Home in the West," "Down the Long, Long Trail," and other songs of British gaiety. Then Henry and the C.O. sang "The Royal King of England" and had to repeat it three times.

The Colonel led the way into another room where there was a roulette table. He had several hundred five-franc pieces for chips. Each man took his turn at banker and everyone played. Henry was lucky. He won 2,000 francs. What good was that? He hadn't spent 200 francs in four months. What good was 2,000? He tried to lose it but he only won more. They were drinking port now, and cognac and whisky. Henry stuck to the port. It was heavy and would put him to sleep. It did. He woke up in the car outside his tent and the chauffeur was shaking him and the C.O. to awaken them. Damn good evening!

The next day Johnny led an uneventful patrol and Henry made plans. He was going to avenge Ben. Rot! Ben was killed in a fair fight. He was simply going to outguess that Fokker leader. He was going to let him see two top flights but not let him suspect the S.E.s. The Fokker leader would be acting as decoy himself. So much the better. He could spring his own trap. He could slap himself in the face with his own shovel.

He went out for an hour in the afternoon to drop little twenty-pound bombs on the Hun back area. Nothing exciting.

The Majors and Flight Commanders of the S.E.s and Dolphins came over. They were all kids younger than Henry, but they had been flying at least two years, a year of it at the front. They didn't like the idea of following a comparatively inexperienced leader. But the decoy had to lead and they were heartily in favour of letting the Camels be the decoys. Nobody wanted to be a decoy. It wasn't safe.

In the end they were satisfied—all but the Dolphins. They refused to go beyond gliding distance from the lines unless there was a dog-fight in progress. Their motors were bad and they had forced landings on every patrol. They would start on the patrol with fifteen planes. Maybe they would get ten up to 22,000 feet. Maybe— no promises. That's where the Dolphins had the advantage. They were no good down low.

Then the Majors and Flight Commanders descended upon the bar and the battle raged until dusk. Somebody took them out and threw them in their planes and started up for them.

Henry took off at exactly six next morning. They chose that hour because the Fokkers were sure to be out enjoying the advantage of the sun behind them, and still the sun wasn't high enough to let them get immediately above them.

Henry had four planes behind him. Johnny was 1,000 feet above him with five planes, and Tubby was 1,000 feet above Johnny with six planes. Sixteen little Camels—going out to deliver an invitation to battle.

At 10,000 feet over a ruined town they made a rendezvous with the S.E.s. The S.E.s turned south and continued to climb. The S.E.s worked best at 15,000 feet so they were to stay high up. The Camels were no good above 12,000. At 18,000 were the Dolphins —how many, he couldn't see.

He crossed the lines at 12,000 and was greeted by a bombardment of Archie. Fine—good advertisement! The S.E.s were invisible now. Good! Mustn't let the Huns see them.

He steered straight into Hunland for ten miles, turning, twisting, and peering below and above. Nothing but Archie. Johnny was back three miles and 2,000 feet above him. Tubby was 2,000 feet above Johnny. Then there were the S.E.s, and finally the Dolphins. Just like the steps of stairs. When the fight started the formation would collapse like a house of cards. Woe to the Huns at the bottom!

Henry turned south and held his level. The wind was against him fairly strong so he turned back to the lines. Mustn't get too far over. That Hun leader knows his business.

In ten minutes he saw what he was looking for—four Fokkers 2,000 feet below him. So that was it? The Hun leader wasn't going to take a chance of letting him slip out of his clutches this time. He was going to cut him off from below. He studied the sun, his finger covering the ball of it. There they were! Two layers of them—about ten in each layer several thousand feet above him.

The four were climbing and turned south underneath him. The nerve of it! What an insult—four Fokkers flying under fifteen Camels! He knew it was because they had other machines above him. They were decoys too! All right, a little closer to the lines and he'd give them the surprise of their lives. He'd nail those four first—before the others got down on him—he'd show them what to do with decoys!

The Huns above were drawing nearer, two traps were ready to be sprung. All right, he'd spring it. He warmed his guns, waved to his men, and raised his right arm. Then he put his nose down and throttled back. No zooming now—he was going to stay down with them—dog-fight those four; and he didn't need speed—too much speed and he couldn't shoot straight or get in a long burst.

The four Fokkers saw him coming and were ready. They closed up and turned. Henry took the leader head on. The leader turned and Henry was on his tail in a flash. But before he could get his sights on him another Fokker was firing at him. He saw the tracer bullets streaking by and had to turn quickly. The Fokker stuck on his tail. He circled and turned to shake him off. Where was Johnny? The Fokker was firing again. Pretty close, that! Here were the others! Down came five Camels, guns blazing tracer sparklets and phosphorus. Four Fokkers and ten Camels—but only for a second. Eight more Fokkers dived after the Camels! A Camel was firing at the Fokker on his tail. Good old Johnny! He could tell it was Johnny by his streamer. He saw the Camel go down out of control. Poor Johnny! Good-bye, Johnny. Henry was firing at a Fokker and a Fokker was firing at him when both guns jammed. Damn that Gunnery Officer. He turned on his side, loosed his shoulder yoke, and worked at the stoppages. One clear. Where's that hammer? Bang! The other gun was clear. Where's that top flight?

Five more Camels plunged into the centre of the whirling mass, each man taking a Fokker as he levelled off. Henry saw two planes go down in flames—burning like meteors. So swift was their descent that he could not tell friend from foe. All were firing, twisting, turning. Henry saw a Fokker beneath him and pounced on to its tail. The Fokker half rolled, and he turned quickly on to another. There was that damn sickly yellow phosphorus again in front of him. He looked back. Then came the other eight Huns. Where were the S.E.s? He was too busy to look.

He looked at his altimetre—10,000 feet. He noted his position —ten miles over. A killing for the S.E.s. For God's sake, come on! He saw a Fokker explode and blaze up. Fine. Down went another plane, twisting dizzily and smoking badly. A Camel this time. God, what a fight! Greatest dog-fight in history. He was proud that he had staged it. Beyond his control now—nothing to do but fight his own battle. Another jam—he cleared it and looked above him. There was a Fokker coming down on him. He turned sharply and the Fokker roared by and turned back toward him. Henry noticed that he had a streamer on his rudder—it was the Hun leader! All right—after this scrap one side or the other would have a new leader. Johnny was already gone. He must even up the score.

There were the S.E.s. We've won! My God, there're more Fokkers! Where'd they come from? What a fight! He saw an S.E. and a Fokker collide, head on. A horrible sight. An immediate death was kind—think of the seconds they had to wait as eternity rushed up to them. There were the other Fokkers. Must be fifteen of them. All right—every man for himself. The sky was black with planes and powder. The greatest fight of the War!

Henry and the Hun leader were to the south-east of the fight and 500 yards from it now as they jockeyed for position. Twice they came at each other head on and pulled away in climbing turns at the last fraction of a second before colliding. Nerve the fellow had! Not a shot fired—both were too wary and too cool to waste a foot of altitude for a random shot. A burst of twenty at fifty feet on a man's tail was worth 300 random shots. Henry didn't even glance through his sight. He was watching the Fokker—an ugly square plane with a white nose and a black and white checkerboard fuselage and tail. He made out a skull and crossbones on it. The same fellow! He'd give him a death's head all right. They had closed in now and were circling. The circle was not a hundred feet in diameter and each plane was at the nadir, flat on its side in a vertical bank. Occasionally one would hit the other's backwash and stagger dizzily for a moment, then get back its stride. Not a shot came from either pair of guns.

Henry glanced at the ground. The wind was blowing him farther over; this wouldn't do! All the Hun had to do would be to hold him in a turn, and the wind would do the rest. He must get out of this.

Henry was as cool as if he were playing chess. He had perfect command of every faculty—every resource. He was in the enemy's territory. He had a good plane but a poor motor. The Hun clearly had the better motor for he was gaining a little in height every time.

Henry was thinking calmly: this bird is too good for me—I'll never get him—got to get out of this—can't run for it—he'd get me first crack—can't stay here—other Fokkers will see this fight and come down—then *fini*. Gotta get out of this—this fellow knows his job and he's gaining—he's gaining twenty feet a turn —we're at 7,000—he'll run me into the ground at this rate—he'll get above me—then he's got me. I can come out of this turn, but he'll be on my tail above me. I can half roll and loop, but he'll follow me. Everything I do, he'll do right above me. If I half roll, he'll half roll. Sooner or later he gets me. He'll never fire until he's sure of me. If I go into a spin, so does he. When I come out, he's still on my tail. He can do this all day—damn fine pilot. And he will! Well, I've got to get him. Got to get him! Only one way to do it. It's he or I now. Take a chance. Let him get on my tail— he's going to sooner or later—dive for it and see who can stand the gaff the longest. Then pull the old trick on him—it might work. When I pull up, he'll pull up and wait for a shot. I'll take one when he isn't looking—worth a try—my only hope!

Henry looked at the sun and waited until his back was to it. Then he levelled off and dived toward the lines.

Come on, you sucker, I'll dive until I see your tracer!

He hadn't long to wait. The Hun finished his half circle and dived after him. Henry had a start of 500 feet on him.

The Hun closed it up. Henry turned around as far as his shoulder yoke would let him and watched—300 feet—200 feet—100 feet. He must sit still and take the first burst. He was suddenly cold as he awaited the crack of the spandaus. How good a shot was this Hun? Cool and deliberate he was. Could he hit him with the first burst? He'd soon know. Gotta sit and take it.

140—150—160—175—his airspeed indicator told him. It broke. Crack—crack—crack! There it was—the Hun was making his killing. Now for it! Henry had both hands on the stick and he pulled it back steadily with all his force as he pressed his own trigger. The terrific pressure threw him back into his seat and pressed the breath out of him.

He was looking through his sight now—God what a noise from the wires! He heard one snap—good shot—would his wings stay on? The whole machine shook convulsively as his nose rose, pointed straight up, and continued backward in a loop. Would the Hun see him and pull up or would they collide? Crack! Something pierced his left shoulder. Good shot again!

Then he saw through his sight what he was looking for—the white nose. Both guns were going and he pushed the stick forward to hold his sight on the Hun—just a second, oh, God—just a second! He was upside down now—both guns playing on the white nose.

His nose started to drop—he half rolled and turned quickly—thank God for that shoulder yoke—ouch—how his shoulder hurt! Where was the Hun? There he was—my God, what a zoom! The Fokker was going straight up like an elevator—he must be doing 250—there, he's half rolling—he's—— An icy hand gripped his heart as the wings folded backward and the Fokker turned a somersault in the air and went roaring down not fifty feet from him. He watched it a second and saw it fluttering downward. Too bad—he was losing a friend—a fine fellow—hell of a war!

He was diving toward the lines now with his motor wide open. He must get back quickly. Faster—faster—faster—nothing could catch him now but the angel Gabriel. He tried to look back, but when he moved his shoulder stabbed him. The pain made him sick at his stomach. How was his arm? He could move his arm all right—at least he could land—he could work the throttle. God, what pain! Would he bleed to death before he got back? Probably. He felt he was fainting.

There were the lines, two miles ahead. Should he land in the balloon line while he was still conscious? No. Go on—back where he came from—like Ben did. Die on his own field—that was the way to do it. He could feel the blood running down his back. Was his shoulder blade broken? He tried to move it—the pain made him wince. What about his lung? Pierced? He took a deep breath. More pain. Yes, shoulder and lung. *Fini la guerre!* He was through. He and Johnny—gone the same way! And Ben! Good way to go!

They'd died with their shoes on! All right.

What's the use of the whole thing? Been fighting five months. What for? To get plugged through the shoulder by a better man.

He wondered if he had hit the Fokker or if the Fokker had simply broken up from structural weakness. Nobody would ever know. At least, he was firing at the Fokker. He would get credit for it. Credit? What did he want with any credit? He couldn't take any credit with him where he was going.

He was tired, dog-tired. His mind burned him. Well, it was all over now—he could feel himself getting weak. Could he last it? God, what pain!

Well, this was the end. Suddenly he was frightened—panicky. He didn't want to die. He was young; the wealth of life called to him. He had never been afraid to die—damn it, he wasn't afraid to die now—never had been afraid—he knew he had to die—that was the bargain he had struck with himself as the price of his courage. But he wasn't ready yet to pay the forfeit. He wasn't afraid—only regretful. Now he would never enjoy the fruits of his labours. In the moment of victory he was snatched away. He would die in torture like Ben. He recalled his shrieks of agony. No, he wasn't afraid to die, but he was afraid of pain. He couldn't stand pain. They would probe and cut and sew. He couldn't stand it! Should he dive into the ground now and end it?

This was the end. Why? He had given his life. For what? He couldn't remember. War! A good joke on him. He was a soldier —well, soldiers got killed. Why? So somebody else could get the booty. So the Congressmen's sons could take their feet off their desks and go home and get elected to office eternally. So Wall Street could get 8 per cent. So our grandchildren could be taught a fresh bunch of lies. This was glory. This was the end!

Was this what happened to a drowning man? God, he was so lonely. He didn't want to die. He wanted to scream it so loud that Johnny would hear and yell back to him. Think of the wine he would never drink—the girls he would never kiss—the books he would never read—the music he would never hear! A big monument at home—taps—he felt sorry for himself and the tears came. No, he didn't want to die—he wasn't going to—he must pull himself together! He must fight for his life.

There was the aerodrome. He throttled back and sideslipped in. He landed in a daze. How tired he was!

He taxied up to the hangar. A lot of serious faces—his sergeant at attention—come here—help me out—send for doctor—shot through shoulder—Hun leader did it—then pulled wings off. He noticed all his flying wires were loose and flapping—a narrow escape from crumpling. All right, get me out.

They lifted him out tenderly and laid him on the ground.

" There it is," exclaimed the sergeant; " drilled clean through. Look at the blood."

He was dizzy. They were taking off his helmet and boots and overalls, then his shirt and undershirt. Why didn't they hurry? Here was the doctor. The doctor bent over him and put his hand on his shoulder—he was wiping away the blood——

Henry saw the bloody cloth—blood from his shoulder—his life's blood! Then he fainted.

When he came to he was lying in the shade. The sergeant was sitting beside him fanning him with his hat and holding a wet piece of cloth on his forehead. The pain was all gone and a piece of canvas was thrown over him.

" There, you're all right," the sergeant soothed him. " Those yellow-bellied Heinies can't kill you. We got ten of 'em this morning—five of our men missing. Lie still a minute. You're all right. Your plane's no more good. Every wire loose—full of holes too."

Henry groaned. Why, he didn't know. He was in no pain. He was just tired.

" I guess you got to get a new sergeant," he went on. " I blacked an eye for that damn medical sergeant. He laughed at you. And I nearly busted the doc one too. Damned old sawbones!"

" Laughed at me?" Henry asked, trying to think what he had done that was funny. " Why was he laughing at me?"

" 'Cause you thought you were hit and weren't. If somebody took a shot at that medico he'd run all the way to Calais."

" Not hit? What about my shoulder?"

" You must have reared back something fierce 'cause you jabbed the buckle tongue of your shoulder yoke plumb through your flying suit and dug it an inch under your skin. Must have stayed in the flesh because it's all torn loose. All right, let's go down and get doc to plaster it up. I'd better let one of the other men take you down. I ain't popular in the medical tent right now."

" All right, my boy," the doctor told him as he worked with tape and gauze. "I'm glad it's no worse. But you're through here. No more flying for you for a while. I've been expecting you to break —you can wear out any machine. You had a fine case of dementia. You go to Boulogne this afternoon. I don't know what they'll do to you there—probably two weeks' leave. Good for you—spend all that money you won—all right—trot along, now."

FEAR

by
James Warner Bellah

IT was a little spot, that fear, but it had ached in his heart for months—ever since his first solo flight at Upavon Aerodrome. It had come suddenly one morning like the clean pink hole of a steel-jacketed bullet—a wound to be ashamed of, a wound to fight against, a wound that never quite healed. Always it was there to throb and to pinch like the first faint gnawing of cancer. It came with him to the theatre and rankled his mind: "Enjoy this—it may be your last play." It crept into his throat at meals sometimes, and took away the poor savour that was left to the foods of war-time.

The fear of the men who fly. Sometimes he pictured it as an imp—an imp that sat eternally on his top plane and questioned him on the strength of rudder wires, pointed to imaginary flaws in struts, suggested that the petrol was low in the tank, that the engine would die on the next climbing turn.

It was with him now as the tender that was to take him up to his squadron jolted and bounced its way across the *pavé* on the outskirts of Amiens. The squadron was the last place he had to go to. All the months that were gone had led up to this. These were the wars at last. This was the place he would cop it, if he was to cop it at all.

He shrugged. Anyway, he had had his four days in London and his ten days idling at Pilot's Pool before the squadron sent for him. He braced one shoulder against the rattling seat and reached in his tunic pocket for a cigarette. Mechanically he offered one to the driver. The man took it with a grubby finger.

"Thankee, sor-r."

He nodded and lighted both cigarettes with the smudge of his pocket lighter. Anyway, he was not flying up to 44. That was one flight saved. Funny, that fear—how it came and went like the throb of a nerve in an open tooth. Sometimes the spot was large, and filled his whole being; then again it would shrink to a dull ache, just enough to take the edge from the beauty of the sunrise and the sparkle from the wine of the moon.

There had been a time when it had jumped in every fibre of his soul. He had been a cadet officer then, with only twelve solo hours in the air, under the old rough-and-tumble system of learning to fly. Spinning at that time was an unsolved mystery to him, a ghastly mystery that had meant quick death in a welter of blood, flecked with splinters. Fred McCloud had gone that way, and Johnny Archamboult. For weeks afterward, Johnny's screams had rung in his ears like a stab of pain, until the mere smell of petrol and fabric dope made the fear crawl into his throat and strangle him. Somehow he had kept on with the rest, under the merciless scourge that lashed one on to fly—and the worse fear of seeing cold scorn in the eyes of the men who taught the lore of thin cloud miles.

The tender twisted and dodged along the hard mud ribbon that ran like a badly healed cicatrix across the pock-scarred face of the fields. Gnarled and bleak, they were fields that had held the weight of blood-crazed men—still held them in unmarked graves, where they had fallen the year before under the steel flail. He had heard stories from his older brother about those fields—the laughing brother who had gone away one day and returned months later without his laugh, only to go away again, not to come back. He had seen pictures in the magazines—— But somehow no one had caught their utter bleakness as he saw it now.

The riven boles of two obscene trees crouched and argued about it on the lead-grey horizon, tossing their splintered arms and shrieking, he fancied, like quarrelling old women in the lesser streets of a village. Close to the roadway, there were a torn shoe and a tin hat flattened like a crushed derby. Poor relics that even salvage could see no further use in. Farther off, a splintered caisson pointed three spokes of a shattered wheel to the sky, like a mutilated hand thrown out in agony. He was seeing it for himself now.

No one could smile at the cleanness of his uniform again and say : " Wait till you get out. When I was in France——" He was out himself now. In a day or so he would go over the line with loaded guns. His instructors at the training 'drome—thin-jawed men with soiled ribbons under their wings—had done no more, and some of them had done less. The thought braced him somewhat. They had seemed so different—so impossible to imitate—those men. Their war had always been a different one from his; a war peopled with vague, fearless men like Rhodes-Moorehouse and Albert Ball and Bishop, the Canadian; men who flew without a thought for themselves.

It occurred to him with a start that theirs was the same war as his now. Twenty-five miles ahead of him, buried somewhere in rat runs, between Bapaume and Cambrai, it went on and on, waiting for him to come—waiting to claw and maim and snuff him out when he did come. It had seemed so far away from him in England. When he was at ground school he had seen it as a place where one did glorious things—he was young, pitifully young—a place that one came back from with ribbons under one's wings, with nice clean scratches decently bandaged. And he had been slightly offended at his brother's attitude—at the things his brother had said of the staff. Then he had gone to Upavon to learn to fly. He had soloed for the first time, and the spot of fear had crawled into his own heart.

They were rattling into the broken streets of a tottering town

—a town that leered at them and grimaced through blackened gaps in its once white walls. There was a patched-up estaminet with a tattered yellow awning that tried bravely to smile.

" Albert," said the driver.

The new pilot nodded. Some sapper officers were loitering in the doorways of the café. Their uniforms were faded to a rusty brown and reinforced with leather at the cuffs and elbows. Their buttons were leather, too, to save polishing, and their badges were a dull bronze. He looked down at his white Bedford-cord breeches and the spotless skirts of his fur-collared British warm—privileges of the flying corps that men envied. Baths, clean clothing, and better food. The P.B.I.'s idea of heaven. They called flyers lucky for their privileges and cursed them a little bit for their dry beds and the wines they had in their messes, miles behind the line.

The new pilot wondered if they knew what it meant to be alone in the stabbing cold with no one to talk to, no one to help you, nothing between you and the ground save a thin, trembling fabric of cloth and wire and twenty thousand feet of emptiness. That was his fear—emptiness—nothingness—solitude. Those men under the awning could die in company. Not so himself—alone, screaming into the cloud voids, with no one to hear, no one to help, staring with glazed eyes and foam-flecked lips at the emptiness into which one hurtled to death miles below. The price one paid for a bath! He remembered seeing Grahame-White fly at Southport before the War. People had called him an intrepid aviator. The new pilot laughed harshly inside his throat and stared out across the bare fields.

The car topped a slight rise and turned sharply to the left. The driver pointed his grubby finger. " They be comin' in from after-noon patrol," he said. " Yonder is aerodrome."

There were three flat canvas hangars painted a dull brown, and a straggling line of rusty tin huts facing them from across the narrow landing space—like a deserted mining village, shabby and unkempt. As he watched, he saw the last machine of the afternoon patrol bank at a hundred and fifty feet and side-slip down for its landing. In his heart he could hear the metal scream of wind in the flying wires. A puff of black smoke squirted out in a torn stream as the pilot blipped on his engine for one more second before he came into the wind and landed. By the time the tender rolled up to the dilapidated squadron office, the machine had taxied into the row of hangars and the pilot was out, fumbling for a cigarette with his ungloved hands. A thin acrid smell of petrol and carbonised castor oil still hung in the quiet air between the shabby huts. Snow in large wet flakes commenced to fall slowly, steadily.

The new pilot climbed down from the tender, tossed his shoulder haversack beside his kit-bag, and pushed open the door of the squadron office. The Adjutant was sitting on his desk top, smoking and talking to someone in a black leather flying coat and helmet—someone with an oil-streaked face and fingers still blue and clumsy from the cold.

"Paterson, sir, G. K., Second Lieutenant, reporting in from Pilot's Pool for duty with the 44th."

The Adjutant raised a careless finger in acknowledgment. "Oh yes. How do? Bring your log books?"

"Yes, sir."

"Chuck 'em down. D'ye mind?"

Paterson laid them upon the desk top, still standing to attention. The Adjutant smiled. "Break off," he said. "We're careless here. This isn't cadet school."

The new pilot smiled and relaxed. "Very good, sir."

"That's better," said the Adjutant; "makes me feel more comfortable. Just give me a note of yourself now." He reached for a slip of paper. "G. K. Paterson, Two Lt. Next of kin?" Paterson gave his father's name. "Age?"

"Eighteen and four-twelfths."

"Good!" said the Adjutant. "You'll find an empty cubicle in B Block—that's the middle line of huts. You're lucky. Roof only leaks in three places. I'll have your duffel trekked over shortly."

The man in the flying coat blew upon his numbed fingers and smiled. "I'm Hoyt," he said. "Skipper of C Flight. I'm going to take you now, before A gets after you." He turned to the Adjutant. "That's all right, isn't it, Charlie? Tell 'em I intimidated you." He grinned.

The Adjutant shrugged. "Right-o!"

"Come on," said Hoyt. "I'm in your hut block. I'll show you your hole."

They went out into the snow flurry. Mechanics were fussing in little knots around the five tiny machines that had just landed, lining them up, refilling them, and trundling them into the brown musty hangars.

"Le Rhône Camels," said Hoyt. "We've just been over around Cambrai taking a look-see."

Inside one of the hangars, as they passed, Paterson saw something that drew a thin, wet gauze across his eyeballs. On a rough bench just beside the open flap sat a man with his eyes closed and his lips drawn tightly into a straight bluish line. His flying coat was rolled up behind his head for a pillow, and his tunic had been unbuttoned and cut away from his left shoulder. The white of his flesh showed weirdly in the gloom, like the belly of a dead fish. Just below the shoulder, the white was crumpled and reddened as if a clawed paw had been drawn across it. One man was holding his other hand, while another probed and cleaned and dabbed with little puffs of snowy cotton that turned quickly to pink and then to a deep brown.

Hoyt shrugged. "Lucky man. That's Mallory. He was Number Four this afternoon. We never saw a thing. Just happened. Funny." And he smiled. "That's why I was so keen to get you. Can't tell how long it will be before Mallory gets around again, and I've got one vacancy in the flight already." He shrugged. "You'll see a lot of that here—get used to it. It doesn't mean a thing as long as you get back alive."

Paterson looked at him sharply. He wanted to ask him how many didn't get back alive. He wanted to know what had caused the other vacancy in the flight. But people didn't ask those things. People merely nodded casually and went on.

"I suppose not," he said. They tramped on across the aerodrome.

"Here we are," said Hoyt. He kicked open the hut door and groped down the dark passageway, with Paterson after him. Presently he pushed back another door and yanked at a tattered window curtain.

The new pilot saw a tiny room, with two washstands, a cot, a folding chair, and a cracked mirror. In a corner were his kit-bag and haversack. He pulled out his own cot and chair and set them up; meanwhile Hoyt threw himself down on the other cot and let his cigarette smoke dribble straight upward into the gloom of the pine-raftered roof. Presently he spoke.

"This is a queer war," he said; "full of queer things, and the queerest of these is charity." He laughed in the darkness, and the tip of his cigarette became suddenly pink as he drew the smoke into his lungs. "What was your school?"

"Winchester," said Paterson.

"Right," said Hoyt. "Remember your first day? This is it over again. They've fed you up on poobah at your training 'drome and down at the Pool. They always do. It's part of the system. Just take it for what it is worth and forget the rest. If you want to know anything, come to me and I'll tell you as well as I can. I've been here three months. When I came, I came just as you did to-day, pucka green and afraid to the marrow—afraid of uncertainty. You get over that shortly.

" Our job is a funny one, and we're not here for ourselves, and we're not here to be heroes or to get in the newspapers. The V.C.s are few and far between." He raised himself upon his elbow. " I'm not preaching self-abasement and a greater loyalty to a cause that is right, mind you. I don't know anything about causes or who started the War or why, and I don't care. I'm preaching C Flight and the lives of five men.

" You saw Mallory over at the hangar. It was teamwork that put him there in his own M.O.'s hands. Not much, perhaps "— the cigarette described a quick arc in the darkness—" just a slight closing in of the formation—a wave of somebody's hand—somebody else dropping back and climbing above him to protect his tail from any stray Huns that might 've waylaid him on the way home. That's what I mean. *Esprit de corps* is a cold, hard phrase. Call it what you like. It's the greatest lesson you learn. Never give up a man." Hoyt laughed. " They call me an old woman. Perhaps I am. Take it or leave it.

" Slick up a bit and come into my hutch while I scrape off the outer layer of silt. Dinner in half a tick and I'm as filthy as a pig." He vaulted up from the cot and punched his cigarette out against the sole of his boot. At the door he paused for a moment.

" Ever have wind up?" he asked casually.

Paterson stiffened against the question and the small spot of fear danced within him. " No," he said firmly. Hoyt shrugged. " Lucky man." And he went out into the passage-way.

At dinner he met the rest of the squadron and the other men in C Flight. Mallory, very pale, with his arm slung in a soft pad of bandages, sat beside him. They were coming for him later to take him down to the base hospital. Phelps-Barrington sat on the other side of Mallory, mourning the fact that the wound was not his, that he might get the inevitable leave to follow. Phelps-Barrington took Paterson's hand with a shrug and asked how Marguerite was in Amiens. "What? You didn't meet Marguerite on your way through? 'Struth!" MacClintock sat across the table beside Hoyt —MacClintock, too young to grow a moustache, but with a deep burr that smelled of the heather in the Highlands and huge pink knees under his Seaforth kilts, muscles like the corded roots of an oak. The other man in the flight, Trent, was down with mild flu. He was due back in a week or so from hospital.

There was a wild argument on about the dawn patrol the next morning. Paterson listened to the fragments of talk that flew like sabre cuts across the glasses:

"He's in a red tripe. I don't give a damn for Intelligence. Saw him this morning myself. Same machine Mac and I had that brush with down at Péronne."

"The next time they'll get an idea for us to strafe a road clear to Cologne for them. What are we—street cleaners?"

"So I let go a covey of Coopers and turned for home. They had it spotted for a battery over at 119 Squadron. I saw the pictures. Right pictures, but wrong map squares as usual. That crowd can't tell a battery from a Chinese labour-corps inclosure. I'd rather be a staff officer than a two-seater pilot."

"Steward, a whisky-soda for Mr. MacClintock and myself. Have one, Hoyt? You, Paterson?"

Cruel, thin, casual talk clicking against the teeth in nervous haste; the commercial talk of men bartering their lives against each tick of the clock; men caught like rats in a trap, with no escape but death or a lucky chance like Mallory's. Caught and yet denying the trap—laughing at it until the low roof of the mess shack rumbled with the echo; drowning it in a whisky for the night.

Afterward, Hoyt came down the passage with him to his room —Hoyt, with his face cleaned of the afternoon's oil and his eyes slightly bright with the wine he had taken.

"We're relieved to-morrow on account of casualties," he said. "I'll tick you out early and we'll go joy riding—see what we can teach each other." He smiled. " 'Night."

Paterson undressed slowly and threw back the flap of his sleeping bag. He ran his fingers softly down the muscles of his left arm. Automatically they stopped at the spot Mallory had been hit. He stretched his thumb from the arm to his heart—seven inches. He shrugged. Nice to go that way. Clean and quick. He sat upon the edge of his cot and pulled on his pyjama trousers. Oh, well, this was the place—the last place he had to go to. This was the cot he would sleep his last sleep in. If it weren't a lonely job! That chap in the mess who wouldn't be a two-seater pilot for anything. If he could only feel like that. If he could only feel Hoyt's complacency. Hoyt, with his calm smile and the two little ribbons under his wings. Military Cross and the Legion of Honour, and three months before he had been green—pucka green!

Paterson blew out the light and turned in. Hoyt was a good fellow—damned decent. Outside he could hear Phelps-Barrington's voice muffled by the snow: "Come on, snap into it! Tender for Amiens! Who's coming?" The yell died in the roar from the car's engine.

Paterson lay for a moment thinking; then suddenly he reached for his pocket flash, snapped it, and stared nervously at the empty cot across the room. There was no bedding on it, nor any kit tuck-ed under it; only the chair beside it, and the cracked mirror.

He got up and padded over in his bare feet. Stencilled on one corner of the canvas there was a name—J. G. H. Lyons. There had been no Lyons introduced to him in the mess. Perhaps he was on leave. Perhaps he had flu with Trent and was down at the base. The spot of fear in his heart trembled slightly and he knew sud-denly where J. G. H. Lyons was. He was dead! Somewhere out in the snow, miles across the line, J. G. H. Lyons slept in a shat-tered cockpit.

The door behind him opened softly. It was Hoyt, in pyjamas. "Got a cigarette?" he asked casually.

Paterson turned sharply and grinned. "Right-o," he said. "There on the table."

Hoyt took one and lighted it. "Can't sleep," he said. "Come in and take Mallory's cot if you want to. I've some new magazines and I can tell you something about our work here until we feel sleepy."

Hoyt was a good fellow—damned decent.

The cold wet mist lay upon the fields like a soft veil drawn across the face of an old woman who had died in the night. Me-chanics, with their balaklavas pulled down across their ears, were running about briskly to keep warm—kicking chocks in front of under-carriage wheels, snapping propellers down with mighty leaps and sweeps until the cold engines barked into life and settled to deep concert roaring. Dust and pebbles, scattered by the backwash, swept into the billowing hangars in a thin choking cloud that pat-tered against the canvas walls. Hoyt's machine trembled and crept out of the line, with Phelps-Barrington after it. Trent, who had come back from the base the day before, taxied out next.

Paterson waved to the mechanics to pull out his own chocks. They yanked mightily on the ropes, and he blipped his motor with his thumb. Behind him and to the left came Yardley, the new man who had come up from Pool to fill Mallory's place. Then MacClintock, sitting high in his cockpit, rushed out with a roar and a swish of gravel. MacClintock was deputy leader.

Hoyt waved his hand in a quick nervous sweep, and the flight started. Through the mist they roared with their engines howling into sharp echo against the hut walls. A moment later tails whipped up and wheels bounced lightly upon the uneven ground. Then Hoyt's nose rose sharply and he zoomed into the air in a broad climbing turn, with the five others after him in tight formation.

Paterson glanced at his altimeter—five hundred feet. He looked ahead and to the left. There was Bapaume in its raggedness, half drowned in the mist. Suddenly Phelps-Barrington's machine burst into rose flame and every strut and wire trembled like molten silver—the sun. He could see the red rim just peeping up ahead of him and he was warmer for the sight of it. Below, under the rim of his cockpit, the ground was still wrapped in its grey shroud.

They were climbing up in close formation. The altimeter gave them four thousand feet now. He glanced to the left. Yardley waved. Yardley was going through the agony of his first patrol over the line—the same agony he had gone through himself the week before. Only Yardley seemed different, somehow—surer of himself—less imaginative. He was older, too. Behind them, Mac-Clintock, the watch-dog, was closing in on their tails and climbing above them to be ready to help if the Hun swooped from behind unexpectedly.

There were clouds above—grey blanket clouds that came together in a solid roof, with only a torn hole here and there to show the blue. Bad clouds to be under. Hoyt knew it and kept on climbing. Almost ten thousand feet now. The ground below had cleared slowly and thrown off most of its sullen shroud. Here and there, in depressions, the mist still hung in arabesque ruffles like icing in a confectioner's window or the white smoke of a railway engine.

The line was under them now, running south and east like a jagged dagger cut, in and out, in and out across the land, not stopping for towns, but cleaving straight through their grey smudgy ruins with a cold disregard and a ruthless purpose. The first day he had seen it, it had seemed a dam to him; a breakwater built there to hold something that must not flow past it; a tourniquet of barbed wire twisted and held by half the world that the blood of the other half might not flow. Some day something would break and the whole thing would give way for good or evil. Curiously, now, like Hoyt, he didn't care which. And suddenly he knew how his older brother had felt, on that last leave, and he had called him unsporting in the pride of his youthful heart!

Hoyt was still climbing. Thin wraiths of cloud vapour groped awkwardly for the six tiny Camels, like ghost fingers, trying desperately to stop them and hold them from their work. Paterson glanced again at Yardley. He had been glad when Yardley came. He was still green himself, but Yardley was greener. It helped buck him up to think about it.

The line was behind them now. Hoyt turned south to pass below the anti-aircraft batteries of Cambrai, and presently they crossed the tarnished silver ribbon of the Somme-Scheldt Canal. Mechanically, Paterson reached for his Bowden trigger and pressed it for a burst of ten shots to warm the oil in his Vickers gun against the bite of the cold air. Then he clamped the joy-stick between his knees and reached up for the Lewis gun on his top plane.

His throat closed abruptly, with a ghastly dryness, and his knees melted beneath him. The wing fabric beside his gun was ruffling into torn lace and he could see the wood of the camber ribs splintering as he watched! For a moment he was paralysed, then frantically he whipped around in his seat and swept the air above him. Nothing. There was the torn fabric and the staring rib and nothing else. MacClintock was gone. Yardley was still there, lagging, with the smoke coming in puffs and streaks from his engine. Then Hoyt turned in a wild climb to the left. Phelps-Barrington dipped his nose suddenly and dived with his engine full on, and at once, where there had been only six Camels, the sky was full of grey machines with blunt noses and black crosses.

Blindly he pressed his Bowden trigger and fired into the empty air, blindly he dived after Phelps-Barrington. Somewhere to the left he saw a plume of black smoke with something yellow twisting in the sunlight on its lower end. A blunt nose crossed his propeller—into his stream of bullets. He screamed and banked wildly, still firing. He saw Hoyt above him. He forgot the machine in front and reached for his Lewis to help Hoyt. He tried to wait—something about the outer ring of the rear sight—but his fingers got the better of him and he fired point-blank.

As quickly as it had begun it ended. There was Hoyt circling back, and two other Camels to the left and below him—four of them. They closed in on Hoyt and he wondered where the two others were. He looked for them—probably chasing after the Huns. He could see dots to the southward—too far away to make out the markings. Hoyt had signalled the washout and they were headed back across the line. Funny those two others didn't come. He wondered who they were. Probably Phelps-Barrington and MacClintock, hanging on to the fight until the last. They worked together that way. He had heard them talk in the mess about it. They'd be at it again to-night, and to-night he could join them for the first time. He'd been in a dog fight! Shot and been shot at!

The spot of fear shrank to a pin-point.

The brown smudge of the aerodrome slid over the horizon. He blipped his motor and glided in carefully. No use straining that top wing—no telling what other parts had been hit. No use taking chances.

Hoyt was standing beside his machine with his glove off, staring at his finger-nails. Phelps-Barrington was climbing out. Paterson taxied in between them. The man in the fourth machine just sat and stared over the rim of his cockpit. Phelps-Barrington walked slowly across to Hoyt and laid a hand on his shoulder. Hoyt shrugged and stuffed his bare hand into his coat pocket. Paterson sat with his goggles still on and his throat quite dry. The man in the fourth machine vaulted out suddenly, ripped off his helmet and goggles and hurled them to the ground. It was Trent.

He climbed out of his own machine and walked over toward Hoyt. Phelps-Barrington, who had a wild word for all occasions —Phelps-Barrington, who led the night trips to Amiens—was silent. When Paterson came up he shrugged and scowled ferociously.

"Is it you, Pat?" said Hoyt. "Thought it was Yardley."

"'Struth!" said Phelps-Barrington. "Let's go and have a drink."

Paterson thrilled as the man slipped an arm through his. For one awful moment he had thought——

"Well," Hoyt said, "those things will happen." And he shrugged again.

"I saw dots to the southward," said Paterson. "Maybe they'll be in later."

"No, little Rollo," said Phelps-Barrington. "They won't be in later or ever. I saw it with my own eyes—both in flames. I thought it was you, and until Trent landed I thought he might be Mac. But I was wrong. Let's shut up and have a drink!"

Then suddenly he knew, and his mind froze with the ghastliness of the thought. If he'd been quicker—if he'd turned and climbed above Yardley when he saw him lagging, with the smoke squirting from his hit motor—he could have saved him. If he had kept his eyes open behind instead of dreaming he might have saved MacClintock, too. In a daze, he stumbled after Phelps-Barrington. That's why Trent had hurled his helmet to the ground and walked off. That's why Hoyt had shrugged and said : "Those things will happen." It was his fault—his—Paterson's. He'd bolted and lost his head and fired blindly into the empty air. He hadn't stuck to his man. He had let Yardley drop back alone to be murdered.

"Look here, P.-B.," he muttered, "I'm not drinking." He wanted to be alone—to think. So quick it had all been.

Phelps-Barrington grabbed his arm and pushed him stumbling into the mess shack. Trent was slumped down at the table with his glass before him, thumbing over a newspaper. He raised his head as they came in. " Two more of the same, steward—double."

They sat down beside him, and Phelps-Barrington reached for a section of the paper.

" It says here," said Trent, " that Eva Fay didn't commit suicide. Died of an overdose of hashish she took at a party in Maida Vale the night before."

The steward brought the glasses. Trent raised his and looked at Paterson. " Good work, son."

Paterson stared at him in amazement. Trent sipped his whisky and went on reading as if he had never stopped. Some time later, Paterson left them and went down to the flight office to find Hoyt. The thought of the morning still bothered him, in spite of Trent's words, and he wanted to clear it up. Hoyt smiled as he came in. " Washed the taste out in Falernian?" he asked.

"Some. Look here, skipper—this morning—what about it?"

"What about it?"

"My part—I was fast asleep. I saw Yardley lagging, and I had a moment to cross above him, but I lost my head, I'm afraid, and went wild."

The smile faded and Hoyt laid down his pencil. "Do you really think you could have saved him?"

"He was behind me already when I saw him lagging, just as you climbed and P.-B. dived."

"Then you couldn't have helped him, because Mac was done for when I saw him and climbed, and half a tick after I climbed, P.-B. saw Yardley burst into flames. There you are."

"But if I'd kept my eyes back instead of trusting to Mac?"

"Look here," said Hoyt, "no man can keep his eyes on everything. Something always happens in the place he isn't looking. Bear that in mind and forget this morning. You've seen a dog fight from the inside and lived. Take it easy. You're not here to do everything. You're here to stick to us. You might have run away. Remember that and be afraid of it. Remember if you get away by leaving a pal—he may live to come back. Then you'll have to face him, and engine trouble is a poor excuse.

"Trouble with you youngsters is that you've been fed up on poobah. And the myth of the fearless air fighter. Put it out of your mind. There's no such thing. Some are less afraid than others. Some are drunker—take your choice. Class dismissed." Hoyt grinned. "Go get cleaned up. We'll jog into Amiens for tiffin. Tender in half an hour. Tell Trent and P.-B."

They spent most of the afternoon at Charlie's Bar with some of the men from the artillery observation squadron. For dinner they went to the Du Rhin and the glasses flowed red. Afterward, in another place, there was a fight, as usual, and chairs crashed like match sticks, until whistles sounded outside and the A.P.M.'s car, siren screaming, raced up the street. They poured out into the alleyway and ran, leaving the waiter praying in high, shrieking French.

Trent had a bottle with him. They rode all the way home singing and shouting to high heaven, forgetting that there were two empty chairs in the mess and that there might be more to-morrow.

> Take the cylinders out of my kidneys,
> Take the scutcheon pins out of my brain,
> Take the cam box from under my backbone
> And assemble the engine again!

They were good fellows—Billy Hoyt, P.-B., Pat, and Ray Trent. Have 'nother li'l' drink.

They roared along like a Juggernaut, with the exhaust splitting the night air. Sometimes they were on the road and sometimes they were off. No one cared so long as they kept hurtling into the darkness.

Phelps-Barrington was fast asleep. Pat woke him up at the aerodrome and tumbled him into the hut.

They stumbled over a kit-bag in the doorway. P.-B. straightened up suddenly. "Good-bye, Mac, old lad, sleep tight."

Trent kicked the bag out of the way. "Damned Adjutant! Take P.-B. in with you, Pat. I'm bunking with the skipper. Might have the decency to take Mac's kit over to squadron office and not leave it lying around the passage. 'Night."

Paterson was quite sober. He tumbled P.-B. into bed and stood for a moment at the open window, staring out across the ground mist that billowed knee high in the faint night breeze. He rested his elbows on the sill and hid his face in his trembling hands. If he could only be like the others—casual—calloused. If he had less imagination—more sand—stamina—something. MacClintock had planned this night himself, at breakfast. Yardley had left a letter addressed and stamped on his window sill.

Paterson's mind jumped miles to the eastward. He saw the two blackened engines lying somewhere in the bleak fields beyond, ploughed into the ground, with their mats of twisted wires coiled around them in a hideous trap.

Their families would get word to-morrow. "Missing," it would read. And then later: "Previously reported missing, now reported killed in action." And to-morrow—perhaps his own family. Why can't it be quick?

There was a noise behind him. Someone fumbling at the door latch—Hoyt. "Had this bit left. Bottoms up! Quick!" He took the glass and drained it. The liquor bit into his veins and burned him. Hoyt set his own glass down on the washstand with a sharp click. "Get into bed now, you idiot. Good-night."

Spiked drink. Hoyt was a good fellow—damned decent. Do anything for Hoyt. Never let Hoyt go. Like my brother—before the War. Good old Hoyt. And he sank suddenly into a dreamless fuddle of sleep.

The weeks crawled on slowly. Paterson felt like a man climbing a steep ladder. Each day was a rung behind him. Each new rung showed an infinite number still ahead, waiting for him to go on, luring him with their apparent safety, waiting for him to reach the one rotten rung that would do him in. Some day he would reach it, and it would crack under him, or his fingers would slip and hurtle him into the abyss under his charred engine.

Offensive patrols and escort for the artillery observation squadron filled their time, with sometimes a road strafe to vary the monotony. These he liked best, for some quaint reason—perhaps because there was less space to fall through. Sometimes there would be a battalion on those roads—a battalion to scatter and knock down like tin soldiers on a nursery floor. Quite impersonal. They were never men to Paterson. Like dolls they ran and like dolls they sprawled awkwardly where they fell.

P.-B. and Trent and Hoyt carried him through somehow. Mallory was back again, but Mallory never counted much with him. P.-B. and Trent and Hoyt were a bulwark. They meant safety. It was good to wake up at night and hear P.-B. snoring on the other cot, to know that Hoyt and Trent were asleep in the next cubicle. It was good to see them stamping to keep warm before the patrol took off in the half light of early morning. So different from one another and yet so alike underneath. Hoyt was nearer his kind than the two others. Tall and spindly like his brother, with a straight, thin nose that quivered slightly at the nostril when he was annoyed. Hoyt, who smiled and sanctioned the childish depravity of little P.-B., but never quite met it with his own, although always seeming to, on the night trips to Amiens. Trent, glowering and quiet, with a keen hatred for everything political that he learned in the offices of the London and South-Western before the War, when the Army to him had meant young wastrels swanking the Guards' livery in the boxes of theatres—wastrels who had died on the Charleroi Road three years before.

Suddenly, from one of his mother's letters, he found that he had been in France almost three months. He stiffened with the thought and remembered what Hoyt had told him that day he had come: "I've been here three months. When I came, I came just as you did to-day—pucka green." He knew then that all his hopes were false. He was the same to-day as he had been that first day. He would always be the same. The spot of fear would always be with him. Some day it would swell and choke him and his hands would function without his frozen brain. He should never have tried to fly. He should have gone into the infantry as his brother had. Too much imagination—too little something. In three months he had learned the ropes, that was all; how to fire and when to fire, where the Archie batteries were near Cambrai, how to ride a cloud and crawl into it—nothing more.

The weeks went on, creeping closer and closer to the twenty-first of March—the twenty-first of March—and with them the feeling crept into Paterson's heart—a feeling that something frightful was to happen. Things had been quiet so long and casualties had been few. C Flight hadn't been touched in weeks. He brooded over the thought and slept badly. He went to Amiens with P.-B. more frequently. If it was to be any of the three, he knew he wouldn't be able to stand it. His bulwark would crumble and break and he would break with it. On the dawn patrols, those few minutes before they climbed into the cockpits and took off were agony: " This will be the day. It must be to-day. We can't go on this way. Our luck will break."

One day when they were escorting 119, four dots dived on them from behind and he knew suddenly what he would do. Stark, logically, the thing stood before him and beckoned through the wires of his centre section. If a shot hit his plane, he would go down. They were far over the lines, taking 110 on a bombing show. He would wabble down slowly, pushing his joy-stick from side to side in a slow ellipse as if he were out of control. Then he would land and run his nose into the ground and be taken prisoner. The others would see him and swear that he'd been hit— and he wouldn't do it until his machine had been hit. That for his own conscience's sake and for the years he would have to live afterwards.

But A Flight, behind and far above, saw the dots and scattered them, and the chance was gone.

Then day by day he waited for another. He knew now that he

would do it at the first opportunity. He slept better with the thought, and the minutes seemed shorter now while he waited at dawn for his bus to be run out. All the details were worked out in his mind. If any one of the three were close to him, he'd throw up his hands wildly before he started down. They'd see that and report it. Then when he landed he'd pull out the flare quick and burn his machine so that they would think he had crashed and caught fire. It was so easy!

He spent less time with P.-B. now. Somehow the old freedom was gone. Somehow Hoyt wasn't the same to him either. He was working with three strangers he had never really known—three casual strangers he would leave shortly and never see again.

On the morning of the fourteenth of March the caller turned C Flight out suddenly, without warning, about an hour after P.-B. and Trent had returned from Amiens. A special signal had come in from wing headquarters. B Flight had the regular morning patrol, but there was to be an additional offensive patrol besides. A Flight had morning escort and the dusk patrol. That meant C for the special. Paterson could hear Hoyt swearing about it next door. P.-B., across the room, uttered a mighty curse and rolled over. Paterson got him a bucket of cold water and doused his feverish head in it. Trent and Hoyt were still cursing pettishly in the next cubicle.

Sleep-stupid, the four of them stumbled into the mess for hard-boiled eggs and coffee. Mallory and the new man, Crowe, were already eating, white-faced and unshaven. They slumped down beside them in silence.

In silence, they trooped across the dark aerodrome, buttoning their coats and fastening helmet straps against the cold wretchedness of the March wind. The machines were waiting for them in a ghostly line like staring wasps that had eaten the food of the gods and grown to gigantic size.

They climbed in and taxied out mechanically. B Flight had already left on the regular dawn patrol. They blipped their motors and roared away, leaving their echo and the sharp smell of castor oil behind on the empty 'drome.

Hoyt led them south to the crumpled ruins of Péronne and out to the line, climbing high to get the warmth of the sunlight that began to tint the clouds above them. They were going over to Le Cateau and beyond. Intelligence wanted pictures to confirm certain reports of new Hun shell dumps and battery concentration. The photographic planes were to go out and get them under escort as soon as there was enough light. As additional precaution, offensive patrols were to be kept up far over the enemy's lines to insure the success of the pictures. They passed the sullen black stain that was Le Câtelet and turned to the eastward. The ground was already light and the camera busses would be starting.

Hoyt took the roof at eighteen thousand feet and skirted the cloud wisps, watching below for customers. Paterson watched P.-B. anxiously. He had been roaring drunk an hour before. Groggy and drunk still, probably. He closed in a trifle and climbed above him, but P.-B. waved him down and wiggled his fingers from the end of his nose.

He looked ahead and down at Trent. Trent had been drunk, too, but he was steady now, sawing wood above and slightly behind Hoyt.

Then, suddenly, beyond Trent and far below, he saw a Hun two-seater alone. The old stunt. Hoyt shifted and pulled up his nose to climb above it and wait. Trent followed him up. Somewhere above that two-seater, and a half-mile behind, there would be a flight of Hun scouts skulking under the clouds, waiting to pounce on whoever dived for the two-seater. Hoyt knew it for a decoy. Paterson knew it. They would climb above the cloud edge, circle back, and catch the Hun scouts as they passed underneath.

Paterson trembled slightly. This was his chance at last. There'd be a long dive and a sure fight from behind, and in the mix-up he'd wabble down and out of the War via Lazaret VI in Cologne. He glanced around to see if Mallory was above him, and suddenly, out of the corner of his eye, he saw P.-B. shove his nose full down and throw himself into a straight dive for the decoy bus.

He gazed and shouted "No!" into the roar of his engine, P.-B., in a nasty temper and half fuddled, didn't smell the trick. There was one awful second, while Crowe closed up into P.-B.'s place and Hoyt banked to wait above for the Hun scouts to pounce down on the Camel.

P.-B. fired, pulled up, and dived again, far below them. The Hun two-seater banked sharply and came up and over in an Immelmann turn to get away. P.-B. caught it halfway over and a trickle of smoke swept out from its engine. Then in an instant Hoyt dived, with the rest of C Flight after him.

The next thing Paterson knew there were two Huns on his tail and a stream of tracer bullets pecking at his left wing. He pulled back on his stick and zoomed headlong up under Mallory. So close he was for a second that he could see the wheels turning slowly on Mallory's undercarriage and almost count the spokes glinting in the sunlight where the inside canvas sheathing had been taken off.

Mallory pulled away from him in a quick climbing turn and the Huns passed underneath, banking right and left. Paterson picked the left-hand one, thundered down on him in a short dive, and let go a burst of ten shots into the pilot's back. He saw the pilot's head snap sideways and his gloved hands fly up from the controls. Then Mallory dived over him after the other one. He turned in a wild split-air and followed Mallory.

There were more Huns below him and to the left, with two of the C Flight Camels diving and bucking between them. He raced furiously into a long dive, picked the nearest, and opened fire again in short, hammering bursts. His Hun wabbled and started down awkwardly in long sweeps. He picked another, still farther below, and pushed his stick forward until the rush of air gagged him. Wildly he fired as he ploughed down on it, and the chatter of his guns stabbed through the roar of his engine. He yelled like a madman, shot under the Hun, pulled up sharply, and fired into its grey mud-streaked belly. There was a fan of scarlet flame and a shock that tossed him to one side. He stalled and whipped out into a spin. Far below him he could see the decoy two-seater trailing a long plume of reddish smoke and flopping, wings over, toward the floor.

Then, suddenly, he saw his chance to wabble down and get away. He ruddered out of the spin and ran his stick once through the slow ellipse he had planned. But somehow he had to force himself to do it. There wasn't the relief he had expected. He looked back. Three C Flight machines were still above him, fighting madly—P.-B., Trent, and Hoyt. No—not this time. He pulled his stick back and climbed up. There were five Huns circling the Camels. It was a long shot, but he fired at the nearest and came up under the tail just as one of the Camels hurtled into a nose dive, twisted over, and snapped off both wings. He saw the pilot's arms raised wildly in the cockpit and no more.

Blood streamed into his mouth. He had torn his lips with his teeth in the excitement. The warm salty tang mounted to his brain. His goggles were sweat-fogged. His fingers ached with their pressure on the joy-stick, and his arm was numb to the elbow. In a spasm of blind hatred, he fired. Tracers raced across his top plane and struck with little smoke puffs that ripped the fabric into ribbons. His own bullets clawed at the Hun above him and fanged home.

He threw himself up and over in an Immelmann turn and came under the next, still firing. He let go his stick and jerked his Lewis gun down its sliding mount on his top plane. It fired twice and jammed. He yanked madly at the cocking lug, but it stuck halfway. He hurtled down again in another spin. The ground swept around in a quick arc that ended in clouds and more Hun busses. He caught at his thrashing joy-stick. Again the ground flashed through his centre section struts in a brown smudge, with the blaze of the sun hanging to one end of it. Then there was a Camel above him and a Camel below him. He closed in on the one below and squinted at the markings. Hoyt. He looked up at the other Camel, but the numerals on the side of its fuselage were hidden with a torn flap of fabric. Together, the three turned westward and started back.

Presently, near the line, the bus above him wabbled and dipped its nose. He stared at it. It went into a long, even glide that grew slowly steeper as he watched. He looked down for Huns. There were none. The glide became a dive, the dive twisted into an aimless spin, like the flopping of a lazy swimmer turning over in shallow water. The spin flattened and the Camel whipped out upside down, stalled, snapped out again, and again spun downward in that ghastly slow way. Over and over, only to whip out, stall and spin again. It was miles below him now. Nothing to do. Fascinated, he watched it as he followed Hoyt's tail. It was a mere dot now, flashing once or twice in the sun as it flopped over and over. Close to the ground now—closer. Then, suddenly, a tiny sheet of pink flame leaped up like the flash of a far beacon. That was all.

Hoyt was side-slipping below him, and he saw his own aerodrome under the leading edge of his bottom wing. He followed Hoyt down. They landed together and taxied slowly in toward the hangars. They stopped side by side and climbed out stiff-legged. Paterson looked down and saw that his right flying boot was torn and flayed into shreds across the outer side. There was a jagged fringe on the skirt of his coat where the leather had been ripped into ruffles. Dumbly, he looked back into his cockpit. The floor boards were splintered and the wicker arm of his seat was eaten away. He shrugged and walked over toward Hoyt. There was blood on the rabbit fur of Hoyt's goggles, blood that oozed slowly down and dripped from his chin piece in bright drops.

" Cigarette? "

Paterson gave him one. They walked into the flight office and slumped into chairs. Hoyt ripped off his helmet and dabbed at the scratch on his cheek. " I'm glad you got out, Pat," he said absently.

Then the fear spot broke and spattered into the four corners of Paterson's soul. He sprang up trembling, with his fists beating the air.

" The dirty lice! " he screamed. " They've killed P.-B.! They've killed Trent! D'y' hear me, Hoyt?—they've killed 'em! They're gone! They'll never come back! They've—— "

Hoyt's voice came evenly, calmly, through his screaming. "Steady, boy! Steady! You can't help it. No one can. Steady, now! "

A mat of white oil-splotched faces stared at them from the open doorway that led into the hangar. The boy turned wildly. " Clear out! " he shrieked. They vanished, open-mouthed. Hoyt drew him down into a chair. " No, Hoyt, no! Can't you see? P.-B. and you and Trent have meant everything to me. I can't go on. I've fought this thing till I'm crazy." Hoyt reached quickly and slammed the door. " I've fought it night and day! " He threw up his arms hopelessly and covered his face with his shaking hands.

Hoyt put his hand on his trembling shoulders and patted them. "Steady, now! Steady! None of that!" he said awkwardly.

Paterson's head whipped down across his sprawled arms on the desk top and the sobs tore at his throat in great gusts that choked him. "Oh, God!" he sobbed. "What's it all about, Hoyt? What's the use of it?"

"Steady, son! I don't know. Nobody knows. It just happened, as everything happens. It's much too late to talk causes. We're here and we know what we have to do. That's enough for us. It's all we have anyway, so it must be enough." He took his blood-soaked cigarette from his mouth and hurled it into a corner. It landed with a soft spat.

Someone knocked at the door. "Come in." It was the runner from squadron office. He saluted. "Yes?" said Hoyt.

The man glanced at Paterson's face and snapped his eyes quickly back to the Captain's.

"Beg pardon, sir," he said. "Squadron's just been signalled through wing. One of the C Flight machines came down near B Battery, the 212th."

"Who was it?" asked Hoyt.

"Lieutenant Mallard, they reported it, sir. That'll be Lieutenant Mallory, sir, won't it?"

"Yes." Hoyt's voice was quite flat. "Thank you."

The man saluted again and shut the door. Hoyt dabbed at his cheek and reached into his desk drawer for another cigarette. Paterson stood up suddenly and grabbed his arm. "Listen, skipper!" Hoyt's eyes met his calmly. "I'm going to tell you something. I'll feel better if I do. I've been a weak sister in this flight. I've planned for days to go down and let myself be taken prisoner —to get out of it all. I've been sick of it—sick of it, d'y' hear, until I couldn't think straight. I wanted to get out alive. I wanted to get away in any way I could. This morning I broke. I let go and started down——"

Hoyt smiled. "Your trouble, Pat, is that you think you're the only person in this jolly old war."

Paterson stared at him. "But I did! I started down, out of it, this morning!"

"How'd you get here?" asked Hoyt.

"But if I hadn't broken for that moment this morning——"

"That's a lie!" snapped Hoyt. "You're talking poobah! I know how those things happen. If P.-B. hadn't gone down after the two-seater they'd all be here now; and by the same reasoning, if my aunt wore trousers she'd be my uncle. The important thing is that it's you and me now and nothing else matters. We'll have four brand-new men to whip into shape to-morrow, and whatever you think of yourself, you've got to do it. I can't do much, for I'll be ahead, leading. You'll be behind them and you'll have to do it all. They'll be frightened and nervous and green, but the job's to be done. Understand? You've got to goad them on and get them out of trouble and watch them every minute, so that in time they'll be as good as P.-B. and Trent—so that when their turn comes they can do for other green men what P.-B. and Trent did for you. Do you see now what this morning has done for you?" He paused for a moment, and then, in a lower tone: "Afraid? Who isn't afraid? But it doesn't do any good to brood over it."

C Flight did no duty the next day, nor the day following. Hoyt went up to the 212th and identified Mallory for burial, while Paterson flew back to the Pool for the replacement pilots and a new Camel for Hoyt.

In Amiens he heard the first whispered rumours of what was going to happen. Intelligence was ranting for information. Everybody had the story and nobody was right. The hospitals were evacuating as fast as possible. Fresh battalions were being hustled up. It wasn't a push. Anyone could tell that with half an eye. Something the Hun was doing. The spring offensive a month earlier this year. G.H.Q. was plugging the gaps frantically, replacing and reinforcing and wondering where the hammer would fall and what it would carry with it. Hence the pictures that had cost the lives of P.-B. and Trent. The air itself trembled with uncertainty, and rumours flew fast and thick.

Paterson flew back with the four new pilots and brought the rumours with him. Hoyt had more to barter in exchange. The talk ran riot at dinner.

"It's a Hun push, all right, but where, nobody knows. We'll have word in a day or so, but it'll be wrong whatever it is, mark what I say!"

And then on the evening of the twentieth things started. A signal came for the Major just as they sat down to mess. He went out and presently called out the three flight commanders. When they came back they took their places thoughtfully. Silence trembled in the room like the hush that precedes the first blasting stroke of a great bell in a cathedral tower. The Major swept his eyes down the board.

"You will remain at the aerodrome to-night, gentlemen, and remain sober. Officers' luggage is to be packed and placed on lorries which Mr. Harbord is providing for that purpose." He paused for a moment. "This is a precautionary move, gentlemen. We are to be ready to retire at a moment's notice. Flight commanders have the map squares of the new aerodrome. You can take that up later among yourselves." He leaned back in his chair and beckoned to the mess sergeant. "Take every officer's order, sergeant, and bring me the chit."

The talk broke in a wild flood that roared and crackled down the length of the table. The tin walls trembled with the surge of it and the echoes broke in hot discord among the rough pine rafters. Offensive patrols for all three flights, to start at five minutes to 4 a.m. Air domination must be maintained. Wing's instructions were to stop everything at all costs. Go out and fight and shut up. Somebody presented the Adjutant with the sugar bowl and asked him if he had his umbrella for the trip back. The Adjutant had spent eighteen days without soles to his boots in 1914. He and the medical officer stood drinks for the squadron.

About ten o'clock, Hoyt called the five men of C Flight into his hut. "To-morrow, something is going to happen, I'm afraid, and you've got to meet it without much experience. What I want you to understand is simply this: You've got Pat and you've got me. Follow us and do what we do. We won't let you down so far as it is humanly possible. If the flight gets split up in a dog fight, then fight your way out two and two—and go back to the new 'drome two and two. Don't go separately. Further "—he paused —"if anything happens to me "—Paterson looked up at him quickly and something tugged sharply at his heart; Hoyt went on quietly—" take your lead from Mr. Paterson. You'll be Number 5, Darlington. You'll climb up as deputy leader. And if anything happens to Pat, then it's up to you to bring the rest home." He smiled. "There is a bottle of Dewar's in this drawer. Take a snifter now, if you want it, and one in the morning. It's for C Flight only. Oh yes, one more thing: The fact that we're moving back to a new aerodrome seems to indicate that staff thinks nothing can stop the Hun from breaking through. The fact that nothing can stop the Hun seems to indicate that, for the nonce, we are losing our part of the War. If the thought will help you—it's yours without cost."

The caller rapped sharply and threw back the door. Paterson leaped to his feet half asleep and pushed back the window curtains. The clouds were down to about four hundred feet, lowering in a grey mass over the mist on the aerodrome. He went into the next cubicle and turned Hoyt out. Hoyt sat up on the cot edge and ran his hand across his forehead.

"Stop the caller," he said. "Let's see what's what before we turn everybody out." They shrugged into their flying coats and groped down the passage to the Major's cubicle in the next hut block.

"Let 'em sleep," said the Major. "Can't do anything in this muck. Turn out one officer in each flight to watch for the break and to warn the rest. Send Harbord to me if you see him wandering about."

They woke up the skippers of A and B Flights and told them the news. Paterson took the watch for C. He turned up his coat collar and went out. It was cold and miserable in the open, and the chill crept into his bones. The smoke from his cigarette hung low about him in the still air.

Presently to the eastward there came a low roar. He looked at his wrist watch. The hands pointed to six minutes to four o'clock. The ground trembled slightly to the sound of the distant guns and the air stirred in faint gusts that pulled at blue wraiths of his cigarette smoke. The push had started. His muscles stiffened at the knees as he listened. The first shock of the guns was raw and sharp in the quiet air; then it settled into a lower, full-throated rumble like the heavy notes of an organ growling in an underground basilica. Now it rose again in its greater volume—rose steadily, slowly, as if it were a colossal express train hammering down the switch points at unthinkable speed. Presently it soared to its highest pitch and held the blasting monotony of its tone. The minutes ticked off, but the guns never faltered in their symphony of blood. At 4.35 one pipe of the organ to the south-eastward cut out suddenly and almost immediately began again, closer than before. Again it broke as he listened, and crept nearer still.

He walked down the line of huts, thrashing his arms and blowing on his cold hands. An impersonal thing to him, yet he shivered slightly and stared upward at the low clouds. Men out there to the eastward were in it. The suspense was over for them. And suddenly he found himself annoyed at the delay, annoyed at the fog and clouds above, that kept him on the ground. He wanted to see what was going on—to know. He turned impatiently and went into the mess. The sergeant brought him coffee, and presently Muirhead of A Flight came in with Church of B.

"It's on," Church said absently. "I suppose this fog means hell up the line."

They drank their coffee and smoked in silence. The sound of the guns crept nearer and nearer, and one by one the rest of the squadron drifted in for breakfast.

Hoyt sat down next to Paterson. "I don't like it," he said. "Something is giving way up there." He went to the window and looked out. "Clouds are higher," he said, "and the fog's lifted a bit. What do you think, Major?"

They crowded out of the mess doorway and stood in an anxious knot, staring upward. It was well after six o'clock.

"All right"—the Major turned around—"get ready to stand by."

C Flight collected in a little knot in front of Hoyt's Camel, smoking and talking nervously. Paterson kept his eyes on Hoyt and stamped his feet to get the circulation up. A strange elation crept into his veins and warmed him. In a moment now—in a moment. Awkward waiting here. Awkward standing around listening to Darlington curse softly and pound his hands together.

Somewhere behind him on the road, a motor-bike roared through the mist, and then to the southward a shell crashed not a thousand yards from the 'drome, and the echo of it thumped off across the fields. Darlington jumped and stared at the mushroom of greasy black smoke. A moment more—a moment now. Paterson reached over and tapped Darlington's sleeve. " Keep your guns warm, old boy." Darlington nodded fiercely.

The Major climbed into his cockpit and a mechanic leaped to the propeller. The engine coughed once and the propeller snapped back. The mechanic leaped at it again. It spun down and melted into a circle of pale light. Everyone was climbing in. Hoyt flicked his cigarette away sharply and put a leg up into his stirrup.

They were taxi-ing out into the open ground, with the mechanics running after them. Presently they could see the road. Paterson stared at it in amazement. It was brown and crawling with lorries and troops. Something had happened! A Flight, with the Major, sang off across the ground and took the air together in a climbing turn. B Flight waited a brief second and followed. Out of the corner of his eye Paterson could see the mess sergeant climbing up on the lorry seat beside Harbord, the equipment officer. Then Hoyt waved his hand. Mechanics yanked at the chock ropes and waved them off. They blipped their motors and raced out after Hoyt.

At five hundred feet they took the roof in the lacy fringe of the low clouds. Bad, very bad, Paterson thought. He ran his thumb across the glass face of his altimeter and his globe became wet with the beaded moisture. He could hardly see Darlington's tail. Ahead of them the clouds were a trifle higher. Hoyt led them up and turned northward. Murder to cross the line at that height, with the barrage on. Darlington was lagging a bit. Afraid of the clouds.

He dived on Darlington's tail and closed him up on Number 3. Darlington glanced back at him and ducked his head.

Hoyt was circling back now in a broad sweep. Over there somewhere was Cambrai. He looked up for an instant just in time to see the underside of a huge plane sweep over him. He ducked at the sight of the black crosses, but the plane was gone before he could whip his Lewis gun into action. Almost immediately one corner of his windshield ripped away and the triplex glass blurred with a quick frosting of a thousand cracks. He cursed into the roar of his motor and kept on.

They were higher now, but the visibility was frightful—like flying in a glass ball that had been streaked with thick, dripping soapsuds. Here a glimpse and a rift that closed up as soon as you looked; there a blank wall, tapering into tantalising shreds that you couldn't quite see beyond. He fidgeted in his cockpit and turned his head from Hoyt, below him, to the grey emptiness behind. Nothing.

Presently Hoyt banked around, and following him, the compass needle on Paterson's instrument board turned through a half circle. They were going back toward the south again and climbing still higher. An even thousand feet now—just under the rising, ragged clouds. He felt a drop of rain strike his cheek where his chin piece ended. It bit his skin like a thorn and stung for seconds afterward. His goggles were fogging. He ran a finger up under them and swept the lenses.

Then, in a breath, it happened. A grey flash swept down out of the clouds in front of the formation. Hoyt zoomed to avoid it. The Hun zoomed, and they came together and melted into each other in a welter of torn, rumpled wings and flying splinters. Something black and kicking rose out and disappeared. The cords stood out in Paterson's neck and his throat closed. Somewhere his stomach leaped and kicked inside of him, trying to get out, and he saw coffee dripping from the dials of his instruments.

In a second he had thrown his stick forward and gone down into Hoyt's place. He didn't dare look—he couldn't look. He was screaming curses at the top of his voice and the screams caught in his throat in great sobs. His goggles were hopelessly fogged. He ripped them off. Behind him the four new men closed in tightly, with Darlington above them as deputy leader.

There was blood again on his lips. He pulled back his stick and climbed. There, somewhere in the clouds, were the men who had done it! All right! All right! His eyes stung and wept with the force of the wind, and his cheeks quivered under the lash of the raindrops. With his free hand, fist clenched, he pounded his knee in stunned anguish until his muscles ached. Hoyt! Hoyt! Then he saw what he wanted, and dived down furiously at the shape in the mist. Bullets tore at his top plane and raked across the cowling behind him. He closed on the Hun and sent it spinning. There was another—three—five—nothing but Huns. He dived in between them. Fine! He was screaming again and firing. He forgot he was flying. The joy-stick thrashed crazily between his knees, and the ground and the clouds were a muddy grey scarf that swept from side to side across his eyes. Guns were the thing. Once, in a quick flash, he saw tiny men running upside down through the ring sight of his Lewis gun—the gun on his top plane —funny.

His wrists ached and his fingers were quite dead against the Bowden trigger. No, not that; that's a Camel—Darlington. He grabbed at his joy-stick and pulled it back. Funny how hard it was to pull it. Another Camel swept in beside him, and another, with startling suddenness. It had been a long time now—a long time. Somebody had been afraid once and there had been a man named Hoyt. No, Hoyt was dead. Hoyt had been killed days before. Must have been P.-B. P.-B. was probably in Amiens by now. He'd left in the tender at six o'clock. And always his guns chattered above the roar of his engine.

Abruptly, the cross wires of his centre section raced up to him from a great distance and stopped just before his eyes. He wondered where they had been all this time. He stared past them into the light disc of his propeller, and again the rain lashed into his face and stung him. He caught at the kicking joy-stick and held on to it with both hands—but one hand fell away from it and wouldn't come back. With an effort he pulled back his stick to climb up under the clouds again. Must be up under the clouds. Must wait and get more Huns. Funny things, Huns. Clumsy, stupid grey things you shot at and sent down. Go home soon, rest a bit, and get some more. He laughed softly to himself. Joke. Funniest thing in the world.

The centre section wires clouded up before his eyes and started to race away from him. Here! That's bad! Can't fly without centre section wires. He chuckled a bit over that. Absurd to think of flying without centre section wires! Come back here! You come back!

Just as his eyes closed, he saw a streak of roadway flicker through the struts of his left wing. There were faces on it quite close to him —faces that were white and staring; faces with arms raised above them. Funny. He whipped back his joy-stick with a convulsive jerk, and then his head crashed forward and he threw up his arm to keep his teeth from being bashed out against the compass.

It was very dark—dark except for a dancing blue light far away. He moved slightly. Something cool touched his forehead.

" All right," he muttered; " that's all right now. You just follow me." Someone whispered. He opened his eyes and stared into the darkness. "No," he said quite plainly. "I mean it! Hoyt's dead. I saw him go down."

He felt something sharp prick his arm. "You've got the new aerodrome pin-pointed, haven't you?" he asked.

A soft voice said: "Yes. Sh-h-h!"

"No," he said, "I can't. Darlington's alone now, and I've got to go back. They're green, but they're good boys." He moved his legs to get up. "There's a bottle of Dewar's——"

"No," said the voice beside him.

"Oh yes," he said quietly. "Really, this is imperative. I know I crashed."

A stealthy languor crept across his chest and flowed down toward his legs. He thought about it for a moment. "I ought to go," he said pettishly. "But I'm so tired."

"Yes," said the voice. "Go to sleep now."

"Right-o," he said. "You call a tender and wake—me—half—an—hour." He was quiet for a moment more and then he chuckled softly. "Tell 'em it's poobah," he said sharply.

"All right," said the voice. "It's poobah."

His breathing became quiet and regular, and footsteps tiptoed softly down the ward away from his bed.

FLYING SCHOOL, 1914

by
Richard Euringer

FISCHER had mounted two of the "new" L.V.G.s. One of them had been got ready by Schwink and Sirry; the other one, that dark brown old box, which Captain Wirth had already refused to take over, was for Lieutenant Murner. It stood next to the smart L.V.G., looking like a mangy old pack camel. There was something rather touching about it. We tapped all its parts, inside and out. A home must be found for it somewhere. Someone will crash in it, but anyway it will turn up again at No. 4 school, having passed in due course through Schools 1 to 3.

Meanwhile the nimble Faberle had completed his maiden flight and reported a safe return.

Then Holzbock had to have a trial. I asked him seriously whether he would not rather have some more instruction. I got into the old "camel," whose stern was supported by trestles, showed him how to start it, what he had to do when he banked, and the natural position of the undercarriage. He did not seem to be listening. He did not laugh when I made a joke. At first he was all dazed; then he seemed to be quite apathetic. What would happen to him if I sent him away? I sent one of my men, who got a disease on leave, back to his regiment, as I had told the men I should. Six weeks later he was shot.

Fly, Holzbock, for Christ's sake, fly!

What would happen to this old brown box if I sent it back to the G.V., my first war machine: L.G.V.—Otto 43, constructed 1914. Fischer will think I'm mad, but I must find the hole, dating from Ungewitter's time, when a shot went through the strut above Houthoulst Forest . . . the strut was replaced a long time ago. But there can't be any doubt about it. In my old log-books there must be some record of handing over. That's the plane in which we hoped to take Calais, although there were already rumours that the French had surrounded Lille; the plane from which, at the battle of Ypres, we reported the Vormezeel battery which was silenced by our guns. That was the time when the 6th Bavarian reserve division took Wytschaete, lost it, and took it again. Above a bank of clouds, fearing that I was over enemy territory, I once flew as far as Oudernade, much too far east, and even then slipped back into the clouds, because the little flag over the church tower looked suspiciously French. By Jove! that was a time. The English were constantly throwing fresh forces into the line; it was touch and go with Italy. Our dump was suddenly moved back, and one of the squadron's motor lorries was missing for days. The windows in the Rue du Capt. Ferber shook with the gun-fire, until finally, with the help of our bomb dropper, the last panes went, and were replaced with cardboard. "The Russians are marching on Konisberg," so the natives said, from whom we requisitioned beer, hens, vegetables, blankets, and mica-celluloid *pour jongler des bonbons.* (Gestures had to do service for French.) There isn't the slightest trace left on my poor old flounder of the improvised bomb-dropping apparatus. It all went smash in the show of November 12.

Under this very tank, wedged in between the motor and the observer's seat, I have seen a man's feet nearly sawn off at the ankles in an effort to disentangle him from the fuselage. No, not under this tank. That one was somewhat rusted, dented like a sardine tin. This motor, my respected Captain Bohm, my dear Murner, my worthy Fruhholtz and Fischer, Sirry, and Schwink; no, not this one, but a motor like it, had to be dug out of the earth with spades. . . . Château Bondue was the place. A pleasant little country seat, the château of the Counts de la Serre, full of history, a Flanders mansion—that was later, of course, but it's all the same. In order to conceal the hangar, the skipper felled two of the magnificent elms, which, rising above thick blackberry bushes, closed in a feudal park, in the centre of which Southern fruits sunned themselves on baroque sandstone statues. The old Count, an 1870 veteran, stood by bareheaded, heard the mighty trees groan and saw the foliage come crashing down, and nodded slightly ever after, a nodding that was a little timorous and a little proud, but not without goodwill towards the barbarians, who protected his priceless china against bomb splinters, and gave a certified inventory of his buried silver to the authorities, and with whose flying exploits he soon felt himself associated as an old soldier, a nobleman, and a sportsman. But all this was also later.

At that time—the period following on November 10, the front seemed to be actually heaving under the devastating gun-fire. Pilots understood none of the details of what was happening, but the observers suddenly had an important air. Divisional headquarters wanted to keep a tighter hand on the pilots, and so the squadron was soon on the move. With our workshop, four hangars, and the greater part of the men, the squadron commander set out to find a little château. It was pouring with rain, and those days made us familiar with Flanders mist. Two machines were smashed up. Clods of mud flew round the cockpit; the tyres stuck to the earth. We stood about, stamping in the mud, but the mist would not sink, and would not rise. The squadron commander sent us the ominous message that he had found a château . . . that was late in the evening. During the night the mist cleared before a gale. Towards midnight the stars shone out clearly, but the driving clouds passed in close formation across the sky above a burning village. Two hours later the tent-poles were bending,

as the storm drove the clouds along. Meteorologically it was uncanny. The Prussians turned the men out. As the wind was tugging at the tent-pegs, there was a risk that the tent might fly
away. That night a couple of grapnels were pulled up. The heavy
planes bellied and flapped, whenever a bit of canvas slipped open.
The wind howled and whistled round the entrenchments. In the
morning Captain Brauer's anemometer registered fourteen kilometres per second. Impatience produced a sinking feeling in our
stomachs. It was difficult to imagine just what would happen if
a plane were to attempt to fight against the storm. If the propeller should jam, as it whirled about the clods of earth, one
would be hurled by the gale against the ramparts and then whirled along like a scrap of paper, whipped by the wind.

There was a roaring and a shaking; the rage of the bombardment made such a savage accompaniment to the soughing of the
trees and the fury of the upper elements, that we found ourselves
suffering from acute pains in the stomach. After one such interlude two men of the squadron to which we were attached opened
a tent and pushed their machines out. . . . Did they really in-
tend to fly? When one gives the lead, others usually follow it!

Was a lead necessary? Ungewitter ran to get his helmet and
rifle. I shouted after him: "Bring my helmet and coat. . . ." My
voice did not carry. A man ran after him.

If the Prussians had a shot at it, why not others?

Men hung on to all the struts. The roar of the propellers was
drowned in the gale. Men struggled to hold the planes down and
rammed pegs into the ground.

Prussians have always taken the lead, and others have followed.
It needed no special skill to stagger along right behind them.
Besides, we knew now what was up. I had been at the High Com-
mand on the evening before the battle. Crown Prince Rupprecht

was standing there, very pale. Though only a junior officer, I had gathered that if we were now held up the winter weather would prevent any further progress. In the East the Russians were moving in enormous numbers into our country. Ungewitter did not return. I sent some men after him, who reported that he was engaged with the artillery commander.

The first machine hardly moved along the ground, for the hurricane lifted her over the trees. The wind shrieked in the fuselage, but the machine made no progress forward, she only went higher. Mysteriously she shot up, a thing without weight, and hung as though attached by ropes, her propeller digging into the air, while the next machine followed hard on her track. Then I saw no more. Savagely the storm tore at the tent. Ungewitter staggered up, threw me my gear, and shouted that the skipper had telephoned that he was being pressed by Divisional H.Q.: Couldn't we fly? He had reported it was impossible. What did we think about it?

To that there could be but one answer.

One machine came down again. That didn't matter to us now.

As that machine was being stowed away, Captain Brauer came along and signed to give it up. With a neck-breaking, gull-like action he trundled the other machine into the open space and pancaked.

"That's finished it!" shouted Brauer. "We'll only crash."

If he'd come up to us and lifted us out of the cockpit I should probably have been grateful to him. It would have been a back door through which one could have slipped with some kind of decency. But, as it was, he merely said: "I have forbidden you gentlemen to go up."

And our skipper asked us what we thought.

To that I found no reply.

So we staggered up. It was not pleasant. But after five frightful minutes we knew at any rate that it was feasible. The Prussians had made it possible, and my old box stood it; that ancient contraption, which was like a silver fish with its frosted aluminium cockpit. We sang wild songs of rage and defiance at the storm. The citadel whirled away below us. It was more dangerous to plane down than to fight one's way right through to the more stable layers of the air.

The enormous Ypres salient was spread out below under a haze of the smoke from the guns. Dark fragments of cloud, like cotton-wool whales, surged at us, 600 metres off. We topped them, gleaming white over the swollen shadows, which they dragged across the map of the landscape. We had to drop Verey lights over Warneton. Warneton lay somewhere below. That old bus knew how to jump about. After 1,200 metres the grey mist suddenly disappeared for a few moments and a gleam of daylight showed through the uncertain darkness. I pressed on upwards; over the massed clouds, out of the haze of streaming mist into the elemental hurricane. When at 1,600 metres the rainbow gloriole of the propeller rose from the waving cloudscapes into the glacial blue of a clearer zone, a couple of shell cloudlets, fired at random, floated in the air quite prettily, but neither eye nor field-glasses could pierce the cloudbank, whose brilliant surface contrasted with the murky flashes of gun-fire.

Francis kept waving his map and gesticulating: we were too comfortable; it was no good, we had to go through the " snow " again. . . . As, with an invocation to the deity, I dashed at the next cloudbank, we saw our own plane rushing at us, rainbow-hued. Then we were swallowed in the darkness. . . .

For an hour we laboured; we revelled in lift sensations. I had only one anxiety, that my friend with the meteorological name would fall out. He did indeed drop his sixteen-pointed star on to the fighting ant-heap below, but—truth to tell—we had not much to show for our labour. We swooped and planed; the storm buffeted us, but the battle owed us nothing on that day of wind and danger, November 12.

Checkmated, we returned home. Home behind Comines and Warneton, in a toy château, surrounded by waving elms, set in a park.

Damnation! What we wanted was a landing-place!

I was beginning to feel angry.

We banked steeply downwards, setting our teeth. There was not a patch to land on. Only a narrow strip of rough ploughed land between the park and the stunted willows. The gale was behind us. We planed down. (It seemed to me that the head wind counterbalanced the weight of the machine.) A gust from the flank pushed the tail of the machine down towards the branches; trees drifted by.

The bus slipped along an avenue with elms on the right and stunted willows on the left; caught, broke away, soared upwards, banked again with the wind behind, and sheered off again for the ploughed field, a mere strip of molehills between the park and the willows.

I saw the danger and understood what was happening. But I was no longer interested as to exactly how I should land in front of the château.

With a kind of malicious joy I realised what was going to happen. . . . The left wing brushed the tree-tops and crumpled up like a paper bag. With a sudden windmill action the machine swerved and the tail went up, straight in the air like the fin of a whale. I saw a broken branch rushing at my left goggle, close to the eye. The glass smashed. I laughed. My eye was saved!

Cautiously, I opened my eye.

I never felt the landing. The machine dived straight down into the brambles with a force that buried the motor right up to the third cylinder. For long afterwards I heard the crashing and splintering of framework, fuselage, and branches. My belt was torn as we bumped, and I was thrown head downwards into the brambles. Wedged between the motor and the tank, I hung there, head downwards. I felt very sick.

Men rushed up with picks and shovels and began the work of extricating us. Suddenly there was a piercing yell. Francis wanted to curse but couldn't think of anything to say. He collapsed exhausted on top of me, his legs dangling behind him.

In their eagerness to get him free they had sawed at his ankles. He was moaning at the loss of his left leg.

I lost my Francis. They packed him off home. Later I gave him his little Iron Cross in hospital (for a rifle encounter with two British Bristols). Afterwards he became an accomplished pilot.

What about the machine? It was an extraordinary sight. The carriage was the only thing on it that hadn't lost any parts. It stretched its wheels up into the air. Perhaps the same wheels that you admired on the old flounder here. No, those are rubber tyres. Perhaps the axle was the same, if it hasn't been repeatedly smashed up since then. They attached new wings, antediluvian in all conscience, made up of God knows what old patches of linen. The old belt had been torn away—the one that almost burst my stomach muscles—but it had been given a new belt. No scrap of linen, no cable, strut, beam, spar, nut, bolt, or screw survived, but by some miracle it was the same machine.

The old flounder nursed a great secret. It was a giant ship but a very short time ago. Someone cut out a bloodstained piece of cloth and worked on it the number 4. There it lay, felled, but not dead, a memorial; its own War memorial.

L.V.G.—B.43. . . . Old tin Lizzie! My black-brown flounder. It was an old box, but the old box was new. Not a patch of the original was left after all its crashes. And the machine was there still.

Get your knees around it, my dear Murner, pack yourself into this new machine, which is your first, and solve the mystery! Between heaven and earth, spinning as though to crash, man and machine together; you will then understand the miracle of flight.

AT SEA

THE TALE

by
Joseph Conrad

OUTSIDE the large single window the crepuscular light was dying out slowly in a great square gleam without colour, framed rigidly in the gathering shades of the room.

It was a long room. The irresistible tide of the night ran into the most distant part of it, where the whispering of a man's voice, passionately interrupted and passionately renewed, seemed to plead against the answering murmurs of infinite sadness.

At last no answering murmur came. His movement when he rose slowly from his knees by the side of the deep, shadowy couch holding the shadowy suggestion of a reclining woman, revealed him tall under the low ceiling, and sombre all over except for the crude discord of the white collar under the shape of his head and the faint, minute spark of a brass button here and there on his uniform.

He stood over her a moment masculine and mysterious in his immobility before he sat down on a chair near by. He could see only the faint oval of her upturned face and, extended on her black dress, her pale hands, a moment before abandoned to his kisses and now as if too weary to move.

He dared not make a sound, shrinking as a man would do from the prosaic necessities of existence. As usual, it was the woman who had the courage. Her voice was heard first—almost conventional —while her being vibrated yet with conflicting emotions.

"Tell me something," she said.

The darkness hid his surprise and then his smile. Had he not just said to her everything worth saying in the world—and that not for the first time!

"What am I to tell you?" he asked, in a voice creditably steady. He was beginning to feel grateful to her for that something final in her tone which had eased the strain.

"Why not tell me a tale?"

"A tale!" He was really amazed.

"Yes. Why not?"

These words came with a slight petulance, the hint of a loved woman's capricious will, which is capricious only because it feels itself to be a law, embarrassing sometimes and always difficult to elude.

"Why not?" he repeated, with a slightly mocking accent, as though he had been asked to give her the moon. But now he was feeling a little angry with her for that feminine mobility that slips out of an emotion as easily as out of a splendid gown.

He heard her say a little unsteadily, with a sort of fluttering intonation which made him think suddenly of a butterfly's flight:

"You used to tell—your—your simple and—and professional —tales very well at one time. Or well enough to interest me. You had a—a sort of art—in the days—the days before the War."

"Really?" he said, with involuntary gloom. "But now, you see, the War is going on," he continued in such a dead, equable tone that she felt a slight chill fall over her shoulders. And yet she persisted. For there's nothing more unswerving in the world than a woman's caprice.

"It could be a tale not of this world," she explained.

"You want a tale of the other, the better world?" he asked, with a matter-of-fact surprise. "You must evoke for that task those who have already gone there."

"No. I don't mean that. I mean another—some other—world. In the universe—not in heaven."

"I am relieved. But you forget that I have only a five days' leave."

"Yes. And I've also taken a five days' leave from—from my duties."

"I like that word."

"What word?"

"Duty."

"It is horrible—sometimes."

"Oh, that's because you think it's narrow. But it isn't. It contains infinities, and—and so——"

"What is this jargon?"

He disregarded the interjected scorn. "An infinity of absolution, for instance," he continued. "But as to this 'another world' —who's going to look for it and for the tale that is in it?"

"You," she said, with a strange, almost rough, sweetness of assertion.

He made a shadowy movement of assent in his chair, the irony of which not even the gathered darkness could render mysterious.

"As you will. In that world, then, there was once upon a time a Commanding Officer and a Northman. Put in the capitals, please, because they had no other names. It was a world of seas and continents and islands—"

"Like the earth," she murmured bitterly.

"Yes. What else could you expect from sending a man made of our common, tormented clay on a voyage of discovery? What else could he find? What else could you understand or care for, or feel the existence of even? There was comedy in it and slaughter."

"Always like the earth," she murmured.

"Always. And since I could find in the universe only what was deeply rooted in the fibres of my being there was love in it too. But we won't talk of that."

"No. We won't," she said, in a neutral tone which concealed

perfectly her relief—or her disappointment. Then after a pause
she added : "It's going to be a comic story."

"Well——" he paused too. "Yes. In a way. In a very grim
way. It will be human, and, as you know, comedy is but a matter
of the visual angle. And it won't be a noisy story. All the long
guns in it will be dumb—as dumb as so many telescopes."

"Ah, there are guns in it, then! And may I ask—where?"

"Afloat. You remember that the world of which we speak had
its seas. A war was going on in it. It was a funny world and terribly in earnest. Its war was being carried on over the land, over the
water, under the water, up in the air, and even under the ground.
And many young men in it, mostly in ward-rooms and mess-rooms
used to say to each other—pardon the unparliamentary word—
they used to say, ' It's a damned bad war, but it's better than no
war at all.' Sounds flippant, doesn't it?"

He heard a nervous, impatient sigh in the depths of the couch
while he went on without pause :

"And yet there is more in it than meets the eye. I mean more
wisdom. Flippancy, like comedy, is but a matter of visual first-im-
pression. That world was not very wise. But there was in it a
certain amount of common working sagacity. That, however, was
mostly worked by the neutrals in diverse ways, public and private,
which had to be watched; watched by acute minds and also by
actual sharp eyes. They had to be very sharp indeed, too, I can
assure you."

"I can imagine," she murmured, appreciatively.

"What is there that you can't imagine?" he pronounced soberly.
"You have the world in you. But let us go back to our Commanding Officer, who, of course, commanded a ship of a sort. My tales
if often professional (as you remarked just now) have never been
technical. So I'll just tell you that the ship was of a very ornamental

sort once, with lots of grace and elegance and luxury about her. Yes, once! She was like a pretty woman who had suddenly put on a suit of sackcloth and stuck revolvers in her belt. But she floated lightly, she moved nimbly, she was quite good enough."

"That was the opinion of the Commanding Officer?" said the voice from the couch.

"It was. He used to be sent out with her along certain coasts to see—what he could see. Just that. And sometimes he had some preliminary information to help him, and sometimes he had not. And it was all one, really. It was about as useful as information trying to convey the locality and intentions of a cloud, of a phantom taking shape here and there and impossible to seize, would have been.

"It was in the early days of the War. What at first used to amaze the Commanding Officer was the unchanged face of the waters, with its familiar expression, neither more friendly nor more hostile. On fine days the sun strikes sparks upon the blue; here and there a peaceful smudge of smoke hangs in the distance, and it is impossible to believe that the familiar clear horizon traces the limit of one great circular ambush."

"Yes, it is impossible to believe, till some day you see a ship not your own ship (that isn't so impressive), but some ship in company blow up all of a sudden and plop under almost before you know what had happened to her. Then you begin to believe. Henceforth you go out for the work to see—what you can see, and you keep on at it with the conviction that some day you will die from something you have not seen. One envies the soldiers at the end of the day, wiping the sweat and blood from their faces, counting the dead fallen to their hands, looking at the devastated field, the torn earth that seems to suffer and bleed with them. One does, really. The final brutality of it—the taste of primitive passion—the fero-

cious frankness of the blow struck with one's hand—the direct call
and the straight response. Well, the sea gave you nothing of that,
and seemed to pretend that there was nothing the matter with the
world."

She interrupted, stirring a little.

"Oh yes. Sincerity—frankness—passion—three words of your
gospel. Don't I know them!"

"Think! Isn't it ours—believed in common?" he asked anxiously, yet without expecting an answer, and went on at once. "Such
were the feelings of the Commanding Officer. When the night
came trailing over the sea, hiding what looked like the hypocrisy
of an old friend, it was a relief. The night blinds you frankly—
and there are circumstances when the sunlight may grow as odious
to one as falsehood itself. Night is all right.

"At night the Commanding Officer could let his thoughts get
away—I won't tell you where. Somewhere where there was no
choice but between truth and death. But thick weather, though it
blinded one, brought no such relief. Mist is deceitful, the dead lu-
minosity of the fog is irritating. It seems that you *ought* to see.

"One gloomy, nasty day the ship was steaming along her beat
in sight of a rocky, dangerous coast that stood out intensely black
like an Indian-ink drawing on grey paper. Presently the Second-in-
Command spoke to his chief. He thought he saw something on
the water, to seaward. Small wreckage, perhaps.

"'But there shouldn't be any wreckage here, sir,' he remarked.

"'No,' said the Commanding Officer. 'The last reported sub-
marined ships were sunk a long way to the westward. But one
never knows. There may have been others since then not reported
nor seen. Gone with all hands.'

"That was how it began. The ship's course was altered to pass
the object close; for it was necessary to have a good look at what

one could see. Close, but without touching; for it was not advisable to come in contact with objects of any form whatever floating casually about. Close, but without stopping or even diminishing speed; for in those times it was not prudent to linger on any particular spot, even for a moment. I may tell you at once that the object was not dangerous in itself. No use in describing it. It may have been nothing more remarkable than, say, a barrel of a certain shape and colour. But it was significant.

" The smooth bow-wave hove it up as if for a closer inspection, and then the ship, brought again to her course, turned her back on it with indifference, while twenty pairs of eyes on her deck stared in all directions trying to see—what they could see.

" The Commanding Officer and his Second-in-Command discussed the object with understanding. It appeared to them to be not so much a proof of the sagacity as of the activity of certain neutrals. This activity had in many cases taken the form of replenishing the stores of certain submarines at sea. This was generally believed, if not absolutely known. But the very nature of things in those early days pointed that way. The object, looked at closely and turned away from with apparent indifference, put it beyond doubt that something of the sort had been done somewhere in the neighbourhood.

" The object in itself was more than suspect. But the fact of its being left in evidence roused other suspicions. Was it the result of some deep and devilish purpose? As to that all speculation soon appeared to be a vain thing. Finally, the two officers came to the conclusion that it was left there most likely by accident, complicated possibly by some unforeseen necessity; such, perhaps, as the sudden need to get away quickly from the spot, or something of that kind.

" Their discussion had been carried on in curt, weighty phrases,

separated by long, thoughtful silences. And all the time their eyes
roamed about the horizon in an everlasting, almost mechanical effort of vigilance. The younger man summed up grimly:

" ' Well, it's evidence. That's what this is. Evidence of what we
were pretty certain of before. And plain too.'

" ' And much good it will do to us,' retorted the Commanding
Officer. ' The parties are miles away, the submarine, devil only
knows where, ready to kill; and the noble neutral slipping away to
the eastward, ready to lie!'

" The Second-in-Command laughed a little at the time. But he
guessed that the neutral wouldn't even have to lie very much. Fellows like that, unless caught in the very act, felt themselves pretty
safe. They could afford to chuckle. That fellow was probably chuck-
ling to himself. It's very possible he had been before at the game
and didn't care a rap for the bit of evidence left behind. It was a
game in which practice made one bold and successful too.

" And again he laughed faintly. But his Commanding Officer
was in revolt against the murderous stealthiness of methods and
the atrocious callousness of complicities that seemed to taint the
very source of men's deep emotions and noblest activities; to cor-
rupt their imagination which builds up the final conceptions of
life and death. The suffered——"

The voice from the sofa interrupted the narrator.

" How well I can understand that in him! "

He bent forward slightly.

" Yes. I too. Everything should be open in love and war. Open
as the day, since both are the call of an ideal which it is so easy, so
terribly easy, to degrade in the name of Victory."

He paused; then went on:

" I don't know that the Commanding Officer delved so deep as
that into his feelings. But he did suffer from them—a sort of dis-

enchanted sadness. It is possible, even, that he suspected himself of folly. Man is various. But he had no time for much introspection, because from the south-west a wall of fog had advanced upon his ship. Great convolutions of vapours flew over, swirling about masts and funnel, which looked as if they were beginning to melt. Then they vanished.

" The ship was stopped, all sounds ceased, and the very fog became motionless, growing denser and as if solid in its amazing dumb immobility. The men at their stations lost sight of each other. Footsteps sounded stealthy; rare voices, impersonal and remote, died out with resonance. A blind white stillness took possession of the world.

" It looked, too, as if it would last for days. I don't mean to say that the fog did not vary a little in its density. Now and then it would thin out mysteriously, revealing to the men a more or less ghostly presentment of their ship. Several times the shadow of the coast itself swam darkly before their eyes through the fluctuating opaque brightness of the great white cloud clinging to the water.

" Taking advantage of these moments, the ship had been moved cautiously nearer the shore. It was useless to remain out in such thick weather. Her officers knew every nook and cranny of the coast along their beat. They thought that she would be much better in a certain cove. It wasn't a large place, just ample room for a ship to swing at her anchor. She would have an easier time of it till the fog lifted up.

" Slowly, with infinite caution and patience, they crept closer and closer, seeing no more of the cliffs than an evanescent dark loom with a narrow border of angry foam at its foot. At the moment of anchoring the fog was so thick that for all they could see they might have been a thousand miles out in the open sea. Yet the shelter of the land could be felt. There was a peculiar quality in

the stillness of the air. Very faint, very elusive, the wash of the rip-
ple against the encircling land reached their ears, with mysterious
sudden pauses.

" The anchor dropped, the leads were laid in. The Commanding Officer went below into his cabin. But he had not been there
very long when a voice outside his door requested his presence on
deck. He thought to himself : 'What is it now?' He felt some impatience at being called out again to face the wearisome fog.

" He found that it had thinned again a little and had taken on
a gloomy hue from the dark cliffs which had no form, no outline,
but asserted themselves as a curtain of shadows all round the ship,
except in one bright spot, which was the entrance from the open
sea. Several officers were looking that way from the bridge. The
Second-in-Command met him with the breathlessly whispered information that there was another ship in the cove.

" She had been made out by several pairs of eyes only a couple
of minutes before. She was lying at anchor very near the entrance
—a mere vague blot on the fog's brightness. And the Commanding Officer by staring in the direction pointed out to him by eager
hands ended by distinguishing it at last himself. Indubitably a
vessel of some sort.

" 'It's a wonder we didn't run slap into her when coming in,'
observed the Second-in-Command.

" 'Send a boat on board before she vanishes,' said the Commanding Officer. He surmised that this was a coaster. It could
hardly be anything else. But another thought came into his head
suddenly. 'It is a wonder,' he said to his Second-in-Command,
who had rejoined him after sending the boat away.

" By that time both of them had been struck by the fact that the
ship so suddenly discovered had not manifested her presence by
ringing her bell.

"'We came in very quietly, that's true,' concluded the younger officer. 'But they must have heard our leadsmen at least. We couldn't have passed her more than fifty yards off. The closest shave! They may even have made us out, since they were aware of something coming in. And the strange thing is that we never heard a sound from her. The fellows on board must have been holding their breath.'

"'Ay,' said the Commanding Officer thoughtfully.

"In due course the boarding-boat returned, appearing suddenly alongside, as though she had burrowed her way under the fog. The officer in charge came up to make his report, but the Commanding Officer didn't give him time to begin. He cried from a distance:

"'Coaster, isn't she?'

"'No, sir. A stranger—a neutral,' was the answer.

"'No. Really! Well, tell us all about it. What is she doing here?'

"The young man stated then that he had been told a long and complicated story of engine troubles. But it was plausible enough from a strictly professional point of view and it had the usual features: disablement, dangerous drifting along the shore, weather more or less thick for days, fear of a gale, ultimately a resolve to go in and anchor anywhere on the coast, and so on. Fairly plausible.

"'Engines still disabled?' inquired the Commanding Officer.

"'No, sir. She has steam on them.'

"The Commanding Officer took his Second aside. 'By Jove!' he said, 'you were right! They were holding their breaths as we passed them. They were.'

"But the Second-in-Command had his doubts now.

"'A fog like this does muffle small sounds, sir,' he remarked. 'And what could his object be, after all?'

" ' To sneak out unnoticed,' answered the Commanding Officer.
" ' Then why didn't he? He might have done it, you know.
Not exactly unnoticed, perhaps. I don't suppose he could have
slipped his cable without making some noise. Still, in a minute or
so he would have been lost to view—clean gone before we had
made him out fairly. Yet he didn't.'

" They looked at each other. The Commanding Officer shook
his head. Such suspicions as the one which had entered his head
are not defended easily. He did not even state it openly. The
boarding officer finished his report. The cargo of the ship was of
a harmless and useful character. She was bound to an English port.
Papers and everything in perfect order. Nothing suspicious to be
detected anywhere.

" Then, passing to the men, he reported the crew on deck as the
usual lot. Engineers of the well-known type, and very full of their
achievement in repairing the engines. The mate surly. The master
rather a fine specimen of a Northman, civil enough, but appeared
to have been drinking. Seemed to be recovering from a regular bout
of it.

" ' I told him I couldn't give him permission to proceed. He said
he wouldn't dare to move his ship her own length out in such
weather as this, permission or no permission. I left a man on board,
though.'

" ' Quite right.'

" The Commanding Officer, after communing with his suspicions for a time, called his Second aside.

" ' What if she were the very ship which had been feeding some
infernal submarine or other?' he said in an undertone.

" The other started. Then, with conviction:

" ' She would get off scot-free. You couldn't prove it, sir.'

" ' I want to look into it myself.'

" 'From the report we've heard I am afraid you couldn't even make a case for reasonable suspicion, sir.'

" 'I'll go on board all the same.'

" He had made up his mind. Curiosity is the great motive power of hatred and love. What did he expect to find? He could not have told anybody—not even himself.

" What he really expected to find there was the atmosphere, the atmosphere of gratuitous treachery, which in his view nothing could excuse; for he thought that even a passion of unrighteousness for its own sake could not excuse that. But could he detect it? Sniff it? Taste it? Receive some mysterious communication which would turn his invincible suspicions into a certitude strong enough to provoke action with all its risks?

" The master met him on the after-deck, looming up in the fog amongst the blurred shapes of the usual ships' fittings. He was a robust Northman, bearded, and in the force of his age. A round leather cap fitted his head closely. His hands were rammed deep into the pockets of his short leather jacket. He kept them there while he explained that at sea he lived in the chart-room, and led the way there, striding carelessly. Just before reaching the door under the bridge he staggered a little, recovered himself, flung it open, and stood aside, leaning his shoulder as if involuntarily against the side of the house, and staring vaguely into the fog-filled space. But he followed the Commanding Officer at once, flung the door to, snapped on the electric light, and hastened to thrust his hands back into his pockets, as though afraid of being seized by them either in friendship or in hostility.

" The place was stuffy and hot. The usual chart-rack overhead was full, and the chart on the table was kept unrolled by an empty cup standing on a saucer half full of some spilt dark liquid. A slightly nibbled biscuit reposed on the chronometer case. There

were two settees, and one of them had been made up into a bed
with a pillow and some blankets, which were now very much
tumbled. The Northman let himself fall on it, his hands still in
his pockets.

"'Well, here I am,'" he said, with a curious air of being surprised at the sound of his own voice.

"The Commanding Officer from the other settee observed the
handsome, flushed face. Drops of fog hung on the yellow beard
and moustaches of the Northman. The much darker eyebrows ran
together in a puzzled frown, and suddenly he jumped up.

"'What I mean is that I don't know where I am. I really don't,'
he burst out, with extreme earnestness. 'Hang it all! I got turned
around somehow. The fog has been after me for a week. More
than a week. And then my engines broke down. I will tell you
how it was.'

"He burst out into loquacity. It was not hurried, but it was insistent. It was not continuous for all that. It was broken by the
most queer, thoughtful pauses. Each of these pauses lasted no more
than a couple of seconds, and each had the profundity of an endless meditation. When he began again nothing betrayed in him the
slightest consciousness of these intervals. There was the same fixed
glance, the same unchanged earnestness of tone. He didn't know.
Indeed, more than one of these pauses occurred in the middle of
a sentence.

"The Commanding Officer listened to the tale. It struck him
as more plausible than simple truth is in the habit of being. But
that, perhaps, was prejudice. All the time the Northman was speaking the Commanding Officer had been aware of an inward voice,
a grave murmur in the depth of his very own self, telling another
tale, as if on purpose to keep alive in him his indignation and his
anger with that baseness of greed or of mere outlook which lies

often at the root of simple ideas.

"It was the story that had been already told to the boarding officer an hour or so before. The Commanding Officer nodded slightly at the Northman from time to time. The latter came to an end and turned his eyes away. He added, as an afterthought :

"'Wasn't it enough to drive a man out of his mind with worry? And it's my first voyage to this part, too. And the ship's my own. Your officer has seen the papers. She isn't much, as you can see for yourself. Just an old cargo-boat. Bare living for my family.'

"He raised a big arm to point at a row of photographs plastering the bulkhead. The movement was ponderous, as if the arm had been made of lead. The Commanding Officer said, carelessly :

"'You will be making a fortune yet for your family with this old ship.'

"'Yes, if I don't lose her,' said the Northman gloomily.

"'I mean—out of this war,' added the Commanding Officer.

"The Northman stared at him in a curiously unseeing and at the same time interested manner, as only eyes of a particular blue shade can stare.

"'And you wouldn't be angry at it,' he said, 'would you? You are too much of a gentleman. We didn't bring this on you. And suppose we sat down and cried. What good would that be? Let those cry who made the trouble,' he concluded with energy. 'Time's money, you say. Well—*this* time *is* money. Oh! isn't it!'

"The Commanding Officer tried to keep under the feeling of immense disgust. He said to himself that it was unreasonable. Men were like that—moral cannibals feeding on each other's misfortunes. He said aloud :

"'You have made it perfectly plain how it is that you are here. Your log-book confirms you very minutely. Of course, a log-book may be cooked. Nothing easier.'

"The Northman never moved a muscle. He was gazing at the floor; he seemed not to have heard. He raised his head after a while.

"'But you can't suspect me of anything,' he muttered, negligently.

"The Commanding Officer thought: 'Why should he say this?'

"Immediately afterwards the man before him added: 'My cargo is for an English port.'

"His voice had turned husky for the moment. The Commanding Officer reflected: 'That's true. There can be nothing. I can't suspect him. Yet why was he lying with steam up in this fog—and then, hearing us come in, why didn't he give some sign of life? Why? Could it be anything else but a guilty conscience? He could tell by the leadsmen that this was a man-of-war.'

"Yes—why? The Commanding Officer went on thinking: 'Suppose I ask him and then watch his face. He will betray himself in some way. It's perfectly plain that the fellow *has* been drinking. Yes, he has been drinking; but he will have a lie ready all the same.' The Commanding Officer was one of those men who are made morally and almost physically uncomfortable by the mere thought of having to beat down a lie. He shrank from the act in scorn and disgust, which was invincible because more temperamental than moral.

"So he went out on deck instead and had the crew mustered formally for his inspection. He found them very much what the report of the boarding officer had led him to expect. And from their answers to his questions he could discover no flaw in the log-book story.

"He dismissed them. His impression of them was a picked lot; have been promised a fistful of money each if this came off; all slightly anxious, but not frightened. Not a single one of them likely to give the show away. They don't feel in danger of their life.

They know England and English ways too well!

"He felt alarmed at catching himself thinking as if his vaguest suspicions were turning into a certitude. For, indeed, there was no shadow of reason for his interferences. There was nothing to give away.

"He returned to the chart-room. The Northman had lingered behind there; and something subtly different in his bearing, more bold in his blue, glassy stare, induced the Commanding Officer to conclude that the fellow had snatched at the opportunity to take another swig at the bottle he must have had concealed somewhere.

"He noticed, too, that the Northman on meeting his eyes put on an elaborately surprised expression. At least, it seemed elaborated. Nothing could be trusted. And the Englishman felt himself with astonishing conviction faced by an enormous lie, solid like a wall, with no way round to get at the truth, whose ugly murderous face he seemed to see peeping over at him with a cynical grin.

"'I dare say,' he began suddenly, 'you are wondering at my proceedings, though I am not detaining you, am I? You wouldn't dare to move in this fog?'

"'I don't know where I am,' the Northman ejaculated earnestly. 'I really don't.'

"He looked around as if the very chart-room fittings were strange to him. The Commanding Officer asked him whether he had not seen any unusual objects floating about while he was at sea.

"'Objects! What objects? We were groping blind in the fog for days.'

"'We had a few clear intervals,' said the Commanding Officer. 'And I'll tell you what we have seen and the conclusion I've come to about it.'

"He told him in a few words. He heard the sound of a sharp

breath indrawn through closed teeth. The Northman with his hand on the table stood absolutely motionless and dumb. He stood as if thunderstruck. Then he produced a fatuous smile.

"Or at least so it appeared to the Commanding Officer. Was this significant, or of no meaning whatever? He didn't know, he couldn't tell. All the truth had departed out of the world as if drawn in, absorbed in this monstrous villainy this man was—or was not—guilty of.

"'Shooting's too good for people that conceive neutrality in this pretty way,' remarked the Commanding Officer, after a silence.

"'Yes, yes, yes,' the Northman assented, hurriedly—then added an unexpected and dreamy-voiced 'Perhaps.'

"Was he pretending to be drunk, or only trying to appear sober? His glance was straight, but it was somewhat glazed. His lips outlined themselves firmly under his yellow moustache. But they twitched. Did they twitch? And why was he drooping like this in his attitude?

"'There's no perhaps about it,' pronounced the Commanding Officer sternly.

"The Northman had straightened himself. And unexpectedly he looked stern too.

"'No. But what about the tempters? Better kill that lot off. There's about four, five, six million of them,' he said grimly; but in a moment changed into a whining key. 'But I had better hold my tongue. You have some suspicions.'

"'No, I've no suspicions,' declared the Commanding Officer.

"He never faltered. At that moment he had the certitude. The air of the chart-room was thick with guilt and falsehood braving the discovery, defying simple right, common decency, all humanity of feeling, every scruple of conduct.

"The Northman drew a long breath. 'Well we know that you

English are gentlemen. But let us speak the truth. Why should we love you so very much? You haven't done anything to be loved. We don't love the other people, of course. They haven't done anything for that either. A fellow comes along with a bag of gold. . . . I haven't been in Rotterdam my last voyage for nothing.'

"'You may be able to tell something interesting, then, to our people when you come into port,' interjected the officer.

"'I might. But you keep some people in your pay at Rotterdam. Let them report. I am a neutral—am I not? . . . Have you ever seen a poor man on one side and a bag of gold on the other? Of course, I couldn't be tempted. I haven't the nerve for it. Really I haven't. It's nothing to me. I am just talking openly for once.'

"'Yes. And I am listening to you,' said the Commanding Officer quietly.

"The Northman leaned forward over the table. 'Now that I know you have no suspicions, I talk. You don't know what a poor man is. I do. I am poor myself. This old ship, she isn't much, and she is mortgaged too. Bare living, no more. Of course, I wouldn't have the nerve. But a man who has nerve! See. The stuff he takes aboard looks like any other cargo—packages, barrels, tins, copper tubes—what not. He doesn't see it work. It isn't real to him. But he sees the gold. That's real. Of course, nothing could induce me. I suffer from an internal disease. I would either go crazy from anxiety—or—or—take to drink, or something. The risk is too great. Why—ruin!'

"'It should be death.' The Commanding Officer got up, after this curt declaration, which the other received with a hard stare oddly combined with an uncertain smile. The Officer's gorge rose at the atmosphere of murderous complicity which surrounded him, denser, more impenetrable, more acrid than the fog outside.

"'It's nothing to me,' murmured the Northman, swaying visibly.

"'Of course not,' assented the Commanding Officer, with a great effort to keep his voice calm and low. The certitude was strong within him. 'But I am going to clear all you fellows off this coast at once. And I will begin with you. You must leave in half an hour.'

" By that time the Officer was walking along the deck with the Northman at his elbow.

"'What! In this fog?' the latter cried out huskily.

"'Yes, you will have to go in this fog.'

"'But I don't know where I am. I really don't.'

" The Commanding Officer turned round. A sort of fury possessed him. The eyes of the two men met. Those of the Northman expressed a profound amazement.

"'Oh, you don't know how to get out.' The Commanding Officer spoke with composure, but his heart was beating with anger and dread. 'I will give you your course. Steer south-by-east-half-east for about four miles and then you will be clear to haul to the eastward for your port. The weather will clear up before very long.'

"'Must I? What could induce me? I haven't the nerve.'

"'And yet you must go. Unless you want to——"

"'I don't want to,' panted the Northman. 'I've had enough of it.'

" The Commanding Officer got over the side. The Northman remained still as if rooted to the deck. Before his boat reached his ship the Commanding Officer heard the steamer beginning to pick up her anchor. Then, shadowy in the fog, she steamed out on the given course.

"'Yes,' he said to his officers, 'I let him go.'"

The narrator bent forwards towards the couch, where no movement betrayed the presence of a living person.

" Listen," he said forcibly. " That course would lead the North-man straight on a deadly ledge of rock. And the Command-ing Officer gave it to him. He steamed out—ran on it—and went down. So he had spoken the truth. He did not know where he was. But it proves nothing. Nothing either way. It may have been the only truth in all his story. And yet. . . . He seems to have been driven out by a menacing stare—nothing more."

He abandoned all pretence.

" Yes, I gave that course to him. It seemed to me a supreme test. I believe—no, I don't believe. I don't know. At the time I was certain. They all went down; and I don't know whether I have done stern retribution—or murder; whether I have added to the corpses that litter the bed of the unreadable sea, the bodies of men completely innocent or basely guilty. I don't know. I shall never know."

He rose. The woman on the couch got up and threw her arms round his neck. Her eyes put two gleams in the deep shadow of the room. She knew his passion for truth, his horror of deceit, his humanity.

" Oh, my poor, poor——"

" I shall never know," he repeated sternly, disengaging himself, pressed her hands to his lips, and went out.

S.O.S. OFF LIBAU

by
Gerhard Von Gottberg

CAPTAIN BORK, the flotilla commander of the small cruiser *Stolp*, scarcely turned as the orderly came up. He took the chit with a curt nod and laid it on one side.

Things went on as before. There was the heavy, rhythmic throbbing of the engines and an occasional light step on deck. Nothing else to suggest that they were pushing full steam ahead for Libau . . . in the middle of the War . . . straight for the jaws of the Russians.

The old Captain, with his grey, pointed beard and his blue eyes under bushy, white brows, was not thinking of that either. Leaning back, he was reading his son's letter. A deep furrow marked his brow, for what was in the letter caused him to compress his lips sternly. The son was asking his father to support and send on to the Admiral his application for leave. His young wife was very ill; she was shortly to become a mother. . . . As he read the letter, Captain Bork felt something like resentment rising up in him. After all, they were at war. Was there such a thing as a private life for a sailor, an officer? Surely one had to become a piece of the iron Colossus on which one rode, with whose iron heart one throbbed. Was there any room left for thoughts of wife and child?

But his son had written about this; he begged and prayed; he was torn in two; if only he could get away for three days, while his ship was in dock; he would miss nothing. . . .

Captain Bork felt the resentment within him, like a lump, growing and solidifying, against his own son. Treating it as an official chit, he minuted in the margin of the note: "No. If it were peace-time I would concur. Your wife must sacrifice herself like all the women at home. And you also." In the same straight, firm handwriting he addressed the envelope:

" To the Imperial German First Lieutenant at Sea,
Herr Hans-Werner Bork,
c/o H.M.S. *Oranien*."

He was going to ring for the orderly, when it occurred to him that, as they were steaming for the enemy, no post would be forwarded until their return, and there was no question of telegraphing.

The last wireless message caught his eye, and he read it again: "U. 05 . . . U. 011 . . . with *Carola* to Rendezvous L. on 16th November steaming 3·50 knots. H.M.S. *Oranien* with *Herzogin* and *Minerva* have put out four knots to-day."

A grim smile passed over his face as he laid the note aside and took up his cap. At last they were at the enemy again; at last they had got orders to go full steam ahead. After this endless hanging around in harbours and round the coast, they had craved for a real battle like a starving man for bread.

Similar thoughts were passing through the mind of the spare, weather-beaten Commander, who was ploughing the seas with his half flotilla of torpedo-boats, several knots ahead of Captain Bork. Occasionally the crest of a wave would scud over the bridge, and occasionally the young Commander would mutter: " The Russians will be surprised when we bung up their own hole for them."

Great as was the joy of the officers and men on the cruisers and torpedo-boats that they were to be in action, the sturdy skippers, who were ploughing along in the wake of the *Stolp* in their clumsy steamers filled with cement, were still more delighted at being actually privileged to take part in a show, even if it were only as commanders of hulks which in a few hours were to be sunk in the harbour entrances of Libau.

Night came on. Port watch was at fighting stations, starboard watch in hammocks, when suddenly drum and bugles sounded . . . a warning, rousing note. There was a hurrying and running below; a few moments later the last rating was at his station. But there was still a constant restlessness; each man was running over in his mind his duties and tasks in the battle. The munition elevators were tested, reserve ammunition was passed up to the gun-turrets.

With quiet precision the reports came in: " Artillery ready. Machines and auxiliary machines ready."

The first officer made a short round of inspection, and was able to report to the Commander: " Ship cleared for action."

A blizzard set in, driving clouds of snow over the sea and a damp cold that crept into the bones.

But the men on the bridge did not feel it. Every nerve was tense with expectation. Russian territorial waters had been entered. At any moment from the dark skirting of forest a few miles off there might burst a hail of steel; at any moment the enemy might unloose his overwhelming fury against the small German squadron. He must know that there were only a few obsolete ships in the Baltic, that every modern ship was in the North Sea, ready for the first fight with England.

Captain Bork gave a sly smile of satisfaction; the blizzard was just right for him to steal through unobserved. It was a matter of complete indifference to him that visibility was so bad that one could only just see one's hand before one's face. With map and compass he would be able to make Libau according to the time-table. And he was not worrying about his three torpedo-boats ahead. He knew he could rely upon their young Commander as he could upon himself. The snow, moreover, had one great advantage: friend " Russki " would certainly find it snugger to sit over his grog in a warm guard-house than to risk getting rheumatism keeping watch on the dunes.

On they went, but at a very easy pace. It would be no good arriving off Libau while the block ships were still staggering along somewhere in the Baltic.

There was silence on the bridge. Captain Bork was not given to words. With short nods he noted that everything was in order, and concurred in the instructions to be given. A man who has spent thirty years aboard ship has no use for unnecessary talk. His second-in-command thought likewise, and had modelled himself on the dry manner of his chief.

Below decks there was a breathless silence. Only now and again, when a man returned from a short lookout on deck, quick voices asked for news. There was the keenest excitement, a vibrant tension that only iron wills could restrain.

They knew that the battle demanded a complete sacrifice of self. Only a few would be in the thick of things, only a few would be up on deck to see the action. But everywhere there was quiet confidence and a firm belief in the Commander. The sailors in the munition chamber far below the water-level, the stokers at the boilers, the men at the munition elevators—they asked few questions, for each man knew his own job and each man knew that his failure might bring disaster upon them all.

Everywhere confidence was the note. It was the Prussian tradition. One must stand up to superior force, one must fear nothing . . . except God.

Activity increased on the bridge; field-glasses were raised, the first and second officers exchanged comments, but the captain seemed not to hear.

A sharp squall of wind had cleared the air, revealing a few fluttering snowflakes, and then, in the distance . . . somewhere afar off in the desolation of the night . . . a flickering of tiny lights. Libau!

They had passed the torpedo-boats, for they were now going at full speed. Now the goal was reached. Through the snow and the darkness they moved relentlessly on.

H.M.S. *Stolp* was alone. Fate had dealt out the cards, and the men were ready to take a sailor's chance, a fighting chance. None of them, from the Captain to the youngest stoker, was ignorant of the dangers that were ahead.

At any moment batteries might roar at them from the edge of the forest, from concrete bastions, from hollows in the dunes; at any moment they might be greeted by the first salute of Russian battleships and destroyers. And at Libau the British U boats E. 1 and E. 9 were expected to slip through; eager to join in sounding the death-knell of German men, if . . .

But this " if " was slow in materialising.

Captain Bork was standing on the bridge, watch in hand. The torpedo-boats and their block ships must by now be in position, their secret work must have been begun.

A runner dashed up to the bridge, and stood at attention before the Captain: " S.O.S. wireless from *Oranien,* sir. ' We are torpedoed. Our position is . . . Help urgently needed.' "

And, as though this wireless message were the signal for the enemy, there was a sudden roar . . . far away in the distance . . . a tearing and a crashing. From somewhere in the night and darkness it swelled up, to sink somewhere in the sea . . . whirling, monstrous fountains were hurled from the surface of the water.

Not a muscle twitched in the Captain's face. In iron composure he stood on the bridge. Yet there was a struggle going on within his breast, the more terrible because it must be fought out in silence, because it might not find expression.

For the Admiral's orders read: "Libau is to be blocked at all costs and whatever happens. The enemy must be destroyed."

Within the heart of that hard old man on the bridge the choice clamoured, torturing him almost to madness. Could he send one of the three T. boats to the *Oranien's* assistance, or would that imperil the whole scheme? Every moment was priceless to those men, those comrades of his with his only son among them, fighting for their lives on the doomed ship. He could save them, but between him and them was the monstrous and irremovable mountain of responsibility.

He pulled himself together, forcing himself to a decision. Curtly he shook his head when the first officer asked him for orders. There were none.

They would never understand what this cost him. Never before in any storm had he hesitated to go to the rescue of struggling seamen. But this was his burden, and by him alone could his action be appraised. He only was the judge.

The firing from the land grew in intensity; great charges flogged the boiling sea. One Russian battery after another joined in, but the torpedo-boats were beginning to reply. Far back, over the dark land, there were flashes in the sky. There, where Libau lay, bright metallic lights wandered and flickered, grew broader and stronger. And then a fierce blue-pointed flame shot right up into the sky. The German shells had struck the oil tanks. There was a flaming and a hissing, strange and grotesque, and then, in a moment, the explosion.

Out of the smoke and fire, out of the shadowy outline of the coast, the steel defences thundered their defiance in panic, ever increasing in rage and savagery. The guns of the *Stolp* replied then, slowly and methodically, as though they were on manœuvres.

In the thick of the battle, his eyes fixed on the glare and smoke in front of him, the Captain was suffering the torments of the damned. He was seeing all that was taking place only a few miles away. As a midshipman he had himself been wrecked off the coast of Spain, and the horror of those hours had permeated every fibre of his memory. He knew that the hopes of six hundred desperate men were centred on him, and he was leaving them to the mercy of the Baltic.

In his breast-coat pocket he could feel his son's letter. His own words came back to him with the remorselessness of inescapable destiny—"the fate of the individual is nothing." But his son was still young. Surely he had the right to expect a little joy and happiness from life? Resentfully the old Captain tried to shake off these thoughts, but they refused to leave him; they returned again . . . and yet again . . . to the man who during the next few short hours would allow hundreds of German women to become widows, hundreds of children to be deprived of their fathers.

The mad torment went on in his brain—the conflict between the will to help and the harsh "no" of duty.

The orderly officer came in. " T. 1015 reports that block ships 5, 7, and 9 have been sunk. The south entrance has been completely blocked."

" What about the north entrance?"

" T. 1021 has run aground."

" She must be got off." Bork turned away abruptly and looked at his watch. Another hour and it would be daylight; if the boat were still aground she would be lost, like those others behind, who were now no doubt saying their last " Our Father," and from whom no wireless now came through. The ether was crackling with enemy messages, interfering with any reception.

The night seemed to be alive with demons and furies. Lurid

smoke-clouds flickered over luckless Libau; the flames shot out . . . and for miles along the coast the echoing salvoes of the defending batteries roared, mingled with the thunder of the attackers.

Captain Bork felt these things. But a burden had settled upon his soul—a burden which he would carry with him . . . always . . . until at last he himself found rest somewhere in a sailor's grave.

At last another wireless message was received : " T. 1021 afloat. All the block ships have been sunk as ordered."

Then the Captain turned round : " Wireless to the flotilla : full steam about to the rescue."

In the first grey of morning the ships turned from the coast. They sank into the mist.

Below in the bunkers there was bustle and animation; the sweat poured from the half-naked bodies of the stokers. The boiler doors were red-hot; the shovels keep on rattling to the constant cry of " Stoke up."

All out, they were steaming back. A thick smoke trailed behind, unfurling its pennons over the sea; the body of the cruiser quivered and shook. The torpedo-boats had already disappeared in the morning mist, far ahead; with their 25,000 horse-power engines they had left the poor old *Stolp* behind.

The officers stood in a group on the bridge, struggling with their feelings. The men who stole up to the deck for a breath of fresh air did not perceive their anxiety. Yet there was a feeling of tension over all which they found hard to restrain. All martial pride in their exploit off Libau was forgotten. Six hundred comrades had been sacrificed. But they still hoped and tried to justify their hopes. Perhaps the wreck of the *Oranien* was still struggling somewhere on the sea; perhaps there was still time to save the men.

Another message from the wireless room : " T. 1021 has reached the ship's position. One lifebelt and one cap belonging to the

Oranien have been picked up."

Again the long, suffocating silence on the bridge. Captain Bork acknowledged the message with a curt nod, and said nothing. His short, spare form could be seen standing aside on the bridge, his fists tightly clenched. Dumb and aloof he stared at the sea, which had robbed him of his only child. He knew that he was responsible, and that many men would blame him for a breach of the traditions of the service. But he knew also that he would act again as he had acted that night; that in the death struggle of one nation against another, individual destinies, even if they amounted to thousands of individual destinies, must be sacrificed to the whole if the whole were to live.

They drew nearer to the German coast. Captain Bork had only been below for a few minutes, and he had sent his first officer to join his fellows in the mess. He did not want food or rest, and words were an unbearable torture. He was not yet fully master of himself; later on, when he would be asked to account for his action, he would be himself again.

Once more those mysterious sparks, striking across great distances, reached the *Stolp*. The young wireless operator came on to the bridge, standing radiant before the Captain. He handed him the message : " Have picked up 635 men from the *Oranien*. Ship sunk 7.35 a.m.—H.M.S. *Marienburg*."

Captain Bork read it in silence. Then he flung his hands up to his head, as though the news would make it burst. The other officers watched the grey face of their Commander and his deep-sunken eyes with the light behind them. As he took off his cap they saw that the uncovered hair was ashen white. But still he kept guard over himself, and passed down into his cabin in silence.

The good news had gone through the *Stolp* like a hurricane. The ship's company, which had seemed almost petrified since they left Libau, awoke once more to life. From stoke-holes and engine rooms, fore and aft, the old song arose, the hymn to the God of Prussia:

> You will we serve in loyalty,
> Faithful and unfaltering, living and dead.
> Our lives to you we dedicate,
> Standard of the Fatherland, black and white and red.

Night fell as the *Stolp* reached harbour. She anchored alongside the *Marienburg*, where the rescued had been paraded on deck before marching off the ship.

The night was black, and out in the distance a long-drawn siren keened. But Bork paid no heed to it. He was going to the Admiral on the *Marienburg*, he must explain why he did not . . .

But the Admiral cut him short, holding out his hand.

"I know all about it, Bork. The torpedo-boat Commander has reported already. Your action was completely justified and it will be recognised. I have already made a full report to the Commander-in-Chief, and he is very pleased. . . . But . . . my God, Bork! . . . I should not have liked to be in your place that night. . . ."

The Admiral's voice was jerky, and a queer atmosphere of constraint and oppression had settled in the little room. The face of the Commander of the Marienburg, the Admiral's chief of staff, was pained and serious; the Admiral paused and fidgeted a little.
. . .

Outside the signal of the harbour boat was booming, over their heads shuffled the rescued ship's company as they went off the *Marienburg*. The Admiral was speaking again; his voice was deeper and more subdued, it had lost its fluency: "As I was saying, my dear Bork, you were perfectly right. Your job had to be carried through. What are we, what are individual destinies, when the nation is fighting for its very existence? We are its servants, and sooner or later every one of us must be prepared to answer the call. . . . I know you believe that. . . . The war may take anything from us, even what we hold most dear . . . our lives, our sons. . . ."

Bork looked from one to another. Their faces seemed to be distorted in a red mist—red like the smoke and flames that had danced before his eyes on that fatal night when he had had to make his decision. His hand clutched jerkily at his breast, where he could still feel his son's letter. And then a chill horror came over him, although the sweat stood on his brow.

"For God's sake, Admiral . . . what are you trying to tell me?"

The reply came quietly: "Your son, with eight men, died at his post, having carried out his duty faithfully, remaining with his ship to the last."

Once more the commander of the *Stolp* was master of himself. Firmly and steadily he walked back to his ship, acknowledging mechanically the salutes of the men on the way. As he went into his cabin, the sound of a concertina drifted in from somewhere, playing the sort of melancholy tune that the German sailor always chooses after the heat of the battle.

Silent, aloof, Captain Bork listened. He did not order the player to stop. He thought of his son's young wife, now a widow, and of the unborn child, who would have no father. But, like the tune, all this was remote, afar off. His iron spirit repudiated it, standing up to the salute.

SATIRES OF CIRCUMSTANCE

HONOURS EASY

by
C.E. Montague

WHEN Colin March, a younger son of a famous diplomatist, played in a British Embassy garden abroad his foreign nurse gave him a tortoise. "A useful beast," she explained. "It devours cockroaches; they are its passion."

Colin wanted to see this beneficent passion at work. So he captured one of the Embassy's many cockroaches and put it down in front of the tortoise's nose, like an early Christian presented to a lion. The tortoise eyed the offered feast and mused deeply. The cockroach did not muse. It was a cockroach of action. Without any apparent need for reflection it bolted for cover, like a flash of blackness, right into the tortoise's shell, and hid itself in that profound thinker's armpit.

The cadet of a dynasty of ambassadors was charmed with the cockroach's wit. He filed the whole affair in a pigeon-hole of his cute little mind. As he grew up he would often chuckle to think of it. Piquant parallels would occur to him. For a fox to go to earth under the kennels, for landsmen to go out to sea to escape from a press-gang, for cannon-fodder to hide at the back of the cannon— this was the wit of life put into a kind of practical epigram, salt and impudent. He adored it.

When Colin was twenty the War came. "*C'est beau, ça,*" he said, when he saw what was done on the spot by most of the young men he knew. He was a connoisseur. He could tell a fine gesture. "It makes fools," he said, "of us scoffers. It is as if God had broken loose out of the churches. Little new peers, like my dear cousin

Grax, are becoming patrician. The rich are fairly jumping through the needle's eye, flocks of 'em—sheep at a gap."

Colin was not to be carried off his own feet by any rush to take arms. He made no holy excuses about the omission : his sense of humour saved him from that. The only kind of humbug that it would allow him to practise was humbug conscious and gleeful— not Pecksniff's humbug; only Sganarelle's. It was a vital interest to him, he demurely said, not to be dead. And how could a ruling class rule from the tomb? Might not one honestly praise Father Damien without rushing off to nurse lepers? Besides, his elder brother was badly wounded already; life, he pointed out, might at any moment become vastly more worth living than ever.

And yet the War, and the way that his caste thought about it, were not to be easily talked out of his path. Like lions, they straddled across it; like tortoises, they impended over our quick-witted cockroach. Perhaps he remembered. He seemed to. For one day he spoke to his father, his father spoke to the proper person, and Colin was given a temporary commission for "special employment" in France. From war he thus found refuge in the Army. The cockroach was safe in the tortoise's armpit.

There were many strange "special employments" in France. One special employé wrote tracts upon the duty of desertion for airmen to drop on the enemy's lines. Another kept a country house for visiting magnates to stay at. Another met dying officers' wives at the boat, and whisked them away in fleet cars to the death-bed. All these had something to do. And there were others, who may have done little harm. Colin was one of them : "G.H.Q., Fifth Echelon," was his army address. By day he sat in a tin hut, properly warmed. His casement opened on the Channel's foam. A sergeant-major brought him forms to sign, and said : "The place, sir, for the name is 'ere." He had a telephone soon—a great help in crying off dinner engagements whenever a more amusing one came. He made the right faces when anyone called. He was always game for a round of golf with the Brigadier at Le Touquet. For these duties his qualifications were excellent French and Italian. He may not have borne any physical part in the great westward retreat. But how could he? What good would it do to wade into the sea?

II

For three months Colin had led a life of rude health, brightened by spirited tiffs with other saviours of the country. Ruder disputes going on elsewhere formed a dim, distinguished background for these engaging figures : battles and sieges, the Marne and the Aisne, the fall of Antwerp, the first Battle of Ypres. Colin was highly aware of the value of all this forest distance of tapestried gloom against which his own foreground figure was planted. He knew what was what. All this was romance, like the whining of winds that have blown over deserts of snow when they sniff at night round the house where a person, who knows what is what, lies in bed, with the firelight leaping or musing.

Then came the Deluge. Or, rather, one of the Deluges. Colin would say : " Poor old G.H.Q. was made to be inundated and re-inundated, like Holland, on proper occasions. Or it's like England, with Picts and Brythons and Angles and Normans all rushing it in their turns. All of us here are ex-conquerors, layer on layer of us. First to charge in were the War Office braves, the old hands, the mighty hunters of good jobs before the Lord. I came as a sutler with them. I'm the *jeune premier arriviste*. Then, after three months of the War, the notes of a distant recessional march strike our ears, a thunderous tramping is heard in the east, and there burst in upon us the pick of the old Regulars from the front—oh, not all of them, only those who had found that it was not the right sort of war, and that they had the right sort of friends. Approaching, they took a short run, and fairly butted and rammed their way into shelter, with all their mothers and uncles pushing them hard from behind—fell right in on top of us here with their cavalry spurs and their Guards knickerbockers and buttons and swashing and martial outsides. They were like the saints taking the Kingdom of Heaven by storm. We tried to be nice to them; sat as close as we could to make room; cut our work in two and gave them half, like St. Martin; talked to them kindly and wittily. They only stared. Then I knew them—the poor old Army Class worthies at school. Look at Claude, *par exemple*—his eyes! ' There is no speculation in those eyes'."

Claude Barbason's brain, it may be, was not all air and fire. And Colin was yoked to him now. They bit wooden penholders in the same hut, and perfected a dislike of each other that they had roughed out in peace-time in London.

" Ever see," Colin would pleasantly ask you, " such a good German as Claude? *Tout ce qu'il a de Boche absolument*!" Claude's face indeed, with its pink and white gravity, heavy blue eyes and straw hair, did call up visions of some German officer prisoners. No doubt, he had, through his ancestors, sojourned in England a good thirteen hundred years. Still, you could fancy him, that long ago, full of home thoughts of West Saxony, marching Londonward from the sea, mopping the sweat from pink cheeks and shaking the yellow hair away from china-blue eyes, to see, for the first time, from the Kentish chalk downs, the Thames shining below through the trees.

Claude would take his own part, without positive sparkle, in this commerce in compliments. Colin to him was " the mountebank," with his " bounding cleverness " and his " beastly quotations." Colin, he said, dirtied everything that he touched; he seemed to like rolling himself and everyone else in the mud; he called the scarlet staff tabs—which they were both seeking—the Red Badge of Funk; he said the Job Lot Mess, where they and other odds-and-ends ate, ought to hang out a sign on a board "*Au Ravitaillement des Embusqués*"; he called Fifth Echelon "Chelsea" and "Greenwich"—because, as he idiotically said, it gave a secure and honoured old age to so many young men; he was always dragging in rotten gobbets of verse, with foul under-meanings: "Soldier, rest, thy warfare o'er"; "Keep thou still when clans are arming"; "His tin hat now shall be a hive for bees"—oh, there was no end to his loathsomeness!

"Speak for yourself," Claude often wanted to say. Let the fellow befoul his own nest, and not decent people's. What could an amateur soldier like that know about what a real soldier must feel? Yet Claude's scorching retorts did not get themselves uttered—only something dry and austere, like "I suppose we all get our orders and have to obey them," or, "Well, if you don't mind, I'll get on with my work. There's a war on," said with a reproving stiffness. Then Claude would bite his penholder pretty severely.

III

I fancy it was in the gloom following one of these indecisive engagements with Colin that Claude's eyes were suddenly opened, like Adam's and Eve's, and he saw that, for the high purpose of conflict with Colin, he, Claude, was little better than naked. If, now, he had a ribbon or two on his bosom, all the darts of Colin's flashy, trashy wit would be deflected; Claude would be armour-plated, like capital ships; like generals, he would be able to score without saying a word, just by sitting behind the front of his tunic and letting it tell.

Somebody said in his hearing that night that the King of Alania

—we'll call it Alania—was soon to visit our front. Claude listened. After dinner he cast a long, passionate look at a framed thing that hung on the ante-room wall. It looked from afar like a coloured plate of the full solar spectrum, but it was labelled, "The Ribbons of all the World. Orders of Honour." Yes, an Alanian ribbon was there—a blue one, a beauty! Fie, thought Claude, upon this quiet life in a hut, yoked with an unbeliever. Swiftly he wrote to three uncles of his—wrote as he had not written since the days when he first perceived that the trenches were no place for him.

The uncles were loyal; Claude, if a babe in some ways, was no Babe in the Wood. And they were soldiers, and well placed for doing good deeds to a nephew. One of the three was in actual charge of the plans for giving this Alanian King a good time, *vice* somebody else who was ill.

The King duly came. He was reverentially motored about from meal to meal, well in the rear of our front. And who but Claude sat in state beside the chauffeur, except when he—Claude, not the chauffeur—leapt down to open the door! In this great office Claude bore himself meekly through three dusty midsummer days. On the third evening the King and his British guides, nurses, and gillies of every degree stood somewhat self-consciously grouped at Amiens on one of that city's desolate lengths of low railway platform. The guest was going away. Abruptly the fountain of honour was turned full on, and it played in the twilight.

Nervous and kind, wishful to do the right thing by Britain, but not to keep one of France's trains waiting, the King dealt out stars of Alania with shy expedition to all the British officers who had done anything for him. An A.D.C. stood beside him and fed the blue-ribboned trinkets into the gracious hand. Claude went in last. But even when he was bestarred three stars were visibly left over. The King held one of them, ready to shed. The A.D.C. was still holding an unmistakable brace. Somebody must have miscounted. Or else, as Claude came to believe later, the devil was in it. The fountain of honour looked like slopping over the edge of its basin.

A little way off, in the gathering dusk, three British officers, not attached to the King's party, were standing—perhaps awaiting the train, perhaps not. The Alanian A.D.C. cast a look towards them. Then he looked at the King and drew the King's eyes towards the trio. The King nodded. "There iss," he said sweetly, "no British officer who iss not worthy." The red-eyed train for Paris was now clanking out of the tunnel into the station. "Quick, please!" said the King, in Alanian.

The three unpremeditated vessels of the royal grace were informed. And the angel of this annunciation was Claude. To his unaffected distaste he found, on approach, that one of the three was Colin. Still, Claude's not to reason why, at any rate until later. He delivered royalty's summons. In three minutes the three remainder stars had settled into their new, fortuitous homes, the King had peace in the quickening train, and Claude had briefly let himself go on the question of unearned increment, and was hearing a little from Colin about the divine super-equity of the ruling that he who had borne the burden and heat of three full days' work in the vineyard should not receive more than he who had wrought for one hour only.

"An hour!" objected the literal Claude. "Why, you only paraded for pay!"

"Absolutely," said Colin. But he was too modest. That dramatic scene at the station had really taken some skill and pains to bring off. Drama, they say, is the art of preparation.

Claude simmered and fumed. "Anyhow," Colin said like an angel, "it has all ended happily."

"Not that I wanted," Colin explained to me later, "this acrid

Alanian blueblob. Red is the only wear, to my mind, on this obscene khaki. Still, one has to take life as it comes. So I went to the
station. I even took other trouble. Why should I have to, though?
Why should Claude have to eat dust all over the Pas de Calais before he can stick what he likes on his coat? Let's have Free Trade
in all ribbons. Then they'd give real distinction. A man would
write himself down just what he is by the things he'd put on. All
the born base-wallahs would put up three rows on the spot, if
they'd not got them now. The Samurai at the front would take
care to wear nothing—they'd be like the patriciate we're getting in
England at last, the fellows who won't take the peerages. I should
wear dozens, but I'd be an artist about it. I'd paint like a Rubens
and wear my own picture. I'd start from that deep Russian red
with the bottomless lustre—the Cross of St. George, or what is it?
—and fight it out in that key all the summer. Oh, I see red; I can
hear it—whole chords of red, peals of it. Isn't any Grand Duke
ever coming this way?"

IV

None came. But some bird of the air must soon have carried to
Colin the news that a mission of British officers, heroes of Mons
and the Marne, was about to visit the Russian front. For Colin
wrote, swiftly and well, to the proper person in London. He had
heard that for this mission ten hard-bitten fighters were needed;
they had to have manners, know French, and be able to carry their
wine. Colin answered the call of his country the moment he got
it to come to him. It was, he saw, no case for delay. Empires perish.
Before such another call came, the Russians might have a republic,
and no decorations about, like the poor Yanks, and then—too late,
the saddest words in life, too late. Plenty of time, later on, for Colin
to prosecute his conquests in France. He took his stand now with

the nine other courteous and capacious linguists.

In holy Russia the primitive virtue of hospitality was so ardently practised that Colin came back crying out for a separate peace. Only a cure at Marienbad, he declared, could patch up his old body for heaven. No mere London season, he vowed, had ever made such demands upon the digestive force of the celebrants as this Muscovite joy-ride. Still, that profoundly lustrous red ribbon was his.

He brought back, besides, a lot of good stories. One was about a Japanese Colonel, another guest of the Tsar's. In a Russian trench this child of the sunrise had strayed from the side of his guides and fallen in with four Russian privates. They were good lads from the country, simple but careful. They were not sure whether the War was still the old one with Japan or another. Anyhow, they considered it safer to kill a loose Jap. The faithful souls did it, and Colin declared that the consequent Russian apologies to Japan were a classic for young attachés to study, apart from their primary worth as light fiction. Richer still in comedy was the Japanese Government's plight. For, by way of good manners, it had to pretend to believe that the murder was not got up by the Tsar. And, to keep up this pose, a Russian staff Captain, the guide who had not succeeded in keeping the Japanese Colonel alive, had to be given a Japanese Order.

"That gaud," said Colin to the Job Lot Mess, "was a treasure, a sovereign prince of enamels. We ought to make more of the Japs. We ought to shift the whole war farther East. We might hold all the gorgeous East in fee. Churchill is right."

V

Claude did not hear this address upon strategy. Claude, too, had gone East, though less far. When left alone in the hut he had thought deeply about A.D.C.s. Peace, perfect peace, was their lot in this war. They toiled not, neither did they fight; yet honour found them; beauty fell, as it were, from the air, and was caught upon their tunics. Claude, as the New World says, figured upon it. Then he acted. Nature may not have made him expressly for action; rather, perhaps, for the contemplation of himself in some becoming light. But Colin's own devout self was not surer than Claude of the efficacy of prayer, directed to the right quarter. Had not he, too, seen the Red Sea cut in two for his safety, and passed across dry? And now the right quarter was clear. It was that bachelor uncle of Claude's who had lately got the command of a corps. "Claude is descended," Colin explained, "from a long line of bachelor uncles. All Barbasons are. That's why they're so rich."

On the second day of the Battle of Loos Claude rallied round this beneficent uncle. The new A.D.C. took the place of a wild young peer who had gone mad and swindled and lied his way back to the head of an equally wild Irish platoon, then diminishing in the lost battle. The uncle told Claude about this eccentric: "Damn little fool! I'd just been thinking of putting him up for an M.C. I hope *you'll* know when you're well off." Claude did. Like Issachar, he "saw that rest was good." And the corps headquarters were pleasant. There would he see no enemy but winter and rough weather; and these are not lethal in well-built châteaux. "Fritz has got a new gun," I was once told by an infantry private in that corps, "as will carry thirty-eight miles." "Goowan," another put in, "that ain't nothing. He's got a gun would hit our corps H.Q." The corps, as a whole, felt sure its commander was safe.

To this essential of safety a nephew's love added several subsidiary blessings. Claude laboured, as in God's sight, to get the General's coffee milk really boiled and not just heated—a test of capacity which the General knew to be crucial. "If a man," as he said, "can't get a little thing like that right, he'll never win battles." Neither did Claude disdain to make sure that the General's boots were done just as he liked them. Of myrrh and frankincense less material Claude offered unstintingly all that his talents allowed. He was not as many A.D.C.s are. Some of the most contumacious of men are those who do little personal things for the great. Valets to emperors, ushers to Solons, batmen to heroes—too often nothing is great to such men, and nobody either. Nearly all the most mutinous blasphemy that was talked during the War was talked in the A.D.C. rooms of the mighty. But Claude revered his chief. To him his uncle was one in whom the soul of "the real army" lived on, pestered, indeed, but still nobly unswamped by the rag, tag, and bobtail of Kitcheners and Territorials. Claude could feel for the corps commander. Had he not too, for long months, endured the manners of Colin, the New Army man, in the wilderness?

To those who knew what most people did not, the uncle was known as The Derby Winner, or, more succinctly, The Crook. He had come out to France in command of a division. The first time it went into action his genius miscarried and lost a mile of ground and half his men. It was only then that the General showed his full speed. Some said he had leapt into a waiting aeroplane the moment the battle was lost. Anyway, he was in London incredibly soon, and seeing the proper person about a mark of distinction so signal that, when the bad news came in, it would look silly to turn round and give him a post on the shelf. Still, the news came in the end; some of these things will get out, whatever you do. Clearly The Crook was not born to command divisions. So he was given a corps to command, and the corps was now in the line, in a pretty hot corner, expiating this stroke of humour in high places. The Crook, however, cannot have been a wholly bad man. He must have had some natural affection. Claude had not served him a month when the uncle sent up his name for a Military Cross. "You'll get it too," he told him. "Whenever these lists of recommendations look a bit long to the people upstairs they start lopping off names from the tail-end and work up. So I've wedged yours in near the middle, well up."

Claude knocked off work for the day, he was so moved. He went to lie on his bed, to get at more leisure the feel of the full warmth of Fortune's benediction upon him. All things were well. Through the tall window, across the bejewelled dewy grass of the park, he could see a white road and troops on it: a New Army battalion—he could tell that; they had no smartness—marching up to the front, to go into the line, the undersized men bending under their packs, to ease the cut of their straps on the shoulder, and chorusing one of their contumacious songs of mock funk:

> Oh my! I don't want to die;
> I want to go home.

Then the road was vacant and white for a time, till a wailing of bagpipes arose, and a kilted battalion, dwarfed to the size of a company, hove into sight, marching the opposite way—four little companies like platoons, and few officers anywhere; the pipes skirling some fearful lament, almost animal, like a moaning or keening of primitive women over their dead; the men with a stiff, savage gait of sombre defiance—scorn of the enemy they had smashed, of the staff that had thrown Scottish valour away, of the non-Scottish troops that had failed on a flank, of the non-Scottish commander-in-chief that had loosed the fool battle.

Claude was no great hand at reading that sort of print. Still, he did make out something. War was the great game; he saw that more clearly than ever; he saw, too, how great beyond all other wars was this war, how much more important a business to shine in. And, gosh! what a facer this M.C. would be for the Mountebank!

VI

It was " at the front," of all places, that this blow fell upon Colin; not quite at the place where the smell of rotting meat hung all that autumn, but still pretty near it—at a brigade headquarters. It counted all right for his purpose.

After his travels in Russia, Colin had felt it was time he became a full G.S.O., a staff officer proper. Base was the slave who remained for ever merely " attached to " the staff. But so many Colins had felt this before, and had carried their point so completely, that scandal was feared. To avert it, a ruling had gone forth that all G.S.O.s appointed thenceforth must have had some trench service. Poor Colin, to compass his end, had to take kit for a whole fortnight's stay in a new brigade commander's charmless dug-out, and listen in candle-lit frowst to the banalities talked by the Brigadier, brigade Major, staff Captain, and some odds-and-ends of medicine, signals, and the Church. Each of these, he found, had some two things to say about life, and three jokes, so that the conversation of each was a sort of recurring decimal of five places. Each of them watched, with bitter foreknowledge, the countless revolutions of the others' antique decimals. One day, however, Colin heard a new thing.

A Major, an acting battalion commander, had come in to tea. He knew the Brigadier well, and, like a good soldier, he was blaspheming the great for the sweat that they will often give you for nothing. " Hardly a fortnight ago, sir," he said to his host, " just before you came to us, a corps order came round to say some foreign devils—the Japs, I believe—had sent a wad of their ' Crosses for Valour '—sort of V.C.s—one for the absolute ace—any rank—in each British corps. Every C.O. was to pick out the hottest man-eater he got for the corps to select the tip-topper. I took days at the job, worried my officers, ricked my own brain with being judgmatic. I sent in a beauty at last—a sergeant. He'd got cut off in a post with five men and had held up the Boches for two days till we got him away. He'd had a broken arm all the time—a great fellow! All the other C.O.s in the corps ran their prize tigers, too, for all they were worth. No good. It was all waste of time. The Cross never got past the corps. An A.D.C. got it, a fellow just up from the base—Barton, Brabazon, Brasner; some name like that."

" The ribbon was—what colour, sir?" Colin asked.

"Mouldy bluish, I heard," said the Major, " like Stilton."

"I think the name," Colin said, " must be Barbason."

"That's right," said the Major, suddenly interested in Colin. "You know him?"

"I thought everyone did," said Colin, the man from the centre of things, almost severely. Ignorance seems, at times, as if it must almost be affectation.

"We're pretty provincial out in these parts," said the Brigadier softly. Colin laughed, and looked at the Brigadier with new respect. Colin could take with good humour any rebuke that had wit.

"What has this beggar done?" the Major vindictively asked him.

"He doesn't exactly *do* things," said Colin. " He *wears* them. Like me. Only he goes in for blue. He has just got an M.C. That's three different blues on his coat—a whole Blue Ribbon Army. No arrangement in blue, like a Whistler, but more chaste and natty— a glove fit of the blues. He's Little Boy Blue, and he blows his own horn." Where other people get cross, Colin becomes a few degrees more copiously vivacious.

The two seniors looked at each other. The dull plum ribbon of the Victoria Cross was the only one on the Brigadier's tunic. The Major had fought well in three battles, and he had not even one. The Brigadier pointed to where a bar of ruddy Oriental radiance, that no Western loom could have made, glowed on Colin's breast, next to the lustrous Russian crimson. " That's pretty," the Brigadier said.

" It should be," said Colin; " it's old, and Chinese. I won it by running away."

" Now, now———" The Brigadier, as a Colonel, had often had to curb the plunging modesty of subalterns.

" No idle boast, sir," said Colin. " Some Chinese Moltke came to G.H.Q. I was told to ' take the old euchre-player away out of this—anywhere—up to the front and get him shot over.' So we set off in a car for the front. The Far East didn't like the idea. Nor did the West. But pride ruled our will. We got down four miles from the front and walked on up a road that felt naked and cocked up right into the air. Then the trouble came. There was a sort of *émeute* going on in the air. A flock of white puff-balls was stray-ing about the blue sky, always advancing by having a new puff break out on ahead of it. Then something venomous fell into the road, six feet away, and hissed in a puddle—a thing like a bolt, or a nut, from the blue."

The Brigadier put in a note : " A chip from one of our own Archie shells."

" No doubt, sir," said Colin. " I did not examine. I fell back. So did my lovely charge. Let nobody say a Chinese cannot run. The man who could beat me that day to the car must have been an Achilles. As we sped home my companion gave thanks, and made promises : first to God, then to me for my lead. He was a faithful fellow ! *Ecce signum* !" Colin touched the beautiful new ribbon on his bosom.

An orderly came in for his kit. His trench service was over. When he had gone the two elder officers stared at each other. Simple souls abounded on our front and near it. Else how could we have won ?

VII

Honours, as old-fashioned whist players say, were now easy—three all. But March had the pull in one way. For he was first to be back at the base, the honoriferous seaboard, washed by such tides as a man may take at the flood and be led on to fortune. "Always stick to the base in a war," a fatherly Regular on the Q. side once advised him; "don't be led away by love of excitement. Most of the good things go to the base at the end of a war, and most of the big chances come to it now." But Colin needed no man's help to see a church by daylight.

Colin's prestige at the seats of the mighty was rising. The Chinese hero had lauded, in august ears, Colin's daring and skill as a guide to the front. But the next call on his gifts was to be for a virtue more distinctively Christian. Appendicitis had suddenly smitten another illustrious guest of our army, a Spanish-American Marshal, a neutral, and therefore more to be cherished than an ally. While he lay sick unto death in an inn at Bruay the British officer who had led him about in the time of his health, and who hated the sight of natural deaths, was telephoning all day to beg that some bedside mannerist might be sent up to carry on smoothing the pillow, *vice* himself. "The Dago only wants," he said, "a sort of Angel in the House."

Colin was offered this errand of mercy. He pondered. A long time ago he had tried for some days to learn Spanish; he might find he could talk it a little now if he tried. And that Russian story showed how from the pure and unpolluted flesh of deceased foreign officers violet and other beautiful colours may spring. Possibly red. Red, he hoped. He looked carefully into the same coloured plate on the ante-room wall at which Claude had once tenderly gazed. Yes, both the Aureate Harvest (with Swords) and the Bleeding

Heart (with Swords, too) had red ribbons. The sick must be visited. Colin accepted.

He was back at the sea in eight days, better thought of than ever.
His choice of official wreaths to put on the coffin, his turning of
phrases on those little cards that are tied to the wreaths, were felt
to have aided the cause. Spanish-America, too, must have felt he
had done the thing well. For in due time the Aureate Harvest came
in as the other kindly fruits of the earth do for the use of her Colins.

"A somewhat ghoulish business," said Claude, when this just
award was gazetted. Claude, at the time, was just back from the
corps. The uncle's drafts upon Britain's man-power had grown so
exacting that he was transferred to a more august job, where any
diminutions he made in the population of these islands would be
less violently observable. Colin said he was changed from a fatal
accident into an obscure mortal disease. Anyhow, he had no use
for Claude any longer; nor had Claude for him. Restored to the
coast, Claude was working out a new way of fighting the Germans,
a quite new engine of war. It was to have a great vogue, this new
weapon. It could be used almost anywhere except in a regiment. It
was called "the reorganisation of the establishment" of the department or unit of which the reorganising person had charge.

Even in those early days the G.H.Q. heaven was one that had
many mansions. They were of all sizes, and growing like melons
—so fast that in some of them little time could be found for any
work except settling where everybody should sit. Officers in command of departments, sub-departments, and sections, and sections
and sub-sections of sub-departments would draft and re-draft plans
for the further sub-division of each into two or more parts, according to the earliest and best biological precedents, each of the new
parts to be as important as the existing hole, each, therefore, to be
commanded by an officer of as high rank as the existing com-

mander of the whole, with the natural corollary that the existing commander should get a step of promotion in order to have proper authority over these branch subordinates, all of whose labours he would have to superintend if the draft should be approved. Claude, now a Captain, was senior officer at the Sink, as his and Colin's little department was called by its irreverent neighbours. At first the Sink had been Colin; then Colin and Claude; six officers, doers of miscellaneous odd jobs, now reposed within it; there were a score of attendant orderlies, clerks, and chauffeurs. Why not cut it in two and house the two portions apart, with Claude to co-ordinate the exertions of both, as a G.S.O. 2 and a Major? Claude fell to work on a draft, fortified with a kind of genealogical tree to establish the lawful descent of disciplinary power over each of his expected twins, all the way down from the commander-in-chief. While he was writing the draft and drawing the tree he sometimes felt more apt to the sword than to the pen. But he stuck to the pen gamely.

VIII

Something, I think, must have made Colin suspicious. Perhaps he saw Claude writing with an abnormal fluency. Or, of course, he may just have had a pricking in his thumbs. Anyhow, like the intelligent dog whom God has taught to scent in good time his master's intention to drown him, Colin took himself off before Claude's draft was approved by the proper person. My next letter from Colin was from a ducal, delectable house in Mayfair:

"You see, they have combed me out of the trenches. Is it that I am seconded, or what is the term used by you militarists? *Tout court*, England hath need of me here. I work in this weatherproof house, the new Ministry of Liaison. No, I am not the Minister—only his eyes and ears, or a portion of these, and of his understanding. A *raison d'être* for the

Ministry is being prepared. Meanwhile it offers asylum to young men of quality fleeing from Military Tribunals. Rods of the houses of signatories to Magna Charta rush in daily and cling to the horns of the altar. It is a dock-leaf planted by merciful nature where the nettles grow."

It seems that some gifted Scottish statesman, out of a job at the time, had been going up and down with a dirk, as it were, in his stocking, till all the statesmen in office wanted to find him something nice to play with, lest he should stick the knife into one of their wames. To save life in this way the Ministry of Liaison was founded, and this man of mettle was placed at its head. The Ministry was " to co-ordinate the functions of various administrative departments."

Colin wrote to me later :

"My reverence for this foundation grows. In this kicked ant-heap of a Europe it must be about the last abode of peace on earth and of goodwill towards men, all men.

> Nae German lays his scaith to us,
> We ne'er did ony harm.

"To us the harried Anglo-German flies, and we make him a confidential clerk or an interpreter. Here he spends happy days of Government time in writing letters to London newspapers, mostly to ' show up the Hun in our midst.' Like mediæval monasteries, we cherish through a dark and bloody age the endangered graces of life. Here, in the best types of chair, sleep the brave; here knit or crochet the fair, or, within seemly limits, carry on with the brave.

> Liaison our name;
> And I will not deny,
> In respect to the same,
> What that name might imply.

" A free, gallant life. To take me to the club, to lunch, my country has a car like Tennyson's full tide that 'moving, seems asleep.' Not a speck in the sky, except passing thoughts of what Claude may be up to. Are we not members one of another, and, if aught befall him, shall I not feel?"

Under that peaceful surface considerable forces were stirring. For nearly three years our Napoleons, Alexanders, and Cæsars had been collecting merited marks of distinction. The skill of collectors had almost outgrown the supply of colligible matter. The most skilful were wearing about every ribbon there was; they had gained the whole world, and unless the world were enlarged they might as well bid an early farewell to the neighing steed and shrill trump and go home. To keep their ardour from going the way of the former warmth of the moon, as well as for other good reasons, the O.B.E was invented.

The new species of laurel was sent, very justly, in bulk to the Ministry of Liaison, to show how well the sender had done in creating a Ministry so worthy of reward. But Colin, through some unfortunate slip, was not on the list of those whom the King, on first thoughts, delighted to honour. He wrote to me :

" They must have put me down third reserve only. The stones that these builders reject! Still, I was jammed in, head of a corner, later. Three high-stomached civilians, who work with us here, rejected the bauble, with a slight wave of the hand. I commend, I can even envy them. A civilian is free; he may guard his own honour. But to us soldiers, you know, an order's an order; mine not to make reply. In I went, third wicket down. With canine loyalty I wagged an unoffended tail, and accepted my one-third of the crumbs that had fallen from the table of the proud."

You see, Colin, to my mind, had no real humbug about him, as I understand humbug. He had not the lie in his soul. He did not tell lies to himself, nor really very many to anyone else. Humbug was Claude's special subject, not his. Colin's special subject was reds, and for that plummy red of the O.B.E. ribbon there was a place ready in his heart, or about a couple of inches above it.

The danger of being saddled with some undesirable job, as a vicegerent of Claude's, had now had time to blow over, and Colin began to hear the great wars and the tented or hutted field call him again. One month of tactful importunacy in the right place and he was gone, now in the full rosy red of a G.S.O., with the red and blue brassard of G.H.Q. too—with every guarantee, in fact, of life, liberty, and the pursuit of happiness. To begin with, he travelled from London in the uncrowded staff train, after his luncheon, instead of rising at six in the morning to catch the common, crammed leave train, like the ruck of regimental officers. These, on their way back to be killed, were carried off early to cool their heels for half a day at Folkestone till the staff train should arrive at the pier and its occupants have time to dig themselves on all the best sites on the boat. "A kindly precaution," said Colin that night in the new mess at Bligny, to which he found himself carried away by the car that awaited him on the quay at Boulogne—"one of the many kindly precautions we take to set the moribund free from too much love of living."

Colin found Claude commanding at Bligny. Such a find might not seem elating. But it inspired Colin at dinner that night with a fine mischievous brightness. Taking a quick look at Claude now and then, to see how the stimulant worked, Colin rattled on about that slouching file of *condamnés,* the infantry and artillery subalterns coming back from their leave, trailing up the steep gangway at Folkestone on to the deck, with all their lumpish kits on their backs, and their eternal pipes and mud-sick uniforms, and looking awkwardly round them, shy among all the seated staff people, for some solid object to sit on.

Claude rose to the fly; his face lit up a little when Colin played on his sense of the "New Army bounders'" social deficiencies. Yes, he had noticed those fellows—anyone would—when he last went on leave. "Appalling crowd of navvies!" He felt himself, for the moment, in quite warm agreement with Colin—with what he took to be Colin. Colin described to me later this tender reunion. "You should have heard him!" said Colin. "Claude is simply so much natural born prey for irony. He is like one of the little guinea-pigs that they give to the snakes at the Zoo. A plain shirker like me is almost decent beside him. I only deny Christ right out —I frankly skulk by the fire while He's getting crucified. Claude would sneer at the cut of the clothes that Christ wore on the Cross. We're the two thieves, but Claude is the one that sniggered. 'Bill Sikeses in Sam Brownes'—that's what the little rodent calls the fellows that he and I have deserted. 'Really rather awful,' he says —'these new officers. Quite five-sixths of them the sort of people you'd expect to touch their caps to you in civil life.' Imagine the lice on one of our Tommies finding fault with the Tommy's pedigree! Then he remembered that he was an acting Major, and also the only Regular there, so he quenched his familiar smile, like the ass in the play, with an austere regard of control."

I had never seen Colin angry before. Any common vexation only made him more gaily ironical. He may be cutting jokes in heaven yet when Claude lies howling.

IX

So far our two heroes had had to work, if only an hour, for all they got. The next thing to come in was, as Colin vulgarly said, a bit of a war bonus.

For months our gallant London Press had felt a painful dearth of " hero stunts " and " sob stories." Lord Jellicoe had meanly preferred the continued existence of his fleet to the proper provision of good matter for " scare heads." Heroic editors began to shake their heads over Sir Douglas Haig's want of " snap," " go," and "punch" in maintaining the daily ration of thrills for bald men in armchairs at home. Pending the proper measures for " gingering up" these commanders there might be some market still for a little emotionalising about the old stunt of " the heroes of Mons." Just to fill up the gap, why not a " whirlwind campaign " for giving a special medal or star to the few living men who had stemmed the German rush upon Paris in 1914?

It was rather a daring piece of stop-gappery. Legends of Mons were wilting already under the first rays of the higher criticism. Irreverent people at home were comparing the casualties of 1914 with the rates at which a gifted old Regular staff had since extinguished so many New Army battalions. It had leaked out that in that infant war of 1914 there had been no bombardments that would not now seem like seasons of relative rest and release from the true, high-pressure hells of the later dispensation. Heartless rationalists had begun to reflect that perhaps it was not really so much more meritorious to join the Army in times of deep peace, to get off the streets or to escape harder and grimier work, than it was to join it when joining meant embracing, almost at once, the fairest chance of an early death that had ever smiled on British recruits; that to the old Regular officers, in especial, the war had not brought the surrender of worldly good things, of beloved work or the plans and hopes of their lives, but a suddenly opened prospect of these happinesses—more pay, quicker promotion, a paradise of professional opportunity, and, after the one great toss-up with death in 1914,

safety and ease in the odour of certified glory for most of those who
had not lost the toss.

Still, it was a cheap " stunt." It needed no telegraphing; it could
be " done in the office." And there was no risk of actions for libel
and of " exemplary damages," as in " stunts " of detraction against
great Generals and Admirals and Ministers and leaders of industry
who failed in their several ways to act up to the needs of stunt presses. So the stunt Press took courage, and ranted and gushed, boom-
ed and bleated and shrilled. And, the War Office having no courage to take, the Mons Star was invented when nearly all the men
who might have deserved it were dead. Thus do the Colins and
Claudes of this world build better than they know. They fight
with their back to the walls of good bedrooms against every foe
that would take a job from them, and at the close of the long day,
or earlier, some unsought meed is added unto them, besides all
that they seek.

Alike in gaining this guerdon, our two pretty men were not alike
in the emotions raised by its possession. Colin crowed with frank
joy at the scandal. Scandals, he said, were too few in these colour-
less times. Scandal was only a reverberation of adventure, the fum-
ing of timid mobs when taller spirits hustled and pushed their way
through. Wherever a high plume had stirred in the world, and big
throws had been made and the costly unreason of romance had
been properly prized, scandal had smoked up to heaven like dust
from winning chariot-wheels. This wisdom of life he imparted to
Claude, adjuring him also not to misuse the new ribbon. Blue at
one end and red at the other, and all shaded, watered, transitional
and connective—why, it was clearly sent by Heaven for purposes
of liaison, to hitch on the garden of gentians, forget-me-nots, helio-
trope and cornflower that had first bloomed on Claude's tunic to
any later sallies he might meditate in red, green, even black. Only

let Claude beware of minding the foolish orders issued by poker-fed Generals, men blind to the arts, as to the order in which ribbons should be arranged on the martial bosom. Imagine Velasquez or Tintoret laying his colours on in obedience to General Routine Orders! "No; blue to blue, red to red, each after its kind arrange we them."

Claude hated all such talk. Raffish gammon, only fit for a Radical hairdresser! If the King thought it good enough to honour a man, what loyal soldier would jeer or belittle? Claude had the Old Army's fine sense of relative values well lodged in his soul. Gazetted awards were no mere measures of worth: they were worth itself, crystallised, capitalised. "Perhaps it isn't easy," he said to Colin, with solemn concessiveness, "for other people to understand what these things mean to a soldier."

Somehow Colin did not seem so confounded by this as he ought to be. Instead, he only looked at Claude as if Claude were a curious exhibit in a museum, and this wounded afresh Claude's soldierly consciousness of his own irreproachable normality. Claude felt at these times an intense and burning wish that Colin were not the son of a peer. The craving was almost physically painful, like retching. If Colin were scrubby by birth, somehow the world would seem more coherent.

But all this was an interlude. Back now to the grim realities of the War.

X

War hath her triumphs of company-floating no less deserving renown than peace's. Claude had drafted and drawn to some purpose. With help from on high the Sink had become thrice itself, not merely twice, and one of these three Sinks alone was more capacious than the great original. Unhappily, Claude had not secured command of the whole trinity. Some more majestic bird of prey, a G.H.Q. Colonel, had dropped like a stone out of the upper sky, somewhere close to the sun, and stuck his claws firmly into Claude's kill. But, subject always to this depredator, Claude received the fattest of the three distinct commands which owed him their being.

At Bligny he could not quite say what most of his six officers did. He felt surer about the chauffeurs. One of the officers he suspected of plans for salvaging solder from old bully-beef tins—a low job. He fancied another to be the minute early embryo of a demobilisation unit. A third was in unmistakable travail, writing a novel. A fourth seemed to have something to do with some of the Army's visitors from abroad. A fifth moved obscurely about in a dim borderland between letters and war; rumour said that he " smuggled the dope " into papers at Amsterdam and Madrid—" a Wolff in sheep's clothing, you know," Colin told me. The sixth was said to be sure that if only the War went on long enough we should end it decisively at last by feeding all the outer world's " movies " with the right stuff, and to this happy issue it was hoped that he was making some larger contribution than anyone saw. Anyhow, they all kept moving. Cars were there for all, and petrol failed not. How was Claude to check the things they did or left undone? He walked, unpolluted by such inquisitive cares, among the mysteries of his command.

The place itself had amenity. It was a white, classical pre-Revolution château in a hollow between two chalk downs and beside a trout stream. G.H.Q., with its possibly critical eyes, was safely far off. No one at G.H.Q. cared about Bligny. It was a mere trousers-button, a thing to be put out of mind until it should, hang it, come off. Claude " ran his own show," and as it and everything in it were things without precedent there was no binding routine; he might fashion the show after his own image. And, in the course of nature, some honour accrued to every head of a show in the course of a year, and where would Colin be then?

Colin, also, asked himself that. No specific job had been given him yet. He had only been dumped on Bligny because there was no valid reason for dumping him anywhere else. There he lay down to sleep of a night and rose up of a morning to ring for a car and roll off to visit some proper person and bring to his mind the parable of the Importunate Woman. This time he had quite a long run in the rôle of that excellent female, And, like her, he got there at last. He prayed himself into a job—not, he felt, one that was quite what it should be. Still, it was not at Bligny; it was at G.H.Q. proper, near the heart of the rose. And so Colin rolled off for good, as it seemed.

He left Claude sitting rather moodily in his "office"—the absent Comtesse de Bligny's boudoir. Claude always sat there for several hours a day. It was the bridge of his ship, and a captain looks best on the bridge. He was moody, because in these last weeks he had found that, however little a Captain may do on his bridge, he may still make some sort of a mess. Two or three times he had almost had to act in some way or other, to take an absolute plunge, adopting one course and rejecting another. That was the trouble; alternatives were like horses : he couldn't guess which was a winner. So Claude had tried hard each time to take either both courses or none, and now some captious god in the G.H.Q. heaven was not taking this so well as he might. Rumours of grand muddles at Bligny began to circulate in Olympus. " Silly little devil!" Colin was soon to hear a dangerous Brigadier-General say of Claude. " Of two evils, choose both—that's his idea."

In giving the Bligny billet to Claude the proper person concerned had not entertained extravagant hopes. Barbason, he had said at the time, wasn't a flyer; still, he was clearly fed-up with the job he had had before. And the new Bligny show was too much of a pearl to cast before any New Army swine. So the proper person had hoped as hard as he could about Claude, and then had looked the other way as hard as he could, hoping no harm would come. But Claude made a truly wonderful mess of it all. What made things worse was the way that opportunities for making messes were growing. The show itself grew, as everything grew in that tropical army. More and more officers came after Colin had gone. The work of some of these had all sorts of civilian connections. Visitors came, British and foreign, some of them famous, some subterraneanly powerful, some open-eyed and quick-witted. They went away, all over the earth, telling funny stories of croppers that Claude had come in his kingdom. Colin heard some of them. Faint but disturbing echoes of horrid laughter found their way round, even to Claude. He grew angry, first, at all this vulgar demand for the unsoldierly cleverness that fools called efficiency. But he grew anxious, too, for G.H.Q. had been weak before now in the face of the howlings of beasts; men had been thrown to the wolves. To be safe, he supposed he must get in some brainy bounder as an assistant at Bligny.

With mingled pride and embarrassment, Claude found, on reflection, how few brainy bounders he knew. Colin was much the brainiest of the few—a beast, but a clever beast. And Colin, he fancied, was only marking time just at present. Claude gallantly fought down his natural aversion, went to see Colin, and found him sparkling with health and good-humour after three hours' squash rackets. Claude set forth his proposition frankly. The trout fishing at Bligny was not surpassing, but it was good. There was some work, it was true, but no coolie work of routine to be done on the nail, as at G.H.Q. proper, and no office hours. No Generals came blowing in to inspect. All the great people from London, who ran things, came through the place sooner or later. Colin would meet them at Bligny. A clever devil like him would put it all over them, so as to do himself no end of good.

There was certainly something in that, Colin thought. He thought a good deal. The tall ship of his warlike career had lately been lying becalmed, and Heaven knew how much longer these doldrums might last. He knew that Claude had been slipping up, with good comic effect. He might slip up more, and then—yes, there were good troubled waters at Bligny; there might be a little good fishing, besides that for the trout. He temporised and prepared.

While, for some weeks, he continued to do so, things went no better at Bligny. G.H.Q. rocked with mirth at Claude's misadventures. Pedantic precisians began to ask how this entertainment helped to beat Germany. Comic paragraphs crept into London and Paris newspapers. Somebody asked a sarcastic question in Parliament. Then at last it was felt that Claude had to go. But some of the great and wise were sorry for Claude. They felt he had his points. Nosing civilians had hounded him out of his job. The like might happen to anyone. So the wise and the great said he should stay for a month more, and meanwhile be given a little something to make him feel better. Claude's D.S.O. was the most piquant thing in the next list of rewards for special gallantry and devotion. A month after this piece of justice appeared in the *Gazette* Claude got his orders to hand over the Bligny command—yea, to hand it over to the forethoughtful Colin.

"You know why I'm unstuck," Claude said to his officers when the blow fell. "Because March is a New Army man. Some ticks in the Press have been blowing hot air about the 'Regular Army trade union,' saying it corners all the good jobs—that sort of bilge. So some New Army man has got to be jumped into something—any old job—just to have him ready to show. All very well if there

weren't a war on. But how're we to win if they're always taking
the heart out of the backbone of the Army?" Claude, you see, was
no great commander of metaphors, either. "I know one thing,"
he continued: "I'm not taking any hand in this ramp."

To keep this vow not to touch pitch, Claude, strictly speaking,
did not "hand over" to Colin at all. He never explained to Colin
the work of the place, the lie of the land, the things that had to be
seen to. A stand had to be made against all this handing over to
the unworthy, so Claude felt, and went out for the day in his car.
He did this every day of the week during which he was to hand
over, Colin and he being both in the house. He breakfasted early
so as not to see Colin. Towards the end of one of these last break-
fasts some tactless officer let fall a hint that a few tips about the
routine of the show might help the new commander to vanquish
the Germans.

"No! let him rip," said Claude, with an air of stern virtue. "If
he slips up, all the better—show that wars are not won by sham
soldiers."

Colin came in at the moment, and Claude left it at that, and
finished his coffee inflexibly. Already his car stood at the door; another long day's service to the petrol trade had dawned. He gone,
Colin frankly commended his love of the road and of his kinsfolk.
"It's time he hopped round," Colin said to the rest of the table,
"and talked to those uncles." No "reserve" or "discretion" for
Colin. War, he said, was quite enough of a morgue, anyhow, without that.

XI

For the next two months Colin was kept pretty busy. The chase
engaged him by day. He rode a great many partridges down on
the swelling chalk hills, where the air and turf were divine. A
sterner task was teaching an Irish retriever how to course hares. At

night, any time he could spare from French billiards and bridge, he employed in making up war arrears of light reading. Unto his officers he did as he would that his superiors should do unto him. "*Continuez, mes enfants,*" he would benignantly say to them, whatsoever they did. After a Claude, he said, the land ought to have rest for some years. As to the men, he quoted distinguished authorities on the subject of "trusting the lads." He owned that he desired his command to have the charms of an ancient and untended garden, diverse and engaging with wayward, self-sowing flowers, unmarred by the desolating militarist symmetries and uniformities of geometric "carpet" flower-beds. In short, even as Claude had trusted, Colin "ripped."

He ripped so visibly and audibly that, long before the next harvest of decorations had time to come in, he was, even in G.H.Q.s clement eyes, "ripe for booting," as Claude elatedly said. And booted he was, in his turn. But to boot Colin was like booting a large polygonal stone. It might hurt. Not for nothing had Colin practised all his social charms at Bligny for the last two months. Many visitors—editors, politicians, miscellaneous powers of light or of darkness—had gone back to England enslaved by Colin's little ways. One enamoured magnate had said before going away: "If any old fool in the Army tries to get in your way, let me know." Colin had formed a Prætorian Guard, upside down—a little band of lusty civilians ready to hustle an army.

At Colin's cry for help his trusty bravoes fell to work like firemen. They pulled long wires, spread sinister rumours, warned proper persons, and made incipient booming sounds through certain megaphones of the Press which were known to be capable of giving forth, when in full blast, the most horrific bellowings. Nervous superior officers sought to appease Colin with long leave at home. He only used it to prime his redoubtable backers with nastier facts and more vitriolic suggestions.

You see, he was in quite a strong position : he had no regiment to be bundled back to; his unit was " General List "; so he might win, but he could not be smashed—he was dormy. He took up high ground—that the " Old Army Gang " had pushed him out by jade's tricks; that, if he had to go back to civil life now with a black mark to his name, some of those wanglers must howl for it. Then he would moderate slightly this rhadamanthine tone, and would temper justice with mercy : if they had the sense to rub out the black mark, he would not be vindictive. But he must have something done to prove to the world that he had done his duty and not been turned down in disgrace.

" Oh, give him his blasted M.C. and be done with it," somebody said at last, looking up from an office table at somebody else.

" Afraid we can't, sir," said somebody else. " This new rule, you know, sir—about keeping M.C.s for things done in action."

" Oh, damn! D.S.O., then."

" Very good, sir."

So Colin left with a new red and blue stain on his coat, and none at all on his character as a soldier. He bore no grudge against his persecutors. He was too deeply amused. What tickled him most was that he was the very last, he believed, of all the old-world D.S.O.s, the men to whom the gaud came, like the Garter, with " no damned merit about it." A rule came into force, almost immediately after, that D.S.O.s were not to be given any longer for telephoning or clerking, or any other mode of escape from the Germans; they were all to be for the mere hack-work of fighting.

" I'm like the last Groom of the Posset," said Colin, " or Clerk of the Royal Backstairs. I'm the Last British Wolf. I ought to be stuffed, when I die, and bought for the nation, and put up on the Horse Guards Parade. It has a kind of brain, you know, the dear old Regular Army; its madness has method. For three years of war all of it gorges itself with these D.S.O.s—I mean all of it that is not busy fighting. Meanwhile it invents the M.C., and settles on that also, till every unconscientious objector in France has got one or both. Then it sees all the Vandals and Goths of the New Army approaching the sanctuaries, so up goes this rule. It hath a twofold operation, like old Falstaff's drinks—keeps out any future staff crowd, and runs up the stock for the crowd who got in on the ground-floor. Look at my own little investment. Every new D.S.O. from this day forth will only prove more and more what a terrible fellow I was in the trenches."

I found that Claude, too, gave the new regulation his blessing. We met and dined, on my way back from a leave, at the splendid new G.H.Q. Officers' Club at Montreuil. Presently the benign operation of Louis Roederer 1906 slightly unlaced and unbuttoned the fine Prussian greatcoat and boots of Claude's mind.

"I seriously think," he seriously said, "that at least a large proportion of these decorations ought to be given for purely physical acts of valour. Otherwise they may lose caste, as it were, in the sight of the public. You may say to me, 'Why not just do our duty and let the public be damned?' Still, the public is there, and it's only fair to ourselves to mind, in some slight degree, what it thinks. When I got my own D.S.O. and M.C. I knew myself, and I think my friends knew, that I had earned them. But how is the public to know, or even to guess? All you can do to help it, and make the most hard-earned distinctions worth having, is to keep them connected, in people's minds, with the more obvious sorts of good work—front-line stunts and so on, the only things, I suppose, that the man in the street can understand about soldiering."

I tried to work this clear in my mind, assisted by the illuminating radiance of the H.A.C. band, the foaming grape of Eastern

France, and the beautiful W.A.A.C. waitresses dressed as comic-opera gitanas—all rendered curiously intoxicant by the sound of the rain on the roof and the imminence of my return to a little wet home in the earth of the salient. "So the bread of the children," I construed, thinking aloud, " ought to be sometimes—rather often —given to dogs, because somehow its being half-eaten by dogs makes it still more nice for the children."

"I don't call those brave fellows in the trenches dogs," said Claude somewhat distantly. He had a way of talking about the trenches, to us who lived in them, that made us feel it must only be in some incomplete unreal sense that we lived there at all; whereas in a spiritually higher and more valid sense he, the authentically rugged soldier, abode there himself, so that, in the sight of Heaven, his were war's thorns and ours her roses.

"Nor I," said I, "really," somewhat discomfited. I scarcely ever touch irony without getting into some mess and showing up badly.

Claude, still severe, said : " And I wouldn't exactly call the staff children."

" Nor I," said I, feeling I must have been rude.

" Then I don't see your point," Claude austerely pursued.

" No?" said I, still believing that somewhere or other I had one, but not feeling quite sure. And how could one waste in ill-humour the last night of music and light, the shine of clean glasses and white tablecloths?

XII

I next heard of Claude from Colin, in London. A portion of me had gone the way of all flesh in the salient, and Colin came to liven me up in a desolate Belgravian palace used as a hospital. Colin never grudged the War Office's time to any work of good nature. Some men took it all for themselves.

"You've not heard about Claude?" he answered my question. "Why, Claude has entered into his kingdom. Claude has done the impossible, the unthinkable—found a new seam, a very Bonanza, where the most piercing eyes in the Army had only seen level sand. You know how all the princes and counsellors of the earth go out to visit Douglas Haig. D. H. believes they must all be longing to get sniped and bombarded, just because he likes it himself. So, in pure kindness of heart, he puts them into a car and packs them off for long days at the front. But Claude really knoweth man's heart. He has found them a way of escape—some sort of ' safety-first ' apparatus, no one quite knows what—whether it's a quiet shebeen in the wilds of the Somme, where they can lie *perdu* all day till it's time to go home, or a whole dummy battlefield, well out of harm's way, with old German helmets and rifles lying about for the visitors to absorb as war souvenirs. Some brain-wave like that."

Perhaps I looked puzzled. How could a mere acting Major have so happy a thought, and no Colonel or General knock him down and take it away and use it himself?

"Oh, Claude worked the flotation all right," Colin assured me. "Claude knew his chief, Blunt, was a fool—with a temper. So he unfolded his little idea at nine on a morning when old Blunt was looking his cheapest and blackest.

" 'Think it a good idea, do you?' said Blunt. 'Well, I think it a damn bad idea, so you shall work it out yourself—and don't come whining to me when you've failed.' Can't you imagine him saying it?"

Yes, I knew that dodge of drowning new-born reformers like kittens in bucketfuls of detail.

"Of course," Colin said sagely, "Blunt was right in a way. If you're a downy old serpent, you don't want any infant Hercules kicking about. And yet Blunt was a fool. Claude had got him on

the ground hop, just as he'd planned. For then he was able to go
right on with his plan of the funk-hole. He did, and now this contraption of his is the envy of all G.H.Q. They say the proud and
the great of this world are tumbling over each other to get in at
the door. I hear that unless you're of royal blood, or a premier,
Claude becomes quite short and dry with you. Once he had two
live Kings and two Queens in the place, all at once—all the Court
cards in one hand—the sort of thing people write to the *Field*
about. When he comes home from the wars he'll sell his visitors'
book and buy land and live on his rents. When the august go away
they always give him an order apiece before stepping into the car.
His Legion of Honour is said to be lost in the crush. It's thought
the ribbons will soon go all round his back, like a gym belt, in a
broad band. I fear it can't last, though."

"Why?" said I. "Are there not enough Kings in the world?"

"When a rather small hen," said Colin, "finds a large hunch
of bread in the run, is a welter-weight cock to look on unmoved?
Is Blunt, because he has been a fool once, to be a fool always? Believe me, he suffers remorse for his harshness to Claude. He will
say: 'I have sinned.' He will undo the past. He will reorganise
the establishment. Claude will be in the outer darkness, and Blunt
will feed all the auriferous geese out of his own lily hand."

XIII

Then Colin talked about himself. He always had frankness, almost to the point of disease. He was, he said, eaten by care, because he had never yet failed to overtrump little Claude, and now
little Claude had played such a whacking big trump. Colin said he
had known an old woman once, in the country, who died of lying
awake at night fearing the patchwork quilt of the old woman next
door was getting on faster than hers. Colin avowed he was hag-

ridden too, with the thought of that textile mosaic on Claude's bosom expanding swiftly and inexorably. Things, he said, must be thought out, lest he should die.

With Colin, to think was to talk; his thought worked best along a kind of paper-chase track of vivid words laid for the pursuing intellect by the forerunning tongue. So there he sat, by my bed, and made more picturesquely clear, to himself as well as to me, the thing that had struck him most in all his war travels across Northern France between the coast and our front—how, as he went east, the ribbons on passing men's breasts seemed always to die down and wither, just as the corn and the roses did, by the road, till on the wastes of thistle and poppies where the shell-fire began you would seldom see a decorated man. He thought, aloud, of that Brigade H.Q. where he had slept for a resonant fortnight— his nearest point of approach to the firing line. That thrice-wounded Major there had not had a ribbon at all. None of the officers and men who had come in to that place from the actual front had had any. Colour had only begun to break forth again where, on Colin's way back to the sea, he had passed a Divisional H.Q. five miles farther west—"first streaks of auroral rose breaking out," Colin said, "only—not in the east. No stars in the east; precious little dayspring to visit it—

In front the sun climbs slow, how slowly,
But westward, look, the land is bright!

"And then it was only at corps headquarters, twenty miles farther away from the fight, that the real thing came, all the flora of valour well out, the 'high midsummer pomp,' and so forth, fully on. The Army H.Q. again, when I got there, seemed like the tropics. I've worked it out that on the average the number of ribbons a British officer gets in this war varies in direct proportion to the square of his distance from the front. It's a 'law,' like the laws about heat and the conservation of energy."

I knew he hadn't worked it out before; he was only doing it now, led on by his own talk, that wildly intuitive advance-guard of his marching mind. And then, from ascertained facts, unquestionable laws, he went on visibly to speculate. Why should the working of any such law of nature as this—a law of the nature of man—be interrupted by any mere physical accident such as a sea? Was it not of the very nature of things that the London clays should be to the payable sands of Boulogne and the rich quartz rock of Montreuil as these soils were to the utter deserts of Ypres and La Bassée? All civilisation, the great world movement, had always been westward. Was not human experience now confirming this scientific hypothesis?—rain ribbons as it might in maritime France, it poured in Whitehall. That was the centre of things; there all the fountains of honour played most freshly and amply, unexhausted as yet with watering the thirsty fields of France.

Colin left me in rather a hurry at last. He had seen a great light. Things had come clear. He had to be off and withdraw his application for fresh employment in France. Not there, but on British soil, must Claude be outshone.

The job that Colin, under this new inspiration, sought from the proper person, and presently got, was, I fancy, that of a kind of occasional A.D.C. to be lent to august foreigners passing through town on their way to visit our front. Princes and Premiers, Marshals and Admirals, Colin saw them safe through the great wicked city. Claude might draw on them later, but Colin tapped the stream nearer its source. He had his reward. When I caught sight of him next the thin red lines across his tunic had been—well, reinforced.

This narrative has to end without any climax. If it were fiction it might, no doubt, culminate in some one superlative masterpiece of acquisition by one or other of its heroes. But life does not work in that way : we constantly have to put up with the ineffectiveness of truth. The two seemed to pass out of my sight like two racing yachts on a day of light airs. First one of them would catch a little local breeze and skim away with a lead, and then would run into some patch of dead air while the other would pick up a puff and be carried ahead, to be then becalmed in his turn. I heard they looked most beautiful, with three full rows of ribbons apiece, like commanders-in-chief, and that people turned round to look at them in the street, marvelling that men so young should have had time for so much valour.

DEAD ALIVE

by
Henri Barbusse

DURING the War, as the result of various wounds, I passed through a good many hospitals. I was at Breteuil, and at Chartres, and at Courville, and at Brives. The inside of Plombières Hospital saw me too—saw enough of me, I may add, after a brief stay, for I did not live in odour of sanctity with the black-robed nuns, with the supervisors and orderlies in cassocks of blue. Their uniforms were blue, but their faces were ruddy with health, for one and all, from the highest to the lowest, were vicars in ordinary life.

But I now wish to speak of another matter—of an evening we spent, sick and wounded side by side, round the stove which battled with November, in the large ward upstairs.

Our talk was of misery, wrongs, and crimes. Every survivor floating on the surface there had his own true story to tell. During these evenings, I collected the stories of many eye-witnesses, which I afterwards used in my books. And if those pages have sometimes moved the reader, it was because they woke to life some vibration of the living truth, like those violins which, old fables say, stirred the heart-strings of all listeners, not because an artist had made them, but because somebody's soul was imprisoned within them.

One of the speakers—I shall call him Peter—said this:

"There was a man dead alive once—lived after he was shot. And to prove it, I'll give him name—Waterlot Francis.

"They shot him all right—it was up against a haystack. But after his execution he was as fit as a fiddle."

Peter told us the story; it began with a picture of exhaustion and despair.

Round Meaurs, near Sézanne, the soldiers of 327th Line Regiment were supporting the 270th, which held the front lines. On the night of September 5th and 6th, 1914, they were on the lookout in the outskirts of a wood.

These were Peter's words :

"They had chucked themselves down on the ground on the edge of this wood and were snoozing beside their haversacks—just like 'em they looked. Leave was given that night to sleep, fully equipped. You bet they slept; ever since war broke out these chaps from the North, who had been in the Belgian retreat, had had a rough time of it. Worn out they were. What with tramping this way and that, and then the long march backwards, they had had that too. Always on their feet, always tied to their haversacks like walking packs of troubles, always goaded on, always on the watch, always damned. And they were already played out when, three days before this, the great offensive began, and piled on the agony.

"So there they were, sleeping in the dark, dead beat and dead still, and truce hung for a moment over this half-cemetery of soldiers.

"But up at the front, in the firing line, there was dirty work. The German armoured cars had managed to get in on top of the French trenches and were pouring lead into them. Taken by surprise and completely staggered, the 270th chaps, N.C.O.s ahead, gave ground, left the trench, and streamed back. They reached the wood, and the 327th, who were lying on the ground asleep, were stirred up by the feet of these men wandering through the night with the enemy's fire close on their heels. So then they blinked an eye, stood up, shook themselves into life. They saw, as well as eyes could see in the dark, these ghosts hurrying by! No N.C.O. had thought fit to stay with the men. Discipline was gone. And so, of course, up they got, away they went with the flowing tide.

" But this panic (as you know, a panic has something mechanical about it, like a railway engine, and it can't be stopped all at once when steam's up and it's for running off the lines)—the panic didn't last long. The nightmare vanished with the first streaks of light. The men belonging to the 327th formed up again in Lachies village, and there were a good three hundred now, beginning to look around for their regiment and yawning.

" But, worse luck for them, who should come trotting that way but General Boutegourd.

" General Boutegourd was in command of the 51st Division. And he was *the* brute of brutes.

" You'll understand," said Peter, " that if I give him that name when there are dozens of first-rate candidates among general officers commanding, it is because there are pretty good reasons.

" He had the heaviest hand and sharpest tongue of all leaders. He would clap his revolver on you on the least provocation, and was always talking of wiping out French soldiers (because, you see, he wouldn't have nearly such a good chance with the German soldiers). He often would hit laggards and slow-coaches himself with his cane, and we all know that that same cane stopped our fellows in Guignicourt from drinking the water which the inhabitants had put out in buckets along the side of the street for them to drink. If you gave way to temptation, down on your shoulders, whack! came the cane of this little god almighty (who didn't feel thirsty or else was frightened and wanted to hop it still quicker). And many other things he's done, of which he shall hear more.

" So this was the General, complete with staff, who ran into the lads of the 327th in Lachies Street.

" ' Who are these men?' shouted brassy brass hat, in a fury already.

" He questioned one.

"'What's that you say? Looking for your regiment? You don't catch me with that story. You're deserters. Pick me out six men and a corporal, and shoot them on the spot.'

"Used as the General Staff was to saying Amen to all the utterances of this pontiff whose cap was so stiff with gold braid, the officers now pulled a long face and took upon themselves to say:

"'Excuse us, sir, but that can't be done.'

"To be brief, they pointed out that things weren't quite so simple as that: these men had not abandoned their posts, for they hadn't been in action. They were resting in the rear, and had been swept back in the night, with no leaders to control them in the general panic. Besides, before shooting seven men they must sentence them, and before sentencing them try them, and that was exactly what courts-martial were for. Two honourable men, Colonel Vezat and Major Richard Vitry (which proves that we must never generalise and talk about 'the officers' *en bloc*), submitted these arguments to ears which did not understand, then begged, implored this Grand Mogul creature who held life and death in his hands.

"All for nothing. He had seven men chosen by lot and separated out. He stopped there to see it done. He enjoyed this retribution of master on slave. He also enjoyed saying No to one of the seven who dropped on his knees and begged for mercy, crying out that he had five children.

"Apparently he had the law on his side. All that's needed is for an old campaigner to be taken with a craze for murdering. Never mind whether there's any justifiable reason for the whim or even no reason at all; up he comes, scoops up seven chance men out of a crowd, and says: 'To the stake with them.' It's down in the Regulations; and that in a country which pretends to have some respect for the fighting soldier, where one old fellow who com-

mands some attention has declared that soldiers *have* rights, and
where some funny fools have also claimed rights, actually known
as *les Droits de l'Homme,* for *all* men.

"But if the law's an ass, well, it's the lookout of the people who
are fools enough to be had that way. What I can't understand is
how a man who's done a job like that can walk about in the street
and show his nose anywhere without getting spat at by decent
people, and getting his head knocked off by someone more decent
still.

"They packed the seven of them into some old barn, and next
day, at dawn, a detachment took them out into the fields, to find
a haystack to stand them up against.

"About a mile from the village they found one that would do.
They lined them up."

At this point someone interrupted Peter, the teller of the story
and said, or rather moaned out, as in a dream:

"How is it that men can always be found ready to kill their
comrades?"

Peter merely answered:

"They're found all right.

"Well, they lined them up, asked for their handkerchiefs, and
bandaged their eyes. The detachment lined up, rifles and all. The
command was given: 'Fire!'

"The squad obeyed because they were miserable worms and
hadn't the pluck to be men. But though they obeyed the order,
they felt it, you know, and they shut their eyes the way kids do as
they pulled the trigger.

"After this magnificent salvo, they set about finishing them off.
A regimental sergeant-major, true to army tradition, stepped forward revolver in hand. He blew out the brains of two. One of the
victims, the father of five, cried out as his skull opened up. Then

the R.S.M. had enough. They say he wept because he couldn't stick it. So he didn't go any further. There are fellows like that. They do all the harm they can in their execution of their b——y duty, then they stop when they've had enough. They're better chaps than the rest, some say. I don't see it. He ought to have had enough before he began.

"When the word to fire was given, one of the seven fell like a log and never stirred again. So he had fallen, as I might say, just a tiny bit too soon, a split second before the bullet came along. The man opposite him hadn't seen him when he fired because he shut his eyes, and the Adjutant hadn't spotted him, either, because he'd only finished off the two first in the row, feeling sick.

"When the firing squad pushed off, this man was astonished to find he wasn't dead. He felt himself carefully, and made sure he wasn't the least bit dead. He crawled away to hide himself for a bit on t'other side of the stack, just like a miserable stunned bird, then got up on his feet and ran off like mad, straight ahead.

"An hour after, those passing saw six bodies instead of seven under the haystack. Five only were corpses; the sixth had simply been wounded—fractured thigh. They picked him up and dressed him.

"As for the hale and hearty one, he ran all night and fetched up next day in some billets. 'Who's this old bird?' said the fellows there. His hair had actually gone white (though he was a fair-haired chap and only twenty-seven), which proved to me that this going-all-white-in-a-moment business doesn't only happen in novels (for once, then, a thing that happened in the War agrees with the stories in books)!

"In the billets he made a clean breast of the whole affair—a foolish thing to do. But they didn't hand him over; they took him on in the regiment, as supernumerary. They couldn't put his name on the roll or give him a number, for by the Regulations he was dead, and a 'dead deserter' at that (for that's what they call them officially). So he was the odd soldier of the 233rd Line Regiment. And he used to shake like a leaf when he thought how they might fetch his case up into daylight and put matters straight by killing him properly. Meanwhile he was put with the ensign bodyguard, a job that keeps you safe, as you're never in the firing line.

"He was a miner, and belonged to Montigny-en-Gohelle. He had been mobilised on the 3rd of August, the very day his wife was giving birth to their firstborn; but he'd never seen the baby, as it was born in the afternoon and he had to leave in the morning. I know the names of the other six, too, and could tell you them. There were even one or two like Hubert; his relations got a military medal, a military cross, and a mention in despatches out of it, for at headquarters they had discovered what a dastardly business it was and wanted to hide it up with ornaments. But I shan't mention anyone but Waterlot."

One of the circle made bold to say :

"Don't you go giving his name like that, old chap. The less known about it all, the better for him, eh?"

"Fat lot he cares about it all, the poor blighter," returned Peter, "seeing as how he was knocked out by a shell later on, and properly. Don't you worry.

"It was this way. One day his new regiment ran across his old regiment, at some cross roads. He simply couldn't resist the desire to go back. Funny thing the way a man hangs on to the number of his regiment, as if it meant something. So once again he did his job as a soldier. And it isn't in reason that a plain infantryman who does his job from the start of the war in a fighting regiment should keep on his legs for long (though it has been known). Once he was seriously wounded, and got patched up and went back to the job that men don't ask for. But on the 16th June in '15, during the Artois offensive at Hébuterne, a shell mopped him up for good and all.

"And who knows? Perhaps the poor blighters who sent up that shell were poor blighters just like him—p'r'aps the men in that firing squad were too—although it's true they were *told* to do murder, in a language that wasn't their own. Anyway, killed he was at last, by his own kind."

"Sure he was," we all murmured in chorus.

IN HOSPITAL

IN ANOTHER COUNTRY

by
Ernest Hemingway

IN the fall the War was always there, but we did not go to it any
more. It was cold in the fall in Milan and the dark came very
early. Then the electric lights came on, and it was pleasant along
the streets looking in the windows. There was much game hanging outside the shops, and the snow powdered in the fur of the
foxes and the wind blew their tails. The deer hung stiff and heavy
and empty, and small birds blew in the wind and the wind turned
their feathers. It was a cold fall and the wind came down from the
mountains.

We were all at the hospital every afternoon, and there were
different ways of walking across the town through the dusk to the
hospital. Two of the ways were alongside canals, but they were
long. Always, though, you crossed a bridge across a canal to enter
the hospital. There was a choice of three bridges. On one of them
a woman sold roasted chestnuts. It was warm standing in front of
her charcoal fire, and the chestnuts were warm afterward in your
pocket. The hospital was very old and very beautiful, and you entered through a gate and walked across a courtyard and out a gate
on the other side. There were usually funerals starting from the
courtyard. Beyond the old hospital were the new brick pavilions,
and there we met every afternoon and were all very polite and interested in what was the matter, and sat in the machines that were
to make so much difference.

The doctor came up to the machine where I was sitting and
said: "What did you like best to do before the War? Did you
practise a sport?"

I said: "Yes, football."

"Good," he said. "You will be able to play football again better than ever."

My knee did not bend and the leg dropped straight from the knee to the ankle without a calf, and the machine was to bend the knee and make it move as in riding a tricycle. But it did not bend yet, and instead the machine lurched when it came to the bending part. The doctor said: "That will all pass. You are a fortunate young man. You will play football again like a champion."

In the next machine was a Major who had a little hand like a baby's. He winked at me when the doctor examined his hand, which was between two leather straps that bounced up and down and flapped the stiff fingers, and said: "And will I too play football, Captain-doctor?" He had been a very great fencer, and before the War the greatest fencer in Italy.

The doctor went to his office in a back room and brought back a photograph which showed a hand that had been withered almost as small as the Major's before it had taken a machine course, and after was a little larger. The Major held the photograph with his good hand and looked at it very carefully. "A wound?" he asked.

"An industrial accident," the doctor said.

"Very interesting, very interesting," the Major said, and handed it back to the doctor.

"You have confidence?"

"No," said the Major.

There were three boys who came each day who were about the same age I was. They were all three from Milan, and one of them was to be a lawyer, and one was to be a painter, and one had intended to be a soldier, and after we were finished with the machines sometimes we walked back together to the Café Cova, which was next door to the Scala. We walked the short way through the communist quarter because we were four together. The people hated us because we were officers, and from a wine-shop someone would call out, "A basso gli ufficiali!" as we passed. Another boy who walked with us sometimes and made us five wore a black silk handkerchief across his face because he had no nose then and his face was to be rebuilt. He had gone out to the front from the military academy and been wounded within an hour after he had gone into the front line for the first time. They rebuilt his face, but he came from a very old family and they could never get the nose exactly right. He went to South America and worked in a bank. But this was a long time ago, and then we did not any of us know how it was going to be afterward. We only knew then that there was always the War, but that we were not going to it any more.

We all had the same medals, except the boy with the black silk bandage across his face, and he had not been at the front long enough to get any medals. The tall boy with a very pale face who was to be a lawyer had been a Lieutenant of Arditi and had three medals of the sort we each had only one of. He had lived a very long time with death and was a little detached. We were all a little detached, and there was nothing that held us together except that we met every afternoon at the hospital. Although, as we walked to the Cova through the tough part of town, walking in the dark with light and singing coming out of the wine-shops and sometimes having to walk into the street when the men and women would crowd together on the sidewalk so that we would have had to jostle them to get by, we felt held together by there being something that had happened that they, the people who disliked us, did not understand.

We ourselves all understood the Cova, where it was rich and warm and not too brightly lighted, and noisy and smoky at certain hours, and there were always girls at the tables and the illustrated papers on a rack on the wall. The girls at the Cova were very patriotic, and I found that the most patriotic people in Italy were the café girls—and I believe they are still patriotic.

The boys at first were very polite about my medals and asked me what I had done to get them. I showed them the papers, which were written in very beautiful language, and full of *fratellanza* and *abnegazione,* but which really said, with the adjectives removed, that I had been given the medals because I was an American. After that their manner changed a little toward me, although I was their friend against outsiders. I was a friend, but I was never really one of them after they had read the citations, because it had been different with them and they had done very different things to get their medals. I had been wounded, it was true; but we all knew that being wounded after all was really an accident. I was never ashamed of the ribbons, though, and sometimes, after the cocktail hour, I would imagine myself having done all the things they had done to get their medals; but walking home at night through the empty streets with the cold wind and all the shops closed, trying to keep near the street lights, I knew that I would never have done such things, and I was very much afraid to die, and often lay in bed at night by myself afraid to die, and wondering how I would be when I went back to the front again.

The three with the medals were like hunting-hawks; and I was not a hawk, although I might seem a hawk to those who had never hunted; they, the three, knew better and so we drifted apart. But I stayed good friends with the boy who had been wounded his first day at the front because he would never know now how he would have turned out; so he could never be accepted either, and I liked him because I thought perhaps we would not have turned out to be a hawk either.

The Major, who had been the great fencer, did not believe in bravery, and spent much time while we sat in the machines correcting my grammar. He had complimented me on how I spoke Italian, and we talked together very easily. One day I had said that Italian seemed such an easy language to me that I could not take a great interest in it; everything was so easy to say. " Ah, yes," the Major said. "Why, then, do you not take up the use of grammar?" So we took up the use of grammar, and soon Italian was such a difficult language that I was afraid to talk to him until I had the grammar straight in my mind.

The Major came very regularly to the hospital. I do not think he ever missed a day, although I am sure he did not believe in the machines. There was a time when none of us believed in the machines, and one day the Major said it was all nonsense. The machines were new then and it was we who were to prove them. It was an idiotic idea, he said, " a theory, like another." I had not learned my grammar, and he said I was a stupid, impossible disgrace, and he was a fool to have bothered with me. He was a small man and he sat straight up in his chair with his right hand thrust into the machine and looked straight ahead at the wall while the straps thumped up and down with his fingers in them.

"What will you do when the War is over, if it is over?" he asked me. "Speak grammatically!"

"I will go to the States."

"Are you married?"

"No, but I hope to be."

" The more of a fool you are," he said. He seemed very angry. " A man must not marry."

"Why, Signor Maggiore?"

"Don't call me Signor Maggiore."

"Why must not a man marry?"

"He cannot marry. He cannot marry," he said angrily. "If he is to lose everything, he should not place himself in a position to lose that. He should not place himself in a position to lose. He should find things he cannot lose."

He spoke very angrily and bitterly, and looked straight ahead while he talked.

" But why should he necessarily lose it?"

" He'll lose it," the Major said. He was looking at the wall. Then he looked down at the machine and jerked his little hand out from between the straps and slapped it hard against his thigh. " He'll lose it," he almost shouted. " Don't argue with me!" Then he called to the attendant who ran the machines: " Come and turn this damned thing off."

He went back into the other room for the light treatment and the massage. Then I heard him ask the doctor if he might use his telephone and he shut the door. When he came back into the room I was sitting in another machine. He was wearing his cape and had his cap on, and he came directly toward my machine and put his arm on my shoulder.

" I am so sorry," he said, and patted me on the shoulder with his good hand. " I would not be rude. My wife has just died. You must forgive me."

" Oh——" I said, feeling sick for him. " I am *so* sorry."

He stood there biting his lower lip. " It is very difficult," he said. " I cannot resign myself."

He looked straight past me and out through the window. Then he began to cry. " I am utterly unable to resign myself," he said, and choked. And then crying, his head up looking at nothing, carrying himself straight and soldierly, with tears on both his cheeks and biting his lips, he walked past the machines and out the door.

The doctor told me that the Major's wife, who was very young and whom he had not married until he was definitely invalided out of the War, had died of pneumonia. She had been sick only a few days. No one expected her to die. The Major did not come to the hospital for three days. Then he came at the usual hour wearing a black band on the sleeve of his uniform. When he came back, there were big framed photographs around the wall of all sorts of wounds before and after they had been cured by the machines. In front of the machine the Major used were three photographs of hands like his that were completely restored. I do not know where the doctor got them. I always understood we were the first to use the machines. The photographs did not make much difference to the Major because he only looked out of the window.

RÉCHOUSSAT'S CHRISTMAS

by
Georges Duhamel

R ÉCHOUSSAT repeated in a shrill, strained voice : "I tell you, they're not coming after all."

Corporal Têtard turned a deaf ear to this. He was sorting out his stock on a table : lints, oil, rubber gloves reminiscent of the fencer, probes enclosed in a tube like vanilla cornets, a basin of enamelled sheet-iron resembling a big bean, and a bulging vase with a wide gaping mouth, looking like nothing at all.

Réchoussat affected an air of indifference. "They needn't come if they don't wish to. Anyway, I don't care."

Corporal Têtard shrugged his shoulders. "But I tell you they will come," he said.

The wounded man obstinately shook his head. "Not here, old boy, nobody 'll come here. All those who visit downstairs never come up here. I'm only telling you. I don't really care, you know."

"You may be sure they will come."

"Really, I don't know why I have been placed here alone in the room."

"Probably because you must have quiet."

"Whether they come or not, it's all one to me."

Réchoussat frowned to show his pride, then he added, sighing : "You can begin now with your bag of tricks."

As a matter of fact Corporal Têtard was ready. He had lighted a candle-end and in one movement drew back the sheets.

Réchoussat's body was revealed, extraordinarily thin, but Têtard scarcely noticed it, and Réchoussat had for three months now been fairly accustomed to his misery. He knew quite well that to have a piece of shell in the back is a serious matter, and that, when a man's legs and abdomen are paralysed, he is not going to recover quickly.

"Feeling better?" asked Têtard in the course of his operation.

"Yes," he replied. "Now it's six o'clock and they haven't come. Good thing! I don't mind."

The corporal did not reply; with a weary expression he rubbed together his rubber gloves. Riveted to the wick, the candle-flame leaped and struggled, like a wretched prisoner yearning to escape and fly up alone in the blackness of the room, and beyond, higher, higher, in the winter sky, in regions where the sounds of the war of men are no longer heard. Both the patient and the orderly watched the flame in silence, with wide-open vague eyes. Every second a gun, far away, snapped at the panes, and each time the flame of the candle started nervously.

"It takes a long time! You're not cold?" asked Têtard.

"The lower part of my body does not know what cold means."

"But it will, one day."

"Of course it will. It's dead now, but it must become alive again. I am only twenty-five; it's an age when the flesh has plenty of vigour."

The corporal felt awkward, shaking his head. Réchoussat seemed to him worn out; he had large sores in the places where the body rested on the bed. He had been isolated in order that his more fortunate comrades should be spared the sight of his slow, dragging death.

A long moment went by. The silence was so oppressive that for a moment they felt their small talk quite inadequate. Then, as if he was continuing a mental discussion, Réchoussat suddenly remarked:

"And, you know, I'm so easily satisfied. If they came for two minutes only."

"Hush!" said Têtard. "Hush!"

He leaned, listening, towards the door. Obscure sounds came from the passage.

"Ah, here they are!" said the orderly.

Réchoussat craned his neck. "Bah! No, I tell you."

Suddenly a wonderful light, rich in reflections of gold and crimson—a strange fairy light—filled the passage. The wall in front stood out; ordinarily as pale as December woods, now it suddenly exhibited the splendour of an Eastern palace or of a princess' gown. In all this light there was the sound of happy voices and of laughter. No one could be heard singing, yet the light itself seemed to be singing a magnificent song. Réchoussat, who could not move, stretched his neck the more vigorously, and raised his hands a little above the sheets, as if he wanted to feel this beautiful sound and light.

"You see, you see!" said Têtard. "I told you they would come."

Then there was a big blaze. Something stopped before the door; it was a tree—a real fir-tree from the forests, planted in a green box. There were so many Chinese lanterns and pink candles hanging from its branches that it looked like an enormous torch. But there was something grander to come; the wise and learned kings now entered. There was Sorri, a Senegalese gunner, Moussa, and Cazin. Wrapped in cloaks from Adrianople, they wore long white beards made of cotton wool.

They walked right into Réchoussat's room. Sorri carried a little packet tied with ribbon. Moussa waved aloft two cigars, and Cazin a bottle of champagne. The three of them bowed punctiliously, as they had been told, and Réchoussat found himself suddenly with a box of chocolates in his right hand, two cigars in his left, and a glass of foaming wine on his little table.

"Ah, boys! No, no; you're joking, boys."

Moussa and Cazin laughed. Sorri showed his teeth.

"Ah, boys!" repeated Réchoussat, "I don't smoke, but I'm going to keep the cigars as a souvenir. Pass me the wine."

Sorri took the goblet and offered it as if it were a sacred cup. Réchoussat drank it gently and said:

"It's some wine! Good stuff!"

There were more than a score of faces at the door, and they all smiled at the gentle naïve Réchoussat.

Afterwards, a veritable sunset! The wonderful tree receded, jolting into the passage. The venerable kings disappeared, with their flowing cloaks and their sham beards. Réchoussat still held the goblet and gazed at the candle as if all the lights existed there. He laughed, slowly repeating, "It's some wine!" Then he continued to laugh and never said a word.

Quite gently the darkness entered the room again and lodged itself everywhere, like an intimate animal disturbed in its habits.

With the darkness something very sad insinuated itself everywhere, which was the odour of Réchoussat's illness. A murmuring silence rested on every object like dust. The face of the patient ceased to reflect the splendour of the Christmas tree; his head sunk down, he looked at the bed, at his thin, ulcerated legs, the glass vessel full of unclean liquid, the probe, all these incomprehensible things, and he said, stammering with astonishment:

"But . . . but . . . what is the matter then? What is the matter?'

AFTER THE WAR

ARMISTICE

by
H.M. Tomlinson

THE tumult of that year, desperate and stupefying, lessened. We had leisure to breathe again. The Germans were expended. Ludendorff had gambled with his last reserves, and he had lost. The threatening colossus suggested by his name dissolved in vapour. His armies, wasted in spendthrift recklessness, stood dangerously upon an enlarged front. Behind them was a nation which had stoutly endured starvation within frontiers locked fast by the war fleets of its enemies while hope maintained it. Hope had gone. It saw starkly a reality which no device of words could hide. The victories of its heroes had brought it to this; and the Americans, who could never cross the seas, were in fact in France, ready to begin a new war. Foch and Haig struck back rapidly alternating blows at the disheartened German front. Germany collapsed.

The guns would cease fire on this November day, so we were told. It was true, maybe. We had been told many things. Now They who ruled everything, even what we should read and know, even the number of potatoes we should eat—They who had taken so much from us, for our good, that only ashes were left, They said the guns would cease to fire. We hoped so. But it was late.

It was a quiet winter morning. The perspective of the long trial was too deep. Nothing could be seen in it now, nothing but the wan sky over the Thames. We waited, lethargic, hardly believing. It was near the hour. London was still. Then a rocket burst over the river.

The end! That was the end of it!

A window was flung open. Someone was cheering across the street. Syrens began to hoot on the river. The whistles of locomotives kept up their whistling. There was shouting and singing below. I looked out. The city was erupting. An Australian soldier sat on the roof of a cab with a nurse on his lap. People were flooding from every door; clouds of papers and official forms fell over the cheering crowds from the windows of offices; the street already was a congested, tumultuous torrent of released people.

When I turned to the room my own office was deserted. It was oddly quiet. The staff had dropped everything and had gone. Discipline had departed to sing and dance elsewhere. One had better join it, perhaps?

But as I made for the door, there, only just visible in the shadow of a recess, was an old bowler hat on a peg. It was ancient with dust. It was ridiculously out of fashion. I stood and looked at it. That was Charley Bolt's old hat. He left it there, to go to war, four years ago. It seemed very much by itself. I got out a pipe; took a chair; I might just as well keep it company, on such a day.

"THE WATCH ON THE RHINE"

by
Ared White

AS the first scattering notes of the division's lately improvised marching song rose from tired throats up near the head of the trudging column, Corporal McGee reached instinctively for the big silver watch that hung on a heavy link chain in the upper bellows pocket of his blouse just under his bright new Croix de Guerre. He consulted the faded dial of the ancient timepiece ostentatiously.

"Seven o'clock by Heinie's watch," he announced in a voice loud enough to be heard by the seven sullen members of his squad. "Seven o'clock. Another hour 'n' a half yet to hike!"

There was a groan as of protest at this needless reminder of the hour.

"Ah, perk up and take the gaff smilin'," he bantered them. "Ain't you gettin' the Rhine for a Christmas present? Another ten days by Heinie's watch and you'll be in soft billets eatin' Boche poison with your Christmas pork 'n' beans."

"Wish you'd throw Heinie's watch in the Rhine!" muttered someone disgustedly.

The song up ahead began to gather form. Dragging feet that sloshed through thin mud and scraped over rough cobblestones along the endless course of sinuous grey kilometres that led to the Rhine lifted a bit less heavily as the rollicking refrain swept through the ranks. Battalion and company officers smiled wearily or pretended not to hear. Anything had warrant enough that would bring spirit back into their leg-weary men.

> The General got the Croix de Guerre,
> *Parlez vous,*

The General got the Croix de Guerre,
Parlez vous,
The General got the Croix de Guerre,
The son of a gun was never there,
Hinky, dinky, *parlez vous!*

It rose, like a wind at sea, from an eddying swirl among a few squads to a rhythmic storm hurled into the grey dreariness of the dying day by the strong lungs of six thousand men. Feet began dragging in cadence to the music. Shoulders that had drooped nearly to the waist under the heavy full field packs began rising higher. A bugler who a moment before had been all but staggering in exhaustion found strength to trumpet a crude accompaniment, using the five tones of his bugle scale to catch a chord here and there. Another bugler picked it up, and another. The march to the Rhine suddenly became, for the moment, all but a blithesome promenade.

Presently taut arms arose fully extended above the heads of the Majors who sagged wearily in saddles at the heads of battalions. It was the signal for the hourly halt. Barely half an hour had passed since the last halt; but dusk was gathering swiftly and who could know for certain that the new divisional commander himself might not dash back along the line at any moment in his military limousine to note the progress of this record hike of forty kilometres to-day. The song died out as suddenly as it had commenced as the men fell gratefully in their tracks at the sides of the road for ten minutes' surcease from the day's gruelling advance. Regimental commanders breathed easier. It was one thing to have one of this fighting division's allotment of French war crosses given to the new divisional commander, who had joined them from some imposing staff assignment after the Armistice had been duly signed.

It might prove another thing should that new divisional commander, in the course of the division's march to the Rhine, learn the men's opinion of the transaction as perpetuated in song. The music might be well enough for the men's marching morale; but then it might not, at the same time, stir the General's fancy in a way that would be good for the morale of the brigade, regimental and battalion commanders, anon, when they were part of the American watch on the Rhine.

Corporal McGee, sitting on his unslung pack while his men lay motionless about him, got out the big silver watch again and held it before him as the hands ticked swiftly toward that instant when he must get them back in column again. He invariably found some excuse for bringing the timepiece into use when the song was in the air. To him the watch was his alibi—a reminder to his squad that his own Croix de Guerre had not been issued to him with the ration or passed to him by some obsequious staff person.

"Five minutes more to go, by Heinie's watch!" he announced with forced airiness, heroically putting aside an impulse to cast himself alongside his men on the wet ground and pass into slumber.

"Wish you'd left that Boche clock where you got it from," grumbled a private, without raising his weary head from the ground. "It's allus takin' the joy out o' life."

"One minute left to go—get ready!" the corporal cautioned them, taking his own place manfully in the road, ready for the gruff chorus of "fall in" that presently would come from the officers.

He put the big silver watch carefully back in the bellows pocket of his coat under the Croix de Guerre. The watch had validated his war cross again. It had shielded his own decoration from the devilish innuendo of that song. Since the appearance, and instant popularity, of the musical satire on the General's cross, Corporal

McGee had found the silver watch a source of comfort and gratification, as well as of utility. It was a grim token of the manner
in which he had served, one whose mortal glory no mere song
might dim. It was symbolical of that breathless moment in the
crimson Argonne when he had gone ahead of his platoon to engage a German machine-gun crew hand-to-hand, vanquishing them
with the bayonet in a desperate encounter against odds.

On one of his antagonists—the one he had vowed was the size
of two ordinary men—he had found the ancient silver timepiece.
Its owner had the watch chained to his belt, apparently for ready
consultation against the moment when he need hold his position
no longer and might retire to a place of greater security following
the retreating German riflemen. Now the watch could not have
been slow. It kept excellent time. Corporal McGee, in the momentary frenzy of battle that sometimes seizes individuals and endows
them with the courage of a dozen men, simply had been ahead of
schedule.

The corporal had cleaned his bayonet in the mud and slipped
the watch remorselessly into his pocket. He was robbing no one.
The German would have no further use for it. The corporal took
it as one imbued with the common practices of the battlefield
might take a spiked helmet or a Luger pistol or a sawtooth bayonet.
Thoughts of its one-time owner and his untimely end haunted the
corporal as little as a rabbit's foot or sealskin sacque might fret its
possessor. War begets its own peculiar conscience in such matters.
And this silver watch, with the name engraved in German script
inside the heavy hunting case, was a souvenir such as only a first-
class fighting man might hope to possess by means other than pur-
chase. Non-combatants, denizens of deep command dug-outs,
might win the Croix de Guerre by rank or favour—but how were
they to validate their crosses in the eyes of the combatant men?

"Snap into it—keep movin' there!" Corporal McGee fumed, as the members of his squad took their places beside him in the long sluggish column that moved off grudgingly in that eternal sloshing and scraping of heavy feet that were moving toward the Rhine.

"Are they goin' to hike us clean on to Berlin without stoppin' for sleep?" a private of his squad demanded querulously.

"Another two hours by Heinie's watch and you'll all be tucked away in a nice Boche feather bed—sleepin' with one eye open to keep Heinie's wife from stickin' a knife in between your ribs," he cheered them.

"Two hours more o' this an' I'll be lyin' dead 'longside the road," groaned another member of the squad.

Corporal McGee felt his first concern that one or two of his squad might give up the hike and join the footsore and weak of will who made up the ambulance and truck-riding slackers. Not a single member of his company had so disgraced himself. The corporal shuddered at the thought of such dishonour coming to his own squad.

"Ah, you birds just think you're gettin' tired out," he bantered them. "You ain't even had good leg exercise yet to-day!"

His own feet came out of the thin mud heavily, each of them seeming to weigh more than the sixty-pound pack on his back; and he all but winced every time one of his raw feet struck a submerged cobblestone in the muddy road. But sense of responsibility fed his sinews and strengthened him in carrying his own fatigue while laughing at the others. And it fed his strength, this laughing at the others, and cheering them on; attesting his own superiority of moral and physical fibre which a leader must have.

"Bet I could talk you buddies into hikin' all night an' all to-morrow an' the only kick you'd make was when I asked you to stop to rest or eat!" he challenged them whimsically, intent on keeping the thought fixed in their minds that they really were far from exhausted.

"I'll bet ye another five kilometres and ye'll need a ambulance fer the second squad," came a vacant threat from the ranks.

"But supposin'," chuckled the corporal, "supposin' I'd jus' give the order ' squads right about ' and informed you the Watch on the Rhine was all off an' we was startin' back to Brest to catch a Christmas boat home, what'd happen?"

"It'd take a darned fast horse to keep up with me," announced one of the squad.

"You said somethin', buddy," came a voice from the squad in rear. "I could do it to Brest in nothin' flat if they'd only turn me loose and gimme the road."

"That's different. Course we could do that," echoed someone in his own squad.

"You all agree?" Corporal McGee asked them.

"It wouldn't be a march, it'd be a stampede," another averred feelingly. The others muttered their assent.

Corporal McGee chuckled triumphantly. There had been method in his queries.

"Then it all goes to prove you birds ain't as tired as you might be," he charged them. "It's mostly homesickness just like you had it last year at Christmas time when you'd nothin' to do but lay around billets. Now cut out your dream stuff and quit laggin'. Come on now, snap into it. Ain't you gettin' the Rhine for Christmas—an' maybe a slit throat!"

Corporal McGee's diagnosis which he had emphasized thus to his own advantage as squad leader, was flawless. The War was over. In the minds of the men who fought it, the conflict ended November 11. Up to the hour of eleven o'clock of that greatest of days in human experience they had been sombre supermen, baiting a death-dealing Frankenstein in its lair with little thought of what life might hold for them when this desperate mission were ended —if it should ever end. Life was too insecure, and the demands of duty too sacred, to reckon deeply with the future. And at fifteen minutes after the hour of eleven they were so many homesick men and boys with their thoughts upon home, and Christmas; reckoning the chances of getting to the base ports and back home in civvies again for Christmas Day. What a Christmas present!

The unfailing grape-vine, greatest of army communications, had brought their home-bound orders to the ——th Division every day after the Armistice until that dismal hour when the crushing official orders actually arrived with the calamitous information that they were crossing the Rhine, rather than the Atlantic, for Christmas Day of 1918.

General and Colonels—and an occasional Major—might find a thrill in the thought that "Die Wacht Am Rhine" was going to have a new set of works—American works; even in the leading of a victorious army on past Coblenz to Berlin itself, or around the world for that matter. But for the butcher boys, clerks, farm hands, students, brokers, artists, and artisans who made up the ranks a more dismal disaster could not come into their lives at Christmas time.

Fifteen miles a day they had marched in the early stages of the advance—an easy hike, readily completed before noon. With the four other veteran combat divisions that had been taken from the flower of the brilliant Liggett's fighting First Army to make up the invading Third Army, their advance was by "bounds," which is to say that they marched three days or so and rested an equal period in cities along the route, billeting with the natives in accordance with carefully wrought military plans. In France, and throughout that borderland where France and Germany merged into an area whose populace had cultivated the art of enthusiastic welcome for conqueror, whoever he might be, their march was one triumphal procession, noisy throngs packing the streets and countryside waving flags and cheering *Vive les Américaines* or *Vive les Allies.*

Now they had entered into the true Rhineland whose allegiance to the Kaiser had paid its full toll of sons and gold into the Prussian cause, and the olive drabbed columns were met with a sodden, almost sullen indifference. Sober faces peered discreetly from behind closed windows. Conquered were looking with dire forebodings, if not with smouldering venom, upon conqueror. The advance guard was reinforced. Strong connecting groups were put out to maintain liaison with other allied columns marching on parallel routes to the north and south in readiness for instant deployment. The security measures were those of an advance in the face of the enemy. Occasional glimpses were to be had of the shattered German war machine as its jaded rearguards faded sullenly into the grey distance barely ahead of the American advance parties. Anything might happen.

Only an occasional old man appeared on a street corner in the villages to watch the Americans parade by at rigid attention; flags flying at the head of regiments in the main column behind the advance guards, bands blaring American march music. Old men, and the ubiquitous small boy, the latter drawn to the bands in small droves as by a magnet and trooping fearlessly along, big-eyed and beaming; stirred by the thrumming drums and throbbing brass, thrilling innocently to the compelling rhythm of " Stars and Stripes For Ever " quite as if it had been some Teuton martial quickstep proclaiming " *Deutschland Über Alles!* "

To-day's historic march of forty kilometres had begun at daybreak. It would bring the division late at night through the final stage of the long hike. To-morrow and the next day, and perhaps the day after that, the men would rest in billets near the west bank of the Rhine, replace worn-out uniforms, shoes, and impedimenta, and then sweep on across to the east shore of the haughty river into the heart of Rhenish Prussia, a spic-and-span bit of fighting mechanism bent on seeing to it that the Kaiser's hosts made good the hard terms of the Armistice they had signed.

Heinie's watch, which Corporal McGee found occasional vindication in quoting, had ticked off two heavy hours before the fatigue-driven column tumbled into German billets at the end of the final "bound." And its stocky little hour hand had completed six revolutions of the ancient dial before the column, now rested and fully outfitted, found the proud old Rhine rolling humbly under their democratic American feet as they trod, route step, toward the beckoning spires of Coblenz in that moment of pulsating magnificence when the Stars and Stripes rose suddenly over stern old Ehrenbreitstein, replacing the Prussian red, white, and black—and all that those colours symbolised by way of evil omen to the world.

"The thing ain't as wide as the Hudson," announced someone disparagingly.

If the men in the ranks had been fired for the moment by the portentous significance of their arrival at the Rhine, their sense of the dramatic moment which thrilled a continent at home quickly gave way to the spirit of badinage which the now humble stream itself aroused. It had been forbidden them that they scoff at persons and things along the route of march. Not that the feelings of their broken foemen mattered—but such a show is not of a well-disciplined army. The river, however, was an inanimate thing even though it did seem to echo of the one-time splendour of the vaunted Hohenzollerns.

"It's a crick 'longside the Miss'sippi," another soldier proclaimed.

"I wouldn't trade a quart of the muddy ol' Missouri fer the whole thing," another insisted with feeling.

"Gimme the Columbia fer mine," chorused a soldier from the far West; and the rivers of America followed in quick succession.

A warning order came snapping down the column and brought them back to the serious business at hand. The moment was at hand when they would cross into the great Prussian city itself. The new division commander would add to the import of the occasion, and to his own martial traditions, by personally reviewing this division as it set foot east of the Rhine. His large red command flag with its two white stars could be seen unfurled in the distance, just beyond the bridge-approach on the Coblenz side. The men began checking their accoutrement and blouse-buttons. A few lapsed into a gentle humming of the division marching song, brought to their vagrant minds by proximity of the new division commander; but officers quickly suppressed them with sharp words of reprimand or caution. This was no time for such foolishness.

Corporal McGee, at the first humming notes, instinctively reached for the big silver watch that hung on a heavy link chain in the upper bellows pocket of his blouse, in full vindication of his own bright new Croix de Guerre.

"Right on time, fellows," he announced plausibly. "Right here to the dot. An' say, fellows, ever stop to think that Heinie's watch's back on the Rhine—with me carryin' it? Let 'em write a song about that if they want to!"

The division snapped into its best military stride as it swept from the bridge with a magnificent "eyes right" for the sternvisaged new division commander who stood reviewing them with arms folded and a brooding martial air that hinted of "Napoleon at Friedland"; then on through the principal business section of Coblenz with every man putting himself into the business of presenting a proud and lasting spectacle of armed superiority before the awed eyes of a conquered host. The Germans had laughed a year ago, had they? Well, let them take a close-up of these despised American volunteers and see what it was that had amused them so. Let them laugh now if there was humour left in their souls! The thought was expressed in the demeanour of every marcher as feet rose and fell with perfect unison, shoulders dipped with a splendidly co-ordinated rhythm and eyes looked hard and fast straight to the front in those files that covered off as perfectly as if they had been laid by field transit.

The streets were all but empty except for the inevitable old folks and the everlasting small boys; but the invaders sensed the thousands of eyes that were observing them carefully, and estimating them anxiously, from behind windows and curtains. Let all such form their own opinion as to whether such men might be temporised with; whether isolated treachery, poison in food and knife-thrusts in the dark might be indulged in with impunity!

At the end of an interminable parade, when the populace must have been duly impressed, the columns broke into regiments, then into battalions, companies, and finally on down into squads as the elaborate billeting plans unfolded; and such men as had been selected for duty within the city itself marched off to present themselves at the homes which were to receive and shelter them.

Corporal McGee brought his own squad to an impressive halt, late in the afternoon, in front of a plain-appearing stone house in the residential district. It was one of an endless row of houses, all alike, of the kind occupied by the better middle class, two stories and attic, distinctive only in the possession of steep slate roof and green shutters. Before presenting his billeting ticket, the corporal faced his men impressively and gave them their final instructions.

"Remember, fellows, no fraternisin' with the enemy. Get that! That's one thing the Cap'n won't stand for. Remember we're dealin' with the enemy. What's more, we're conquerors an' we got to act our part. The Cap'n says we're to keep our hats on in the house even when wimmin folks is present. You ain't to say 'thanks' for nothin' they try to do for you. Wear sidearms all the time an' if any of 'em tries to knife you—well, you knows what to do without bein' told. Now then, in we goes!"

He strode firmly to the door and rapped decisively.

A middle-aged woman, thin, grey, and with a cold reserve in her careworn face, answered the summons. She reached in a dignified, detached way for the billeting ticket that Corporal McGee held out to her; then paused suddenly, hand extended without taking the ticket, the while she stood staring at the members of the squad who were assembled in wide-eyed expectancy about the door stoop. Her expression changed to one of startled surprise as she looked slowly from one to the other as if she had been suddenly confronted by some unbelievable phantom.

"What's matter, marm—don't you like the looks o' my crew?" broke in the corporal nervously, turning to look at the squad as if to learn what caused her sudden change of humour. "Not a bad bunch o' lads if they ain't ruffled."

She turned with a start to the corporal, looking at him with wide puzzled eyes, then took the billeting ticket without looking at it.

"Why, you are just a few liddle boys, no different much as mein Heinrich," she exclaimed in a voice that reflected her perplexity and seemed to carry a measure of sudden and unexpected approval of them.

She threw the door wide open confusedly, still staring from one to the other, and led them silently to their sleeping-places on the second floor. Three rooms, the billeting ticket called for—and there were three comfortable rooms with two large feather beds in each room, rug carpets on the floor, a few pictures on the walls and other evidences of homelike luxury such as belonged to a cherished but dimly remembered past existence. While they laid out their meagre possessions from their packs and prepared to make themselves comfortable in their temporary German domicile, she bustled back and forth dragging large rocking-chairs into the rooms and adding bits of bric-à-brac as if under a sudden impulse to minister further to their comfort.

"Is it you haf hunger?" she asked them suddenly when they were settled and she had finished rearranging their rooms.

The suggestion found instant response.

"Hungry's right—hungry enough to eat a slab o' raw salt pork," exclaimed Corporal McGee spontaneously.

"I haf some nice cakes und some tea should make if you will wish for it," she tempted them, with a friendly smile.

"Cakes!" exclaimed one of the squad. "Is they any such thing in the world! If they is lead me to 'em. It's sure be a life-saver, Mrs.——"

"Fenstermacher—Frau Fenstermacher," she supplied the name. She bustled out of the room and downstairs; and members of the squad could hear distinctly the exquisite music of clattering chinaware as the spread was being made ready for them. It was late afternoon. The noon meal had consisted of two heavy sandwiches, designed to carry them through the last brief hike across the Rhine and tide their stomachs over until the company messes were set up to ladle out hot food late that evening. As for cake, it had vanished entirely from their lives that same day the Statue of Liberty sank into the hazy skyline behind them. Cake and war had remained persistent strangers throughout the length and breadth of France.

"Think of real cake and tea," Corporal McGee fairly gloated, betrayed for the moment by his treacherous appetite; for in common with the other youngsters of twenty-two and under who made up the bulk of the fighting forces, and all of Corporal McGee's squad, his stomach had found few moments of actual delight in this thing of war. The veneer of discipline swept him suddenly and rescued him from his peril. He jumped to his feet and faced his squad sternly, remembering his duty.

"Put on you hats, you birds—what did I tell you about how you was to act!" he ordered them, covering his own head abruptly by way of example.

"Your cake und tea it is ready—and I haf found some cold poultry," came the inviting voice of Mrs. Fenstermacher from below.

Corporal McGee held the others in the room with an abrupt warning order of his hand. Then he marched manfully and with true martial stride out into the hall, downstairs, and faced Mrs. Fenstermacher, hat in hand again.

"Where are der oder liddle boys?" she smiled lightly. Her kindly face and the sight of cakes and viands on the table nearly swept the corporal from his course.

"Thank you—thank you, Mrs. Fenstermacher—but we can't put you to a lot of fuss over us," he stammered. "Besides, it ain't——"

"It's not any troubles," she said earnestly. "It will gif me pleasure to see you liddle boys eat. Come, die tea it will cold get."

The corporal, recovering himself in his habit of obeying orders, dashed his recalcitrant hat back on to his head and blurted out the worst.

"We ain't allowed to fraternise with the enemy," he said thickly, and turned quickly back upstairs as if in search of a refuge, leaving Frau Fenstermacher to look after him in pained wonderment.

"Now you fellows pretty near stubbed your toe first rattle," he cautioned his squad once he had assembled them in his own room and closed the door.

"If it's agin orders to eat a piece of cake with a nice old German lady, then this is goin' to be a fine Christmas package they handed us," protested one of the squad.

"And I'll bet she sure can make cake," spoke up another of the disgusted seven. "She looks just like Sergeant Billie Walters' mother back home and she made the best cakes in the world—next to my own mother."

"Yes, an' for all you knows the old lady'd slip a few pinches of rat poison in the tea and then where'd we all be? The Cap'n 'd know right away we hadn't followed orders and we wouldn't even get a decent military funeral. We got to remember that these folks is our enemy and we can't mix with 'em," the corporal warned them.

But if Frau Fenstermacher's cake and tea went untouched that afternoon; if the corporal and his squad wore their hats and their sidearms about the place when they were there during the off-duty hours of the next few days, the end of a week found these precautionary habits laid aside almost entirely; and Mrs. Fenstermacher's cake had a habit of disappearing as quickly as it was baked.

Not only in Corporal McGee's squad, but among squads wherever billeted, the nightly relations became more those of host and guest. Neither conquered nor conqueror measured up to previous expectations of one another. Living under the same roof seemed to bring the amazing discovery to them that all were mere human beings, moved by similar impulses and attributes. The Americans, strangely enough, neither pillaged, plundered, nor pushed people arrogantly off the sidewalks into the streets. Moreover, they were a cheerful, kindly lot among whom women and children were quite safe. Why, their own Teuton troops had not behaved themselves so much as gentlemen and been such tolerant and tractable billet guests!

"These Americans are not savage beasts as we had been led to expect," was the word that went around among the civilian populace at the end of a week of nervous observation.

"These Heinies are not going to stick knives in our backs while we're asleep—they're a mighty hospitable lot and don't rob us the way the French did," was the American estimate that passed from mouth to mouth in the billets at the end of the week of watchful observation.

"Propaganda!" cautioned the French high command sharply, bringing pointedly to the attention of the American high command the reports of French liaison officers that a spirit of flagrant, if not open, fraternisation with the enemy was springing up between the German populace and American soldiers.

"Those artful Huns are laying it on thick trying to win the hearts of the American soldiers and gain favour at the peace table," shouted the British War Office, urging that the practice be wiped out summarily.

New and rigid orders came out forthwith against fraternising with the enemy. They were emphasised at officers' assemblies and passed on down through every channel of command to the squad leaders themselves, who carried them to the men in the billets.

Corporal McGee carried his orders to his own squad with righteous indignation at their derelictions, reflecting the spirit that had come on down to him from the higher command with unerring precision and spirit, as becomes a squad leader. He saw the thing in its proper light now that it had been made clear to him. Chevrons had come to him within a month after he left his job as an apprentice brickmaker to help win the war, and he always had taken his responsibility seriously, carrying out his orders without fear or maudlin sympathy for those who were wont to complain of military exactitude.

"Let me warn you birds again," he admonished them, "this fraternising' with the enemy has got to stop right now."

"Seems to me you've been eating your share of the enemy's cake," retorted Private Jones, the most outspoken of the squad, whose first year at college, interrupted by the War, had given him critical propensities.

"New orders has come to-day and I want this fraternisin' cut out," the corporal asserted himself. "We got to remember we're conquerors and not get too gay with the natives."

"Don't being conquerors rank us a piece of cake and cup of tea once in a while," persisted Private Jones, encouraged to debate the matter by the sympathetic attitude of his buddies and the past culpability of his corporal. "'Specially when the enemy's a nice old mother who says she's adopted us and wants us to be happy while we're at her house."

"It's Boche propaganda," affirmed Corporal McGee. "The Cap'n told us all about it. He got it straight from the Colonel, who got it right from the General himself."

"Stuff!" sneered the squad spokesman.

"It's not stuff neither," Corporal McGee affirmed. "I been

thinkin' it over on the way up here and it is kinda odd the way these Heinies are treatin' us. What should this old lady want to make us a lot of cakes and feed us all the time if she didn't have some motive? She's got her orders from the Kaiser direct if we only knew the truth. The Cap'n said as much about all of 'em. He says we can't make friends out of our enemies and get away with it."

"Stuff!" persisted the obdurate Jones. "Don't we know what's got under the feelings of Mrs. Fenstermacher. The only thing that's puzzlin' us is that she don't want to put rat poison in the cake."

"What you mean?"

"Didn't she get confidential with us the other night," Private Jones narrated feelingly, "and tell us she had three boys of her own in this War—and that none of 'em came back—an' that they were all just kids—an' the last of 'em killed in the Argonne fracas! And wasn't there tears come into her eyes when she tells us that she was expecting a lot of long-bearded cut-throats and—when she saw us come up she said that except for the uniform we might 've been her own boys coming back home. And she says to us—she likes to imagine we are her boys back in the house again and she wants to take care of us until we go back where we'll have our own mothers. That may sound like propaganda to the Cap'n or it may sound like mush to you, Corporal McGee, but not to us that was there and heard her say it."

Corporal McGee swallowed hard and sat in wide-eyed reflection for some minutes, debating Private Jones' disclosure against the Captain's stern warning. Mothers were really baffling creatures. He never had been able to fathom the strange feelings akin to awe that they had awakened back in the training camps when they had revealed themselves to him as hallowed beings who alone seemed to sound the depths of tragedy and scale the heights of courage that went into this sombre business of sending an army of their boys away to battle. There came into his memory the grim pathos of a brave smile he had seen, time and again, following some lad from his mother's face until the troop train was lost in the distance. Then see her break and fall! The memory of mothers he had seen at the troop trains had come up before him suddenly to haunt him in battle when youngsters he had known fell.

He put the picture out of his mind suddenly. What had that to do with fraternising with the enemy? he demanded of himself. Why permit his squad to be taken in further by organised propaganda intended to disarm their suspicions and gain their favour for no good purpose? There was no craftiness of which these Germans were not capable. He had his orders and he would assert them.

"You birds talk like you ain't growed up," he charged them.

"If you're a growed-up sample then I never want to be one," retorted Private Jones.

"All I got to say," the corporal replied stubbornly, sensing the unsympathetic attitude of his squad, "you'd better not let me catch you fraternisin' with the enemy. Take your own chances if you quit bein' soldiers—an' if you get in the hoosegow don't ask for no sympathy from yours trooly. I can't be here every second to watch you—but after this watch your step when I'm around!"

"Then all I got to say to the corporal is that you're kiddin' yourself out of a mighty fine Christmas dinner right here in this billet," Private Jones asserted disgustedly.

The Christmas spirit had been in the air for a week. Everyone sensed it without realising very definitely just what it was until the day was hard upon them. Christmas was a day to reckon with this year, for the bounty of peace was hung in the world's stocking. Christmas was no longer a hollow mockery, even though it brought sad memories and heavy hearts in its wake. It held at least a glad portent for Christmas days to come, Christmas days when the gaping wounds and blinding hurts of war were as nearly healed as the miracle of time can heal them. The spirit of Christmas must have been at bottom of this fraternisation that winked covertly at stern orders; the spirit that nurtured goodwill among men along with the peace that now had come in just ahead of the Yuletide.

Corporal McGee's squad, less Corporal McGee, decided to make it a day. Frau Fenstermacher herself had invited them to a Christmas dinner, to be held in the evening behind closed doors, after they had returned from their own company mess. Private Jones had suggested a Christmas tree. The others had fallen in with the spirit of the enterprise avidly. It would help drive away the ominous blue devils of gloom that had invaded their division at Christmas time a year ago and gnawed at the entrails of strong men and boys. These same haunting blue devils were in the offing now and they could be counted upon to haunt the camps at Christmastide until those camps were a thing of black memory.

Corporal McGee scoffed at the idea and flatly refused to have anything to do with such an affair. He shut the squad off from telling him too much of their plans. What he did not know would not hurt his conscience as corporal. If they were intent on making fools of themselves behind his back—it was their affair. He could not remain eternally at the billet and spy upon their every move. And he was not the kind to report his whole squad in to the Captain.

"I'm goin' up to Bonn for the Christmas ball-game and root for our bunch while they clean up on the Canucks," he told them gruffly. "I'm gettin' back home here about ten o'clock and leavin' it to you not to do nothin' you shouldn't do!"

"Don't be a saphead," Private Jones badgered him. "We're having a real Christmas to-morrow. Ma Fenstermacher's having in a few little kids that's minus dads as a result of this War, and we're giving 'em some chocolate tins from the commissary and we got some dolls and sleds and skates for 'em. Then Ma Fenstermacher's going to——"

"You can't get away with that stuff—that's fraternisin' with the enemy." Corporal McGee answered warmly. "What'd the Cap'n say if he——"

"Cap'n shucks," laughed Private Smith, the youngest member of the squad, a red-faced cherub of sixteen. "He's in about the same fix you'se in on this fraternisin' business, I guess."

"What do you mean?" demanded the corporal.

"Didn't me and Jonesey run into him this afternoon? We goes into a store to buy some dolls and skates. We just git started when in waltzes the Cap'n. We hid out fast behind a counter—and what does the Cap'n do but buy a half-dozen dolls and some skates, tin soldiers and a lot of truck, lookin' around nervous like at the door every minute. Then he has 'em wrapped up and carries 'em out in the company mailbag actin' just like he was pullin' off a bank stick-up. What's that but fraternising? Or maybe you think he was gettin' them dolls for his dear little pet corp'rals and sergeants."

"If he bought them things it was to send to his own kids at home," protested Corporal McGee loyally. "You wouldn't catch the Cap'n fraternisin' with the enemy after the way he laid it out to us about these Dutch."

"You're right that no one'll catch him," asserted Private Smith acridly. "Leave that to him. But just the same the Cap'n's goin' to fraternise—and German kids 'll be playin' with that sackful o' toys before Christmas is over."

"Well, anyhow," retorted Corporal McGee bluntly, "you ain't goin' to see me taken in by none of this Boche propaganda and rewardin' these Dutch for killin' off our buddies by given' 'em a nice Christmas present. And you birds better be in your feather beds when I get in from Bonn at ten o'clock."

He stalked from the room with an air of washing his hands of the whole affair and leaving them alone to their perilous and treasonable folly.

From a Third Army truck driver who made the long supply haul up the Rhine to regiments billeted in the Rhenish hill lands the squad secured a small fir-tree for five marks. They smuggled it into their billet late at night, hidden in shelter halves and ponchos lest their premeditated plan of fraternising with the enemy awaken the ready suspicions of the military police.

"Nice Christmas spirit," grumbled Private Jones when the tree was safely inside. "Nice Christmas spirit when you got to sneak around about it like robbin' somebody's watermelon patch."

But the Christmas spirit lost nothing of its zest for all its perils; and it was with something akin to bubbling youthful enthusiasm that the seven temporarily transplanted youngsters strung popcorn and devised coloured paper ornaments for the tree under Frau Fenstermacher's skilful instructions. No blue devils should haunt them this Christmas. It was really not such a bad Christmas after all. They would put nothing on the tree for one another. The monthly war wage of privates, after the allotments for Liberty bonds and what-not had been deducted, put a strain upon their combined resources in buying dolls and trinkets for the youngsters that Frau Fenstermacher was to have in for the evening. And besides, they had bought for her a Christmas surprise—a warm new cape of real cloth, not cheap ersatz material, at the staggering cost of seventy marks.

"I was just thinkin'," ruminated Private Smith when their Christmas arrangements had been completed and they were assembled upstairs in their billet ready for bed on Christmas Eve, " I was just thinkin' that I'm gettin' more kick outa this Christmas than if the tree was goin' to be loaded with things for me alone, like it used to be back home. And none of us gettin' a thing either."

"Don't be too sure none of us ain't getting a thing," Private Jones rejoined cynically. "If they catch us romping around that tree with that old lady and these kids the whole bunch of us is likely to get about six months in the hoosegow for fraternisin' with the enemy."

When Corporal McGee approached his billet, glum and blue from a dismal, cheerless Christmas which not even the drubbing his buddies gave the Canadians at Bonn served to dispel, his ears were greeted by the unmistakable sound of revelry. The squad was trying to sing a discordant ensemble that served nevertheless to herald their high spirits. It enraged him that they not only had ignored taps but were cavorting thus noisily at ten o'clock on Christmas night in open fraternisation with the enemy. As he entered the hall of the billet in high wrath and firm purpose, he found that the door to the living-room shut off the merriment. He pounded officiously on the door. Mutual disgrace could only come of such conduct should the noise come to the attention of the military police. He would assert his authority at once.

Frau Fenstermacher had answered the door and seized him irresistibly by the arm before he could announce his stern humour. She bustled him quickly inside to the table that was littered with the remnants of cakes and tempting viands, and upon which stood two half-empty bottles of Rhine wine which she had served up after the custom of the country. His squad gathered about him on the instant in noisy and effusive greeting. Corporal McGee remained inflexible.

"I thought I told you birds to be in bed by ten o'clock," he raged, ignoring Frau Fenstermacher's tender of a chair. He left his hat on his head, set at an arrogant angle.

"The children's gone with their dolls 'n' things but you shoulda seen 'em—eyes big as saucers and they had the time o' their lives," effused Private Smith, unaffected by the corporal's martial austerity. "Say 'n' you ought to see what we give Ma Fenstermacher!"

Another member of the squad brought the cape gaily from a chair in the corner of the room and had her put it on for inspection. The corporal did not look.

"Nice bunch—fraternisin' with the enemy an' me up to Bonn rootin' for our buddies while they clean up the Canucks!" he sneered unyieldingly.

Frau Fenstermacher took him in hand firmly, removing his hat and seating him in spite of himself at the table before an uncut layer cake and a glass of wine with an expertness that bespoke long practise and expert knowledge in the art of handling stubborn striplings. In a few moments his overcoat was off and his grumbling silenced for the moment. She led him off into a discussion of the game at Bonn and clapped her hands with delight at the news that the Americans had won over their Canadian allies. In the finesse of her skill in bringing him into something of the spirit of the merry squad she chanced presently to inspect his Croix de Guerre with an intimate and friendly interest.

"Und that pretty medal is for being a goot soldier in der wars?" she asked him guilelessly.

Private Jones leaped from his seat on the instant and raised his hand to the members of the squad.

"All together fellows," he announced hilariously. "All together—the division song. Sing!" As he led off the others picked up the air and words and carried the song through waggishly as if in answer to Frau Fenstermacher's inquiry.

> The General got the Croix de Guerre,
> *Parlez vous,*
> The General got the Croix de Guerre,
> *Parlez vous,*
> The General got the Croix de Guerre,
> The son of a gun was never there,
> Hinky, dinky, *parlez vous!*

Corporal McGee reddened as he arose and reached instinctively for the big silver watch that hung on a heavy link chain in the upper bellows pocket of his blouse just under his bright new Croix de Guerre. As they ended the song with a jeering laugh he drew the watch forth and consulted the faded dial of the ancient timepiece ominously.

"That'll be all for you birds this night," he muttered decisively. "It's ten-fifteen by Heinie's watch—time for bad boys to be tucked in bed. All upstairs, you birds. Snap into it!"

The sight of Frau Fenstermacher, suddenly frozen to a stark staring statue, her face white as death, swept upon them in the next instant. Her eyes were fixed upon the ancient timepiece that Corporal McGee held in his hand; and as he made to put it back in his pocket she laid her hand upon his wrist.

"Where did you came by it?" she asked in a low voice that trembled with some strong emotion.

"What—you mean that clock?" said the corporal airily. "I took it off a bull elephant of a——"

He stopped speaking suddenly, his voice arrested by an intuition that Frau Fenstermacher's tragic manner aroused. He turned quickly to another explanation.

"Why, I—I got that there watch from—from one o' them big French pawnbrokers—down there at Nancy—for ten francs," he stammered. "Why?"

"It was mein liddle Heinrich's," Frau Fenstermacher whispered simply, taking the watch and pressing it pathetically to her lips.

She opened the hunting case and held it up before them.

"See," she whispered, pointing to the inscription in German script. "It is der name of his fadder also. Heinrich. He haf it at Sedan und he gif it to liddle Heinrich, to bring him safe back from der wars like it did for his fadder. But no, it was not so for mein liddle Heinrich. Some low Frencher kilt mein Heinrich und took his watch."

The Christmas gaiety in the German billet was replaced by the noisy ticking of the clock over the mantel. Corporal McGee stood gaping in the throes of a sudden rending revelation. Frau Fenstermacher no longer puzzled him. She was disclosed—the mother of a soldier.

"Maybe," he said when he could direct a voice that seemed intent on choking him, "maybe you'll—let me give it back to you—for a Christmas present."

PRENTICE

by
Gerald Bullett

O NE is always running across them, these survivors of the dark age. They serve to remind one of the incredible fact that the War really did happen. It was in a public-house not too remote from Fleet Street that I met Jimmy Prentice again, all that was left of him. From his dark corner he stood eyeing me speculatively over the rim of his glass. He lacked an arm, and the livid scar that ran diagonally across his face, breaking the nose in two, lent him a sinister appearance. It was small wonder that I did not at first recognise him, and small wonder that as soon as I recalled his name there flashed into my mind a vision of George Leek. My last sight of Prentice had been at a casualty clearing-station behind Vimy. Then, his face had been swathed in bandages, his eyes shaded, his tortured body strapped to a bed. A whole man feels awkward in the presence of such disaster. What could one offer by way of con-solation to a man permanently disfigured and disabled? Jimmy Prentice had no more than his share of vanity: that I knew well enough. But, when all is said, many of us would rather lose a limb than have our likeness destroyed. Disablement is disablement, and there's an end of it; but the face, be it plain or handsome, is one's very self, the living and outward sign of whatever lurks within, and its disfigurement involves, in some sense, a loss of identity. Prentice, therefore, was the victim of a double outrage, and I was frankly afraid to learn how he was taking it.

"Here's a pal come to see you," said the medical orderly. To me he whispered: "Only two minutes."

"Well, Jimmy," said I, taking the plunge, "you've got a Blighty one this time, old cock."

For a few seconds he made no answer. Seeing his lips move I bent over him.

"Who's there?" said the grey lips.

I told him my name. "You remember me, don't you?"

He grunted assent. "Bit dizzy, that's all. Yes, corp, I got a plateful all right. But nothing to what Old George got. Old George Leek."

This was a dangerous subject. Prentice and Leek had been inseparable friends ever since I had known them. They came from the same street in Camberwell, but had never met there—a circumstance that not only drew them together but provided them with an inexhaustible subject for conversation and debate. They were for ever delightedly comparing notes about music-halls and cinemas they had both frequented and "tarts" they had both known; and it seemed to them marvellous that with all they had in common they might never have become acquainted but for the War. "S'pose you never come across a feller called Spink, George? 'Im what used to keep a lil paper-shop down the 'Igh Street? What, you knew 'im! Fency that now! You knew old Spink!" It seemed too good to be true that Leek had actually bought cigarettes from old Spink. To the bond of these common memories, which gave to Prentice and Leek an illusive grasp upon our vanished civilisation, there was added, during the long alternation of action and so-called rest, the bond of incessant companionship. In the rest camp they pooled their wits against the sergeant-major, shamelessly dodging fatigues whenever they could; in the trenches they generally contrived to occupy the same dug-out. Once, once only, they went over the top together; more than once, squatting side by side, a shirt spread over each lap, they competed in the slaughter of lice.

In this kind of tournament Prentice was generally the victor, though Leek ran him close enough to give a zest to the betting. They were an oddly assorted pair, and there was something correspondingly odd in their relationship. Prentice was—and is—a small, wiry fellow, whereas Leek had a biggish, clumsy body and a red moon face. Through Leek's composition ran a streak of singular simplicity, and, from the very first, little Prentice stood to him *in loco parentis*. Prentice, in fine, mothered Leek, as one might mother an awkward schoolboy : cheered him when he was down, steered him when he was drunk, and from motives purely sanitary kept him away from brothels. All this, whether at first or second hand, was common knowledge in the platoon; and it provided me with a good reason for wishing to discourage further mention of Leek. Jimmy Prentice had lost more than a friend : he had lost his child.

"George caught it a lot worse than me," murmured the man on the bed, and seemed to wait for my comment.

"I know," said I. "But your own little packet'll see you home, Jimmy, well out of this. That's what you've got to think of."

"Yes, I'm fixed up for duration. Not arf I ain't." There was curiously little tone in his words. "I'm a lucky one, corp, there's not a doubt of it. But old George Leek—you oughter seen old George and what they done to 'im, corp. You ought, struth!"

In point of fact I had seen George Leek, and was busy trying to forget the sight. It had confirmed me in the belief that war is an untidy method of settling differences of opinion. I felt a tide of sickness rising in me again, and so, remembering the orderly's injunction, hastened to make my farewells.

"Well, good luck, Jimmy. You'll be back in Camberwell soon, you know."

It was a stupid blunder, as I realised the moment it had passed my lips. I could not shake hands with him; I dared not so much as lay a finger upon that immobile mass of pain. A touch, had it been possible, would have expressed more for me than my feeble speech, and I was exasperated to be denied it. Yet I was glad his eyes were masked when he said, still without tone : " No more Camberwell for old George."

II

These were the memories that stirred in my subconsciousness the other day when I caught sight of Jimmy Prentice flashing mute questions at me over his glass of bitter. I walked over to where he stood.

"I'm sure we've met before. Was it in France?"

"Shouldn't wonder," he said, with a crooked grin. "Prentice, my name, sir."

"Of course!" I remembered everything. "And mine——"

"Oh, I know *you* right enough," said Prentice, more at his ease. "I been lookin' at you this last *ten* minutes."

"Let's go and sit down—over there," I said. "We can talk in comfort."

We began drinking together and talking over old times. It was not at first very easy going. He began by being cursedly deferential, till I almost wished for another war that should get us back on the old, easy terms. But soon he thawed; told me what pension he got in consideration of his lost arm, and wondered whether the Government would consent to take the other at the same price. My own contributions to the talk were somewhat halting, because I could not get the idea of George Leek out of my head, and yet was afraid to introduce him into the conversation. This obsession must have made me appear absent minded, and the consciousness of appearing so added to my embarrassment.

Over his fourth glass Prentice grew pensive. "I s'pose," he said suddenly, "you wouldn't remember that chap Leek I used to knock about wiv—fat sort of feller wiv a red face?"

"I remember him very well. He got knocked out in the same scrap, didn't he?"

"The same straff," corrected Prentice. "Crawling round on your belly and holding what Jerry sent over. Not much scrap about it. Georgie Leek, he was a fair knock-out for getting into trouble. You din know 'im well, did you, corp? Not to *say* well?"

"Only by sight," I admitted. "I know you two were always together."

"You've got it," Prentice assured me. "Always together we were. And need be, what's more. Would you believe it, 'e come from the same street as me, did George Leek, and we never knew nuffin of it till we got out there. There was suthin about George I couldn't 'elp liking. 'E was like a blessed infant in some ways, though never what you'd call a fool, if you get me. And yet I dunno. One day 'e dragged me up out of a shell-'ole in the middle of a big strarf, and you'd never guess what for. 'Ello, Jimmy,' he 'ollers down to me, 'you missin' a good thing down there, matey. Jest you kim up 'ere a minute.' Course, I tell 'im to go to 'ell, but in the end I 'ad to go up so as to make 'im take care of 'isself. 'Now you jest listen,' says George, cocking 'is 'ead a one side very senti-mental. 'Why don't you take cover?' I asks him, mild as milk but the least bit sarcastic. 'I've 'eard that ullyballoo before to-day.' But there wasn't no arguing wiv George. 'No,' says 'e. 'I din mean listen to Jerry. We've all 'eard '*im*. Listen agin.' Then I 'eard what 'e mean—right up in the sky there was a bleedn lil skylark sing-ing like one o'clock. It made me feel queer, but I din let on to George. 'Come to that, I've 'eard *that* before,' I tells 'im, pretty short. So I had, too, moren once. But that was George all over. He was soft, there's no getting away from it. Did 'e ever tell you about 'is girl Ada?"

I shook my head, and Prentice launched at once into a long and highly circumstantial account of George's girl Ada. George had carried in his wallet six or seven photographs of Ada; and Ada was nominated as sole beneficiary in the last Will and Testament that George had laboriously scrawled in the back of his paybook. Prentice could not deny that she was a pretty piece, but he would have it that she was not the girl for George. George, a hopeless romantic, was very much in love; and Ada, it appeared, had neither difficulty nor compunction in playing ducks and drakes with him. It was George's trouble, Prentice told me, that he never had anyone to look after him properly, and him a chap that needed more looking after than most. His own mother, for example, was nothing but an 'Oly Terror. Poor George had conceived the first and last passion of his life when he was a mere warehouse lad with I don't know how few shillings a week. Even that meagre wage, whatever it was, was pitilessly seized by his mother, and George provided with a minute fraction of it for his daily expenses, so that he was quite unable to pay Ada those little delicate attentions— cinemas and fish suppers—that courtship demands. But the time came when he got promotion, accompanied by an increase in salary of sixpence a week. This good fortune he determined to conceal from his mother. Thereafter, for ten consecutive weeks, he secreted a sixpenny piece in the tail of his shirt. Then he made an appointment with Ada. For that great occasion, said Prentice, George got himself up regardless. He even went so far as to change into a clean shirt. Ada's disgust, when he confessed to having left his money behind, can be imagined, though I gathered from Prentice that she did not put George to the trouble of imagining it. The lover crawled home with his tail between his legs, and faced the second dose of music as best he could. By the fire stood his mother, a picture of wrath. On the mantelpiece, as his guilty eyes were quick to see, was a neat little pile of sixpences. " Come 'ere, yer cunning little bastard!" cried mother. " Well, mum," retorted George, with more spirit than one would have given him credit for, " you ought to know."

" And then," said Prentice, " she clouted 'im—a feller, mind you, what could have squeezed 'er silly 'ead off wiv 'is finger and fumb. I'd like to catch *my* muvver at sech tricks. But that," added Prentice, lapsing into his refrain," that was old George all over, soft, soft as pap. As for that Ada, she was a dirty bit of goods and no mistake. Cadgin' and crawlin' and naggin' 'im all in once. Spend· in' 'is rhino, and orf wiv other chaps the same day. And did 'e ever learn better? Not 'im. You dunno George if you think 'e learned better, corp. Leaf after leaf he wasted runnin' around after that Ada, the lil bitch; and if ever he got so much as arf an hour's 'and 'olding on the top of a bus 'e thought isself lucky. The things 'e used to tell me. ' You're a good boy, George,' she'd say to 'im, laughing up 'er sleeve at 'im or my name's not James Prentice; ' there's no one I'd trust like I trust you, George.' 'E din know the first word about wimmin, and that's a fact, corp. Used to make me fair mad to 'ear 'im. She trusted 'im, did she! When he tell me that I jest up and tell '*im* suthin. I tell 'im what she was and what would do 'er good, and, bleeve me or bleeve me not, 'e wouldn't speak to me for a couple of days. Still, I din take offence. Can't take offence wiv a soft bloke like that. Someone got to look after 'im, and me being from the same street—well, I took the job on, any old 'ow. Cleaned 'is buttons and 'elped 'im wiv 'is clobber when we was in billets, and made 'im keep 'is 'ead down when we wasn't. And I 'ad to be sharp sometimes. 'Ad to pretend I thought the world of 'is girl Ada. When 'e got blotto down at a base camp this talk of Ada was the on'y thing ud keep 'im out of mischief. Course I got a bit short wiv 'im time and agin. I was sorry arterwards. 'Your girl Ada,' I tell 'im once, 'she'll be the deaf of me, George, and of you too, shouldn't wonder.' That's what I told 'im, corp, and I wasn't far out—about 'im, any'ow."

Our glasses stood empty before us on the little round table at which we sat. Prentice declared that he had had enough. He refused my invitation to lunch, but agreed that a snack from the counter would do us both good. When I returned with a plate of sandwiches, I asked him to explain in what sense Ada had been the death of George Leek. Whereupon he promptly withdrew his remark. He admitted generously that Ada couldn't help it, poor girl. If George chose to be such a noodle—well, it wasn't really her lookout. What he had meant was that if George hadn't been so soft about that girl he might never have gone back to get them field-glasses.

"What field-glasses?" I asked. "This is the first I've heard of them."

It was, said Prentice, like this here. The company, as I very well knew and no one better, had been holding a very exposed part of the front line. The relief was due in an hour and a half, but the enemy had got our position perfectly sighted and were sending over the best they had got. Their best proved very good indeed. When one in every ten of us had been suitably mutilated the order came through that we were to abandon the position. Its importance, we were led to understand, had been exaggerated, and the men that were to relieve us had been sent elsewhere. The retirement was orderly but hurried, and in the hurry George Leek left behind him a pair of field-glasses entrusted to his care by O.C. Lewis guns.

"Blimey," said Leek, "I'm going back for them, Jimmy."

Prentice, who was slightly wounded, contented himself with a volley of oaths in disparagement of this suggestion. To carry it into effect involved crawling five hundred yards on one's belly in to a shell-swept area.

"And me wallet too," said Leek. "I've left me wallet behind, paybook and all."

At this Prentice took alarm. He knew, as well as George did, what was in that wallet. "Nah, George," he said urgently, "stay where y'are, boy. No gal's worf it, let alone her photer."

But the ineffable George was already on his way. A few minutes later they heard, even above the shriek of artillery, a devastating human scream.

III

Prentice paused in his narration and stared for several seconds at the dregs in his glass.

He said presently: "Course I oughta stopped 'im. But I wasn't quick enough, that's all about it, and I'd caught a lil packet in me thigh, what's more. Any'ow, when we 'eard that scream we 'ad to go and see about it. So me and another bloke—Evans, they called 'im—started orf. Oh yes, we got there all right. And we seen George Leek, not arf we didn't. Tell you straight, I never seen sech a sight. 'Ow 'e could scream at all wiv arf 'is face gorn beats me. But scream 'e did, and never stopped a moment cep to get 'is breaf back. Lyin' on 'is back all knocked to pieces, 'e was. Tell you straight, corp, I din like it. 'Come on, Evans,' says I. 'We got to get 'im out o' this.' So Evans takes 'old of 'is 'ead, and me 'is legs, and—Gawstruf, they twisted all ways! Then George, old George Leek, 'e opened 'is eyes and seen me lookin' at 'im. And suddenly 'e stop 'is row and jest stared up at me. Looked at me sorta sick, as though I'd 'it 'im. Then 'is mouf moved, and 'e said, straight to me, wiv a sort of whistle in his voice, and a sorta sob: 'Jimmy . . . Crysake do us in!' Well, it was a fair knock-out, I dunno what to do. 'Im all to pieces like that and still alive. No gettin' 'im back. And whizz-bangs all round us—merry 'ell."

Prentice's voice wavered and was silent. I did not dare to look up, but presently I asked: "And what did you do?"

"Well," said Prentice, slightly surprised by the question, "what could I do? 'Crysake do us in!' says old George. So I out wiv me jack-knife and cut 'is bloody froat. 'E was a good pal to me."

The clock struck. It was three. The barman, who had already uttered several times his warning chant, "Time, gentlemen, please!" now came to reinforce his persuasions. Prentice, before yielding up his glass, drank off the muddy dregs that from time to time during his narrative he had so sadly scrutinised. We got up and sauntered into the street, where, facing each other for a parting word or two, we heard the tavern key turn against us.

THE BLIND LIEUTENANT

by
Georg Grabenhorst

THIS hour of solitude in the evening before dinner, lying on one of the comfortable deck-chairs in the park, was exceedingly pleasant. The noisy afternoon concert, the wandering about amongst chattering and laughing people, was over; the nervous tension of disjointed conversations, casual greetings from acquaintances over tea-drinking, on the landing-stage, or the tennis tournament, was over too. That tension in its essence was not related at all to these daily commonplaces, to those chance contacts that left him always with a certain painful sense of exclusion: it was simply between him and her, the woman next to him there, with whom he felt happy and in harmony as long as he was alone with her, but who seemed to escape him and to become a stranger, indeed part of that very strangeness itself, as soon as he was amongst other people with her.

It was not jealousy that caused the blind man—blinded in a war which was carefully not mentioned or was glossed over with polite phrases—to feel his separation from the loved one who could see. It was not suspicion that gradually came between them, at any rate not that anxious, jealous suspicion so common between human beings. His feeling for her was too sincere and too sure for that. He was too grateful and too certain of his love for Lena, perhaps too lacking in passion. No, the tension between them, of which he was becoming increasingly aware, was of a different kind. In his lonely hours he was tortured by the helpless consciousness of that chasm across which bridges might be thrown—bridges of love and compassion, of gratitude, of understanding, and willingness for sacrifice, but which nevertheless remained a chasm in all its terrible profundity, with two eternally separate worlds on either side.

It was good to rest in the park, in a place where the hotel guests rarely came, to recline in the shadow of the acacias and lime-trees, whose faint odours were wafted to him from time to time. This evening repose soothed him, and though his thoughts now always returned to his insoluble problem, he heard the call of the thrush and the roar of the sea, and the sweet melody of children's voices occasionally borne upon the breeze.

It was good to rest here alone, for once unprotected, to enjoy a brief escape from that constant care and consideration, that solicitude which would soon drive him to despair. He had grown silently to hate this solicitude; not for one second was he free from it; everything that happened round about him, all actions and words and even thoughts were falsified and spoiled by it. All emotion was diluted by it and its savour was lost. Everyone handled him with a cautious gentleness, like the sisters in hospital. On no account might he be hurt; everything must be kept from him that might remind him of the gulf which separated him from the rest of the world. He was honest enough to admit to himself that there had been a time when he accepted all this as an alleviation of his lot, grateful for the remoteness, for this soft, pseudo-life that was being carried on beyond his dead eyes. There had been a time when he regarded the obliteration of this world as an elevation, the darkness before him as a herald of light, and the selfless love of this woman as a grace that he did not deserve, that no one could deserve, a grace that gave meaning to the meaningless, and imposed the profound duty to bear and overcome the intolerable. There were still times when he felt like that. But there were also the more frequently recurring periods in which he was overcome by this terrible knowledge of the uselessness of it all, of the ghastly weariness of the sacrifices of love, the unspeakable satiety of that futile solicitude, which slowly confirmed in him the suspicion that fundamentally, under the guise of love and sympathy, it was a *reproach*. A secret, hidden reproach, an enmity of the blood that never came into the open.

An enmity of the blood? He reflected upon the meaning of this. Did such an enmity exist between him and her? Was blood not passion, and was not passion insignificant in their union, outside their genuine mutual love that nothing could affect?

No; it was not that. His love for this woman was not without passion; that had played its part in the magnetic current that flowed between them and gave them those high moments of satisfaction and liberation. True, passion had not been the determining factor, nor the first attraction between them. The first contact had lain within a realm to which passion was almost foreign, in a spirituality such as only the deep common sorrow for men and events, the deep common struggle to find some footing, some fresh start after terrific world events, could produce. This universal impulse had been *their* start, the beginning of their common life, their love. His convalescence, slow and difficult, had been *her* convalescence; as a sister she had stood by him in hospital, and so now she stood by him in life, remaining with him, his friend and companion, and finally his wife. Passion had not been the deciding factor, but he felt at this moment only too clearly that passion had become important, that it was inextricably woven into their common life, their love; that it was impossible to disregard, to discard it. He felt only too well that they had both grown different, that, as all the suffering of that chaotic period receded into the distance, their spirits had been readjusted to admit again old, forgotten, and repressed claims, which were sometimes terrifying in their insistence, intensified to a vehemence that made her ashamed, and which they both sought vainly to conceal.

Perhaps it was for this reason that he found her considerateness, her undiminished or indeed increased solicitude, so painful; it seemed that the latent reproach was developing into a suppressed resentment—a resentment against the fetters which destiny had cast about her during a period that was over and done with, and which stood like a debt in an old ledger, for which it was unfair to hold her responsible.

He knew that it was in him and not in her that this thing had begun; this craving for what they were missing, this outbreak of longing and desire buried under mountains of spiritual suffering. It was he who had first felt those promptings that grew more insistent and more desperate as he became increasingly aware of their deceptive futility. He had first roused *her*. It was he who had roused her out of the dim feeling of self-sacrifice, out of that quiet little world of renunciation into the tumult of the great, self-confident world outside. It was he who had pressed out amongst men, into the pleasures of travel and society. It was he who had wished to come to this noisy, popular seaside resort in which he had felt unhappy from the first, save when he was alone with her, in her sitting-room, or on the balcony overlooking the sea. He would lean against the balcony until far into the night, listening to the monotonous song of the breakers beneath him, beating up against the massive, protruding walls of the hotel, sometimes driving their spray right up to him. He excepted, too, that hour after the afternoon concert, which he could spend alone here in the park, resting in his deck-chair under the acacias, meditating as he listened to the thrush, to the distant sound of the sea and to occasional children's voices on the sand. Yes, he excepted that hour, short though it was.

For to-day it was at an end. He already heard the door on the glass verandah open and steps on the gravel—those steps that approached him much too quickly, cutting into his peaceful loneliness so that he would have to nerve himself again to the tension of human contacts. He perceived that there were different steps—those unmistakable steps of hers, and those of a stranger already familiar to him, little though they concerned him. His nerves were becoming too sensitive, his hearing too perceptive, nor could he do anything to prevent it.

Lena had met Herr van Huelst in the lounge. She had spent the whole afternoon in his motor-boat.

"Isn't the air intoxicating? One can positively taste it."

"What a strong smell the acacias have!" said Lena—"almost too strong. Weren't you getting bored?"

As he made some reply, taking Lena's arm as they make their way back to the hotel along the gravel path, he was thinking: "Why don't you say that the sky is burning blue, that you can hardly bear to look as the gulls dive into it until they are only little points of silver in the azure gold? Why don't you say all this? why do you keep it to yourselves and make a secret of it? Why do you shut me out of this world a second time? Why do you let me feel my isolation in trying to conceal it from me? Is it not the same fear of admission, the same covert reproach, the same false forgiveness of the unforgivable between us?"

At the dining-room door they met the retired civil servant, who tapped him on the shoulder. "Hullo, my dear Lenz! How are you? This is delightful—quite exceptional luck. Of course you'll join me? I'll get a table. We'll have a comfortable corner to ourselves with a nice bottle of wine."

Am I his patient? Lenz reflected. Am I still the wounded officer in bed 16? What right has he to inquire after my health so urgently, to call me "my dear fellow," to invite me to share his bottle of wine? He knows, of course, the dear, kind old gentleman, that the others, who are young and healthy, want to dance and flirt; they have their own world. We two are out of the running—one over sixty with his gout, and the other poor devil a war casualty, blinded. We two are suited to one another; we, too, have our world! Our world, our little bottle of wine!

Although these thoughts passed through his mind he made some pleasant remark, shook hands with the old gentleman, who returned the pressure with interest, and took Lena's arm again. As they entered the dining-room, he turned to Herr van Huelst— why doesn't he go on Lena's right, why do they go out of their way to take him between them?—"You come, too, Herr van Huelst, won't you? My wife has a passion for dancing, and I shall be dining at Carey's table. Anyhow, you'll be a better partner than I shall."

He said this quite casually, as though it were the most commonplace thing in the world, and Herr van Huelst answered in the same careless fashion. But the blinded officer, holding on to the arm of his beautiful wife, was not taken in. He knew that it was not all so easy, so matter of fact, as the three of them were pretending. He knew that it was a tacit admission of the worlds that lay between them, of the involuntary alliance, of the involuntary enmity, of the treason in the blood. Yes, it amounted to treason; those two could hardly look at each other without blushing because of the secret between them, the secret which Lenz knew, which he had almost blurted out. Why didn't they admit it? Why persevere in this lying solicitude? Why? Why?

But they went on eating, with Herr van Huelst talking brightly about his travels in Africa, telling anecdotes at which they all laughed, while Lena, untiring as ever, offered him smoked salmon or pâté or a little more coffee. Now, as always, Lenz tried to handle his knife and fork as skilfully as possible, not to upset anything, to be normal, inconspicuous. He could hear the waiter passing backwards and forwards, and the snatches of conversations drifting in from other tables. He wondered what all these people looked like; he tried to picture them as he listened politely to Herr van Huelst, laughing in the right places, and saying: "That's really priceless." But all the time there was the same thought at the back of his mind—the feeling that they were being noticed, pointed out. "You see that blind man over there?" they were saying. "Frightfully sad. The wife's a charming woman, and that man seems quite smitten with her. Oh yes, a nice fellow, an attaché in the Diplomatic Service. Well, you can't blame her. She's got a right to ask something more out of life, a young and pretty woman like that, tied to a blind man. It must be simply ghastly. Still, he'll give her something else to think about . . . tied to a blind man . . . what can he do for her . . . what can he know about her feelings, cut off from the world outside . . ."

He took the piece of fruit that Lena had prepared for him. Oh yes, he knew what they said—the poor blind devil knew. He knew all about that world outside; he felt its beauty and variety as only the man who has once shared in it and is now cut off from it can know or feel. But those memories that might have consoled him were poisoned by his longing to bridge the unfathomable chasm between them. It was not mere rebellion or jealousy. His love for her was too sincere for the intrusion of that vulgar emotion. And he knew only too well that the attaché didn't really matter, no man could really matter. It was their *world* that they had lost, that world through which they had set out so happily together. But it was no use. He could do nothing. He always came back where he started.

Dinner was over; he went out on Lena's arm into the lounge, where they stood around, chatting, smoking, talking politics or business, discussing one of the inevitable crises discovered nightly by the evening papers. Herr van Huelst went off to change for the party, and they also went back to their room.

Lena put out his things—shirt, collar, and tie. She filled the basin, laid out the towels and the shaving brushes, placed his hair-brushes and comb conveniently by.

"I can manage now, thanks," he said, and he opened the door on to the verandah. A cool breeze came up from the sea.

"Are you sure you want to go, dear? Won't it be too much for you? If you'd rather we stayed quietly here . . ."

What was that misgiving, he wondered, as the door closed on the echoes of her voice? Was it that guilty consciousness, not hers, not Lena's own particular consciousness, but the shamefaced con-sciousness of all those people who asked him to parties, who were agreeable, kind, and attentive to him? Was it not that widespread conspiracy of guilty consciousness, he wondered, that made life so unbearable? And was it worth while? For her, who had loved and married and watched over him, for him, for all the others? Was it worth anything at all? Was not their pain as great as his? Did they not struggle and torment themselves, perhaps, even more than he? How could he know? He didn't know. He knew noth-ing of their endeavours, of their failures, or their victories. Was it bearable any longer? By him? By her? Was it? Was it?

He leant over the rail of the verandah, drinking in the sharp, salt sea air.

Should he allow it? Ought he to accept this continual sacrifice? Did anything justify it? Which of their two worlds had the greater right, the greater justification? Her world, the living world, bril-liant, various, and unfettered, or his world of darkness and isola-tion? *Hers, not his.* Why had he hesitated? Why did he not sur-render since he could never win? Why did he not give her up to the world—the world to which she had a right, the whole vast world of loving and hating, heat and cold, beauty and ugliness, sickness and health, life and death? Why did he hesitate?

The breakers were rolling up in the little bay; the secret surges of the deep were awakening to life, their sound swelling, their waves mounting, higher and higher, in impatient expectation.

There was a voice rising within him, cold and dark and swelling like the rising tide. "Do not trouble any more," it said: "you have thought about it long enough. To-day is just the same as yesterday, and to-morrow will be just the same as to-day. There will always be a kind old gentleman to offer you, as your world, a little bottle of wine. There will always be a little something for you everywhere, an armchair to lie in, a little rest, a little weariness, a little sorrow, and a little joy. A little of everything, always a little of everything. *But never again anything whole and complete.* She will always put out your things for you, she will always be kind and affectionate, she will always be patient, and she will always stay by you, as often and as long as you wish. But there will always be someone else—this man or another—to whom she cannot talk without blushing, without feeling disloyal, without feeling the hampering fetters of the bond. Life will be denied to her, and she will always feel it struggling. It will be buried alive, stifled, renounced with pain and longing. Is that good enough for the woman you love? Isn't she worth this sacrifice? Isn't she worthy of a fuller life? Square the account with her now, this very day, this very hour. Reckon it up no more, cease weighing and measuring; do it, do it *blind. Do it; think no longer.*"

He listened at the door for a moment. Then he leaned further over the railings, further and further still. Was she calling him? He let himself drop.

In his last seconds of consciousness as he fell through the air the staggering doubt assailed him.

"Lena, Lena, what have I done? Don't you love me, Lena? Enough to defeat everything? Don't you love me just as I am, blind and lonely, in my ruined, darkened world? Are you not bound to it even more indissolubly than I, linked by those bridges of solicitude and sacrifice? Does not your love transcend our narrow separate worlds and fuse them into a greater world than either? I have only been thinking of myself when I thought I was thinking of you; I am wrenching away what I thought I was giving; I am cheating you when I thought I was serving you; I am destroying what I wished to set free. It's too late, Lena. Too late now. I was wrong."

ONE HUNDRED PER CENT

by
Leo V. Jacks

UNCLE HENRY flicked the reins over the black mare, and shifted his quid of Union Leader. "What 'd you think of all the speechifyin' at the Crossin'?"

As any dutiful fifteen-year-old nephew would, I said it was good. The Crossing is a town of a thousand inhabitants, and, like many such towns, it takes its Fourth of July undiluted. When there is any Americanism to be dispensed, the Crossing always gulps a liberal dose.

This ideal rural festival had just terminated after a barbecue in the grove, many tubs of pink lemonade, firecrackers till hell wouldn't hold them, and of course some perspiring orators. Now it was sundown, and Uncle Henry and I were on our way home. The yeomen had milled around all day in the hot sun, red-faced, panting, and happy. They enjoyed everything.

The chief speaker was the Honourable J. O. Coughlin, our Congressman, and if he didn't twist the British lion's tail, and pull all the feathers out of the Austrian eagle—— He gave the French hell for not paying their war debt, and the crowd said he ought to know, for he was there in '18.

He talked at great length about the gallantry of our boys in the War, and he told a story of a very brave Y. secretary who had run out into No Man's Land, or some place, under the fire of eighty-four machine-guns and several regiments of the Bavarian Guard to rescue some wounded soldier. While this story was being related, I heard Uncle Henry swearing under his breath, and I thought maybe a mosquito had bitten him. Mr. Coughlin told none of his own brave deeds. I suppose he was too bashful.

As I studied him, I couldn't help thinking that he would be a dangerous man in a fight, for he was big and heavy, and he looked strong enough to put an awful push behind a bayonet. Then, too, he had an air of embattled virtue which indicated that when he was roused he could be terrible. It was a mighty good thing for our district that we had such a man to protect the public interests. And, yet, he had an ingratiating way; tall, with a fair, full face, and bright, trusting blue eyes, and a great hand-shake. He dressed very well.

A young boy is a natural-born hero-worshipper. You know how quickly he will construct a heroic character out of any big man he admires, and how badly he feels when he sees the feet of clay. I'll never forget the story of the Chicago White Sox trial, and the newsboy's wail when Joe Jackson fled from the court-room with his hands over his face: "Say it ain't true, Joe, say it ain't true."

The mayor had introduced Coughlin as a veteran of many battles, who had gone into politics to purify them. I didn't see any medals on him, but he was probably modest and left them at home. The mayor said, anyway, that he had been in some desperate battles, so, like any youngster, I watched the big man with a good deal of admiration and not a little awe. I'd made up my mind that on our way home I'd quiz Uncle Henry about those battles.

Uncle Henry is thin-faced, and always clean-shaved. He has bright grey eyes and a retiring way. He is five feet nine, and he limps a little when he walks. He got a shrapnel bullet in his left foot at the Fond des Meszeires, and didn't go to the hospital.

So, you see, he is an alumnus of the A.E.F., and a clever one, too, and a skilled manipulator of the esteemed soixante-quinze. Now, as we jogged along, he hummed gently over the exploits of the mademoiselle from Bar-le-Duc, and the old farm-waggon rattled. Uncle Henry rolled his quid reflectively and ruminated for a moment. Then he spat accurately at a thirteen-striped gopher that darted out of the rut just in time to escape the encroaching wheels.

"Fourth of July speeches don't mean nothin', kid," he observed. "The politicians—and that goes for Coolidge and Coughlin, and ninety-nine per cent. of the men holding offices that they got by votes—they don't care a rap for the common people, or the soldiers either, spite of all they talk about battles, and brave boys, and all that."

"Well, if the politicians don't appreciate what the boys did in France, the people did," I said. "They've elected some of these fighting soldiers to good jobs. There's Mr. Coughlin——"

"Yeah? Well, if the people feel that way, they sure show their appreciation of the fighting man in strange ways.

"Now, I recall a fellow in our battery, and he was—— But I'll tell you all about him.

"When our brigade started up to the Marne in July, the dope had it that there would be a big battle. It came, too. Well, this fellow, a handsome blond with blue eyes and very fair hair, whom you can call Spicks or Sticks, or some such thing, was a cannoneer.

"In the middle of the last night, when we were getting close to the front, and we could hear the guns booming and see the red flashes on the sky-line, it began to rain cats and dogs, and what with all the mud and confusion, and the trampling, and the troops jammed up in the cross roads, and the black darkness, Sticks or Wicks lost his way, and went somewhere else. Damned if we didn't have to go into action without him.

"Our brigade was in fighting at Fresnes, and Courmont, and the Croix Rouge Farm, and Chamery, and Dravegny, and old Death Valley, where we buried a lot of our good men, and so on, from July 30th to August 24th. You'd think, now, wouldn't you, that a rabid patriot who was just yearning to kill him a few Germans would have found his way up to the front, and rejoined his regiment in the course of twenty-six consecutive days of hard fighting?

" But Sticks or Bicks couldn't find his way. By day the thunder of the guns could have guided him somewhat, and at night you could see the sky all lit up like the mouth of hell and fiery red for miles around Hangar Claudin, and Fismes, and Fismettes. But he didn't see or hear. From where we lost him it was only a ten-mile walk to Courmont, and many's the time we hiked thirty miles between sundown and sunrise, so the distance couldn't have bothered him much.

" But, anyway, on August 25th we were pulled out of the Aisne-Marne entertainment, and started elsewhere. And our boys went along feeling pretty chirrupy, because they had it that we were bound for a rest-camp. Soldiers are optimistic cusses. They still think a rest-camp means rest.

" Well, sir, second day on the road we ran right into Ticks or Spicks, and there were tears in his big blue eyes as he told First Lieutenant Finnegan, who happened to be our commanding officer because the Captain had been killed by a shell, how hard he'd been hunting for us, and what a rocky time he'd had away from the battery, and, gee! couldn't he have something to eat? He was damn near starved.

" So the Looie rode back to the rolling-kitchen, and he said to the cooks: 'This poor son of something is in an awful fix. Can you give him a little snack?'

" They said they could, and they did.

" For the next three days Spicks or Hicks was one of the most diligent boys I ever laid my two eyes on, and he certainly made some of our prize duty-dodgers look like what they were. He chopped wood for the kitchen, and worked at this and that, and he begged Sergeant Nixon to give him back his old job on the seventy-five.

"On August 27th came a God-awful hike. All day and no let-up. Top speed. Night fell. Some of our men began to get pretty leg-weary. The old horses groaned, and panted, and cursed in horse and the Colonel made every son get down and walk.

"The country we were passing through looked tough. Fields all shell-holes, and the houses in ruins. Besides, you don't go to rest-camps on twenty-four-hour forced marches. Finally, about three in the morning we began to see the old red flashes and hear the guns. We didn't know where we were, but we knew there was a hell of a battle going on, and that was the reason for all the hurry. We were slated for a nice juicy job, probably right in the front row.

"Then it rained. Ye gods, how it rained! But at last our column, blistered and tottering and groaning and cursing and starvation-hungry, pulled up under some trees in a meadow to take a final inventory before we stepped in where the water was deep.

"Then somebody discovered that Sticks was missing. Lost again. By God, that boy had tough luck! He always got lost when there was a battle in the offing.

"The great Oise-Aisne drive is all history now. We had a wild time in company with the First Moroccan Division. They're the greatest soldiers in the world. I take off my hat to those North Africans.

"Our division lost a lot of men, but we took all our objectives, and buried our dead, and, finally, our brigade came out on the 6th of September, after about nine days of real big league battling.

"We were marching down the old sunshiny road toward the Forest of Retz when here came Sticks. Lord! he was a sorry-looking mess, but he was sorrier when Lieutenant Finnegan clapped eyes on him. 'Jesus-God!' Finnegan roared. 'Donner und Blitzen! Sacre nom du chien! Get me a pair of handcuffs quick!'

"And if he didn't grab that Sticks in a hurry, I hope to spit in your mess-kit.

"Believe it or not, Sticks had had a lot of hard luck. Practically all the hard luck in the A.E.F. There were tears in his eyes while he told about it, and Finnegan couldn't make him shut his mouth. And, believe me, he begged hard, and argued.

"For a while nobody really believed that he got lost the second time, but if you keep at a story long enough you can make some people swallow it. And, of course, we didn't have any handcuffs. What 'd you do with handcuffs in a regiment of field artillery?

"So Finnegan had to let him go. But the officers were disgusted, and some of the enlisted men that 'd had their friends or relatives killed said Spicks should be made an example of, and they talked about court-martial.

"You'd think, maybe, with all that hanging over his head, Picks would have deserted in dead earnest. But he didn't. He wore his air of injured virtue day and night. He was humbler than ever, and more diligent. He cut wood, and he didn't have to be told. He worked hard for the cooks, and he stuck to the battery like a leech. And all the time he protested innocence, and swore his disappearance had been an accident pure and simple. He may have been pure, but he was not so simple.

"We went to a damn rest-camp in the Haute-Marne, where we did everything but rest, and before there was time for a court-martial, before there was time for anything but one or two good drunks, the whole brigade was hustled away to Verdun. The underground telegraph said that all the battles fought up to date would shrink into nursery rhymes alongside what was coming.

So we tightened our harness, and oiled the guns, and ate everything we could get. We never let the War interfere with our appetites. And every night we went legging it in thirty-mile hikes up through the Bar-le-Duc country, past Eurville-Bienville, and on to Esnes.

"It rained every night, and lots of the boys fell down by the road just plumb paralysed, and every morning our column was thinner than the day before. And all day long the cripples would come staggering into camp, and the cooks fed them, and helped them along. We had good cooks.

"On the morning of September 23rd we limped into the Bois de Brocourt. The rain stopped, and at six o'clock the sun shone. Lord! that was a beautiful morning. Some birds were singing, and the grass and leaves were sprinkled with raindrops shining in the light. There were little sunny meadows all around. Lieutenant Finnegan said that when breakfast was over, and the horses fed and groomed and watered, we could sleep all day.

"When we lined up for mess, there was no Sticks at the kitchen. The head cook, Jones, said that Sticks was with them some time during the night, and then again, all of a sudden, he wasn't there. Just like that.

"Lieutenant Finnegan never said a word, but his face got as hard as a steel trap, and I figured it 'd be the firing-squad for Sticks if we ever caught him again. So we went blithely, and from September 26th to November 11th the Meuse-Argonne drive was on, forty-seven days of continuous battling in a country that 'd make the Dismal Swamp look like a public playground.

"And our regiment fought in most of that fight, because we saw thirty-nine consecutive days of the fun. When they brought us out at last we could just totter, and that was all. Clothes in rags, equipment busted, guns blown up. Seventy-five per cent. of the old horses were dead, seventy-two per cent. of the men killed, wounded, or gassed.

"Nobody laughed, or joked, or talked. They just walked along, glassy-eyed. When it was time to rest, they rested, and when the guides said 'Go,' they got up passively, and went. Thirty-nine days in the Meuse-Argonne without a break. Ask anybody that was there.

"After a week or two we'd hobbled down into the neighbour-hood of Neuville-sur-Orne, and damned if we didn't walk right on to Private Sticks. And, believe it or not, he got lost on that hike to Verdun. He smiled a wan smile when they took him to the guard-house. He said it was tough treatment for a poor boy who was trying to do his duty, and had had misfortunes. But the M.P. snapped him off, and said that the Y. was also doing its duty, and having misfortunes.

"Our regiment wasn't really a hard-hearted crowd, and nobody hated Sticks, though they all despised him. But you'd think we were a lot of Pontius Pilates from the way he behaved toward us. He got six months in the brig, and the guards cuffed him around a lot, but he was damned lucky he didn't get shot.

"When we finally came back to America, old Finnegan said: 'Turn the blankety-blank son of a skunk loose, and let him go.' So Sticks chirked up immediately. I heard he worked 'em for an honourable discharge."

The plodding team was beginning to descend into the old hol-low around grandfather's farm, and we could hear the crows caw-ing in the woods, and some squirrels barking in the great cotton-woods overhead.

"Gee," I said, "that fellow was a dirty yellow coward, and I wouldn't trust him with anything. What made you think of him, Uncle Henry?"

" Oh, I *saw* him—at the Crossin'."

" You did?" I cried. " Who is he?"

Uncle Henry got rid of his quid of Union Leader, and flicked the reins sharply over the black mare before he answered : " Why, our honourable Congressman, J. O. Coughlin."